Lecture Notes in Business Information Processing 601

LNBIP reports state-of-the-art results in areas related to business information systems and industrial application software development – timely, at a high level, and in both printed and electronic form.

The type of material published includes

- Proceedings (published in time for the respective event)
- Postproceedings (consisting of thoroughly revised and/or extended final papers)
- Other edited monographs (such as, for example, project reports or invited volumes)
- Tutorials (coherently integrated collections of lectures given at advanced courses, seminars, schools, etc.)
- Award-winning or exceptional theses

LNBIP is abstracted/indexed in DBLP, EI and Scopus. LNBIP volumes are also submitted for the inclusion in ISI Proceedings.

Emanuele Laurenzi · Barbara Re ·
Hans Friedrich Witschel
Editors

Hybrid Intelligence in Business

25th International Conference, BIR 2026
Olten, Switzerland, October 7–9, 2026
Proceedings

Springer

Editors
Emanuele Laurenzi
FHNW University of Applied Sciences
and Arts Northwestern Switzerland
Olten, Switzerland

Barbara Re
University of Camerino
Camerino, Italy

Hans Friedrich Witschel
FHNW University of Applied Sciences
and Arts Northwestern Switzerland
Olten, Switzerland

ISSN 1865-1348 ISSN 1865-1356 (electronic)
Lecture Notes in Business Information Processing
ISBN 978-3-032-38497-3 ISBN 978-3-032-38498-0 (eBook)
https://doi.org/10.1007/978-3-032-38498-0

This Springer imprint is published by the registered company Springer Nature Switzerland AG
The registered company address is: Gewerbestrasse 11, 6330 Cham, Switzerland

Preface

Business Informatics applies digital technologies to improve the efficiency and effectiveness of complex organisations. It draws on information systems, computer science, artificial intelligence, the social sciences, and business administration, among other disciplines. The International Conference on Perspectives in Business Informatics Research (BIR) is an established venue that brings together researchers from these fields.

BIR 2026, the 25th edition of the conference, was organised by the School of Business of the University of Applied Sciences and Arts Northwestern Switzerland (FHNW) and held on 7–9 October 2026 in Olten, Switzerland—the first BIR edition held in Switzerland.

The central theme of BIR 2026 was "Hybrid Intelligence in Business", which explored how human expertise and creativity can be complemented by intelligent solutions from informatics and AI to strengthen organisational capabilities.

Emanuele Laurenzi from the FHNW School of Business, Switzerland, served as General Chair, while Barbara Re from the University of Camerino, Italy and Hans-Friederich Witschel from the FHNW School of Business, Switzerland, served as Program Committee Chairs.

The conference received 56 submissions from 22 countries. As is customary at BIR, papers underwent a rigorous single-blind review. The 2026 Program Committee comprised 67 reviewers from 26 countries, and each paper typically received three reviews. Of the 56 submissions, the Program Committee accepted 28 as full papers (an acceptance rate of 50%) and six as short papers (a combined acceptance rate of 61%). All accepted papers were presented at the conference. The papers in these proceedings cover different aspects of the discipline, focusing mainly on AI opportunities and challenges, AI applications and use cases in business, business intelligence, business and information systems development, cybersecurity, and knowledge management and traceability.

The conference featured four keynote talks.

Frank van Harmelen, professor of artificial intelligence at the Vrije Universiteit Amsterdam, the Netherlands, delivered a talk titled "Hybrid AI: AI systems that collaborate with people instead of replacing them" on hybrid intelligence, focusing on AI systems that collaborate with people rather than replace them. He stressed that such systems must be able to adapt to changes in the team and the environment, which requires them to model the people they work with (a "theory of mind"), act on moral values, and explain themselves. The talk set out a research agenda for hybrid intelligence that differs substantially from the research agenda for autonomous AI, presented early results from researchers worldwide, and illustrated use cases for hybrid intelligence across different sectors of society.

Hans-Georg Fill, professor of business informatics and vice president of the Department of Informatics at the University of Fribourg, Switzerland, delivered a talk titled "AI or not AI: From Uncertainty to Fact and the Role of Conceptual Modeling". He analysed the developments of generative AI from the perspective of business informatics and examined their implications and trade-offs along two dimensions—training and education, and research and product innovation—from the perspectives of both academia and industry. By revisiting how uncertainty emerged in the history of abstraction, he identified potential anchors of stability and illustrated the role conceptual modelling can play in this context.

Christian Lichka, board member of the BOC Group, an international leader in enterprise management systems, delivered a talk titled "Model your Business. Architect its Intelligence. How Enterprise Digital Twins Close the Contextual AI Gap". Lichka emphasised the value of enterprise models in the era of generative AI and presented an industry perspective on the model-based Digital Twin of the Organisation, stressing that it serves as the shared language connecting human judgement with intelligent systems, and business strategy with IT reality. He then elaborated on hybrid intelligence as a paradigm that emerges from this shared language, where human insight and machine reasoning find a common structure to think, decide, and transform together.

Toni Wäfler, professor at the FHNW School of Applied Psychology, Switzerland, where he established the Institute "Humans in Complex Systems", delivered a talk titled "How to Combine Humans and AI Smartly". Wäfler highlighted the negative effects AI can have on human work behaviour: people tend to accept suboptimal AI results without questioning them, so their expertise erodes, while faster and more polished output inflates their sense of competence. AI can also hollow out jobs by taking over their core creative and problem-solving tasks and leaving humans only to supervise, which lowers motivation, causes cognitive overload, and reduces job satisfaction, all of which increase error rates. He argued that companies can avoid these effects only by jointly designing and optimising humans, technology, and organisation in their mutual interdependencies, and presented criteria and methods being developed at FHNW for this purpose, drawing on projects such as AI4SME.

Following the conference tradition, the first day was dedicated to satellite events: workshops, tutorials, and the Doctoral Consortium.

The Doctoral Consortium, chaired by Hanlie Smuts from the University of Pretoria, South Africa, and Robert Andrei Buchmann from Babeş-Bolyai University of Cluj-Napoca, Romania, offered doctoral researchers a stimulating environment to discuss their ideas and progress with experts from the BIR community.

Raimundas Matulevičius from the University of Tartu, Estonia, and Fabrizio Fornari from the University of Camerino, Italy, chaired the workshops and tutorials. Five workshops were organised: the 2nd International Workshop on Digital Technologies for Smart and Sustainable Buildings (DTSSB 2026), the 2nd Workshop on Challenges and Opportunities in Digital Transformation (CODiT 2026), the 11th Workshop on Managed Complexity (ManComp 2026), the 3rd Workshop on Domain-Specific Modeling Methods and Tools – Exchange of Experience and Knowledge of OMiLAB Nodes (OMiLAB-KNOW 2026), and the 16th Workshop on Business and IT Alignment (BITA 2026).

Bohdan Haidabrus from Riga Technical University held a tutorial titled "Hybrid Intelligence in Lean-Agile Enterprises: AI-Augmented Delivery at Scale", in which he showed how Hybrid Intelligence, with AI augmenting rather than replacing people, can strengthen Lean-Agile practices at scale, from portfolio planning and flow optimization to quality assurance and continuous improvement.

The BIR Industry Bridge, a new format introduced this year and chaired by Emanuele Laurenzi and Manuel Renold from the FHNW School of Business, Switzerland, brought together industry leaders and academic experts to discuss the adoption of AI across industries and the implications of the emerging hybrid intelligence paradigm.

Piermichele Rosati from the FHNW School of Business, Switzerland, and the Universitat Politècnica de València, Spain, served as Web Chair, while Jessica Piccioni from the University of Camerino, Italy, Arianna Fedeli from the Gran Sasso Science Institute, Italy, and Devid Montecchiari from the FHNW School of Business, Switzerland, served as Publicity Chairs.

We thank Marite Kirikova from Riga Technical University, Latvia, and the members of the BIR Steering Committee for their continued support and guidance during the organisation of the conference. We thank all authors who submitted their papers, the Program Committee members for their timely reviews, the keynote speakers for their inspiring talks, and the organisers of the workshops and the Doctoral Consortium for their dedication.

We are grateful to our sponsor, The BOC Group, for their generous support. We also thank the Springer team for their prompt support in producing these proceedings and for their continued partnership with BIR, an important factor in the conference's longevity.

Finally, we sincerely thank the FHNW local team—Jaelle Fuchs, Lea Matter, and the student volunteers—for supporting the organisation of the event and looking after all conference participants.

July 2026

Emanuele Laurenzi
Hans Friedrich Witschel
Barbara Re

Organization

General Chair

Emanuele Laurenzi	FHNW - University of Applied Sciences and Arts Northwestern Switzerland, Switzerland

Program Committee Chairs

Hans Friedrich Witschel	FHNW - University of Applied Sciences and Arts Northwestern Switzerland, Switzerland
Barbara Re	University of Camerino, Italy

Steering Committee

Robert Buchmann	University of Cluj-Napoca, Romania
Björn Johansson	Linkoping University, Sweden (Co-Chair)
Dimitris Karagiannis	University of Vienna, Austria
Mārīte Kirikova	Riga Technical University, Latvia (Chair)
Raimundas Matulevičius	University of Tartu, Estonia
Jyrki Nummenmaa	University of Tampere, Finland
Malgorzata Pańkowska	University of Economics, Katowice, Poland
Andrea Polini	University of Camerino, Italy
Václav Řepa	Prague University of Economics and Business, Czech Republic
Kurt Sandkuhl	Rostock University, Germany
Janis Stirna	Stockholm University, Sweden
Benkt Wangler	University of Skövde, Sweden

Program Committee

Jan Aidemark	Linneaus University, Sweden
Gundars Alksnis	Riga Technical University, Latvia
Saïd Assar	Institut Mines-Telecom Business School, France
Per Backlund	University of Skövde, Sweden
Peter Bellström	Karlstad University, Sweden
Tomáš Bruckner	Prague University of Economics and Business, Czech Republic

Robert Buchmann	Babeş-Bolyai University of Cluj Napoca, Romania
Witold Chmielarz	University of Warsaw, Faculty of Management, Poland
Rebecca Deneckere	Centre de Recherche en Informatique, France
Chiara Di Francescomarino	DISI - University of Trento, Italy
Antinisca Di Marco	University of L'Aquila, Italy
Hans-Georg Fill	University of Fribourg, Switzerland
Hector Florez	Universidad Distrital Francisco Jose de Caldas, Colombia
Ana-Maria Ghiran	Babes-Bolyai University of Cluj-Napoca, Romania
Knut Hinkelmann	FHNW University of Applied Sciences and Arts Northwestern Switzerland, Switzerland
Ebba óra Hvannberg	University of Iceland, Iceland
Mojca Indihar Štemberger	University of Ljubljana, Slovenia
Mubashar Iqbal	University of Tartu, Estonia
Amin Jalali	Stockholm University, Sweden
Manfred Jeusfeld	University of Skövde, School of Informatics (IIT), Sweden
Björn Johansson	Linköping University, Sweden
Shahrzad Khayatbashi	Linköping University, Sweden
Marite Kirikova	Riga Technical University, Latvia
Janne J. Korhonen	Aalto University, Finland
John Krogstie	Norwegian University of Science and Technology, Norway
Michael Le Duc	Mälardalen University, Sweden
Moonkun Lee	Chonbuk National University, South Korea
Sotirios Liaskos	School of IT, York University, Canada
Francisco J. Lopez-Pellicer	University of Zaragoza, Spain
Audrone Lupeikiene	Vilnius University Institute of Mathematics and Informatics, Lithuania
Andreas Martin	FHNW University of Applied Sciences Northwestern Switzerland, Switzerland
Raimundas Matulevičius	University of Tartu, Estonia
Charles Møller	Aarhus University, Denmark
Andrea Morichetta	University of Camerino, Italy
Jacob Nørbjerg	Copenhagen Business School, Denmark
Jyrki Nummenmaa	Tampere University, Finland
Malgorzata Pankowska	University of Economics in Katowice, Poland
Victoria Paulsson	Linkoping, Sweden
Jens Myrup Pedersen	Aalborg University, Dept. of Electronic Systems, Denmark

Pierluigi Plebani	Politecnico di Milano, Italy
Paul Pocatilu	Bucarest University of Economic Studies, Romania
Geert Poels	Ghent University, Belgium
Andrea Polini	University of Camerino, Italy
Henderik A. Proper	TU Wien, Vienna, Austria
Manuel Renold	FHNW University of Applied Sciences and Arts Northwestern Switzerland, Switzerland
Václav Řepa	University of Economics, Prague, Czech Republic
Ben Roelens	Open Universiteit, Ghent University, Belgium
Christian Sacarea	Babes-Bolyai University, Romania
Kurt Sandkuhl	The University of Rostock, Germany
Ulf Seigerroth	Jönköping University, School of Engineering, Sweden
Manuel A. Serrano	ALARCOS Research Group. UCLM, Spain
Hanlie Smuts	University of Pretoria, South Africa
Janis Stirna	Stockholm University, Sweden
Frantisek Sudzina	Aalborg University, Denmark
Ann Svensson	University West, Sweden
Torben Tambo	Aarhus University, Denmark
Pedro Valderas	Universitat Politècnica de València, Spain
Filip Vencovský	Prague University of Economics and Business, Czech Republic
Gianluigi Viscusi	Linköping University, Sweden
Gatis Vītols	Latvia University of Life Sciences and Technologies, Latvia
Hans Weigand	Tilburg University, Netherlands
Anna Wingkvist	Linnaeus University, Sweden
Alfred Zimmermann	Reutlingen University, Germany
Iryna Zolotaryova	Simon Kuznets Kharkiv National University of Economics, Ukraine

Workshops Co-chairs

Fabrizio Fornari	University of Camerino, Italy
Raimundas Matulevičius	University of Tartu, Estonia

Doctoral Consortium Co-chairs

Robert Buchmann	University of Cluj-Napoca, Romania
Hanlie Smuts	University of Pretoria, South Africa

Hybrid AI: AI Systems that Collaborate With People Instead of Replacing Them

Frank van Harmelen
Vrije Universiteit Amsterdam

Frank van Harmelen's talk on hybrid intelligence focuses on AI systems that collaborate with people instead of replacing them. He discusses the importance of building AI systems that can adapt to changes in the team and environment by employing a "theory of mind", instill moral values, and be explainable. The talk outlines a research agenda for hybrid intelligence (which is substantially different from the research agenda for autonomous AI), presents early results from researchers worldwide into hybrid intelligence and presents a variety of use-cases for Hybrid Intelligence in different sectors of society.

AI or Not AI: From Uncertainty to Fact and the Role of Conceptual Modeling

Hans-Georg Fill
University of Fribourg, Switzerland

In many areas of science and practice, generative AI is currently regarded as a paradigm shift. This means that existing boundaries are being overthrown or must at least be reconsidered. However, this comes at the cost of uncertainty and the necessity to validate generated results. In this talk, we will analyze these developments from the perspective of business informatics and examine the implications and trade-offs. Our analysis will encompass two distinct dimensions: training and education, as well as research and product innovation, and will be conducted from the perspectives of academia and industry. By revisiting the emergence of uncertainty in the history of abstraction, we aim to identify potential anchors of stability and illustrate the potential role of conceptual modeling in this context.

Model Your Business. Architect Its Intelligence. How Enterprise Digital Twins Close the Contextual AI Gap

Christian Lichka
BOC Group, Switzerland

Organisations are facing enormous pressure to change — faster, smarter, and with fewer resources. Volatile markets, shrinking margins, ever-tightening regulation, and the disruptive force of Generative AI are reshaping industries simultaneously, leaving little room for decisions based on gut feeling or fragmented information. This is exactly where enterprise models prove their worth — and where their role is growing, not fading. A model-based Digital Twin of the Organisation — integrating Business Process Management, Enterprise Architecture, and Governance, Risk & Compliance — serves as the shared language connecting human judgment with intelligent systems, and business strategy with IT reality. Built on this foundation, organisations can move beyond static documentation: modelling the enterprise as it is, analysing the impact of change before it happens, simulating alternatives, and ultimately predicting outcomes with confidence. At the same time, AI amplifies every step — assisting in model creation, enriching context, and generating decision-relevant insight at a scale no human team could match alone. The implications for enterprise modeling are clear: Hybrid Intelligence does not emerge from AI alone — it emerges from the shared language of enterprise models, where human insight and machine reasoning find a common structure to think, decide, and transform together.

How to Combine Humans and AI Smartly

Toni Wäfler
FHNW School of Applied Psychology, University of Applied Sciences and Arts Northwestern, Switzerland

AI is changing work and hence human behavior at work. As research shows, the impact on human work behavior can be negative. For example, humans tend to accept suboptimal results from AI without critically questioning them. As they stop thinking, their own thinking skills arc no longer trained, and hence their expertise erodes. To notice this is difficult for them, since work is completed more quickly with AI and the results appear more professional. As a consequence, the subjective sense of competence increases, while the actual competence declines. At work, this causes an increase in errors. AI can also hollow jobs, i.e. erode the essence of work, as for example coders report. When AI takes over the creation of programs and humans are left only to supervise and monitor, the job loses its essence. Yet it is this essence that makes the job interesting in the first place. It involves solving novel problems and developing implementation strategies. As a result, those affected report a loss of motivation, cognitive overload, and a decline in job satisfaction. This, too, contributes to an increase in error rates. Companies must prevent such negative effects of AI if they rely on the motivation and commitment of their employees as well as on their professional expertise and practical experience. This can only be achieved if humans, technology, and organization are considered in mutual interdependencies and jointly optimized by design. For this, the School of Applied Psychology FHNW is developing criteria and methods. The keynote presentation reports from corresponding projects as e.g. AI4SME.

Contents

Short Papers

Design of Hybrid Intelligence Systems and Processes

From Human-AI Task Allocation to Accountable Process Design:
Modelling Concerns for Responsible Hybrid Intelligence

Vincent A. Balau[1], Marianne Schnellmann[1(✉)], and Henderik A. Proper[1,2]

[1] TU Wien, Vienna, Austria
marianne.schnellmann@tuwien.ac.at
[2] HU University of Applied Sciences, Utrecht, The Netherlands

Abstract. Artificial Intelligence (AI), particularly sub-symbolic AI (e.g. Large Language Models, and Generative AI), is increasingly integrated into knowledge-intensive business processes. Yet, responsible Human-AI collaboration remains insufficiently supported by enterprise and process modelling approaches. Prior work on task allocation between human and AI actors provides limited support to express ethical and governance-related concerns when both actor kinds jointly contribute to process outcomes. Building on a structured literature review, this paper derives modelling concerns for responsible hybrid intelligence in business processes. The analysis is grounded in four determinants of Human-AI task allocation: structural logic, interpretive and contextual nuance, risk and accountability, and multi-agent collaboration dynamics. From these, we derive concerns of accountability, human oversight and automation boundary, explainability, fairness, trust and competence as well as data governance and auditability. We discuss how these translate into modelling requirements for business process and enterprise modelling approaches, using BPMN and ArchiMate as examples. The paper contributes a conceptual bridge between responsible AI and process design, shifting attention from task allocation to accountable process modelling.

Keywords: Human-AI Collaboration · Task Allocation · Process Modelling

1 Introduction

Artificial Intelligence (AI), particularly sub-symbolic AI (e.g. Large Language Models, and Generative AI), is increasingly integrated into knowledge-intensive business processes. Consulting reports from e.g. the Boston Consulting Group [1] and McKinsey [20] describe AI as one of the most consequential technologies of our time. However, they also reveal a persistent gap between adoption and business value: while 60% of firms report only minimal gains and 88% report regular use, only around 6% capture meaningful enterprise value [1,20]. Existing

E. Laurenzi et al. (Eds.): BIR 2026, LNBIP 601, pp. 3–19, 2027.
https://doi.org/10.1007/978-3-032-38498-0_1

explanations attribute this gap to organisational factors such as weak leadership, fragmented implementation, or unclear transformation roadmaps.

The research reported in this paper, based on [3], addresses a more specific design problem: *before organisations can manage AI adoption, they must understand which tasks are suitable for AI.* This is particularly relevant in knowledge-intensive processes where human and AI actors contribute jointly. Organisations often lack clarity on what to delegate, what to automate or augment, and where the boundaries of responsible integration lie. Accordingly, this paper investigates how Human-AI collaboration can be structured to be effective and responsible, commonly framed through task allocation. Prior research has examined which work can be formalised, which work requires human judgement, and how risk and trust shape work distribution [4,10,12,19,23]. This literature is relevant as task allocation strongly influences process design and system requirements [11].

Nevertheless, task allocation alone does not resolve the underlying design problem: *knowing that a task should be AI-supported does not specify what must be made visible, governed, or controlled in implementation.* This limitation is most evident in knowledge work. Knowledge-intensive processes are characterised by ambiguity, contextual dependence, tacit knowledge, and interpretation rather than rule-based execution [2,8]. Hybrid Human-AI arrangements are therefore rarely reducible to substitution logic, but instead involve shifting responsibility, delegated reasoning, justified decisions, and constraints from fairness, privacy, or governance requirements.

These issues are central to responsible AI, yet not systematically reflected in enterprise and process modelling languages. Such models structure change, assign roles, communicate responsibilities, and support design decisions prior to implementation. While enterprise and process modelling languages like Business Process Model and Notation (BPMN) [15] and ArchiMate [22] can represent activities, actors, systems, and flows, they do not explicitly capture accountability, human override conditions, explainability requirements, or audit trail retention. Thus, responsible AI often remains a narrative requirement rather than a modelled design property.

In line with this, this paper focuses on the following primary research question: *Which modelling concerns should be considered when human and AI actors jointly perform knowledge-intensive business processes?* We are furthermore concerned with the questions: (1) *which concerns emerge from literature on Human-AI task allocation and responsible AI*, and (2) *how these can be translated into modelling requirements for modelling languages such as BPMN and ArchiMate.* Building on [3], we conduct a structured literature review and interpret results from a modelling perspective. The paper contributes: (1) four determinants of responsible Human-AI task allocation, (2) six modelling concerns for hybrid intelligence, and (3) implications for business process and enterprise modelling. In doing so, it shifts attention from who performs tasks to how Human-AI collaboration is represented, governed, and analysed. The remainder of this paper is organised as follows. Section 2 discusses task allocation, knowledge work, and responsible AI. Section 3 outlines the research design. Section 4 presents modelling concerns. Section 5 reflects on their implications for BPMN and ArchiMate. Finally, Sect. 6 concludes the paper and outlines future work.

2 Background

Human-AI Collaboration in Business Processes – Business Process Management (BPM) provides a starting point to analyse responsible hybrid intelligence, understood here as Human-AI collaboration under explicit accountability, oversight, and governance conditions. A business process consists of interrelated activities, events, actors, and decisions that lead to a valuable outcome [11]. Within the life cycle, task allocation belongs to process redesign. However, hybrid Human-AI arrangements challenge the assumption that tasks are assigned to single participants, since work may involve AI-generated recommendations, human verification, and subsequent execution by other actors.

The concept of *task-technology-fit* (e.g. [13]) suggests that performance depends on the fit between task demands and technological capabilities. For AI-enabled knowledge work, allocation should therefore be guided by task structure, cognitive requirements, context, and process embedding, rather than by technological availability alone, while also accounting for technical, social, and organisational requirements [12].

Research on Human-AI collaboration shows that hybrid work extends beyond substitution, covering trust and workload [10], augmented intelligence [25], cognitive function distribution [21], and multi-agent coordination [27]. A recent systematic literature review by Senjic et al. [19] similarly identifies task allocation, communication, interaction, and cognitive augmentation as interdependent enablers of Human-AI team effectiveness. Together, these works frame responsible Human-AI collaboration as a process design problem rather than a purely technical one. We build on this perspective, but shift the focus from team effectiveness to modelling concerns for process and enterprise models.

Knowledge Work, Context, and Responsible AI – Knowledge work differs from routine automation because it depends on interpretation, judgement, non-routine reasoning, tacit knowledge, unstable goals, and social or ethical nuance [2,8,17]. For AI design, this means that automation is limited not only by computational feasibility but also by contextual and normative requirements.

This challenge is reflected in task complexity, opacity, and generative AI research, which show that automation suitability, transparency, and output quality remain limited in knowledge-intensive settings [6,7,23,26].

Responsible AI literature frames these issues as governance concerns. In high-risk contexts, accountability, fairness, explainability, and human oversight become central, as risk and stakeholder harm constrain automation decisions and task complexity and opacity affect fairness [4,23]. Studies on trust calibration and deskilling further show that failures may arise from over-reliance, premature rejection, or loss of human competence [5,9,10]. Responsible Human-AI collaboration requires design choices that make such concerns visible and governable.

A Modelling Perspective on Responsible Hybrid Intelligence – From a modelling perspective, business process and enterprise models support abstraction, communication, and analysis. BPMN represents tasks, flows, events, and roles, while ArchiMate captures relations between actors, applications, information, and governance across abstraction levels.

However, these languages do not explicitly capture responsible AI concerns. They indicate roles and system support, but not whether human review is required, outputs must be explainable, decisions are fairness-sensitive, or accountability remains with a specific role. In practice, such concerns are often handled through informal annotations or external governance rather than explicit model constructs. This creates a gap between two sources of literature. Research on Human-AI task allocation and responsible AI identifies when judgement, oversight, and governance are required. Process and enterprise modelling, however, require explicit constructs for such insights to inform design. This paper addresses this gap by reinterpreting task allocation literature as a source of modelling concerns for responsible hybrid intelligence.

3 Research Design

This paper follows an exploratory, conceptual design based on a structured literature review guided by Kitchenham and Charters [14]. The aim is not to provide exhaustive coverage of all AI-related work redesign literature, but to derive modelling concerns for responsible Human-AI collaboration from research on task allocation, knowledge work, and responsible AI. Prior task-allocation research is used as an entry point and reinterpreted from a process and enterprise modelling perspective. The guiding question is not only which actor should perform a task, but what must be represented and governed when humans and AI jointly contribute to knowledge-intensive business processes.

Review Scope – To define the scope, we applied the Population, Intervention, Comparison, Outcome, and Context (PICOC) framework [16]. The *population* comprises human workers and AI agents in knowledge-intensive processes. The *intervention* refers to approaches for allocating and coordinating work between them. The *comparison* covers human-only, AI-only, and hybrid execution. The *outcomes* include principles, decision factors, and design guidance for responsible Human-AI task allocation and process redesign. The *context* consists of knowledge-intensive processes shaped by expertise, tacit knowledge, judgement, and accountability.

Search Strategy – The literature base was developed through a multi-stage search process. Firstly, an expert-guided seed paper strategy established an initial perspective on AI-enabled work redesign. Secondly, semantic discovery broadened the scope beyond citation chains and keyword searches. Thirdly, database searches were conducted in IEEE Xplore, ACM Digital Library, and the

Table 1. Search strings

IEEE Xplore:
```
((("Document Title":"Task Allocation in Human Machine" OR "Document
Title":"Task Allocation" OR "Document Title":"Process Automation" OR
"Document Title":"Workflow Automation" OR "Document
Title":"Human-machine Hybrid Augmented Intelligence")
AND
("Abstract":"AI" OR "Abstract":"artificial intelligence" OR
"Abstract":"agents" OR "Abstract":"Human Machine")
AND
("Abstract":"knowledge-intensive" OR "Abstract":"business process" OR
"Abstract":"workload" OR "Abstract":"task allocation")))
```

ACM Digital Library:
```
[[Abstract: "design guidelines"] OR [Abstract: "design principles"]
OR [[Abstract: "framework"] AND [Abstract: "conceptual model"]]] AND
[[Abstract: "artificial intelligence"] OR [Abstract: "ai"] OR
[Abstract: "generative ai"] OR [Abstract: "llm"]] AND [[Abstract:
"business process"] OR [Abstract: "knowledge work"] OR [Abstract:
"workflow management"]]
```

AIS Electronic Library:
```
("Human-AI" OR "Hybrid Intelligence") AND "Task Allocation" AND
"Business Process"
```

AIS Electronic Library. Finally, backward snowballing traced foundational concepts and relevant theoretical sources. Search strings were adapted per database; see Table 1.

Inclusion and Exclusion Criteria – The database of results was filtered using inclusion and exclusion criteria. Included papers had to be peer-reviewed journal or conference articles, written in English, and published after 2019. They also had to address at least one relevant topic, such as Human-AI task allocation, AI-supported knowledge work, responsible AI integration, process redesign, or hybrid collaboration design guidance. Papers were excluded if they focused on physical robotics, hardware, sensors, edge computing, battery optimisation, or purely technical benchmarks without transferable modelling insights.

Selection Process – Across the three databases, 115 records were identified. Titles and abstracts were screened for relevance to Human-AI task allocation, knowledge-intensive processes, responsible AI integration, and system design. Fourteen papers were selected for full-text review, of which six were retained for providing transferable concepts such as risk-informed delegation, cognitive automation suitability, task complexity, opacity, trust, or multi-agent coordination. Three additional papers from seed and semantic discovery were included to strengthen conceptual coverage. The final corpus consists of nine core papers covering risk-centred redesign, adaptive allocation, automation assessment, Human-AI coordination, task decomposition, fairness, opacity, augmented intelligence, generative AI in knowledge work, and multi-agent role allocation [4,10,12,18,21,23,25–27].

Synthesis Procedure – The selected papers were analysed using a synthesis matrix (see the appendix of [3]) and coded along six categories: task and context definition, task-related factors, human-related factors, AI/system-related factors, allocation logic, and design principles. This enabled a comparison of task suitability for AI support, human judgement, or hybrid execution. Rather than counting concept frequencies, the coding aimed to identify recurring issues relevant to Human-AI task allocation and its representation in process and enterprise models. The synthesis identified four cross-cutting determinants: task structure, contextual nuance, risk and accountability, and collaboration dynamics. These determinants were then reinterpreted from a modelling perspective by asking what each issue implies for allocation, what conventional models would leave implicit, and what must be represented to support accountability, oversight, explainability, fairness, trust calibration, competence preservation, and data governance, including auditability. This shifted the focus from task allocation as assignment to modelling concerns.

4 Results

Responsible Human-AI collaboration is not a binary choice between human and machine execution. The literature review identifies four determinants that shape task allocation and process redesign (Sect. 4.1) and, from a modelling perspective, reveal six modelling concerns (Sect. 4.2). Implications for BPMN and ArchiMate are discussed in Sect. 5.

4.1 Determinants of Responsible Human-AI Task Allocation

Structural Logic of a Task – Structural logic refers to the degree to which a task can be formalised, decomposed, and executed reliably by an AI system, depending on task complexity, cognitive requirements, agency shifts, and data conditions [12,21,23,25]. Tasks with explicit rules, stable inputs, and clearly defined outcomes are easier to automate, whereas tasks with ambiguous evidence, competing goals, contextual dependencies, or fragmented data require human involvement or hybrid forms of augmentation.

Task complexity is a central aspect of structural logic. Building on earlier task complexity theories of [7] and [24], Vimalkumar et al. [23] distinguish between five levels of increasing complexity: simple, problem, decision, judgement, and fuzzy tasks. Across this typology, increasing complexity corresponds to decreasing task determinacy. Simple and problem tasks have clearer goals and solution paths, which makes them more suitable for automation. Decision, judgement, and fuzzy tasks involve multiple possible outcomes, uncertain evidence, or evolving problem definitions. In such cases, automation cannot be treated as a purely technical question, because the system must be guided by a goal that reflects organisational priorities, stakeholder interests, or normative trade-offs.

A related perspective concerns the decomposition of tasks into cognitive functions and agency layers. Stohr and O'Rourke [21] distinguish between core cognitive functions, which are more suitable for automation because they rely on data-intensive or computational processing, and symbiotic cognitive functions, which depend on ambiguity, subjective judgement, or experience-based interpretation. Similarly, Xiang and Yu [25] distinguish between intention, reasoning, decision, and action layers. Reasoning and action layers often offer automation potential, while intention and decision layers remain sensitive because they involve goal definition, value trade-offs, and responsibility for consequential outcomes. Together, these perspectives show that task allocation should not only ask whether an entire task can be automated, but which parts can be delegated to AI, which require augmentation, and where human judgement must remain part of the process.

Finally, automation feasibility depends on the data landscape of the task. AI-supported execution is limited when relevant data is unavailable, fragmented, outdated, restricted, or difficult to represent digitally. As tasks become more complex, they often depend on unstructured information, tacit knowledge, or knowledge distributed across organisational silos [12]. This is particularly relevant in knowledge work, where much organisational data is messy or unstructured [26]. Data readiness is therefore not separate from structural logic, but part of the feasibility of AI support.

Structural logic indicates whether AI support is technically plausible, but not whether it is responsible. Even structurally simple tasks may require human control when embedded in sensitive or high-risk contexts.

Interpretive and Contextual Nuance – Interpretive and contextual nuance captures whether the relevant meaning of a task can be represented in data, including contextual understanding, tacit knowledge, social awareness, or moral judgement beyond formal task execution. In knowledge work, important aspects of a task are often implicit, unstable, or embedded in professional experience, including unspoken rules, social dynamics, emotional signals, cultural expectations, or domain-specific knowledge.

This determinant highlights the risk of contextual blindness. An AI system may identify statistical patterns in data but fail to understand their situated meaning. A task may therefore appear suitable for automation while still producing inadequate outcomes if its value depends on contextual interpretation. The Plant Jammer case analysed by Schroder et al. [18] illustrates this point: although the AI system could generate many recipe combinations, human food scientists were needed to judge whether these combinations were balanced, palatable, and meaningful for users. In this configuration, the AI contributed computational scale, while humans supplied tacit and sensory judgement.

A similar issue appears in AI-supported knowledge work. Yun et al. [26] show that generative AI can help organise large amounts of information and identify recurring topics, but may struggle with emotional nuance, personal relevance, or the situated interpretation of specific wording. For example, a human expert may recognise frustration, hesitation, or urgency in a customer transcript in ways that cannot be reduced to textual pattern recognition alone. Human involvement remains important when the quality of an outcome depends on interpretation rather than information processing alone.

Contextual nuance is also connected to goal definition and the relational setting of work. Xiang and Yu [25] argue that every task begins with an intention layer, where the goal of the task is defined. If this goal is ambiguous, changes over time, or depends on stakeholder circumstances that are not represented in the data, an AI system may optimise for the wrong objective. This is particularly relevant in knowledge work, where objectives are often shaped through interaction with clients, patients, users, or other stakeholders. In such cases, task allocation cannot be based only on whether AI can process the available data. It must also consider whether the system can respond appropriately to shifts in meaning, purpose, and context. Contextual nuance is not limited to how information is interpreted. It also includes social presence and relationship requirements, which Engel et al. [12] identify as factors that reduce the suitability of a task for cognitive automation. In domains such as consulting, healthcare, education, or public services, human interaction may itself be part of the value delivered.

Interpretive and contextual nuance serve as boundary conditions for automation. Where contextual, social, emotional, or moral understanding is central to the value or legitimacy of an outcome, AI is more appropriate as an augmenting actor than as a substitute for human judgement.

Risk and Accountability – While structural logic assesses automation feasibility and contextual nuance addresses situated meaning, risk and accountability address the consequences of failure. Even structurally simple, low-context tasks may require human oversight if errors could harm stakeholders or create legal, organisational, or ethical consequences.

Bidar et al. [4] approach task allocation from a risk-informed perspective, where risk refers to the potential harm that an AI application may cause to stakeholders. They distinguish between limited-risk tasks, whose errors are unlikely to cause direct or irreversible harm, and significant-risk tasks, which may affect stakeholders' well-being, safety, rights, or access to essential services. This distinction is particularly relevant in public-sector contexts, where affected individuals often cannot choose an alternative provider and are directly exposed to the consequences of automated decisions. The Dutch "toeslagen-affaire" illustrates how over-reliance on such decisions can create serious stakeholder harm [4].

The central implication is that the criticality of a task determines how much human control must be preserved. Full automation is more defensible when potential errors are limited and recoverable. When the risks are high, AI may still support the task, for example, by processing data or generating recommendations, but human oversight becomes necessary to preserve accountability. This applies especially to high-reliability tasks, which may not require high expertise but still involve significant risk, and to wicked tasks, which combine high expertise requirements with high stakeholder impact [4]. In both cases, allocation decisions must ensure that responsibility for the outcome can be clearly assigned.

Risk also arises from the technical properties of AI systems. Vimalkumar et al. [23] show that increasing task complexity is often associated with increasing algorithmic opacity. As tasks move from simple to fuzzy, the models required to process them may become less transparent, making it harder to reconstruct how an output was produced and whether the procedure was fair. Drawing on [6], such opacity can stem from organisational secrecy, technical complexity, or high-dimensional optimisation that exceeds human interpretability. This links complexity, opacity, and fairness. As model opacity increases, procedural fairness becomes harder to assess, while tasks with multiple possible outcomes increase the risk of biased or unequally distributed results [23]. In high-risk judgement or fuzzy tasks, hidden bias and limited explainability make full substitution problematic. Human involvement is needed not only to monitor AI outputs, but also to provide an accountable decision point.

Risk and accountability define a threshold for responsible task allocation. AI may support reasoning by identifying patterns, producing predictions, or generating recommendations. However, when decisions have legal, ethical, or social consequences, final authority should remain with a human actor or institution that can justify, contest, and take responsibility for the outcome.

Multi-agent Collaboration Dynamics – Multi-agent collaboration dynamics concern how human and AI actors interact once tasks are decomposed and distributed across several agents. In knowledge work, AI systems may generate recommendations, humans may validate or contextualise them, while other actors may execute the resulting decision. Task allocation reshapes not only task execution, but also handovers, responsibilities, and coordination within the process.

This determinant captures the collaboration overhead that emerges when several agents contribute to a shared outcome. A decomposition that appears feasible at the level of individual sub-tasks may still fail if the interaction between agents is poorly designed. Bidar et al. [4] show that AI-supported redesign can shift human roles from direct execution to supervision, validation, exception handling, or contextual interpretation, with organisational consequences beyond technical task execution.

Trust calibration is a central challenge in such arrangements. Xiang and Yu [25] identify trust as a key issue in human-machine hybrid intelligence, while Dubois and Le Ny [10] model trust as a dynamic variable that changes through interaction with AI systems. Trust influences whether human actors accept, question, ignore, or override AI outputs. Over-trust may lead to insufficient scrutiny, while under-trust may prevent useful AI support. Both undermine the intended allocation logic. Long-term reliance on AI may also lead to deskilling, where humans lose the ability to assess or take over tasks that were previously part of their expertise [26].

Coordination between agents is equally important. Human and AI actors may operate with different goals, constraints, and forms of reasoning. If responsibilities are unclear, work may be duplicated, neglected, or handed over in a form that the next actor cannot use effectively. Zhang et al. [27] show that allocation must therefore consider not only individual capabilities, but also how well agents perform together. From a process-design perspective, this makes handovers, escalation points, and responsibility boundaries central modelling concerns.

Finally, Human-AI collaboration creates privacy and data-integrity risks at the interfaces between agents. Information must move across actors, systems, and organisational boundaries, creating risks of unauthorised access, data misuse, incomplete transfer, or loss of contextual information. This is particularly relevant in knowledge work, where sub-tasks often involve sensitive client data, internal organisational knowledge, or personal information, while data required for automation may be fragmented, restricted, or poorly documented [12].

Multi-agent collaboration dynamics act as an allocation constraint in their own right. Even structurally automatable, contextually limited, and low-risk tasks may be unsuitable for hybrid execution if they create excessive coordination costs, weak accountability boundaries, trust issues, or data-interface risks.

4.2 Derived Modelling Concerns

Building on the four identified determinants, we derive six modelling concerns that process and enterprise models should make explicit for responsible hybrid intelligence. The synthesis translates these determinants into modelling needs: structural logic and contextual nuance point to explainability and fairness, especially where complexity and limited transparency are involved; risk and accountability point to accountability and human oversight; collaboration dynamics point to trust calibration and competence preservation; and data conditions point to data governance and auditability. Table 2 summarises these concerns, their rationale, and their modelling implications.

Accountability and Human Oversight – Accountability and human oversight arise primarily from the risk and accountability determinant. High-risk tasks constrain what can responsibly be delegated to AI, even when parts of the reasoning are technically automatable [4]. For modelling, it is therefore not sufficient to show that a human actor is involved in the process. Models should indicate where responsibility is anchored, who may accept or reject AI-supported outcomes, and when escalation or override is required. This distinction is important because "human-in-the-loop" is often treated as a generic safeguard, even though monitoring, validating, approving, and deciding imply distinct accountability structures.

Table 2. Derived modelling concerns for responsible hybrid intelligence

Concern	Rationale	Modelling implication
Accountability	AI-supported outcomes require assigned answerability, especially in high-risk contexts.	Represent the role accountable for accepting, rejecting, or justifying outcomes.
Oversight and automation boundary	Human review, approval, or override may be required despite AI-supported reasoning.	Distinguish automated tasks, AI recommendations, approvals, escalation, and override paths.
Explainability	Human validation requires understandable and evidence-linked AI outputs.	Indicate required rationale, confidence information, evidence, or alternatives.
Fairness	Limited transparency may hide bias or unequal treatment.	Mark fairness-sensitive decisions and attach monitoring, review, or audit requirements.
Trust and competence preservation	Hybrid work may fail through over-reliance, under-reliance, or deskilling.	Identify tasks requiring active human engagement, manual checks, or competence retention.
Data governance and auditability	AI-supported work depends on legitimate data use and traceability.	Represent restricted data flows, access controls, logs, and retained decision traces.

Explainability and Fairness – Explainability and fairness emerge from the interaction between structural complexity, algorithmic opacity, and risk [6,23]. Where humans validate AI recommendations, models should indicate required rationale, confidence information, evidence, or alternatives. Without such information, human oversight may be formally present but practically ineffective. Fairness-sensitive decision points should likewise be made visible, especially where AI-supported decisions may systematically affect stakeholder groups. Modelling fairness does not mean reducing it to a technical metric, but identifying where bias monitoring, review, audit, or contestability mechanisms are required.

Trust Calibration and Competence Preservation – Trust calibration and competence preservation stem from multi-agent collaboration dynamics. Hybrid Human-AI work may fail through over-reliance, where users accept AI outputs uncritically, or under-reliance, where useful AI support is rejected [5,10]. Models should indicate where AI outputs may be accepted, actively reviewed, or handed over between human and AI actors. Trust is dynamic and changes through experience with AI behaviour. Long-term automation may additionally weaken the human ability to verify, recover, or take over tasks [9]. For this reason, models should make visible where active human engagement, periodic manual checks, or competence retention are necessary.

Data Governance and Auditability – Data governance and auditability concern the data conditions and traces required for responsible AI-supported work. Hybrid Human-AI processes require information to move across actors, systems, and organisational boundaries, creating privacy, integrity, and compliance challenges [12,25,26]. In high-risk settings, organisations may need to reconstruct which data was used, which recommendation was generated, who reviewed it, and what final decision was taken. Models should go beyond ordinary data flows by representing access controls, logging obligations, retained decision traces, and audit-relevant evidence.

Together, these concerns answer the research question by identifying modelling-relevant properties that emerge from Human-AI task allocation and responsible AI literature. Responsible hybrid intelligence requires models to represent not only task execution but also the conditions that make Human-AI collaboration accountable, explainable, fair, governable, and auditable. This includes making explicit who is accountable, where human control is required, what explanations are needed, where fairness must be monitored, how trust and competence are preserved, and how data use remains traceable.

5 Discussion

The six modelling concerns can be translated into three broader modelling requirements for business process and enterprise modelling approaches, such as BPMN and ArchiMate. While the concerns identify what must be considered in responsible Human-AI collaboration, the modelling requirements describe what a modelling approach should be able to make explicit. These requirements are: (R1) representing allocation and control explicitly, (R2) representing evaluation and justification conditions, and (R3) representing sustaining and governance conditions. For each requirement, BPMN and ArchiMate offer complementary modelling possibilities.

R1: Represent Allocation and Control Explicitly. The first modelling requirement concerns the explicit representation of task allocation, accountability, and human oversight. A hybrid process model should not merely show that a human and an AI system are both involved in a process. It should indicate which parts of the process are automated, where human intervention is required, who has the authority to accept or reject an AI-supported outcome, and where escalation or override paths exist.

In BPMN, this can be implemented by distinguishing between service tasks for AI-based execution, user tasks for human review or approval, and gateways or escalation events for cases that require manual intervention. Lanes can be used to separate human actors, AI services, and organisational roles. Boundary events, escalation events, and alternative paths can serve as override mechanisms or require mandatory human intervention. Annotations or task markers can further indicate whether a task is fully automated, AI-supported, or human-controlled.

In ArchiMate, the same requirement can be represented by linking business roles, business processes, application services, and governance responsibilities. For example, an AI scoring function can be modelled as an application service used by a business process, while the accountable case officer is represented as a business role assigned to the final decision. Requirements or constraints can specify that certain decisions must remain under human authority. This makes the automation boundary visible not only at the task level but also at the enterprise responsibility level.

R2: Represent Evaluation and Justification Conditions. The second modelling requirement concerns the conditions under which AI outputs can be evaluated, justified, and challenged. This requirement follows from the concerns of explainability and fairness. When humans are expected to validate AI recommendations, the model should indicate which kind of explanation, evidence, or monitoring is required for that validation to be meaningful.

In BPMN, this can be implemented by attaching data objects, annotations, or additional review tasks to AI-supported activities. For example, an AI recommendation task may produce not only a recommendation, but also a confidence score, rationale, supporting evidence, or a list of alternative options. A following human review task can then be modelled as depending on these outputs. Fairness-sensitive decision points can be marked through annotations, groups, or explicit monitoring tasks. When bias checks are required, the process may include a separate audit or review before the final decision is made.

In ArchiMate, explainability and fairness can be represented through requirements, principles, constraints, assessments, and stakeholder concerns. An AI application service may be linked to a requirement such as "provide interpretable rationale" or "enable contestability of automated recommendations". Fairness-sensitive decisions can be connected to stakeholder groups, governance principles, and compliance requirements. This allows explainability and fairness to be modelled as situated obligations attached to specific services, decisions, or information objects, rather than as abstract properties of the AI system as a whole.

R3: Represent Sustaining and Governance Conditions. The third modelling requirement concerns the long-term sustainability and governability of hybrid Human-AI collaboration. This includes trust calibration, competence preservation, data governance, and auditability. A responsible model should make visible whether human oversight can remain effective over time, whether relevant human competences are preserved, how sensitive data flows through the process, and how contested decisions can later be reconstructed.

In BPMN, this can be implemented by modelling forced review points, periodic manual execution, competence-retention tasks, logging activities, restricted data flows, and audit-relevant events. For example, a process may include a mandatory human review for a sample of otherwise automated cases to prevent over-reliance and preserve human judgement. Decision traces can be represented through data objects or data stores that capture the AI recommendation, the explanation provided, the human decision, and the final action taken. Data access restrictions can be indicated through annotations, message flows, or separate subprocesses for data validation and logging.

In ArchiMate, this requirement can be represented by connecting business roles, capabilities, application components, data objects, access constraints, and governance principles. Human competence preservation can be modelled through capabilities, roles, and training-related requirements. Data governance can be represented by linking information objects to application components, access constraints, and compliance requirements. Auditability can be modelled by relating decision records, application services, business processes, and governance roles. This enterprise-level view is important because responsible hybrid intelligence depends not only on the execution of individual process steps, but also on organisational capabilities, data governance, and compliance structures.

Together, these three modelling requirements show how the six concerns can be translated into modelling practice. BPMN is particularly useful for representing the operational execution of hybrid work: which activities are automated, where human intervention occurs, what evidence is required for review, and how exceptions or escalations are handled. ArchiMate is better suited to representing the enterprise context in which this process is embedded: which roles are accountable, which AI services are used, which information objects are accessed, which capabilities are required, and which governance constraints apply. The point is not that every concern must be encoded in one notation in the same way. Rather, responsible hybrid intelligence requires that these concerns be made explicit within the modelling environment.

To illustrate how the three requirements work together, consider an AI-supported public-service eligibility assessment. A conventional process model may show application intake, AI-based scoring, human review, final approval, and notification. A responsible hybrid process model would additionally mark the scoring task as AI-supported, assign final accountability to the case officer, require explanations for contested recommendations, provide override paths, identify fairness-sensitive decisions, and retain decision traces for audit. At the enterprise level, the same case could link the accountable role, the AI application service, the relevant information objects, the fairness principle, and the audit requirement.

This translation from concerns to modelling requirements clarifies the paper's contribution. The literature on Human-AI task allocation primarily asks which actor should perform which type of work and under which conditions. This paper argues that such allocation decisions imply a second-order modelling problem: once a hybrid configuration is selected, process and enterprise models must reflect the governance properties that make this configuration accountable, understandable, and auditable.

6 Conclusion

This paper has developed a conceptual foundation for modelling responsible hybrid Human-AI collaboration in knowledge-intensive business processes. Rather than proposing a complete modelling language extension, it identifies modelling concerns that can inform future extensions, viewpoints, and analysis mechanisms for approaches such as BPMN and ArchiMate. The central implication is that responsible AI integration should be reflected already at the modelling stage, not only during implementation or post-hoc governance.

The paper contributes a three-step conceptual bridge: four determinants explain what shapes responsible Human-AI task allocation, six modelling concerns identify what must be made explicit, and three modelling requirements indicate how process and enterprise modelling approaches should support such representation. This shifts attention from task allocation as a question of who performs work to process design as a question of how Human-AI collaboration can be represented, governed, and analysed.

The study has several limitations. First, it is conceptual and literature-based. The proposed concerns were derived from a selected set of literature sources and have not yet been empirically validated with practitioners. Second, the framework remains notation-agnostic. Although BPMN and ArchiMate were discussed as relevant modelling approaches, no formal metamodel, syntax extension, or tool implementation is provided. Third, the underlying literature focuses mainly on bounded forms of AI-supported work, while emerging agentic systems may introduce more dynamic forms of task allocation, process adaptation, and decision autonomy.

Future work should focus on operationalising the proposed concerns. A first step would be to develop concrete modelling constructs, annotations, or viewpoints for BPMN and ArchiMate. A second step would be to evaluate these constructs empirically through expert interviews, modelling workshops, or case studies. Finally, future research could develop analysis mechanisms that detect missing accountability, insufficient explainability, unmarked fairness-sensitive decisions, or weak auditability in hybrid Human-AI process models.

References

1. Apotheker, J., et al.: The Widening AI Value Gap: Build for the Future 2025. Global study, Boston Consulting Group (2025). Accessed 29 Mar 2026. https://media-publications.bcg.com/The-Widening-AI-Value-Gap-Sept-2025.pdf
2. Autor, D.: Polanyi's Paradox and the Shape of Employment Growth. Working Paper 20485, National Bureau of Economic Research (2014). https://doi.org/10.3386/w20485

3. Balau, V.A.: Balancing the workload between digital and human actors in Knowledge Work. Bachelor's thesis, TU Wien, Vienna, Austria (2026). https://doi.org/10.5281/zenodo.20051128
4. Bidar, R., Someh, I., Rinta-Kahila, T., Williams, K., Indulska, M., Ryan, I.: Redesigning Work with Artificial Intelligence. Technical report, The University of Queensland; SAP Institute for Digital Government, Brisbane, Australia; Canberra, Australia (2023). https://doi.org/10.14264/6428cca
5. Buçinca, Z., Malaya, M.B., Gajos, K.: To trust or to think: cognitive forcing functions can reduce overreliance on AI in AI-assisted decision-making. Proc. ACM Hum.-Comput. Interact. **5**(CSCW1) 188, 1–21 (2021). https://doi.org/10.1145/3449287
6. Burrell, J.: How the machine 'thinks': understanding opacity in machine learning algorithms. Big Data Soc. **3**(1), 205395171562251 (2016). https://doi.org/10.1177/2053951715622512
7. Campbell, D.J.: Task complexity: a review and analysis. Acad. Manag. Rev. **13**(1), 40–52 (1988). https://doi.org/10.5465/amr.1988.4306775
8. Coombs, C.R., Hislop, D., Taneva, S.K., Barnard, S.: The strategic impacts of Intelligent Automation for knowledge and service work: an interdisciplinary review. J. Strat. Inf. Syst. **29**(4), 101600 (2020). https://doi.org/10.1016/j.jsis.2020.101600
9. Crowston, K., Bolici, F.: Deskilling and upskilling with AI systems. Inf. Res. Int. Electron. J. **30**(iConf), 1009–1023 (2025). https://doi.org/10.47989/ir30iconf47143
10. Dubois, C., Le Ny, J.: Adaptive task allocation in human-machine teams with trust and workload cognitive models. In: 2020 IEEE International Conference on Systems, Man, and Cybernetics, SMC 2020, Toronto, ON, Canada, 11–14 October 2020, pp. 3241–3246, IEEE (2020). ISBN 978-1-7281-8526-2. https://doi.org/10.1109/SMC42975.2020.9283461
11. Dumas, M., La Rosa, M., Mendling, J., Reijers, H.A.: Fundamentals of Business Process Management, 2nd edn. Springer, Berlin (2018). ISBN 978-3-662-56509-4. https://doi.org/10.1007/978-3-662-56509-4
12. Engel, C., Elshan, E., Ebel, P., Leimeister, J.M.: Stairway to heaven or highway to hell: a model for assessing cognitive automation use cases. J. Inf. Technol. **39**(1), 94–122 (2024). https://doi.org/10.1177/02683962231185599
13. Goodhue, D., Thompson, R.L.: Task-technology fit and individual performance. MIS Q. **19**(2), 213–236 (1995). https://doi.org/10.2307/249689
14. Kitchenham, B.A., Charters, S.: Guidelines for performing systematic literature reviews in software engineering. Technical Report. EBSE 2007-001, Keele University and Durham University Joint Report (2007). Accessed 20 Dec 2007. http://www.dur.ac.uk/ebse/resources/Systematic-reviews-5-8.pdf
15. OMG: Business process model and notation (BPMN), Version 2.0. Technical report, Object Management Group, Needham, Massachusetts, USA (2011). Accessed 11 June 2026. http://www.omg.org/spec/BPMN/2.0/
16. Petticrew, M., Roberts, H.: Systematic Reviews in the Social Sciences: A Practical Guide. Blackwell Publishing, Oxford (2006). https://doi.org/10.1002/9780470754887
17. Polanyi, M.: Personal Knowledge: Towards a Post-Critical Philosophy. University of Chicago Press, Chicago (1958)
18. Schroder, A., Constantiou, I.D., Tuunainen, V.K., Austin, R.D.: Human-AI collaboration – coordinating automation and augmentation tasks in a digital service company. In: 55th Hawaii International Conference on System Sciences, HICSS 2022, Virtual Event/Maui, Hawaii, USA, 4–7 January 2022, pp. 1–10. ScholarSpace (2022). https://doi.org/10125/79355

19. Senjic, P., Bitsch, G., Braun, A.: Enabling complexity: a systematic literature review on task allocation, communication, interaction, and augmentation in human-AI teams. In: Longo, F., Solina, V., Francalanza, E. (eds.) Proceedings of the 7th International Conference on Industry of the Future and Smart Manufacturing (ISM 2025), La Valletta, Malta, 12–14 November 2025, Procedia Computer Science, vol. 277, pp. 2135–2144. Elsevier, Amsterdam (2026). https://doi.org/10.1016/j.procs.2026.02.251
20. Singla, A., Sukharevsky, A., Hall, B., Yee, L., Chui, M., Balakrishnan, T.: The State of AI in 2025: Agents, Innovation, and Transformation. Technical report, McKinsey & Company (2025). Accessed 29 Mar 2026. https://www.mckinsey.com/~/media/mckinsey/business%20functions/quantumblack/our%20insights/the%20state%20of%20ai/november%202025/the-state-of-ai-2025-agents-innovation_cmyk-v1.pdf
21. Stohr, A., O'Rourke, J.: Through the cognitive functions lens - a socio-technical analysis of predictive maintenance. In: Ahlemann, F., Schütte, R., Stieglitz, S. (eds.) WI 2021. LNISO, vol. 47, pp. 182–197. Springer, Cham (2021). https://doi.org/10.1007/978-3-030-86797-3_13
22. The Open Group: ArchiMate 3.2 Specification. Van Haren, Zaltbommel, The Netherlands (2023). ISBN 1-957866-02-4
23. Vimalkumar, M., Gupta, A., Sharma, D., Dwivedi, Y.K.: Understanding the effect that task complexity has on automation potential and opacity: implications for algorithmic fairness. AIS Trans. Human-Comput. Interact. **13**(1), 104–129 (2021). https://doi.org/10.17705/1thci.00144
24. Wood, R.E.: Task complexity: definition of the construct. Organizat. Behav. Human Decis. Processes **37**(1), 60–82 (1986). https://doi.org/10.1016/0749-5978(86)90044-0
25. Xiang, C.G., Yu, Z.: Human-machine hybrid augmented intelligence: human-machine relationship, collaboration and mutual enhancement. In: Proceedings of the 2023 China Automation Congress (CAC), Wuhan, China (2023). https://doi.org/10.1109/CAC59555.2023.10451218
26. Yun, B., Feng, D., Chen, A.S., Nikzad, A., Salehi, N.: Generative AI in knowledge work: design implications for data navigation and decision-making. In: Yamashita, N., et al. (eds.) Proceedings of the 2025 CHI Conference on Human Factors in Computing Systems, CHI 2025, Yokohama, Japan, 26 April–1 May 2025, pp. 634:1–19, ACM, New York City (2025). ISBN 979-8-4007-1394-1. https://doi.org/10.1145/3706598.3713337
27. Zhang, X., Zhu, Z., Li, Y., Zhu, H., Sun, Y., Zhou, X.: Role-based human-machine collaboration task-allocation strategy in multiagent environment. IEEE Trans. Human-Mach. Syst. **55**(5), 799–808 (2025). https://doi.org/10.1109/THMS.2025.3591603

Automation-Induced Complacency as a Dual Suppressor of Hybrid Intelligence: Evidence from GenAI Literacy and Critical AI Evaluation Among Citizen Developers

Silvio Menezes[1](✉) and Karla Menezes[2]

[1] Instituto Português de Administração de Marketing, IPAM Lisboa, Lisboa, Portugal
silvio.menezes@universidadeeuropeia.pt

[2] Polytechnic University of Setúbal, School of Business and Administration, 2914-503 Setúbal, Portugal
karla.menezes@esce.ips.pt

Abstract. Hybrid Intelligence (HI) depends on humans who can engage AI systems critically, not merely fluently. This paper addresses whether automation-induced complacency, the tendency to accept AI outputs uncritically, undermines HI at its foundation by suppressing the very competencies, GenAI literacy and critical AI evaluation, that HI requires, rather than only degrading interaction outcomes. This gap matters for business informatics because current IS alignment and training strategies assume literacy growth is sufficient for effective human-AI collaboration; if complacency instead erodes literacy itself, that assumption fails. Drawing on a field study of 108 individuals engaged in sustained human-GenAI interaction over 14 weeks as citizen developers, we test five hypotheses linking complacency, GenAI literacy, critical AI evaluation, and data literacy self-efficacy (DLSE). Complacency is negatively associated with both GenAI literacy and critical AI use, and its effect on analytical self-efficacy is partly transmitted through reduced literacy (29.8% of the total effect), supporting a cascade suppression mechanism. Notably, GenAI literacy is not significantly associated with critical evaluation, suggesting that functional competence and critical judgment may develop as separable capacities. These findings reframe complacency as a competency-development risk, not only a performance risk, with direct implications for how HI systems, IS alignment strategies, and citizen-developer training should be designed to explicitly cultivate critical evaluation rather than assume it follows from functional fluency.

Keywords: Hybrid intelligence · Automation-induced complacency · GenAI literacy · Critical AI evaluation · Data self-efficacy

1 Introduction

Hybrid Intelligence (HI), the seamless integration of human expertise and intelligent information systems, has emerged as a central paradigm for business informatics research [1]. Effective HI requires not only capable AI systems but humans who can engage with

E. Laurenzi et al. (Eds.): BIR 2026, LNBIP 601, pp. 20–29, 2027.
https://doi.org/10.1007/978-3-032-38498-0_2

them critically, calibrate their trust appropriately, and leverage AI outputs for superior decision-making. Yet a fundamental risk threatens this human side of the equation: automation-induced complacency.

Automation-induced complacency, the tendency to uncritically accept AI-generated outputs and delegate cognitive effort to automated systems, has long been identified as a risk in human-automation interaction [2, 3]. With the proliferation of generative AI (GenAI) tools across professional domains, this risk extends beyond safety-critical systems into everyday knowledge work, IS use, and business decision support. In the context of hybrid intelligence, where humans and AI systems are expected to complement each other's strengths, complacency may undermine the human component of HI, reducing the very literacy and critical capacity that makes human-AI collaboration effective.

This paper addresses a critical empirical gap: does automation-induced complacency suppress not only the outcomes of human-AI interaction, such as analytical self-efficacy [4], but also the competencies that enable effective HI, namely GenAI literacy [5] and critical AI evaluation [6]? We investigate this through a field study in which 108 individuals engaged in sustained human-GenAI interaction over 14 weeks, creating approximately 572 functional IS prototypes as citizen developers [7, 8], a naturalistic HI setting where humans leverage GenAI to perform IS tasks traditionally requiring enterprise systems.

We make three contributions to HI and business informatics research. First, we provide the first empirical evidence that automation-induced complacency is negatively associated with GenAI literacy, revealing a cascade suppression mechanism that directly threatens HI capability. Second, bootstrapped mediation demonstrates that 29.8% of complacency's effect on analytical self-efficacy is transmitted through reduced GenAI literacy, quantifying the potential HI capability cost of complacency. Third, the findings suggest that GenAI literacy and critical AI evaluation may represent distinct competencies, with direct implications for HI system design and IS alignment. RQ: Does automation-induced complacency suppress not only interaction outcomes but the GenAI literacy and critical evaluation competencies that HI itself requires? Sect. 2 reviews HI, complacency, and literacy research; Sect. 3 develops the five hypotheses tested; Sect. 4 describes the citizen-developer field setting and measures; Sect. 5 reports the hypothesis tests that directly answer this question; Sect. 6 discusses implications for HI system design and IS alignment; Sect. 7 concludes.

2 Theoretical Background

2.1 Hybrid Intelligence, Human-AI Interaction, and the Citizen Developer Context

Hybrid Intelligence systems are designed to leverage the complementary strengths of human and artificial intelligence [1]. In business informatics, HI manifests in ERP, CRM, SCM and decision support contexts where AI augments human analytical capacity, and success depends on how well human and AI contributions are combined for a given task [22]. Effective HI requires humans who can formulate appropriate AI queries, critically evaluate AI outputs, and integrate AI-generated insights with contextual business knowledge; the human component of HI, AI literacy, critical evaluation, and analytical confidence, is a first-order research concern for business informatics [9]. The citizen developer, a non-technical professional creating functional applications using low-code/no-code and GenAI tools [7, 8], provides a naturalistic setting for this research: iterative prompt formulation, output evaluation, and IS prototype refinement mirror the human component requirements of broader HI systems in business [16, 17], making citizen developer settings ecologically valid for studying HI capability formation and the risks that undermine it.

2.2 Automation-induced Complacency as an HI Risk

Automation-induced complacency, originally documented in aviation and process control [2], refers to the tendency to over-rely on automated systems, accepting their outputs without critical scrutiny. Merritt et al. [3] validated the Complacency Potential Rating Scale (CPRS), establishing complacency as a stable individual trait predicting unsafe cognitive delegation. Dual Process Theory [10] provides the mechanism: complacency activates fast, heuristic System 1 processing, suppressing the slow, analytical System 2 engagement necessary for critical evaluation. In HI contexts, complacency manifests as uncritical acceptance of AI-generated outputs, failure to cross-check recommendations, and progressive delegation of reasoning to the system. Cognitive Load Theory [11] predicts that such offloading prevents the formation of internal cognitive schemas, including the literacy schemas that constitute the human component of HI.

2.3 GenAI Literacy and Critical AI Evaluation

AI literacy has been conceptualised as a multidimensional competency encompassing understanding, using, evaluating and creating with AI systems [12, 13]. The GAILS instrument [5] operationalises GenAI literacy through prompt optimisation, output evaluation, and critical calibration. A theoretically critical distinction exists between functional GenAI competence, formulating effective prompts and interacting with AI tools, and critical AI evaluation, systematically questioning outputs, cross-checking with alternative sources, and calibrating trust by task [6]. Whether these develop together or independently in HI contexts is an open empirical question with direct implications for HI system design.

2.4 Data Literacy Self-Efficacy as an HI Outcome

DLSE, the confidence to identify, evaluate, and interpret data, has been validated as a key IS competency outcome grounded in Social Cognitive Theory [4, 14]. In HI contexts, it represents the human analytical confidence that enables effective use of AI-generated insights, a core capability for business IS alignment [15].

3 Research Model and Hypotheses

The research model positions automation-induced complacency as a dual suppressor of HI capability: directly inhibiting GenAI literacy and critical AI evaluation, and indirectly reducing DLSE through literacy suppression. The model integrates Cognitive

Load Theory [11], Dual Process Theory [10], and Social Cognitive Theory [14] within an HI capability framework. Five hypotheses are derived and the model is presented in Fig. 1:

H1: Automation-induced complacency is negatively associated with GenAI literacy.
H2: Automation-induced complacency is negatively associated with critical AI use.
H3: GenAI literacy is positively associated with critical AI use.
H4: GenAI literacy mediates the relationship between automation-induced complacency and DLSE.
H5: DLSE is positively associated with critical AI use.

H1 and H2 derive from Cognitive Load Theory: complacent individuals who offload reasoning to AI develop fewer internal schemas, reducing both functional literacy and critical evaluation capacity. H3 tests whether functional and critical capacities co-develop in HI contexts. H4 tests the cascade mechanism: complacency → reduced literacy → reduced analytical self-efficacy. H5 tests whether analytical confidence enables critical AI engagement.

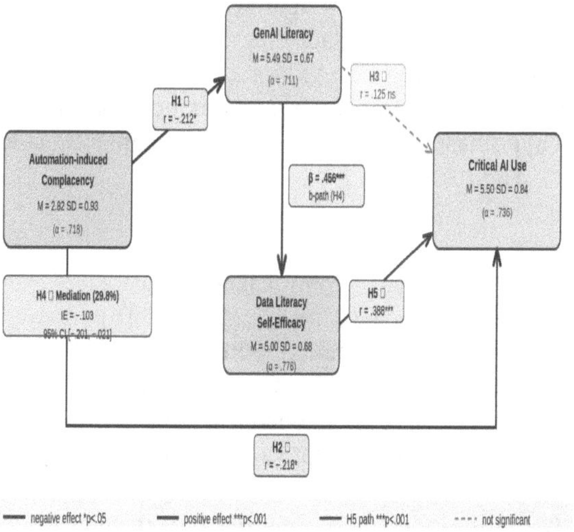

Fig. 1. Research model. Automation-induced complacency as dual suppressor of GenAI literacy (H1) and critical AI use (H2). H4: GenAI literacy mediates complacency → data SE (IE = −.103, 95% CI [−.201, −.021]). H3 not supported. Dashed = not significant. $^{*}p < .05$; $^{***}p < .001$.

4 Methodology

4.1 Field Setting and HI Context

The study was conducted in an applied IS course at a Portuguese higher education institution. Over 14 weeks, participants used GenAI tools (V0 Vercel, Replit, Lovable) to create approximately 572 functional IS interface prototypes, operational, analytical, and decision-support, using real business datasets and iteratively refined prompts. This citizen developer setting was adopted because institutional access to enterprise systems (ERP, CRM, SCM) was unavailable; GenAI prototyping provided a naturalistic HI environment for studying sustained human-GenAI interaction. The inverted activity model, artefact first, analysis second, theory third, follows Experiential Learning Theory [17].

4.2 Sample and Procedure

A post-experience cross-sectional survey was administered at semester end. Of 118 responses, 108 were retained after excluding 10 that failed an embedded attention check (exclusion rate 8.5%). Sample: four groups (n = 30, 31, 27, 20); 81% aged 18–23; 80% reported daily or weekly prior AI use; self-reported digital proficiency M = 4.48, SD = 0.88 (1–7 scale). According to institutional enrolment records for the four groups, gender composition was 60.6% male and 39.4% female (course-level data, not linked to individual survey responses, preserving respondent anonymity); all participants were enrolled in Management (Gestão) undergraduate degree programmes, yielding a disciplinarily homogeneous, single-domain sample. Participation was voluntary and anonymous. The instructor-researcher role constitutes a potential conflict of interest, acknowledged as a limitation. Note on data reuse: the dataset was originally collected for a companion study (under review) examining GenAI literacy as a predictor of DLSE. The present paper applies a distinct theoretical framework, automation complacency as HI capability suppressor, and tests hypotheses not examined in the companion study.

4.3 Measures

All constructs were measured on 7-point Likert scales (1 = strongly disagree, 7 = strongly agree). GenAI Literacy (4 items): GAILS [5] (α = .711, CR = .827). Automation-induced Complacency (4 items): CPRS [3] (α = .718, CR = .832). Critical AI Use (4 items): Lee and See [6] (α = .736, CR = .836). Data Literacy Self-Efficacy (4 items): DLSES [4] (α = .776, CR = .856). Discriminant validity: HTMT [18] maximum = 0.683, below 0.85 threshold, discriminant validity supported across all construct pairs.

Table 1. Construct descriptive statistics and reliability (n = 108).

Construct	M	SD	α	CR
GenAI Literacy	5.49	0.67	.711	.827
Automation-ind. Complacency	2.82	0.93	.718	.832
Critical AI Use	5.50	0.84	.736	.836
DLSE	5.00	0.68	.776	.856
HTMT max = 0.683 (below 0.85 threshold)				

5 Results

5.1 Descriptive Statistics

Participants reported high GenAI literacy ($M = 5.49$, $SD = 0.67$) and critical AI use ($M = 5.50$, $SD = 0.84$), moderate-to-high DLSE ($M = 5.00$, $SD = 0.68$), and low automation-induced complacency ($M = 2.82$, $SD = 0.93$). The low complacency mean indicates participants did not perceive themselves as uncritical AI users, though variance was sufficient to detect its effects. Table 1 presents full descriptive statistics.

5.2 Hypothesis Testing

Table 2 presents results. H1 was supported: complacency is negatively associated with GenAI literacy ($r = -.212$, $p = .027$), the first empirical demonstration of this HI capability risk. H2 was supported: complacency is negatively associated with critical AI use ($r = -.218$, $p = .023$). H3 was not supported: GenAI literacy is not significantly associated with critical AI use ($r = .125$, $p = .197$), suggesting that functional and critical capacities may be empirically separable, an important consideration for HI design. H5 was supported: DLSE is positively associated with critical AI use ($r = .388$, $p < .001$).

Table 2. Hypothesis testing results.

Hyp	Path	r/IE	p/95% CI	Result
H1	Complacency → GenAI Literacy	− .212	p = .027	Supported *
H2	Complacency → Critical AI Use	− .218	p = .023	Supported *
H3	GenAI Literacy → Critical AI Use	+ .125	p = .197	Not supported
H4	Mediation GenAI (Comp → DLSE)	IE = − .103	CI[−.201, − .021]	Supported ***
H5	DLSE → Critical AI Use	+ .388	p < .001	Supported ***
—	GenAI Literacy → DLSE	+ .522	p < .001	Reference path

5.3 Bootstrapped Mediation (H4)

Bootstrapped mediation (5,000 resamples) confirmed H4. The a-path (complacency → GenAI literacy, $r = -.212$, $p = .027$) and b-path (GenAI literacy → data SE controlling complacency, $\beta = .456$, $p < .001$) were both significant. Indirect effect: $IE = -.103$, 95% CI [−.201, − .021], excluding zero, confirming significant mediation. GenAI literacy mediates 29.8% of complacency's total effect on DLSE. The mediation results support the proposed cascade mechanism: higher complacency is associated with lower GenAI literacy, which in turn is associated with lower analytical self-efficacy, quantifying the potential HI capability cost of complacency.

6 Discussion

6.1 Complacency as an HI Capability Risk, The Cascade Mechanism

The most novel finding is H1 ($r = -.212$, $p = .027$): automation-induced complacency is negatively associated with GenAI literacy. Combined with H4 (29.8% bootstrapped mediation), this reveals that complacency undermines HI capability through a cascade: complacent individuals who accept AI outputs without critical engagement develop diminished GenAI literacy, which in turn reduces DLSE. Consistent with Cognitive Load Theory [11], offloading cognitive effort to AI prevents formation of the internal schemas that constitute literacy itself. For business informatics, this has a direct implication: complacency is not merely a performance risk in HI systems, it is a competency development risk that degrades the human component of hybrid intelligence over time.

6.2 Separability of Functional Competence and Critical Evaluation

The non-significant H3 ($r = .125$, ns) is the most significant finding for HI system design. Higher self-reported GenAI literacy was not significantly associated with stronger critical evaluation behaviours in this sample. Functional AI literacy and critical AI evaluation may be distinct capacities with different developmental antecedents; this is consistent with evidence that different styles of GenAI use produce divergent learning outcomes even under similar task exposure [21]. This implies that HI systems and IS alignment strategies focused exclusively on functional proficiency, teaching users to prompt effectively, without cultivating critical evaluation will produce technically capable but analytically dependent human partners, amplifying rather than counteracting complacency effects.

6.3 Data Self-Efficacy as an Enabler of Critical AI Engagement

H5 ($r = .388$, $p < .001$) suggests analytical self-confidence facilitates critical AI engagement. Individuals who trust their own data analytical capacity are more likely to compare AI outputs with alternative sources. For HI design, this implies that building DLSE, through applied dataset work, iterative IS prototyping, and analytical practice, may be an indirect pathway to developing critical AI evaluation, even when direct literacy training does not achieve this.

6.4 Implications for Business Informatics and IS Alignment

Four concrete implications follow for designing and deploying GenAI-powered HI systems. First, HI capability assessments should screen for complacency potential alongside GenAI literacy: since the two are negatively correlated ($r = -.212$), and complacency alone is directly associated with reduced critical AI use (H2) while GenAI literacy alone is not (H3, ns), literacy scores overstate readiness for HI roles, and organisations risk deploying functionally fluent but analytically complacent users into decision-support contexts. Second, IS alignment for ERP, CRM, and SCM environments that embed GenAI copilots should build complacency-mitigating interaction design into the system itself, such as mandatory justification prompts before accepting AI recommendations, confidence-calibrated flags when an output diverges from historical baselines, and periodic trust audits in which users justify recent AI-assisted decisions to a supervisor or peer. Third, because the findings suggest that functional competence and critical evaluation may be empirically distinct capacities (H3, ns), citizen-developer and low-code training programmes cannot assume that teaching prompt fluency will produce critical evaluators; curricula should explicitly scaffold critical evaluation as a distinct competency, for example through structured exercises requiring users to identify AI errors, compare outputs against alternative sources, and document why an output was accepted or rejected. Fourth, the cascade mechanism identified in H4 suggests that literacy-building interventions have indirect protective value for analytical self-efficacy: IS training that strengthens GenAI literacy may partially buffer users against the erosive effect of complacency on downstream data confidence, making literacy training a leverage point even where complacency itself is difficult to intervene on directly.

6.5 Limitations

Key limitations: (1) cross-sectional design prevents causal inference; (2) single-institution sample limits generalisability; (3) all constructs are self-reported, raising common method bias concerns and a more specific validity risk: self-assessed competence may not track actual competence, and individuals with lower actual critical-AI-use skill may systematically overrate it (a Dunning-Kruger-type pattern), which could attenuate or distort the H3 and H5 relationships reported here; future work should complement self-report with behavioural or task-based measures of critical evaluation; (4) AVE below 0.50 for two constructs warrants CFA confirmation; (5) instructor-researcher conflict of interest despite anonymisation; (6) data shared with a companion paper, with distinct hypotheses and analyses here; (7) the citizen-developer prototyping task may not generalise to other HI settings, since non-technical participants have limited capacity to verify the code GenAI tools produce, making prior technical knowledge a plausible unmeasured confound on the relationships tested; (8) course-level gender composition (60.6% male, 39.4% female) is reported, but the sample is disciplinarily homogeneous, drawn entirely from Management undergraduate programmes, limiting generalisation to other academic or professional domains; the 81% concentration in the 18–23 age range further limits generalisation beyond early-career users.

7 Conclusion

This paper showed that automation-induced complacency is associated with reduced GenAI literacy (H1) and reduced critical AI use (H2), and is indirectly associated with lower DLSE through literacy suppression (H4; 29.8% bootstrapped mediation). The non-significant H3 suggests that functional AI competence and critical AI evaluation may be empirically distinct capacities and that functional proficiency alone should not be assumed to translate into critical evaluation behaviour, a finding with direct implications for HI system design, IS alignment, and business informatics research. The cascade suppression mechanism identified here represents a new theoretical contribution:

in hybrid intelligence contexts, complacency does not merely impair performance outcomes, it erodes the literacy infrastructure that makes human-AI collaboration effective. Future work should replicate with larger multi-institutional samples, adopt longitudinal designs, conduct CFA-based measurement validation, and extend to professional and organisational HI deployment contexts.

Acknowledgments. Use of Generative AI: The authors used artificial intelligence tools (Claude, Anthropic) to assist in verifying the use of the English language and formatting of the article. The authors assume full responsibility for the research design, data collection, statistical analysis, and all conclusions presented.

Disclosure of Interests. The authors have no competing interests to declare that are relevant to the content of this article. The instructor-researcher dual role disclosed in the Limitations section is a methodological consideration addressed through anonymisation and voluntary participation, not a financial or personal competing interest.

References

1. Dellermann, D., Ebel, P., Söllner, M., Leimeister, J.M.: Hybrid intelligence. Bus. Inf. Syst. Eng. **61**(5), 637–643 (2019). https://doi.org/10.1007/s12599-019-00595-2
2. Parasuraman, R., Manzey, D.H.: Complacency and bias in human use of automation: an attentional integration. Hum. Factors **52**(3), 381–410 (2010). https://doi.org/10.1177/0018720810376055
3. Merritt, S.M., et al.: Automation-induced complacency potential: development and validation of a new scale. Front. Psychol. **10**, 225 (2019). https://doi.org/10.3389/fpsyg.2019.00225
4. Kim, J., Hong, L., Evans, S.: Toward measuring data literacy for higher education: developing and validating a data literacy self-efficacy scale. J. Am. Soc. Inf. Sci. **75**(8), 916–931 (2024). https://doi.org/10.1002/asi.24934
5. Liu, X., Zhang, L., Wei, X.: Generative artificial intelligence literacy: scale development and its effect on job performance. Behav. Sci. **15**(6), 811 (2025). https://doi.org/10.3390/bs15060811
6. Lee, J.D., See, K.A.: Trust in automation: designing for appropriate reliance. Hum. Factors **46**(1), 50–80 (2004). https://doi.org/10.1518/hfes.46.1.50_30392
7. Richardson, C., Rymer, J.R.: New Development Platforms Emerge for Customer-Facing Applications. Forrester Research, Cambridge (2014)
8. Sahay, A., Indamutsa, A., Di Ruscio, D., Pierantonio, A.: Supporting the understanding and comparison of low-code development platforms. In: Proceedings of the 46th Euromicro Conference on Software Engineering and Advanced Applications, pp. 171–178. IEEE (2020). https://doi.org/10.1109/SEAA51224.2020.00036
9. Ng, D.T.K., Leung, J.K.L., Chu, S.K.W., Qiao, M.S.: Conceptualizing AI literacy: an exploratory review. Comput. Educ. Artif. Intell. **2**, 100041 (2021). https://doi.org/10.1016/j.caeai.2021.100041
10. Kahneman, D.: A perspective on judgment and choice: mapping bounded rationality. Am. Psychol. **58**(9), 697–720 (2003). https://doi.org/10.1037/0003-066X.58.9.697
11. Sweller, J.: Cognitive load during problem solving: effects on learning. Cogn. Sci. **12**(2), 257–285 (1988). https://doi.org/10.1207/s15516709cog1202_4
12. Long, D., Magerko, B.: What is AI literacy? Competencies and design considerations. In: Proceedings of CHI 2020 (2020). https://doi.org/10.1145/3313831.3376727

13. Hwang, G.J., Xie, H., Wah, B.W., Gašević, D.: Vision, challenges, roles and research issues of artificial intelligence in education. Comput. Educ. Artif. Intell. **1**, 100001 (2020). https://doi.org/10.1016/j.caeai.2020.100001
14. Bandura, A.: Self-efficacy: toward a unifying theory of behavioral change. Psychol. Rev. **84**(2), 191–215 (1977). https://doi.org/10.1037/0033-295X.84.2.191
15. Grover, V., Chiang, R.H.L., Liang, T.-P., Zhang, D.: Creating strategic business value from big data analytics: a research framework. J. Manag. Inf. Syst. **35**(2), 388–423 (2018). https://doi.org/10.1080/07421222.2018.1451951
16. Lieberman, H., Paternò, F., Klann, M., Wulf, V.: End-user development: an emerging paradigm. In: End User Development, pp. 1–8. Springer, Heidelberg (2006). https://doi.org/10.1007/1-4020-5386-X_1
17. Kolb, D.A.: Experiential Learning: Experience as the Source of Learning and Development. Prentice-Hall, Upper Saddle River (1984)
18. Henseler, J., Ringle, C.M., Sarstedt, M.: A new criterion for assessing discriminant validity in variance-based structural equation modeling. J. Acad. Mark. Sci. **43**(1), 115–135 (2015). https://doi.org/10.1007/s11747-014-0403-8
19. Kasneci, E., et al.: ChatGPT for good? On opportunities and challenges of large language models for education. Learn. Individ. Differ. **103**, 102274 (2023). https://doi.org/10.1016/j.lindif.2023.102274
20. Fornell, C., Larcker, D.F.: Evaluating structural equation models with unobservable variables and measurement error. J. Mark. Res. **18**(1), 39–50 (1981). https://doi.org/10.2307/3151312
21. Lehmann, M., Cornelius, P.B., Sting, F.J.: AI meets the classroom: when do large language models harm learning? (2024). https://doi.org/10.2139/ssrn.4941259
22. Vaccaro, M., Almaatouq, A., Malone, T.: When combinations of humans and AI are useful: a systematic review and meta-analysis. Nat. Hum. Behav. **8**(12), 2293–2303 (2024). https://doi.org/10.1038/s41562-024-02024-1

Human-AI Co-capability in the Public Sector: Agility Gains, Performance Benefits, and Work-Life Trade-Offs

Gideon Mekonnen Jonathan[1](✉), Foluso Ayeni[2], Deden Witarsyah[3], and Erik Perjons[1]

[1] Department of Computer and Systems Sciences (DSV), Stockholm University, Borgarfjordsgatan 12, 16455 Kista, Sweden
{gideon,perjons}@dsv.su.se
[2] Metro State University, 1501 Hennepin Avenue, Minneapolis, MN 55403, USA
foluso.ayeni@metrostate.edu
[3] Faculty of Computer Science, Universiti Tun Hussein Onn Malaysia, Parit Raja, Malaysia
deden@uthm.edu.my

Abstract. Artificial intelligence (AI) is reshaping public sector work, yet its effects on workforce capability and subsequent employee and organisational outcomes remain insufficiently theorised, particularly in non-Western settings. Drawing on dynamic capability theory and the job demands–resources (JD-R) tradition, we propose and test a model of AI-enabled workforce augmentation using partial least squares structural equation modelling (PLS-SEM). Using survey data from 326 UAE public sector employees, we find that AI use intensity and smart system capability are jointly associated with AI-augmented work practices, which in turn are positively associated with workforce agility (β = .48, 95% CI [.36, .59]), work performance (β = .51, [.40, .62]), and—indirectly through agility—digital transformation (indirect β = .19, [.12, .27]), while being negatively associated with work–life balance (β = −.18, [−.29, −.06]). Two-stage moderation analyses indicate that organisational support attenuates the negative association with work–life balance, whereas leadership amplifies agility gains. Marker-variable and full-collinearity diagnostics suggest that common method bias is unlikely to drive the results, and Gaussian-copula tests did not indicate detectable endogeneity among the focal antecedents. Because the design is cross-sectional, we interpret these paths as robust associations rather than causal effects. The study contributes to dynamic capability theory by conceptualising workforce capability as a human–AI co-capability and provides evidence that AI augmentation functions simultaneously as an enabling resource and a source of employee demands in the public sector.

Keywords: Artificial intelligence · Workforce augmentation · Dynamic capabilities · Human–AI collaboration · PLS-SEM · Public sector · Work–life balance

E. Laurenzi et al. (Eds.): BIR 2026, LNBIP 601, pp. 30–45, 2027.
https://doi.org/10.1007/978-3-032-38498-0_3

1 Introduction

Artificial intelligence (AI) is reshaping work in public sector organisations at a pace that is increasingly difficult to match with existing conceptual frameworks. The results of empirical studies indicate that governments are embedding AI into decision support, citizen-facing services, and back-office operations to improve efficiency and service quality [1,2]. As AI systems become more deeply integrated into everyday administrative and professional tasks, understanding how they reshape public sector work is of growing relevance for both research and practice.

Despite this momentum, theoretical understanding of how AI relates to workforce capability remains limited. The extant literature typically frames workforce agility as a human-centric dynamic capability that enables organisations to adapt and to support digital transformation [5,6]. This framing assumes that technology is external to capability—something employees adapt to rather than work with. However, scholars argue that such an assumption is increasingly untenable in AI-enabled environments. The rationale is that AI systems actively participate in work by generating insights, interpreting data, and recommending decisions [7,8]. Consequently, work outcomes are no longer produced by human capability alone but emerge from recursive human-machine interaction—what we conceptualise as AI-augmented work.

This theoretical gap is compounded by an empirical one. A closer look at prior research on AI in the public sector has largely focused on adoption barriers and governance challenges, devoting comparatively little attention to how AI transforms everyday work practices and employee experience [9,10]. When performance effects are examined, evidence is drawn predominantly from private-sector and Western contexts [11], limiting generalisability to public administrations operating under distinct institutional logics such as accountability, bureaucratic rigidity, and legacy infrastructures [2]. Moreover, Moreover, the limited body of research addressing employee well-being reports contradictory findings, with AI potentially reducing workload while simultaneously intensifying demands and blurring work-life boundaries [7,12]. We argue that, taken together, these gaps leave us with an insufficient understanding of how AI-enabled work practices simultaneously shape workforce capability and employee outcomes in public sector settings.

The aim of this study is to propose and empirically test a theoretical model of AI-enabled workforce augmentation in the public sector. We examine the organisational and technological antecedents of AI-augmented work; its associations with workforce agility, work performance, and work-life balance; and the moderating roles of organisational support and leadership. Using partial least squares structural equation modelling (PLS-SEM) [13] on survey data from 326 public sector employees, the study advances theory by conceptualising workforce capability as a human-AI co-capability, offers empirical evidence for the dual—simultaneously enabling and demanding—nature of AI augmentation, and identifies the organisational conditions that are associated with whether AI's benefits are realised and its costs contained.

The study was conducted in the United Arab Emirates, where the National Strategy for AI 2031 positions the country as a global leader in AI adoption and has driven large-scale deployment of AI systems across federal agencies, healthcare, and law enforcement [3,4]. This combination of ambitious policy commitments and concentrated national investment makes the UAE a highly informative—yet still underexplored—setting for examining how AI is reshaping public-sector workforces.

2 Theoretical Background and Hypotheses Development

2.1 Dynamic Capability Theory, Human–AI Collaboration, and AI-Augmented Work

Dynamic capability theory explains how organisations adapt to changing environments through sensing opportunities, seizing them through investment, and transforming resources and routines [5,6]. Workforce agility is commonly viewed as a key micro-foundation of these capabilities because agile employees identify emerging demands, acquire new skills, and adapt work practices in response [16–18]. Dynamic capabilities emerge when such adaptive behaviours become coordinated, codified, and embedded in organisational workflows, allowing individual-level routines to aggregate into organisation-level sensing, seizing, and transforming capacity [6,16]. In public sector organisations, workforce agility is particularly consequential because digital transformation efforts are often constrained by institutional rigidity, regulatory requirements, and legacy systems [2,19]. Prior research therefore identifies agile workforces as critical enablers of technology adoption and digital change in government settings [20]. However, these accounts largely treat agility as a purely human capability—an assumption that becomes increasingly difficult to sustain as AI systems move from peripheral tools to active participants in work processes.

A growing stream of research conceptualises AI as a collaborative partner in cognitive work rather than as a passive technology. Jarrahi [8], for example, describes human–AI symbiosis in which humans contribute contextual judgement and ethical reasoning while AI contributes computational scale and pattern recognition. Raisch and Krakowski [7] similarly distinguish between automation and augmentation, arguing that organisations increasingly derive value from complementary human–AI interactions rather than substitution. Empirical research further suggests that human–AI combinations can outperform either humans or AI acting alone in a range of administrative and decision-making tasks [21].

Building on this literature, we define *AI-augmented work* as the recursive co-production of work outcomes by employees and AI systems, characterised by reciprocal adjustment, emergent practices, and a redistribution of cognitive labour within the human–AI dyad. This individual-level construct differs from organisational AI capability, which captures a firm's broader ability to deploy and leverage AI resources [9], and from AI use measures that primarily capture frequency or intensity of use rather than the nature of human–AI interaction

[11]. In public sector contexts, AI is typically deployed to support rather than replace civil servants in judgement-intensive and citizen-facing activities, making augmentation a particularly relevant lens for understanding how AI reshapes everyday work practices [10,21].

2.2 Antecedents and Outcome Effects of AI-Augmented Work

According to the extant literature, two antecedent conditions are likely to determine whether work becomes AI-augmented. First, *AI use intensity*—the frequency and comprehensiveness of AI integration into daily tasks—facilitates augmentation through the development of habituated human-machine routines [22]. Technology-in-practice research shows that sustained engagement with digital systems embeds technology into work through behavioural adaptation and interpretive learning [23]. As AI use intensifies, work increasingly becomes co-produced by humans and AI, rather than merely supported by technology [11]. Second, *smart system capability*, encompassing accuracy, reliability, responsiveness, adaptability, and explainability, conditions whether AI can be meaningfully integrated into work practices. Information systems success research identifies system quality as a primary determinant of effective use outcomes [24], with unreliable or opaque systems eroding trust and prompting avoidance, while high-capability systems support workflow integration and reduce cognitive burden [25]. Thus, we posit:

H1: *AI use intensity is positively associated with AI-augmented work practices.*

H2: *Smart system capability is positively associated with AI-augmented work practices.*

AI-augmented work is expected to shape multiple employee outcomes. First, it is likely to be associated with stronger workforce agility by strengthening employees' capacity to sense, respond, and adapt—core components of dynamic capability micro-foundations [6]. By automating routine cognitive tasks, AI can free attentional resources for higher-order adaptive problem solving [21], while data-driven recommendations can improve sensing by enabling faster detection of patterns and emerging demands [20]. Adaptation in AI-augmented environments thus extends beyond individual skill acquisition to the human–AI dyad itself, as employees learn to direct, interrogate, and selectively override AI outputs. Thus, we posit:

H3: *AI-augmented work practices are positively associated with workforce agility.*

Second, AI-augmented work is expected to be associated with higher work performance. AI may support performance by automating repetitive tasks, increasing information-processing capacity, and generating insights that exceed unaided human cognition [9,11]. Experimental evidence indicates that AI assistance can improve performance in public sector tasks, particularly under conditions of high task complexity [21]. Large-scale observational studies similarly report productivity gains among AI-assisted employees, though primarily in private-sector contexts [11]. Thus, we posit:

H4: *AI-augmented work practices are positively associated with work performance.*

Third, AI-augmented work may have adverse implications for employee well-being. The job demands–resources (JD–R) framework conceptualises technologies as potential job resources that reduce effort and support performance, but also as job demands that generate technostress, cognitive overload, and boundary blurring [14,15]. Empirical research supports this dual characterisation: AI efficacy is associated with engagement and satisfaction, while AI-related stress is independently linked to emotional exhaustion and work–family conflict [12]. In public sector contexts characterised by mandated AI adoption and high performance expectations, these demand effects may dominate. Thus, we posit:
H5: *AI-augmented work practices are negatively associated with work–life balance.*

Agile workforces are further expected to be associated with digital transformation, understood as the ongoing reconfiguration of organisational processes, structures, and capabilities to exploit digital technologies [26]. By adopting new workflows, acquiring digital skills, and reallocating effort in response to technological change, agile employees enable transformation initiatives [5,20]. In the public sector, workforce agility may be particularly important for overcoming institutional inertia that often stalls transformation efforts [2], with empirical evidence suggesting that employee adaptability is associated with transformation outcomes more strongly than technology investment alone [19]. Thus, we posit:
H6: *Workforce agility is positively associated with digital transformation outcomes.*

2.3 Boundary Conditions: Organisational Support and Leadership

Finally, organisational and managerial conditions are likely to moderate the effects of AI-augmented work. JD–R theory predicts that job resources buffer the strain associated with increased job demands [14,15]. Organisational support—through training, managerial assistance, and protective policies—constitutes a critical job resource in AI-augmented environments [27]. Empirical evidence indicates that perceived organisational support moderates the relationship between AI-related demands and employee well-being outcomes [12], suggesting that supportive contexts can mitigate the boundary-blurring and overload effects of AI augmentation. Thus we posit:
H7: *Organisational support attenuates the negative association between AI-augmented work practices and work–life balance.*

Leadership represents a complementary boundary condition. Transformational leaders influence how employees interpret AI, frame it as an opportunity rather than a threat, and legitimise experimentation with AI-enabled work practices [16]. In public sector contexts, where institutional conservatism may dampen enthusiasm for AI adoption, leadership that models AI engagement and articulates a coherent vision for AI-enabled work is likely to be particularly consequential for translating AI-augmented work practices into workforce agility [4]. Thus, we posit:

H8: *Leadership strengthens the positive association between AI-augmented work practices and workforce agility.*

Based on the above, we propose the theoretical model depicted in Fig. 1. AI use intensity and smart system capability are positioned as antecedent conditions associated with the depth and quality of AI-augmented work practices. These practices are in turn modelled as antecedents of three direct outcomes: workforce agility, work performance, and work–life balance. Workforce agility is modelled as an antecedent of digital transformation, completing a mediated path. Organisational support is hypothesised to moderate the AI-augmented work → work–life balance relationship; leadership is hypothesised to moderate the AI-augmented work → workforce agility relationship.

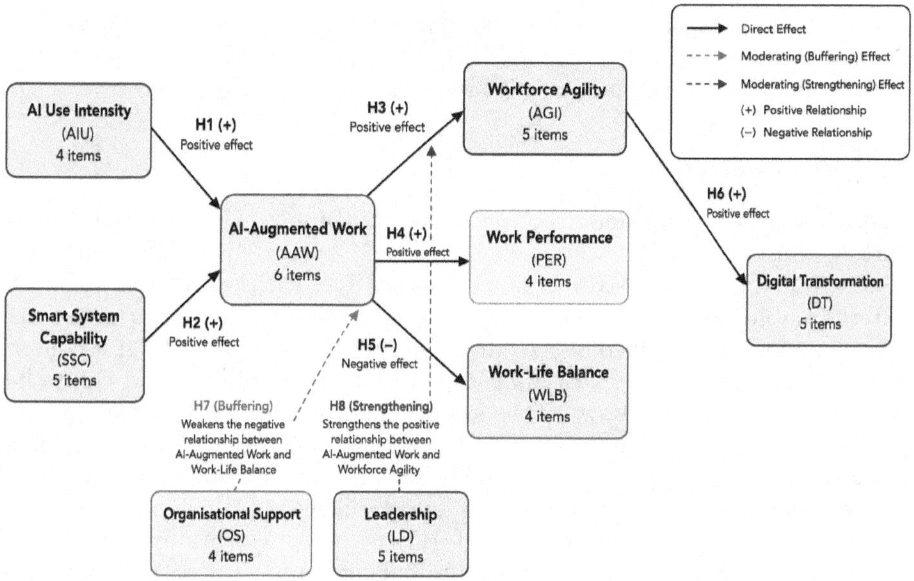

Fig. 1. Proposed Theoretical Model of AI-augmented workforce capability.

3 Methodology

3.1 Research Context, Sampling, and Data

The study was conducted with the public sector workforce of the United Arab Emirates (UAE). Given that its comprehensive national AI strategy mandates AI integration across healthcare, education, transport, and public administration, we argue that the UAE provides a salient empirical setting for our study [3]. Despite the attention given to AI adoption and related policy implementation, quantitative research on AI use within public sector workforces across the Gulf

Cooperation Council (GCC)—comprising Bahrain, Kuwait, Oman, Qatar, Saudi Arabia, and the UAE—remains scarce [4].

Data were collected using purposive sampling supplemented by snowball referral to recruit UAE public sector employees with substantive AI-use experience. Initial respondents were drawn from federal and emirate-level entities known for early AI adoption and asked to refer eligible colleagues. Participants were required to work in a UAE public sector organisation and have used AI systems for at least six months. Of 842 invitations and referrals, 372 questionnaires were returned (44.18% response rate); after removing incomplete responses and failed attention checks, the final sample comprised $N = 326$ respondents. The sample included both national and expatriate employees with varied organisational tenure and AI experience. Full demographic details are provided in the online supplementary material. Informed consent was obtained, no personally identifying information was collected, and the English-language survey was piloted with 10 respondents excluded from the final sample. The sample size comfortably exceeded recommended thresholds for PLS-SEM [29].

3.2 Measurement

All constructs were measured using reflective multi-item scales with seven-point Likert response formats (1 = strongly disagree; 7 = strongly agree). Items were adapted from validated instruments where available, with wording adjustments to fit the public sector and AI context; the full measurement instrument and source mapping are provided in the online supplementary material. AI use intensity items were adapted from Brynjolfsson et al. [11] and Mikalef and Gupta [9]. Smart system capability drew on the system quality framework of DeLone and McLean [24], extended with explainability items adapted from Enholm et al. [25]. AI-augmented work was operationalised using a newly developed scale grounded in Raisch and Krakowski [7], Jarrahi [8], and Orlikowski [23]. Workforce agility items were adapted from Sherehiy et al. [17] with refinements from Gong and Ribiere [20]. Work performance, work–life balance, and digital transformation items were adapted from Zhang et al. [21], Chuang et al. [12], and Vial [26] and Zuiderwijk et al. [19], respectively. Organisational support was measured using the short form of Eisenberger et al. [27], and leadership using the transformational leadership component of the Multifactor Leadership Questionnaire [31].

3.3 Development and Validation of the AI-Augmented Work Scale

Because AI-augmented work is central to the model and no established measure captures the recursive, dyadic mode of human–AI co-production we theorise, we developed a dedicated scale following established scale-development guidance [41]. An initial pool of items was generated from the conceptual definition and its theoretical anchors [7,8,23], each item targeting a defining facet of the construct (integration of AI into tasks, AI support of decision-making, AI-shaped work practices, reciprocal adaptation, joint production of outcomes, and AI influence on task prioritisation). Prior to estimating the PLS-SEM measurement model, we conducted an exploratory factor analysis (EFA) on the AI-augmented work items, which returned a single dominant factor with all items loading cleanly above .70 and no problematic cross-loadings, supporting the unidimensionality of the construct. The construct's psychometric properties were then confirmed in the full measurement model (Sect. 4), where it met all reliability, convergent-validity, and discriminant-validity thresholds.

3.4 Analytical Procedure

Analyses were conducted using SmartPLS software 4 [30] following established PLS-SEM guidelines [13]. The measurement model was evaluated for internal consistency reliability (Cronbach's α, Dijkstra-Henseler's ρ_A, composite reliability), convergent validity (average variance extracted), and discriminant validity using the heterotrait-monotrait ratio [33]. Structural models were estimated using 10,000 bootstrap resamples to obtain bias-corrected and accelerated 95% confidence intervals for direct, indirect, and conditional effects. Moderation hypotheses were tested using the two-stage approach [34], with conditional effects examined at ± 1 standard deviation of the moderator. Mediation was assessed using bootstrapped confidence intervals following Sarstedt et al. [35]. Predictive relevance was evaluated using Stone-Geisser's Q^2 via blindfolding and out-of-sample assessment using PLSpredict [36]. Endogeneity was assessed using the Gaussian copula approach applied to non-normally distributed antecedents [37]. Common method bias was examined using Harman's single-factor test, the marker-variable technique [32], and full-collinearity variance inflation factors [38]; detailed diagnostics are reported in the online supplementary material.

4 Results

4.1 Measurement Model

Our analysis indicates that all constructs in our theoretical model exceed conventional thresholds for internal consistency (α, ρ_A, CR $> .87$), convergent validity (AVE $\geq .71$), and discriminant validity (HTMT $\leq .74$; full matrix in the online supplementary material). Indicator loadings ranged from .76 to .92 and were all significant at $p < .001$ (Table 1).

Three complementary common method bias diagnostics converged. Harman's single-factor test indicated that a single factor accounted for 27.4% of total variance (below the 50% threshold). The marker-variable analysis [32] returned an average correlation of $r = .04$ between the office-layout marker and the substantive constructs (range $-.06$ to .09); marker-adjusted partial correlations changed no path coefficient by more than .02. The full-collinearity VIF approach [38] returned VIFs in the range 1.46–2.83 across all constructs, well below the 3.3 conservative threshold. Together these diagnostics provide stronger evidence against substantive CMB than Harman's test alone [28]. Full diagnostic detail is in the online supplementary material.

Table 1. Measurement model results

Construct	Items	α	ρ_A	CR	AVE	Loadings
AI Use Intensity	4	.91	.92	.94	.79	.82–.91
Smart System Capability	5	.90	.91	.93	.72	.79–.88
AI-Augmented Work	6	.92	.93	.94	.73	.81–.89
Workforce Agility	5	.90	.91	.93	.73	.80–.89
Work Performance	4	.91	.92	.94	.79	.84–.91
Work–Life Balance	4	.87	.88	.91	.71	.76–.88
Digital Transformation	5	.92	.93	.94	.77	.83–.92
Organisational Support	4	.89	.90	.92	.74	.78–.89
Leadership	5	.91	.92	.93	.73	.80–.89

Note. Thresholds: α, ρ_A, CR $> .70$; AVE $> .50$ [13].

4.2 Structural Model, Mediation, and Moderation

Table 2 reports direct, conditional, and indirect effects with BCa 95% confidence intervals and f^2 effect sizes. All eight hypothesised paths are statistically significant in the expected direction. AI use intensity ($\beta = .36$, [.25, .47]) and smart system capability ($\beta = .42$, [.30, .54]) are jointly associated with 52% of variance in AI-augmented work, with system capability the stronger antecedent—consistent with the proposition that system quality is a prerequisite for meaningful augmentation. AI-augmented work is positively associated with work performance ($\beta = .51$, [.40, .62]; $R^2 = .61$) and workforce agility ($\beta = .48$, [.36, .59]; $R^2 = .52$), and negatively associated with work–life balance ($\beta = -.18$, [$-.29$, $-.06$]; $R^2 = .28$). Workforce agility is positively associated with digital transformation ($\beta = .39$, [.26, .51]; $R^2 = .39$). Among controls, prior AI experience (in months) was significantly associated with AI-augmented work ($\beta = .11$, [.01, .21]); organisational tenure showed a marginal positive association with workforce agility ($\beta = .09$, [.00, .19]). Age, gender, education, sector type, and nationality were not significant in any structural equation, and adding sector and nationality as covariates in robustness checks did not change any path coefficient by more than .02.

The indirect effect of AI-augmented work on digital transformation through workforce agility is significant ($\beta_{\text{indirect}} = .19$, [.12, .27]); the direct effect freed in a competing model is non-significant ($\beta = .07$, 95% CI [$-.04$, .18]),indicating an indirect-only mediation pattern, with a substantial proportion of the association operating through workforce agility (VAF $= 0.73$) [35]. Figure 2 visualises the estimated structural model with standardised coefficients.

Two-stage moderation analyses confirm both interaction hypotheses (Table 3). Organisational support attenuates the negative AI-augmented work $\rightarrow$ work–life balance association: the simple slope is strong at low support ($\beta = -.31$, $p < .001$), moderate at the mean ($\beta = -.18$, $p < .01$), and non-significant at high support ($\beta = -.05$, $p = .47$). Leadership amplifies the

Table 2. Structural and conditional effects

Path (Hypothesis)	β	**BCa 95% CI**	f^2
AI Use Intensity → AI-Augmented Work (H1)	.36	[.25, .47]	.19
Smart System Capability → AI-Augmented Work (H2)	.42	[.30, .54]	.27
AI-Augmented Work → Workforce Agility (H3)	.48	[.36, .59]	.30
AI-Augmented Work → Work Performance (H4)	.51	[.40, .62]	.35
AI-Augmented Work → Work–Life Balance (H5)	−.18	[−.29, −.06]	.04
Workforce Agility → Digital Transformation (H6)	.39	[.26, .51]	.18
AI-Aug. Work × Org. Support → WLB (H7)	.21	[.10, .32]	.05
AI-Aug. Work × Leadership → Agility (H8)	.19	[.08, .30]	.04
Indirect effect: AI-Aug. Work → Agility → Digital Transformation	.19	[.12, .27]	—
Control: Prior AI experience → AI-Augmented Work	.11	[.01, .21]	.02

Note. 10,000 BCa bootstrap resamples. f^2: .02 small, .15 medium, .35 large [13]. Two-stage moderation [34]. Mediation: VAF = 0.73, indicating that a substantial proportion of the total effect operates through workforce agility [35].

positive AI-augmented work → workforce agility association: the simple slope is moderate at low leadership ($\beta = .31$, $p < .01$), strong at the mean ($\beta = .48$), and very strong at high leadership ($\beta = .62$; both $p < .001$).

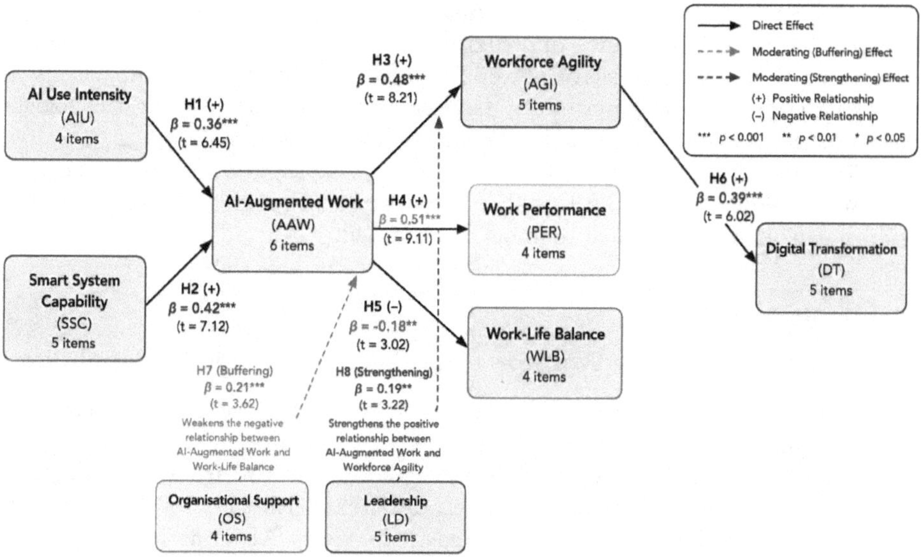

Fig. 2. Structural model results of the PLS-SEM analysis (standardised coefficients; $^{**}p < .01$, $^{***}p < .001$).

Table 3. Simple slopes for moderation effects

Moderator level	β	BCa 95% CI	p
AI-Augmented Work → Work–Life Balance, conditioned on Organisational Support			
Low (−1 SD)	−.31	[−.43, −.19]	< .001
Mean	−.18	[−.29, −.06]	< .01
High (+1 SD)	−.05	[−.17, .08]	.47
AI-Augmented Work → Workforce Agility, conditioned on Leadership			
Low (−1 SD)	.31	[.19, .43]	< .01
Mean	.48	[.36, .59]	< .001
High (+1 SD)	.62	[.49, .74]	< .001

4.3 Predictive Relevance and Endogeneity

Stone–Geisser Q^2 values via blindfolding (omission distance 7) were positive for every endogenous construct (AI-Augmented Work = .39; Workforce Agility = .37; Work Performance = .47; Work–Life Balance = .19; Digital Transformation = .27), indicating acceptable predictive relevance. Out-of-sample predictive power was assessed via PLSpredict with $k = 10$ folds and 10 repetitions [36]: construct-level Q^2_{predict} values were positive for all endogenous constructs, and indicator-level PLS-SEM RMSEs were lower than the linear-model benchmark for all indicators of performance and agility and for a majority of indicators of work–life balance and digital transformation, indicating medium-to-high out-of-sample predictive power (detailed indicator-level comparisons in the online supplementary material). Gaussian-copula tests [37] for the exogenous antecedents returned non-significant copula terms (copula$_{\text{AI use}}$: $\beta = .04$, $p = .31$; copula$_{\text{system capability}}$: $\beta = -.03$, $p = .47$), suggesting no evidence of detectable endogeneity in the tested relationships, although the cross-sectional design means causal inference remains constrained.

5 Discussion

5.1 AI Augmentation, Workforce Agility, and Dynamic Capability

The strong association between AI-augmented work and workforce agility ($\beta = .48$; $R^2 = .52$) suggests that agility in AI-enabled environments may arise not only from employees' individual adaptive capacity but also from the quality of their interaction with AI systems. This is consistent with the growing literature on human–AI collaboration, which increasingly views AI as an active participant in cognitive work rather than a passive technological tool [7,8]. Whereas dynamic capability theory traditionally locates agility in human actors and routines [5,6,17], the present findings suggest that adaptation may increasingly emerge through recurring patterns of collaboration between employees and AI systems. This interpretation aligns with Jarrahi's [8] notion of human–AI symbiosis, in which humans contribute contextual judgement while AI contributes analytical capacity and computational scale. It also resonates with Raisch and Krakowski's [7] argument that organisations increasingly operate within an augmentation rather than a pure automation logic. In practical terms, adaptation in AI-enabled workplaces appears to involve not only acquiring new skills but also learning how to direct, interpret, challenge, and integrate AI-generated outputs into everyday work practices.

The positive associations of both AI use intensity ($\beta = .36$) and smart system capability ($\beta = .42$) with AI-augmented work further highlight the importance of distinguishing between technology adoption and technology integration. Consistent with technology-in-practice perspectives [23], repeated engagement with AI appears to facilitate the development of stable human–AI routines, while system quality characteristics such as reliability, responsiveness, and explainability provide the conditions under which such routines can develop [24,25]. The stronger association observed for smart system capability suggests that meaningful augmentation depends not only on how frequently AI is used but also on whether employees perceive the technology as sufficiently capable and trustworthy to incorporate into their work practices.

5.2 The Dual Character of AI Augmentation

The combination of a strong positive association with work performance ($\beta = .51$), a similarly strong association with workforce agility ($\beta = .48$), and a negative association with work–life balance ($\beta = -.18$) highlights the dual character of AI augmentation. Rather than producing uniformly positive or negative outcomes, AI appears to function simultaneously as a productivity-enhancing resource and as a source of additional demands. This pattern is consistent with the augmentation perspective of Raisch and Krakowski [7] and with JD–R-inspired arguments that technologies can act as both resources and demands within the same work environment [12,14,15].

The positive performance association converges with evidence from several contexts. Zhang et al. [21] report performance gains associated with AI-enabled work in public-sector settings, while Brynjolfsson et al. [11] document substantial productivity improvements among AI-assisted employees in the private sector. Although these studies differ in context, method, and outcome measures, the convergence of findings suggests that AI augmentation can improve employees' ability to process information, complete tasks, and respond to work demands. The present findings indicate that similar patterns may also be observed within public-sector environments characterised by administrative complexity and ongoing digitalisation efforts.

The significant indirect association between AI-augmented work and digital transformation through workforce agility ($\beta = .19$, 95% CI [.12, .27]) provides further insight into how these benefits may emerge. Consistent with dynamic capability theory [5,6] and prior public-sector research [19,20], the findings suggest that digital transformation is associated less with technology adoption itself than with employees' capacity to modify routines, workflows, and behaviours in response to technological change. Workforce agility therefore appears to be an important pathway through which AI augmentation becomes linked to broader transformation outcomes.

At the same time, the negative association with work–life balance is consistent with concerns that AI can introduce new pressures into the workplace. JD–R theory proposes that technologies may simultaneously reduce effort and create additional demands [14,15]. In AI-enabled environments, increased expectations regarding responsiveness, monitoring, information processing, and continuous availability may offset some of the efficiency gains provided by automation and decision support. This interpretation is consistent with the findings of Chuang et al. [12], who show that AI-related efficacy and AI-related stress may coexist. Because the present study did not directly examine engagement or exhaustion mechanisms, the results are best viewed as consistent with rather than a direct test of JD–R theory.

5.3 Boundary Conditions: Organisational Support and Leadership

The moderation results provide a more nuanced understanding of when the consequences of AI augmentation are most likely to emerge. Organisational support substantially altered the association between AI-augmented work and work–life balance. The negative relationship declined from $\beta = -.31$ under low support to a non-significant $\beta = -.05$ under high support. Consistent with JD–R theory [14,15], organisational resources appear capable of buffering strain associated with increased technological demands. This finding also aligns with Chuang et al. [12], who identify supportive organisational environments as an important factor shaping employee responses to AI-related demands.

The moderation pattern suggests that the well-being consequences of AI augmentation are not fixed properties of the technology itself. Rather, they appear partly contingent on the organisational environment in which AI is implemented. Training, managerial assistance, workload management, psychological safety, and explicit boundary-setting practices may therefore help employees realise the benefits of AI while limiting associated strain.

Leadership played a complementary role. The relationship between AI-augmented work and workforce agility increased from $\beta = .31$ under low leadership to $\beta = .62$ under high leadership. This pattern is consistent with arguments that organisational adaptation depends not only on technological resources but also on managerial cognition, strategic intent, and the ability to mobilise change [16]. Leaders who actively legitimise AI use, encourage experimentation, and frame technological change as an opportunity may strengthen employees' willingness and ability to integrate AI into their work practices. Taken together, the moderation results suggest an asymmetric pattern in which organisational support primarily mitigates the costs of AI augmentation, whereas leadership primarily amplifies its benefits.

5.4 The UAE Context: Culture, Workforce Composition, and Institutional Conditions

Several characteristics of the UAE context help illuminate the observed relationships. First, the workforce represented in the study is highly multinational. The robustness analyses indicate only limited differences between national and expatriate employees, suggesting that the substantive relationships are relatively stable across groups despite potentially different experiences and interpretations of AI-enabled work.

Second, cultural characteristics associated with the UAE may help explain the strength of the moderation effects. Prior research characterises the region as relatively high in power distance and collectivism [39]. In such contexts, employees may be more responsive to signals from leaders regarding appropriate technology use, helping explain the strong leadership effect. Similarly, collectivist norms may increase the salience of organisational support by reinforcing expectations of reciprocity and institutional care. Although the present data cannot directly test these mechanisms, the observed patterns are broadly consistent with these cultural interpretations.

Third, the UAE's ambitious national AI agenda and extensive public-sector investment in AI create conditions that differ from many voluntary or experimental adoption settings [3,4]. When AI adoption is actively promoted and embedded within organisational strategy, both the benefits and pressures associated with AI may become more pronounced. This institutional context may therefore help explain why AI augmentation is associated simultaneously with strong performance and agility gains and measurable work–life balance costs. More broadly, the findings suggest that the consequences of AI adoption are shaped not only by technological characteristics but also by the institutional and policy environments in which implementation occurs.

References

1. De Sousa, W.G., de Melo, E.R.P., Bermejo, P.H.D.S., Farias, R.A.S., Gomes, A.O.: How and where is artificial intelligence in the public sector going? A literature review and research agenda. Gov. Inf. Q. **36**(4), 101392 (2019)
2. Wirtz, B.W., Langer, P.F., Fenner, C.: Artificial intelligence in the public sector–a research agenda. Int. J. Public Adm. **44**(13), 1103–1128 (2021)
3. UAE Government: UAE National Strategy for Artificial Intelligence 2031. National Programme for Artificial Intelligence (2018)
4. Almheiri, H.M., Ahmad, S.Z., Khalid, K., Ngah, A.H.: Examining the impact of artificial intelligence capability on dynamic capabilities, organizational creativity and organization performance in public organizations. J. Syst. Inf. Technol. **27**(1), 1–20 (2025)
5. Teece, D.J., Pisano, G., Shuen, A.: Dynamic capabilities and strategic management. Strateg. Manag. J. **18**(7), 509–533 (1997)
6. Teece, D.J.: Business models and dynamic capabilities. Long Range Plan. **51**(1), 40–49 (2018)

7. Raisch, S., Krakowski, S.: Artificial intelligence and management: the automation-augmentation paradox. Acad. Manag. Rev. **46**(1), 192–210 (2021)
8. Jarrahi, M.H.: Artificial intelligence and the future of work: human-AI symbiosis in organizational decision making. Bus. Horiz. **61**(4), 577–586 (2018)
9. Mikalef, P., Gupta, M.: Artificial intelligence capability: conceptualization, measurement calibration, and empirical study on its impact on organizational creativity and firm performance. Inf. Manag. **58**(3), 103434 (2021)
10. Sun, T.Q., Medaglia, R.: Mapping the challenges of artificial intelligence in the public sector: evidence from public healthcare. Gov. Inf. Q. **36**(2), 368–383 (2019)
11. Brynjolfsson, E., Li, D., Raymond, L.R.: Generative AI at work. Q. J. Econ. **140**(2), 889–942 (2025)
12. Chuang, Y.-T., Chiang, H.-L., Lin, A.-P.: Insights from the job demands-resources model: AI's dual impact on employees' work and life well-being. Int. J. Inf. Manag. **83**, 102887 (2025)
13. Hair, J.F., Hult, G.T.M., Ringle, C.M., Sarstedt, M.: A Primer on Partial Least Squares Structural Equation Modeling (PLS-SEM), 3rd edn. Sage, Thousand Oaks (2022)
14. Demerouti, E., Bakker, A.B., Nachreiner, F., Schaufeli, W.B.: The job demands-resources model of burnout. J. Appl. Psychol. **86**(3), 499–512 (2001)
15. Bakker, A.B., Demerouti, E.: Job demands-resources theory: taking stock and looking forward. J. Occup. Health Psychol. **22**(3), 273–285 (2017)
16. Teece, D.J., Peteraf, M.A., Leih, S.: Dynamic capabilities and organizational agility: risk, uncertainty, and strategy in the innovation economy. Calif. Manag. Rev. **58**(4), 13–35 (2016)
17. Sherehiy, B., Karwowski, W., Layer, J.K.: A review of enterprise agility: concepts, frameworks, and attributes. Int. J. Ind. Ergon. **37**(5), 445–460 (2007)
18. Jonathan, G.M., Reychav, I.: People powering digital transformation in the public sector: cultivating workforce agility. In: Proceedings of the 2025 Computers and People Research Conference, pp. 1–9 (2025)
19. Zuiderwijk, A., Chen, Y.-C., Salem, F.: Implications of the use of artificial intelligence in public governance: a systematic literature review and a research agenda. Gov. Inf. Q. **38**(3), 101577 (2021)
20. Gong, C., Ribiere, V.: Understanding the role of organizational agility in the context of digital transformation: an integrative literature review. VINE J. Inf. Knowl. Manag. Syst. **55**(2), 351–378 (2023)
21. Zhang, W., Yu, Y., Dai, S.: AI-enabled workforce: performance improvements in public sector tasks of varying innovative work behavior. Public Manag. Rev. 1–36 (2025)
22. Murray, A., Rhymer, J., Sirmon, D.G.: Humans and technology: forms of conjoined agency in organizations. Acad. Manag. Rev. **46**(3), 552–571 (2021)
23. Orlikowski, W.J.: Using technology and constituting structures: a practice lens for studying technology in organizations. Organ. Sci. **11**(4), 404–428 (2000)
24. DeLone, W.H., McLean, E.R.: The DeLone and McLean model of information systems success: a ten-year update. J. Manag. Inf. Syst. **19**(4), 9–30 (2003)
25. Enholm, I.M., Papagiannidis, E., Mikalef, P., Krogstie, J.: Artificial intelligence and business value: a literature review. Inf. Syst. Front. **24**(5), 1709–1734 (2022)
26. Vial, G.: Understanding digital transformation: a review and a research agenda. J. Strat. Inf. Syst. **28**(2), 118–144 (2019)
27. Eisenberger, R., Huntington, R., Hutchison, S., Sowa, D.: Perceived organizational support. J. Appl. Psychol. **71**(3), 500–507 (1986)

28. Podsakoff, P.M., MacKenzie, S.B., Lee, J.-Y., Podsakoff, N.P.: Common method biases in behavioral research: a critical review of the literature and recommended remedies. J. Appl. Psychol. **88**(5), 879–903 (2003)
29. Kock, N., Hadaya, P.: Minimum sample size estimation in PLS-SEM: the inverse square root and gamma-exponential methods. Inf. Syst. J. **28**(1), 227–261 (2018)
30. Ringle, C.M., Wende, S., Becker, J.-M.: SmartPLS 4. SmartPLS GmbH, Bönningstedt (2024)
31. Bass, B.M., Avolio, B.J.: MLQ Multifactor Leadership Questionnaire: Technical Report. Mind Garden, Palo Alto, CA (1995)
32. Lindell, M.K., Whitney, D.J.: Accounting for common method variance in cross-sectional research designs. J. Appl. Psychol. **86**(1), 114–121 (2001)
33. Henseler, J., Ringle, C.M., Sarstedt, M.: A new criterion for assessing discriminant validity in variance-based structural equation modeling. J. Acad. Mark. Sci. **43**(1), 115–135 (2015)
34. Becker, J.-M., Ringle, C.M., Sarstedt, M.: Estimating moderating effects in PLS-SEM and PLSc-SEM: interaction term generation × data treatment. J. Appl. Struct. Eq. Model. **2**(2), 1–21 (2018)
35. Sarstedt, M., Hair, J.F., Nitzl, C., Ringle, C.M., Howard, M.C.: Beyond a tandem analysis of SEM and PROCESS: use of PLS-SEM for mediation analyses. Int. J. Mark. Res. **62**(3), 288–299 (2020)
36. Shmueli, G., et al.: Predictive model assessment in PLS-SEM: guidelines for using PLSpredict. Eur. J. Mark. **53**(11), 2322–2347 (2019)
37. Park, S., Gupta, S.: Handling endogenous regressors by joint estimation using copulas. Mark. Sci. **31**(4), 567–586 (2012)
38. Kock, N.: Common method bias in PLS-SEM: a full collinearity assessment approach. Int. J. e-Collaborat. **11**(4), 1–10 (2015)
39. Hofstede, G.: Culture's Consequences: Comparing Values, Behaviors, Institutions, and Organizations Across Nations, 2nd edn. Sage, Thousand Oaks (2001)
40. Huang, L., Zhao, Y.: The impact of AI literacy on work-life balance and job satisfaction among university faculty: a self-determination theory perspective. Front. Psychol. **16**, 1669247 (2025)
41. MacKenzie, S.B., Podsakoff, P.M., Podsakoff, N.P.: Construct measurement and validation procedures in MIS and behavioral research: integrating new and existing techniques. MIS Q. **35**(2), 293–334 (2011)

Brigitta: A Multi-agent LLM System for Business Process Modeling Using Mermaid Diagrams

Tomáš Bruckner(✉), Jan Černý, Oleg Svatoš, and Filip Vencovský

Prague University of Economics and Business, Prague, Czechia
{bruckner,jan.cerny,oleg.svatos,filip.vencovsk}@vse.cz

Abstract. Business process modeling notations such as BPMN, EPC and UML impose expertise barriers on domain practitioners. This paper presents Brigitta, a multi-agent system that investigates Mermaid diagram notation as a concise, machine-readable carrier of business meaning for Large Language Model (LLM)-assisted process modeling. We examine whether LLMs can maintain business context across multiple diagram types: flowcharts, class diagrams, and state diagrams, and perform meaningful modifications based on natural language instructions, without access to conversational history. The system employs a client-side multi-agent architecture comprising an Orchestrator for skill selection, specialized Skill agents for diagram generation, and a Validator for output quality assurance. The server functions solely as a secure proxy to the LLM API. An empirical evaluation across business scenarios demonstrates that the approach maintains cross-model consistency and handles both complex and incremental modifications effectively. We discuss implications for stateless context design, skill decomposition, and the viability of lightweight diagram notations as LLM knowledge representation.

Keywords: Business Process Modeling · Large Language Models · Mermaid Diagrams · Multi-Agent Systems · Agent Skill · Orchestration · Natural Language Processing · Model Consistency

1 Introduction

Business process modeling is a foundational activity in enterprise analysis, information systems design, and organizational improvement [1]. Established notations such as Business Process Model and Notation (BPMN) [21], Unified Modeling Language (UML) [26], and Event-driven Process Chains (EPC) [13] provide rigorous formalisms for capturing process logic, organizational roles, and data flows. The principles of consistency among individual models, such as process models, ontologies, and state diagrams, are also described in detail [25].

Recent advances in Large Language Models (LLMs) have opened new possibilities for lowering these barriers. LLMs demonstrate increasing capability in

E. Laurenzi et al. (Eds.): BIR 2026, LNBIP 601, pp. 46–62, 2027.
https://doi.org/10.1007/978-3-032-38498-0_4

understanding natural language descriptions and generating structured outputs, suggesting potential for automated or semi-automated transformation of informal business descriptions into formal models [6]. However, several fundamental research questions remain insufficiently explored in the literature:

Context Representation: Can concise, text-based diagram notations effectively carry sufficient business meaning for LLMs to maintain context and reason about interconnected models across multiple modeling perspectives?

Incremental Modification: Can LLMs meaningfully modify existing diagrams based on natural language instructions, handling both comprehensive restructuring and targeted partial changes while preserving existing model structure?

Skill Decomposition and Consistency: Can modeling work be decomposed among specialized agents, each responsible for a distinct diagram type, while maintaining overall cross-model consistency – particularly in the absence of conversational history?

This paper presents Brigitta[1], a prototype multi-agent system designed to investigate these questions. Brigitta uses Mermaid diagram notation [19,31] as the exclusive carrier of business context, testing whether this lightweight, text-based format can serve as effective knowledge representation for LLM-assisted modeling. The system operates without conversational history, relying solely on the current state of Mermaid diagrams as context for all reasoning and modification tasks.

The idea behind this approach emerged during the practical implementation of LLM-assisted modeling in an enterprise-level low-code platform [32], where existing approaches introduced challenges related to the large scale of the context and the difficulty of decomposing it into subtasks while maintaining reliability and consistency.

1.1 Research Questions

The design and evaluation of Brigitta are guided by the following research questions:

RQ1: Can LLMs maintain business context encoded in the concise form of Mermaid diagrams (flowchart, class diagram, state diagram) and utilize this context for subsequent modeling and modification tasks?

[1] The software is temporarily available at https://brigitta.pages.dev, for access contact authors.

RQ2: Are LLMs capable of meaningfully modifying diagrams based on natural language instructions for both complex (multi-diagram) and partial (single-diagram) changes while preserving existing model structure?

RQ3: Can the orchestration of specialized modeling skills maintain consistency across multiple diagram types without access to conversational history, relying exclusively on diagram state as context?

1.2 Contributions

The principal contributions of this work are as follows:

1. **A novel multi-agent architecture** for business process modeling that uses Mermaid diagrams as the sole context carrier, eliminating dependence on conversational history.
2. **An empirical investigation** of LLMs' ability to maintain, reason about, and modify business models represented in multiple interconnected diagram types.
3. **A working prototype** demonstrating the feasibility of client-side orchestration with server-only proxy functionality, contributing to discussions on privacy-preserving LLM application design.

The remainder of this paper is structured as follows: Sect. 2 reviews related work in LLM-assisted modeling, multi-agent systems, and diagram-based knowledge representation. Section 3 details the system architecture. Section 4 describes the implementation. Section 5 presents the evaluation methodology and results. Section 6 discusses findings, implications, and limitations. Section 7 concludes the paper.

2 Related Work

2.1 LLM-Driven Generation of Business Process Models from Natural Language

The translation of natural language descriptions into formal process models has emerged as a central application of large language models (LLMs) in business process management. A foundational concern across this body of work is the expertise barrier imposed by dominant notations such as BPMN and UML, which have historically restricted process modeling to trained specialists [12, 18, 33]. Several systems address this barrier by positioning LLMs as intermediaries that convert unstructured text directly into syntactically valid BPMN artefacts.

Kourani [15] established a benchmark for this approach, proposing a framework with prompting strategies and an error-handling mechanism that supports exporting models in standard notations including BPMN and Petri nets. Subsequent work refined this pipeline: Hörner et al. [11] proposed a systematic framework for BPMN generation from process descriptions, combining prompt design with quality assessment, and Ružižka and Štancel [27] evaluated GPT-based synthesis of BPMN from text specifications, analysing the tool's effectiveness in transforming process descriptions into visual BPMN models. Shbita [30] introduced MermaidSeqBench, a benchmark to evaluate how well large language models generate specifically Mermaid sequence diagrams from natural language descriptions.

A recurring finding is that LLM performance on BPMN generation degrades with text length and structural complexity. Boujmil and Chebil [5] addressed this directly by fusing NLP preprocessing pipelines with LLM generation through prompt-guided fusion, achieving improved handling of long and semantically dense process descriptions. Similarly, Li et al. [17] developed domain-adapted language models for the extraction and BPMN generation from Chinese procedural texts. Drakopoulos et al. [10] conducted an evaluation of five LLM-powered BPMN generation tools using a structured quality framework covering clarity, correctness, and completeness, finding that current tools produce diagrams with missing steps, inconsistent logic, or modeling rule violations. The democratisation potential of these approaches is widely noted: Wenger et al. [33] specifically frame LLM-based BPMN generation as a means to lower participation thresholds for non-technical domain practitioners, a theme that directly motivates the Brigitta system examined in the present paper.

2.2 Multi-agent and Agentic Architectures for Process Modeling

Increasing attention has been paid to multi-agent architectures as a means of overcoming the limitations of single-LLM process modeling pipelines. The core intuition is that decomposing the modeling task across specialised agents (each responsible for a defined sub-problem) reduces error propagation and enables modular quality assurance. Xu et al. [34] instantiate this logic in a dual-agent hierarchical reasoning framework for industrial BPMN modeling, in which an analysis agent decomposes user requirements into a structured report that guides a separate modeling agent. Sai and Rinderle-Ma [29] extend agentic generation to regulatory text processing, presenting a fully automated approach that generates BPMN 2.0 process models from regulatory documents such as the GDPR.

Agent orchestration has also been explored in conversational and interactive settings. Klievtsova et al. [14] demonstrate AutoBPMN.AI, a system in which an orchestrating agent manages iterative dialogue with the user to refine process models incrementally. Alayón et al. [3] report a multi-modal pipeline applied to justice administration workflows, generating BPMN diagrams automatically from video recordings of process explanations. Ait et al. [2] take a complementary direction by proposing a BPMN extension to formally represent human-agent collaborative workflows, recognising that agentic systems are themselves increasingly the subjects of process modeling rather than merely its instruments. The Brigitta architecture described in this paper aligns with this trend, employing a client-side orchestrator, domain-specialised skill agents, and a dedicated validator: a decomposition that mirrors the agent role structures identified across the literature as most effective for quality-assured diagram generation.

2.3 Conversational and Interactive Process Modeling Interfaces

A significant strand of the literature moves beyond batch generation to explore conversational and direct-manipulation interfaces that allow users to iteratively construct and modify process models through natural language. Köpke and Safan [16] introduced the BPMN-Chatbot, Safan and Köpke [28] subsequently extended this system to BPMN-Chatbot++, adding support for collaboration diagrams with data annotations. Licardo et al. [18] present BPMN Assistant, an enterprise-oriented tool that combines conversational input with structured output validation, targeting non-technical business analysts as its primary users.

The challenge of maintaining contextual coherence across conversational turns is a recurring concern in this literature. Hörner [12] is developing an LLM-based conversational framework that enables users to generate and iteratively evolve BPMN models. Pardo Gutierrez et al. [23] present a direct manipulation interface that combines natural language input with visual editing affordances. Radhakrishnan [24] addresses SME practitioners with limited documentation culture by designing a conversational AI system that elicits tacit process knowledge and externalises it as BPMN. Möller [20] contributes a conceptual framework for assessing the comprehensibility of process models produced through manual, automatic, and semi-automatic means, providing evaluation criteria relevant to any conversational generation system including Brigitta. Critically, none of these systems explores stateless context design (the explicit exclusion of conversational history from LLM context) as an architectural principle, which is a distinguishing feature of the Brigitta approach.

2.4 Lightweight and Alternative Diagram Notations as LLM Knowledge Representations

While BPMN dominates the literature as the target notation, a smaller but growing body of work examines whether alternative, lighter-weight notations may be more suitable for LLM-assisted process modeling. The underlying argument is that BPMN's expressiveness comes at the cost of syntactic complexity that strains LLM token budgets and increases the likelihood of structural errors [5,10]. Balamwar et al. [4] explore XML and OWL ontological serialisations of BPMN as machine-readable intermediary formats, demonstrating that structured representations enable more reliable downstream reasoning and simulation generation. Dolha et al. [8,9] investigate multi-modal and RDF-serialised BPMN representations, finding that semantic serialisation improves LLM interpretability of process structures, particularly for retrieval-augmented generation scenarios.

These findings collectively suggest that structured but accessible representations and targeted evaluation are critical prerequisites for reliable LLM-based process modeling, and that the question of optimal output notation remains open, creating an opening for lightweight alternatives such as Mermaid, the focus of the Brigitta system, which offers a text-native, concise syntax amenable to both LLM generation and human inspection.

2.5 Research Gap

The reviewed literature demonstrates substantial progress in LLM-based business process modeling, yet several gaps remain unaddressed. First, the overwhelming majority of systems target BPMN as the exclusive output notation, leaving largely unexplored whether lightweight, text-native alternatives such as Mermaid can serve as effective carriers of business semantics for LLM-assisted modeling. Second, despite the prevalence of conversational interfaces, no prior work explicitly investigates stateless context design, that is, whether LLMs can maintain meaningful business context across multiple diagram types without access to conversational history. This is a practically important question for deployments where session state cannot be assumed. Third, cross-diagram consistency (the capacity of a system to produce coherent flowchart, class, and state representations of the same underlying process) has not been evaluated in the existing literature. Finally, while multi-agent architectures have been proposed, client-side skill decomposition that keeps the server as a stateless LLM proxy has not been examined as an architectural pattern. The present paper addresses these gaps through the Brigitta system.

3 System Architecture

3.1 Architectural Overview

Brigitta follows a client-side orchestration architecture in which all prompt assembly, context management, validation, and diagram rendering occur within the browser. The server functions exclusively as a secure proxy to the LLM API, validating access credentials and enforcing Cross-Origin Resource Sharing (CORS) policies. This architectural decision reflects two design principles: (1) minimizing server-side processing to reduce latency and infrastructure costs, and (2) keeping business context client-side to address potential data sensitivity concerns in enterprise modeling scenarios.

The user interacts with the system through a browser-based chat interface. User input is received by the Orchestrator agent, which analyzes the request against available skill descriptions and determines which specialized skills to invoke. Selected Skill agents then process the request, receiving the complete business context (all current Mermaid diagrams) alongside the user's natural language instruction. The Validator agent assesses each skill's output for format compliance and quality. Valid outputs are integrated into the business context and rendered as diagrams.

3.2 Agent Architecture

The system employs three distinct agent types, each with a clearly defined role in the modeling workflow.

Orchestrator Agent. The Orchestrator serves as the entry point for all user interactions. It receives the user's natural language input alongside descriptions of all available skills and the current business context (all existing Mermaid diagrams). Based on semantic analysis of the user's intent against skill descriptions, the Orchestrator determines which skills are relevant and returns a JSON array of skill names to execute. If the input does not match any skill's domain, the Orchestrator returns a guidance message directing the user toward appropriate input formulation. The Orchestrator does not perform any modeling itself; its function is purely analytical and routing-oriented.

Skill Agents. Three specialized Skill agents handle diagram generation and modification:

- *Flowchart Skill:* Models business process flows as Mermaid flowcharts, capturing tasks, decision points, and control flow sequences.
- *Class Skill:* Models business ontology as Mermaid class diagrams, identifying entities, attributes, and relationships.
- *State Skill:* Models entity lifecycles as Mermaid state diagrams, capturing states, transitions, and triggering events.

Each Skill agent receives the complete business context (all three diagram types, where they exist) alongside the user's request. This cross-context provision is a deliberate design choice enabling each skill to maintain awareness of the broader modeling landscape. Skills are defined as Markdown files with a standardized structure comprising description, inputs, outputs, rules, and output examples (see Appendix A for an example).

Validator Agent. The Validator assesses whether a Skill agent's output meets expected format and quality criteria. It receives the skill's output and the skill's defined output criteria, returning a binary assessment (valid/invalid). Invalid outputs trigger a single retry with an additional instruction requesting valid Mermaid notation. The binary validation approach was chosen for implementation simplicity; we discuss its limitations in Sect. 6.

3.3 Context Management: Diagram-Only State

A defining architectural decision is the exclusive use of Mermaid diagrams as context. Unlike conversational LLM applications that maintain chat history [22], Brigitta's context consists solely of:

- Current flowchart (if one has been created)
- Current class diagram (if one has been created)
- Current state diagram (if one has been created)

No conversational history, no prior user messages, and no intermediate reasoning traces are preserved or provided to the LLM. This design directly addresses RQ1 and RQ3 by testing whether concise diagram notation can carry sufficient business meaning for LLM reasoning without supplementary conversational context.

The context is maintained as session state in the browser and can be exported to the clipboard for external persistence. This session-only persistence model reflects the system's positioning as a research prototype rather than a production tool.

3.4 Processing Pipeline

The complete processing pipeline for a single user request proceeds as follows:

1. **Input reception:** The user submits a natural language request through the chat interface.
2. **Orchestration:** The Orchestrator analyzes the request against skill descriptions and current context, selecting relevant skills.
3. **Skill execution:** Each selected skill is invoked with the complete business context and the user's request. Skills are executed sequentially.
4. **Validation:** Each skill's output is assessed by the Validator. Invalid outputs trigger one retry with corrective instruction.
5. **Context update:** Valid outputs replace the corresponding diagram in the business context.
6. **Rendering:** Updated diagrams are rendered using Mermaid.js and displayed to the user.

4 Implementation

4.1 Technology Stack

Brigitta is implemented as a vanilla JavaScript web application deployed on Cloudflare Pages, reflecting a deliberate choice to minimize framework dependencies and maximize deployment simplicity:

- **Frontend:** HTML5, CSS3, vanilla JavaScript (no frameworks)
- **Backend:** Cloudflare Pages Functions (serverless proxy)
- **LLM:** Claude Sonnet 4.6 (Anthropic) via OpenRouter API
- **Diagram rendering:** Mermaid.js v10 (CDN-delivered)

The serverless proxy pattern ensures that API credentials are never exposed to the client while adding minimal latency. All business logic, including prompt construction, context management, and validation, executes client-side.

4.2 Skill Definition Format

Skills are defined as Markdown files stored in `/public/skills/*.md` with a standardized (but not enforced) structure:

```
# skill-name
## Description
Brief description of the skill's purpose and capabilities.
## Inputs
- Description: Natural language input
- Business Context: Current Mermaid diagrams
## Outputs
Expected output format and constraints.
## Rules
- Specialization rules
- Consistency requirements
- Best practices
## Output Example
Example of expected output.
```

This Markdown-based skill definition approach enables rapid skill modification and extension without code changes, supporting iterative research and experimentation.

The application code itself does not address the content of the models or their rules in any way. Everything is defined using natural language or diagram-as-code examples in Markdown files, which makes it possible to continuously refine and modify the expected behavior. When using standard LLM models, any natural or modeling language supported by the respective LLM can be employed; therefore, the approach is not limited to either the English language or Mermaid-based models.

Consistency rules are handled in the same manner - they are either described textually or left to the discretion of the LLM. Each agent associated with a particular skill has access to all models within the context and may therefore adjust its output to ensure consistency with the others. Whether to prioritize consistency or changes requested by the user can again be specified through rules expressed in natural language or dynamically modified during the conversation.

4.3 Orchestrator and Validator Mechanism

The Orchestrator receives a structured prompt containing the user's message, available skills with their descriptions, and the current business context (all existing diagrams). It is instructed to return JSON in one of two formats, one for skill assignment and one for inputs that do not match any skill's domain. The JSON-only output constraint ensures reliable programmatic parsing without natural language interpretation. Principles of orchestration are described in natural-language Markdown file, similarly to the skills. If no initial context provided, orchestrator invokes all skill in specified order.

The Validator receives the skill's output and the skill's defined output criteria, returning 1 if the output is valid (syntactically correct Mermaid notation meeting the skill's criteria defined in skill expected output), and 0 if the output violates expectations.

Invalid outputs trigger a single retry with an appended instruction: "Please provide valid Mermaid notation." The single-retry limit prevents infinite loops while providing the LLM an opportunity to self-correct. The user is informed in the chat about a potentially incorrect format and may, at their discretion, request a correction.

5 Evaluation

5.1 Methodology

We conducted a structured evaluation to assess Brigitta's capabilities across the three research questions. The evaluation employed a scenario-based testing approach, presenting the system with realistic business modeling tasks of varying complexity and measuring output quality along three dimensions:

1. **Initial modeling quality:** Accuracy and completeness of diagrams created from natural language descriptions.
2. **Incremental modification fidelity:** Ability to modify existing diagrams based on partial instructions while preserving unrelated structure.
3. **Cross-model consistency:** Maintenance of referential integrity across flowchart, class diagram, and state diagram (e.g., entities referenced in the flowchart appear in the class diagram; states referenced in the process flow appear in the state diagram).

All tests were conducted using Claude Sonnet 4.6 via OpenRouter. Each scenario was executed three times to assess determinism, though we note that LLM outputs are inherently stochastic.

5.2 Test Scenarios

We designed seven scenarios of increasing complexity, each comprising an initial modeling request followed by incremental modification requests (Restaurant Billing, HR - Hiring, HR - Employee offboarding, Timber extraction from the forest, Processing a complaint, General order-to-cash and Asset management). The team members executed the given scenarios, adaptively adjusted the flow of conversation, and monitored whether the outcomes met expectations in terms of modification and consistency. Based on this, the skills were continuously adjusted and fine-tuned until the expected results were achieved. Additional tests were conducted through informal application testing during development and prompt tuning. Part of one of the tests is described here in detail as an example:

Scenario Restaurant Billing Process. textbfInitial request: "Model a restaurant billing process."

Results: The system correctly generated all three diagram types. The flowchart was direct with one branching (cash or card payment). The class diagram identified four entities (Bill, Guest, Payment, Receipt) with appropriate attributes and relationships. The state diagram captured the Bill lifecycle through states Issued → Presented to Guest → Disputed → Payment method selected → Paid with correct transitions.

Incremental Request: "Add the ability to split a bill among guests."

Results: The flowchart captured both payment paths (individual and group) with appropriate decision logic. It was correctly extended with a "Calculate Individual Share" task. The class diagram added a `splitRatio` attribute to the Bill entity. The state diagram correctly remained unchanged, as the split payment mechanism does not alter the Bill lifecycle. This demonstrates appropriate selectivity in modification (RQ2).

Incremental Request: "But every guest pays only its own consumption."

Results: The flowchart was changed to a cycle where every guest is asked to pay its consumption until total bill amount is exhausted. The class diagram introduced a specific GuestBill for every guest and a relationship to Bill. The state diagram chose the entity to describe from Bill to GuestBill and the states slightly changed to match flowchart. Cross-model consistency was maintained: the Discount entity appeared in both the class diagram and was referenced in the flowchart's decision logic (RQ1, RQ3).

5.3 Summary of Findings

Key observations include:

Context Maintenance (RQ1): LLMs effectively maintained business context across all three diagram types throughout the evaluation. Entities, states, and process steps introduced in earlier requests were correctly referenced in subsequent modifications.

Modification Capability (RQ2): The system handled both complex (multi-diagram) and partial (single-diagram) modifications. Incremental changes preserved existing structure while correctly integrating new elements. The system demonstrated appropriate selectivity, modifying only diagrams relevant to the request.

Consistency without History (RQ3): Cross-model consistency [25] was maintained across all scenarios despite the absence of conversational history. The diagram-only context proved sufficient for the LLM to reason about inter-model relationships.

Orchestrator Accuracy: The Orchestrator correctly identified appropriate skills for all test requests, including distinguishing between single-skill and multi-skill invocations.

5.4 Limitations Observed

Several limitations emerged during evaluation:

Determinism: While outputs were semantically consistent across runs, syntactic variation was observed (e.g., different attribute ordering in class diagrams). This reflects inherent LLM stochasticity.

Complex Modifications: When a single request required changes to multiple interconnected elements within one diagram, occasional inconsistencies appeared (e.g., a new state referenced in the flowchart but not defined in the state diagram). These were rare and typically resolved on retry. In some cases, the consistency had to be enforced by user request, especially when not all skills were executed.

Validation Granularity: The binary validation mechanism occasionally passed outputs with minor quality issues (e.g., suboptimal naming conventions) that a more nuanced validator would catch. The results were always corrected after intuitive additional request by user.

6 Discussion

6.1 Mermaid as a Context Carrier

Our results provide empirical evidence that Mermaid notation can effectively serve as a concise carrier of business meaning for LLM context (RQ1). Three properties of Mermaid contribute to this effectiveness:

Compactness. Mermaid's text-based syntax conveys substantial modeling information within a compact representation. A typical business process with 10–15 tasks, 4–6 entities, and 5–8 states requires about 600–800 - well within the context window of modern LLMs. Brigitta conversation for creating such model needs approximately 6 000–9 000 input tokens and 1 000–2 000 output tokens in 7–15 iterations. This compactness enables all three diagram types to be provided simultaneously, supporting cross-model reasoning. For comparison: A similar adjustment, while maintaining context with a complete JSON template exported from a low-code platform, consumed about 2 million tokens.

Structural Enforcement. Mermaid's syntax enforces a consistent structural representation. Unlike free-text descriptions, which may vary in organization and terminology, Mermaid diagrams impose a canonical structure that reduces ambiguity in LLM interpretation.

Semantic Parseability. LLMs demonstrate capability in parsing Mermaid semantics, correctly interpreting entity relationships, state transitions, and process flows. This aligns with findings on LLMs' code comprehension capabilities [7].

However, we note that Mermaid's expressiveness is lower than that of BPMN or UML. Advanced BPMN constructs (e.g., compensation handlers, complex gateways, message flows) and UML constructs (e.g., activity partitions, composite structures) lack direct Mermaid equivalents. This trade-off between compactness and expressiveness represents a fundamental design tension that practitioners must navigate based on their modeling requirements.

6.2 Skill Decomposition and Orchestration

The division of modeling work among specialized skills proved effective for maintaining focus and quality within each modeling perspective (RQ3). Each Skill agent, receiving the complete business context but instructed to modify only its assigned diagram type, demonstrated appropriate domain focus while maintaining cross-model awareness.

The Orchestrator's skill selection accuracy was high across all test scenarios, correctly identifying which skills were relevant to each request. This suggests that skill descriptions, when sufficiently discriminative, can serve as effective routing signals for LLM-based orchestration.

The sequential execution model (as opposed to parallel execution) was chosen to ensure that each skill's output is available as context for subsequent skills within the same request. This ordering dependency is a deliberate design choice that prioritizes consistency over speed.

6.3 Stateless Design Implications

The absence of conversational history, while initially appearing as a limitation, offers several advantages that merit discussion:

Deterministic Behavior. Given the same diagram state and the same user request, the system produces semantically equivalent outputs (though with syntactic variation due to LLM stochasticity). This determinism supports reproducibility and debugging – valuable properties in both research and practice. However, overly creative results may arise if the user's request is vague.

Context Efficiency. By eliminating conversational history, the entire context budget can be allocated to business-relevant information (the diagrams). This is particularly valuable for complex models that approach context window limits.

Simplified Architecture. The stateless design eliminates the need for conversation management, message ordering, and history compression – all of which add complexity and potential failure modes.

However, this design also entails limitations. The system cannot leverage conversational context to resolve ambiguous references (e.g., "add that feature to the previous entity" requires the entity to be identifiable from diagrams alone). It also cannot learn from or adapt to user preferences across interactions. These limitations suggest that hybrid approaches – combining diagram state with selective conversational context – may offer a productive direction for future work.

6.4 Architectural Positioning

Brigitta's client-side orchestration with server-only proxy positioning represents a distinct point in the design space of LLM applications. Unlike fully server-side architectures (which centralize processing but raise data privacy concerns) or fully client-side architectures (which require API key exposure), Brigitta's hybrid approach keeps sensitive business context client-side while protecting API credentials server-side. This positioning is particularly relevant for enterprise modeling scenarios where business processes may contain confidential information.

6.5 Threats to Validity

We acknowledge several threats to the validity of our evaluation:

Internal Validity: The evaluation was conducted by the system's developer team, introducing potential bias in scenario design and output assessment. Independent evaluation by domain experts would strengthen validity.

External Validity: The evaluation employed a limited set of scenarios in a few domains. Generalizability to other domains, larger models, and more complex modification patterns remains to be established.

Construct Validity: Our quality assessment criteria (completeness, consistency, selectivity) were evaluated qualitatively. Formal metrics for cross-model consistency and modification fidelity would enable more rigorous assessment.

Single Model Dependency: All tests used a single LLM (Claude Sonnet 4.6). Results may not generalize to other models with different capabilities and limitations.

6.6 Future Work

Several directions for future work emerge from this study:

Comprehensive user studies with domain experts to evaluate usability, output quality, and the system's effectiveness in lowering modeling barriers.

Formal consistency metrics for quantifying cross-model consistency, enabling systematic comparison across approaches.

Enhanced validation with multi-dimensional quality assessment (syntax, semantics, consistency, completeness) rather than binary validation.

Integration into a low-code platform as a real industrial implementation.

Other modeling languages integration to test of languages and model types.

7 Conclusion

This paper presented Brigitta, a multi-agent system for LLM-assisted business process modeling that uses Mermaid diagrams as the exclusive carrier of business context. Through a structured evaluation across three business scenarios, we investigated three research questions concerning LLMs' ability to maintain diagram-based context, perform meaningful modifications, and maintain cross-model consistency without conversational history.

Our findings indicate that Mermaid notation can effectively carry business meaning for LLM context (RQ1), that LLMs can meaningfully modify diagrams for both complex and partial changes (RQ2), and that orchestration of specialized skills can maintain cross-model consistency in a stateless design (RQ3).

While limitations exist – including single-model dependency, binary validation, and the expressiveness constraints of Mermaid notation – the results provide a foundation for future research on LLM-assisted modeling. The system's working prototype demonstrates feasibility and suggests promising directions for both research and practical application.

Acknowledgment. The development of Brigitta was supported by the Operational Programme Technology and Applications for Competitiveness (OP TAK), project No. CZ.01.01.01/01/24_062/0007594, co-funded by the European Union.

References

1. van der Aalst, W.M.P.: Business process management: a comprehensive survey. Int. Scholarly Res. Notices **2013**(1), 507984 (2013). https://doi.org/10.1155/2013/507984
2. Ait, A., Izquierdo, J.L.C., Cabot, J.: Towards modeling human-agentic collaborative workflows: a bpmn extension. In: Lecture Notes in Computer Science. Springer, Heidelberg (2026). https://doi.org/10.1007/978-3-032-04190-6_22

3. Alayón, S., Martín, C., Torres, J., Bacallado, M., Aguilar, R., Savirón, G.: Transformation of verbal descriptions of process flows into business process modelling and notation models using multimodal artificial intelligence: Application in justice. CMES - Comput. Model. Eng. Sci. (2026). https://doi.org/10.32604/cmes.2025.073488
4. Balamwar, A., Raj, A., Mitra, R., Das, D., Tiwari, M.K., Prabhu, V.: Bpmn-driven ai framework for simulation model generation and performance modelling for supply chain networks. In: Proceedings of the International Conference on Artificial Intelligence, Computer, Data Sciences, and Applications (ACDSA 2026). IEEE (2026). https://doi.org/10.1109/ACDSA67686.2026.11468135
5. Boujmil, I., Chebil, W.: Improving bpmn model generation from texts through a prompt-guided fusion of nlp and llm approaches. In: K-CAP 2025 – Proceedings of the 13th Knowledge Capture Conference. ACM (2025). https://doi.org/10.1145/3731443.3771362
6. Brown, T.B., et al.: Language models are few-shot learners. Adv. Neural. Inf. Process. Syst. **33**, 1877–1901 (2020)
7. Chen, M., Tworek, J., Jun, H., Yuan, Q., Pinto, H.P.D.O., Kaplan, J.: Evaluating large language models trained on code. arXiv preprint arXiv:2107.03374 (2021)
8. Dolha, D.N., Buchmann, R.A.: Generative ai for bpmn process analysis: experiments with multi-modal process representations. In: Business Process Management Workshops. Lecture Notes in Business Information Processing. Springer, Heidelberg (2024). https://doi.org/10.1007/978-3-031-71333-0_2
9. Dolha, D.N., Buchmann, R.A.: Experimental assessments of retrieval-augmented conversational agents interpreting rdf-serialized bpmn models. In: Lecture Notes in Business Information Processing, Springer, Heidelberg (2026). https://doi.org/10.1007/978-3-032-04375-7_18
10. Drakopoulos, P., Malousoudis, P., Nousias, N., Tsakalidis, G., Vergidis, K.: Do llms speak bpmn? An evaluation of their process modeling capabilities based on quality measures. Computation **14**(1) (2026). https://doi.org/10.3390/computation14010010
11. Hörner, L.F., Möller, M., Reichert, M.: Automatically generating bpmn 2.0 process models from natural language process descriptions: challenges, framework, quality assessment. Bus. Inf. Syst. Eng. **68**, 59–83 (2026). https://doi.org/10.1007/s12599-025-00983-x
12. Hörner, L.F.: Towards an llm-based conversational framework for business process modeling: research approach and preliminary results. In: Lecture Notes in Business Information Processing. Springer, Heidelberg (2025). https://doi.org/10.1007/978-3-031-94590-8_34
13. Keller, G., Nüttgens, M., Scheer, A.W.: Semantische prozessmodellierung auf der grundlage„ereignisgesteuerter prozessketten (epk)". In: Scheer, A.W. (ed.) Veröffentlichungen des Instituts für Wirtschaftsinformatik. Heft 89, Saarbrücken (1992)
14. Klievtsova, N., Ehrendorfer, M., Mangler, J., Rinderle-Ma, S.: Autobpmn.ai: conversational process modeling and automation. In: CEUR Workshop Proceedings (2025)
15. Kourani, H., Berti, A., Schuster, D., van der Aalst, W.M.P.: Process modeling with large language models. In: Enterprise, Business-Process and Information Systems Modeling, Lecture Notes in Business Information Processing, vol. 511, pp. 229–244. Springer, Cham (2024). https://doi.org/10.1007/978-3-031-61007-3_18
16. Köpke, J., Safan, A.: Introducing the bpmn-chatbot for efficient llm-based process modeling. In: CEUR Workshop Proceedings (2024)

17. Li, S., et al.: Structured extraction and bpmn generation from Chinese procedural texts via hybrid attention-based domain language models. IEEE Access (2025). https://doi.org/10.1109/ACCESS.2025.3611811
18. Licardo, J.T., Tankovic, N., Etinger, D.: Bpmn assistant: an llm-based approach to business process modeling. Appl. Sci. **16**(5) (2026). https://doi.org/10.3390/app16052213
19. Mermaid.js: Mermaid documentation (2024). https://mermaid.js.org/
20. Möller, M.: Towards the comprehensibility of manually, automatically, and semi-automatically created process models: a conceptual framework. In: Lecture Notes in Business Information Processing. Springer, Heidelberg (2025). https://doi.org/10.1007/978-3-031-94590-8_35
21. Object Management Group: Business process model and notation (bpmn) version 2.0. OMG Specification (2011)
22. OpenAI: Chat completions api documentation (2024). https://platform.openai.com/docs/
23. Pardo Gutierrez, S., Alrabie, L., Di Fede, G., Vitali, M., Andolina, S.: A direct manipulation interface for llm-based process modeling. In: CHItaly 2025 – Proceedings of the 16th Biannual Conference of the Italian SIGCHI Chapter. ACM (2025). https://doi.org/10.1145/3750069.3755960
24. Radhakrishnan, U.: Documenting sme processes with conversational ai: from tacit knowledge to bpmn. In: IET Conference Proceedings (2025). https://doi.org/10.1049/icp.2025.3640
25. Řepa, V., Svatoš, O.: Fundamentals of Business Architecture Modeling. The Enterprise Engineering Series, 1 edn. Springer, Cham (2024).https://doi.org/10.1007/978-3-031-59035-1
26. Rumbaugh, J., Jacobson, I., Booch, G.: The Unified Modeling Language Reference Manual, 2nd edn. Addison-Wesley, Boston (2004)
27. Ružička, M., Štancel, M.: Synthesis of bpmn models from text specification using gpt model. Acta Polytechnica Hungarica **23**(2) (2026). https://doi.org/10.12700/APH.23.2.2026.2.3
28. Safan, A., Köpke, J.: Bpmn-chatbot++: Llm-based modeling of collaboration diagrams with data. In: CEUR Workshop Proceedings (2025)
29. Sai, C., Rinderle-Ma, S.: Agentic generation of process models from regulatory texts. In: Lecture Notes in Computer Science. Springer, Heidelberg (2026). https://doi.org/10.1007/978-3-032-15538-2_21
30. Shbita, B., Ahmed, F., DeLuca, C.: Mermaidseqbench: an evaluation benchmark for nl-to-mermaid sequence diagram generation (2026). https://arxiv.org/abs/2511.14967
31. Sveidqvist, K.: Mermaid (2026). https://github.com/mermaid-js/mermaid, computer software. Accessed 16 May 2026
32. Team assistant: Team assistant – low-code platform for business process management (2026). https://www.teamassistant.app/en/home/. Accessed 17 May 2026
33. Wenger, S., Spahic-Bogdanovic, M., Martin, A.: Large language models for democratizing business process modeling: Bpmn model generation and style guide adherence. In: Communications in Computer and Information Science. Springer, Heidelberg (2025). https://doi.org/10.1007/978-3-031-78255-8_22
34. Xu, Q., Zhang, Y., Tang, H., Ran, Q., Gao, H., Xu, Y.: H2a-bpmn: a hierarchical and hybrid agent framework for industrial bpmn automated modeling. In: Lecture Notes of the Institute for Computer Sciences, Social Informatics and Telecommunications Engineering. Springer, Heidelberg (2026). https://doi.org/10.1007/978-3-032-21171-2_10

Extending Business Process Modelling for Ad-Hoc Adaptability

Eliana Felice[1] and Knut Hinkelman[1,2](✉)

[1] FHNW University of Applied Sciences and Arts Northwestern Switzerland, Windisch, Switzerland
knut.hinkelmann@fhnw.ch
[2] OMiLAB NPO, Berlin, Germany

Abstract. Business process modelling and execution approaches restrict runtime adaptability when unplanned decisions are needed. Enabling both adaptability and control can avoid inefficient workarounds, foster innovative solutions, and align with situational demands. This work addresses this limitation by introducing a modelling extension for Business Process Model and Notation (BPMN) that enables controlled ad hoc process adjustments. Process executors can change process behavior at runtime through predefined flexibility attributes without compromising compliance or efficiency. The extension integrates adaptive capabilities directly into BPMN models rather than introducing a new modelling paradigm, ensuring compatibility with existing modelling environments.

Following the Design Science Research, design principles were derived from an analysis of a concrete case from a financial institution and expert interviews A metamodel containing the necessary elements was developed using the ADOxx platform. Additionally, an adapted process execution procedure was designed. The design principles and the BPMN extension were evaluated in a workshop, with a primary focus on usability, applicability, and efficiency.

Keywords: BPMN · Business Process Flexibility · Process Adaptability

1 Introduction

In a fast-changing business environment, companies must be able to adapt their business processes to unforeseen events and evolving circumstances [1, 2]. The evolution from rigid to flexible process design reflects a growing demand for adaptability not only in modelling languages but also in the tools that support execution. Without sufficient process adaptability, organizations risk using inefficient workflows or wasting resources on frequent redesigns [3] with negative influence also on compliance, and process quality [4] and potential innovation benefits [5].

It is a common observation that processes often are not executed or "lived" as they are defined. Recent studies have shown that deviations, also known as workarounds, are driven by three motivational factors: psychological aspect and the need for autonomy [4], organizational and cultural support [5] and technical and procedural hurdles caused by system rigidity [6].

E. Laurenzi et al. (Eds.): BIR 2026, LNBIP 601, pp. 63–79, 2027.
https://doi.org/10.1007/978-3-032-38498-0_5

In practice, many business processes exhibit a hybrid character and require a certain degree of situational flexibility [7]. Despite ongoing efforts to support runtime flexibility, current modelling approaches remain limited to predefined design-time deviations [3, 8]. Unforeseen adaptations are often implemented retrospectively or entirely outside of standardized workflows [5, 9]. The lack of embedded flexibility becomes evident in numerous domains like investment approvals [10] and healthcare, where structured administrative procedures intersect with flexible, expert-driven medical processes [11].

Common execution platforms for business processes provide only limited support for ad hoc runtime adaptation lacking semantic task interpretation, context awareness, and validation mechanisms to support user-driven adaptations [2, 12]. Event-Condition-Action (ECA) rules allow flexible model process execution by specifying conditions under which a task can be skipped, but they lack a graphical visualization [13] The Case Management Model and Notation (CMMN) also enables the modelling of events and conditions for tasks [14, pp. 6 & 32–36]. It additionally distinguishes between planned and discretionary tasks. The user can individually decide to execute a discretionary task, but cannot deviate from the planned flow. Both approaches, however, are not compatible with the Business Process Model and Notation (BPMN), which is widely used in enterprises. This leads to the following research question:

"How can business process modelling be extended to enable ad hoc adaptability while ensuring efficiency and compliance in process execution?"

Section 2 provides a literature review covering categorizations of process flexibility and techniques for ad-hoc adaptation of process execution. Section 3 explains the applied research methodology. Section 4 describes the practical requirements covering the problem understanding of the applied Design Science Research strategy. Section 5 explains the modeling extension of BPMN satisfying the requirements as well as specification for process execution. After describing the evaluation of the artefact in Sect. 6, the contribution and future research is described in Sect. 7.

2 State of the Art

2.1 Categories of Process Structure and Flexibility

Determining when workarounds are appropriate requires an understanding of the degree of process structure. A common distinction is between structured processes, cases, and ad hoc processes [10, p. 14]. Szelągowski and Lupeikiene [15] further divide cases differentiating the process structure into four categories:

- **Structured static processes***:* Fixed and fully known sequence.
- **Structured processes with ad-hoc exceptions:** Process flows with allowed deviations predefined points.
- **Unstructured processes with predefined fragments:** Only parts of the flow can be planned in advance.
- **Unstructured processes without a defined sequence:** Adhoc process that cannot be described in advance.

Although in real processes the distinction between structured processes and ad hoc parts is often unclear [7], companies usually model structured business processes that allow limited ad hoc adaptations during process execution [16]. For example, in the travel planning process, travel approval is required before a flight or accommodation can be booked. In an era of highly dynamic pricing models, this traditional approach prevents cheap accommodation, or flight offers from being booked before approval has been granted. Therefore, an opportunity will be missed [17].

Various taxonomies attempt to capture the timing and nature of flexibility. Schonenberg et al. [18] categorize process flexibility by possible changes to model elements. *Flexibility by design* enables alternative execution paths during the design. *Flexibility by deviation* allows temporary deviations during runtime. *Flexibility through underspecification* enables adding missing information to an incomplete process model at runtime. Finally, *flexibility through change* encompasses modifying the process model during execution, whether for individual process instances or the entire model. Martinho et al. [3] classify adaptations based on the characteristics of *anticipation* (planned versus ad hoc), *duration* (temporary versus permanent), *swiftness* (immediate versus deferred) and *extent* (incremental versus revolutionary) (Table 1).

Table 1. Process Flexibility based on Martinho et al. (2015) and Schonenberg et al. (2008)

	Extent	Duration	Swiftness	Anticipation
Flexibility by design	–	Permanent	–	Planned
Flexibility by deviation	–	Temporary	Immediate	Ad hoc
Flexibility through under-specification	–	Temporary or permanent	Immediate	Planned or Ad hoc
Flexibility through change	Incremental or Revolutionary	Temporary or permanent	Immediate or deferred	Planned or Ad hoc

A step further toward the self-adaptation of business processes encompassing six central dimensions [2]: *Monitoring* involves collecting and processing contextual information, often using sensors or models. *Detection* identifies the need for adaptation, whether reactive or proactive. *Planning* involves designing adaptations at various levels of the process. *Acting* refers to the technical implementation of adaptations. The *meta-dimension* assesses the maturity of solutions, including their implementation and validation.

2.2 Existing Adaptation Techniques

For the analysis of practical approaches for enabling runtime adaptation we distinguish between planning-based and modelling-based techniques.

Planning-Based Techniques. Rule-based approaches rely on predefined rules, often ex-pressed as if-then logic, to dictate how processes respond to specific conditions at runtime [2]. One of the earliest contributions of rule-based approaches proposed the so-called generative planning [19]. The method aimed to generate schedules context-sensitively at runtime while maintaining process integrity.

Event-Condition-Action (ECA) rules have been shown to be suitable for modelling business processes [13]. ECA rules enable decisions based on predefined conditions, increasing flexibility as almost any type of event and condition can be utilized. However, the lack of visualization leads to unclear dependencies, complicates the management of complex processes, and limits transparency.

To address some of these shortcomings, the Object Management Group (OMG) introduced the Case Management Model and Notation (CMMN), which combines a planning and modelling-based approach. CMMN distinguishes between planned tasks, which follow predefined logic, and discretionary tasks, which enable users to respond more flexibly to varying process situations. Task sentries contain events and conditions but still do not visualize them. Therefore, CMMN has been criticized for its limited readability and its challenges in handling unforeseen exceptions in practical applications [8].

Marrella et al. [1] and Bucchiarone et al. [20] argue that rule-based systems lack the flexibility required in dynamic, unpredictable environments because all potential exceptions and their responses must be predefined at design time. In response, they introduce the frameworks like Madapt [20] and SmartPM [1] to enable automated, context-sensitive adaptations at runtime. Madapt uses artificial intelligence (AI) driven planning to generate subprocesses at runtime, providing context-aware, goal-driven adaptation similar to [19]. SmartPM [1] supports runtime adaptation through automated planning, Situation Calculus, and AI, enabling flexibility without predefined rules. Limitations include difficulties with complex requirements, incomplete information, and tasks with multiple effects [21].

The proactive and automated process adaptation of [22] is based on predictions of potential issues. The system automatically adjusts without user intervention when violations, but few BPMN engines support such mechanisms [22].

Modelling-Based Techniques. Modelling-based approaches use graphical or formal process models to explicitly define workflows and activities, including possible variants and paths. BPMN integrates ad hoc decisions through so-called ad hoc subprocesses, which can be executed during the process for predefined activities and, therefore, limit user flexibility.

CF4BPMN [3], extends BPMN by enabling process designers to specify which process elements can be modified at runtime, providing controlled flexibility making it suitable for cases where complete freedom is not desired.

The business logic in the Knowledge Work Designer [7] appears as a structured process in BPMN and an unstructured case plan in CMMN, which are combined into the Business Process and Case Management Notation BPCMN.

The Collective Adaptive System [23] extends the Business Process Execution Language (BPEL) to include abstract activities which are only filled with concrete activities at runtime or during deployment - either manually by pausing the instance and waiting for human intervention or automatically by retrieving process fragments from a repository. Compared to the previous approaches, CAS represents a flexible but less controlled strategy, highlighting the trade-off between adaptability and governance in modelling-based systems.

The Challenge of Run-Time Flexibility. Business Process Management Systems (BPMS) enable the design, analysis, execution, and monitoring of business processes based on explicit process models [24]. Classic BPMS provides only limited support for runtime process adjustments [2]. In particular, the possibility of ad hoc adjustments by process executors themselves has hardly been implemented to date. In practice, changes are often made manually and outside of standardized processes, which is time-consuming, prone to errors and does not allow for scaling. Unflexible processes often lead to workarounds [5, 25]. These restrictions are particularly problematic in less predictable, knowledge-intensive processes, where flexibility plays a central role [2].

The analysis of 47 implementations of 47 BPMS tools showed that only three of them enable executable BPMN interpretations, and even then, the systems only work with considerable restrictions highlighting that potential extensions for flexibility are rarely used in practice. [12]. Process models still lag behind operational reality [26]. Many BPMS struggle to cope with the complexity and variability of real-world processes. The lack of ad hoc flexibility remains particularly critical. Ongoing processes can rarely be adapted on the fly, as traditional architectures strictly separate modelling from execution. In addition, current self-adaptive systems are often simplistic, reactive, and instance-focused [2]. These solutions lack semantic reasoning, traceability, and validation mechanisms and rarely address dynamic, knowledge-intensive or emergent processes. As a result, current BPMN-based systems offer insufficient support for ad hoc flexibility in complex, unstructured scenarios.

As shown, current BPMSs lack integrated approaches that support ad hoc process adaptation without compromising efficiency and compliance. This leads to the research problem dealt with in this paper.

3 Research Methodology

The research followed a Design Science Research (DSR) strategy distinguishing the five phases outlined by Kuechler and Vaishnavi (2008). Following pragmatism as a research philosophy we applied a multimethod qualitative approach. To ensure practical relevance, real-world use cases were analyzed. First, three semi-structured interviews were conducted with professionals from three different organizations. Then three processes at a Swiss bank were investigated, in which employees have to deal with unstructured, context-dependent situations. Triangulating insights from the literature, expert perspectives, and process analysis workshop enables the study to identify and categorize practical requirements for ad-hoc adaptability and to explore weaknesses of current technologies.

From the triangulation of empirical and theoretical requirements design principles were derived that guided a conceptual extension of BPMN 2.0 and adaptation of the execution procedure. The modeling extension was then implemented using the ADOxx0F[1] metamodeling platform. The development process followed an internal iterative approach in which the artefact was repeatedly refined to ensure consistency with the design principles.

As the developed artefact represents a conceptual and technical design prototype rather than a fully integrated workflow system, an evaluation in a real organizational environment was not feasible. Therefore, a *qualitative ex post workshop (focus group) evaluation* was conducted as an appropriate alternative. Such an approach is consistent with Hevner and Chatterjee [27 p. 119], who suggest analytical or observational evaluations when real-world implementation is not yet possible.

4 Practical Requirements for Ad-Hoc Adaptability

The objective of the phase of problem awareness was to identify (1) the demands in practice for ad hoc business process adaptability and (2) the key limitations of existing business process modelling languages in enabling ad hoc adaptability without compromising compliance and efficiency.

4.1 Practical Demands for Ad Hoc Business Process Adaptability

Expert interviews with three process management specialists from different organizations were conducted. All three experts have been working in Business Process Management (BPM) for many years and bring diverse perspectives: The first interviewee was a senior consultant specialized in BPM who works closely with clients in the areas of modelling, risk management, regulatory and compliance in the financial sector. Interviewee 2 was a BPM Lead Manager with in-depth knowledge of the three OMG standards (BPMN 2.0, CMMN and DMN). Interviewee 3 was a Professional Business Automation Consultant, focusing more on process automation primarily using CMMN and BPMN. The core statements of the participants demonstrated high consistency, so no additional interviews were conducted.

The triangulation of literature, workshops and interviews reveals four central requirement dimensions:

- **Balance of structure and flexibility:** Systems should combine strong support and standardization with the ability to make ad hoc adjustments (e.g. skipping or reordering tasks). This reflects Regev and Wegmann [16] who emphasize stable process components with controlled adjustability.
- **User-oriented adaptability:** Modular structures must enable both simple and complex processes to be tailored to the process executor needs without violating regulations. This confirms the multidimensional adaptability [2].

[1] https://adoxx.org

- **Efficient execution:** Integration of tools, automated data transfers, instant document generation and transparent status reports are crucial to avoid media breaks, redundancy and inefficiency. Otherwise, workarounds emerge, as confirmed in the literature [6, 25, 28].
- **Adaptive compliance:** Compliance must not be seen as a restriction but as supportive guidance. Employees seek controlled flexibility rather than full autonomy, as emphasized by [3]. This notion of controlled flexibility aligns with the principle of acting by opportunity [19], empowering employees to act autonomously within a structured, compliant environment.

Interviews further revealed that short-lived processes vary more strongly, while long-term ones are more stable, but complex processes require many exceptions. Ad hoc cases are often not modelled upfront and only become visible in practice. The interviews also make it clear that processes must be modelled with sufficient flexibility from the outset, in line with the concept of flexibility by design [18]. At the same time, modelling and reality often diverge due to different detail levels, communication gaps, and delays. Employees, therefore, need autonomy to make adjustments, as well as clear roles and frameworks to ensure compliance. In relation to the flexibility dimensions outlined in Sect. 2.1, the findings indicate a preference for structured processes with ad hoc exceptions [15] or for flexibility by deviation during runtime [18]. These are characterized by their temporary, immediate and ad hoc nature, as described by Martinho et al. [3].

It appeared that in practice, there is a high demand for flexible, customer-oriented and efficient processes that reliably meet regulatory requirements. Ad hoc adaptability is regarded as a necessary skill for dealing with exceptional cases, individual customer needs and dynamic process situations. The degree of flexibility required depends both on the level of process structure and the type of flexibility needed.

4.2 Key Limitations of Existing Approaches for Ad-Hoc Adaptability

Interviews revealed that BPMN 2.0 has limited capabilities when it comes to enabling ad hoc adaptability without compromising efficiency or compliance:

- **No real support for unforeseen adaptability:** Existing approaches or ad hoc adaptability are based almost exclusively on predefined mechanisms such as ad hoc subprocesses in BPMN, CF4BPMN, CMMN, BPCMN or ECA rules [3, 7, 8, 13]. Even more advanced solutions, such as SmartPM and Madapt, rely on fully modelled contextual knowledge or do not extend existing modelling languages [20, 21].
- **Workarounds as a risky standard practice:** In reality, exceptions are usually addressed through process variants, tool-specific mechanisms or manual workarounds. The interviewees add that this entails considerable risks. While workarounds promote short-term problem-solving and can even ensure efficiency gains or process continuity in individual cases, they can easily develop into unofficial standards that can lead to data inconsistencies, a lack of traceability, and compliance, legal, and financial risks. A finding that is also found in the literature [4, 5, 29].
- **Risks associated with runtime adjustments:** Although modern tools based on BPMN allow changes to running processes, interview partners say these pose considerable risks to the stability and consistency of active process instances. This is in line

with literature stating that BPMS offer only limited flexibility, low semantic depth and little support for runtime adjustments, which means they cannot cope with the complexity of real, dynamic business processes [2, 12, 26].

- **Complexity due to additional standards:** Supplementary notations such as CMMN or DMN expand the range of expression but increase complexity and slow down adjustments. A point of criticism that is emphasized both by practitioners and in the literature [8].

It appeared that the existing modelling languages and tools currently meet these requirements only to a limited extent. Although BPMN is established as a standard, it does not provide sufficient support for unforeseen ad hoc adaptability to ongoing processes. In practice, this leads to risky workarounds that jeopardize efficiency, compliance and quality. There is therefore a discrepancy between practical requirements and technological possibilities, which underlines the need for further development of BPMN.

The identified requirements and limitations highlight a discrepancy between practical needs and existing technological capabilities demanding for new approaches that enable more robust and flexible process modelling.

5 Ad Hoc Adaptation of BPMN

5.1 Extensions of BPMN

Given that BPMN is a standard for practice of business process management systems, a promising approach is to extend the existing BPMN 2.0 standard to create additional means of expression for restricted ad hoc scenarios instead of creating a new modeling paradigm. The adaptations focus on activities, as they represent the primary executable elements and gateways that support complementary decision-making capabilities. To make the flexibility visible for process modeler and executor, new markers were added that make deviations from the prescribed execution order remain visible, interpretable, and semantically grounded within the BPMN 2.0 model.

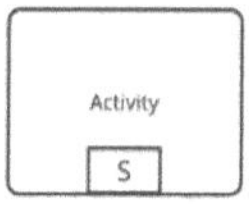

Skip – This mechanism allows activities to be skipped (S*: Skip = true*) if they are not required for a specific instance. Skipped activities are removed from the worklist and not executed later. Before completion, a final validation ensures that all skipped tasks have been reviewed or justified

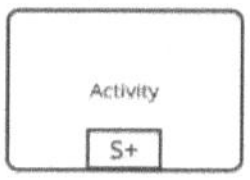

Skip under the Conditions – A refinement of the skip mechanism is conditional skipping (*S+: SkipUnderCondition = true: This task may be skipped if X is met*), in which the omission of an activity is bound to predefined conditions, such as a fulfilled business rule, a low-risk case classification, or supervisory approval. Conditional skipping thereby provides structured, rule-governed flexibility without modifying the control-flow structure.

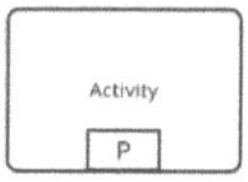

Postpone – The postpone execution mechanism (*P: Postpone = true*) allows activities to be deferred and temporarily placed in the worklist. Postponed tasks must be completed before the process can be finalized, ensuring that mandatory steps remain auditable and are not overlooked.

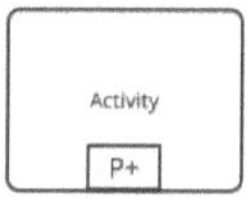

Postpone under Conditions – Analogous to conditional skipping, the conditional delay (*P+: PostponeUnderCondition = true: This task may be postponed if X is met*) mechanism restricts the postponement of an activity to predefined conditions. Postponing a task is therefore only permissible when clearly specified contextual requirements are met. These rules are embedded in the activity, ensuring that postponement remains controlled, transparent, and semantically grounded.

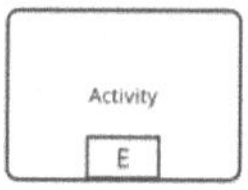

Earlier Execution – Certain activities may be executed before their assigned position (*E: ExecutedEarlier*) in the process. Early-completed tasks are recorded in the worklist to prevent duplicate execution. When the normal process flow reaches the activity, the workflow engine detects the prior completion and skips it while maintaining traceability. A final validation ensures that no mandatory activities were omitted. Only tasks explicitly marked for early execution may use this mechanism.

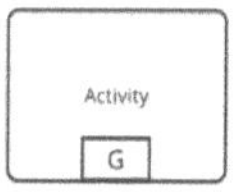

Goal-based Earlier Execution – A related mechanism links an activity to a defined goal condition (*G: GoalAchieved = true*). When the process reaches the activity, the workflow engine checks whether the goal has already been fulfilled. If so, the activity is automatically marked as completed without explicit execution, enabling implicit early execution.

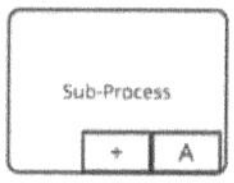

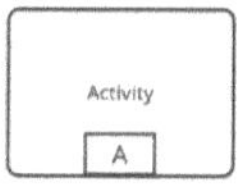

Alternative Execution – This extension supports alternative execution paths by defining substitute activities that fulfil the same logical purpose. A task may be linked to an alternative (A= Alternative), allowing a predefined substitute to replace the primary activity. Unlike BPMN ad hoc subprocesses, which enable open-ended and user-driven flexibility but are insufficient when user freedom must be controlled, this mechanism defines explicit and controllable substitution relationships between tasks.

The concept of discretionary tasks in CMMN [14, pp. 5–6] was not adopted in this work, as it belongs to a different modelling notation and introduces complexity by mixing BPMN and CMMN

User-driven Gateways – They may be used to enable authorized users to select predefined execution options at runtime. Such gateways make the distinction between the standard process path and permitted deviations explicitly visible within the control flow. User-driven gateways offer flexibility only within predefined options and require greater modelling effort to ensure that each deviation path is correctly represented.

Rule-based Gateway – Rule-based gateways can be used to in-corporate technical and compliance-related decision logic directly into the process flow. Such gateways determine whether a case follows the standard or an exceptional path based on predefined rules (*if specialCase = true, then activate deviation path*).

While user-driven and rule-based gateways provide a high degree of control, they also increase model complexity when numerous exceptions and alternative paths must be represented..

Several of the proposed flexibility mechanisms rely on the ability to track the status of the activities. Their semantics are explained using the concept of a central worklist, which workflow engines use to control execution and ensure traceability and validation. The worklist records all affected activities throughout process execution and ensures that they are systematically validated before the process instance is completed.

The consolidated view in Table 2 summarizes how the selected extensions support flexible yet compliant process execution. The table provides a structured overview of each mechanism, including its advantages and limitations.

The proposed BPMN extensions provide a structured and semantically grounded way to model controlled runtime flexibility directly within the notation. To operationalize these mechanisms in a real workflow environment, it is essential to analyze the execution procedure and propose adaptations that support the extended semantic.

5.2 Implementation of the Modelling Language

The metamodel for the BPMN extension was implemented using the ADOxx metamodeling platform (See Footnote 1), which provides both a development environment for modelling language extensions and a modelling toolkit for applying and visualizing the resulting artefact (Fig. 1).

Table 2. Proposed Extension Mechanisms

Mechanism	Advantages	Limitations
Skip/Skip under the condition	• High flexibility • Rule-based control • Reduce unnecessary work	• Requires validation to prevent unjustified skipping/postpone-ment • Conditional rules must be defined
Postpone/Postpone under the condition	• Retains mandatory tasks • Supports controlled flexibility	
Earlier execution	• Supports opportunistic work • Prevents redundant execution	• Requires validation
Goal-based earlier execution	• Prevents redundant execution • Supports opportunistic work	• Requires clearly defined and verifiable goal conditions • Implicit flexible
Alternative execution	• Modular adaptability • Supports contextual variations	• Alternative must be clearly modelled • Grouping required

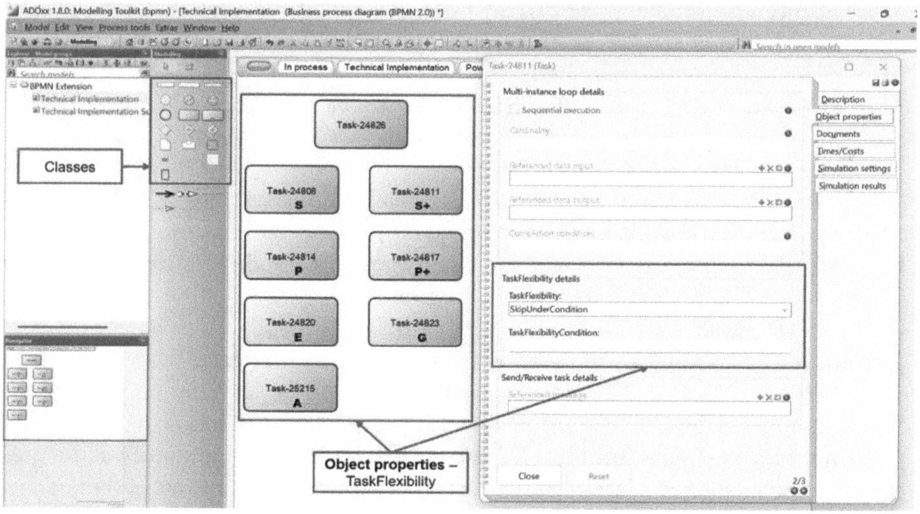

Fig. 1. ADOxx Modelling Toolkit TaskFlexibility

5.3 Adaptation of the Execution Procedure

Modelling extensions alone are insufficient if the execution engine does not support them (Geiger et al. 2018). Any extension to the flow objects of a modelling language must be accompanied by corresponding adaptations in the execution environment to ensure that the intended semantics are correctly operationalized. This section outlines adaptations required in the workflow engine that enables the execution of the BPMN extensions introduced in Sect. 5.1. The execution logic for the user task in this thesis explicitly relies on a worklist, consistent with standard BPMN implementations. Building on BPMN execution procedure, the following modifications (written in *italics*) are necessary to support the BPMN extensions:

- **Follow the sequence flow:** Tokens move along the defined sequence flow, thereby controlling the process's flow.
- **Activation of tasks:** As soon as an activity (task) receives a token, it is activated.

  For automated tasks, the system executes them immediately.
  For human tasks (user tasks), they are added to the worklist.

  - ***Skip:*** *The engine immediately records it as skipped and proceeds with the next step. If a task is skipped, it must be reviewed and justified.*
  - ***Skip under condition:*** *The engine evaluates the associated condition. If the condition is met, the task is marked as skipped under the condition; otherwise, it remains active in the worklist.*
  - ***Postpone:*** *The task is deferred and remains in the worklist with the status postponed. Execution is possible at any later time before instance completion.*
  - ***Postpone under condition:*** *The engine evaluates the postponement condition. If fulfilled, the task is postponed; otherwise, it must be executed immediately.*
  - ***Earlier execution:*** *If the task was already completed earlier in the process, the activation triggers a check of the worklist. The engine recognizes prior completion and automatically bypasses the task.*
  - ***Goal-based earlier execution:*** *Upon activation, the engine evaluates whether the task's goal condition is already satisfied. If so, the task is marked as completed without further action.*
  - ***Alternative execution:*** *If the task has defined alternatives, the engine evaluates the alternative subprocess and displays the primary task alongside all permissible substitute activities. Once the user selects an alternative, the corresponding activity is activated instead of the original task.*

- **Execution and completion of tasks**: When a human task is selected from the worklist and executed, it changes from ready to active in the lifecycle. After processing, the task is completed, and the associated token is passed on to the following item(s).
- **Continuation and termination of the process**: The process continues as long as tokens are available. A process ends when all the following points are given:

  All started activities have been completed.
  No more tokens are active.
  No more events are waiting to be triggered.
  All tasks on the worklist are completed:

  - *In case of skipped tasks, they are reviewed and justified.*

- *In the event of early execution, tasks are verified to ensure no mandatory activities have been omitted.*

Taken together, these adaptations provide the execution-level logic required to technically realize the proposed BPMN extensions and thereby enable flexible task behavior at runtime.

6 Evaluation

A *qualitative ex post workshop (focus group) evaluation* was conducted. This method allowed an in-depth examination of expert feedback regarding the artefact's *usability*, *applicability*, and *efficiency*.

The qualitative feedback gathered during the workshops was analyzed to identify strengths, limitations, and areas for improvement regarding both the artefact and the underlying design principles. This empirical investigation represents an *ex post validation*, providing external confirmation of the artefact's utility and the contextual relevance of the design principles in real-world business process scenarios.

The evaluation was conducted in a workshop with four process management experts from a Swiss bank, who were not involved in the previous workshop to minimize confirmation bias and ensure the independence of the evaluation. This participant composition captured complementary perspectives on the design principles and the developed artefact. During the workshop, the participants reviewed and critically discussed the formulated design principles and applied and critically discussed the developed BPMN extensions for modelling ad hoc adjustments to previously analyzed business processes (see Sect. 4.1).

The evaluation focused on assessing the design principles, verifying their clarity, completeness, and relevance as perceived by practitioners. It examines whether the principles sufficiently capture the requirements for enabling adaptive process execution. In terms of internal validity, the evaluation employed a coherent and appropriate methodology for the artefact's early development phase. The qualitative workshop helped to clarify the perspectives of process executors and modelers. However, the results are based mainly on personal views rather than measurable data. In terms of external validity, the results mainly reflect the environment at the specific bank, where the overall maturity level of process management is relatively low. The scenarios tested were realistic but limited in scope and complexity. To confirm the broader applicability of the BPMN extension and design principles, future evaluations in different organizations or more dynamic environments would be helpful.

Despite these limitations, the selected evaluation criteria of usability, applicability, and efficiency provided a clear and consistent framework. Nevertheless, these criteria focus mainly on qualitative aspects. Evaluating quantitative metrics, such as modelling time or error rates, in future studies could improve the reliability and comparability of results.

7 Conclusion

7.1 Contribution

The study shows that BPMN can be meaningfully extended through targeted metamodel extensions that embed flexibility attributes and conformity constraints directly into the notation. This integration enables controlled, rule-based adjustments at runtime without requiring additional modelling languages or compromising the model's simplicity. The developed BPMN extension addresses all four dimensions in an integrated manner.

- **Modelling extension:** Enhances the BPMN 2.0 metamodel without introducing a new language.
- **Ad hoc adaptability:** Implements flexibility attributes enabling controlled process adaptations directly within the model.
- **Efficiency:** Embeds flexibility into the BPMN structure, removing the need for external work-arounds and reducing modelling and execution complexity.
- **Compliance:** Defines rule-based, auditable conditions governing deviations, ensuring transparency and regulatory compliance.

Regarding the classifications discussed in Sect. 2.1, the developed BPMN extension primarily addresses *structured processes with ad hoc exceptions* [15] and *case-oriented processes* [10], in which a stable process structure is maintained while controlled deviations are permitted. In terms of flexibility types, it mainly provides *flexibility by design* and partially supports *flexibility by deviation* [18]. According to the dimensions of [3] these adaptations are planned (defined during design), typically immediate (selected at runtime), often temporary but potentially permanent at the instance level, and generally incremental (applied locally to tasks or subprocesses).

In addition to the adhoc processes or inclusive gateways in BPMN or the CF4BPMN extension, the presented adaptations also allow changes in the order of process execution by even performing tasks earlier than planned (acting by opportunity). While higher levels of self-adaptation [2], such as automated monitoring, proactive detection, or autonomous execution are not yet addressed, the extension provides a solid foundation for advancing BPMN towards more context-aware and self-adaptive process execution.

The design principles bridge the gap between flexibility and governance in business processes and can serve as a basis for future research on adaptive process design. The artefact itself operationalizes these principles by extending the BPMN metamodel, demonstrating how controlled flexibility can be embedded directly into a standard notation.

7.2 Open Questions and Future Research

Although the research confirmed the feasibility and conceptual soundness of the proposed BPMN extensions, there are some suggestions for improvement. The current solution focuses on the modelling level and proposes adapting the execution procedure. Future research should therefore investigate how the proposed flexibility constructs can be operationalized within workflow engines to enable real-time adaptation and automatic compliance checking.

Although the artefact supports predefined flexibility (flexibility by design), it does not yet allow for spontaneous deviations at runtime (flexibility by deviation). Participant feedback further indicated a need for greater user guidance and system support. Future research should therefore explore how user-centered technologies, such as process mining or AI-based assistance systems, can enable controlled ad hoc adaptability while maintaining compliance and usability for non-technical users.

Acknowledgments. We thank Hypothekarbank Lenzburg for providing the case.

Disclosure of Interests. The authors have no competing interests to declare that are relevant to the content of this article.

References

1. Marrella, A., Mecella, M., Halapuu, P., Sardina, S.: Automated process adaptation in cyber-physical domains with the SmartPM system (short paper). In: 2015 IEEE 8th International Conference on Service-Oriented Computing and Applications (SOCA), pp. 59–64 (2015). https://doi.org/10.1109/SOCA.2015.18
2. Oukharijane, J., Chaâbane, M.A., Said, I.B., Andonoff, E., Bouaziz, R.: An assessment taxonomy for self-adaptation business process solutions. Data Knowl. Eng. **155**, 102374 (2024). https://doi.org/10.1016/j.datak.2024.102374
3. Martinho, R., Domingos, D., Varajão, J.: CF4BPMN: a BPMN extension for controlled flexibility in business processes. Procedia Comput. Sci. **64**, 1232–1239 (2015). https://doi.org/10.1016/j.procs.2015.08.509
4. de Vargas Pinto, A., Beerepoot, I., Maçada, A.C.G.: Encourage autonomy to increase individual work performance: the impact of job characteristics on workaround behavior and shadow IT usage. Inf. Technol. Manag. **24**(3), 233–246 (2023). https://doi.org/10.1007/s10799-022-00368-6
5. Soffer, P., Outmazgin, N., Hadar, I., Tzafrir, S.: Why work around the process? Analyzing workarounds through the lens of the theory of planned behavior. Bus. Inf. Syst. Eng. **65**(4), 369–389 (2023). https://doi.org/10.1007/s12599-023-00802-1
6. Zainuddin, E., Staples, S.: Developing a shared taxonomy of workaround behaviors for the information systems field. In: 2016 49th Hawaii International Conference on System Sciences (HICSS), pp. 5278–5287 (2016). https://doi.org/10.1109/HICSS.2016.652
7. Hinkelmann, K.: Business process flexibility and decision-aware modeling—the knowledge work designer. In: Karagiannis, D., Mayr, H.C., Mylopoulos, J. (eds.) Domain-Specific Conceptual Modeling, pp. 397–414. Springer, Heidelberg (2016). https://doi.org/10.1007/978-3-319-39417-6_18
8. Zensen, A., Küster, J.:. A comparison of flexible BPMN and CMMN in practice: a case study on component release processes. In: 2018 IEEE 22nd International Enterprise Distributed Object Computing Conference (EDOC), pp. 105–114 (2018). https://doi.org/10.1109/EDOC.2018.00023
9. Goldstein, A., Johanndeiter, T., Frank, U.: Business process runtime models: towards bridging the gap between design, enactment, and evaluation of business processes. Inf. Syst. E-Bus. Manag. **17**(1), 27–64 (2018). https://doi.org/10.1007/s10257-018-0374-2
10. Gadatsch, A.: Grundkurs Geschäftsprozess-Management: Analyse, Modellierung, Optimierung und Controlling von Prozessen, 9th edn. Springer eBooks (2020). https://doi.org/10.1007/978-3-658-27812-0

11. Domingos, D., Martinho, R., Varajão, J.: Controlled flexibility in healthcare processes: a BPMN-extension approach. In: Cruz-Cunha, M., Miranda, I., Martinho, R., Rijo, R. (eds.) Encyclopedia of E-Health and Telemedicine, pp. 521–535. IGI Global Scientific Publishing (2016). https://doi.org/10.4018/978-1-4666-9978-6.ch040
12. Geiger, M., Harrer, S., Lenhard, J., Wirtz, G.: BPMN 2.0: the state of support and implementation. Futur. Gener. Comput. Syst. **80**, 250–262 (2018). https://doi.org/10.1016/j.fu-ture.2017.01.006
13. Knolmayer, G., Endl, R., Pfahrer, M.: Modeling processes and workflows by business rules. In: van der Aalst, W., Desel, J., Oberweis, A. (eds.) Business Process Management. LNCS, vol. 1806, pp. 16–29. Springer, Heidelberg (2000). https://doi.org/10.1007/3-540-45594-9_2
14. OMG. Case Management Model and Notation (CMMN). Object Management Group (2016). https://www.omg.org/spec/CMMN/1.1/PDF
15. Szelągowski, M., Lupeikiene, A.: Business Process management systems: evolution and development trends. Informatica **31**(3), 579–595 (2020). https://doi.org/10.15388/20-INFOR429
16. Regev, G., Bider, I., Wegmann, A.: Defining business process flexibility with the help of invariants. Softw. Process: Improvement Pract. **12**(1), 65–79 (2006). https://doi.org/10.1002/spip.301
17. Fahland, D., Koschmider, A., Laune, R.: Prozessmanagement und Process-Mining: Grundlagen. De Gruyter Oldenbourg (2020). https://doi.org/10.1515/9783110500165
18. Schonenberg, M.H., Mans, R.S., Russell, N.C., Mulyar, N.A., Van Der Aalst, W.M.P.: Process flexibility: a survey of contemporary approaches. In: Dietz, J.L.G., Albani, A., Barjis, J. (eds.) Advances in Enterprise Engineering I, vol. 10, pp. 16–30. Springer, Heidelberg (2008). https://doi.org/10.1007/978-3-540-68644-6_2
19. Hinkelmann, K., Karagiannis, D.: Context-sensitive office tasks a generative approach. Decis. Supp. Syst. **8**(3), 255–267 (1992). https://doi.org/10.1016/0167-9236(92)90018-K
20. Bucchiarone, A., Pistore, M., Raik, H., Kazhamiakin, R.: Adaptation of service-based business processes by context-aware replanning. In: 2011 IEEE International Conference on Service-Oriented Computing and Applications (SOCA). 2011 IEEE International Conference on Service-Oriented Computing and Applications (SOCA), Irvine, CA, USA (2011). https://doi.org/10.1109/SOCA.2011.6166209
21. Marrella, A.: Automated planning for business process management. J. Data Semant. **8**(2), 79–98 (2018). https://doi.org/10.1007/s13740-018-0096-0
22. Ghahderijani, A.Y., Karastoyanova, D.: Autonomic process performance improvement. In: 2021 IEEE 25th International Enterprise Distributed Object Computing Workshop (EDOCW), pp. 299–307 (2021). https://doi.org/10.1109/EDOCW52865.2021.00061
23. Sáez, S. G., Andrikopoulos, V., Hahn, M., Karastoyanova, D., Weiß, A.: Enabling reusable and adaptive modeling, provisioning & execution of BPEL processes. In: 2015 IEEE 8th International Conference on Service-Oriented Computing and Applications (SOCA), 51–58 (2015). https://doi.org/10.1109/SOCA.2015.13
24. van der Aalst, W.M.P.: Process-aware information systems: lessons to be learned from process mining. In: Jensen, K., Aalst, W.M.P. (eds.) Transactions on Petri Nets and Other Models of Concurrency II: Special Issue on Concurrency in Process-Aware Information Systems, pp. 1–26. Springer, Heidelberg (2009). https://doi.org/10.1007/978-3-642-00899-3_1
25. Davison, R.M., Wong, L.H.M., Ou, C.X.J., Alter, S.: The coordination of workarounds: insights from responses to misfits between local realities and a mandated global enterprise system. Inf. Manag. **58**(8), 103530 (2021). https://doi.org/10.1016/j.im.2021.103530
26. Szelągowski, M., Berniak-Woźny, J.: BPM challenges, limitations and future development directions – a systematic literature review. Bus. Process. Manag. J. **30**(2), 505–557 (2024). https://doi.org/10.1108/BPMJ-06-2023-0419

27. Hevner, A., Chatterjee, S.: Design research in information systems: theory and practice. In: Design Research in Information Systems. Integrated Series in Information Systems, Vol. 22. Springer US (2010). https://doi.org/10.1007/978-1-4419-5653-8_1
28. Wibisono, A.: Workarounds arise from a brokerage structure in the organisation: case study insights. Procedia Comput. Sci. **234**, 741–747 (2024). https://doi.org/10.1016/j.procs.2024.03.060
29. Ross, K., Sean, S., Jim, B., Vijay, K.: Workarounds to computer access in healthcare organizations: you want my password or a dead patient? In: Studies in Health Technology and Informatics (2015). https://doi.org/10.3233/978-1-61499-488-6-215

BPMN-Based RPA Projects Modeling and Analysis Method

Andrei Pavel(✉), Ana-Maria Ghiran, and Robert Andrei Buchmann

OMILAB@UBB-FSEGA and Business Informatics Research Center, Faculty of Economics and Business Administration, Babeş-Bolyai University, 58-60 T. Mihali Street, 400591 Cluj-Napoca, Romania

andrei.pavel.ro@gmail.com, {anamaria.ghiran, robert.buchmann}@econ.ubbcluj.ro

Abstract. During the last decade, RPA (Robotic Process Automation) has gained significant popularity as a transformative force in enterprise digitalization projects. However, the practice has been largely platform-driven and detached from traditional business process management, the BPM lens being applied rather retrospectively. In the authors' regional outsourcing hub, RPA projects are defined around the licensed platform that facilitates the actual development of bots. This pragmatic view is based on the RPA promise of reduced operational costs, but not all business processes are suitable for this transformation. Elements of the traditional BPM lifecycle return in specific forms, e.g. new approaches to process querying and reporting. The transition from identifying a potential RPA candidate project to a successful and scalable one can be complex, relying on traceable semantics that consider both the process structure and key performance indicators - these can be integrated by means of domain-specific conceptual modeling, extending process modeling standards that lack the specificity needed to support the phases of the RPA project lifecycle. This paper proposes a BPMN extension in tandem with Generative AI recommendations, tailored to bridge the gap between traditional business process modeling and RPA project management. The work follows a metamodeling approach and a Design Science process to produce a hybrid BPMN-RPA modeling method informed by the concrete needs of RPA practice as well as by the design-oriented research tradition on BPMN extensions.

Keywords: Robotic Process Automation · RPA lifecycle · BPMN · Business process management

1 Introduction

Robotic Process Automation (RPA) has emerged as a critical component in enterprise automation and digital transformation [1]. Even in the age of Generative AI, it remains the basis for workflow and orchestrations, with many RPA platforms being rebranded as AI workflow managers and agentic orchestrators (see [2]). Indeed, the desideratum of automating procedural work remains relevant as a complement to the stochastic behavior of generative AI [3, 4], or in tandem with symbolic knowledge representation - for

E. Laurenzi et al. (Eds.): BIR 2026, LNBIP 601, pp. 80–96, 2027.
https://doi.org/10.1007/978-3-032-38498-0_6

process knowledge [5], for work systems contextualization of processes [6] and even for RPA-specific bot logic [7]. Beyond the execution concerns that dominate the RPA landscape, this practical-oriented field is also subjected to business process management (BPM) concerns e.g. regarding the maintenance of process repositories, gap analysis, prioritization decision-making. However, RPA platforms have been less interested in such aspects, forcing automation projects to center on bot development, leaving teams to handle project management through legacy approaches from software development projects, and less as business process reengineering projects.

Rather recently, considerations for business process analysis and design were raised as an afterthought in the RPA vendor discourse, with some new resources introduced as explicit support – e.g. a BPMN modeler recently added to UiPath [8], or a process analysis framework added to the vendor's training programs [9]. The business process modeling scientific community started investigating the RPA phenomenon rather retrospectively, with recent design propositions and conceptualizations [10] following already in-place wide adoption and practice, rather than offering prescriptive knowledge. These are signals that the pragmatic and the scientific facets of RPA are converging - perhaps with a detour induced by agentic AI, towards which RPA products gravitate as orchestration engines. This paper proposes a *model-driven RPA management method* that reflects this convergence trend – on a project management level and in design-time scope, rather than as run-time support. The work contributes a novel BPMN extension that bridges the gap to RPA management needs, combined with semantic traceability and GenAI recommendations based on project knowledge gathered in a modeling environment. BPMN has been chosen as a starting point for (a) *an ideological reason* – to close a gap between traditional BPM and RPA by leveraging potential BPMN familiarity; (b) *a scientific reason* – to enrich the landscape of BPMN extensions [11] with a pragmatically relevant domain specificity, and (c) *a pragmatic reason* – the availability of a BPMN open source implementation for ADOxx, as part of the Bee-Up educational tool [12]. The BPMN execution semantics are not involved here, as RPA bots are still expected to be developed on vendor-specific platforms, therefore the proposed treatment is hereby positioned as a knowledge capture approach in support of decision-oriented phases of the RPA management lifecycle.

The work is organized as a Design Science project [13] with a DSML engineering subprocess in its Development and Demonstration phases based on the AMME (Agile Modeling Method Engineering) [14] methodology. AMME is a framework for tool development on the ADOxx metamodeling platform [15] - an established platform across many DSML projects [16] and across the OMILAB Community of Practice [17].

2 Background and Problem Statement

2.1 RPA Project Management Challenges

RPA still serves as a mature and *deterministic* approach to deploying more efficient processes by replacing human work with robotic agents acting across heterogeneous system interfaces, operating consistently, continuously and at scale [18]. The execution scope must be complemented by design & analysis methods that precede technology-focused bot development and can support evaluation efforts and decision-making.

RPA project management is often performed in an ad-hoc manner, using in-house tools and metrics inherited from legacy practices from agile software projects. Especially in the outsourcing-centric environment of the authors, business process management cultures are lacking, most resources being allocated to engineering and execution under the incentive or threat of back-shoring also signaled in recent surveys [19]. The lack of comprehensive process documentation at local RPA service providers has made it difficult to assess the automation potential for a specific RPA customer. Decision makers tend to focus on very specific KPIs e.g. return of investment (ROI) or implementation effort, and analysis is done at financial level, lacking traceability to granular business processes being automated, failing to reflect the transformative impact.

In over 5 years of involvement with RPA projects in the region, we encountered two stakeholder groups with divergent objectives: (a) decision makers that must assess whether an investment in an RPA project is reliable and effective; (b) RPA COE (Centers of Excellence) consultants whose role is to propose and promote the suitability of a certain project for automation. Both groups heavily rely on subjective judgments and financial evidence detached from process granularity, or overly simplified representations of a process (i.e. flowchart sketches), often agnostic of standards like BPMN.

Vendors like UiPath [2] outlined a lifecycle for RPA projects comprising several stages: it starts with the submission of potential automation ideas (the *Idea* phase) or their derivation from a specific ideation approach (e.g. Design Thinking), followed by the *Assessment* and *Qualification* phases in which feasibility, risks and expected benefits are evaluated, before the UiPath platform is actually engaged in development. The *Idea* phase is often illustrated through screen captures and screen recordings of the manual process, capturing a manual performer's work experience on small tasks but failing to give a full overview of the use case in its enterprise context. Consequently, the automation analysis is narrow-scoped and incomplete, often leading to poor performances in subsequent steps, e.g. *Implementation* and *Live*. In some cases, such recommendations are enhanced with encouragement towards BPMN modeling (commonly replaced with improvised flowcharting) - an explicit recognition of a need for process analysis frameworks and even process mining [20] adopted from traditional Business Process Management, but this is still done in a disconnected manner that keeps neglecting an enterprise-wide integrated view on business process interdependencies.

This is the gap that our work aims to fill through a model-based demonstrator – centered around BPMN but with the potential to be extended towards enterprise architectures. Standard modeling practices such as those based on BPMN can formally and granularly represent the process fragments targeted for automation and their dependencies, but they do not provide support for risk assessment, benefits or impact in the organization [21]. Therefore, this paper aims to build on the complementarity between traditional BPMN modeling and RPA project management. As design-oriented work, it contributes a BPMN modeling extension that integrates KPIs and model-driven GenAI recommendations into BPMN diagrams, supporting more informed and comprehensive decision making during the *Assessment* and *Qualification* phases of the RPA lifecycle.

2.2 The Problem Context: RPA Project Phases

The reality of RPA projects we came in direct contact with is characterized by pilot projects that pose major issues when they must expand across the entire enterprise – scaling and complexity management requires process knowledge that is both granular and remains traceable as it scales. For this, RPA vendors promote structured development lifecycles, governance frameworks and dedicated Centers of Excellence but are less interested in providing system analysis tooling. Although each vendor might use their own terminology, project management methodologies are rather similar: e.g. UiPath [2] proposes a lifecycle composed of the following stages that are interpreted in our outsourcing environment as follows:

1. **Idea** – automation ideas are submitted by selected stakeholders, and duplicates are filtered out. Ideas that can't be automated are rejected and the rest advance. No process catalog/repository is assumed to exist – ideas come from ideation workshops (brainstorming, Design Thinking) or are directly submitted as a response to a frustration or inspired by a cost saving proposition.
2. **Assessment** – ideas are assessed to understand their scope and the technology required to implement them. Assessments depend on how articulated ideas are and how convincing the savings benefits. The AsIs vs ToBe gap analysis and structural process reengineering should come into place in a BPM culture, but typically weakly structured process sketches and Powerpoint slides become the basis for assessment, lacking streamlining to quantitative indicators that typically originate somewhere else than in process simulations and performance indicators.
3. **Qualification** – In this phase, automation decision-makers prioritize and pick the automation ideas they want to move forward with.
4. **Implementation** – The ToBe automated process steps are designed based on current documentation that often does not even have a process form (screen recordings, shadowing of human workers, think aloud protocols). A solution design is put in place and the developers start building the actual bot. Testers will test the solution and document their activities managed as a software development project. An end-to-end legacy process description with enterprise dependencies is not always available prior to implementation, the modeling mostly focus on the ToBe evolution and propositions, but even those lack in terms of machine-readability, traceability and comparability. The architectural dependencies in the overall process or enterprise architecture are obscured or discovered as obstacles are met.
5. **Go-Live** – After the automation is built and tested, it can be moved into a production environment, followed by monitoring and quality assurance efforts.

In the *Assessment* and *Qualification* phases, a significant effort is spent on formalizing the process to be carried out in order to reduce ambiguity and uncertainty. This has been also reported by literature [22], and is confirmed by our own experience with planning RPA projects in the absence of a BPM culture, strictly from a service/engineering provider stance or as reaction to back-shoring initiatives. Although automation use cases are evaluated in detail, the criteria again reveal a software development or workload management perspective: presence of structured data, rule-based logic in isolation (around a decision), IT systems dependencies, work volume and frequency. Work system viewpoints are missing or unsupported, even those pertaining to traditional business process management systems and the BPM lifecycle. Stakeholders are looking into potential time savings and alignment with the enterprise's strategic goals. They may use legacy project management tools to provide a thorough *Assessment* phase output based on backlogs and hierarchical decompositions rather than streamlining, granularity and traceability along workflows. In the *Qualification* step, prioritization typically considers business criticality and estimated implementation effort. The main question that this phase should answer is: "Should this process be automated now?" – considering alternatives and dependencies that propagate across a holistic process map – which only exists where BPM existed as a practice before the uptake of RPA initiatives; in an outsourcing environment where this does not exist, the nature of such projects is highly fragmented and driven by costing considerations.

Several documentation tools are commonly involved, and these may use modeling tools for communication and documentation purposes, including visual flowcharting. In BPM process analysis means more than that, e.g. involving process simulation and process querying. BPMN has become the de facto standard for representing business processes, but even if a process management culture based on it exists, the standard misses RPA-specialized concepts for decision making [21]. The main players in the RPA market provide their own visual design environments as low-code environments - BPMN was not the preferred design language, even though BPMN-based automation/orchestration proved feasible prior to the success of RPA (in products like Camunda [23], Tasky [24] etc.). RPA platforms focus on delivering seamless integration and execution across enterprise system interfaces, promoting the low-code development experience rather than supporting a business process management perspective.

3 Research Objectives

3.1 The Nature of the Design Science Artifact

Domain specific modeling allows the integration of custom semantics, constraints and functionality that can incorporate technological-specificity to achieve streamlining and alignment with practice-specific purposes [25]. Taking the DSML engineering approach advocated in the OMILAB Community of Practice and past projects reported in the literature [16], we use as starting point a BPMN implementation aiming to bridge the gap against use cases identified in the RPA projects lifecycle. More specifically, the objective of this Design Science research (DSR) is to extend BPMN into a modeling method that incorporates aspects relevant to the RPA project lifecycle. This comprises both language extensions (visual and semantic) as well as model-driven functionalities for decision support, with feasibility demonstrated through an ADOxx-based toolkit realized around the existing BPMN metamodel deployment available in Bee-Up [12].

3.2 Comparison with UiPath Automation Hub

To address the project management shortcomings of RPA bot development toolkits, UiPath has recently introduced the Automation Hub [26]. This is a collaborative workspace that allows users to discover and manage automation opportunities in one place. It supports the previously described RPA project lifecycle, especially the prerequisite steps before the Implementation phase. The main feature of Automation Hub is that it centrally captures and manages automation opportunities and process improvements while also allowing prioritization by impact and ROI. It offers a visual way to manage ongoing projects, as well as a collaborative approach to the RPA project lifecycle. Automation Hub uses as main criteria for evaluating a project the ease of implementation (which is required as input from a user) and the automation potential, derived from financial perspective (ROI, savings, etc.). A missing aspect of the Automation Hub is the overview of the process, and a clear delimitation of the automation scope, an AsIs vs ToBe analysis, potential risks at enterprise level and changes in the organization.

4 Research and Application Methodology

This study adopts Design Science Research (DSR) [13] as a general research methodology. AMME (Agile Modeling Method Engineering) [14] was employed as the engineering approach for creating and evolving the BPMN-derived modeling method and model-driven functionality deployed through the ADOxx metamodeling platform. AMME on the other hand is a DSML development methodology that repurposes agile principles for modeling method engineering – oftentimes it is employed as a subprocess of DSR, considering the nature of the proposed artifact. The envisioned application methodology for the proposed method is an augmentation of the RPA lifecycle as depicted in Fig. 1.

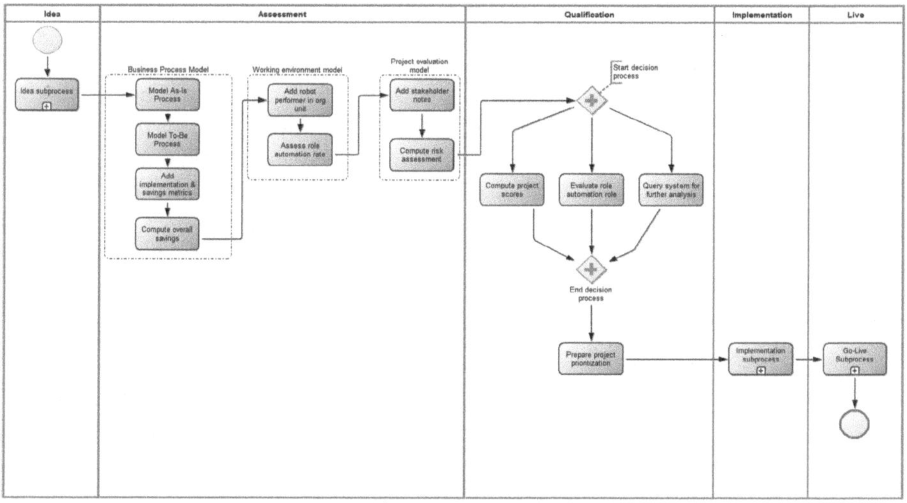

Fig. 1. ToBe workflow of the RPA project lifecycle

The functionalities of the modeling tool are centered towards the *Assessment* and *Qualification* steps of the RPA project lifecycle: labelling AsIs vs ToBe steps for comparability, to showcase how the process would change via RPA automation, computing evaluation metrics on different RPA initiatives, getting GenAI interpretations and assessing the impact of the automation at business unit level. Diagrammatically, the method is based on (a) *Business process models* – BPMN with some project management extensions; (b) *Working environment models* – an intersection between Alter's work system conceptualization [33] and Bee-Up's legacy organizational charts, reflecting the participation of robot workers and the execution roles delegated to them; (c) *Project evaluation models* – a project management view with computation features that aggregate indicators and risks, towards computing a project-level automation score that can be used for prioritization.

5 The Proposed Artifact

5.1 Design Decisions

The DSML consists of three model types depicted in Fig. 2 – legacy concepts that are directly reused (from BPMN and Bee-Up's organization chart) are not shown:

A. **The business process model** – it reuses BPMN concepts to showcase the process steps of the scenarios proposed for automation. The Task object is annotated with implementation and savings attributes, that allow a granular decomposition of the cost-benefit analysis. It also contains the Referenced Task attribute, meant to differentiate those tasks that are common (or different) in the AsIs vs ToBe analysis. The Data Object has also received the same referencing treatment. The specialized Process State aggregation is meant to better group the two states of the depicted process. Visually, the Business Process Diagram also benefits from highlighting, changing colors based on relevant attribute values (to be shown in running examples in Sect. 5.2).
B. **The process evaluation model** – for cataloguing candidate automation projects, aggregate their costs, savings and stakeholder annotations as basis for a prioritization framework. It uses certain elements from the BPMN notation, such as pools that only serve a visual grouping purpose. The RPA Project resource contains attributes that characterize relevant KPIs for the process *Assessment* and *Qualification* phases of the RPA lifecycle. Furthermore, the BPMN Note element was specialized into a Stakeholder Note object, that contains attributes relevant for weighing the notes of stakeholders on a project. As the Process evaluation model works with subprocesses, the element was also specialized using the *Implementation time* and *Frequency per month* attributes.

The *linked_to* connector has the role to aggregate all subprocesses needed to implement a certain RPA Project. A project is typically made up of more "automations", and the possibility to link multiple process fragments to a project opens up other contribution analysis: how would the project look if we automate everything, what if we don't implement x or y fragments – flexible decomposition in process fragments is thus essential. The new element, *RPA _Project* has several attributes with values incorporated in the graphical representation (Fig. 3) for a quicker grasp of the project KPIs. The Stakeholder note is a grey rectangle, that also shows relevant annotations - title, note text and note weight – these are intended to be exposed to and interpreted by an LLM service (OpenAI in current demonstrators acting as an automation recommender).

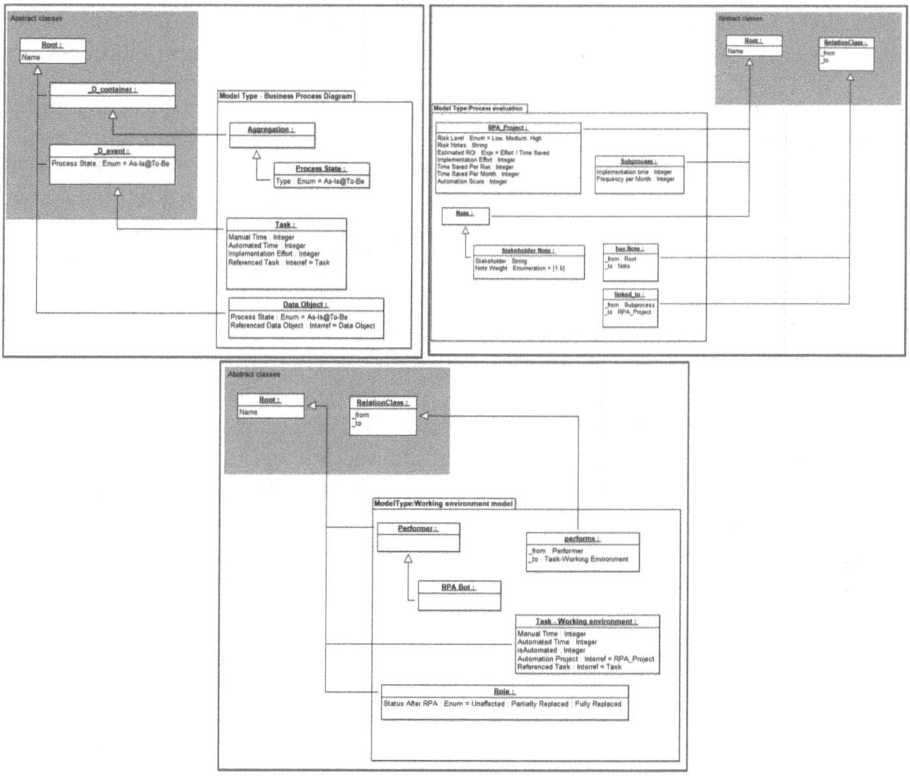

Fig. 2. BPMN extensions (top-left), the Process evaluation metamodel (top-right) and the Work environment extensions (bottom)

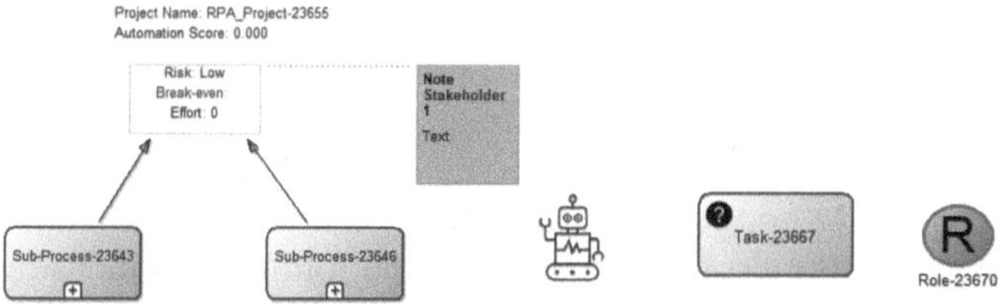

Fig. 3. Mappings to KPIs and stakeholder inputs (left), custom work system elements (right)

C. **The working environment model** – extends the Bee-Up working environment to express the replacement or addition of "bot" workers along human performers and the possibility to connect them to tasks/subprocesses as recommended by the work systems framework [27], therefore it provides a task responsibility mapping beyond the legacy organigram. The model type was specialized to allow an analysis of the automation impact over the organization. The *Role* resource is enriched with a post RPA status that contribute to an automation rate per business unit. The *Performer* was also specialized in a bot worker and, unlike the original Bee-Up organization charts, such elements are connected to convenient process fragments (subprocesses).

Scripted functionalities augment the modeling method with various capabilities. Notable examples are "assessing the risk" for an RPA project and computing project automation scores. To assess the project risk, stakeholders' notes attached to each RPA project resource are aggregated and delegated to a public LLM, together with notes and the weights of the notes. Conflicting notes would automatically lead to a high risk highlighting stakeholder indecisiveness or diverging viewpoints, while also considering the note weights. Automation scores computation will evaluate all RPA candidate projects available in a *Process evaluation* model - mechanism allows the modeler or business analyst to define custom weights for the evaluation criteria (e.g. weight for the project risk, for the implementation effort, time saved per month etc.), enabling the tool to adapt the result to different strategic priorities or contexts. For example, in healthcare environments, automation risks may represent critical factors due to the potential impact on patient safety but in other domains the implementation effort or the projected ROI may be prioritized. A weighted score of the project will reflect the suitability for the organization – to be showcased in a running example.

Annotation scripts further assign some attribute values based on relationship with other elements across modeling canvases or aggregating other attributes. For example, the execution times associated with individual tasks are automatically aggregated to compute the "total execution time" for each task type (these are further used to calculate the "time savings" resulted in adopting the RPA project, which is an important KPI as it provides a direct estimation of operational efficiency gains). Another relevant example is "assessing the automation rate" on business unit level - a metric of interest in RPA projects management reflecting the degree at which human or bot workers perform tasks at granular units levels.

5.2 Feasibility Demonstration

Feasibility and fulfilment of analysis requirements is the main validation criteria of this method in the current iteration, since many of its technical ingredients are inherited from the underlying ADOxx platform (usability, performance) or from the extended Bee-Up implementation (most of the notation). The following demonstration is based on replicating a real case project evolution and analysis needs:

Some RPA project ideas have been submitted for an accounting department subjected to automation. We take as a fulfilled prerequisite the fact that the ideas have been selected, duplicates filtered out, and now several RPA projects have arrived in the Assessment phase. The initial phase presents 3 RPA Projects: invoice processing, budget forecasting and the daily allowance check. Each project is associated with one or more process fragments (Fig. 4). Also, stakeholder notes were gathered during the Idea phase, in ideation meetings. In the *Assessment* phase, the main question that should be answered is "Can this process be automated?". In order to answer this question, the user should model each of the subprocesses and perform an AsIs vs ToBe analysis. We will exemplify how Process Invoices subprocess would look like in such an analysis (Fig. 5, left). The steps taken at this stage are:

- Add the two process state aggregations – AsIs and ToBe – and describe process flow for each;
- Run the "Compute task types" functionality on top of the AsIs process state, then for the ToBe process state. This will modify the name, process state and time saving attributes according to the process state they are currently into;
- Run the "Find referenced tasks" functionality on top of any activity (Fig. 6) which will assess if tasks from both states (ToBe or AsIs) can be referenced by one another, based on task names;
- Reference any tasks that are common between the two states;
- Add the time savings attributes to each of the tasks.

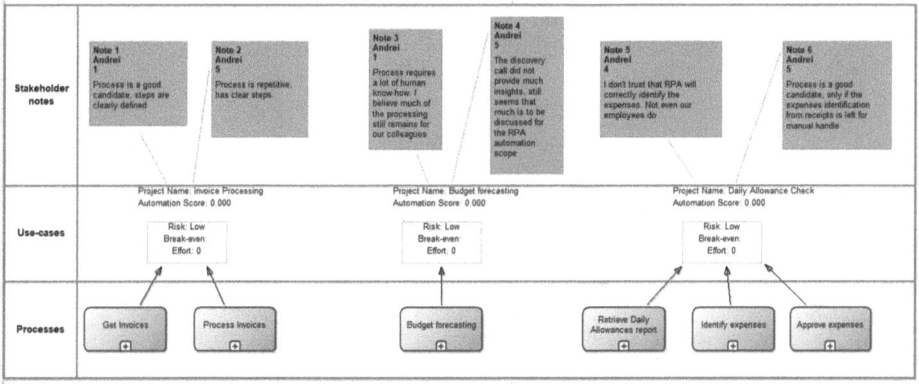

Fig. 4. Initial ideation output

As the *Extract invoice details* task has the same base, but it is found in both AsIs and ToBe states, it will be returned by the Find referenced tasks script (Fig. 6). Time attributes can be configured at task-level using the annotation schema. The Times/Costs > RPA Analysis offers for this the Manual Time, Automated Time and Implementation Effort attributes in the RPA Analysis annotations chapter (Fig. 7).

After configuring all the subprocesses and tasks, the user can return to the Process evaluation model to execute the "time savings computation" script, and the "risk assessment" script. An example of "risk assessment" input and output is depicted in the Fig. 8, as a prompt directed to an LLM service together with stakeholder notes and weights, from which contradictions or SWOT elements can be synthesized. After having computed these KPIs, the user can go on and finalize the assessment step. The process analysis model at this step will look as shown in Fig. 9: The border color indicates a recommendation in the *Assessment* step, by computing a combination between the risk and break-even point. Green marks a very good automation candidate, yellow marks a mediocre automation candidate, and red marks an unsuitable one.

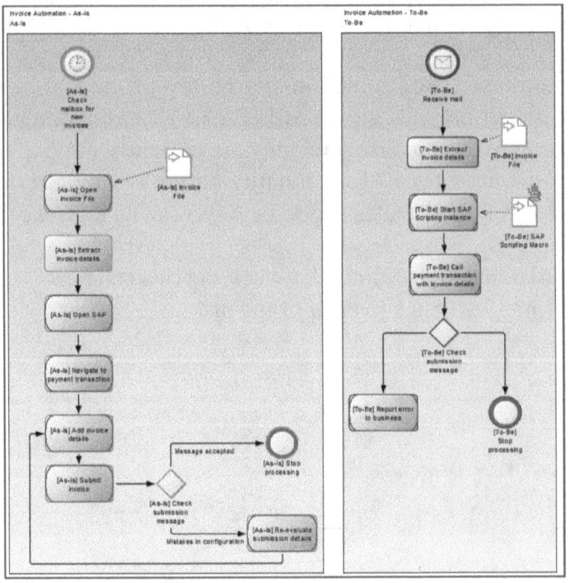

Fig. 5. Example of AsIs vs. ToBe analysis

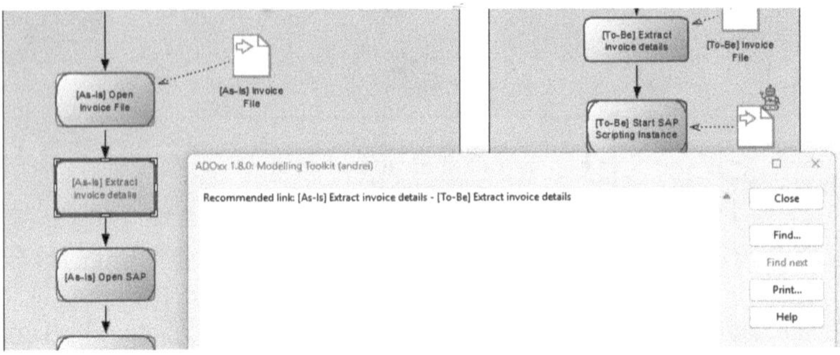

Fig. 6. Result of the Find referenced tasks script

Further down the project evolution, in the *Qualification* phase the following question should be answered: "Which of the previous RPA projects that were identified as suitable for automation should be automated?" The user can now run the compute automation score functionality, which will recommend the projects in the following order: Daily Allowance Check, Budget forecasting and Invoice Processing (based on the values for the automation score computed as a weighted average for risk, implementation effort, break-even in months and time saved per month).

In the *Implementation* phase, the adopted RPA solutions will require an update on the working environment models. Figure 10 shows the post-implementation situation of the projects Daily Allowance Check and Budget forecasting. A business analyst can execute the "role automation rate" functionality available in this model to evaluate the percentage of automated tasks vs. manual ones.

Fig. 7. Attribute configuration example for the Extract invoice details task

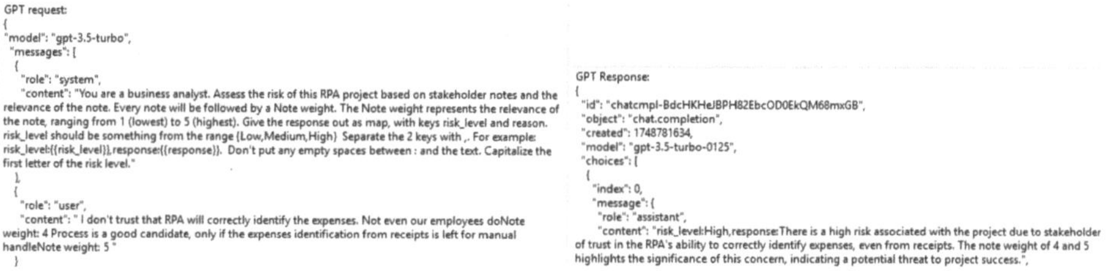

Fig. 8. Input and output of the OpenAI API risk assessment request

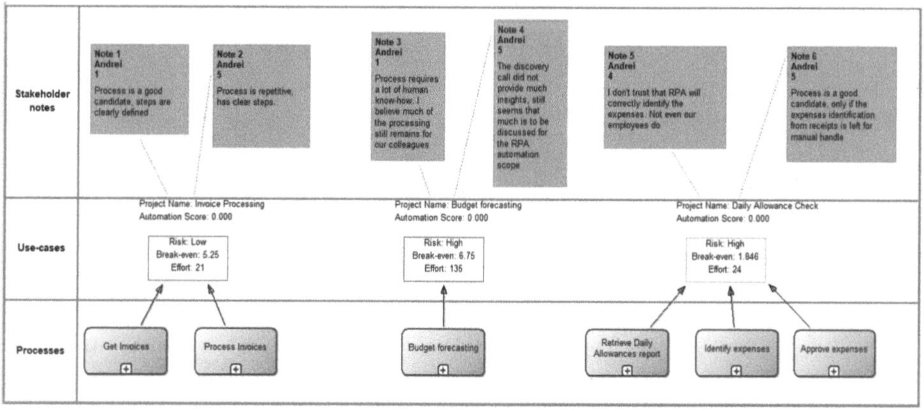

Fig. 9. Process evaluation model during the Assessment phase

Across the interconnected models the built-in query engine of ADOxx enables metamodel-grounded queries thus providing an evaluation perspective similar to the competency questions traditionally employed in ontology engineering. These also open potential for future AI integration with retrieval capabilities in the vein of RAG pipelines but based on the accumulated model repository. Examples of retrieval queries:

Get all subprocesses in a process analysis model that are not referencing any model. AQL query: (<“Sub-Process” >) [?“Referenced subprocess” = “”]

Get all tasks with high implementation effort (greater than 10): (<“Task” >) [?“Implementation Effort” > 10]

Get all RPA projects that are high in cost but provide rapid turnover: (<“RPA_Project” > [?"Estimated ROI” < 7]) AND (<“RPA_Project” > [? “ImplementationEffort” > 100])

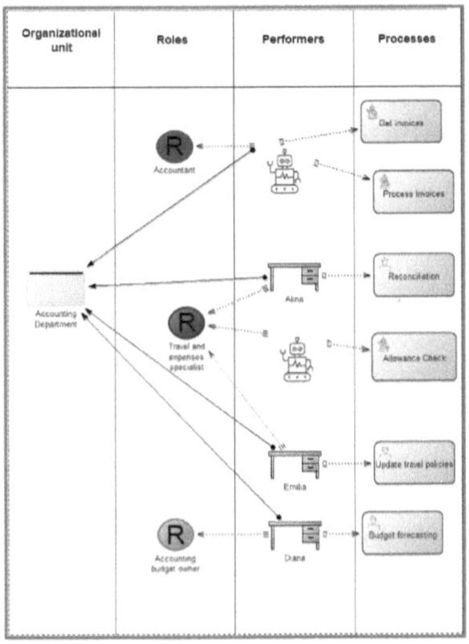

Fig. 10. Post-automation work environment overview

6 Related Works

Völker and Weske [10] initiated design-oriented work for conceptualizing RPA bots, extending into a conceptual framework [28] and even advancing to complexity analysis use cases [29] and to an ontological perspective [30]. Compared to this body of work we are more interested in bridging the gap between traditional BPM and RPA project management, rather than the taxonomical and ontological constituents of bots. Richter et al.[31] propose itsVALUE, a modeling and analysis framework for representing value streams in IT Services. Their motivation resides in the fact that IT Service Management is one of the top drivers of business growth, and enterprises should consider it for gaining a competitive advantage. The goals of this framework are: identification of relevant stakeholders and their values, understanding and defining relationships between values of the stakeholders and lastly defining AsIs and ToBe value streams, associated with adopting an IT service. This topic aligns with the focus of our study, as it similarly explores decision making processes based on stakeholder values and opinions. Lamine et al. [32] propose the concept of Risk-aware Business Process Management, by integrating two traditionally isolated areas: risk management and BPM - they use a taxonomy that includes definitions for risk categories, analysis, relationships and treatment. The proposed artifact is a risk-extended business process model which aims at modeling developments in the event of expected and anticipated risky situations. In project portfolio management, assessing and mitigating risk is essential to informed decision-making. By using a modeling method to visualize and analyze risks, as in our approach, organizations are able to identify uncertainties and can proactively design strategies to address them. The Wanner et al. [33] also concentrate on "process selection" (i.e. which process to automate) and propose computing the economic value of RPA projects. Their approach supports decision making via formulas and indicators but has less emphasis on the visualization component. Agaton and Swedberg [34] acknowledged that BPMN can be used to model the processes of a company but it faces obstacles in capturing data-related aspects of the process or difficulty to model decision points beyond the gateways. These limitations reinforce the need for an RPA-specific modeling approach that could extend BPMN with clearer semantics and measurable evaluation mechanisms.

This work also contributes to the research stream on BPMN extensions recently catalogued in [35]. BPMN extensions have been developed for a long time within the OMILAB Community of Practice employing the same metamodeling platform, with the overall goal of demonstrating directions of expanding the scope of business process management for various domain specificities – multi-protocol IoT data pipelines [36], BPMN-based user experience workflows [7], Design Thinking processes [37], processes contextualized by the Work Systems Framework [6].

7 Conclusions

The paper presents a modeling method and language extension of BPMN to support the Assessment and Qualification phases of RPA projects. The proposed extension is augmented with model-driven functionality developed on the ADOxx metamodeling platform to address limitations in current tools, by integrating BPMN as an RPA documentation approach. This enables a more comprehensive and integrated view of candidate processes, capturing not only the operational steps but also the organizational dependencies or risks. The approach supports two types of business stakeholders that need to converge on the RPA project adoption: decision makers who require evaluations in line with enterprise work systems and RPA consultants who must promote automation opportunities. Future work includes several directions aimed to enhance the robustness and applicability of the proposed modeling method: validation in RPA projects; interoperability with UiPath Automation Hub; support for other steps of the RPA lifecycle, particularly the Ideation phase, where we aim to converge work with recent OMILAB approaches to model-driven Design Thinking [37, 38].

Acknowledgments. This work was developed as part of the first author's master dissertation titled *A Domain-Specific Extension of BPMN for Modeling and Managing RPA Project Portfolios in*

ADOxx - by Andrei Pavel, defended at Babeş-Bolyai University in 2025 under the supervision of Prof. Dr. Robert Andrei Buchmann. The work extends the BPMN implementation of the Bee-Up OMILAB project available at https://bee-up.omilab.org/activities/bee-up/. We are thankful to the Bee-Up authors and to OMILAB NPO for the shared resource.

Disclosure of Interests. The authors have no competing interests to declare that are relevant to the content of this article.

References

1. Willcocks, L., Lacity, M., Craig, A.: Robotic process automation: strategic transformation lever for global business services? J. Inf. Technol. Teach. Cases **7**(1), 17–28 (2017). https://doi.org/10.1057/s41266-016-0016-9
2. UiPath. UiPath: Automation platform for AI-powered business transformation. https://www.uipath.com/UiPath. Accessed 17 Apr 2026
3. Camunda, The benefits of using BPMN with AI agents. https://camunda.com/blog/2025/05/benefits-bpmn-ai-agents/. Accessed 17 Apr 2026
4. Dolha D., Osman C.C., Chiş A.: KM4ESG: BPMN and AI-powered knowledge management platform for ESG analysis and reporting, CAISE 2025 RPE section. In: CEUR WS vol. 4050 (2025). https://ceur-ws.org/Vol-4050/paper01.pdf
5. Bachhofner, S., Kiesling, E., Revoredo, K., Waibel, P., Polleres, A.: Automated process knowledge graph construction from BPMN models. In: Proceedings of DEXA 2022, LNBIP vol. 13426, pp. 32–47. Springer, Heidelberg (2022). https://doi.org/10.1007/978-3-031-12423-5_3
6. Chiş, A., Ghiran, A.M., Buchmann, R.A: WSF4ADO: an ADOxx deployment of the work systems framework. In: Proceedings of CAiSE 2025 Forum. LNBIP, vol. 557, pp. 45–52. Springer, Heidelberg (2025). https://doi.org/10.1007/978-3-031-94590-8_6
7. Uifălean, Ş., Buchmann, R.A.: Low-code browser front-end automation using RDF graphs and a domain-specific language for UX representation. In: Proceedings of RCIS 2025. LNBIP vol. 547, pp.140–155. Springer, Heidelbegr (2025). https://doi.org/10.1007/978-3-031-92474-3_9
8. UiPath Modeler, https://bpmn.uipath.com/. last accessed 2026/04/17
9. UiPath Academy, Process analysis framework https://academy.uipath.com/courses/process-analysis-framework , last accessed 2026/04/17
10. Völker, M., Weske, M.: Conceptualizing bots in robotic process automation. In; Proceedings of ER 2021, LNCS vol. 13011, pp. 3–13. Springer (2021). https://doi.org/10.1007/978-3-030-89022-3_1
11. Cavalcante M., Gonçalves E., Araújo J., Heineck T.: A Catalog of BPMN Extensions, In: Companion Proceedings of ER 2025, CEUR-WS vol. 4099 (2025) https://ceur-ws.org/Vol-4099/forum_paper5.pdf
12. OMiLAB NPO, The Bee-Up Modeling Tool. https://bee-up.omilab.org/activities/bee-up/. Accessed 17 Apr 2026
13. Hevner, A. R., March, S. T., Park, J., Ram, S.: Design science in information systems research. MIS Q. **28**(1), 75–105 (2004). https://aisel.aisnet.org/misq/vol28/iss1/6/
14. Karagiannis, D.: Conceptual modeling methods: the AMME agile engineering approach. In: Informatics in Economy (IE 2016) LNBIP, vol. 273, pp. 3–19. Springer, Heidelberg (2018) https://doi.org/10.1007/978-3-319-73459-0_1
15. ADOxx Documentation. Retrieved from Introduction to ADOxx. https://www.adoxx.org/live/introduction-to-adoxx. Accessed 17 Apr 2026

16. Karagiannis, D., Lee, M., Hinkelmann, K., Utz, W. (eds.): Domain-Specific Conceptual Modeling: Concepts, Methods and ADOxx Tools. Springer, Heidelberg (2022). https://doi.org/10.1007/978-3-030-93547-4
17. OMILAB Community of Practice. https://www.omilab.org/community/. Accessed 17 June 2026
18. Murdoch, R.: Robotic process automation: guide to building software robots, automate repetitive tasks & become an RPA consultant. Richard Murdoch & RPA Ultra (2018)
19. Crişan, E.L., Chiş, D.M., Bodea, E.E., Buchmann, R.: Mechanisms for robotic process automation implementation in organizations: a systematic literature review. J. Adv. Manag. Res. **20**(5), 920–946 (2023)
20. UiPath Process Mining. https://www.uipath.com/product/process-mining. Accessed 17 June 2026
21. Dumas, M., Rosa, L.M., Mendling, J., Reijers, A.H.: Fundamentals of Business Process Management. Springer, Heidelberg (2018) https://doi.org/10.1007/978-3-662-56509-4
22. Jimenez-Ramirez, A., Reijers, H.A., Barba, I., Del Valle, C.: A method to improve the early stages of the robotic process automation lifecycle. In: Proceedings of CAISE 2019, LNCS, vol. 11483, pp. 446–461. Springer, Heidelberg (2019). https://doi.org/10.1007/978-3-030-21290-2_28
23. Camunda, The open platform for agentic orchestration. https://camunda.com/. Accessed 17 Apr 2026
24. Tasky Cloud, All in one BPM Platform. https://tasky.cloud/. Accessed 17 Apr 2026
25. Buchmann, R. A.: The purpose-specificity framework for domain-specific conceptual modeling. In: Karagiannis, D., Lee, M., Hinkelmann, K., Utz, W. (Eds.), Domain-specific Conceptual Modeling, pp. 69–93. Springer, Heidelberg (2022). https://doi.org/10.1007/978-3-030-93547-4_4
26. UiPath Automation Hub: Discover and manage automation opportunities in one place (2025). https://www.uipath.com/product/automation-hub. Accessed 17 Apr 2026
27. Alter S.: Work system theory. overview of core concepts, extensions, and challenges for the future. J. Assoc. Inf. Syst. **14**(2) (2013). https://doi.org/10.17705/1jais.00323
28. Hohenadl, T., Völker, M., Stummeyer, C., Weske, M.: Democratizing robotic process mining: a conceptual framework for user actions, tasks, and RPA bots. In: Proceedings of BPM Forum 2024, LNBIP, vol. 527, pp. 185–199. Springer, Heidelberg (2024). https://doi.org/10.1007/978-3-031-70445-1_12
29. Völker, M., Weske, M.: Measuring complexity of bot models in Robotic Process Automation. In: Proceedings of BPM Forum 2024, LNBIP, vol. 527, pp. 154–168. Springer, Heidelberg (2024). https://doi.org/10.1007/978-3-031-70445-1_10
30. Völker, M., Weske, M.: Ontology-based abstraction of bot models in robotic process automation. In: Proceedings of ER 2023, LNCS, vol. 14320, pp. 239–256. Springer, Heidelberg (2023). https://doi.org/10.1007/978-3-031-47262-6_13
31. Richter, H. D., Lantow, B., Pröpper, T.: itsVALUE: modeling and analysing value streams for IT services. In: Karagiannis, D., Lee, M., Hinkelmann, K., Utz, W. (eds.) Domain Specific Conceptual Modeling: Concepts, Methods and ADOxx Tools, pp. 161–183. Springer, Heidelberg (2022). https://doi.org/10.1007/978-3-030-93547-4_8
32. Lamine, E., Thabet, R., Sienou, A., Pingaud, H.: The integration of risk aspects into business process management: the e-BPRIM modeling method. In: Karagiannis, D., Lee, M., Hinkelmann, K., Utz, W. (eds.) Domain-Specific Conceptual Modeling, pp. 265–284. Springer, Heidelberg (2022). https://doi.org/10.1007/978-3-030-93547-4_11
33. Wanner, J., Hofmann, A., Fischer, M., Imgrund, F., Janiesch, C., Geyer-Klingeberg, J.: Process selection in RPA projects-towards a quantifiable method of decision making. In: Proceedings of ICIS 2019. Association of Information Systems (2019). https://aisel.aisnet.org/icis2019/business_models/business_models/6/

34. Agaton, B., Swedberg, G.: Evaluating and developing methods to assess business process suitability for robotic process automation. Department of Computer Science and Engineering (2018). https://publications.lib.chalmers.se/records/fulltext/255664/255664.pdf
35. Cavalcante M., Gonçalves E., Araújo J., Heineck, T.: A catalog of BPMN extensions. In: Companion Proceedings of ER 2025, CEUR-WS 4099 (2025). https://ceur-ws.org/Vol-4099/forum_paper5.pdf
36. Chis, A., Ghiran, AM.: BPMN extension for multi-protocol data orchestration. In: Karagiannis, D., Lee, M., Hinkelmann, K., Utz, W. (eds.) Domain-Specific Conceptual Modeling. Springer, Heidelberg (2022). https://doi.org/10.1007/978-3-030-93547-4_28
37. Moldovan A., Buchmann R.A.: Towards a process-centric knowledge management capability for design thinking. In: Proceedings of BIR 2025 Workshops, CEUR-WS, vol. 4304 (2025). https://ceur-ws.org/Vol-4034/paper97.pdf
38. Muck C., Palkovits-Rauter S.: Conceptualizing design thinking artefacts: the Scene2Model storyboard approach, In: Karagiannis, D., Lee, M., Hinkelmann, K., Utz, W. (eds.) Domain-Specific Conceptual Modeling: Concepts, Methods and ADOxx Tools, pp. 567–587. Springer, Heidelberg (2022). https://doi.org/10.1007/978-3-030-93547-4_25

The Logic of Processed Events in Human Processes

Václav Řepa(✉)

Prague University of Economics and Business, 130 67 Prague, Czech Republic
repa@vse.cz

Abstract. The paper investigates the logical structure of event processing in human processes, emphasizing the unique characteristics of events defined by their meaning, temporal ordering, and exclusivity. Drawing on the framework of MMABP (a methodological approach prioritizing event granularity based on purpose-driven semantics), the paper formalizes the equivalence between event implication ($\varepsilon \Rightarrow \varphi$) and logical equivalence ($\varepsilon \equiv \varphi$) in human-centric processes. This conclusion arises from the necessity of exclusive, time-ordered resolution in human processes, where disjunctive decisions are modeled as XOR logic. The paper further contrasts this logic with OntoUML's system-centric event modeling, highlighting key differences in event uniqueness, exclusivity, and human-centric focus. By establishing a rigorous, human-centric framework for event processing, the paper provides theoretical foundations for designing event-driven algorithms, ensuring unambiguous resolution in workflows, business processes, and human-machine interactions. The paper also explores implications for process modeling, emphasizing the integration of temporal constraints, exclusive event relationships, and human intent in system frameworks.

Keywords: Human processes · event processing · MMABP · OntoUML · logical equivalence · exclusive disjunction · process modeling

1 Introduction

Human processes - whether business processes, workflows, or task sequences - involve a series of activities managed by humans or machines. These processes are inherently purpose-driven, reflecting human will and requiring unambiguous execution. This paper investigates the logical structure of events within such processes, focusing on how events are defined, processed, and resolved. The central question is: **How does the logic of event processing in human processes differ from traditional logic, and what are the implications of this difference?**

The question arises from the existing gap between current process modelling approaches, in which events play a key role, and relevant theories such as modal and temporal logic, algorithmic theory, and cybernetics. These theories could significantly improve the quality of process modelling through their findings. In order to apply the general findings of the theories to the practical field of process modelling, it is necessary

E. Laurenzi et al. (Eds.): BIR 2026, LNBIP 601, pp. 97–110, 2027.
https://doi.org/10.1007/978-3-032-38498-0_7

to have a **clear understanding of the specific meaning of events in the processes**. The aim of this paper is to make a small contribution to this field.

The paper begins by introducing the background methodology MMABP. Then we definine the core principles of human processes, including the role of negative feedback, the temporal ordering of events, and the exclusivity of disjunctive decisions. In the following section, we derive a formal relationship between logical implication and equivalence in the context of event processing, demonstrating that the implication of events *($\varepsilon \Rightarrow \varphi$)* is equivalent to their logical equivalence *($\varepsilon \equiv \varphi$)*. This conclusion is validated through logical derivations and a truth table analysis.

In the fourth section we then discuss the implications of this conclusion for event processing and consequential methodological aspects like granularity of events in processes, organization of the process system, needed synchronization of processes, and how it retroactively influences modeling of the process flow.

In Sect. 5, we pay special attention to the differences in the understanding of events in business processes and in OntoUML as a representative of an ontology-driven approach to events. A correct understanding of this difference is crucial for grasping the MMABP Philosophical Framework as a methodological basis for event processing presented in this paper.

2 Theoretical Framework

A general methodological background of the presented approach is the Methodology for Modeling and Analysis of Business Processes (MMABP) [11]. MMABP approach is defined in the **Philosophical Framework for Business System Modeling** [11, 12], which was developed to capture all essential aspects of the real world that should be reflected in an information system. Since information systems aim to provide accurate and up-to-date representations of a business system, a general and universal understanding of reality is required. This framework is thus related to multiple disciplines, including philosophy and logic, to achieve preciseness, correctness, and broad applicability.

The framework is based on two fundamental phenomena:

- **being**
- **behavior**

and two fundamental perspectives:

- The **system** (static) view.
- The **particular** (temporal) view.

Being describes what exists or can exist in the real world, including objects, their properties, and relationships. It can be formally expressed using **modal logic**.

Behavior represents actions and events caused by real-world actors, such as goal achievement, and is described using **process-oriented models**.

The **system view** provides a static perspective of the whole system, focusing on structure and relationships while abstracting from time.

The **temporal view** focuses on events and changes over time, describing specific parts of the system through sequences of actions.

Combining these dimensions yields four basic model types (see Fig. 1):

- Model of **Real World Modality** – static view of being (objects and relationships) traditionally called a **conceptual model**. MMABP uses the **UML Class Diagram** [10] for this model.
- Model of **Real World Causality** – temporal view of being (object states and transitions). MMABP calls this model a model of an **object life cycle** and uses the **UML State Chart** [10] for this model.
- Model of **Collaboration** – static view of behavior (processes and their cooperation) MMABP calls this model a **process map** and uses the **TOGAF Event Diagram** [16] for this model.
- Model of **Acting** – temporal view of behavior (action sequences within processes). MMABP calls this model a **process flow model** and uses the **BPMN** [9] for this model.

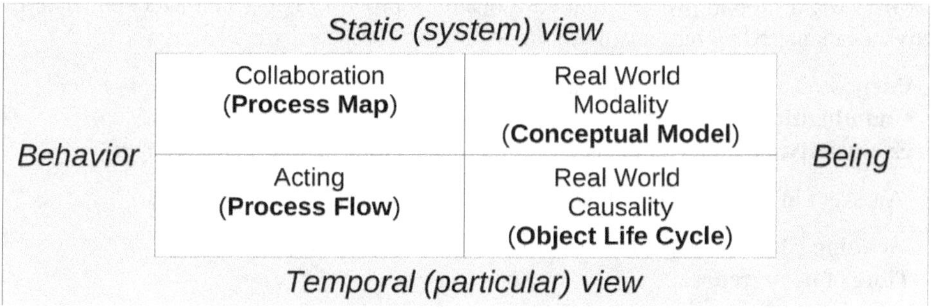

Fig. 1. Kinds of business system models in MMABP.

In business process modeling, MMABP addresses two key challenges:

The need to model not only individual **process flows** but also the overall **system of processes** (the Global Process Model or Process Map).
The need to model processes as **intentional, goal-driven** activities.

The Global Process Model views processes as parts of a process system that cooperate through services. It captures processes as objects with attributes (e.g., goals, customers) and relationships, enabling a clear distinction between key and support processes. However, most methodologies and approaches - especially BPMN [9] - focus mainly on the internal flow of a single process and provide only limited support for modeling inter-process relationships. For instance, the collaboration diagram in BPMN (using pools and lanes) does not adequately represent the system-wide structure.

To address this limitation, BPMN should be complemented by object-oriented approaches, such as the Eriksson-Penker UML extension [5], which distinguishes between:

- a **global - system view** (interactions among processes), and
- a **detailed - behavioral view** (detailed execution of a single process).

Another critical aspect is **intentionality**. Business processes are inherently goal-oriented and must be understood as purposeful behavior. This implies the presence of

feedback mechanisms [13], where process outputs are continuously adjusted based on inputs from the environment to ensure alignment with goals.

A key modeling implication of a natural process intentionality is the concept of a **process state** - a point where the process waits for external input before continuing. This reflects the need to synchronize process execution with real-world events. While some methodologies (e.g., IDEF [8], Eriksson/Penker [5], WfMC [15], Petri Nets [14] etc.) somehow support this concept, BPMN does not explicitly include process states. In BPMN is only possible to represent process state indirectly, as a general synchonization construction (via so-called 'parallel AND gateway', for example see Fig. 2).

3 Human Processes and Event Semantics

In MMABP, a human process (called a business process) is defined as a sequence of activities managed by humans, with the following characteristics:

- **Purpose**: The process has a goal set by a human actor.
- **Unambiguity**: Events are resolved in a unique, time-ordered sequence.
- **Exclusivity**: Disjunctive decisions about events are exclusive (XOR logic).

An event in a process is defined by two essential attributes:

- **Meaning** (the role of the event in the context of the process purpose).
- **Time of occurrence**.

Events with the same meaning but different times of occurrence are treated as distinct, ensuring a unique sequence in the process flow.

Processing of events thus has to cover both their essential parts. Particular events processed by the process differ in the meaning and/or in the moment of occurrence. Even the events with the same meaning occurring in different moments must be in the process regarded as different. This is caused by the fact that the process represents an algorithm, which places all processed events in the timeline in an unambiguous sequence. Thus, the ordering of particular events in the particular process is unambiguous. Consequently, this fact makes any decision about the occurrence of events unambiguous. Looking from the point of view of the logic of decision expressions, ***one can see any disjunctive decision about events in the process as exclusive***. The request for the unambiguity of an algorithm does not admit more than exactly one correct option in such a decision.

Using the Boolean terminology, any disjunctive decision about events in the process is an XOR (exclusive OR) decision [2]. Different events must occur in different moments and thus just one of them can be the first one. The situation, when more than one disjunctive options in the decision about events can be correct, is not acceptable in the process.

The special feature of the logic of processed events discussed above has important consequences for the meaning and processing of events. These consequences are discussed below. In the following text, we use the symbols **P** and **Q** to represent general operands in general logic expressions, and the symbols ε and φ to represent operands in logical expressions within the domain of processed events.

3.1 Formal Derivation

In traditional logic, implication is defined as:

$$(P \Rightarrow Q) \Leftrightarrow \neg P \vee Q \tag{1}$$

In the context of human processes, the exclusivity of event resolution leads to a revised definition of the ***Event implication***:

$$\varepsilon \Rightarrow \varphi \Leftrightarrow \neg\varepsilon \veebar \varphi \tag{2}$$

The exclusivity of event resolution in human processes leads to the use of ***exclusive OR*** (XOR) logic. The exclusive disjunction ($P \veebar Q$) is defined as:

$$P \veebar Q \Leftrightarrow (P \vee Q) \wedge \neg(P \wedge Q) \tag{3}$$

In the context of event processing, this operation is used to model disjunctive decisions. Based on definition (3), we then can accommodate definition (2) to the domain of ***processed events***:

$$\varepsilon \Rightarrow \varphi \Leftrightarrow (\neg\varepsilon \vee \varphi) \wedge \neg(\neg\varepsilon \wedge \varphi) \tag{4}$$

Applying De Morgan's laws [3], this simplifies to:

$$\begin{gathered} \varepsilon \Rightarrow \varphi \Leftrightarrow (\neg\varepsilon \vee \varphi) \wedge (\varepsilon \vee \neg\varphi) \\ \varepsilon \Rightarrow \varphi \Leftrightarrow (\varepsilon \Rightarrow \varphi) \wedge (\varphi \Rightarrow \varepsilon) \\ \varepsilon \Rightarrow \varphi \Leftrightarrow \varepsilon \equiv \varphi \end{gathered} \tag{5}$$

The formula (5) expresses the conclusion that in the the field of events in human processes, the ***implication of events ($\varepsilon \Rightarrow \varphi$) is equivalent to logical equivalence ($\varepsilon \equiv \varphi$).***

3.2 Truth Table Validation

A truth table Tab 1 [2, 4] is provided to validate the equivalence between implication and equivalence in the context of event processing. The table shows that the results of $\varepsilon \Rightarrow \varphi$ and $\varepsilon \equiv \varphi$ are identical, confirming the formula $\varepsilon \Rightarrow \varphi \Leftrightarrow \varepsilon \equiv \varphi$.

Table 1. Truth Table validation of the correctness of formula (5).

ε	$\neg\varepsilon$	φ	$\neg\varepsilon \veebar \varphi$	$\varepsilon \equiv \varphi$
0	1	0	1	1
1	0	0	0	0
0	1	1	0	0
1	0	1	1	1

As the values in the columns for both compared logical expressions are the same, we can regard the formula (5) being a tautology.

The truth-table validation demonstrates consistency with the previous definitions, it verifies the internal logical consistency of the formalization. Nevertheless, it does not by itself establish the broader theoretical validity of the equivalence claim.

The theoretical validity of the equivalence follows from the ontological definition of business events adopted by MMABP. Since a **business event** is defined as an occurrence that causes a **meaningful transition in the intentional behavior** of a process, the notions of **business event and process state transition are semantically equivalent**. The logical proof therefore confirms, rather than establishes, an equivalence that is already grounded in the ontology of intentional processes. This ontological justification is also supported by a practical example in following sections and shortly discussed in the conclusions section.

4 Implications for Event Processing in Human Processes

Formula (5) as a result of the reasoning in the previous section, leads to the conclusion:

In the logic of processed events, the ***operation of logical implication means logical equivalence***: $\varepsilon \Rightarrow \varphi \Leftrightarrow \varepsilon \equiv \varphi$, where ε and φ are processed events.

This conclusion significantly influences the understanding of the natural meaning of events in processes. The formula above can be interpreted as follows: if event ε implies the event φ then both are actually the same event. In other words, ***there is nothing like an implication relationship of two events in processes but only either their identity or divergence***.

The equivalence of implication and equivalence in event processing has profound implications:

- **Events must be distinct** in time or meaning to avoid ambiguity.
- **Implication is not a relational concept** but a condition of identity.
- **Processes must enforce strict temporal ordering** to ensure unambiguous resolution.

4.1 Applications in Process Modeling

Business processes are inherently goal-driven (intentional). This means that a business process cannot simply be regarded as a sequence of actions; it is a **controlled behavior aimed at achieving a specific goal** [13]. To ensure that the goal can be reached, the process must continuously monitor and adjust its behavior, this is where feedback becomes essential.

In this context the feedback refers to the mechanism by which a process **compares** its current state and outputs with the desired goal, and **adjusts** its subsequent actions based on this comparison. This is typically **negative feedback**, meaning it reduces deviations from the goal[1].

In a business process the feedback represents:

[1] See [13] for an explanation of the general validity of this essential cybernetics rule.

- **Goal definition**. Every process has a defined goal (e.g., "deliver order correctly and on time").
- **Execution and outputs.** The process produces outputs (e.g., shipped order, delivery status).
- **Environmental input (feedback signal).** The environment provides information about the outcome, for example customer confirmation or complaint, delivery delay notification or quality check result, etc.
- **Adjustment of behavior**. Based on this input, the process adapts its next steps. For example, it may reprocess order, escalate an issue, or change the execution path, etc.

Without this loop, the process would be just **blind execution**, not **goal-directed behavior**.

A key implication is that **inputs do not occur only at the start** of a process. Instead, **intermediate inputs** occur during execution and influence the next steps. They are essential for maintaining alignment with the goal.

These inputs are what make the process adaptive and intelligent, rather than static.

To properly handle feedback, the process must include **states** where it pauses execution, waits for relevant input, and consequently decides how to proceed.

These states represent synchronization points with the environment, moments where feedback is evaluated. Examples are: Invoice sent (waiting for payment confirmation), Order proposal placed (waiting for customer approval), etc.

Process states are not actions, but **control points driven by feedback.**

For example of the process states and process steps (i.e. indicated process parts between the states) see Fig. 2.

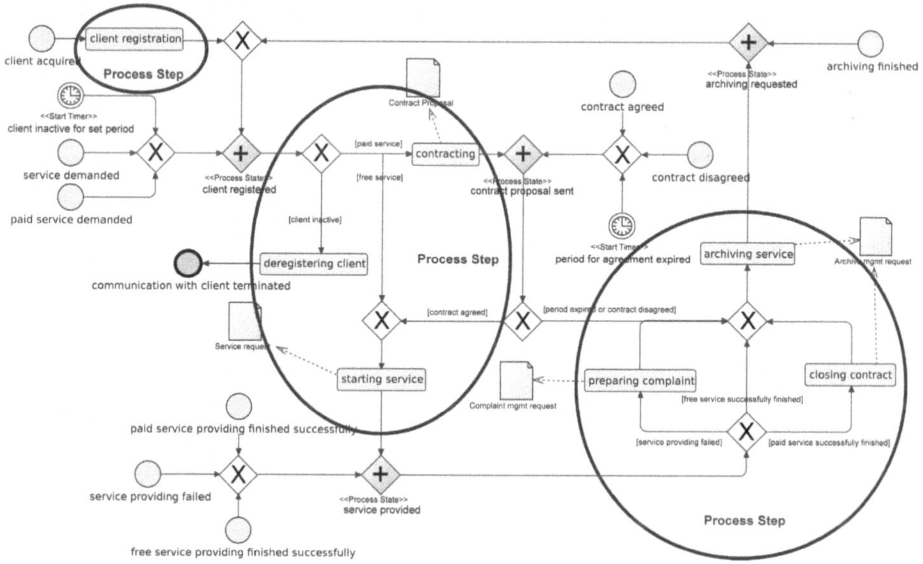

Fig. 2. Example of the *Client Management* process flow model (MMABP methodology).

Figure 2 shows how the events actually define the process structure. The process contains four **process states** (see the AND gateways in gray). The structure of activities between two following process states (or between the process start and the first state, or between the last state and the process end) represents one **process step**. Note that all activities between two states mutually exclude each other, they represent one decision tree. Therefore, they all can be regarded as just one process step since in the process execution only one of them is performed. The structure of the process is thus actually defined by the events expected in the process and their meanings in the context of the process goal.

The presented approach to the business process modeling distinguishes MMABP from many modeling approaches such as BPMN [9], which emphasize flow of activities but ignore the need for feedback loops and process states. As a result of such an approach processes appear linear, which contradicts the nature of a real-world processes that are **cybernetic systems with continuous adjustment**.

4.2 Teleological Granularity of Events in a Human Process

One of the key problems that has to be solved during the process modeling is achieving the proper **granularity of events**. Regarding the broad, general understanding of events, there is a need for a methodological rule that unambiguously determines the correct level of detail in a business process model. MMABP brings that rule based on a teleological nature of a business process derived from the root of cybernetics [13].

In MMABP, the granularity of an event is not defined only by time or physical occurrence, but by its **meaning within a business process**, i.e., by its **purpose (telos)**

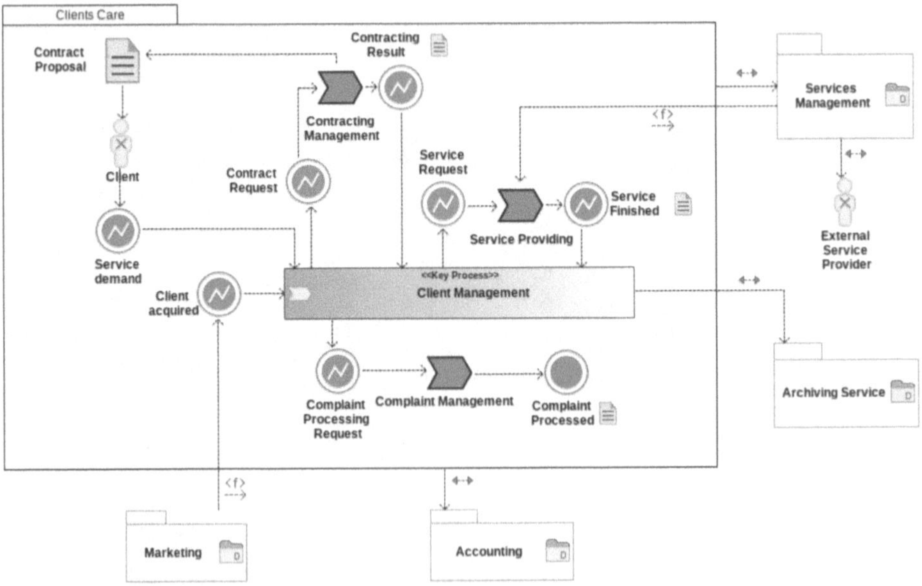

Fig. 3. Example of the MMABP Process Map (TOGAF Event Diagram).

in relation to the **process goal**. In other words, an event is "atomic" not because it is indivisible in time, but because it is indivisible from the perspective of achieving the process goal.

The key determinants of an event granularity are:

- the **goal** of the process, and
- the **role** the event plays in progressing toward that goal.

Thus, an event is defined at the level where it has a **clear business meaning**, and it triggers or influences **intentional behavior** within the process.

For example let us consider the *Client Management* process (Fig. 2) as a key process of the *Clients Care* enterprise function, as shown in the Process Map (Fig. 3). We can see there the *client acquired* starting event, which indicates that the process focuses on the client throughout its entire life cycle (from a business perspective, this means its life as a client). We can also see there the events that occur during the client's lifetime as a client, representing its actions such as *service demanded* or *contract agreed.* Other events represent the actions of supporting processes such as *service providing finished* or *archiving finished*. Each event obviously represents a point in time, not an interval. Each event is also tied to the process purpose: *provide the client with services throughout its entire life cycle.* These are events in a process / teleological sense because they have clear **business meaning** and are relevant to the **process goal / purpose**.

The required level of detail for an event is then determined by its role in the process. From this point of view, several events with different meanings should be regarded as the same event if they form a single subject of the decision determining the next process step. Conversely, if the process has to distinguish between the different aspects of a broadly defined event, it may be necessary to divide it into several different events, each requiring a different alternative process reaction.

For example in the *Client Management* process, the particular service provided to the client is only represented by the events *service providing finished successfully* or *service providing failed*. There are no events representing details of the service providing, such as *service providing started*, *service providing interrupted*, *service problem solved*, etc. This is because *Service providing* support process (see the Process Map in Fig. 3) is responsible for providing the service, while the *Client Management* process is only responsible for managing its result. Thus, even though the meanings and times of occurrence of the aforementioned detailed events are different, from the perspective of the *Client Management* process, they all form a single subject of the decision determining the next process step. From this point of view, the only relevant time point is the end of the service provision. During the service provision, the *Client Management* process is inactive, waiting in its *service provided* process state. On the other hand, after the contract proposal has been sent, the process must distinguish between the events *contract agrees* and *contract disagreed,* since they require different reactions. Even though they may be represented by a single event *client's response* accompanied by information about the decision (agrees/disagrees), process also has to take into account the third possible event: *period for agreement expired.* Without a proper reaction to this event, the set of necessary process reactions would be incomplete[2]. In general, the possibility of zero external action must be taken into account in almost all process states. Such an event differs from regular events (which MMABP refers to as *ad hoc events*) in that it does not represent any external action. Therefore, the process itself has to model it as a *timer* (see Fig. 2).

5 Event Understanding in Human Processes Versus OntoUML

OntoUML [6, 7] is a modeling language that integrates ontologies with UML (Unified Modeling Language) [10], enabling the representation of complex systems. Formal definition of OntoUML is based on the Unified Foundation Ontology (UFO). Similarly to MMABP, also OntoUML distinguishes between two basic dimensions of the real world – structure and behavior, which leads its to two foundation ontologies. Ontology of endurants UFO-A [6] represents an ontology of things (structure), and ontology of perdurants UFO-B [1] represents an ontology of events (behavior over time). OntoUML is the best representation of a conceptual modeling methodology that also focuses on modeling behavior, and therefore, it can be used to compare with the MMABP's understanding of events in terms of modeling human (business) processes. Such a comparison is important for achieving a thorough understanding of the specific meaning of events in human processes, which is necessary for their methodologically correct modeling.

This section provides a brief comparative analysis of the concept of events in human processes, as defined in the paper, and the event modeling in **OntoUML**, a formalism used for modeling complex systems. While both frameworks address events in the context of processes, they differ in their assumptions, constraints, and applications. This section explores these differences, highlighting how the paper's logic of events applies to human-centric processes and contrasts it with OntoUML's system-centric approach.

5.1 Event Modeling in Human Processes

In this paper, events in human processes are defined as **temporally ordered, unambiguous, and exclusive entities** (phenomena). Key characteristics include:

1. **Temporal Uniqueness**: Events are distinguished by their time of occurrence, ensuring a strict, unambiguous sequence in the process.
2. **Exclusivity**: Disjunctive decisions about events (e.g., "which event occurs next") are exclusive (XOR logic), as only one event can be valid at a given moment.
3. **Semantic Identity**: The logical implication of events ($\varepsilon \Rightarrow \varphi$) is equivalent to their identity ($\varepsilon \equiv \varphi$), reflecting the necessity of resolving events as distinct entities in time or meaning.
4. **Human-Centric Purpose**: Events are tied to human intent, with processes defined by human will and goals.

[2] The completeness of the necessary process reactions in the process state is a crucial methodological requirement of the MMABP, which distinguishes it from many current process modelling approaches that neglect this aspect.

This logic is rooted in the **algorithmic nature of human processes**, where events must be resolved in a deterministic, time-ordered sequence to ensure correctness. This framework is particularly relevant to **business processes, workflows, and human-machine interactions**, where human oversight is critical.

5.2 Event Modeling in OntoUML

In OntoUML, events are modeled as **occurrences** that trigger changes in a system, often with the following features:

1. **Generalized Event Types**: Events in OntoUML are categorized into types such as ***signal events, time-based events,*** *or* ***condition-based events***, depending on their triggering mechanism.

   Signal and time-based events correspond to the two essential types of event in MMABP: ***ad-hoc event***, and ***timer***. Condition-based event does not fulfill the definition of event in a human process since it miss the temporal dimension. It actually presumes the existence of the decision as a part of some process, which makes it a fully-fledged event. It means there must be another reason for such a decision in the process, either internal (timer) or external (ad-hoc event), which in terms of the events-identity rule presented in this paper represents its special meaning in the process.
2. **Temporal Flexibility**: In OntoUML, events are not strictly time-ordered in the same way as in this paper. They can occur in parallel or sequentially, depending on the system's constraints.

   Events in OntoUML are temporally flexible thanks to the absence of a temporal dimension, which is a basic condition of its system-orientation.
3. **Non-Exclusive Decisions**: Disjunctive decisions made over OntoUML models may allow for multiple events to occur simultaneously or in overlapping timelines, unless explicitly constrained by the model. This is another effect of a temporal independence of OntoUML models already discussed in the previous paragraph and also mentioned in the following paragraph as abstraction and flexibility.
4. **System-Centric Scope**: Events in OntoUML are part of a ***broader system model***, which may include different kinds of processes, without a strict emphasis on human intent. OntoUML is designed for ***system-level modeling***. Its event model is ***more abstract, flexible***, and ***temporally independent***, allowing for multiple events to coexist or interact in complex ways.

Table 2 summarizes key differences and similarities of understanding events in human process modeling (represented by MMABP) and in system modeling (represented by OntoUML).

The MMABP event model is tailored for processes, where **unambiguous resolution** is critical. In contrast, OntoUML's event model is more general, system-oriented, and thus allowing events to occur in parallel or in non-deterministic ways. For example, in a business process (human-centric), an event like "Payment Received" must be uniquely resolved at a specific time. In a distributed system, multiple events (e.g., "Order Placed" and "Inventory Updated") may occur concurrently since it naturally covers multiple parallel processes.

Table 2. Event understanding in human processes and OntoUML - key differences and similarities.

Aspect	Human Processes	OntoUML (System Modeling)
Event Uniqueness	Strictly time-ordered, **unambiguous sequence**	Flexible temporal ordering; **events may overlap**
Exclusivity	Disjunctive decisions are **exclusive** (XOR)	Disjunctive options **may overlap** (OR)
Event Identity	Events must be distinct in time or meaning	Events may share meaning but differ in timing
Logical Implication	$\varepsilon \Rightarrow \varphi \Leftrightarrow \varepsilon \equiv \varphi$ (events are equivalent if implied)	$\varepsilon \Rightarrow \varphi$ is a general implication, not necessarily identity
Human-Centric Focus	Events are tied to **human intent** and purpose	Events are part of a **system model**, not necessarily human-centric
Application Context	Business processes, workflows, human-machine systems	Ontologies. Complex systems

The conclusion that $\varepsilon \Rightarrow \varphi \Leftrightarrow \varepsilon \equiv \varphi$ is a theoretical constraint for human processes, ensuring that **events are resolved as distinct entities (phenomena)**. OntoUML does not enforce this equivalence, allowing for events to be logically related without being identical.

Events in human processes are **driven by human intent**, with processes defined by human goals. OntoUML, on the other hand, models events as parts of a system dynamics, which is independent of a human oversight.

The event model presented in this paper provides a ***rigorous, human-centric framework*** for processes where unambiguous resolution is critical. OntoUML, by contrast, offers a ***flexible, system-centric approach*** that accommodates complex, non-human-centric systems.

This section underscores the importance of ***contextual modeling*** in event understanding, highlighting how the paper's logic applies to human processes while OntoUML serves broader system modeling needs.

6 Conclusions

This paper redefines the logic of event processing in human processes, demonstrating that the implication of events ($\varepsilon \Rightarrow \varphi$) is logically equivalent to their identity ($\varepsilon \equiv \varphi$). This conclusion arises from the necessity of exclusive, time-ordered resolution in human processes. The derived equivalence has significant implications for the design of process models, algorithmic systems, and the understanding of human intentionality in computational systems.

The key implications of the presented understanding of events for modeling processes are as follows:

Events are semantically loaded, meaning that not all real-world happenings become process events, but only those **relevant to the goal** are modeled.

The granularity of events is context-dependent. The same real-world occurrence may be either one event in one process or multiple events in another.

Events define process structure (see Fig. 2). Process flow transits between its different **states**. Each process state is a **synchronization point**, at which the process flow sychronizes with an external influence represented by **events**, which the process uses as **feedback triggers** delivering to the process an important information to be used for the decision about the proper process reaction.

A teleological rule that determines the appropriate level of detail helps to avoid over-modeling. It shows that there is no need to capture low-level technical events but rather focus on **business-relevant milestones**, which the events actually represent in the process.

The key distinction from other approaches are as follows:

In **temporal logic**, an event is understood to be something that happens at a specific point in time. Its granularity is therefore either **time-based** or **system-based**. However, the main problem with this concept is that it is often too fine-grained and meaningless for business modeling. In **OntoUML / UFO-B** an event is a perdurant, something that is **extended in time**. Its granularity is ontological, meaning it is based on the identity and structure of events. OntoUML focuses on what kind of event it is in reality. While this strong ontological grounding is generally valuable, it is not necessarily aligned with business purpose. It may distinguish events that are irrelevant for process control.

In UFO-B, events bring about situations and situations define state changes, while In MMABP, business events are those events that are relevant to process intentionality. Therefore MMABP specializes the general ontological notion of event by adding the teleological criterion. This gives an independent justification beyond Boolean logic.

In the teleological view of **MMABP**, an event is defined as a **meaningful change** that is **relevant to achieving a goal**. Its granularity is purpose-driven and based on the importance of the event for the process. Such events correspond to decision points and define process states and transitions, thereby structuring intentional behavior represented by the process. In this conception a business process is a **feedback-controlled system** that continuously adapts its behavior to achieve a goal under changing conditions.

An event in MMABP is not an arbitrary occurrence in time but a real-world occurrence that is relevant to achieving the process goal. Consequently, **the occurrence becomes an event if and only if it causes a meaningful transition in the intentional behavior of the process**.

Acknowledgments. The paper was supported by the Faculty of Informatics and Statistics, Prague University of Economics and Business.

Disclosure of Interests. The author has no competing interests.

References

1. Almeida, J.P.A., Falbo, R.A., Guizzardi, G.: Events as entities in ontology-driven conceptual modeling. In: Laender, A.H.F., Pernici, B., Lim, E.-P., De Oliveira, J.P.M. (eds.) Conceptual Modeling. pp. 469–483. Springer, Cham (2019). https://doi.org/10.1007/978-3-030-33223-5_39

2. Boole, G.: An Investigation of the Laws of Thought, on Which are Founded the Mathematical Theories of Logic and Probabilities. Walton and Maberly, London (1854)
3. De Morgan, A.: Formal Logic; or, The Calculus of Inference, Necessary and Probable. Taylor and Walton, London (1847)
4. Enderton, H.: A Mathematical Introduction to Logic, 2nd edn. Harcourt Academic Press (2001). ISBN 0-12-238452-0
5. Eriksson, H.-E., Penker, M.: Business Modeling with UML: Business Patterns at Work. Wiley, New York Weinheim (2000)
6. Guizzardi, G.: Ontological foundations for structural conceptual models. Centre for Telematics and Information Technology. Telematica Instituut, Enschede, The Netherlands (2005)
7. Guizzardi, G., Botti Benevides, A., Fonseca, C.M., Porello, D., Almeida, J.P.A., Prince Sales, T.: UFO: unified foundational ontology. AO **17**, 167–210 (2022). https://doi.org/10.3233/AO-210256
8. National Institute of Standards and Technology: Integration Definition for Function Modeling (IDEF0). Federal Information Processing Standards Publication 183 (1993)
9. Object Management Group. Business Process Model and Notation, Version 2.0 (2011)
10. Object Management Group. Unified Modeling Language (UML), Version 2.5.1 (2017)
11. Řepa, V., Svatoš, O.: Fundamentals of Business Architecture Modeling. Springer, Cham (2024). https://doi.org/10.1007/978-3-031-59035-1
12. Řepa, V.: Philosophical framework for business system modeling. In: 2023 IEEE 25th Conference on Business Informatics (CBI), pp. 1–6. IEEE, Prague (2023). https://doi.org/10.1109/CBI58679.2023.10187427
13. Rosenblueth, A., Wiener, N., Bigelow, J.: Behavior, purpose and teleology. Phil. Sci. **10**, 18–24 (1943). https://doi.org/10.1086/286788
14. van der Aalst, W.M.P.: The application of petri nets to workflow management. J CIRCUIT SYST COMP. **08**, 21–66 (1998). https://doi.org/10.1142/S0218126698000043
15. Workflow Management Coalition: Workflow Process Definition Language (WPDL/XPD). WfMC-TC-1016-P (1999)
16. The Open Group. The TOGAF® Standard, Version 9.2. The Open Group (2018)

Ethical, Responsible, and Accountable AI and Digital Trust

Digital Trust in Health Data Sharing: A Value Sensitive Design Approach

Pascal Moriggl(✉), Janine Jäger, and Mario Bonic

School of Business, Institute for Information Systems, University of Applied Sciences and Arts Northwestern Switzerland FHNW, Windisch, Switzerland
pascal.moriggl@fhnw.ch

Abstract. The increasing use of digital technologies for the exchange of health data offers significant opportunities to advance personalized healthcare, medical research, and system efficiency, but also raises critical concerns related to trust, privacy, and ethical responsibility. This study addresses a research gap in conceptualizing and operationalizing digital trust within the design of health data sharing technologies. Guided by value-sensitive design (VSD), we conducted a mixed-method study that combined a survey of 124 participants with semi-structured interviews with five digital healthcare experts to identify essential values to foster digital trust in the sharing of health data. The findings indicate that transparency, data privacy, security, and user control are the values most prioritized, while the willingness to share data decreases when data collectors are not a direct care provider or when data are highly personal. Based on the findings, 28 norms and 74 design requirements were derived as actionable guidance to embed digital trust in health data sharing technologies. The study concludes that digital trust in the sharing of health data is based on transparency, consent, and user control and is shaped by perceptions of fair value exchange. These findings offer a foundation for designing trust-based health data sharing systems, thereby supporting more ethical, reliable, and user-accepted digital health ecosystems.

Keywords: Data Sharing · Digital Health · Digital Trust · Value Sensitive Design

1 Introduction

The collection and sharing of health data has become integral to healthcare care, driving advances in patient care, research, and system efficiency. Digital health is heavily based on data from mobile devices (mHealth), electronic health records (EHR), telehealth, or insurance sources [9, 10, 18, 24]. Its goal is to create a seamless cycle: from patient-generated data, through analysis by professionals and devices, to patients as actionable information [12, 24].

Despite this potential, digital health raises concerns, especially around trust in the sharing of health data [2, 16]. Trust, a complex and multidimensional concept [14, 26], is essential to overcome risk and uncertainty in digital interactions.

E. Laurenzi et al. (Eds.): BIR 2026, LNBIP 601, pp. 113–126, 2027.
https://doi.org/10.1007/978-3-032-38498-0_8

Although people increasingly express their willingness to share health data, this is conditional on data security, anonymity, and prevention of misuse [2,8,18]. In Switzerland, for example, two thirds of people trust hospitals, half trust government authorities, but far fewer trust insurance or pharmaceutical companies [18]. Thus, the willingness to share data is closely related to institutional trust [8].

Value-sensitive design (VSD) is a possible approach to embedding values in technology design and fostering trust by identifying stakeholder values and translating them into design requirements [4,22]. Researchers argue that trustworthy digital health initiatives must go beyond privacy protection, fostering a culture of trust through user-centric approaches [8,10,24]. This study therefore aims to develop standards and design requirements for technologies that share health data based on trust-related values using VSD as a guiding framework.

1.1 Trust in Digital Environments

Digital trust can be described as the extent to which operators, consumers, buyers, partners, and other stakeholders rely on an organization's ability to protect data and the privacy of individuals [17]. It has also been defined as the confidence of stakeholders in the competence of actors, technologies, and processes to establish reliable and secure business networks [15]. From a blockchain perspective, [19] digital trust has been conceptualized as the ability of users to apply heuristics that balance security and privacy and reflect their level of confidence. The concept of digital trust also emerges in the context of open innovation and industry 4.0 technologies [15].

Taken together, these perspectives illustrate that digital trust is a complex and multifaceted construct without a universally agreed-upon definition. It encompasses confidence in organizational data protection and privacy practices, in the competence of actors and technologies to establish secure networks, and in the reliability of systems leveraging emerging technologies such as blockchain. Digital trust is commonly characterized by values such as transparency, reliability, and adherence to norms and regulations, which are essential to foster trust in digital interactions. Unlike interpersonal trust in a traditional sense, digital trust must account for the absence of physical interaction and the potential for falsified or manipulated information in digital environments.

Despite a general willingness of people to share health data [1,18], lack of trust reduces this willingness and hinders progress in healthcare care [8]. Establishing trust is more complex in the digital world than in the social world, as communication depends on human and technological components, lacks visual cues, and is vulnerable to falsified information or fake identities [26]. Adapting societal trust to digital contexts, therefore, remains a significant challenge.

Nevertheless, fostering a culture of digital trust is essential for advancing digital health, with public confidence in data being a key priority [24]. Although prior research has identified bottlenecks [2,16] and conceptualized trust across different contexts [6,11,13,20], there is a gap in translating trust-related values into specific design requirements. This research is based on the assumption that design requirements for digital trust in health data sharing technologies can be effectively specified using Value Sensitive Design.

1.2 Value Sensitive Design

Value-sensitive design (VSD) is a principled approach to embed values of ethical importance into technology design [4,22]. It provides a systematic, theory-based methodology that integrates values throughout the design process by combining three complementary forms of investigation: conceptual, empirical, and technical (Fig. 1).

Conceptual investigations identify direct and indirect stakeholders and clarify the values at stake [3,5]. Empirical investigations involve stakeholders directly, using methods such as surveys, interviews, or observations to examine how values are prioritized and negotiated in practice [4]. The technical investigations then analyze or design technological features to determine how they support or constrain these values [4].

A key contribution of VSD is its explicit consideration of ethical values (e.g. privacy, accountability, autonomy, trust) alongside usability concerns, recognizing that technology design inherently balances multiple, sometimes conflicting, human values [4]. The approach emphasizes iterative refinement, translating values into norms and then into concrete design requirements [23]. This approach enables the design of systems that account for cultural and contextual differences while upholding widely recognized ethical commitments.

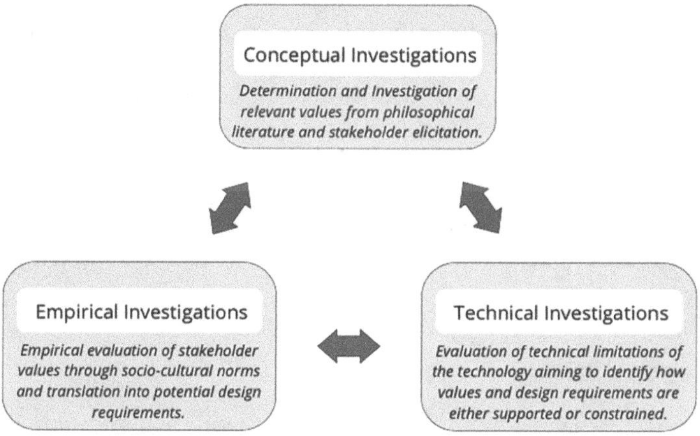

Fig. 1. Value Sensitive Design Framework [21].

1.3 Research Objectives

This study applies Value Sensitive Design (VSD) to address the challenge of integrating values relevant to digital trust into the design of technologies to share sensitive health data. It examines how digital trust can be conceptualized in this context and how stakeholder values can be translated into the corresponding norms and design requirements.

Accordingly, the study pursues three main objectives. First, it seeks to conceptualize digital trust in the context of health data sharing by reviewing relevant scientific literature and identifying stakeholders for empirical investigation. Second, it aims to derive norms for designing healthcare data sharing technologies by eliciting values from stakeholders and situating them within the broader literature on trust and health data sharing. Third, it focuses on translating these values into norms and design requirements. In doing so, the study provides guidance for the development of trust-centered health data technologies and contributes to future research in digital health.

This study has several limitations. First, it focuses on stakeholder values and trust-related factors for the sharing of digital health data rather than on specific technologies or other influencing factors in digital health. Second, the empirical findings are limited by the use of a non-representative survey sample drawn exclusively from Switzerland and by the small number of expert interviews, which constrain the breadth of perspectives, particularly from indirect stakeholders. Finally, the values, norms, and design requirements identified in this study are not intended to be exhaustive and may vary across different cultural, institutional, and data-sharing contexts.

2 Methodology

This study applied VSD [4] to identify values relevant to digital trust in the sharing of health data and translated them into norms and design requirements for associated technologies. The work was structured according to the three phases of VSD: conceptual, empirical, and technical investigation. The eleven trust-related values were identified through a structured literature review conducted during the conceptual phase of the Value Sensitive Design (VSD) process. Following VSD, this phase synthesizes relevant theoretical and empirical literature to identify stakeholder values that subsequently guide the empirical investigation.

2.1 Conceptual Phase

A literature review was conducted to establish a theoretical foundation for digital trust in the sharing of health data and to identify relevant stakeholders. From this review, the core values associated with trust in digital health technologies were derived using a deductive approach across the domains of digital health, sensitive health data sharing, general trust, and Value Sensitive Design.

Although prior studies indicate a relatively high willingness to share sensitive health data [1,2,18], a lack of trust in data-sharing initiatives reduces this willingness [8]. Building a culture of trust in digital environments is essential to ensure benefits for all stakeholders and to advance digital health, with public trust in the use of health data being a central priority [24].

To address this gap in digital trust, this research aims to develop norms and design requirements that allow integration of trust-related values into system design. For this research, values are defined as what individuals or groups consider important in life [4]. The key trust-related values identified through the literature review include willingness to share data, competence, integrity, benevolence, privacy, control, data security, transparency, accountability, reliability, and understandability [6,11,13,20]. Translating these values into norms and design requirements provides a structured approach to addressing the identified research gap.

Based on the literature, this study defines digital trust in the sharing of health data as a set of values that becomes important when health data is exchanged within technology-mediated cooperative relationships under conditions of uncertainty.

2.2 Empirical Phase

A mixed-method approach was applied to prioritize and specify identified values and derive corresponding norms and design requirements.

Survey: The survey aimed to explore the values of direct stakeholders (individuals that would potentially use health data sharing technologies) and to better understand if and under what conditions individuals are willing to share their personal health data in digital form. The anonymous online questionnaire was structured based on the values identified as relevant to digital trust in the sharing of health data. Participants were recruited via convenience sampling. The instrument measured the perceived importance of the 11 trust-related core values (e.g., privacy, transparency, competence) using Likert scale items, prioritization tasks, and demographic questions. A total of 124 participants (N = 124) completed the questionnaire, of whom n = 74 (59.68%) were male, n = 49 were female (39.52%) and n = 1 (0.81%) preferred not to disclose their gender. Regarding age distribution, the majority of respondents (63.71%, n = 79) were 25–34 years old, followed by 20.97% (n = 26) of the sample being 35–44 years old. A smaller proportion of participants belonged to the 55–64 age group (7.26%, n = 9), followed by the 45–54 age group (4.84%, n = 6). The youngest age group, 18–24 years, represented only 3.23% (n = 4) of the sample.

Interviews: The semi-structured interviews aimed to specify the values of indirect stakeholders, particularly organizations involved in the collection and exchange of health data. In total, five interviews were conducted with experts possessing extensive knowledge of the healthcare sector and experience with the topic of health data sharing. The participants represented diverse professional backgrounds in digital health and data-driven research. They included a Technical Department Head for Clinical Data Platform Research at a university hospital, the Global Head of Data, Analytics, and Research at a pharmaceutical company, and the Director of Clinical Bioinformatics at a large research institute. Additionally, two academic researchers participated, who are a lecturer and health technology researcher at a University of Applied Sciences, and a lecturer affiliated with a digital health lab at a university. An interview guide was developed based on the eleven values identified in the literature review and operationalized in the survey. Each interview lasted approximately one hour and was audio-recorded for subsequent transcription and analysis.

2.3 Data Analysis

Survey data were analyzed using descriptive statistics and chi-square tests of independence in IBM SPSS to identify value priorities and examine relationships with demographic variables. The interview transcripts were analyzed using inductive content analysis [25], involving iterative coding, category refinement, and thematic synthesis. The findings were subsequently mapped to the predefined core values to ensure consistency across methods.

2.4 Technical Phase

The findings of the conceptual and empirical phases were synthesized to derive norms and design requirements for trustworthy health data sharing technologies. Although a detailed technical investigation, specifically the translation of these requirements into concrete technical mechanisms, was beyond the scope of this study, it informed the formulation of design requirements and is left for future research. The identified values were translated into norms and design requirements following the framework proposed by Van de Poel (2013) [23].

This process involves a shift from evaluative to prescriptive terms, whereby norms represent appropriate and sufficient responses to values, and end norms specify the capabilities and properties that a technology should embody. Design requirements further refine these norms by detailing the conditions under which they should be realized, including what should be implemented, how, and for what purpose.

3 Results

The results of both the online questionnaire with direct stakeholders (potential users of health data sharing technologies) and the semi-structured interviews with indirect stakeholders (digital healthcare experts and organizations) provide complementary information on the conceptualization of digital trust in health data sharing.

3.1 Key Findings from the Questionnaire

The results of the questionnaire indicate that most respondents are open to sharing their health data under certain conditions. Participants reported multiple motivations, where the most frequently indicated motivation was learning more about personal health (20.96%, n = 83), followed by improved documentation of health-related outcomes (19.44%, n = 77). Other frequent motivations included improving health (18.18%, n = 72) and communication with healthcare providers (17.93%, n = 71). Altruistic motivations were also observed, including contributing to scientific research (10.86%, n = 43) and supporting the development of better health services (8.84%, n = 35).

The majority of the respondents (70.16%, n = 87) reported collecting health data using a smartphone or smartwatch, while 29.84% (n = 37) have not yet participated in this type of data collection. Among participants who reported tracking health-related data, the category of data most frequently recorded (n = 83, 38.25%) was physical activity (e.g., step count, calories burned, exercise). This was followed by cardiovascular data (e.g. heart rate, blood pressure; n = 44, 20.28%) and sleep data (e.g. duration, quality, wake time; n = 39, 17.97%). The less frequently tracked data categories included reproductive health data (n = 27, 12.44%), nutrition data (n = 13, 5.99%) and mental health data (n = 11, 5.07%). In particular, no participants reported tracking clinical or medical data (e.g., glucose levels, chronic disease monitoring).

According to the survey results, direct stakeholders place the highest importance on the values of **Transparency**, **Data Privacy**, and **Accountability**, which were ranked as top priorities among the 11 values related to trust. Participants also expressed a strong preference for explicit consent, the ability to revoke shared data, and notifications regarding data access. When participants were asked to rate the importance of a provider of digital health data sharing solutions adhering to values such as honesty, fairness, and confidentiality, more than half (52.42%, n = 65) rated this aspect as extremely important while additional 22.58% (n = 28) considered it very important. An additional 17.74% (n = 22) regarded it as reasonably important, indicating that over 90% of respondents attribute at least moderate importance to ethical alignment and integrity. Only a small minority considered it only slightly important (4.84%, n = 6) or not important at all (2.42%, n = 3).

Comfort with sharing health data was highest for individual healthcare providers, such as family doctors (M = 4.10, SD = 0.91) and therapists (M = 3.68, SD = 1.09), and lowest for insurance companies (M = 2.15, SD = 1.07), pharmaceutical companies (M = 2.15, SD = 1.13), and technology developers (M = 2.60, SD = 1.10). Willingness to share data also varied strongly depending on the type of data: while sharing of demographic and health metrics was widely accepted, sharing of genetic and mental health data was associated with greater discomfort.

Regarding trust-related values, participants were asked to select the six values they considered most important when using digital health data sharing technologies. Transparency, defined as the ability of users to be informed about the processing of their health data and and corresponding outcomes, was the value selected most frequently (n = 111, 15.55%), followed by Data Privacy (n = 100, 14.01%). In this study, data privacy refers to the ability of users to determine with whom their data are shared and to revoke access if desired. Control over personal health data, defined as the ability to decide whether to share health data at all, and accountability, defined as awareness of the parties involved in data handling and the policies governing data protection, were each selected 92 times (12.89%). Integrity, defined as the perceived alignment of values between user and the technology provider, was also highly valued, with 68 selections (9.52%). All other values were chosen less frequently.

Demographic analyzes (sex, education level, income) did not reveal significant differences in health data collection or willingness to share health data, suggesting that these behaviors were relatively independent of demographic factors in this sample. In general, the results underscore that digital trust is conditional and context-dependent, requiring both technical safeguards and ethical assurances.

3.2 Key Findings from the Interviews

Semi-structured interviews with healthcare experts revealed that organizations handling health data place a strong emphasis on governance, data protection frameworks, and regulatory compliance (e.g., GDPR, DSG). Integrity was described as a central factor in maintaining organizational reputation, and breaches of trust were perceived as highly damaging.

The interviewees consistently emphasized the importance of **co-creating consent processes**, enhancing transparency, and improving patient education. They also identified several systemic challenges, including limited interoperability, insufficient data harmonization, administrative burdens, and varying levels of digital maturity between institutions.

While hospitals and non-profit organizations are generally perceived as more trustworthy, commercial entities face challenges in demonstrating benevolence and avoiding perceptions of commodifying patient data. Experts further highlighted the importance of competence (multidisciplinary teams, technical and legal expertise) and reliability (standardization, interoperability, and long-term accountability mechanisms) as key enablers of trustworthy health data sharing.

3.3 Combined Insights

A comparison of the findings from the two data collection phases reveals a clear alignment between direct and indirect stakeholders.

- Both groups consistently emphasize the central role of **Transparency**, **Privacy**, and **Control** as fundamental conditions for establishing digital trust. However, their perspectives differ in emphasis.
- Direct stakeholders primarily focus on individual autonomy, highlighting the importance of consent, willingness to share data, and the ability to revoke

access.In contrast, indirect stakeholders emphasize systemic and organizational safeguards, such as governance structures, regulatory compliance, and accountability mechanisms.
- Both groups agree on the importance of effective communication and understandability. Direct stakeholders express a need for clear, accessible information, whereas organizations recognize the necessity of tailoring transparency to diverse user groups.
- A notable divergence exists in the perception of **value exchange**: while experts emphasize the broader benefits of data sharing for research and innovation, individuals remain concerned about personal risks, limited direct benefits, and the potential misuse of their data.

Overall, the findings indicate that digital trust in health data sharing is not static but relational and situational. Trust is shaped by factors such as the data-requesting actor, the type of data involved, and the perceived safeguards in place. Across both stakeholder groups, transparency, privacy, accountability, and the ability to exercise control consistently emerge as the most critical values. These insights provide an empirical foundation for the subsequent analysis, in which they are interpreted through the lens of Value Sensitive Design and situated within the broader literature on digital trust.

4 Discussion

In total, 11 values, 28 norms, and 74 tentative design requirements were identified and described to support the development of digital trust in technologies for health data sharing. The identified values are summarized in Table 1.

Table 1. Values for Digital Trust in Health Data Sharing

No.	Value
1	Transparency
2	Data Privacy
3	Willingness to Share Data
4	Accountability
5	Integrity
6	Understandability
7	Reliability
8	Benevolence
9	Competence
10	Purpose
11	Data Security

Organizations that collect and process health data emphasized the importance of establishing a clear value exchange in data sharing, for example through mechanisms such as data monetization, and highlighted the need for more robust concepts to enable its effective and scalable implementation. This perspective was also reflected by potential users, indicating a shared recognition of the importance of perceived benefits in fostering engagement with health data sharing technologies.

At the same time, the findings reveal inherent tensions between stakeholder values, reflecting differing priorities between users and organizations. Key value tensions include the balance between user control and seamless, purpose-driven data sharing, the trade-off between transparency and privacy protection, and the challenge of reconciling user-friendly design with technical complexity and understandability. Addressing these tensions requires the design of health data sharing technologies that offer flexibility and adaptability to diverse user needs and contexts. In particular, systems should enable configurable levels of control and transparency, allowing stakeholders to adjust these features according to their preferences and situational requirements. As the relative importance of values, such as control versus seamless data sharing, may vary across users and organizations, incorporating mechanisms for customization is essential for fostering digital trust.

These value tensions illustrate the need to translate abstract values into concrete norms and design requirements. Table 2 presents the specification of norms assigned to the value transparency as an example of such a translation.

Table 2. Norms for the value transparency

No.	Norms
Norm 1	The digital technology shall provide users with clear and accessible information about how and where users'health data is collected and stored
Norm 2	The digital technology shall disclose with whom users' health data is shared, including the purpose for the sharing, in an understandable format
Norm 3	The digital technology shall inform users about the algorithms used to process their health data, including their purposes and decision-making processes
Norm 4	The digital technology shall provide a log of all activities related to a user's data-sharing account, including when data was accessed, by whom, and for what purpose
Norm 5	The digital technology shall clearly explain how users' health data may be used in the future, including potential secondary uses, research, or sharing with third parties

Transparency was ranked as the most important trust-related value by the participants in the questionnaire. Across all items that characterize transparency, Across all Likert-scale items, respondents consistently emphasized the importance of understanding how their health data are collected and stored, with

Table 3. Design Requirements for Transparency Norms (Req. 1a–5b)

No.	Category	Description
1a	Transparency	Provide visual aids (e.g. infographics or flow diagrams) to illustrate data storage and processing workflows
1b	Transparency	Add an audit feature allowing users to see when and where their data is backed up or transferred
2a	Transparency	Create a "Data Sharing Dashboard" where users can view a list of entities with access to their data, the purpose of sharing, and the duration of agreements
2b	Transparency	Offer exportable reports that summarize data-sharing activity
2c	Transparency	Implement notifications to inform users whenever their data is accessed or shared
3a	Transparency	Include a "How Data is Processed" page with plain-language summaries of algorithms, the type of data processed, and their purposes
4a	Transparency	Develop an "Activity Log" showing timestamped entries of access events, who accessed data, and for what purpose
5a	Transparency	Provide scenario-based explanations to help users understand potential future uses of their data
5b	Transparency	Implement visualization tools (e.g. graphs or timelines) to show the life-cycle of user data

whom they are shared, which algorithms are used to analyze them, what activities are performed on their data, and for what additional purposes they may be used.

The findings of the interviews further reinforce the central role of transparency. Experts emphasized the importance of transparent procedures for health data exchange and the need to tailor communication to different audiences, such as patients and business stakeholders. In particular, they highlighted the need to clearly explain the purpose of data collection, its intended use, and how data are managed and propagated across systems.

Furthermore, quantitative results strongly indicate concerns about data sharing practices ($M = 4.44$) and secondary uses of health data ($M = 4.00$). These findings suggest that potential users are particularly concerned that their data are being shared with third parties without their knowledge. In contrast, the relatively low importance assigned to algorithmic transparency ($M = 3.05$) suggests that participants consider this aspect less critical, possibly reflecting a lack of understanding or concern about how algorithms affect their health data processing. This interpretation is supported by interview insights, which suggest that, while detailed algorithmic transparency can be provided, explanations are typically delivered at a higher level, with a stronger focus on data security. In general, these findings highlight the need to prioritize clear and accessible communication on data sharing practices, storage, and use to address user concerns and improve transparency in health data sharing contexts.

The norms associated with each value were subsequently translated into design requirements, which can serve as a practical guide for the development of health data sharing technologies. Table 3 illustrates this process by presenting the design requirements derived from the norms associated with the value of transparency. A comprehensive list of all the norms and the corresponding design requirements developed in this study is available from Zenodo [7].

5 Conclusion

Although prior research has extensively examined the challenges of sharing sensitive health data and the concept of trust in isolation, limited work has integrated these domains through Value Sensitive Design to systematically derive norms and design requirements for trust-centered health data sharing technologies. This study addresses this gap by combining conceptual and empirical insights to operationalize digital trust in the context of health data sharing. The findings suggest that digital trust is grounded in transparent data-sharing practices, the assurance of informed consent, and the provision of user control over health data before and after disclosure. Furthermore, digital trust is shaped by the perceived fairness of value exchange, which plays a critical role in mitigating uncertainty and perceived risks. Building on these insights, this study conceptualizes digital trust in health data sharing as a set of values that become important when health data are exchanged within technology-mediated cooperative relationships under conditions of uncertainty. By translating the identified values into 28 norms and 74 design requirements, this study makes a methodological and practical contribution by providing actionable guidance for designers, developers, and policy makers aiming to develop trustworthy health data sharing technologies. In doing so, it advances the application of Value Sensitive Design in digital health and offers a foundation for future research on the design and governance of trust-centered digital systems.

References

1. Bochud, M., Currat, C., Chapatte, L., Roth, C., Mooser, V.: High participation rate among 25 721 patients with broad age range in a hospitalbased research project involving whole-genome sequencing – the Lausanne Institutional Biobank. Swiss Med. Weekly **147**(4142), w14528 (2017). https://doi.org/10.4414/smw.2017.14528. https://smw.ch/index.php/smw/article/view/2383
2. Brall, C., Berlin, C., Zwahlen, M., Ormond, K., Egger, M., Vayena, E.: Public willingness to participate in personalized health research and biobanking: a large-scale Swiss survey. PLoS ONE **16**(4 April) (2021). https://doi.org/10.1371/journal.pone.0249141
3. Friedman, B., Hendry, D.G., Borning, A.: A survey of value sensitive design methods. Found. Trends® Hum.–Comput. Interact. **11**(2), 63–125 (2017). https://doi.org/10.1561/1100000015. https://www.nowpublishers.com/article/Details/HCI-015

4. Friedman, B., Kahn, P.H., Borning, A., Huldtgren, A.: Value sensitive design and information systems. In: Doorn, N., Schuurbiers, D., van de Poel, I., Gorman, M.E. (eds.) Early engagement and new technologies: Opening up the laboratory. PET, vol. 16, pp. 55–95. Springer, Dordrecht (2013). https://doi.org/10.1007/978-94-007-7844-3_4
5. Gerdes, A., Frandsen, T.: A systematic review of almost three decades of value sensitive design (VSD): what happened to the technical investigations? Ethics Inf. Technol. **25**(2) (2023). https://doi.org/10.1007/s10676-023-09700-2
6. Hoff, K.A., Bashir, M.: Trust in automation: integrating empirical evidence on factors that influence trust. Hum. Factors **57**(3), 407–434 (2015). https://doi.org/10.1177/0018720814547570
7. Jäger, J., Moriggl, P., Bonic, M.: Digital trust in health data sharing: a value sensitive design approach (2026). https://doi.org/10.5281/zenodo.21327276
8. Kalkman, S., Delden, J.V., Banerjee, A., Tyl, B., Mostert, M., Thiel, G.V.: Patients' and public views and attitudes towards the sharing of health data for research: a narrative review of the empirical evidence. J. Med. Ethics **48**(1), 3–13 (2022). https://doi.org/10.1136/medethics-2019-105651. https://jme.bmj.com/content/48/1/3
9. Kariotis, T., et al.: Emerging health data platforms: from individual control to collective data governance. Data Policy **2**, e13, (2020). https://doi.org/10.1017/dap.2020.14. https://www.cambridge.org/core/journals/data-and-policy/article/emerging-health-data-platforms-from-individual-control-to-collective-data-governance/C2FABA49744B674D157DC5E09E15DDCD
10. Landers, C., Vayena, E., Amann, J., Blasimme, A.: Stuck in translation: stakeholder perspectives on impediments to responsible digital health. Front. Dig. Health **5** (2023). https://doi.org/10.3389/fdgth.2023.1069410
11. Lee, J.D., See, K.A.: Trust in automation: designing for appropriate reliance. Hum. Factors **46**(1), 50–80 (2004). https://doi.org/10.1518/hfes.46.1.50_30392. https://journals.sagepub.com/doi/abs/10.1518/hfes.46.1.50_30392
12. Lingg, M., Lütschg, V.: Health system stakeholders' perspective on the role of mobile health and its adoption in the swiss health system: qualitative study. JMIR mHealth uHealth **8**(5), e17315 (2020). https://doi.org/10.2196/17315. https://mhealth.jmir.org/2020/5/e17315
13. Mayer, R.C., Davis, J.H., Schoorman, F.D.: An integrative model of organizational trust. Acad. Manag. Rev. **20**(3), 709–734 (1995). https://doi.org/10.2307/258792. https://www.jstor.org/stable/258792
14. McKnight, D.H., Choudhury, V., Kacmar, C.: Developing and validating trust measures for e-commerce: an integrative typology. Inf. Syst. Res. **13**(3), 334–359 (2002). https://doi.org/10.1287/isre.13.3.334.81. https://pubsonline.informs.org/doi/10.1287isre.13.3.334.81
15. Mubarak, M.F., Petraite, M.: Industry 4.0 technologies, digital trust and technological orientation: what matters in open innovation? Technol. Forecast. Social Change **161**, 120332 (2020). https://doi.org/10.1016/j.techfore.2020.120332. https://www.sciencedirect.com/science/article/pii/S0040162520311586
16. Ormond, K.E., et al.: What are the bottlenecks to health data sharing in Switzerland? An interview study. Swiss Med. Weekly **154**(1), 3538 (2024). https://doi.org/10.57187/s.3538. https://smw.ch/index.php/smw/article/view/3538
17. Pietrzak, P., Takala, J.: Digital trust – a systematic literature review. Forum Scientiae Oeconomia **9**(3), 59–71 (2021). https://doi.org/10.23762/FSO_VOL9_NO3_4. https://ojs.wsb.edu.pl/index.php/fso/article/view/411

18. Pletscher, F., Lerch, K., Glinz, D.: Willingness to share anonymised routinely collected clinical health data in Switzerland: a cross-sectional survey. Swiss Med. Weekly **152**(2324) (2022). https://doi.org/10.4414/SMW.2022.w30182
19. Shin, D.D.H.: Blockchain: the emerging technology of digital trust. Telematics Inform. **45**, 101278 (2019). https://doi.org/10.1016/j.tele.2019.101278. https://www.sciencedirect.com/science/article/pii/S0736585319307701
20. Solberg, E., Kaarstad, M., Eitrheim, M.H.R., Bisio, R., Reegård, K., Bloch, M.: A conceptual model of trust, perceived risk, and reliance on AI decision aids. Group Organ. Manag. **47**(2), 187–222 (2022). https://doi.org/10.1177/10596011221081238
21. Umbrello, S.: Meaningful human control over smart home systems. Humana.Mente **13**, 40–65 (2020). https://www.semanticscholar.org/paper/Meaningful-Human-Control-Over-Smart-Home-Systems-Umbrello/8e61eae75ed6445074d4ccd59c987dff6a71bf44
22. Umbrello, S., van de Poel, I.: Mapping value sensitive design onto AI for social good principles. AI Ethics **1**(3), 283–296 (2021). https://doi.org/10.1007/s43681-021-00038-3
23. Van De Poel, I.: Translating values into design requirements. In: Michelfelder, D.P., McCarthy, N., Goldberg, D.E. (eds.) Philosophy and Engineering: Reflections on Practice, Principles and Process. Philosophy of Engineering and Technology, vol. 15, pp. 253–266. Springer Netherlands, Dordrecht (2013). https://doi.org/10.1007/978-94-007-7762-0_20
24. Vayena, E., Haeusermann, T., Adjekum, A., Blasimme, A.: Digital health: meeting the ethical and policy challenges. Swiss Med. Weekly **148**(0304), w14571–w14571 (2018). https://doi.org/10.4414/smw.2018.14571. https://smw.ch/index.php/smw/article/view/2433
25. Vears, D.F., Gillam, L.: Inductive content analysis: a guide for beginning qualitative researchers. Focus Health Prof. Educ. Multi-Prof. J. **23**(1), 111–127 (2022). https://doi.org/10.3316/informit.455663644555599. https://search.informit.org/doi/abs/10.3316/informit.455663644555599
26. Yan, Z., Holtmanns, S.: Trust modeling and management: from social trust to digital trust. In: Computer Security, Privacy and Politics: Current Issues, Challenges and Solutions. IGI Global (2007). https://doi.org/10.4018/978-1-4666-2803-8.ch018. https://www.igi-global.com/gateway/chapter/74120

Agency Perceptions and Trust in Generative AI: A Longitudinal Study on Software Engineers

Valentina Curcio[1(✉)] and Olivier Le Van[1,2(✉)]

[1] Cegedim, Lyon, France
{valentina.curcio,olivier.levan}@cegedim.com
[2] Université Paris Saclay, Paris, France

Abstract. Generative AI tools are reshaping software development, yet the mechanisms through which developers build or lose trust in these tools remain poorly understood. Vanneste and Puranam posit that perceiving an AI as agentic affects trust through three mechanisms: enhancing perceived ability, shifting the locus of trust from designer to AI, and amplifying betrayal concerns. This model remains untested, and treats agency as a unitary construct—an assumption not yet examined empirically. To address this gap, we test the three-mechanism model and examine whether agency functions as a unitary construct through a mixed-methods longitudinal field study with 107 software professionals using AI coding assistants (four survey waves; nine semi-structured interviews). The survey confirms the first two mechanisms: agency correlates with perceived ability and trust progressively shifts from the designer to the AI as the primary trustee. The third mechanism, however, is reversed: betrayal cost is positively associated with trust, contradicting the predicted negative relationship. The interviews reveal why: professional users do not perceive agency as unitary. They grant the AI autonomy but deny it intentionality and free will, a distinction drawn by 7 out of 9 interviewees. Because users do not attribute intentional action to the AI, they assign errors to their own prompting and describe potential AI loss as functional dependency rather than betrayal. Agency decomposition thus emerges as a boundary condition for trust models in AI: mechanisms requiring only perceived autonomy (ability enhancement, locus shift) operate as predicted, while betrayal aversion, which presupposes perceived intentionality, is structurally neutralized. These findings suggest that treating agency as unitary may lead to incorrect predictions in populations that differentiate its facets.

Keywords: Generative AI · Trust · Software Development · Agency Perception · Longitudinal Study

1 Introduction

The adoption of generative AI tools in software development has accelerated rapidly, with AI coding assistants such as Claude Code, Cursor and GitHub Copi-

E. Laurenzi et al. (Eds.): BIR 2026, LNBIP 601, pp. 127–144, 2027.
https://doi.org/10.1007/978-3-032-38498-0_9

lot becoming integral to daily workflows [18,42,45]. Developers using AI coding agents to plan and execute multi-step tasks constitute a form of hybrid intelligence [8], in which human judgment and machine capabilities are interleaved. While the effects on productivity have been widely documented [4,8,18,33,46], the question of how developers come to trust these tools, and how that trust evolves over sustained use, remains underexplored. Trust is critical because it governs the extent to which developers rely on AI suggestions, verify AI-generated code, and ultimately integrate AI into consequential decisions. Empirical observations have shown that developers keep only 52% of the original AI suggestions, frequently reviewing their trust judgments in real time [43].

Classical models of organizational trust identify Ability, Benevolence, and Integrity (ABI) as antecedents of trustworthiness [7,31], but generative AI poses a unique challenge: unlike traditional software, large language models blur the boundary between tool and agent, adapting to context, producing unexpected outputs and appearing to reason [1]. It can also exhibit creative [16] and even voluntarily deceptive behaviour toward users [17,20,35], in addition to well-documented hallucination problems.

Vanneste and Puranam [50] provide a theoretical framework to answer a fundamental research question: *Does the degree to which a user perceives an AI as agentic affect how trust is formed and maintained?* They argue that perceived agency, the extent to which an AI is seen as capable of thinking, planning, and acting, affects trust through three mechanisms: (1) enhancing perceived trustworthiness of both the AI and its designer (i.e. the entity providing the AI system, as Anthropic), (2) shifting the relative importance of AI versus designer trustworthiness (locus shift), and (3) amplifying betrayal concerns through betrayal aversion (Fig. 1). Their model has not yet been tested empirically. Software developers constitute a particularly relevant population for such a test, given their sustained, technically informed interaction with generative AI [27].

The present study addresses this gap. We conduct a mixed-methods longitudinal field study with 107 software professionals using commercial generative AI tools in a professional setting, combining four survey waves with nine semi-structured interviews. Our contributions are threefold:

1. We provide the first empirical test of the three-mechanism model in a real-world longitudinal context.
2. While this model treats agency as unitary, recent work [25,49] conceptualizes it as a multifactorial construct. Our findings support this view: the facets of agency identified in the literature, autonomy, intentionality, and free will [3,24,48,50], do not form a unitary construct in our sample. Professional users attribute them independently, granting autonomy while denying intentionality and free will.
3. This non-unity predicts which of the three mechanisms operate: those that require only perceived autonomy are supported, while betrayal aversion, which presupposes perceived intentionality, is not. The qualitative component identifies the mechanisms through which this plays out: users who deny the

AI intentionality attribute errors to their own prompting and frame potential AI loss as dependency on a tool perceived as productive, rather than as betrayal by an intentional agent.

2 Related Works

2.1 Trust: From Human Relationships to AI

The foundational model of organizational trust [31] identifies three antecedents of trustworthiness—Ability, Benevolence, and Integrity (ABI)—and has been extended to human-computer interaction [32]. Applying ABI to generative AI, however, raises new challenges. A meta-review of 562 empirical studies [10] shows that trust formation depends on the interplay between user, AI, and contextual characteristics, and that professional expertise modulates this process, as experts leverage domain knowledge to calibrate trust whereas novices are more susceptible to surface cues. Yet existing frameworks struggle with systems that exhibit adaptive, anthropomorphic behaviors [38]. Features such as perceived task superiority and opacity call for adapted adoption strategies [21], and several authors argue that theories must evolve because generative AI enters previously human-only domains and resists classification as either tool or colleague [37,39]. Moreover, trust in AI is not purely individual: third-party teammates influence trustworthiness perceptions [15], and trust in decision-support AI can develop concurrently with use through boundary spanning [9], challenging the assumption that trust must precede adoption. ABI thus remains a valid lens for capturing trustworthiness perceptions, but requires augmentation with constructs that account for the distinctive nature of AI as a trustee.

2.2 Agency as a Variable in AI Trust

Traditional trust-in-automation research focuses on system reliability and predictability, treating technology as a passive tool whose inner states need not be modelled [28]. Generative AI complicates this framing: modern LLMs exhibit adaptive behaviors as context sensitivity, natural language generation, apparent reasoning, that evoke varying degrees of agency perception in users [19,36,47]. A meta-analysis of 136 studies [30] confirms that the tool-versus-agent distinction matters empirically, with agency-related features (anthropomorphism, autonomous role) driving acceptance differently from tool features (capability, transparency).

Vanneste and Puranam [50] formalize this observation into a theoretical model. They argue that agency perception affects trust through three mechanisms. First, it enhances perceived trustworthiness of both the AI and its designer (the organization that provides the model). Second, it shifts the locus of trust from the designer to the AI itself. Third, drawing on betrayal aversion research [5], it increases the anticipated psychological cost of trust violation when the AI seems capable of intentional action. The question of whether non-agential entities can be genuine objects of trust at all [52] lends conceptual

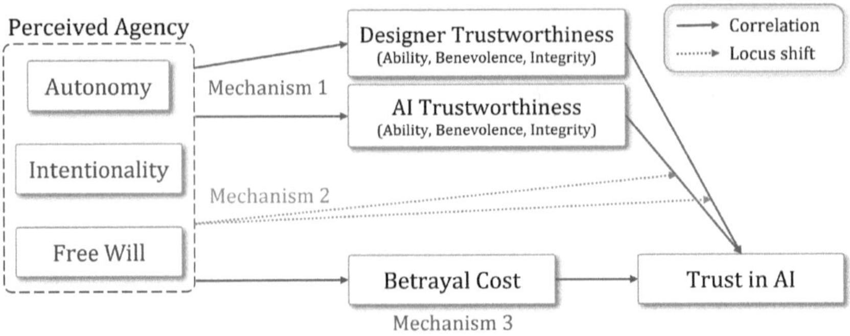

Fig. 1. Theoretical framework (adapted from [50]). Mechanisms 1 and 3 predict positive links from agency to trustworthiness and to betrayal cost; Mechanism 2 predicts a locus shift of trust from designer to AI; betrayal cost is predicted to reduce trust.

weight to this model: the degree to which users perceive an AI as agentic may determine whether they engage in trust or mere instrumental reliance. Empirical work supports this gradient view: higher AI autonomy weakens trust transfer from the creator to the system [44], consistent with the trust shift mechanism theorised by Vanneste and Puranam, while anthropomorphic cues increase trust resilience under reliability degradation [11]. Taken together, these findings position perceived agency not as a binary trait but as a continuous variable that modulates both the antecedents and the pathway of trust formation. Figure 1 summarizes this theoretical framework. The model has since generated active theoretical debate on the respective roles of opacity, explainability, and designers' disclosure choices in shaping perceived agency [23,51], reinforcing the need for empirical tests in specific user populations.

2.3 Trust Dynamics and the Software Development Context

Software development is a particularly informative context for studying trust in AI. Developers interact with AI coding assistants repeatedly, receiving immediate and verifiable feedback [22,42], creating conditions for rapid trust calibration. They also possess technical knowledge of the underlying models, which may shape how they attribute agency, a dimension distinguishing this population from the general public [40,41]. Although cross-cultural research shows that national culture significantly moderates trust antecedents in the general population [10], a survey of 188 software engineers found that habit and performance expectancy drive LLM adoption while cultural values do not significantly moderate the process [26]. Professional identity may explain this specificity: developers across cultures appear to frame their relationship to AI through shared technical expertise rather than national values [27]. Trust in this context is also dynamic: longitudinal research shows that individuals adjust their reliance through experience while rarely deferring fully [29].

A further mechanism shaping trust calibration in this professional context is self-efficacy [2], an individual's belief in their capacity to perform the actions required to achieve a given outcome. In professional settings involving complex tools, those with high task-specific self-efficacy tend to attribute setbacks to controllable input factors rather than to external agents or inherent task difficulty. In AI-mediated software development, this suggests that developers who see themselves as competent prompt authors may systematically attribute AI errors to their own phrasing rather than to model deficiencies. This attributional posture matters because the cognitive landscape developers face is uneven: Dell'Acqua et al. [12] characterise it as a "Jagged Frontier" along which the boundary between AI competence and AI failure is largely invisible. In such conditions, naive reliance can shade into automation bias [34], while a strong sense of prompt-level control may instead sustain active oversight. How these mechanisms unfold over time in sustained professional use remains unexplored.

3 Methods

3.1 Participants and Context

We conducted a longitudinal field study within a large European IT services company. A total of 107 participants responded to at least one survey wave. Among them, 76 held a Claude licence, 12 a Cursor licence, and 19 both. Participants were software developers and IT professionals who had been provided with generative AI coding assistants as part of a company-wide AI adoption initiative. Four monthly survey waves were administered. Because licences were granted progressively and not all participants responded to every wave, sample sizes vary across timepoints: T1 ($n = 91$), T2 ($n = 90$), T3 ($n = 80$), T4 ($n = 68$). Time T is measured relative to each participant's licence attribution date, so that the same T does not correspond to a single calendar date across the sample. The study followed an explanatory sequential design: quantitative results were analyzed first, and semi-structured interviews were then conducted to investigate the principal anomalies that emerged from the survey data.

3.2 Quantitative Component: Survey

Survey Design. Each wave, participants completed an online survey designed to capture trust-related perceptions of their AI coding assistant. The instrument operationalizes the constructs from the Vanneste and Puranam [50] framework: Agency Perception (Autonomy, Intentionality, Free Will), AI Trustworthiness (Ability, Benevolence, Integrity), Designer Trustworthiness (Ability, Benevolence, Integrity), Betrayal Cost, and Trust. All constructs were measured using multi-item scales on 5-point Likert scales (1 = strongly disagree, 5 = strongly agree), following evidence on optimal scale granularity [53], with 9 to 12 items per main dimension. In addition, three baseline moderators were measured at T1 only: Task Complexity, Betrayal Aversion (a dispositional tendency to be averse to betrayal, distinct from the situational Betrayal Cost measured at each wave), and Initial Expectations.

Table 1. Scale reliability (Cronbach's α) across measurement waves.

Dimension	Sub-dimensions	α_{T1}	α_{T2}	α_{T3}	α_{T4}
Agency Perception	Autonomy, Intentionality, Free Will	.53	.69	.71	.61
AI Trustworthiness	Ability, Benevolence, Integrity	.81	.78	.80	.83
Designer Trustworthiness	Ability, Benevolence, Integrity	.81	.84	.89	.89
Betrayal Cost	–	.73	.69	.78	.81
Trust	–	.66	.58	.79	.73

Survey Consistency. Internal consistency was assessed using Cronbach's α at each timepoint (Table 1). AI Trustworthiness (α = .78–.83) and Designer Trustworthiness (α = .81–.89) showed acceptable to good reliability across all waves. Trust varied across waves (α = .58–.79); because trust is the dependent variable and its meaning may genuinely shift as users gain experience, moderate fluctuations in internal consistency are expected and do not compromise the analysis. The Agency Perception composite scale showed lower reliability (α = .53–.71), falling below the .70 threshold at three of four waves, a point we examine in Sect. 4.1. We used it to evaluate the risk of common method bias on all survey items. Since the first factor explained a mere 16.3% of the variance, it falls significantly short of the 50% benchmark required to suggest that a single factor accounts for the majority of the covariance, thereby confirming the robustness of the measurement model.

3.3 Qualitative Component: Semi-structured Interviews

To explore unexpected patterns emerging from the survey data, notably the low internal consistency of the agency scale and a positive association between betrayal cost and trust where theory predicts a negative one (Sect. 4.4), we conducted nine semi-structured interviews (participants P1 to P9), all IT professionals with varied roles (developers, tech lead, compliance officer, manager). Participants were selected to maximize variation in agency coherence (from consistently high scores to divergent sub-dimension profiles) and betrayal patterns (e.g., high betrayal cost with high trust, high betrayal cost with low trust, low betrayal overall). Interviews lasted 25–45 min and covered four themes: AI usage patterns, perceived problems and limitations, agency attribution (autonomy, intentionality, free will), and trust evolution. Transcripts were coded using a purpose-built analysis grid spanning the following dimensions: agency facets (autonomy, intentionality, free will, and whether participants differentiate them), error attribution (self, AI, or designer), betrayal cost (engagement/dependency, perceived exposure), trust dynamics (direction of evolution, triggering events), and the perceived link between agency and betrayal. Coding followed a thematic analysis approach [6]: verbatim quotes were preserved without modification, coding was cross-dimensional (a single passage could feed multiple dimensions), and interviewer utterances were excluded.

4 Results

We first examine the structure of the Agency Perception construct, then test each of the three mechanisms in turn.

4.1 Agency Perception: A Non-unitary Construct

A prerequisite for testing the three-mechanism model is understanding how participants perceive AI agency. Scale reliability analysis already provides a first empirical indication: the Agency Perception composite shows low internal consistency ($\alpha = .53$–$.71$), falling below the .70 threshold at three of four waves, while all other constructs are acceptable (Table 1). This suggests that the three sub-dimensions—Autonomy, Intentionality, and Free Will—do not form a unitary construct.

Inter-correlations between sub-dimensions confirm this. At T1, Autonomy is essentially independent of both Intentionality ($r = .19$, $p = .077$) and Free Will ($r = .02$, $p = .870$), while Intentionality and Free Will are moderately correlated ($r = .34$, $p = .001$). Autonomy remains weakly correlated with the other two facets at T1, T2, and T4 ($r = .02$–$.33$), with the exception of T3 where correlations reach moderate levels ($r = .35$–$.54$). Overall, Autonomy does not consistently cohere with Intentionality and Free Will, undermining the convergent validity of the composite scale.

The semi-structured interviews confirm this pattern: seven out of nine interviewees differentiated the three facets. Autonomy was granted by all participants, consistently scoped to implementation and means rather than goals. **P6**: *"It has autonomous action since it decides to do things on its own."* **P9**: *"I find it autonomous in its research, its implementation choices."* **P2** drew the distinction explicitly: *"The AI will find me a solution... it has autonomy... more on the means than on the result."* **P5** concurred: *"I leave it autonomous on the code itself,"* while retaining architectural control.

Intentionality was denied by 7/9 as belonging to the AI. Participants systematically attributed it either to themselves or to the designer's programming. **P6**: *"There is no intention, except the one I give."* **P1**: *"I wouldn't say intentionality. It tries to answer questions and solve problems."* **P3**: *"I think they're made to satisfy us"*—attributing intent to the designer, not the AI. **P2**: *"For me, no... it's me who frames that."*

Free will was denied by 8/9, reframed as stochastic variability or user error. **P4**: *"It's statistics on the next word."* **P1**: *"I wouldn't say free will, but the way of asking questions."* **P3**: *"I think it's still quite constrained."* **P5**: *"The AI won't tell you, because you didn't ask."*

In sum, participants perceive the AI as autonomous (it acts, produces outcomes, makes implementation choices) but not as intentional or free-willed. We hypothesize that technical literacy may moderate this decomposition: the two participants with the deepest understanding of transformer architecture (P6, P4) produced the sharpest differentiations. This decomposition has direct consequences for each of the three mechanisms tested below.

4.2 Mechanism 1: Ability Enhancement

To preserve comparability with the theoretical model [50], which treats agency as unitary, the following analyses use the composite Agency Perception score. Given the decomposition reported above, this composite should be read as reflecting primarily Autonomy, the sub-dimension universally granted by our participants, while Intentionality and Free Will, attributed less consistently across the sample, contribute more variably to the composite.

The theory predicts that perceiving the AI as agentic enhances perceived trustworthiness, and more specifically that ability should be the primary channel [50]: an AI that appears capable of selecting sub-goals and adjusting to context is judged more competent. Agency Perception is indeed significantly and positively correlated with all six ABI facets at every wave (Table 2), confirming the general prediction. The ability-specific prediction, however, receives only partial support: on the AI side, Ability is the largest or co-largest correlate at T1, T3, and T4, peaking at $r = .65$ (T3), but Integrity tracks closely throughout ($r = .39$–$.58$). On the designer side, Integrity matches or exceeds Ability at most waves. These correlations are consistent with the agency decomposition reported in Sect. 4.1 Ability enhancement requires only that users see the AI as acting and producing outcomes—i.e., perceived autonomy—without requiring perceived intentionality or free will. Since all participants grant autonomy, the mechanism operates as predicted [37,50].

Table 2. Pearson correlations (r) between Agency Perception and the Ability, Benevolence, and Integrity (ABI) sub-dimensions of AI and Designer Trustworthiness.

	Wave	Ability		Benevolence		Integrity	
		r	p	r	p	r	p
Agency → AI Trustw.	T1	.446	<.001	.333	.001	.439	<.001
	T2	.575	<.001	.408	<.001	.577	<.001
	T3	.653	<.001	.378	.001	.567	<.001
	T4	.477	<.001	.404	.001	.392	.001
Agency → Designer Trustw.	T1	.341	.001	.267	.011	.346	.001
	T2	.529	<.001	.387	<.001	.424	<.001
	T3	.362	.001	.406	<.001	.452	<.001
	T4	.367	.002	.393	.001	.417	<.001

4.3 Mechanism 2: Locus Shift

We first examine whether trust is primarily driven by AI or Designer Trustworthiness (Table 3). AI Trustworthiness is the dominant predictor at every wave, growing from $\beta = .40$ ($p = .002$) at T1 to $\beta = .76$ ($p < .001$) at T4, while

Designer Trustworthiness is non-significant at T1–T3 and marginally negative at T4 ($\beta = -.22$, $p = .072$) (Fig. 2a). Notably, Designer Trustworthiness correlates positively with Trust in zero-order terms ($r = .25$–$.46$, all $p < .05$), but this relationship is largely absorbed by its collinearity with AI Trustworthiness ($r = .61$–$.72$; VIF $= 1.60$–2.05): once AI Trustworthiness is controlled, the designer adds no unique predictive value. This pattern holds regardless of the AI tool used (Claude or Cursor).

Table 3. OLS regression predicting Trust from Trustworthiness.

Wave	R^2	AI Trustworthiness		Designer Trustworthiness	
		β	p	β	p
T1	.241	.395	.002	.131	.289
T2	.234	.450	<.001	.049	.694
T3	.374	.568	<.001	.059	.651
T4	.426	.763	<.001	−.218	.072

R^2: explained variance; β: standardized regression coefficient; p: significance level. Sample sizes: T1 = 91, T2 = 90, T3 = 80, T4 = 68.

The theory predicts that as agency perception increases, trust shifts from the designer to the AI. In the full sample, AI Trustworthiness is already the sole significant predictor at T1, suggesting that the designer was never a meaningful trust anchor for most participants. What we do observe is an intensification of AI dominance: the AI Trustworthiness β increases significantly over time (slope $= +.122$/wave, $p = .031$, $R^2 = .94$; Fig. 2a), while the Designer Trustworthiness β decreases and crosses zero at T4.

A subgroup analysis adds nuance. We split participants into High and Low Agency groups based on their T1 Agency Perception score (median split, fixed across waves) and track them over time using the same simultaneous regression (Fig. 2b). In the High Agency group ($n = 55$ at T1), Designer Trustworthiness never carries unique predictive weight (β near zero at all waves), while AI Trustworthiness grows steadily from $\beta = .30$ to .70. These users related to the AI as the primary trustee from the outset. In the Low Agency group ($n = 36$ at T1), by contrast, Designer Trustworthiness is a substantial unique predictor ($\beta = .32$–$.39$) through T1–T3, while AI Trustworthiness remains moderate ($\beta = .24$). At T4, the Low Agency group appears to converge with the High Agency group ($\beta_{\text{AI}} = .72$, $\beta_{\text{Des}} = -.26$), though this observation must be treated as exploratory rather than confirmatory. The reduced sample ($n = 21$) and the pattern of differential attrition raise the possibility that the apparent convergence is an artefact of selective dropout: participants who did not develop AI-centric trust may have been disproportionately lost from the Low Agency group by T4, producing a spurious shift in the aggregate coefficients. We did not formally test whether attrition was random with respect to trust trajectories, and this limits any causal inference about within-person locus change in this subgroup.

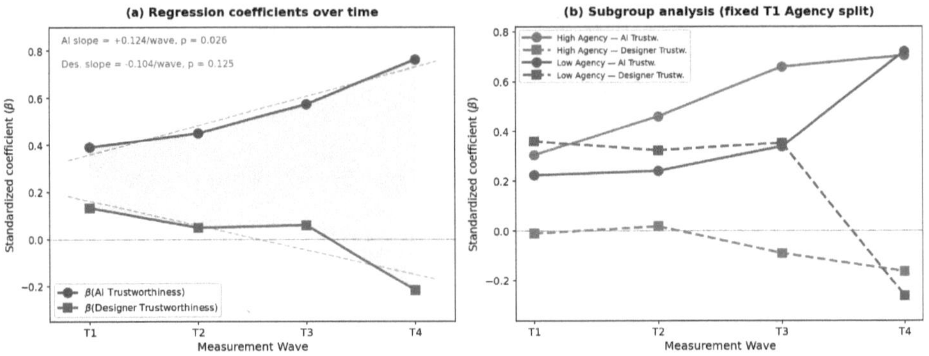

Fig. 2. Trust predictors over time. (a) Standardized β from simultaneous OLS predicting Trust: AI Trustworthiness strengthens significantly over waves while Designer Trustworthiness remains non-significant. (b) Same regression within subgroups (T1 median split on Agency Perception): Designer Trustworthiness carries no unique weight in the High Agency group, but is a substantial predictor through T3 in the Low Agency group before dropping at T4 ($n = 21$).

Taken together, these results suggest that the predicted locus shift manifests less as a gradual transfer and more as a structural asymmetry: for the majority of participants, AI Trustworthiness was the primary trust driver from the outset, and its dominance intensified over time. The subgroup analysis raises the hypothesis that a genuine shift from designer to AI may occur among lower-agency users over time; however, the subsample size at T4 ($n = 21$) and unverified attrition randomness prevent confirmatory inference. This remains an open question for future longitudinal replication with larger and more stable samples. The interviews help explain the structural pattern: most participants did not have a clear mental model of the designer. **P9** found the very concept ambiguous: *"Who is behind it is blurred... Is it the founders of Anthropic, the AI itself, the company?"* **P1** expressed indifference: *"How it works technically—I'd say it doesn't matter, as long as it gives us coherent and roughly correct answers."* **P2** framed the relationship in purely instrumental terms: *"I use it more as a tool."* Only two participants (P4, P6) had an explicit opinion about the designer. **P4** grounded designer trust in perceived transparency: *"He is more serious in terms of morality."* **P6** actively chose an alternative model for his own AI agents based on the designer's identity: *"I prefer to run them with [a French provider]... that way we are sovereign on the matter."* These two cases illustrate that when a mental model of the designer does exist, it can activate the trust pathway predicted by the theory. But for the majority, the designer remains too diffuse a concept to serve as a trust anchor. This pattern may also reflect the study context: participants were assigned their AI tool by the company rather than choosing among providers, in a market where differentiated designer identities have not yet fully emerged.

4.4 Mechanism 3: Betrayal Concerns

Vanneste and Puranam's theory predicts a two-step pathway: agency should increase betrayal cost, which in turn should reduce trust. We test both links (Table 4). The first link is supported from T2 onward ($r = .29$–$.35$, $p < .005$). The second link, however, is reversed: Betrayal Cost is positively associated with Trust at T2 and T4 ($r = .27$–$.36$, $p < .03$), marginally at T1 ($r = .20$, $p = .053$), and non-significant at T3 ($r = .13$, $p = .258$). At no wave is the relationship negative. This directly contradicts the betrayal aversion prediction.

Table 4. Betrayal mechanism: direct correlations.

	n	Agency → Betrayal		Betrayal → Trust	
		r	p	r	p
T1	91	.094	.377	.203	.053
T2	90	.292	.005	.358	.001
T3	80	.349	.001	.128	.258
T4	68	.300	.013	.272	.025

A bootstrap mediation analysis (Table 5) confirms this reversal. In this model, a denotes the effect of Agency on Betrayal Cost, b the effect of Betrayal Cost on Trust (controlling for Agency), c the total effect of Agency on Trust, c' the direct effect (controlling for Betrayal Cost), and $a \times b$ the indirect (mediated) effect. Agency is positively associated with Trust at all waves ($c = 0.75$–1.06), and this relationship is largely direct (c') rather than mediated through Betrayal Cost. The indirect effect is significant at T2 ($a \times b = 0.094$, 95% CI [.003, .228]), but in the positive direction agency increases betrayal cost, which in turn increases trust. At other waves the indirect effect is non-significant. When controlling for Betrayal Aversion, the dispositional trait measured at T1 (see Sect. 3.2), Agency's effect on Betrayal Cost vanishes ($\beta = .03$, $p = .801$) while the trait is a strong predictor ($\beta = .40$, $p < .001$), indicating that betrayal cost is driven by personality rather than agency perception.

Since the positive Betrayal–Trust association directly contradicts the theoretical prediction, we used the semi-structured interviews to investigate the underlying mechanism. Two converging patterns emerged.

Self-attribution of Errors. All nine interviewees predominantly attribute AI failures to their own prompting rather than to the AI itself. Participants spontaneously framed errors as a prompt-quality problem, as exemplified by **P2**: *"They're small errors, but they come more from the prompt,"* **P7**: *"I question*

Table 5. Mediation analysis: Agency → Betrayal Cost → Trust.

	a	b	c'	c	$a \times b$	95% CI
T1	0.203	0.130	0.721	0.747	0.026	[−.031, .114]
T2	0.532	0.176	0.683	0.777	0.094	[.003, .228]
T3	0.710	−0.059	0.957	0.915	−0.042	[−.153, .067]
T4	0.682	0.109	0.716	0.790	0.074	[−.041, .225]

Unstandardized coefficients (scale points). a: Agency → Betrayal; b: Betrayal → Trust (controlling for Agency); c: total; c': direct; $a \times b$: indirect. Theory expects $b < 0$ and $a \times b < 0$.

the prompting rather [than the AI]," and **P4**: *"I tell myself I asked the question badly, I wasn't precise enough, so I'll revise my prompt."* Others generalized the point—**P9**: *"It does what you ask; if you phrase it badly, it performs badly"* and **P3**: *"It's me who uses it, I'm not going to blame the AI."* This consistent self-attribution neutralizes the betrayal pathway: when the perceived source of failure is the user's own input rather than the AI's volition, the conditions for betrayal (such as intentional harmful action by a trusted agent) are not met, and betrayal cost cannot reduce trust.

Functional Dependency Rather than Betrayal Aversion. When asked about losing access to the AI, no participant used terms related to betrayal, deception, or trust violation. Instead, several participants spontaneously framed the relationship in terms of dependency: **P5**: *"You become very quickly dependent,"* **P3**: *"We are dependent on them,"* **P7**: *"It's sad to say, but I think I'd feel a bit diminished... Dependency. I think we shouldn't be dependent."* When asked to elaborate on what losing the tool would mean, the register remained one of withdrawal and productivity loss rather than betrayal: **P5**: *"You go from everything to nothing... like a hangover,"* **P2**: *"Completion time is divided by 10, by 15, by 20... it would be crippling,"* **P4**: *"Without my Claude, I'd go back to the old ways and spend six months to get the answers."* This suggests that the Betrayal Cost scale captures functional dependency rather than aversion to potential betrayal. High dependency naturally coexists with high trust, since both are indicators of successful adoption. Dependence is a construct already developed in automation trust research as the precondition under which a user relies on a tool to achieve goals [28]. Granting autonomy but denying intentionality, our participants keep their dependency "tool-like" rather than exposing them to an agent that could betray them. Unlike Mechanisms 1 and 2, betrayal aversion [5] requires that users perceive the AI as capable of intentional action: a user can only experience betrayal if they believe the AI is capable of acting deliberately. Since our participants deny the AI intentionality (Sect. 4.1), the betrayal pathway is structurally neutralized. We propose that Mechanism 3 [50] requires a boundary condition tied to agency decomposition: the betrayal aversion pathway operates only when users attribute intentionality to the AI, not merely autonomy. A second, intentionality-free route to trust erosion is algorithm aversion: after an observed error, people abandon an algorithm in favour of human judgment, even when it outperforms the human overall [13]. In a later study, Dietvorst et al. [14] mitigate algorithm aversion when humans can introduce modifications into it. Consistent with this, the developer's position as a co-producer who shapes the output through prompting, and the resulting sense of control, has been shown to overcome the aversion.

5 Conclusion

This study provides the first mixed-methods longitudinal field test of the Vanneste and Puranam [50] three-mechanism model linking agency perception to trust in AI, conducted with 107 software developers and IT professionals over four survey waves complemented by nine semi-structured interviews. The findings both support and qualify the theory.

A first result concerns the structure of the agency construct itself: although Vanneste and Puranam treat autonomy, intentionality, and free will as a single construct, in our population these facets do not cohere. Professional users grant the AI autonomy but deny it intentionality and free will, a distinction confirmed by both the low reliability of the composite scale and the interview data. This has direct consequences for each mechanism. Ability enhancement (Mechanism 1) functions as predicted, with agency correlating positively with all facets of trustworthiness. The locus shift (Mechanism 2) manifests not as a gradual transfer from designer to AI but as a structural asymmetry: AI Trustworthiness is the dominant trust predictor from the outset and intensifies over time, while the designer remains largely invisible. Betrayal aversion (Mechanism 3) is not supported: betrayal cost is positively rather than negatively associated with trust. The divergence follows from the decomposition: Mechanisms 1 and 2 require only perceived autonomy, while betrayal aversion presupposes the intentionality this population denies, attributing errors to its own prompting instead. This pattern points to a contextually grounded extension of self-efficacy [2] that we propose to call *prompt-based self-efficacy*: developers who perceive prompt quality as the primary lever of interaction attribute errors to their own phrasing, thereby maintaining a sense of control and structurally neutralizing the conditions for betrayal. The prevalence and boundary conditions of this construct, including whether it weakens as AI systems become more autonomous and prompt-free, warrant dedicated empirical investigation.

The central theoretical contribution is that agency decomposition constitutes a boundary condition for trust models in hybrid intelligence systems. In the developer–AI partnerships studied here, treating agency as unitary obscures qualitatively different dynamics across its facets: autonomy drives the mechanisms that enhance trust, while the absence of attributed intentionality disables, and in fact reverses, the mechanism that would erode it. Returning to the research question: *Does the degree to which a user perceives an AI as agentic affect how trust is formed and maintained?* The answer is yes, but through a differentiated process that the original unitary model does not anticipate: the effect depends on which facet of agency is perceived.

Practical Implications. The dominance of AI Trustworthiness as a trust driver (β = .40 to .76) suggests that organizations deploying AI coding assistants should prioritize demonstrating the tool's competence and consistency. Our data show that Integrity correlates with agency perception as strongly as Ability (Table 2), indicating that predictability and transparency about limitations contribute to building trust, not only raw performance. The subgroup analysis further suggests that onboarding strategies may benefit from differentiation. Users who initially perceive higher AI agency build trust rapidly through direct interaction, whereas users with lower initial agency perception follow a more gradual trajectory in which trust accumulates with sustained experience. Tailoring early-phase support through structured demonstrations, peer endorsement, and guided use cases, may accelerate trust formation in this second group.

Prompt engineering training emerges as a valuable lever, both for improving tool effectiveness and for reinforcing the self-attribution pattern that structurally neutralizes betrayal concerns. However, this same pattern carries a risk: if users systematically attribute AI failures to their own prompting, genuine tool limitations may go unreported. Organizations should complement training with structured mechanisms for distinguishing user error from model deficiencies, preserving a feedback channel that informs both tool selection and workflow design.

Finally, because trust and functional dependency intensify together over time and users do not experience betrayal aversion as a counterweight, these workflows lack a natural self-correcting mechanism against over-reliance. Organizations should monitor dependency levels alongside productivity gains; model transitions or tool disruptions are likely to disproportionately affect long-tenured users, for whom the AI has become deeply embedded in daily workflows.

Limitations and Future Directions. While the main effects are robust across waves, some limitations remain. Sample sizes (n = 68–91) constrain statistical power for subgroup and moderation analyses; the qualitative component ($n = 9$) illuminates mechanisms but cannot establish their prevalence; and four waves capture early adoption rather than long-term equilibria. Attrition is an additional concern: we did not formally test whether dropout was random with respect to agency perception or trust trajectories, and differential loss in the Low Agency subgroup (n = 36 at T1, n = 21 at T4) limits causal inference about the observed T4 convergence pattern for that group.

Among the directions opened by our findings, one stands out: technical literacy may moderate agency decomposition. Participants with deeper knowledge of LLM mechanics produced the sharpest differentiations between autonomy and intentionality, while less technical participants tended to perceive agency more holistically. If this holds, the betrayal aversion mechanism [50] may operate as originally theorized in populations with lower technical literacy, where users are more likely to attribute intentionality to the AI. Future work should test this prediction by including a validated measure of AI technical knowledge, treating agency sub-dimensions as separate variables, and comparing populations that differ in their understanding of AI mechanics.

Disclosure of Interests. The authors are employees of Cegedim, France. They declare to have no competing interests relevant to the content of this article.

References

1. Afroogh, S., Akbari, A., Malone, E., Kargar, M., Alambeigi, H.: Trust in AI: progress, challenges, and future directions. Hum. Soc. Sci. Commun. **11**(1), 1568 (2024). https://doi.org/10.1057/s41599-024-04044-8
2. Bandura, A.: Self-efficacy mechanism in human agency. Am. Psychol. **37**(2), 122 (1982). https://doi.org/10.1037/0003-066X.37.2.122
3. Baumeister, R.F., Monroe, A.E.: Recent research on free will: conceptualizations, beliefs, and processes. Adv. Exp. Soc. Psychol. **50**, 1–52 (2014). https://doi.org/10.1016/B978-0-12-800284-1.00001-1
4. Becker, J., Rush, N., Barnes, E., Rein, D.: Measuring the impact of early-2025 AI on experienced open-source developer productivity. arXiv preprint arXiv:2507.09089 (2025)
5. Bohnet, I., Zeckhauser, R.: Trust, risk and betrayal. J. Econ. Behav. Organ. **55**(4), 467–484 (2004). https://doi.org/10.1016/j.jebo.2003.11.004
6. Braun, V., Clarke, V.: Using thematic analysis in psychology. Qual. Res. Psychol. **3**(2), 77–101 (2006). https://doi.org/10.1191/1478088706qp063oa
7. Calhoun, C.S., Bobko, P., Gallimore, J.J., Lyons, J.B.: Linking precursors of interpersonal trust to human-automation trust: an expanded typology and exploratory experiment. J. Trust Res. **9**(1), 28–46 (2019). https://doi.org/10.1080/21515581.2019.1579730
8. Chen, V., Talwalkar, A., Brennan, R., Neubig, G.: Code with Me or for Me? How increasing AI automation transforms developer workflows. In: Proceedings of the 2026 CHI Conference on Human Factors in Computing Systems. Association for Computing Machinery (2026). https://doi.org/10.1145/3772318.3790850
9. Cui, M., Li, W., Kamoche, K.: Building trust in decision-support artificial intelligence: a boundary spanning perspective. Inf. Syst. J. (2025). https://doi.org/10.1111/isj.70015
10. Dang, Q., Li, G.: Unveiling trust in AI: the interplay of antecedents, consequences, and cultural dynamics. AI & Soc. 1–24 (2025). https://doi.org/10.1007/s00146-025-02477-6
11. De Visser, E.J., et al.: Almost human: anthropomorphism increases trust resilience in cognitive agents. J. Exp. Psychol. Appl. **22**(3), 331 (2016). https://doi.org/10.1037/xap0000092
12. Dell'Acqua, F., et al.: Navigating the jagged technological frontier: field experimental evidence of the effects of artificial intelligence on knowledge worker productivity and quality. Organ. Sci. **37**(2), 403–423 (2026). https://doi.org/10.1287/orsc.2025.21838
13. Dietvorst, B.J., Simmons, J.P., Massey, C.: Algorithm aversion: people erroneously avoid algorithms after seeing them err. J. Exp. Psychol. Gen. **144**(1), 114–126 (2015). https://doi.org/10.1037/xge0000033
14. Dietvorst, B.J., Simmons, J.P., Massey, C.: Overcoming algorithm aversion: people will use imperfect algorithms if they can (even slightly) modify them. Manage. Sci. **64**(3), 1155–1170 (2018). https://doi.org/10.1287/mnsc.2016.2643

15. Erengin, T., Briker, R., de Jong, S.B.: You, Me, and the AI: the role of third-party human teammates for trust formation toward AI teammates. J. Organ. Behav. (2024). https://doi.org/10.1002/job.2857
16. Feuerriegel, S., Hartmann, J., Janiesch, C., Zschech, P.: Generative AI. Bus. Inf. Syst. Eng. **66**(1), 111–126 (2024). https://doi.org/10.1007/s12599-023-00834-7
17. Hagendorff, T.: Deception abilities emerged in large language models. Proc. Natl. Acad. Sci. U.S.A. **121** (2023). https://doi.org/10.1073/pnas.2317967121
18. He, H., Miller, C., Agarwal, S., Kästner, C., Vasilescu, B.: Speed at the cost of quality: how cursor AI increases short-term velocity and long-term complexity in open-source projects. arXiv preprint arXiv:2511.04427 (2025)
19. Heersmink, R., De Rooij, B., Clavel Vázquez, M.J., Colombo, M.: A phenomenology and epistemology of large language models: transparency, trust, and trustworthiness. Ethics Inf. Technol. **26**(3), 41 (2024). https://doi.org/10.1007/s10676-024-09777-3
20. Hicks, M., Humphries, J., Slater, J.: ChatGPT is bullshit. Ethics Inf. Technol. **26** (2024). https://doi.org/10.1007/s10676-024-09775-5
21. Hutzschenreuter, T., Lämmermann, T.: What is your AI strategy? Systematically integrating self-learning technologies into your business strategy. Acad. Manag. Perspect. (2024). https://doi.org/10.5465/amp.2023.0243
22. Khojah, R., Mohamad, M., Leitner, P., de Oliveira Neto, F.G.: Beyond code generation: an observational study of ChatGPT usage in software engineering practice. In: Proceedings of the ACM on Software Engineering, vol. 1, no. FSE, pp. 1819–1840 (2024). https://doi.org/10.1145/3660788
23. Killoran, J., Park, A., Kietzmann, J.: Delineation of reasoning, intentional disclosure, and the potential for harm: an extension of Vanneste and Puranam's "Artificial intelligence, trust, and perceptions of agency." Acad. Manag. Rev. (2025). https://doi.org/10.5465/amr.2024.0193
24. Kim, T., Hinds, P.: Who should I blame? Effects of autonomy and transparency on attributions in human-robot interaction. In: ROMAN 2006-The 15th IEEE International Symposium on Robot and Human Interactive Communication, pp. 80–85. IEEE (2006). https://doi.org/10.1109/ROMAN.2006.314398
25. Kuss, P., Meske, C.: From entity to relation? Agency in the era of artificial intelligence. Commun. Assoc. Inf. Syst. (forthcoming) 1–44 (2025). https://doi.org/10.17705/1CAIS.05626
26. Lambiase, S., Catolino, G., Palomba, F., Ferrucci, F., Russo, D.: Investigating the role of cultural values in adopting large language models for software engineering. ACM Trans. Softw. Eng. Methodol. (2024). https://doi.org/10.1145/3725529
27. Le Van, O., Curcio, V.: From tool to colleague: how AI partnership transforms the developers' identity across cultural boundaries. In: Proc.BIR-WS 2025: BIR 2025 Workshops and Doctoral Consortium, 24th International Conference on Perspectives in Business Informatics Research (BIR 2025), 17–19 September2025, Riga, Latvia (2025). https://ceur-ws.org/Vol-4034/paper75.pdf
28. Lee, J.D., See, K.A.: Trust in automation: designing for appropriate reliance. Hum. Factors **46**(1), 50–80 (2004). https://doi.org/10.1518/hfes.46.1.50.30392
29. Lee, K., Cho, W., Woo, H.G., de Jong, S.: When do individuals believe in themselves rather than in artificial intelligence? Insights from longitudinal investigations in corporate credit-rating contexts. J. Manage. Stud. **63**(2), 399–437 (2026). https://doi.org/10.1111/joms.70009
30. Li, B., Lai, E.Y., Wang, X.: From tools to agents: meta-analytic insights into human acceptance of AI. J. Mark. (2025). https://doi.org/10.1177/00222429251355266

31. Mayer, R.C., Davis, J.H., Schoorman, F.D.: An integrative model of organizational trust. Acad. Manag. Rev. **20**(3), 709–734 (1995). https://doi.org/10.5465/amr.1995.9508080335
32. McKnight, D.H., Carter, M., Thatcher, J.B., Clay, P.F.: Trust in a specific technology: an investigation of its components and measures. ACM Trans. Manag. Inf. Syst. **2**(2), 1–25 (2011). https://doi.org/10.1145/1985347.1985353
33. Pandey, R., Singh, P., Wei, R., Shankar, S.: Transforming software development: evaluating the efficiency and challenges of github copilot in real-world projects. arXiv preprint arXiv:2406.17910 (2024)
34. Parasuraman, R., Manzey, D.H.: Complacency and bias in human use of automation: an attentional integration. Hum. Factors **52**(3), 381–410 (2010). https://doi.org/10.1177/0018720810376055
35. Park, P.S., Goldstein, S., O'Gara, A., Chen, M.K., Hendrycks, D.: AI deception: a survey of examples, risks, and potential solutions. Patterns **5** (2023). https://doi.org/10.1016/j.patter.2024.100988
36. Plaat, A., van Duijn, M., Van Stein, N., Preuss, M., van der Putten, P., Batenburg, K.J.: Agentic large language models, a survey. J. Artif. Intell. Res. **84** (2025). https://doi.org/10.1613/jair.1.18675
37. Ramaul, L., Ritala, P., Kostis, A., Aaltonen, P.: Rethinking how we theorize ai in organization and management: a problematizing review of rationality and anthropomorphism. J. Manage. Stud. (2025). https://doi.org/10.1111/joms.13246
38. Reuter, M., Kirchhoff, B.M., Franke, T., Radüntz, T., Peifer, C.: To trust or not to trust a human (-like) AI—a scoping review and conjoint analyses on factors influencing anthropomorphism and trust. Zeitschrift für Arbeitswissenschaft **79**(3), 402–432 (2025). https://doi.org/10.1007/s41449-025-00481-6
39. Riemer, K., Peter, S., Schwabe, G., Chatterjee, S., Adam, M., Davison, R.M.: Generative AI is neither just another IT artefact nor a colleague: methodological guidance for IS scholarship. Inf. Syst. J. (2025). https://doi.org/10.1111/isj.70027
40. Robles, G., Treude, C., Gonzalez-Barahona, J.M., Kula, R.G.: The role of code proficiency in the era of generative AI. arXiv preprint arXiv:2405.01565 (2024)
41. Roychoudhury, A., Păsăreanu, C., Pradel, M., Ray, B.: Agentic AI software engineers: programming with trust. Commun. ACM **69**(5), 56–58 (2026). https://doi.org/10.1145/3769314
42. Russo, D.: Navigating the complexity of generative AI adoption in software engineering. ACM Trans. Softw. Eng. Methodol. **33**(5), 1–50 (2024). https://doi.org/10.1145/3652154
43. Sabouri, S., et al.: Trust dynamics in AI-assisted development: definitions, factors, and implications. In: 2025 IEEE/ACM 47th International Conference on Software Engineering (ICSE), pp. 1678–1690. IEEE (2025). https://doi.org/10.1109/ICSE55347.2025.00199
44. Saffarizadeh, K., Keil, M., Maruping, L.: Relationship between trust in the AI creator and trust in AI systems: the crucial role of AI alignment and steerability. J. Manag. Inf. Syst. **41**(3), 645–681 (2024). https://doi.org/10.1080/07421222.2024.2376382
45. Santos, H.V.F., Costa, V., Montandon, J.E., Valente, M.T.: Decoding the configuration of AI coding agents: insights from Claude code projects. arXiv preprint arXiv:2511.09268 (2025)
46. Shen, J.H., Tamkin, A.: How AI impacts skill formation. arXiv preprint arXiv:2601.20245 (2026)

47. Suri, G., Slater, L.R., Ziaee, A., Nguyen, M.: Do large language models show decision heuristics similar to humans? A case study using GPT-3.5. J. Exp. Psychol. General **153**(4), 1066 (2024). https://doi.org/10.1037/xge0001547
48. Van Der Woerdt, S., Haselager, P.: When robots appear to have a mind: the human perception of machine agency and responsibility. New Ideas Psychol. **54**, 93–100 (2019). https://doi.org/10.1016/j.newideapsych.2017.11.001
49. Van Lier, M.: Introducing a four-fold way to conceptualize artificial agency. Synthese **201**(3), 85 (2023). https://doi.org/10.1007/s11229-023-04083-9
50. Vanneste, B.S., Puranam, P.: Artificial intelligence, trust, and perceptions of agency. Acad. Manag. Rev. **50**(4), 726–744 (2025). https://doi.org/10.5465/amr.2022.0041
51. Vanneste, B.S., Puranam, P.: Trust and generative artificial intelligence: a reply to Killoran, Park, and Kietzmann. Acad. Manag. Rev. (2026). https://doi.org/10.5465/amr.2024.0397, forthcoming
52. Viehoff, J.: Making trust safe for AI? Non-agential trust as a conceptual engineering problem. Philos. Technol. **36**(4), 64 (2023). https://doi.org/10.1007/s13347-023-00664-1
53. Wakita, T., Ueshima, N., Noguchi, H.: Psychological distance between categories in the Likert scale: comparing different numbers of options. Educ. Psychol. Measur. **72**(4), 533–546 (2012). https://doi.org/10.1177/0013164411431162

Conceptual Modelling of the EU AI Act Towards Trustworthiness and Regulatory Compliance for AI Systems

Ijeoma Faustina Ekeh[1(✉)], Tolulope Ruth Ogundele[2], Raimundas Matulevičius[1], and Joy Mugambi[1]

[1] University of Tartu, Tartu, Estonia
{ijeomafa,rma,mugambi}@ut.ee

[2] Hochschule der Bayerischen Wirtschaft, Munich, Germany
tolulope.ogundele@student.hdbw-hochschule.de

Abstract. The EU AI Act (Regulation 2024/1689) imposes binding technical documentation and trustworthiness obligations on providers of high-risk AI systems, yet provides no structured mechanism for tracing system-level requirements and documentation artefacts to specific regulatory provisions. This paper addresses that gap through a UML-based conceptual meta-model that formally integrates system assets, requirements, trustworthiness principles, AI Act obligations, documentation items, and compliance evidence into a unified and traceable structure. A three-stage traceability methodology grounds the model in operational practice, guiding providers and assessors through model instantiation, requirement-to-obligation linkage, and evidence documentation. Evaluation through dual-system instantiation illustrates the model's applicability across divergent high-risk classification pathways and evidence maturity levels, supporting both documentary conformity review for deployed systems and prospective gap analysis for pre-market systems. The model provides a structured, reusable traceability mechanism that enables providers, notified bodies, and competent authorities to map system-level artefacts to specific regulatory obligations and assess compliance evidence.

Keywords: EU AI Act · Requirements · Trustworthiness · Compliance

1 Introduction

The EU Artificial Intelligence Act [7] establishes the world's first comprehensive horizontal regulatory framework for artificial intelligence [10]. It places legally binding obligations on providers of high-risk AI systems [11]. Among the Act's obligations, Article 11 and Annex IV require providers to prepare, maintain, and supply a single technical documentation set that substantiates the testing, design and monitoring of the system. Additionally, Articles 9 through 15 operationalise a set of trustworthiness requirements, covering risk management, data

E. Laurenzi et al. (Eds.): BIR 2026, LNBIP 601, pp. 145–160, 2027.
https://doi.org/10.1007/978-3-032-38498-0_10

governance, transparency, human oversight, accuracy, robustness, and cybersecurity, against which the system must be evaluated before market placement and throughout its operational life. Although both obligations are specified in the Act, the regulatory framework does not prescribe how providers should organise their internal systems, requirements, and documentation to verify compliance with individual articles [10]. This creates a traceability gap: providers must demonstrate compliance but lack structured guidance on how to link what a system does to the Act's requirements. Existing tooling such as the Assessment List for Trustworthy Artificial Intelligence (ALTAI) [2] and the AI Trustworthiness Assessment framework (AITA) [9] offer self-assessment checklists and assessment process guidance, but they do not provide a formal, reusable representational structure that captures the relationships between a system's assets, its requirements, the trustworthiness principles they address, and the specific AI Act articles [7] requirement they fulfil. Without such a structure, compliance remains an ad hoc documentation exercise rather than a traceable engineering activity. This paper addresses the gap with the following research question: *How can system-level requirements and technical documentation of high-risk AI systems be modelled and traced to demonstrate compliance with the EU AI Act's trustworthiness and technical documentation obligations?* We address this question through three contributions. First, we present a UML-based conceptual model that formally represents the key entities involved in EU AI Act compliance assessment [7]: AI system assets, functional and system-level requirements, trustworthiness principles, system obligations, documentation items, and compliance evidence, along with their relationships. Second, we describe a structured traceability methodology grounded in the model that guides providers through a three-stage process: model instantiation, requirement-to-obligation linkage, and evidence documentation. Third, we demonstrate the model's applicability through a dual-system instantiation across two contrasting high-risk use cases: HireVue, a commercially deployed AI hiring assessment system classified under Annex III point 4, and iCare Central, a research prototype AI-driven assistive device system treated as a prospective Article 6(1) example in conjunction with the Medical Device Regulation (MDR 2017/745) [5]. The two cases were deliberately selected to exercise different high-risk classification pathways and to represent different levels of evidence completeness. The remainder of the paper is structured as follows. Section 2 provides background on the EU AI Act, AI trustworthiness frameworks, and related work. Section 3 presents the conceptual model, the criteria governing its design, and its applicability conditions. Section 4 presents the dual-system instantiation. Section 5 concludes the paper and future directions.

2 Background and Related Works

2.1 EU AI Act: High-Risk Obligations

The EU AI Act [7] introduces a risk-stratified regulatory regime in which the obligations imposed on an AI system depend on its classification [9]. Systems classified as high-risk under Article 6 of the act, either because they fall within the product categories listed in Annex I (such as medical devices regulated under MDR 2017/745) [5] or because they perform functions listed in Annex III (such as employment-related AI, biometric identification, or AI in critical infrastructure), are subject to a set of obligations. For high-risk AI systems, the Act [7] sets out detailed obligations on risk management [Article 9], data governance [Article 10], technical documentation [Article 11 and Annex IV], record-keeping [Article 12], transparency and information to deployers [Article 13], human oversight [Article 14], and accuracy, robustness, and cybersecurity [Article 15]. Article 16 sets out the general obligations of providers, while Article 17 requires providers to establish a documented quality management system. Providers must also undergo conformity assessment [Articles 43, Annex VI-VII] and comply with post-market monitoring and incident reporting duties [Articles 72–75]. Beyond these provider obligations, Article 26 establishes specific duties for deployers of high-risk AI systems.

2.2 AI Trustworthiness

AI Trustworthiness determines whether AI systems can be relied upon ethically, socially or legally. Thus, the concept of AI Trustworthiness predates the EU AI Act but has been significantly shaped by it. The EU High-Level Expert Group on AI (HLEG) [3] defined seven dimensions of trustworthy AI in its Ethics Guidelines: human agency and oversight, technical robustness and safety, privacy and data governance, transparency, diversity and non-discrimination, societal and environmental well-being, and accountability. These dimensions informed the substantive requirements set out in Articles 9–15 of the Act and established a traceable link between ethical principles, such as transparency of AI development, and legal obligations. More recently, ISO/IEC 42001 has emerged as the primary compliance assessment vehicle for AI management systems, structuring organisational obligations in a manner compatible with both the EU AI Act's documentation requirements and the NIST AI Risk Management Framework (RMF). Also, the NIST RMF [6] organises AI risk governance into four functions: Govern, Map, Measure, and Manage. It provides a process-oriented complement to the HLEG's principle-based approach. Although originating in a US policy context, the NIST RMF has been widely adopted by organisations operating across jurisdictions, and its functional structure has been recognised as operationally compatible with the EU AI Act's documentation and risk management obligations, making it relevant to multinational providers subject to the Act. Together, these frameworks provide complementary governance scaffolding but operate at an abstraction level that falls short of the specific documentation and article-level traceability requirements mandated by the EU AI Act. Despite these theoretical developments, several authors have noted that "trustworthy AI" remains operationally vague as a concept [14,16]. Kemmerzell et al. [13] identify a persistent gap between abstract trustworthiness principles and the concrete technical measures that would demonstrate their satisfaction, while Kowald et al. [14] argue that evaluation methodologies for trustworthiness remain inconsistent across domains. This paper's central contribution is a response to precisely this critique [13,14]: by formalising the relationships between trustworthiness principles, system requirements, documentation artefacts, and specific AI Act articles within a structured model, we transform an abstract principle-level assessment into a traceable, artefact-grounded activity.

2.3 Related Work

The present work proposes a UML-based conceptual model for tracing system-level requirements and documentary evidence to specific EU AI Act articles. The following works represent the closest prior attempts to address related problems. Braunschweig et al. [8] introduce the AI Trustworthiness Assessment (AITA) framework, which maps HLEG dimensions to assessment activities and defines coverage metrics. While AITA provides a systematic process, it operates at a checklist level and does not offer a formal representation capable of capturing the traceability relationships between individual system artefacts and specific regulatory articles. The ALTAI self-assessment tool [2] similarly offers structured questionnaires derived from the HLEG guidelines, but is not designed to integrate with system-level technical documentation or to support automated coverage analysis. More recently, Hosseini et al. [12], and Menezes et al. [15] have examined EU AI Act compliance in industrial control systems and healthcare GenAI, respectively, demonstrating domain-specific interpretations of the Act's provisions but without a reusable formal model that generalises across domains. The distinguishing contribution of the present work is a UML-based conceptual model that formally captures the full traceability chain from system asset to functional requirement to trustworthiness principle to AI Act article to documentary evidence, and that is evaluated through instantiation across two contrasting high-risk systems operating under different classification pathways. To our knowledge, no prior work provides a formal, instantiable, multi-class model of this kind that spans both Annex III and Article 6(1) classification routes, as well as the MDR [5] classification route.

3 The EU AI Act Model

This section presents the core artefact of this research: a conceptual model integrating requirements, trustworthiness properties, and EU AI Act regulatory obligations. The model provides a traceable foundation for assessing and documenting trustworthiness assessments under the Act.

3.1 Modelling Approach and Foundations

The model is designed using the Unified Modelling Language (UML) class diagram [1]. UML was selected because its class diagram notation provided a standardised, tool-independent means of representing entities, attributes, and relationships at the level of abstraction needed for regulatory modelling. To ensure "a high level of trustworthiness of high-risk AI systems, those systems should be subject to a conformity assessment prior to their being placed on the market or put into service" [AI Act, Recital 62]. Based on this statement, the modelling decisions are grounded in two foundational sources: the EU AI Act regulatory framework [4], and the trustworthiness dimensions [3].

EU AI Act: The model applies the key provisions of the Act that are applicable to AI systems, along with supporting articles, to provide robust elicitation used for the system. Furthermore, the model incorporates the dimensions of trustworthy AI defined by the **EU's High-Level Expert Group on AI** [3], creating a traceability chain using the technical documentation of AI systems.

3.2 Mapping EU AI Act Requirements and Trustworthiness Dimensions

Figure 1 presents our synthesis of the correspondence between the trustworthiness dimensions defined by the HLEG [3] and the specific articles of the EU AI Act [7] that operationalise each dimension. While the broad correspondence between trustworthiness principles and the Act's provisions has been noted in the literature, the specific article-level mapping, particularly the multi-article coverage of individual trustworthiness dimensions and their representation in a formal model, is an original contribution of this work. For example, in Fig. 1, technical robustness and security primarily correspond to Article 15 [7] (accuracy, robustness, and cybersecurity), but it also draws on Article 9 [7](risk management) and Article 12 [7] (logging), since effective robustness management requires both a risk process and an audit trail. Making these multi-article dependencies explicit is a precondition for complete traceability.

Article	Requirement	Key Obligation	Scope	Trustworthiness Principle
Article 9	Risk Management System	Establish, implement, document and maintain continuous iterative risk management throughout AI system lifecycle	High-risk AI systems	Safety, Risk Management
Article 10	Data and Data Governance	Use high-quality training, validation and testing datasets that are relevant, representative, error-free and complete	High-risk AI systems	Fairness, Non-discrimination, Privacy
Article 11	Technical Documentation	Draw up comprehensive technical documentation per Annex IV before market placement	High-risk AI systems	Transparency, Accountability
Article 12	Record-Keeping	Enable automatic recording of events (logs) over system lifetime for traceability	High-risk AI systems	Transparency, Accountability
Article 13	Transparency and Information to Deployers	Ensure sufficiently transparent operation with clear instructions for deployers	High-risk AI systems	Transparency
Article 14	Human Oversight	Design systems for effective human oversight with appropriate human-machine interface tools	High-risk AI systems	Human Agency, Oversight
Article 15	Accuracy, Robustness and Cybersecurity	Achieve appropriate level of accuracy, robustness and cybersecurity, performing consistently throughout lifecycle	High-risk AI systems	Robustness, Security
Article 16	Obligations of Providers	Ensure compliance with all Section 2 requirements, quality management system, conformity assessment, CE marking	Providers of high-risk AI systems	Accountability, Governance
Article 17	Quality Management System	Establish documented quality management system ensuring compliance with AI Act	Providers of high-risk AI systems	Accountability, Governance
Article 72	Post-Market Monitoring	Establish system to actively and systematically collect, document and analyse relevant data	Providers of high-risk AI systems	Safety, Accountability
Article 73	Serious Incident Reporting	Report any serious incident to market surveillance authorities where incident occurred	Providers and deployers	Safety, Accountability

Fig. 1. Mapping EU AI Act requirements and Trustworthiness dimensions.

3.3 The Conceptual Model

Figure 2 represents the audited artefacts and regulatory actions described in the EU AI Act [4]. The model integrates entities at different abstraction levels because the EU AI Act defines compliance as a socio-technical process involving conceptual principles, legal obligations, organisational actors, activities, and documentary evidence. Rather than treating them as separate entities, the model links them to the end-to-end traceability of the trustworthiness principle, regulatory obligations, and responsible stakeholders to the evidence used to demonstrate compliance.

The `AISystem` describes the architectural composition of the TechnicalDocumentation class. The Requirement is represented by the class `Requirement` containing the attributes 'reqId', a unique identifier for traceability of the requirement, 'description', a textual representation of the requirement, 'Source' (reference to the origin of the requirement), and 'verificationMethod', an enumeration indicating the different approaches on how compliance with the requirement can be demonstrated [Art. 43; Annex VI-VIII; Art. 40]. The technical documentation of the Act [Art. 11 (1–3); Annex IV §1] is represented with `Documentation` class comprising the class `TechnicalDocumentation` [Art. 11], which supports the class `DocumentationItem` (type of documentation) [Annex IV].

The Principles of Ethical AI [Art. 10–15; Annex IV §2–4; Recital 27] are represented by the `TrustworthinessPrinciple` class containing attributes such as 'principleID', taking unique identifiers of the trustworthiness principle, and 'trustworthinessDimension', containing the enumeration of the different principles of trustworthiness. The EU AI Act [4] is represented by the `AIActRequirement` class, which comprises attributes such as 'articleNo', 'paragraph', and 'category' that store information about the act. The provider [Annex V §2] is represented by the `Provider` class, with attributes containing the name, country, registration number, and operations (e.g., *Provider.createDocumentation(doc: TechnicalDocumentation)*) [Art. 11(1–2)].

Other classes to support the EU AI Act compliance assessment of trustworthiness include AI Office/Authority [Art. 54, 59], represented by the `AIOffice` class. The `AIOffice` is expected to receive the report (*AIOffice.receiveReport(report: ComplianceReport*)) [Art. 60, 72–75] and request clarification from the provider (*AIOffice.requestClarificationFrom(provider: Provider)*) [Art. 60, 81]. The Notified Body [Art. 31, 43; Annex VII] represents the `NotifiedBody` that is a notified body or conformity assessment body evaluating AI systems. The class contains attributes such as (*NotifiedBody.conductAssessment(system: AISystem)*) [Art. 43; Annex VI–VII] and (*NotifiedBody.issueCertificate()*) [Art. 49–52; Annex V]. The compliance document [Art. 63–64, Art. 72–75] is represented as `ComplianceReport` and is sent to the AI office (*sendToAIOffice()*) or archived (*archive()*)when no longer in use. The Documentary Evidence [Art 13(2–3)] is represented by the `DocumentaryEvidence` class, which provides the necessary evidence for the verification, recognition, and regular monitoring of the assessment. The class `RegulatoryObligation` [Art 16, 23, 26] represents the legal requirements derived from the Act. It contains three attributes: 'obligation', 'technicalMeasures' (a list of technical measures that implement the obligation), and 'implementationStatus' (a track of the current status of obligation implementation – planned, partial, or complete). The class defines an operation (*RegulatoryObligation.implementMeasure()*) representing the process of implementing the technical measures. Additionally, we added the `Assessment` class to represent the activity performed by the `NotifiedBody` class. The class takes attributes such as 'assessmentId', 'date', 'assessor', and 'coverageScore' (takes the score assigned to each of the requirement coverages). The class poses operations (*Assessment.checkCoverage()*) which prompts the activity of Notified body performed in *conductAssessment(system:AISystem)*. In Fig. 3, we present the mappings of the model to the art and explanations of the elicited component.

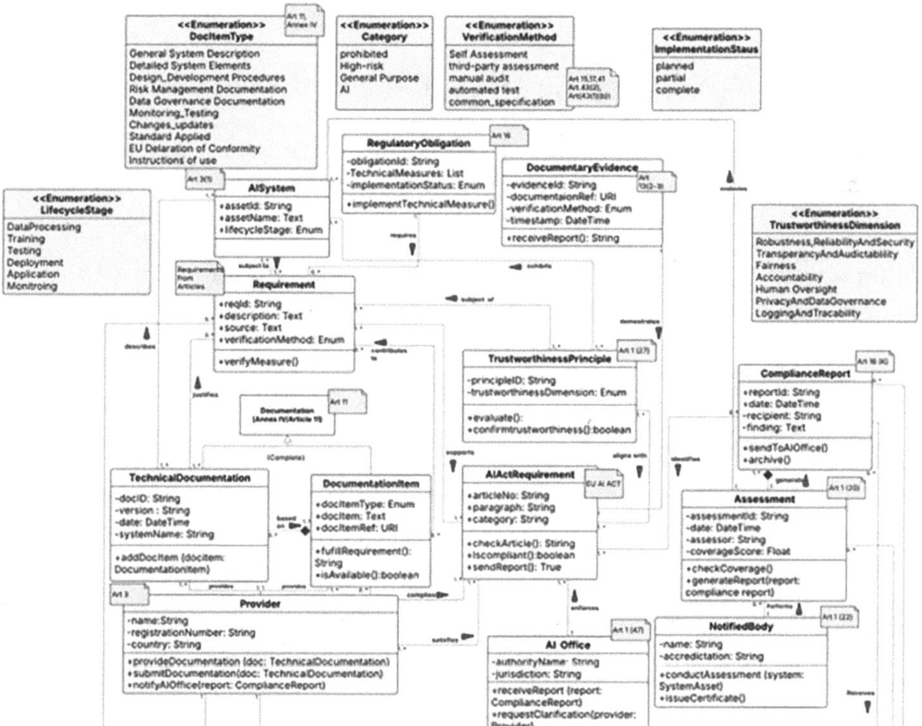

Fig. 2. An EU AI Act model. Expanded view of model here: https://github.com/euaiact-model/trustworthiness-model

3.4 Criteria of Elicitation and Constraints

This section provides the rationale for selecting and representing specific components of the EU AI Act [7] within the conceptual model. We define the modelling constraints that guide the relationships between classes, ensuring the model accurately reflects both the legal framework and practical applicability of AI system trustworthiness assessment.

The EU AI Act [7] is a comprehensive legislative document containing numerous provisions applicable to different categories of AI systems. The conceptual model does not aim to capture the entire Act. Rather, the components were selected based on their relevance to assessing AI trustworthiness, using available technical documentation from AI system providers. Three criteria guided this selection.

Criterion 1: *Relevance to Trustworthiness* Provisions on articles of ethics of AI, addressing one or more dimensions of trustworthy AI. These dimensions correspond to the trustworthiness principles laid down by the EU AI Act and represented in the class diagram.

Criterion 2: *Technical applicability to AI system Architecture* The selected class components of the Act must impose constraints such as the technical documentation of the system development and operation. Only provisions that could be demonstrated through artefacts (such as technical documentation in Art. 11 and Annex IV) are extracted.

Criterion 3: *Relevance to Conformity Assessment* The provisions to ascertain whether providers conform with the Act through conformity assessment processes and verification mechanisms, such as self-assessment by providers or notified body evaluation of the AI system, were considered since they provide the mechanism to validate trustworthiness claims. The following are constraints of the selected provisions of the act.

Constraint 1: *Focus on Technical Documentation* We focused on the requirement of providing technical documentation, as the assessment approach relies on technical documentation provided by the AI system providers.

Constraint 2: *Exclusion of Institutional provisions of the Act* We excluded articles dealing with penalties, market surveillance of the system, institutional governance, and enforcement strategies, as they do not explicitly contribute to the technical evaluation of AI systems.

Constraint 3: *Abstraction of the Conceptual Model* The legal provisions of the act were abstracted into conceptual entities (e.g., AIActRequirement, RegulatoryObligation, DocumentaryEvidence, Assessment) to enable their presentation within the UML class diagram. Thus, some nuances of the regulation's legal text are simplified in the model.

3.5 Applicability of the EU AI Act Conceptual Model

To apply, the proposed model aims to support the structured assessment of AI system trustworthiness based on technical documentation, in accordance with

Model element	AI Act reference	Explanation
AISystem(ID, version, name, description)	Annex IV§1(a–c); Annex V §1	Identifies the AI system: name, version, purpose, provider.
AISystem.assetType	Art. 16, 53; Annex XI	Indicates when the system is built on a specific type of system or model.
Provider(name,registrationNumber, country)	Annex IV §2	Provider identification
Provider.createDocumentation (doc: TechnicalDocumentation)	Art. 11(1-2)	Duty to prepare technical documentation before placing high-risk AI systems on the market and keep it up to date
Provider.submitDocumentation (doc: TechnicalDocumentation)	Art. 11 (2),29	Obligation to supply technical documentation to authorities or notified bodies on request and maintain it for 10 years.
Provider.notifyAIOffice(report: Compliance Report)	Art 60	Obligation for the provider to notify the AI Office when the compliance check is completed and ready to be delivered
TechicalDocumentation(docID, version,date,systemName)	Art. 11(1–3); Annex IV §1	Represents the single set of technical documentation per system version
TechnicalDocumentation. addDocItem (docItem: Documen-tationItem)	Art. 11(1–3); Annex IV §1	Adds the single set of technical documentation per system specification
DocumentationItem (docItemType, docItem,docItemRef)	Annex IV §1(a–f)	This is an enumeration of the specific types, the document text and a URI (if available) of technical documentation expected to be provided
TechnicalDocumentation —> contains DocumentationItem	Art 11(1-2); Annex IV	The required elements must all be present within the documentation
TrustworthinessPrinciple.principleID		Takes a unique identification
TrustworthinessPrinciple. Dimension	Art. 10–15; Annex IV §2–4; Ethics Guidelines	Encodes key compliance aspects (security, robustness, transparency, fairness, oversight, privacy, etc.)
TrustworthinessProperty —> supports AIActRequirement	Art. 10–15	Each dimension is tied to one or more specific AI Act requirements (e.g., security/robustness → Art. 15, oversight → Art. 14)
NotifiedBody(name, accreditation)	Art. 31, 43; Annex VII	Represents a notified body or conformity assessment body evaluating high-risk systems.
NotifiedBody. conductAssessment(system: SystemAsset)	Art. 43; Annex VI–VII	Performs conformity assessment against requirements and technical documentation
NotifiedBody.issueCertificate	Art. 49–52; Annex V	Issue CE certificate and support EU declaration of conformity. One certificate per compliant system version
ComplianceReport (reportID, date, recipient, finding)	Art. 72–75; Art. 63–64	Models internal/official compliance and incident reports; can be used for serious incident notifications and corrective actions.
ComplianceReport -> AIActRequirement	Art. 72–75	Identify which requirement or trustworthiness dimension was assessed or breached
RegulatoryObligation. ImplementTechnicalMeasure()	Art. 16	Represents the process of implementing the required technical measures
DocumentaryEvidence. receiveReport()	Art 13(7), 29(3)	Addresses the evidentiary requirements of the Act

Fig. 3. Mapping of the conceptual model components to the EU AI Act.

the EU AI Act. The proposed model aligns with these technical documentation requirements by linking regulatory obligations to the documentation artefacts that serve as verifiable evidence for trustworthiness evaluations. Concretely, the model applies to AI systems that are classified as high-risk under Article 6 and Annex III and are therefore subject to the obligations in Article 9–15, Article 11 with Annex IV, Article 12, 16, and the conformity assessment and post-market monitoring provisions in Articles 43 and 72–75.

From an operational role perspective, the model primarily supports the activities of providers, notified bodies and competent authorities. Providers use the model to structure their internal requirements for system development, thus preparing, maintaining, and updating the single set of technical documentation required by Article 11 and Annex IV and identifying requirements gaps within the AI system. The model is applicable in contexts where technical documentation and related artefacts are the primary basis for evaluation, such as ex-ante conformity assessment, internal audit and ex-post investigations based on evidence logs and system documentation.

Process of Assessment and Traceability. The assessment process is classified into three stages: preparation and model instantiation, traceability, and assessment. In the preparation and model instantiation stage, the provider provides the technical documentation based on the scope of the system to be assessed. The technical documentation describes how the AI system instantiates its assets. During the traceability stage, the notified body assesses which requirements apply to each asset. Requirements are instantiated from the `Requirement` class, each with a unique identifier, a description of what must be satisfied (e.g., Article 15), and a verification method indicating how compliance will be demonstrated. The next step establishes the link to RegulatoryObligation instances. Each obligation records the specific technical measures that should be available and their current implementation status, and captures each regulation against the AI Act requirement. Also, documenting evidence demonstrating requirement fulfilment. Finally, with the instantiated model, an analysis was conducted to identify missing elements and assess coverage.

4 Scenario Use Case Preliminary Instantiation of Approach

This section demonstrates the applicability of the EU AI Act model through instantiation across two contrasting systems: HireVue, a commercially deployed AI hiring assessment system owned in the United States but placed on the EU market, making it subject to the Act's extra-territorial application provisions, and iCare Central, an open-source AI-driven assistive wheelchair navigation system classified as high-risk under Article 6(1) in conjuction with the Medical Device Regulation (MDR 2017/745) [5]. The two systems were selected to represent contrasting classification pathways and documentation maturity levels. Providers/Deployers of these systems want to assess the trustworthiness dimensions of their AI system in line with the EU AI Act. The assessment process is applied to the two systems used for this case study. As mentioned in Sect. 3.4, the assessment is based on the publicly available technical documentation for these systems. First, the system's assets are extracted from the technical documentation to describe and fill in the expected classes of the EU AI Act model (see Fig. 2). For this study, we are assessing the Act's coverage requirements and aligning them with the trustworthiness principles. HireVue presents us with the system asset "HireVue Assessment Model" called CUSTARD. The technical documentation describes CUSTARD as the model that uses the RoBERTa language model and is further fine-tuned for hiring assessment purposes. For the purpose of the case study, we assessed the compliance of these systems with Articles 9,

10–14 of the EU AI Act. For each requirement, we have conducted an assessment using a self-assessment or manual audit to verify the regulatory obligations for iCare Central and HireVue, including the technical measures implemented to satisfy the Act's requirements and trustworthiness principles.

Figures 5 and 4 present the iCare Central and HireVue instantiations of the EU AI Act model, showing which areas of the assessed articles are covered by the systems and are represented as null where not evidenced. Figure 4 shows how the technical documentation describes the SystemAsset class, represented as the HireVueAssessmentModel (Custard), in accordance with the requirements of Article 13 (Transparency and Provision of Information). During the self-assessment, we reviewed the technical documentation for HireVue to ensure that the CUSTARD assessment model provides clear performance indicators for the job role. When this is unavailable, it is set to null in the RegulatoryObligation class for technical measures applied to comply with this requirement. In the assessment, we found that HireVue indicated they differentiate between the strongest and less promising performers, as evidenced by the product documentation provided. The documentary evidence demonstrates to assessors (e.g., notified bodies) that HireVue, categorised as a high-risk AI system, provides evidence for at least one Article 13 transparency sub-requirement of the EU AI Act and stands as a trustworthy AI system conforming to the trustworthiness principle of transparency on how key indicators for hiring using the CUSTARD Model are achieved. Similarly, Fig. 5 presents the iCare Central assessment, where the technical documentation describes the SystemAsset Class representing the Eye tracker (AI-supported model) and is subject to the Article 15 requirements (Accuracy, Robustness, and Cybersecurity). From the self-assessment, the technical measures were not documented in the technical documentation provided by iCare central on how the eye tracker's accuracy is measured or checked. Due to the unavailability of this evidence for Article 15 (3), the assessment shows that the provider of the Eye tracker (iCare Central) does not comply with this requirement and the trustworthiness principle of accuracy, as regulatory obligations expected to be evidenced in the technical documentation are missing. However, it is important to note that other dimensions of Article 15 (such as robustness and cybersecurity) were evidenced in the assessment[1]

Lessons Learned in the Example. The preliminary instantiation highlights two key points. The success of the proposed EU AI Act model depends on the completeness and quality of system-level technical documentation: where documentation is clear and detailed (as in parts of HireVue), regulatory obligations can be traced and substantiated; when documentation is thin or missing evidence (as it is in iCare Central for some requirements), gaps in compliance and trustworthiness become visible. Additionally, the approach provides practical value by mapping regulatory requirements to trustworthiness principles, enabling an interpretable assessment of AI system behaviour for stakeholders such as auditors and notified bodies.

---

[1] Find the extended instantiation and details of instantiation here: https://github.com/euaiact-model/trustworthiness-model.

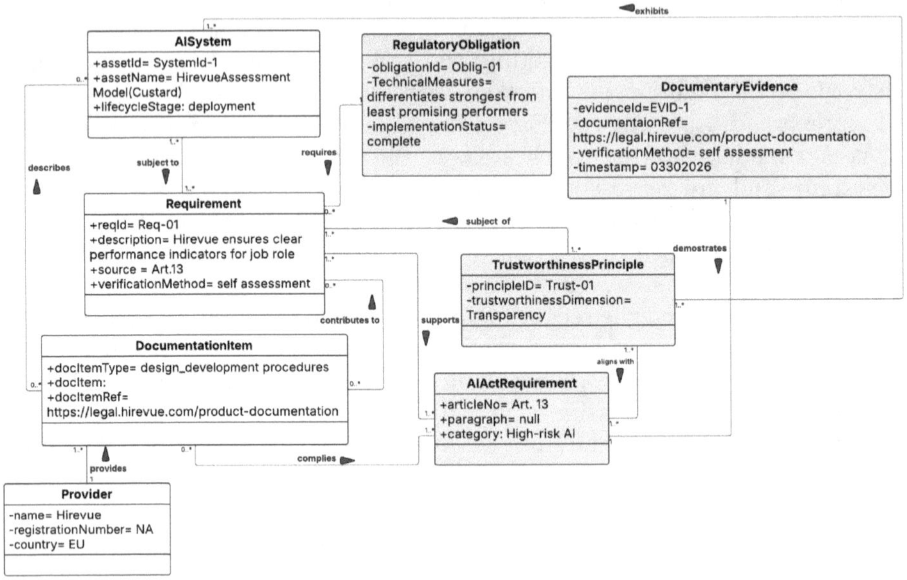

Fig. 4. HireVue instantiation example presenting the compliance traceability of the EU AI Act requirement to trustworthiness with available documentary evidence.

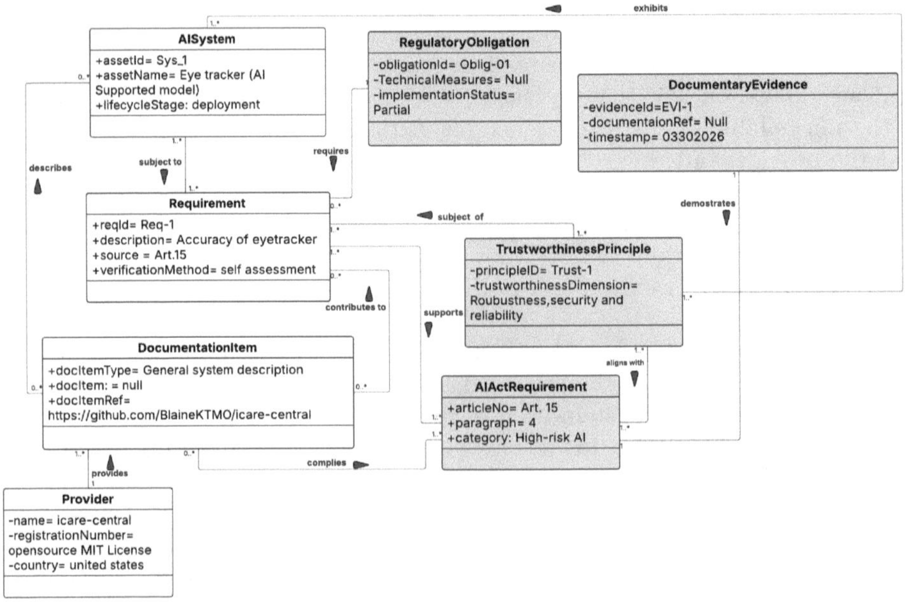

Fig. 5. iCare Central instantiation example presenting the compliance traceability of the EU AI Act requirement to trustworthiness without available documentary evidence.

5 Conclusion, Limitations, and Future Directions

5.1 Discussion

The instantiation was scoped to Articles 9 to 15 and Annex IV, which constitute the core trustworthiness and technical documentation requirements for high-risk AI systems. Articles 16, 26, and other provisions governing provider quality management, deployer responsibilities, and conformity assessment procedures were not instantiated, as the objective was to demonstrate how the model operationalises the traceability mechanism rather than to conduct an exhaustive regulatory audit. The selection of articles should therefore be understood as a deliberate methodological choice to show the model's core capability, not as a claim that these articles represent the complete compliance surface for either system. The assessment was conducted exclusively on publicly available technical documentation. This means the instantiation reflects what providers have disclosed, rather than what has necessarily been implemented. The practical use of the model also raises implementation challenges. Providers may face resource constraints when maintaining article-level traceability, particularly smaller organisations that lack dedicated compliance engineering teams or tool support. Evidence collection is also variable across systems and domains, as some artefacts are available as formal test reports, audit logs, risk management files, or usability studies, while others remain embedded in informal development records or proprietary documentation. This variability affects the granularity and confidence of the resulting compliance assessment. Scalability is another concern, as applying the model across domains such as employment, healthcare, education, and critical infrastructure may require domain-specific evidence templates, terminology mappings, and risk indicators. These challenges do not undermine the model's traceability function, but they indicate that successful adoption requires organisational processes, reusable documentation patterns, and tool-supported model management. The AI Office and Notified Body actor classes were not populated because the assessment was conducted by the research team acting in a self-assessment capacity. Where a formal conformity assessment is conducted by a notified body or reviewed by a competent authority, those actors would be instantiated and their operations engaged accordingly.

5.2 Limitations

The assessment relies entirely on publicly available technical documentation and cannot detect implementation gaps where documentation exists, but organisational practice does not conform to it. The model covers Articles 9 to 15 and Annex IV, but does not address Chapter V obligations for general-purpose AI models (Articles 51 to 56) or the full scope of Article 26 deployer obligations. The model has been evaluated through demonstration but not empirically validated with compliance practitioners, notified bodies, or legal experts, which limits claims of correctness and completeness. The model captures compliance at a point in time and does not reflect the continuous lifecycle nature of obligations under Articles 9, 12, and 72 to 75 of the EU AI Act. Practical adoption may be constrained by provider resources, heterogeneous evidence formats, and the need to adapt evidence mappings to domain-specific regulatory and technical contexts.

5.3 Future Directions

Four directions for extending this work are identified. First, empirical validation with compliance engineers and notified bodies will assess the model's correctness, completeness, and practical usability. Second, the model will be extended to cover general-purpose AI obligations in Chapter V (Articles 51 to 56) and the Article 26 deployer obligation layer. Third, a dynamic, lifecycle-aware extension will be developed to represent continuous compliance obligations and triggered reassessment conditions under post-market monitoring. Fourth, the model will be formalised using the Object Constraint Language or an ontological representation to enable automated coverage queries and tool-supported compliance gap analysis.

5.4 Concluding Remarks

This paper addressed how system-level requirements and technical documentation for high-risk AI systems can be modelled and traced to demonstrate compliance with the EU AI Acty's trustworthiness and technical documentation obligations. The proposed UML-based conceptual model formalises the traceability chain from system asset through functional requirement, trustworthiness principle, and regulatory obligation to documentary evidence, grounded in a three-stage assessment methodology. Evaluation through dual-system instantiation across HireVue and iCare Central demonstrated applicability across divergent classification pathways and evidence maturity levels. The results confirm that structured traceability is both feasible and practically informative, surfacing specific compliance gaps that unstructured documentation review would not systematically identify.

Acknowledgment. The European Union funds this research under Grant Agreement No. 101087529. However, views and opinions expressed are those of the author(s) only and do not necessarily reflect those of the European Union or European Research Executive Agency. Neither the European Union nor the granting authority can be held responsible.

Disclosure of Interests. The authors have no competing interests to declare that are relevant to the content of this article.

References

1. About the Unified Modeling Language Specification Version 2.5.1. https://www.omg.org/spec/UML/
2. Assessment List for Trustworthy Artificial Intelligence (ALTAI) for self-assessment | Shaping Europe's digital future. https://digital-strategy.ec.europa.eu/en/library/assessment-list-trustworthy-artificial-intelligence-altai-self-assessment
3. Ethics guidelines for trustworthy AI | Shaping Europe's digital future. https://digital-strategy.ec.europa.eu/en/library/ethics-guidelines-trustworthy-ai
4. High-level summary of the AI Act | EU Artificial Intelligence Act. https://artificialintelligenceact.eu/high-level-summary/
5. Regulation (EU) 2017/745 of the European Parliament and of the Council of 5 April 2017 on medical devices, amending Directive 2001/83/EC, Regulation (EC) No 178/2002 and Regulation (EC) No 1223/2009 and repealing Council Directives 90/385/EEC and 93/42/EEC (Text with EEA relevance) (2017). http://data.europa.eu/eli/reg/2017/745/oj, legislative Body: CONSIL, EP
6. AI Risk Management Framework. NIST (2021). https://www.nist.gov/itl/ai-risk-management-framework, last Modified: 2025-05-05T13:16-04:00
7. Regulation (EU) 2024/1689 of the European Parliament and of the Council of 13 June 2024 laying down harmonised rules on artificial intelligence and amending Regulations (EC) No 300/2008, (EU) No 167/2013, (EU) No 168/2013, (EU) 2018/858, (EU) 2018/1139 and (EU) 2019/2144 and Directives 2014/90/EU, (EU) 2016/797 and (EU) 2020/1828 (Artificial Intelligence Act) (Text with EEA relevance) (2024). http://data.europa.eu/eli/reg/2024/1689/oj, legislative Body: CONSIL, EP
8. Braunschweig, B., et al.: AITA: AI trustworthiness assessment. AI Ethics **4**(1), 1–3 (2024). https://doi.org/10.1007/s43681-023-00397-z
9. Buscemi, A., Deckenbrunnen, T., Kabir, F., Mishchenko, K., Mowla, N.: Assessing high-risk AI systems under the EU AI act: from legal requirements to technical verification (2025). https://doi.org/10.48550/arXiv.2512.13907, [cs]
10. Ebers, M., Hoch, V.R.S., Rosenkranz, F., Ruschemeier, H., Steinrötter, B.: The European commission's proposal for an artificial intelligence act—a critical assessment by members of the robotics and AI law society (RAILS). J **4**(4), 589–603 (2021). https://doi.org/10.3390/j4040043
11. Finch, W.W., Butt, M.: Gaps in AI-compliant complementary governance frameworks' suitability (for low-capacity actors), and structural asymmetries (in the compliance ecosystem)—a systematic review. J. Cybersecur. Priv. **5**(4), 101 (2025). https://doi.org/10.3390/jcp5040101
12. Hosseini, A.M., Sauter, T., Kastner, W.: Trustworthy AI for security decision-making in ICSs: towards compliance with the EU AI act. In: 2025 IEEE 30th International Conference on Emerging Technologies and Factory Automation (ETFA), pp. 1–4 (2025). https://doi.org/10.1109/ETFA65518.2025.11205756. https://ieeexplore.ieee.org/document/11205756, iSSN: 1946-0759
13. Kemmerzell, N., Schreiner, A., Khalid, H., Schalk, M., Bordoli, L.: Towards a better understanding of evaluating trustworthiness in AI systems. ACM Comput. Surv. **57**(9), 218:1–218:38 (2025). https://doi.org/10.1145/3721976
14. Kowald, D., et al.: Establishing and evaluating trustworthy AI: overview and research challenges. Front. Big Data **7**, 1467222 (2024). https://doi.org/10.3389/fdata.2024.1467222. https://pmc.ncbi.nlm.nih.gov/articles/PMC11638207/

15. Menezes, V.P., Chowdhury, M.J.M., Mahmood, A.: An agentic framework for compliant, ethical and trustworthy GenAI applications in healthcare. In: Proceedings of the 2025 Australasian Computer Science Week, ACSW 2025, pp. 48–54. Association for Computing Machinery, New York (2025). https://doi.org/10.1145/3727166.3727191. https://dl.acm.org/doi/10.1145/3727166.3727191
16. Ryan, M.: In AI we trust: ethics, artificial intelligence, and reliability. Sci. Eng. Ethics **26**(5), 2749–2767 (2020). https://doi.org/10.1007/s11948-020-00228-y. https://pmc.ncbi.nlm.nih.gov/articles/PMC7550313/

Shadow AI, Human Oversight, and Institutional Trust: A Socio-technical Model of Responsible AI Governance in the Public Sector

Gideon Mekonnen Jonathan[1(✉)], Josue Kuika Watat[2], and Erik Perjons[1]

[1] Department of Computer and Systems Sciences (DSV), Stockholm University, Borgarfjordsgatan 12, 16455 Kista, Sweden
{gideon,perjons}@dsv.su.se

[2] HISP Centre, University of Oslo, Gaustadalléen 30, 0373 Oslo, Norway
josuekw@ifi.uio.no

Abstract. Artificial intelligence (AI), particularly generative AI (GenAI), is increasingly embedded in public sector work practices, while accountability and governance mechanisms often lag behind operational realities. This governance–practice gap enables informal and unregulated AI use, commonly termed *shadow AI*, which can undermine transparency, oversight, and institutional legitimacy. Drawing on a socio-technical perspective, this study develops and empirically tests a model explaining how AI governance and organisational practices interact to support responsible AI use. Using partial least squares structural equation modelling (PLS-SEM) on survey data from 214 public sector employees, the study positions shadow AI as a central mediating mechanism linking governance conditions to responsible AI outcomes. The model proposes that governance restrictiveness, socio-technical misalignment, and AI use intensity are associated with increased shadow AI, which in turn is associated with adaptive governance responses. Supported by human oversight and organisational support, these responses foster responsible AI use and enhance perceived organisational legitimacy. The results identify shadow AI as a double-edged mediator: it exerts a negative direct effect on responsible AI use while generating a positive indirect effect through adaptive governance. The findings contribute by operationalising governance dynamics in a predictive structural model, repositioning shadow AI as a diagnostic signal of governance and accountability gaps rather than merely a compliance failure, and providing empirically grounded insights for public sector AI governance. More broadly, the study advances understanding of how organisations can balance control and enablement to promote responsible and accountable AI use.

Keywords: Responsible AI use · AI governance · Shadow AI · Human oversight · Generative AI · Public sector · Trustworthy AI

E. Laurenzi et al. (Eds.): BIR 2026, LNBIP 601, pp. 161–175, 2027.
https://doi.org/10.1007/978-3-032-38498-0_11

1 Introduction

Artificial intelligence (AI) is rapidly reshaping public sector organisations, with governments worldwide investing substantially in AI-enabled services to improve efficiency and citizen outcomes [1,2]. The diffusion of generative AI (GenAI) tools has accelerated this transformation, allowing individual employees to deploy capable systems without specialist knowledge or organisational approval [3,4]. Yet public sector accountability, democratic legitimacy obligations, and legal frameworks governing public decision-making demand a level of transparency that informal AI adoption fundamentally undermines [2,5], and use outside sanctioned channels—increasingly described as *shadow AI*—reduces organisational visibility, disrupts accountability chains, and elevates the risk of non-compliant or ethically problematic outputs [3,6]. This reflects a long-recognised *governance–practice gap* between formal policy and everyday behaviour [7,8], but GenAI's consumer accessibility, monitoring difficulty, and productivity incentives [9,10] render existing frameworks particularly inadequate: when governance is experienced as restrictive or misaligned with task realities, prohibition redirects rather than eliminates the behaviour [11,12].

Despite growing recognition of these dynamics, the literature on public sector AI governance remains predominantly theoretical or qualitatively grounded. Existing frameworks articulate normative principles for trustworthy AI [13,14] and process-oriented accounts describe governance–practice interaction over time [15,16], but quantitative evidence on how specific governance conditions translate into measurable behavioural outcomes is scarce. In particular, the mediating role of shadow AI in linking antecedent governance conditions to adaptive organisational responses, and ultimately to responsible AI use and perceived legitimacy, has not been empirically tested in a structural model.

This study addresses this gap by developing and empirically testing a socio-technical model of AI governance co-evolution in the public sector. Using partial least squares structural equation modelling (PLS-SEM) with a sample of 214 public sector employees, the study positions shadow AI as a central mediating construct linking three antecedent governance conditions—*AI use intensity*, *governance restrictiveness*, and *socio-technical misalignment*—to adaptive governance responses, and examines how those responses, moderated by human oversight and organisational support, produce responsible AI use and, in turn, perceived organisational legitimacy. The study further conceptualises shadow AI as a double-edged socio-technical mechanism that simultaneously undermines responsible use while generating signals that enable governance adaptation.

The study contributes to the extant literature in three analytically distinct respects: (1) it operationalises the concept of AI governance co-evolution in a quantitatively testable structural model; (2) it repositions shadow AI from a dependent variable to a theoretically generative mediating mechanism; and (3) it provides empirically grounded, actionable guidance for public sector AI governance practitioners.

The remainder of the paper is structured as follows. Section 2 develops the theoretical background and hypotheses; Sect. 3 describes the methodology;

Sect. 4 reports the measurement, structural, moderation, and mediation results; Sect. 5 discusses the findings; and Sect. 6 concludes with contributions, implications, and limitations.

2 Theoretical Background and Hypotheses Development

2.1 AI Governance in the Public Sector

AI governance encompasses the structures, policies, and practices guiding the development, deployment, and oversight of AI systems within organisations [2,14]. In the public sector, governance is shaped by legal obligations, democratic accountability, and a mandate to generate public value rather than private benefit [2,5,17], requiring transparency and fairness even where these impose efficiency costs. International frameworks such as the European Commission's Ethics Guidelines for Trustworthy AI [13] and the NIST AI Risk Management Framework [14] articulate principles of transparency, accountability, and human oversight, but presume that policy design translates reliably into behaviour. The well-documented *governance–practice gap* [2,7] between intended and enacted governance challenges this presumption, and AI's distinctive characteristics substantially exacerbate it.

2.2 The Governance–Practice Gap and Shadow AI

The governance–practice gap is amplified for AI because GenAI's accessibility, monitoring difficulty, and productivity incentives create behavioural pressure to adopt tools regardless of formal restrictions [3,9], and employees facing restrictive governance frameworks adopt AI capabilities independently of organisational approval rather than ceasing use altogether. This informal adoption constitutes *shadow AI*: the use of AI tools outside formal governance structures, whether through personal devices, external platforms, or unapproved applications [3,6]. Shadow AI is frequently framed as a compliance failure, and the risks are real: reduced visibility, disrupted accountability, and elevated exposure to errors and legally problematic outputs. Yet it also carries diagnostic value, signalling unmet needs, governance inadequacies, and the insufficiency of sanctioned alternatives—information that can drive productive governance adaptation.

Restrictive governance may paradoxically exacerbate shadow AI rather than suppress it. Reactance theory predicts that perceived threats to behavioural freedom intensify motivation to reclaim the restricted behaviour [11], a dynamic well documented in the information security literature where rigid controls reliably produce workarounds [8]. In public sector settings, lengthy procurement and approval cycles leave employees without sanctioned alternatives for extended periods [2], and shadow IT research confirms that policy stringency is among the most robust predictors of unsanctioned system use [6,12]. As AI use intensity grows, behavioural pressure to seek informal alternatives intensifies correspondingly [9,10]. These mechanisms imply three antecedents of shadow AI: intensive AI use generates capability needs that outstrip sanctioned provision; restrictive governance displaces rather than eliminates use; and policies misaligned with task environments are perceived as illegitimate obstacles [3,15,16]. Thus, we posit:

H1a: *AI use intensity is positively associated with shadow AI.*
H1b: *Governance restrictiveness is positively associated with shadow AI.*
H1c: *Socio-technical misalignment is positively associated with shadow AI.*

2.3 Socio-technical Co-evolution and Adaptive Governance

A socio-technical perspective provides the lens for understanding governance–practice dynamics [15,18]: organisational outcomes emerge not from technology or social structures in isolation but from their continuous, recursive interaction. Governance, on this view, is not a static ruleset but an emergent and adaptive process that co-evolves with the practices it seeks to regulate. As employees adapt AI tools to meet task demands, shadow AI renders policy inadequacies visible and creates conditions for governance adaptation. Institutional theory explains why: when informal practices expose governance failures, normative and mimetic pressures compel organisations to adapt to preserve legitimacy [19,20], and shadow IT incidents are well established triggers for policy revision, enabling platforms, or new oversight mechanisms [12]. Organisational learning theory characterises this as *double-loop* learning, in which the assumptions underlying rules are revised in light of practice [21]. Comparable co-evolutionary dynamics are documented in enterprise systems [16] and platform governance [22] but remain underexplored for AI. Shadow AI, therefore, occupies a theoretically generative position: it mediates between antecedent governance conditions and the adaptive responses those conditions provoke, creating the informational and political conditions for governance adaptation through incidents, near-misses, or managerial discovery. This leads to:

H2: *Shadow AI is positively associated with adaptive governance responses.*

2.4 Responsible AI Use and the Role of Enabling Governance

Adaptive governance mechanisms—updated policies, guidance, training, and enabling platforms developed in response to observed use patterns—create the conditions for responsible AI use by reducing ambiguity and building competencies. Enabling rather than constraining regulatory designs are more effective at producing ethical behaviour because they build intrinsic motivation [2,23], and governance that evolves with practice acquires contextual legitimacy that increases voluntary compliance [20]. Restrictiveness, conversely, drives adoption underground, reducing the visibility needed for oversight and making responsible practices less likely to be observed or reinforced [8]. This dual prediction reflects the competing logics of compliance-based and enabling governance:

H3a: *Adaptive governance is positively associated with responsible AI use.*
H3b: *Governance restrictiveness is negatively associated with responsible AI use.*

Adaptive governance translates into behaviour only where complementary infrastructure exists. Human oversight—managerial review, audit mechanisms, and accountability structures—creates visible consequences for misuse and supplies feedback on output quality [13,14], so the behavioural payoff of any given governance adaptation depends on whether an oversight infrastructure exists to enforce and reinforce it. Where oversight capacity is low, even well-designed adaptive guidance is likely to dissipate before it shapes behaviour; where it is high, the same guidance is converted more reliably into responsible practice, reducing the information asymmetry that otherwise lets irresponsible use go unremedied [26]. Thus, we posit:

H4: *Human oversight positively moderates the relationship between adaptive governance and responsible AI use, such that the positive effect of adaptive governance on responsible AI use is stronger when human oversight is high.*

While shadow AI provokes adaptive governance responses, its immediate effect on responsible practice is detrimental: use outside sanctioned channels reduces the visibility, guidance, and verification structures on which responsible behaviour depends [6,8]. We therefore expect a negative direct relationship between shadow AI and responsible AI use, distinct from the positive indirect path it sets in motion through adaptive governance:

H5a: *Shadow AI is negatively associated with responsible AI use.*

This direct effect is, however, conditional on employee-facing resources. Social cognitive theory holds that self-efficacy mediates between environmental conditions and behaviour, and that organisational support builds self-efficacy through skills and knowledge [24,25]. Training, guidance, and explicit norms therefore buffer the detrimental effect of shadow AI by channelling informal use towards more responsible practices:

H5b: *Organisational support positively moderates the relationship between shadow AI and responsible AI use, such that the negative effect of shadow AI on responsible AI use is weaker when organisational support is high.*

2.5 Responsible AI Use and Institutional Legitimacy

Responsible AI use refers to practices that ensure outputs are accurate, transparent, and aligned with ethical and legal standards. In the public sector, such practices are inextricably linked to institutional legitimacy, understood as the generalised perception that organisational actions are appropriate, just, and trustworthy within socially constructed normative frameworks [20], because when AI influences decisions affecting citizens the opacity of outputs can rapidly erode public trust where accountability is absent or unclear [5,27]. Institutional legitimacy theory holds that organisations earn and sustain legitimacy by visibly conforming to the normative expectations of their environment [19,20]. In democratic contexts, this means demonstrating that AI use is transparent, fair, and subject to meaningful human review. Responsible practices—output verification, disclosure of AI involvement, maintenance of human oversight—instantiate these accountability norms in daily operations, generating the observable signals on which legitimacy judgements rest. Research on public sector digitalisation confirms that procedural transparency and accountability are among the strongest

predictors of citizen trust [5]. Governance frameworks that foster responsible AI use, therefore, generate institutional legitimacy as a downstream benefit:
H6: *Responsible AI use is positively associated with perceived organisational legitimacy.*

Figure 1 summarises the full hypothesised model, integrating the three antecedent governance conditions, the mediating role of shadow AI, the adaptive governance response, the downstream outcomes of responsible AI use and perceived organisational legitimacy, and the moderating effects of human oversight and organisational support.

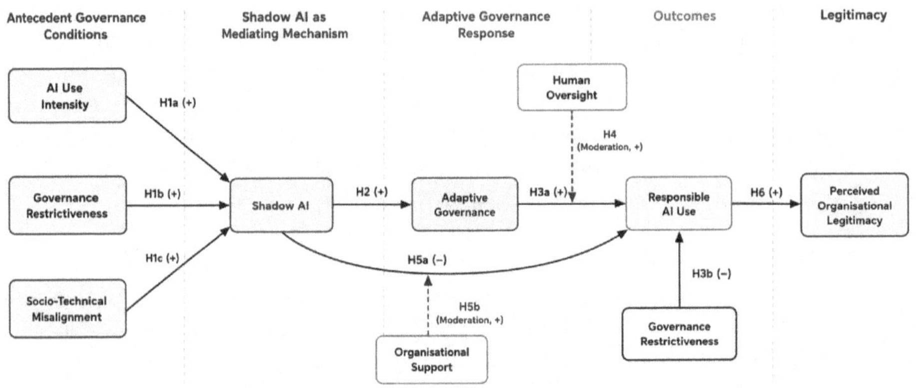

Fig. 1. Hypothesised socio-technical model of AI governance co-evolution.

Solid arrows indicate direct hypothesised effects and dashed arrows the moderating relationships specified in H4 and H5b. Shadow AI is modelled to exert both a negative direct effect on responsible AI use (H5a) and a positive indirect effect via adaptive governance (H2 and H3a). Human oversight moderates the adaptive governance–responsible AI use path (H4), and organisational support moderates the shadow AI–responsible AI use path (H5b); the moderator boxes therefore attach to the relevant paths rather than to the outcome construct directly. Governance restrictiveness appears at two points, reflecting its dual role as a positive antecedent of shadow AI (H1b) and a negative direct predictor of responsible AI use (H3b). All constructs were operationalised as reflective latent variables, consistent with the assumption that their indicators represent manifestations of the underlying constructs. The structural, mediating, and moderating relationships specified in this model are tested empirically in Sects. 4 and 5.

3 Methodology

3.1 Sample and Data Collection

Data were collected via a cross-sectional online survey administered to public-sector employees working in national and local government agencies in Sweden.

The study focused on a single national administrative context, ensuring institutional comparability across respondents. Purposive sampling was employed to target employees with self-reported experience using digital tools in their work, thereby ensuring sufficient variance in AI use behaviour. Participants were recruited via professional networks and organisational mailing lists.

Participation was voluntary and anonymous, and respondents were informed of the study's purpose prior to completing it. After excluding responses with missing data and those failing attention checks, the final analytical sample comprised $N = 214$ employees. Respondents spanned a range of functional roles (administrative, operational, analytical) and organisational levels, providing broad representational coverage of public sector AI use contexts. A post-hoc power analysis confirmed that the sample size exceeded the threshold required to detect medium-sized effects at 80% power for the most complex endogenous construct in the model, namely responsible AI use, which includes both direct effects and interaction terms. This is consistent with established guidelines for PLS-SEM [28].

3.2 Measurement Instrument

All constructs were measured using reflective multi-item scales rated on seven-point Likert scales anchored at 1 (*strongly disagree*) to 7 (*strongly agree*). Constructs were modelled reflectively because the indicators were assumed to represent manifestations of underlying latent variables rather than defining characteristics. Scale items were developed deductively from prior literature and refined through expert review and cognitive pre-testing with five public sector practitioners to ensure clarity, relevance, and content validity. Governance restrictiveness items were adapted from [2], shadow AI items were developed following [3], and responsible AI use items were informed by the NIST AI Risk Management Framework [14]. Human oversight and organisational support items were newly developed for this study due to the absence of validated scales, with particular attention paid to conceptual alignment with the theoretical framework.

The final measurement items are available from the corresponding author upon request.

3.3 Data Analysis

PLS-SEM was employed as the primary analytical technique using SmartPLS, in line with established best-practice guidelines [28]. PLS-SEM was selected for three reasons: it is predictive in orientation, includes multiple mediating and moderating relationships, and contains conceptually complex constructs. Compared with covariance-based SEM, PLS-SEM is better suited to these conditions and does not require multivariate normality. Bootstrapping with 5,000 subsamples was used to estimate standard errors and confidence intervals for path coefficients, and indirect effects were assessed using bias-corrected and accelerated (BCa) 95% confidence intervals. Measurement model quality was assessed using composite reliability (CR), average variance extracted (AVE), Cronbach's alpha, and the HTMT criterion for discriminant validity. Common method bias was evaluated using Harman's single-factor test and Kock's full collinearity assessment [30]. Multicollinearity was assessed via variance inflation factors (VIF), and predictive validity was examined using Stone–Geisser Q^2 statistics.

4 Results

4.1 Measurement Model

As shown in Table 1, the measurement model demonstrates satisfactory reliability and validity across all constructs. Composite reliability values exceed the recommended threshold of 0.70, and Cronbach's alpha values likewise indicate acceptable internal consistency. Convergent validity is confirmed for all constructs, with average variance extracted (AVE) values comfortably surpassing the 0.50 benchmark.

Table 1. Measurement Model Reliability and Validity Statistics

Construct	CR	AVE	Cronbach's α
AI Use Intensity	0.91	0.77	0.85
Governance Restrictiveness	0.88	0.71	0.81
Socio-Technical Misalignment	0.90	0.75	0.84
Shadow AI	0.92	0.79	0.87
Adaptive Governance	0.89	0.73	0.82
Human Oversight	0.87	0.69	0.80
Organisational Support	0.88	0.72	0.83
Responsible AI Use	0.93	0.81	0.89
Perceived Legitimacy	0.94	0.83	0.90

Note. CR = composite reliability; AVE = average variance extracted.

Discriminant validity is supported: all HTMT ratios fall below 0.85 and, per the Fornell–Larcker criterion, the square roots of AVE exceed inter-construct correlations. Harman's single-factor test accounts for 27.3% of variance, well below 50%; because Harman's test is a weak diagnostic, common method bias was further evaluated using Kock's full collinearity approach [30], with all full-collinearity VIFs below the 3.3 threshold. All structural VIFs remain below 3.0, indicating acceptable multicollinearity.

4.2 Robustness and Validity Checks

To further assess the robustness of the estimated PLS-SEM results, a series of diagnostic tests was conducted in line with established best practice recommendations [28], addressing potential threats to internal validity including common-method bias, multicollinearity, and deficiencies in reliability, convergent validity, discriminant validity, and predictive validity. Table 2 summarises these results: all indicators meet accepted thresholds, and positive Stone-Geisser Q^2 values confirm out-of-sample predictive relevance.

Table 2. Summary of Robustness and Validity Checks

Test	Result	Threshold
Common method bias (Harman's)	27.3% variance explained	<50%
Common method bias (full collin.)	Maximum full-collinearity VIF = 3.1	<3.3
Multicollinearity (VIF)	Maximum VIF = 2.7	<3.0
Predictive validity (Q^2)	$Q^2 > 0$ for all constructs	>0.0
Discriminant validity (HTMT)	Maximum HTMT = 0.79	<0.85
Convergent validity (AVE)	Minimum AVE = 0.69	>0.50
Internal consistency (CR)	Minimum CR = 0.87	>0.70

Note. All robustness checks meet standard thresholds for PLS-SEM research.

4.3 Structural Model

Structural estimates (Table 3) are all significant and in the predicted direction. Among the antecedents of shadow AI, governance restrictiveness is strongest ($\beta = 0.41$), followed by AI use intensity ($\beta = 0.32$) and socio-technical misalignment ($\beta = 0.28$), supporting H1a–H1c. Shadow AI strongly predicts adaptive governance ($\beta = 0.47$, H2). Adaptive governance predicts responsible AI use ($\beta = 0.38$, H3a) while governance restrictiveness exerts a negative direct effect ($\beta = -0.22$, H3b). Shadow AI additionally exerts a negative direct effect on responsible AI use ($\beta = -0.31$, H5a), indicating that informal use is directly detrimental to responsible practice independent of the adaptation it provokes. The main effects of the moderator constructs, Human Oversight ($\beta = 0.35$) and Organisational Support ($\beta = 0.12$), are included as required for estimating interaction terms but are not interpreted as separate hypotheses (see Sect. 4.4 for moderation tests). Responsible AI Use strongly predicts perceived legitimacy ($\beta = 0.62$, H6). Explanatory power is acceptable ($R^2 = 0.56$ for responsible AI use; $R^2 = 0.39$ for legitimacy).

4.4 Moderation Analysis

The interaction effects (Table 4) support H4 and H5b. Human oversight positively moderates the adaptive governance–responsible AI use path ($\beta = 0.18$, t = 2.84, 95% CI [0.06, 0.30]), so adaptations translate into responsible behaviour more effectively where oversight is high. Organisational support positively moderates the shadow AI–responsible AI use path ($\beta = 0.15$, t = 2.41, 95% CI [0.03, 0.27]), buffering shadow AI's negative direct effect (H5a) and indicating that support mechanisms partially mitigate the costs of informal use. Both effects are modest but significant.

Table 3. Structural Model Path Estimates

Path	β	t-value	Outcome
AI Use Intensity → Shadow AI	0.32	5.21	Supported (H1a)
Gov. Restrictiveness → Shadow AI	0.41	6.34	Supported (H1b)
Socio-Tech. Misalignment → Shadow AI	0.28	4.87	Supported (H1c)
Shadow AI → Adaptive Governance	0.47	7.12	Supported (H2)
Adaptive Governance → Responsible AI Use	0.38	6.05	Supported (H3a)
Gov. Restrictiveness → Responsible AI Use	−0.22	3.44	Supported (H3b)
Shadow AI → Responsible AI Use	−0.31	4.52	Supported (H5a)
Human Oversight → Responsible AI Use	0.35	5.78	Main effect
Organisational Support → Responsible AI Use	0.12	2.01	Main effect
Responsible AI Use → Legitimacy	0.62	9.11	Supported (H6)

Note. β = standardised path coefficient; bootstrapped t-values from 5,000 subsamples. Paths significant at $p < .001$ except the organisational support main effect, which is significant at $p < .05$. The main effects of moderator constructs (Human Oversight, Organisational Support) are included as required for estimating interaction terms but are not interpreted as separate hypotheses. H4 and H5b are moderation hypotheses tested in Table 4.

Table 4. Moderation Effects

Interaction Term	β	t	95% CI	Outcome
Human Oversight × Adaptive Gov. → Responsible AI Use	0.18	2.84	[0.06, 0.30]	Supported (H4)
Org. Support × Shadow AI → Responsible AI Use	0.15	2.41	[0.03, 0.27]	Supported (H5b)

Note. β = standardised interaction coefficient; t-values and bias-corrected 95% CIs from 5,000 subsamples. Both significant at $p < .05$.

4.5 Mediation Analysis

Because the model positions shadow AI as a mediator, indirect effects were tested explicitly using BCa 95% confidence intervals, with mediation types interpreted following [29]. To establish the form of mediation, a competing model added direct paths from each antecedent to adaptive governance; these were non-significant (all $p > .10$), confirming that antecedents act on adaptive governance only through shadow AI. The shadow AI–responsible AI use path is retained as H5a, so shadow AI's effect on responsible use is only partially transmitted through adaptive governance.

As reported in Table 5, each antecedent exerts a significant positive indirect effect on adaptive governance through shadow AI ($\beta = 0.132$–0.193); with the corresponding direct paths non-significant, this pattern is best interpreted as indirect-only mediation. The effect carries forward serially to responsible AI use via adaptive governance (shadow AI: $\beta = 0.179$; antecedents: $\beta = 0.050$–0.073) and onward to legitimacy ($\beta = 0.111$–0.236).

Figure 2 provides an integrated visual summary of the structural, moderation, and mediation results reported in Tables 3, 4 and 5.

Table 5. Specific and Serial Indirect Effects

Indirect Path	β	95% CI	t
Gov. Restrictiveness → Shadow AI → Adaptive Gov.	0.193	[0.112, 0.281]	4.96
AI Use Intensity → Shadow AI → Adaptive Gov.	0.150	[0.082, 0.225]	4.21
Socio-Tech. Misalignment → Shadow AI → Adaptive Gov.	0.132	[0.071, 0.204]	3.98
Shadow AI → Adaptive Gov. → Responsible AI Use	0.179	[0.108, 0.257]	4.81
Gov. Restrictiveness → Shadow AI → Adaptive Gov. → Responsible AI Use	0.073	[0.041, 0.112]	4.02
AI Use Intensity → Shadow AI → Adaptive Gov. → Responsible AI Use	0.057	[0.030, 0.089]	3.76
Socio-Tech. Misalignment → Shadow AI → Adaptive Gov. → Responsible AI Use	0.050	[0.025, 0.080]	3.54
Adaptive Gov. → Responsible AI Use → Legitimacy	0.236	[0.152, 0.329]	5.24
Shadow AI → Adaptive Gov. → Responsible AI Use → Legitimacy	0.111	[0.064, 0.168]	4.38
Gov. Restrictiveness → Responsible AI Use (total effect)	−0.147	[−0.226, −0.069]	3.71
Shadow AI → Responsible AI Use (total effect)	−0.131	[−0.204, −0.058]	3.55

Note. β = standardised indirect effect; BCa 95% CIs and t-values from 5,000 subsamples; all significant at $p < .001$. The two total-effect rows correspond to competitive mediation (direct and indirect effects of opposite sign).

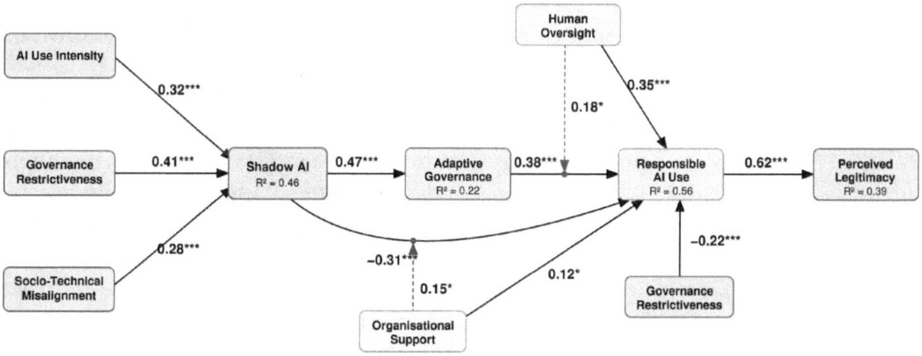

Fig. 2. PLS-SEM structural model and results. Solid arrows indicate direct effects; dashed arrows indicate moderating effects. $^{***}p < .001$; $^{*}p < .05$.

5 Discussion

We interpret the findings against the hypotheses and situate them within the literature on AI governance, socio-technical systems, and public sector legitimacy.

5.1 Antecedents of Shadow AI and the Governance–Practice Gap

Consistent with H1a–H1c, AI use intensity, governance restrictiveness, and socio-technical misalignment are all positively associated with shadow AI, confirming that informal use is systematically shaped by the interaction between behavioural demand and misaligned governance rather than emerging randomly. Governance restrictiveness is the strongest predictor, supporting reactance-theoretic and shadow IT accounts [6,8,11]: when frameworks prioritise prohibition without viable sanctioned alternatives, employees redirect AI use into less visible channels rather than ceasing it. This displacement mirrors established IT-governance patterns [6,12] and substantiates the argument that governance effectiveness depends on alignment with practice rather than stringency per se [16]—a misalignment especially pronounced where public sector procurement is slow and formalised [2].

5.2 Shadow AI as a Serial and Competitive Mediating Mechanism

A central contribution is the demonstration that shadow AI mediates the co-evolution of governance and practice. Consistent with H2, each antecedent exerts a significant positive indirect effect on adaptive governance through shadow AI ($\beta = 0.132$–0.193); because the corresponding direct paths are non-significant, this is indirect-only mediation, validating the socio-technical proposition that informal practices signal organisational adaptation rather than mere compliance failure [15,18]. Shadow AI renders governance inadequacies visible, creating conditions for double-loop learning [21] and the normative pressure to adapt that institutional theory predicts [19,20]. A serial chain extends this to outcomes: shadow AI → adaptive governance → responsible AI use ($\beta = 0.179$) and onward to legitimacy ($\beta = 0.111$).

The most theoretically informative pattern is competitive (inconsistent) mediation [29]. Shadow AI's positive indirect effect via adaptive governance ($\beta = 0.179$) operates against a negative direct effect (H5a), so the channels partially cancel: shadow AI is double-edged, directly eroding responsible use by reducing visibility and verification while indirectly improving it by triggering corrective adaptation. Governance restrictiveness shows the same structure—a negative direct effect ($\beta = -0.220$) only partially offset by a positive indirect effect ($\beta = 0.073$), net $\beta = -0.147$. By positioning shadow AI as a serial and competitive mediator, the study extends the shadow IT literature [6,12] into AI governance and shows how informal use can simultaneously threaten and reshape formal arrangements.

5.3 Restrictive/Enabling Governance and Moderating Infrastructure

Consistent with H3a and H3b, adaptive governance is positively associated with responsible AI use while governance restrictiveness exerts a negative direct effect, supporting claims that enabling designs outperform compliance-based ones

[2,23]: restrictiveness drives adoption underground and limits guidance and oversight [8], whereas adaptive governance reduces ambiguity and supports judgement, verification, and transparency. Support for H4 and H5b shows that complementary infrastructure shapes how this design translates into behaviour. Human oversight strengthens the effect of adaptive governance, consistent with agency theory [26] and normative frameworks treating oversight as foundational [13,14]. Organisational support, per social cognitive theory [24,25], buffers shadow AI's negative direct effect (H5a): training, guidance, and explicit norms equip informal users to act responsibly. Shadow AI is thus not inherently irresponsible—under adequate support its direct cost is mitigated.

5.4 Responsible AI Use and Institutional Legitimacy

Strong support for H6 underscores the institutional stakes of responsible AI use. Drawing on legitimacy theory [19,20], responsible practices function as observable signals of appropriateness and accountability—decisive where AI influences citizen-facing decisions [5]. Linking responsible use to perceived legitimacy extends research on public sector digitalisation [5] and shows that governance which fosters responsible use generates legitimacy as a downstream benefit [2]. Organisations thus face a strategic choice: treat shadow AI as a signal for adaptive learning, or persist with restriction that deepens misalignment and elevates legitimacy risk.

6 Conclusion

AI governance in the public sector emerges through continuous interaction between formal structures and everyday practice rather than static policy design [15,18]. Shadow AI mediates between governance conditions and the adaptive responses that, supported by oversight and organisational support, foster responsible AI use and legitimacy—yet it is double-edged, directly detrimental to responsible use while indirectly beneficial through the adaptation it provokes. These results challenge the prohibition-focused paradigm of much public sector AI governance [2]: echoing the shadow IT and information security literatures [8,12], restriction displaces rather than eliminates undesired behaviour, and effective governance instead requires enabling mechanisms aligned with work practice. Shadow AI is therefore best read not as a failure but as a governance signal informing adaptation. The central implication is that responsible AI governance cannot be achieved through prohibition alone; it requires organisational mechanisms that convert informal use into visible, governable, and accountable practice.

The study makes three contributions: it operationalises AI governance co-evolution in a predictive structural model; it repositions shadow AI from a dependent outcome to a serial and competitive mediating mechanism—both a source of risk and a catalyst for adaptation [6,12,29]; and it integrates socio-technical and institutional theory by linking governance co-evolution to perceived legitimacy

[19,20], connecting governance design to public trust. For practice, the findings suggest a shift from restriction towards enablement: organisations should invest in sanctioned AI pathways genuinely competitive with informal alternatives, strengthen oversight and support infrastructure [13,14], and monitor shadow AI as a diagnostic signal rather than suppressing it.

The results of the study should be interpreted taking the following limitations into consideration. To start with, the data are single-source and cross-sectional: although common method bias was assessed via Harman's test and Kock's full collinearity approach [30], neither common method variance nor causal ordering can be fully excluded, and longitudinal designs are needed to observe co-evolution over time. The model also articulates organisational-level processes but measures them through individual perceptions, so adaptive governance and legitimacy are best read as *perceived*; organisational-level evidence (policy records, audit logs, incident data) and multilevel designs would separate the level of theory from the level of measurement. Moreover, we also recognise that the uniformly positive measurement and structural results may partially reflect the self-reported nature of the survey and respondents' shared understanding of organisational AI practices. Future studies should triangulate perceptual measures with behavioural and administrative data. Finally, the purposive, single-country sample supports institutional comparability but limits generalisability and precludes formal non-response analysis; cross-national replication and attention to micro-level mechanisms—leadership, professional norms, culture—are clear next steps.

References

1. De Sousa, W.G., de Melo, E.R.P., Bermejo, P.H.D.S., Farias, R.A.S., Gomes, A.O.: How and where is artificial intelligence in the public sector going? A literature review and research agenda. Gov. Inf. Q. **36**(4), 101392 (2019)
2. Wirtz, B.W., Langer, P.F., Fenner, C.: Artificial intelligence in the public sector–a research agenda. Int. J. Public Adm. **44**(13), 1103–1128 (2021)
3. Waters-Lynch, J., Allen, D.W., Potts, J., Berg, C.: Shadow user innovation: governing covert generative-AI use for dynamic-capability renewal. Innovation 1–7 (2025)
4. Jonathan, G.M., Han, S.: GenAI in public sector transformation: balancing promise and prudence. In: International Conference on Electronic Government and the Information Systems Perspective. LNCS, pp. 105–121. Springer, Cham (2025)
5. König, P.D., Wenzelburger, G.: Opportunity for renewal or disruptive force? How artificial intelligence alters democratic politics. Gov. Inf. Q. **37**(3), 101489 (2020)
6. Silic, M., Back, A.: Shadow IT: a view from behind the curtain. Comput. Secur. **45**, 274–283 (2014)
7. Heeks, R.: Implementing and Managing eGovernment: An International Text. SAGE Publications (2005)
8. Bulgurcu, B., Cavusoglu, H., Benbasat, I.: Information security policy compliance: an empirical study of rationality-based beliefs and information security awareness. MIS Q. **34**(3), 523–548 (2010)

9. Davis, F.D.: Perceived usefulness, perceived ease of use, and user acceptance of information technology. MIS Q. **13**(3), 319–340 (1989)
10. Venkatesh, V., Morris, M.G., Davis, G.B., Davis, F.D.: User acceptance of information technology: toward a unified theory. MIS Q. **27**(3), 425–478 (2003)
11. Brehm, S.S., Brehm, J.W.: Psychological Reactance: A Theory of Freedom and Control. Academic Press (2013)
12. Furstenau, D., Rothe, H., Sandner, M.: Shadow systems, risk, and uncertainty in organizations. Commun. Assoc. Inf. Syst. **41**(1), 3 (2021)
13. European Commission: Ethics guidelines for trustworthy, AI. Publications Office of the European Union (2019)
14. Artificial Intelligence Risk Management Framework (AI RMF 1.0). National Institute of Standards and Technology. NIST (2023)
15. Orlikowski, W.J.: Using technology and constituting structures: a practice lens for studying technology in organizations. Organ. Sci. **11**(4), 404–428 (2000)
16. Volkoff, O., Strong, D.M., Elmes, M.B.: Technological embeddedness and organizational change. Organ. Sci. **18**(5), 832–848 (2007)
17. Jonathan, G.M., Yalew, S.D., Gebremeskel, B.K., Watat, J.K.: AI adoption in the public sector: organizational readiness and the pursuit of public value. Complex Syst. Inform. Model. Q. **45**, 43–70 (2025)
18. Trist, E.L., Bamforth, K.W.: Some social and psychological consequences of the Longwall method of coal-getting. Hum. Relations **4**(1), 3–38 (1951)
19. DiMaggio, P.J., Powell, W.W.: The iron cage revisited: institutional isomorphism and collective rationality in organizational fields. Am. Sociol. Rev. **48**(2), 147–160 (1983)
20. Suchman, M.C.: Managing legitimacy: strategic and institutional approaches. Acad. Manag. Rev. **20**(3), 571–610 (1995)
21. Argyris, C., Schön, D.A.: Organizational learning: a theory of action perspective. Reis **77**(78), 345–348 (1997)
22. Tiwana, A., Konsynski, B., Bush, A.A.: Platform evolution: coevolution of platform architecture, governance, and environmental dynamics. Inf. Syst. Res. **21**(4), 675–687 (2010)
23. Baldwin, R., Cave, M., Lodge, M.: Understanding Regulation: Theory, Strategy, and Practice, 2nd edn. Oxford University Press (2011)
24. Bandura, A.: Social Foundations of Thought and Action: A Social Cognitive Theory. Prentice-Hall (1986)
25. Compeau, D.R., Higgins, C.A.: Computer self-efficacy: development of a measure and initial test. MIS Q. **19**(2), 189–211 (1995)
26. Eisenhardt, K.M.: Agency theory: an assessment and review. Acad. Manag. Rev. **14**(1), 57–74 (1989)
27. Han, S., Jonathan, G.M.: The contextual edge: LLMs and Sweden's public sector transformation. In: International Conference on Electronic Government, pp. 180–195. Springer, Cham (2025)
28. Hair, J.F., Risher, J.J., Sarstedt, M., Ringle, C.M.: When to use and how to report the results of PLS-SEM. Eur. Bus. Rev. **31**(1), 2–24 (2022)
29. Zhao, X., Lynch, J.G., Jr., Chen, Q.: Reconsidering Baron and Kenny: myths and truths about mediation analysis. J. Consum. Res. **37**(2), 197–206 (2010)
30. Kock, N.: Common method bias in PLS-SEM: a full collinearity assessment approach. Int. J. e-Collaboration **11**(4), 1–10 (2015)

Beyond Observability: Ontology-Based Runtime Governance Validation for Microservice Architectures

Christian Bieri[1,2(✉)], Devid Montecchiari[1], and Andrea Polini[2]

[1] School of Business, FHNW University of Applied Sciences and Arts Northwestern Switzerland, 4600 Olten, Switzerland
christian.bieri@students.fhnw.ch, devid.montecchiari@fhnw.ch

[2] School of Science and Technology, University of Camerino, 62032 Camerino, Italy
christian.bieri@studenti.unicam.it, andrea.polini@unicam.it

Abstract. While microservice architectures (MSAs) offer advantages over monolithic systems, their decentralised, polyglot and highly dynamic nature not only complicates system-wide quality assurance but also renders manual architectural governance validation impractical, increasing the risk of architectural degradation. Although static, dynamic, hybrid and ontology-based analysis approaches exist, they remain fragmented in scope and integration and therefore provide only partial support for automated governance validation. Many severe architectural anti-patterns manifest only during execution and therefore require runtime analysis. Although telemetry data, particularly distributed traces, provide the required runtime information, their use for ontology-based, policy-aware governance validation remains largely unexplored. Consequently, many runtime architectural anti-patterns remain undetected. This paper proposes an ontology-based approach for policy-aware runtime governance validation in MSAs. Traces are semantically lifted into a formal knowledge model and analysed using a policy-aware semantic reasoning layer to detect governance violations during execution. Evaluation using synthetic scenarios and real-world data demonstrates that traces can be transformed into machine-interpretable knowledge for automated detection of architectural anti-patterns. The results show that the proposed approach extends traditional observability towards semantic runtime governance validation.

Keywords: Microservice Architectures · Distributed Tracing · Ontology-Based Reasoning · Architectural Governance · Architectural Anti-Patterns

1 Introduction

Modern software architectures have shifted toward distributed, modular and loosely coupled systems. Building on service-oriented architecture (SOA), MSAs

E. Laurenzi et al. (Eds.): BIR 2026, LNBIP 601, pp. 176–191, 2027.
https://doi.org/10.1007/978-3-032-38498-0_12

apply similar paradigms to smaller, independently deployable services that communicate via lightweight mechanisms [8,12]. While they offer advantages over monolithic systems [12,19,23], their decentralised, polyglot and dynamic nature introduces significant challenges for system-wide reasoning [23].

The resulting fragmentation obstructs a holistic system perspective [1] and makes it difficult to ensure architectural integrity. As a result, architectural and code smells, including critical anti-patterns, frequently remain undetected, particularly when they manifest across service boundaries or emerge only at runtime [18], making the maintenance of MSAs substantially more challenging than in monolithic architectures [7]. While observability makes systems observable by providing insights into their internal state through telemetry data (logs, metrics and traces) [16,24], the aforementioned challenges become particularly severe in large-scale environments, where countless services and complex interaction patterns evolve continuously. In such settings, manual governance validation becomes impracticable, leading to architectural degradation and its consequences, including reduced performance, increased operational costs and diminished reliability [6,20].

Existing approaches to analysing and validating service-based architectures (SBAs), including MSAs, exhibit clear limitations. Static analysis does not capture how users interact with the system at runtime [6,18]. Importantly, many of the most severe and difficult-to-detect architectural anti-patterns manifest exclusively at runtime, remaining entirely invisible to purely static views [18]. This limitation is partially addressed by dynamic analysis, which captures runtime behaviour and provides system-centric, language-agnostic perspectives [4]. However, only very few tools detect such issues, particularly anti-patterns, directly at runtime [18]. Hybrid approaches aim to combine static and dynamic perspectives [5], yet only a limited number of such approaches support the detection of architectural anti-patterns [18].

This reveals a fundamental gap: existing approaches do not provide an integrated solution that (1) transforms trace data into semantically enriched, machine-interpretable knowledge and (2) applies policy-aware semantic reasoning to enable automated runtime governance validation.

Recent work has demonstrated the potential of ontology-based semantic validation for architectural governance and compliance checking in enterprise architecture contexts [13]. At the same time, telemetry has become a standard component of modern observability infrastructures and can be used to support operational monitoring and system diagnostics. Consequently, the potential of runtime telemetry as a machine-interpretable knowledge source for ontology-based, policy-aware governance validation in dynamic MSA environments remains largely unexplored.

Addressing this gap requires combining human expertise with automated reasoning capabilities, aligning with the concept of hybrid intelligence. In this context, human-defined architectural policies must be complemented by machine-executable representations that allow continuous validation at runtime. Ontology-based approaches are particularly promising, as they enable the formal representation of architectural knowledge and support explainable reasoning over heterogeneous data sources.

This paper therefore investigates the following research question: *How can distributed traces be transformed into semantically enriched, machine-interpretable knowledge to move beyond traditional observability towards automated, policy-aware runtime governance validation in MSAs?*

To answer this question, an ontology-based approach is proposed that integrates trace data with policy-aware semantic reasoning to validate architectural governance at runtime. The main contributions of this paper are as follows:

- A trace-based ontology model that formally represents runtime-relevant knowledge in MSAs, enabling semantic interpretation of distributed traces.
- A semantic lifting pipeline that transforms traces into machine-interpretable knowledge, bridging the gap between observability and formal reasoning.
- A policy-aware semantic reasoning mechanism for the automated detection of architectural governance violations at runtime.
- An evaluation demonstrating the correctness, applicability and scalability characteristics of the proposed approach using synthetic and real-world traces.

2 Background and Related Work

This section provides the conceptual foundation for the proposed approach. It reviews ontology- and knowledge-based approaches for reasoning in SBAs and discusses their capabilities and limitations. It also introduces the hybrid intelligence perspective in architectural governance validation, motivating the integration of human-defined policies with automated reasoning. Finally, it identifies the research gap addressed in this paper.

2.1 Ontology and Knowledge-Based Approaches for Reasoning in SBAs

Ontology- and knowledge-based approaches have gained increasing attention in modern computing domains, as they deliver tangible benefits across diverse contexts. These include supporting migration activities [17], facilitating software lifecycle processes from analysis to runtime [11] and enhancing capabilities in cloud computing domains such as security, interoperability and service discovery [3]. Building on this, several ontology- and knowledge-based approaches have been proposed for analysing and reasoning in SBAs.

Filho et al. present IntelliGOV [9], a semantic, rule-based tool for SOA service compliance validation. It uses the Web Ontology Language (OWL) for knowledge representation and combines the Semantic Web Rule Language (SWRL) and the Semantic Query-Enhanced Web Rule Language (SQWRL) to express and validate policies. The approach operates primarily on design-time and configuration artefacts.

Morais and Adda introduce the Ontology of Microservice Architecture Concepts (OMSAC) [14], an ontology for modelling microservice concepts, including principles, patterns and anti-patterns. It is implemented in OWL and provides a structured and extensible knowledge base to support the understanding and exploration of MSAs. It remains largely static and does not incorporate runtime information.

Building on OMSAC, the authors propose x2OMSAC [15], a framework for the semi-automatic population of OMSAC. It instantiates ontology concepts using data from heterogeneous artefacts such as feature models, OpenAPI specifications and deployment descriptors, thereby reducing the manual effort required for ontology population and extending OMSAC. The approach focuses on ontology population and does not support policy-aware reasoning over runtime behaviour.

Kosińska et al. propose the Cloud-Native Ontology (CNOnt) [11], an ontology-based model for representing cloud-native application state. It is implemented in OWL and is populated at runtime using the CNOnt Broker, which constructs individuals from runtime information and static descriptors such as Kubernetes manifests. The approach enables a semantic representation of system state but does not explicitly address architectural governance validation.

Abdelfattah et al. propose Component-based Semantic Dependency (CSD) [2], an approach for identifying hidden semantic dependencies in microservice systems. It constructs component call graphs and applies semantic similarity and machine learning techniques to detect implicit dependencies, operating on static code artefacts.

Several approaches focus on runtime detection of architectural anti-patterns. Soldani et al. present μFreshener [21], which combines static deployment artefacts with dynamic network traffic data to model microservice structures. Gamage and Perera propose Microservice Anti-Patterns Insights Generator (MAIG) [10], which constructs service-dependency graphs from distributed tracing data (OpenTracing/Zipkin) and applies graph-based metrics and visualisations. Similarly, Røhne introduces Granular Hardware Utilization-Based Service Dependency Graph (GHUBS) [20], a multigraph model derived from telemetry data that enables the formal definition and automatic detection of four architectural anti-patterns. These approaches leverage runtime information but rely on graph-based or ad-hoc representations and do not employ ontology-based knowledge representation or provide semantic reasoning capabilities.

2.2 Hybrid Intelligence Perspective

Architectural governance in MSAs can benefit from combining human expertise and automated analysis, suggesting the relevance of hybrid intelligence. In such settings, architectural policies and constraints are typically defined by human experts, while automated systems can support the continuous analysis of runtime behaviour and validation of compliance.

Ontology-based approaches are particularly well-suited to support this paradigm, as they provide a formal and shared representation of architectural knowledge that can be interpreted by both humans and machines. This enables explainable, policy-driven reasoning and facilitates the integration of human-defined architectural intent with automated validation mechanisms.

2.3 Research Gap

However, despite the potential of ontology-based reasoning and hybrid intelligence in supporting architectural governance, existing ontology- and knowledge-based approaches for reasoning in SBAs remain fragmented in scope and integration. Existing approaches typically provide formal knowledge representation through ontologies. Yet, they lack either a runtime perspective (IntelliGOV [9]), an integrated semantic reasoning layer for governance validation (x2OMSAC [15], CNOnt [11]) or both (OMSAC [14]). Conversely, runtime-centric approaches such as GHUBS [20], MAIG [10] and μFreshener [21] analyse system behaviour without ontology-based knowledge representation and semantic reasoning. Other approaches, such as CSD [2], remain limited to static analysis without ontology-based modelling and semantic reasoning.

This fragmentation is summarised in Table 1, which provides an overview of the analysed approaches and their key limitations.

Table 1. Gap analysis of ontology- and knowledge-based approaches for reasoning in SBAs.

Approach	Ontology	Runtime Data	Semantic Reasoning	Gap
IntelliGOV	✓ OWL (SOA compliance)	✗ Design-time artefacts only	✓ SWRL & SQWRL rules	SOA-focused; no runtime data
OMSAC	✓ OWL (MSA concepts)	✗ Static only	✗ Discovery & classification only	No runtime data; no governance reasoning
x2OMSAC	✓ Builds on OMSAC	✓ Semi-automatic population	✗ No reasoning	No semantic governance reasoning
CNOnt	✓ OWL (cloud-native concepts)	✓ Runtime population	✗ No reasoning engine	Not tailored to MSA governance
μ Freshene	✗ Graph-based	✓ Hybrid (static & runtime)	✗ Pattern highlighting only	No ontology; no semantic reasoning
MAIG	✗ Graph-based	✓ Runtime traces	✗ Graph metrics only	No ontology; no semantic reasoning
GHUBS	✗ Multigraph model	✓ Runtime telemetry	✗ Formal detection only	No ontology; no semantic reasoning
CSD	✗ Similarity-based	✗ Static only	✗ ML-based classification	No ontology; no runtime data; no semantic reasoning

Across these approaches, three key limitations emerge. First, ontology-based approaches provide formal knowledge representation but often lack either runtime awareness, an integrated reasoning layer for governance validation or both. Second, runtime-oriented approaches capture dynamic system behaviour. However, they typically rely on graph-based or ad-hoc representations rather than ontology-based knowledge representation and semantic reasoning. Third, existing work does not sufficiently integrate runtime trace data, ontology-based modelling and policy-aware reasoning into a unified framework for architectural governance validation. Recent work has shown the potential of ontology-based validation and semantic reasoning for architecture governance and compliance checking in enterprise architecture contexts [13]. However, applying semantic governance validation to runtime telemetry and distributed traces in dynamic MSA environments remains insufficiently explored.

This paper addresses this gap by proposing an ontology-based approach that integrates trace data with policy-aware semantic reasoning. It enables automated runtime governance validation in MSAs while supporting a hybrid intelligence paradigm through the integration of human-defined policies and automated reasoning. Building on these foundations, the proposed approach extends ontology-based governance validation towards runtime-aware MSA environments. It integrates distributed trace data, semantic lifting and policy-aware reasoning to enable automated runtime governance validation. In doing so, the approach combines runtime observability with explainable semantic reasoning and supports a hybrid intelligence paradigm through the integration of human-defined policies and automated reasoning.

3 Approach

At a high level, the proposed approach consists of three core components: an ontology model (formal knowledge representation, TBox), a semantic lifting process (ontology population, resulting in an ABox) and a policy-aware semantic reasoning layer (governance validation through semantic rules and queries). Together, these components transform runtime trace data into a semantically enriched knowledge base and enable automated governance validation beyond traditional observability. To address the identified limitations, this section presents an ontology-based approach for policy-aware runtime governance validation in MSAs. Figure 1 provides an overview of the proposed workflow. The three core components are described in detail within the following subsections.

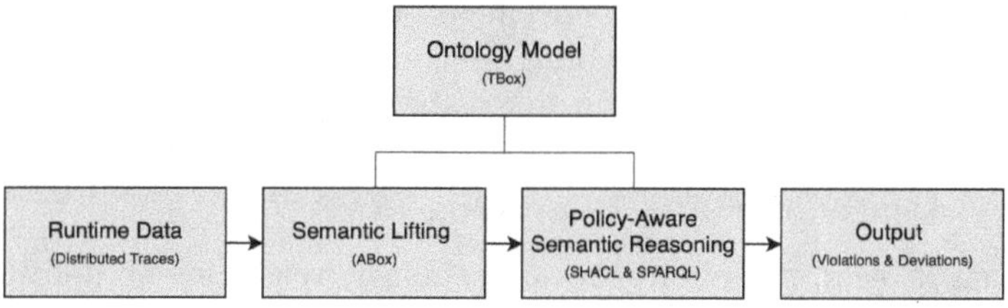

Fig. 1. Overview of the proposed approach for policy-aware runtime validation of architectural governance.

3.1 Ontology Model

The ontology model forms the semantic foundation of the proposed approach, providing a formal and shared representation of runtime-relevant concepts derived from distributed traces. Its primary purpose is to enable a machine-interpretable knowledge model that supports semantic reasoning and the formal evaluation of architectural policies. Rather than modelling the full complexity of the observability domain, the ontology focuses on a minimal yet expressive set of concepts required for governance validation.

Core entities include traces, spans and their associated contextual information, such as resources, scopes, attributes, events and links. These concepts capture both the participating services and the interactions between them. The ontology model is derived from the OpenTelemetry Protocol (OTLP) trace data model and implemented in OWL 2, thereby grounding it in a widely adopted observability standard while enabling formal semantic reasoning. By abstracting from implementation-specific details, it provides a consistent and technology-agnostic view of runtime behaviour.

3.2 Semantic Lifting Process

The semantic lifting process transforms raw trace data into ontology instances. In this step, distributed traces are mapped to ontology concepts, creating individuals that conform to the ontology model and reflect the actual runtime behaviour of the system, thereby instantiating the knowledge base.

This process bridges the gap between telemetry data, particularly trace data, and formal knowledge representation. Instead of merely storing or visualising traces, the approach translates them into a semantically enriched knowledge base that can be systematically queried and analysed. This transformation is essential, as it enables runtime data to be interpreted as formal knowledge rather than raw observability signals. As a result, runtime behaviour becomes accessible to automated reasoning mechanisms.

By relying on the standardised OTLP trace schema, the semantic lifting process remains largely independent of specific programming languages, frameworks and service implementations, enabling a consistent and technology-agnostic transformation of runtime behaviour across heterogeneous and polyglot MSAs.

3.3 Policy-Aware Semantic Reasoning Layer

The reasoning layer applies policy-aware semantic reasoning to detect architectural deviations, operating on top of the ABox. In this context, four anti-pattern definitions (cyclic dependencies, megaservices, inappropriate service intimacy and shared persistence in both its weak and strong forms), derived from established literature [20,22], are considered. The selection is based on two criteria: the perceived harmfulness reported by Taibi et al. [22] and the runtime detectability analysis conducted in this work. Consequently, the selected anti-patterns combine high practical relevance with suitability for ontology-based runtime governance validation.

The selected anti-patterns are formalised as machine-executable queries and inference rules that operate on the knowledge base. These rules are complemented by additional derivation rules that make implicit relationships explicit, thereby enabling the detection of architectural anti-patterns. The reasoning layer is implemented using SHACL rules (SPARQL-based) and SPARQL queries, enabling declarative rule definition and expressive knowledge retrieval over the ontology. Consequently, governance validation is transformed from a manual and retrospective activity into a continuous and automated runtime process.

The approach follows a hybrid intelligence paradigm: architectural policies are defined by human experts, while their validation is performed automatically by the system, enabling scalable and reproducible governance validation while preserving human control over architectural intent.

3.4 Integration in MSAs

The proposed approach is designed to integrate into existing MSAs. It operates as an extension of the telemetry pipeline, where services emit trace data via standard instrumentation and export them to a telemetry backend.

The semantic governance layer consumes these traces, performs semantic lifting and applies policy-aware semantic reasoning as a downstream analysis step. This allows the approach to be deployed without intrusive changes to application code or service architecture.

In this way, the approach extends traditional observability by introducing semantic interpretation and automated reasoning as core capabilities for runtime governance validation, while remaining compatible with existing telemetry pipelines.

3.5 Prototype Implementation

To demonstrate the feasibility of the proposed approach, a prototype was implemented in Python and evaluated in a Kubernetes-based microservice environment equipped with an observability stack based on OpenTelemetry. The research prototype is publicly available in a GitHub repository[1].

Telemetry data from instrumented applications are collected via the OpenTelemetry Collector and made available through the Jaeger tracing backend, from which they are retrieved and subsequently transformed using the semantic lifting process. Data exchange within the telemetry pipeline is based on gRPC. In the prototype, RDFLib is used to implement the ontology population during semantic lifting, conforming to the Trace Ontology.

For governance validation, a SHACL-based reasoning approach using the PySHACL library was implemented to validate architectural constraints. To

[1] https://github.com/ChristianBieri/semantic-runtime-governance-agent. The repository contains the complete research prototype, including the Trace Ontology, semantic lifting pipeline, SHACL rules and SPARQL queries, synthetic test cases, evaluation scripts, and instructions for reproducing the evaluation.

explore alternative reasoning strategies, a triple-store-based approach using GraphDB was also realised, where SPARQL is used both for querying and for expressing inference rules.

The pipeline integrates telemetry collection, semantic transformation and reasoning, thereby enabling end-to-end automated governance validation based on runtime data.

4 Experimental Evaluation

This section evaluates the proposed approach with respect to its ability to enable automated, policy-aware runtime governance validation. It first introduces the evaluation design, followed by an assessment of correctness using synthetic test cases, an analysis of applicability based on real-world trace data and a discussion of performance and scalability considerations.

4.1 Evaluation Design

The evaluation is designed around three dimensions: (1) correctness of governance validation, (2) applicability to real-world trace data and (3) performance and scalability. These dimensions directly reflect the research objective of enabling automated, policy-aware runtime governance validation based on semantically enriched trace data.

To achieve this, the evaluation follows two complementary perspectives. First, controlled synthetic test cases are used to validate the correctness of ontology population and reasoning, ensuring that architectural anti-patterns are reliably detected under well-defined conditions.

Second, real-world trace data collected from the OpenTelemetry Demo application are used to assess the feasibility and applicability of the approach in a realistic microservice environment. It was selected because it represents a decentralised, polyglot microservice application that is fully instrumented with OpenTelemetry, making it well suited for evaluating ontology-based runtime governance validation. Workloads were generated using concurrent users interacting with the system over varying telemetry windows, enabling the collection of distributed traces under realistic runtime conditions.

The evaluation is therefore designed as an exploratory yet systematic assessment, demonstrating both the functional validity of the approach and its practical potential beyond controlled scenarios.

4.2 Correctness of Governance Validation

The correctness of the proposed approach is evaluated using synthetic test cases that model specific architectural scenarios and anti-pattern manifestations. These test cases are designed to represent both valid and invalid system behaviours, enabling a controlled assessment of the reasoning capabilities.

For each scenario, trace data are generated and transformed through the semantic lifting process into ontology instances. The policy-aware semantic reasoning layer is then applied to detect governance violations. As shown in Table 2, the results demonstrate that, under controlled conditions, the approach correctly identifies both structural and interaction-oriented anti-patterns while producing no false positives (FPs).

In addition, the evaluation confirms that the ontology population process accurately reflects the underlying runtime behaviour, providing a consistent and machine-interpretable representation of traces. Together, these findings indicate that the combination of semantic lifting and rule-based reasoning enables reliable governance validation under controlled conditions.

Table 2. Correctness validation using synthetic test cases.

Scenario	Anti-Pattern	Location	Detected	FP
1–5	None (valid cases)	–	–	0
6	Cyclic Dependency	trace-tc06-cycle	Yes	0
7	Megaservice	trace-tc07-megaservice	Yes	0
8	Shared Persistence (weak)	order & billing service	Yes	0
9	Shared Persistence (strong)	account & profile service	Yes	0
10	Inappropriate Intimacy (complex)	trace-tc10-intimacy	Yes	0

4.3 Applicability to Real-World Trace Data

To assess the applicability of the approach beyond controlled scenarios, the evaluation is extended to real-world trace data. In this context, distributed traces collected from the OpenTelemetry demo application, a microservice-based system, are processed through the semantic lifting process and analysed using the reasoning layer. The results demonstrate that the approach can be successfully applied to real-world trace data, enabling the detection of architectural anti-patterns under realistic conditions. Despite the increased complexity and variability of the data, the ontology-based representation provides a consistent abstraction of runtime behaviour, allowing the reasoning process to operate effectively. This confirms that the approach is not limited to synthetic scenarios but can be integrated into existing observability pipelines, thereby supporting governance validation in practical environments. However, the effectiveness of the detection depends on the availability and quality of instrumentation data.

4.4 Performance and Scalability Considerations

The performance of the proposed approach is evaluated by analysing the computational overhead of trace extraction, semantic lifting and policy-aware semantic reasoning. Both trace extraction and semantic lifting scale approximately linearly with increasing trace volume, despite incurring additional computational overhead. This indicates that the transformation of trace data into ontology instances remains feasible for growing data sizes.

In contrast, the SHACL-based reasoning approach exhibits significant scalability limitations. Despite applying optimisation strategies, including ontology size reduction through deduplication and targeted attribute selection, the reasoning process does not scale sufficiently and becomes a performance bottleneck as the dataset grows, rendering the approach unsuitable for practical use in larger telemetry windows (e.g., beyond 300 s in the evaluated setup, depending on trace volume).

The scalability limitations of the SHACL-based approach are primarily caused by repeated graph traversal and constraint validation over increasingly large ontology instances. As trace volume grows, the number of generated RDF triples increases substantially, resulting in higher reasoning overhead during rule evaluation.

To address these limitations, a triple-store-based proof-of-concept implementation using GraphDB was developed. In this approach, the SHACL-based reasoning is replaced by a triple-store-centric strategy, in which SPARQL is used not only for querying results but also for implementing inference rules. In contrast to the SHACL-based approach, the triple-store-based approach benefits from indexing and query optimisation mechanisms provided by GraphDB, enabling more efficient execution of SPARQL-based inference rules.

The dataset sizes and reasoning execution times of both approaches are reported in Table 3, providing the quantitative basis for the scalability comparison.

Table 3. Dataset sizes and execution times used for the scalability comparison of SHACL- and triple-store-based reasoning.

Time Window (s)	# Processed Trace Lines[a]	SHACL-based (s)	Triple-store-based (s)
15	89'585	278.099	0.331
30	180'434	902.135	0.431
60	399'458	3'606.317	0.846
120	902'998	14'876.363	2.965
300	2'669'091	200'963.794	38.006
600	5'342'748	–	187.982
1'200	10'413'325	–	686.313
1'800	15'264'348	–	1'532.430

[a] Reported values represent the average number of processed trace lines across multiple experimental runs for each telemetry window.

Across comparable telemetry windows (15–300 s), the triple-store-based implementation consistently outperformed the SHACL-based approach, achieving speed-ups ranging from approximately 840× to over 5'280×. For telemetry windows beyond 300 s, only the triple-store-based approach was evaluated, as the SHACL-based implementation became impractical because of excessive reasoning execution times. As illustrated in Fig. 2, the triple-store-based approach achieves significantly improved scalability compared to the SHACL-based approach.

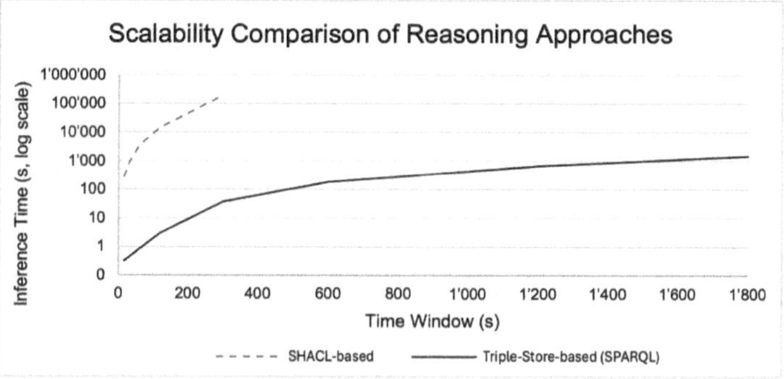

Fig. 2. Scalability comparison of SHACL- and triple-store-based reasoning (log y-axis).

Overall, the evaluation shows that while telemetry extraction and transformation can be handled efficiently, the choice of reasoning approach is critical for achieving scalability in ontology-based runtime governance validation.

4.5 Interpretation of Results

The evaluation results demonstrate that trace data can be effectively transformed into semantically enriched, machine-interpretable knowledge, enabling policy-aware semantic reasoning for the automated detection of architectural governance violations at runtime. This directly addresses the research question by showing that trace data can be utilised beyond monitoring towards actionable governance validation.

The evaluation further confirms that the approach is able to reliably detect architectural anti-patterns and can be applied to real-world trace data, demonstrating its practical feasibility. At the same time, scalability emerges as a critical factor. While trace extraction and semantic lifting scale efficiently, the choice of reasoning mechanism significantly impacts overall system performance, with SHACL-based reasoning showing clear limitations in larger settings. Taken together, the findings support a shift from passive monitoring towards active, policy-driven governance validation.

5 Discussion

The proposed approach demonstrates how semantic technologies can extend traditional observability by enabling machine-interpretable representations of runtime behaviour and policy-aware semantic reasoning. This shifts the role of observability from passive system monitoring towards active governance validation, thereby directly addressing the increasing complexity of MSAs.

From a hybrid intelligence perspective, the approach combines human-defined architectural policies with automated reasoning capabilities. While domain experts define governance rules and constraints, the system continuously transforms runtime data into semantically enriched knowledge. It then evaluates compliance with these policies at runtime, enabling scalable and reproducible decision support. This integration reduces reliance on manual inspection and supports consistent governance validation in dynamic environments. Compared to traditional observability tools, which primarily focus on visualisation and anomaly detection, the proposed approach introduces a formal semantic layer for explainable and policy-driven analysis. By transforming trace data into structured knowledge, it enables reasoning over system behaviour rather than merely observing it. This provides deeper insights into architectural compliance.

In addition, the ontology-based design provides several practical benefits. It enables a shared semantic representation that supports communication across stakeholder roles and facilitates knowledge transfer. Furthermore, the approach is inherently extensible and adaptable. Additional concepts and policies can be integrated as system requirements evolve. By relying on runtime trace data, it remains technology-agnostic and applicable in heterogeneous, polyglot environments. These findings highlight the potential of ontology-based approaches to enhance governance validation in MSAs. However, their effectiveness depends on appropriate reasoning strategies and sufficient data quality, which remain important considerations for practical adoption.

6 Limitations and Future Work

While the proposed approach demonstrates promising results, several limitations arise from design decisions and evaluation boundaries.

First, the approach focuses exclusively on runtime governance validation and is therefore limited to architectural anti-patterns that manifest during execution. Consequently, design-time and code-level issues remain outside its scope. Future work could extend the approach towards hybrid governance validation by integrating static analysis techniques, thereby enabling the detection of architectural issues that are not observable at runtime.

Second, the current implementation supports only a limited set of anti-patterns based on selected definitions from the literature. Future work could expand the anti-pattern catalogue and incorporate alternative or domain-specific formalisations to improve generalisability and applicability across different contexts.

Third, scalability constitutes a key challenge, as trace data can accumulate rapidly in real-world environments and place significant demands on ontology population and reasoning processes. While feasibility is demonstrated under moderate workloads, future work should investigate scalability-oriented optimisations, such as selective ontology population, data reduction techniques and incremental or partitioned reasoning.

Fourth, the evaluation was conducted under controlled conditions and therefore does not fully capture the complexity, scale and variability of production environments. Future work should include large-scale and long-running real-world deployments to assess performance, robustness and integration into operational workflows.

Fifth, the proposed ontology focuses primarily on runtime interaction semantics and does not capture higher-level business or domain semantics, which may limit expressiveness for certain governance policies. Extending the ontology towards multi-view representations, including infrastructure and domain-level perspectives, represents an important direction for future work.

Finally, the effectiveness of the approach depends on the availability and quality of trace data. Incomplete or inconsistent instrumentation can significantly limit system visibility, thereby reducing reasoning accuracy and potentially leading to false negatives in governance validation. Future work could therefore define instrumentation guidelines and best practices to support adoption and ensure sufficient data quality in real-world settings.

Addressing these limitations is a key step towards evolving the proposed approach into a scalable, generalisable and production-ready solution for semantic, policy-aware runtime governance validation in MSAs.

7 Conclusion

MSAs introduce significant challenges for architectural governance due to their decentralised, highly dynamic and polyglot nature, making manual validation increasingly impracticable. At the same time, existing approaches provide only limited support for automated, runtime-aware governance validation.

This paper proposed an ontology-based approach that transforms trace data into semantically enriched, machine-interpretable knowledge and enables policy-aware semantic reasoning for automated runtime governance validation. By combining ontology modelling, semantic lifting and reasoning, the approach extends traditional observability towards actionable, policy-driven analysis.

The evaluation demonstrates that the approach reliably detects architectural anti-patterns, can be applied to real-world trace data and highlights the importance of scalable reasoning mechanisms. Overall, the findings show that combining trace data with ontology-based reasoning extends traditional observability towards policy-aware runtime governance validation.

References

1. Abdelfattah, A.S., Cerny, T.: Roadmap to reasoning in microservice systems: a rapid review. Appl. Sci. **13**(3), 1838 (2023). https://doi.org/10.3390/app13031838

2. Abdelfattah, A.S., Cordes, K.E., Medina, A., Cerny, T.: Semantic dependency in microservice architecture. In: 2025 IEEE/ACM 22nd International Conference on Software and Systems Reuse (ICSR), pp. 44–54. IEEE (2025). https://doi.org/10.1109/ICSR66718.2025.00011
3. Agbaegbu, J., Arogundade, O.T., Misra, S., Damaševičius, R.: Ontologies in cloud computing—review and future directions. Future Internet **13**(12), 302 (2021). https://doi.org/10.3390/fi13120302
4. Al Maruf, A., Bakhtin, A., Cerny, T., Taibi, D.: Using microservice telemetry data for system dynamic analysis. In: 2022 IEEE International Conference on Service-Oriented System Engineering (SOSE), pp. 29–38. IEEE, Newark (2022). https://doi.org/10.1109/SOSE55356.2022.00010
5. Bushong, V., et al.: On microservice analysis and architecture evolution: a systematic mapping study. Appl. Sci. **11**(17), 7856 (2021). https://doi.org/10.3390/app11177856
6. Cerny, T., Taibi, D.: Microservice-aware static analysis: opportunities, gaps, and advancements. OASIcs, Microserv. 2020/2022 **111**, 2:1–2:14 (2023). https://doi.org/10.4230/OASICS.MICROSERVICES.2020-2022.2
7. Dragoni, N., Giallorenzo, S., Lafuente, A.L., Mazzara, M., Montesi, F., Mustafin, R., Safina, L.: Microservices: yesterday, today, and tomorrow. In: Present and Ulterior Software Engineering, pp. 195–216. Springer, Cham (2017). https://doi.org/10.1007/978-3-319-67425-4_12
8. Dragoni, N., Lanese, I., Larsen, S.T., Mazzara, M., Mustafin, R., Safina, L.: Microservices: how to make your application scale. In: Petrenko, A.K., Voronkov, A. (eds.) PSI 2017. LNCS, vol. 10742, pp. 95–104. Springer, Cham (2018). https://doi.org/10.1007/978-3-319-74313-4_8
9. Filho, H.M.T., Azevedo, L.G., Siqueira, S.W.M.: IntelliGOV - a semantic approach for compliance validation of service-oriented architectures. J. Univ. Comput. Sci. **22**(8), 1048–1071 (2016). https://doi.org/10.3217/jucs-022-08-1048
10. Gamage, I.U.P., Perera, I.: Using dependency graph and graph theory concepts to identify anti-patterns in a microservices system: a tool-based approach. In: 2021 Moratuwa Engineering Research Conference (MERCon), pp. 699–704. IEEE (2021). https://doi.org/10.1109/MERCon52712.2021.9525743
11. Kosińska, J., Brotoń, G., Tobiasz, M.: Knowledge representation of the state of a cloud-native application. Int. J. Softw. Tools Technol. Transfer **26**(1), 21–32 (2024). https://doi.org/10.1007/s10009-023-00705-2
12. Lewis, J., Fowler, M.: Microservices: a definition of this new architectural term (2014). https://martinfowler.com/articles/microservices.html
13. Montecchiari, D.: Ontology-based validation of enterprise architecture principles. Appl. Sci. **15**(7), 3352 (2026). https://doi.org/10.3390/app15073352
14. Morais, G., Adda, M.: OMSAC - ontology of microservices architecture concepts. In: 2020 11th IEEE Annual Information Technology, Electronics and Mobile Communication Conference (IEMCON), pp. 0293–0301. IEEE (2020). https://doi.org/10.1109/IEMCON51383.2020.9284892
15. Morais, G., Adda, M., Hadder, H., Bork, D.: x2omsac - an ontology population framework for the ontology of microservices architecture concepts. In: Rocha, A., Adeli, H., Dzemyda, G., Moreira, F., Colla, V. (eds.) Information Systems and Technologies, vol. 800, pp. 263–274. Springer, Cham (2024)
16. OpenTelemetry: What is opentelemetry? https://opentelemetry.io/docs/what-is-opentelemetry/

17. Oumoussa, I., Saidi, R.: The ontology-based mapping of microservice identification approaches: a systematic study of migration strategies from monolithic to microservice architectures. Computers **14**(4), 133 (2025). https://doi.org/10.3390/computers14040133
18. Parker, G., et al.: Visualizing anti-patterns in microservices at runtime: a systematic mapping study. IEEE Access **11**, 4434–4442 (2023). https://doi.org/10.1109/ACCESS.2023.3236165
19. Richards, M.: Microservices vs. Service- Oriented Architecture. O'Reilly Media, Sebastopol (2016)
20. Røhne, A.L.: Architectural anti-pattern identification and mitigation in microservice applications based on telemetry. Master's thesis, Universiteit van Amsterdam (2023)
21. Soldani, J., Muntoni, G., Neri, D., Brogi, A.: The μTOSCA toolchain: mining, analyzing, and refactoring microservice-based architectures. Softw. Pract. Exp. **51**(7), 1591–1621 (2021). https://doi.org/10.1002/spe.2974
22. Taibi, D., Lenarduzzi, V., Pahl, C.: Microservices anti-patterns: a taxonomy. In: Bucchiarone, A., et al. (eds.) Microservices, pp. 111–128. Springer, Cham (2020). https://doi.org/10.1007/978-3-030-31646-4_5
23. Velepucha, V., Flores, P.: A survey on microservices architecture: principles, patterns and migration challenges. IEEE Access **11**, 88339–88358 (2023). https://doi.org/10.1109/ACCESS.2023.3305687
24. Wickramasinghe, S.: Telemetry 101: an introduction to telemetry. https://www.splunk.com/en_us/blog/learn/what-is-telemetry.html

Toward a Layered Model of Security Risk Management Artefacts in Organisational Cybersecurity

Naomi Chinenye Ogu and Vjatšeslav Antipenko(✉)

University of Tartu, Üikooli 18, 50090 Tartu, Estonia
{naomi.chinenye.ogu,vjatseslav.antipenko}@ut.ee

Abstract. Organisations increasingly rely on security frameworks, standards, and methods to manage cybersecurity risks, yet the relationships between these artefacts remain conceptually fragmented. Existing literature frequently uses these concepts interchangeably, while the growing complexity of cyber threats continues to expose gaps between compliance-driven governance and operational resilience. This paper addresses these issues through a systematic literature review of 23 peer-reviewed studies published between 2015 and 2026 following the Kitchenham methodology. The study examines how organisations select security artefacts, how these artefacts evolve, and what organisational impacts they produce. The findings reveal that security risk management artefacts operate within a layered governance structure consisting of strategic frameworks, compliance-oriented standards, and operational methods. To explain this relationship, the paper introduces the *Cascade of Implementation Model.* In addition, the study proposes a four-level *Hierarchy of Evolution Maturity* to classify how security artefacts evolve through adaptation, fusion, and layering. The review shows that while more than half of the analysed studies propose evolved or hybridised artefacts, none demonstrate long-term empirical validation in operational organisational environments. The findings also highlight tensions between compliance and agility, as well as limited integration of socio-technical factors within current security governance research. The paper identifies the gap between conceptual innovation and operational validation as a major challenge for future cybersecurity governance research.

Keywords: Security risk management · Cybersecurity governance · Systematic literature review

1 Introduction

As organisations become increasingly dependent on interconnected digital infrastructures, information security and cybersecurity risk management have evolved from isolated technical concerns into central components of organisational governance. Contemporary cyber threats are no longer limited to opportunistic

E. Laurenzi et al. (Eds.): BIR 2026, LNBIP 601, pp. 192–208, 2027.
https://doi.org/10.1007/978-3-032-38498-0_13

attacks against individual systems; they increasingly target complex organisational ecosystems, critical infrastructure, and operational technology environments [33]. Ransomware campaigns, supply chain attacks, and large-scale disruptions now affect not only financial assets, but also organisational continuity, public trust, and societal resilience.

The vulnerability of digitally dependent societies to large-scale cyber disruption is not a recent phenomenon. The 2007 cyber attacks against Estonia demonstrated how coordinated attacks against public institutions, financial systems, and government communication channels could disrupt national digital infrastructure at scale [17]. Since then, the threat landscape has continued to evolve rapidly. Malware families such as GameOver Zeus and CryptoLocker illustrated how cybercrime increasingly combines technical sophistication with financially motivated extortion models capable of affecting hundreds of thousands of systems globally [13,36]. These developments have reinforced the need for organisations to adopt structured and adaptive approaches to security risk management.

To address these risks, organisations rely on a wide range of security governance instruments, including frameworks, standards, and operational methods. However, despite the growing maturity of cybersecurity governance, organisations continue to face what recent literature describes as a *compliance-security paradox* [8]. Security programmes frequently prioritise compliance with standards and audit requirements, yet compliance alone does not necessarily translate into operational resilience against evolving cyber threats [8]. In practice, many organisations continue to implement security governance as static control-checking exercises rather than as adaptive and iterative risk management processes.

A major source of this problem is the lack of clear alignment between strategic governance objectives and operational security execution. High-level governance frameworks often define organisational security goals without specifying how to translate them into technical implementation practices. At the same time, operational methods are frequently deployed in isolation from broader governance structures. This disconnect creates difficulties for organisations attempting to integrate governance, compliance, and operational security into a coherent risk management approach.

The problem is further complicated by conceptual ambiguity within both academic literature and professional practice. Terms such as *security framework*, *security standard*, and *security method* are often used interchangeably despite serving different organisational purposes [35]. According to ISACA, frameworks primarily support governance and strategic alignment, while standards establish prescriptive compliance baselines and methods provide operational procedures for executing security tasks [18,19]. Nevertheless, these distinctions are frequently blurred in both research and industry discourse [35].

A similar ambiguity exists between the concepts of *information security* and *cybersecurity*. Information security broadly concerns the protection of information assets in both physical and digital forms, whereas cybersecurity focuses more specifically on protecting interconnected digital systems, networks, and technologies from electronic threats [8,30]. Although related, these concepts operate at different scopes and governance levels. The lack of conceptual clarity surrounding these artefacts and domains complicates organisations' ability to select and integrate appropriate security instruments based on their operational context, technical maturity, and resource constraints.

Recent research increasingly attempts to address these challenges through hybrid, adaptive, and context-aware approaches to security risk management. Examples include integrating governance frameworks with agile software development practices [21], developing dynamic risk analysis frameworks [31], and incorporating socio-technical perspectives into healthcare cybersecurity governance [14]. While these approaches demonstrate growing interest in adaptive security governance, their maturity and empirical validation remain unclear. Much of the literature focuses on conceptual integration or controlled demonstrations, with limited evidence regarding long-term operational deployment in live organisational environments.

Consequently, the primary focus of this paper is to address the gap between conceptual design and operational validation in security risk management artefacts. To achieve this objective, the study conducts a systematic literature review ($N = 23$, 2015–2026) following the Kitchenham methodology [22]. The primary focus is supported by the following sub-research questions:

- **SRQ1:** How do organisations choose between security standards, methods, and frameworks?
- **SRQ2:** How have organisations' security frameworks, standards, and methods evolved?
- **SRQ3:** What are the impacts of security frameworks, standards, and methods on organisations?

The remainder of this paper is structured as follows. Section 2 presents the research method, while Sect. 3 introduces the conceptual foundations. Section 4 and Sect. 5 present the findings, Sect. 6 discusses their implications for organisational cybersecurity governance, and Sect. 7 concludes the paper with directions for future research.

2 Research Method

This study applies a systematic literature review (SLR) to examine how security risk management (SRM) artefacts are selected, structured, and evolved within organisational cybersecurity governance. The review follows the evidence-based guidelines proposed by Kitchenham [22] and focuses on the relationship between frameworks, standards, and methods across organisational and operational contexts.

2.1 Search Strategy

The literature search was conducted using the Web of Science (WoS) and Scopus databases. These databases were selected for their broad coverage of peer-reviewed research in information systems, software engineering, cybersecurity governance, and risk management.

The search query was designed to identify studies that discuss security frameworks, standards, and methods in risk management settings. Boolean operators were used to capture literature addressing the interaction, integration, or layering of multiple security artefacts across organisational environments. The following query was applied:

```
(risk management frameworks OR risk management standards OR
risk management methods) AND (security frameworks OR
cybersecurity frameworks) AND (security standards OR
cybersecurity standards) AND (security methods OR
cybersecurity methods)
```

The initial search returned 556 publications, comprising 225 from Web of Science and 331 from Scopus.

2.2 Study Selection and Quality Assessment

A two-stage filtering process was used to refine the initial search results into a relevant and consistent review corpus [22].

In the first stage (Filter 1 summarised in Table 1), inclusion and exclusion criteria were applied to titles and abstracts. The review was restricted to English-language peer-reviewed journal articles and conference papers published between 2015 and 2026. This period extends the information systems security risk management baseline established by Ahmed [3] and captures more recent developments associated with cloud computing, cyber-physical systems, ransomware, and adaptive cybersecurity governance.

Table 1. Filter 1: Study Selection Criteria

Inclusion Criteria	Exclusion Criteria
Published between 2015 and 2026	Duplicate record
Written in English	Grey literature (e.g., white papers, reports, theses, editorials, abstracts only)
Peer-reviewed journal article or conference paper	Retracted publication
Addresses cybersecurity or information security risk management	Not focused on organisational security risk management
Full text available	Does not discuss security frameworks, standards, or methods

During the initial screening stage, duplicate records, grey literature (e.g., white papers, technical reports, theses, editorials, and abstract-only publications), retracted studies, publications outside the scope of organisational security risk management, studies that did not discuss security frameworks, standards, or methods, and records without accessible full text were excluded. These criteria ensured that only peer-reviewed studies relevant to the research objectives proceeded to the quality assessment stage. Application of Filter 1 reduced the corpus from 556 to 158 papers.

In the second stage (Filter 2 summarised in Table 2), the remaining studies underwent full-text review and quality assessment. Studies were retained if they:

- addressed information security or cybersecurity risk management,
- discussed at least one security framework, standard, or method,
- described a transparent research process, and
- provided an analytical or empirical contribution relevant to the research questions.

Importantly, the review intentionally retained conceptual and unvalidated artefacts alongside empirically evaluated studies. Excluding conceptual proposals would have biased the review toward mature artefacts and limited the ability to analyse how new SRM approaches emerge and evolve over time [22].

Table 2. Filter 2: Quality Assessment Criteria

Quality Criterion	Requirement for Inclusion
Relevance to security risk management	The study must address information security or cybersecurity risk management
Security artefacts discussed	The study must include at least one framework, standard, or method
Adaptability or evolution	The study must discuss adaptation, maturity, evolution, or provide substantive insight into the state of the art
Methodological transparency	The research process must be described clearly
Knowledge contribution	The study must provide analytical or empirical contribution relevant to SRM artefacts

Following quality assessment and full-text review, 23 studies remained and formed the final synthesis corpus used in this study. Table 3 summarises the filtering process.

2.3 Primary Review Corpus

The final synthesis corpus spans diverse organisational and industrial domains, including healthcare, critical infrastructure, software engineering, aviation, automotive systems, industrial IoT, and enterprise governance.

Table 3. Systematic Literature Review Filtering Process

Review Stage	WoS	Scopus	Total
Initial search results	225	331	556
Filter 1: Inclusion/exclusion criteria	109	49	158
Filter 2: Quality assessment and full-text review	14	9	23

Table 4. Primary Review Corpus ($N = 23$)

ID	Study	Domain	Main Artefact(s)
1	Hemanidhi & Chimmanee (2017) [16]	Military Operations	CRA, NIST SP 800-115, ISO 31000
2	Sánchez et al. (2025) [31]	Cross-organisational Risk	MARISMA, ISO/IEC 27001, MAGERIT V3
3	Kirpitsas & Pachidis (2026) [21]	DevOps Governance	KIBO, Scrum, COBIT 2019, DevOps
4	Mortágua et al. (2024) [29]	Network Authentication	EAP-OAUTH, IEEE 802.1X, OAuth 2.0
5	Mizrak & Akkartal (2024) [27]	Aviation Security	DEMATEL-QSFS
6	Gabriel et al. (2017) [15]	Industrial Safety Systems	FRGM, NIST CSF, ISA84, ISA99
7	Cho & Kim (2025) [9]	Defense Industry	NIST RMF, MITRE ATT&CK, PASTA
8	Malaivongs et al. (2022) [25]	Cybersecurity Rating	CTI, ISO/IEC 27001, PCI DSS
9	Sawangphol et al. (2024) [32]	Security Visualisation	SecSAGE, NIST CSF
10	Metin et al. (2024) [26]	SMEs	PDCA Architecture, COBIT, NIST SP 800
11	Bita et al. (2025) [6]	Autonomous Vehicles	ISO 26262, ISO/SAE 21434
12	Moreira et al. (2021) [28]	Security Evaluation	MCDA-C, NIST CSF
13	Khan et al. (2022) [20]	Automotive CPS	Residual Risk Framework, ISO/SAE 21434
14	Andersson et al. (2025) [5]	Air Traffic Management	ISO/IEC 27005, NIST 800-30
15	Ewoh et al. (2025) [14]	Healthcare Security	STS Theory, NIST CSF
16	Sheik et al. (2023) [34]	Autonomous Vehicles	TARA, STRIDE, DREAD
17	Abualsauod (2025) [1]	Industrial IoT	ISO 27001, ISO 30141
18	Machal (2024) [24]	AI Medical Systems	FMEA, Fault Tree Analysis
19	Ardebili et al. (2024) [2]	Critical Infrastructure	ISO 31000, NIS 2
20	Al-Dosari & Fetais (2023) [4]	SME Cybersecurity	OCTAVE-S, CRAMM, SQUARE
21	El Arab et al. (2025) [10]	AI Healthcare Governance	IA^2TF
22	Shahzadi et al. (2025) [33]	Healthcare Ransomware	NIST CSF
23	Lake et al. (2024) [23]	XR Healthcare	NIST CSF, STRIDE

Table 4 summarises the 23 primary studies included in the review, together with their operational domains and the main security artefacts investigated.

2.4 Threats to Validity

Following Wohlin et al. [38], the study considered construct, internal, external, and reliability validity.

Construct validity concerns whether the operational measures used in the study accurately represent the concept under investigation. In this review, the central construct was the evolution of SRM artefacts. To reduce interpretive ambiguity, evolution was operationalised through the four-level Hierarchy of Evolution Maturity introduced in Sect. 3.

Internal validity relates to hidden causal factors that may influence the results. Because this study is based on a literature synthesis rather than an experimental evaluation, it does not make causal claims about the effectiveness of specific artefacts. Instead, it analyses patterns, relationships, and distributions identified across the reviewed literature.

External validity concerns the extent to which the findings generalise beyond the reviewed corpus. The review was restricted to peer-reviewed studies indexed in Web of Science and Scopus, which means the findings reflect publicly available academic research rather than proprietary industry practices or confidential organisational implementations. In addition, healthcare and automotive systems are comparatively overrepresented due to the strong regulatory and safety focus within those sectors.

Reliability addresses the consistency of data extraction and classification. Since coding and classification were conducted by a single researcher, interpretive bias remains a potential limitation. To mitigate this risk, the study used transparent search criteria, explicit filtering stages, and a structured synthesis matrix to support reproducibility.

3 Conceptual Foundations

To analyse how security risk management (SRM) artefacts are used and evolve in organisational cybersecurity governance, it is first necessary to distinguish between the core categories of artefacts used in practice. Prior literature notes that the terms *framework*, *standard*, and *method* are frequently used interchangeably despite serving different governance and operational functions [35]. Drawing on definitions from ISACA, NIST, and the reviewed literature [18,19,30,35], this paper separates SRM artefacts into three functional layers.

3.1 Security Risk Management Artefacts

Security risk management artefacts are grouped into three distinct categories based on their governance role, level of prescription, and operational purpose.

- **Security Frameworks:** Security frameworks provide high-level and generally non-prescriptive guidance for managing organisational security risks [19]. They define governance structures, strategic objectives, and broad control areas that align security activities with business goals [26]. Frameworks primarily define *what* organisations should address rather than *how* controls should be implemented. An example of such is the NIST Cybersecurity Framework (NIST CSF) [28].
- **Security Standards:** Security standards translate governance objectives into formal and measurable requirements [18,35]. They establish compliance baselines, certification criteria, and implementation requirements intended to ensure consistency and auditability across organisations and sectors. Examples include ISO/IEC 27001 [25] and ISO/SAE 21434 for automotive cybersecurity [20].

- **Security Methods:** Security methods are procedural or technical approaches used to execute specific security functions or risk assessment tasks [5,37]. They provide operational mechanisms for identifying, analysing, and evaluating risks within a broader framework or standard environments. Examples include STRIDE [23], OCTAVE-S [4], and FAIR [37].

3.2 Hierarchy of Evolution Maturity

To analyse how SRM artefacts evolve, this paper introduces a four-level *Hierarchy of Evolution Maturity*. The hierarchy classifies studies according to the degree of structural modification and empirical validation demonstrated by the proposed artefact.

- **Level 0 – No Evolution (Application Only):** Existing frameworks, standards, or methods are applied without structural modification [28,34]. The contribution is limited to application or contextual use [24].
- **Level 1 – Conceptual Evolution:** A new or modified artefact is proposed through conceptual integration, layering, or synthesis, but without empirical validation [14,32]. These studies remain theoretical or architectural proposals [6,26].
- **Level 2 – Demonstrated Evolution:** A novel or hybrid artefact is demonstrated through worked examples, simulations, synthetic datasets, or case illustrations [16,20,31]. However, the artefact is not validated through long-term operational deployment [21].
- **Level 3 – Validated Evolution:** The artefact is empirically validated in a real organisational setting through longitudinal deployment, comparative evaluation, or extensive practitioner-based assessment [22,38].

The hierarchy provides the analytical lens used in the following sections to evaluate how SRM artefacts evolve from conceptual proposals into operationally validated organisational instruments.

4 Results: The Cascade of Implementation

The synthesis of the reviewed studies ($N = 23$) reveals that security risk management artefacts are not used as isolated tools, but as interconnected layers within organisational cybersecurity governance [4,15]. Across the literature, frameworks, standards, and methods repeatedly appear in a vertical relationship in which strategic objectives are translated into compliance requirements, which are then operationalised through technical procedures.

This paper conceptualises this relationship as the *Cascade of Implementation Model* (Fig. 1). The model describes security risk management as a layered process that moves from strategic governance to operational execution [21].

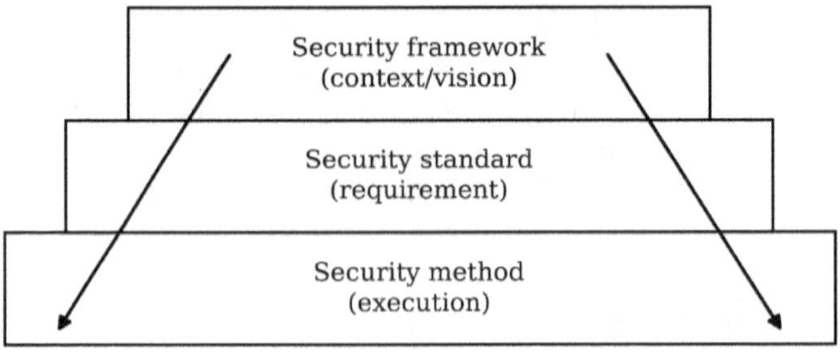

Fig. 1. The Cascade of Implementation Model.

4.1 Strategic Layer: Frameworks

At the top of the cascade are security frameworks. Frameworks provide strategic direction by aligning security objectives with organisational governance, risk appetite, and business priorities [19,26]. Rather than prescribing technical controls, frameworks define the governance structures and processes organisations should establish to manage security risks [31].

The review also highlights limitations of large enterprise frameworks, such as the NIST Cybersecurity Framework (CSF). Several studies note that extensive documentation and complex control mappings can create cognitive and operational challenges during implementation [28,32]. As a result, recent work has explored visualisation tools and adaptive framework designs intended to improve usability and support dynamic threat environments [31,32].

4.2 Compliance Layer: Standards

The middle layer of the cascade consists of security standards. Standards translate strategic governance objectives into measurable and auditable requirements [18,35]. Unlike frameworks, standards are prescriptive and are frequently tied to regulatory compliance, certification, or sector-specific operational requirements.

The literature demonstrates that standards are often adopted due to external regulatory pressure [2,10]. Critical infrastructure organisations, digital service providers, and healthcare systems must comply with regulatory mandates such as the European Union's NIS 2 Directive and healthcare-specific data protection requirements [2,10]. In safety-critical domains such as automotive engineering, standards including ISO/SAE 21434 function as mandatory baselines for cybersecurity and functional safety assurance [6,20].

4.3 Operational Layer: Methods

At the base of the cascade are security methods. Methods provide the operational mechanisms for executing security activities such as threat modelling, vulnerability assessment, and risk calculation [7,37]. They operationalise the requirements established by standards and the governance objectives defined by frameworks [5,23].

The reviewed studies show that method selection is strongly influenced by organisational resource constraints, including budget, technical expertise, and implementation complexity [4,15]. Small and medium enterprises (SMEs), for example, often prefer lightweight qualitative methods such as OCTAVE-S because they require fewer resources and less documentation overhead [4].

The findings also indicate that organisations select methods based on operational efficiency and cost optimisation. Gabriel et al. [15] demonstrate this through the Funnel Risk Graph Method (FRGM), which acts as a low-cost filtering mechanism that reduces the need for more resource-intensive quantitative assessments.

The cascade model illustrates that security risk management depends on the interaction between all three layers. Frameworks provide strategic direction, standards establish compliance baselines, and methods enable operational execution. Together, these layers connect organisational governance objectives with technical security implementation.

5 Results: Evolution of Security Risk Management Artefacts

To examine how security risk management artefacts evolve over time, the 23 primary studies were classified using the four-level Hierarchy of Evolution Maturity. The results show that the literature is dominated by conceptual proposals and limited demonstrations, while rigorous real-world validation remains largely absent.

5.1 Distribution of Maturity Levels

The reviewed studies are unevenly distributed across the maturity hierarchy. Of the 23 papers, 10 studies (43%) were classified as Level 0, meaning they applied existing frameworks, standards, or methods without structurally modifying them [2,4,5,9,10,23,24,28,33,34]. These studies primarily focused on application, evaluation, or literature synthesis.

Four studies (17%) were classified as Level 1 conceptual evolution [6,14,26,32]. These papers proposed new or modified artefacts through integration, adaptation, or theoretical synthesis, but did not validate them through practical implementation or case-based demonstration.

The remaining nine studies (39%) were classified as Level 2 demonstrated evolution [1,15,16,20,21,25,27,29,31]. These studies demonstrated new or hybrid artefacts using simulations, worked examples, synthetic datasets, or controlled evaluation scenarios.

Importantly, none of the reviewed studies achieved Level 3 validated evolution. No paper demonstrated longitudinal empirical validation within a live organisational environment. Table 5 summarises the classification of the reviewed studies.

Table 5. Distribution of Evolution Maturity Levels

Maturity Level	Number of Studies	Percentage
Level 0 – No Evolution	10	43%
Level 1 – Conceptual Evolution	4	17%
Level 2 – Demonstrated Evolution	9	39%
Level 3 – Validated Evolution	0	0%

5.2 Mechanisms of Evolution

The reviewed studies reveal two recurring mechanisms through which SRM artefacts evolve: *fusion* and *layering.*

Artefact fusion combines multiple frameworks, standards, or theoretical approaches into a unified artefact. For example, the MARISMA framework integrates ISO/IEC 27001 with MAGERIT V3 to produce a context-aware risk management framework [31]. Similarly, Ewoh et al. [14] combine Socio-Technical Systems (STS) theory with the NIST CSF to address healthcare cybersecurity from both technical and organisational perspectives.

Layering and stacking extend existing artefacts by embedding additional methods or controls within them. Khan et al. [20], for instance, integrate attack trees and flow graphs into ISO/SAE 21434 to address residual risk quantification. In software governance, the KIBO method combines COBIT 2019 with Scrum and DevOps practices to support continuous auditing within agile development environments [21].

These findings suggest that SRM evolution is largely driven by attempts to adapt existing governance structures to emerging operational and technological requirements.

5.3 The Validation Gap

The most significant finding from the maturity analysis is the absence of Level 3 validated evolution across the reviewed literature. Although many studies propose integrated or adaptive artefacts, few evaluate them in live organisational settings over extended periods.

Most Level 2 studies rely on simulations, synthetic datasets, worked examples, or controlled case environments rather than real operational deployments [1,20]. For example, Abualsauod [1] evaluates an integrated IoT governance framework using publicly available industrial datasets rather than data collected from an active enterprise environment.

This reliance on simulations and isolated demonstrations indicates a gap between conceptual innovation and operational validation. The literature, therefore, remains stronger at proposing new SRM artefacts than at demonstrating their long-term organisational effectiveness.

6 Discussion

The findings reveal that security risk management artefacts operate within a layered governance structure, but also expose several unresolved organisational and socio-technical challenges. By combining the Cascade of Implementation Model with the Hierarchy of Evolution Maturity, the review provides insight into how organisations select, adapt, and operationalise security artefacts in practice.

6.1 Selection Drivers (SRQ1)

The review shows that organisations select frameworks, standards, and methods based on a combination of regulatory, operational, and organisational pressures rather than a single decision factor [2,4]. This finding directly addresses **SRQ1**, which examined how organisations choose between security frameworks, standards, and methods.

External regulatory pressure is a major driver of standards adoption. Regulations such as GDPR and the NIS 2 Directive require organisations in critical sectors to implement formal cybersecurity controls and compliance mechanisms [2,11,12]. In sectors such as healthcare, transport, and critical infrastructure, compliance requirements strongly shape the selection of security artefacts.

At the same time, operational context influences the selection of methods and frameworks. High-risk environments such as military systems and cyber-physical infrastructures often require specialised approaches that go beyond generic governance frameworks [16].

The findings also highlight the role of organisational resource constraints. Large enterprises are generally able to implement complex standards and governance architectures, while SMEs tend to favour lightweight and qualitative methods that reduce implementation overhead [4]. In addition, several studies identify usability and cognitive complexity as important practical concerns, particularly in large frameworks such as the NIST CSF [32].

6.2 Evolution and the Validation Gap (SRQ2)

The review demonstrates that SRM artefacts are evolving primarily through integration, fusion, and layering. More than half of the reviewed studies proposed some form of structural modification intended to improve adaptability, automation, or operational flexibility [21,31]. These findings directly address **SRQ2**, which examined how security frameworks, standards, and methods evolve over time.

The reviewed studies reflect a broader shift away from static, compliance-oriented security models toward more adaptive, context-aware governance approaches [31]. However, the findings also reveal a significant imbalance between conceptual innovation and empirical validation. While many studies demonstrate technical feasibility through simulations or controlled examples, none provide long-term validation in operational enterprise environments.

This gap suggests that the field currently produces more conceptual architectures than operationally verified governance solutions [1,20]. As a result, organisations may struggle to assess the long-term effectiveness, scalability, or maintainability of newly proposed SRM artefacts before adoption.

6.3 Organisational Impacts and Governance Challenges (SRQ3)

The findings also address **SRQ3**, which examined the organisational impacts of security frameworks, standards, and methods. The literature reports both operational benefits and governance-related challenges associated with SRM adoption.

Several studies document measurable organisational improvements, including reduced security incidents, improved uptime, and more efficient information retrieval [1,32]. At the same time, maintaining compliance with overlapping standards and regulatory frameworks introduces substantial implementation and resource burdens, particularly for SMEs and resource-constrained organisations [2,4].

A recurring challenge across the literature is the tension between traditional governance structures and modern software delivery practices [21,26]. Conventional security governance models are typically designed around periodic audits, documentation-heavy controls, and relatively stable operational environments. These assumptions conflict with agile development environments characterised by rapid release cycles and continuous deployment pipelines.

Hybrid approaches such as KIBO attempt to address this tension by integrating governance checkpoints directly into agile workflows [21]. However, the lack of large-scale empirical validation means it remains unclear whether these integrations genuinely improve governance efficiency or simply add operational complexity.

6.4 Socio-technical Blind Spots

Finally, the review highlights a strong technical bias across the SRM literature. Most frameworks, standards, and methods focus primarily on technical safeguards, compliance controls, and risk calculation mechanisms [5,6,29]. Compared with the organisational, behavioural, and human dimensions of cybersecurity, comparatively little attention is given to them.

This limitation becomes particularly important in Cyber-Physical-Social Systems (CPSS), where security failures often emerge from interactions between technology, organisational processes, and human behaviour rather than from isolated technical weaknesses alone [2,14].

Only a small number of studies explicitly address this socio-technical dimension. Ewoh et al. [14], for example, integrate Socio-Technical Systems theory with the NIST CSF to account for organisational workflows and human interaction within healthcare environments. The limited number of such studies suggests that socio-technical integration remains underdeveloped within current SRM research.

7 Conclusion and Future Research

This paper examined the contemporary landscape of organisational SRM artefacts through a systematic literature review of 23 peer-reviewed studies published between 2015 and 2026. The primary objective was to address the gap between conceptual design and operational validation in security risk management artefacts.

The findings show that frameworks, standards, and methods function as interconnected layers within organisational cybersecurity governance rather than as isolated instruments. To explain this relationship, the paper proposed the *Cascade of Implementation Model*, conceptualising SRM artefacts as a layered structure of strategic frameworks, compliance-oriented standards, and operational methods.

To assess how SRM artefacts evolve, the paper also proposed the *Hierarchy of Evolution Maturity*. Although many studies introduce new or hybrid artefacts through fusion, integration, and layering, none achieved Level 3 validated evolution. Most evolved artefacts remain limited to conceptual proposals, simulations, worked examples, or controlled demonstrations rather than long-term organisational deployment.

Overall, the review indicates that SRM research is stronger in conceptual innovation than empirical validation. While organisations increasingly require adaptive and context-aware governance models, the evidence supporting many proposed artefacts remains limited.

The review also identified broader governance and socio-technical challenges. Organisations select SRM artefacts in response to a combination of regulatory pressure, operational context, resource constraints, and implementation complexity, while the literature remains predominantly focused on technical controls, giving comparatively little attention to organisational behaviour and human factors.

Future research should therefore prioritise the operational validation of evolved SRM artefacts in practical organisational settings, strengthen the integration of socio-technical perspectives within cybersecurity governance, and examine the trade-offs between security effectiveness, compliance requirements, operational complexity, and implementation costs. Advancing these areas is essential if SRM artefacts are to evolve from conceptual governance models into practically validated instruments of organisational resilience.

Acknowledgement. This research is supported by the European Union under Grant Agreement No. 101087529. Views and opinions expressed are, however, those of the author(s) only and do not necessarily reflect those of the European Union or European Research Executive Agency. Neither the European Union nor the granting authority can be held responsible for them.

References

1. Abualsauod, E.H.: ISO-based framework optimizing industrial internet of things for sustainable supply chain management. Sustainability **17**(14), 6421 (2025). https://doi.org/10.3390/su17146421
2. Aghazadeh Ardebili, A., Lezzi, M., Pourmadadkar, M.: Risk assessment for cyber resilience of critical infrastructures: methods, governance, and standards. Appl. Sci. **14**(24), 11807 (2024). https://doi.org/10.3390/app142411807
3. Ahmed, N.: Deriving security requirements from business process models. Doctoral dissertation, University of Tartu (2014). https://dspace.ut.ee/items/18d50203-ff20-4356-bd89-b4704ae5b367
4. AL-Dosari, K., Fetais, N.: Risk-management framework and information-security systems for small and medium enterprises (SMEs): a meta-analysis approach. Electronics **12**(17), 3629 (2023). https://doi.org/10.3390/electronics12173629
5. Andersson, S., Bergström, E., Lundgren, M., Bernsmed, K., Bour, G.: Information security risk management tools in the air traffic management domain: what are practitioners' needs? Inf. Secur. J.: Glob. Perspect. **34**(6), 561–578 (2025). https://doi.org/10.1080/19393555.2025.2498472
6. Bita, I.M., Hovemann, A., Dumitrescu, R.: Resilience-by-design: standard-based definition of resilience and identification of action fields for the systems design of mobility system. Proc. Design Soc. **5**, 2781–2790 (2025). https://doi.org/10.1017/pds.2025.10292
7. Borky, J.M., Bradley, T.H.: Protecting information with cybersecurity. In: Effective Model-Based Systems Engineering, pp. 345–404. Springer (2018). https://doi.org/10.1007/978-3-319-95669-5_10
8. Cheimonidis, P., Rantos, K.: Dynamic risk assessment in cybersecurity: a systematic literature review. Future Internet **15**(10), 324 (2023). https://doi.org/10.3390/fi15100324
9. Cho, H., Kim, S.: Threat modeling for the defense industry: past, present, and future. IEEE Access **13**, 53276–53304 (2025). https://doi.org/10.1109/ACCESS.2025.3550337
10. El Arab, R.A., Al Moosa, O.A., Sagbakken, M.: Economic, ethical, and regulatory dimensions of artificial intelligence in healthcare: an integrative review. Front. Public Health **13**, 1617138 (2025). https://doi.org/10.3389/fpubh.2025.1617138
11. European Union: Regulation (EU) 2016/679 of the European parliament and of the council of 27 April 2016 (general data protection regulation) (2016). https://eur-lex.europa.eu/eli/reg/2016/679/oj/eng
12. European Union: Directive (EU) 2022/2555 on measures for a high common level of cybersecurity across the union (nis 2 directive) (2022). https://eur-lex.europa.eu/eli/dir/2022/2555
13. EUROPOL: International action against 'gameover zeus' botnet and 'cryptolocker' ransomware (2014). https://www.europol.europa.eu/media-press/newsroom/news/international-action-against-gameover-zeus-botnet-and-cryptolocker-ransomware
14. Ewoh, P., Vartiainen, T., Mantere, T.: Sociotechnical cybersecurity framework for securing health care from vulnerabilities and cyberattacks: scoping review. J. Med. Internet Res. **27**, e75584 (2025). https://doi.org/10.2196/75584
15. Gabriel, A., Shi, J., Ozansoy, C.: A proposed alignment of the national institute of standards and technology framework with the funnel risk graph method. IEEE Access **5**, 12103–12113 (2017). https://doi.org/10.1109/ACCESS.2017.2718568

16. Hemanidhi, A., Chimmanee, S.: Military-based cyber risk assessment framework for supporting cyber warfare in Thailand (2017)
17. Herzog, S.: Revisiting the Estonian cyber attacks: digital threats and multinational responses. J. Strategic Secur. **4**(2), 49–60 (2011). https://doi.org/10.5038/1944-0472.4.2.3
18. ISACA: Standards, guidelines, tools and techniques. ISACA J. **1** (2020), https://www.isaca.org/resources/isaca-journal/issues/2020/volume-1/standards-guidelines-tools-and-techniques
19. ISACA: ISACA glossary (nd). https://www.isaca.org/resources/glossary
20. Khan, A., Bryans, J., Sabaliauskaite, G.: Framework for calculating residual cybersecurity risk of threats to road vehicles in alignment with ISO/SAE 21434. In: Applied Cryptography and Network Security Workshops, vol. 13285, pp. 235–247. Springer (2022).https://doi.org/10.1007/978-3-031-16815-4_14
21. Kirpitsas, I., Pachidis, T.: Kibo, a new hybrid software development method with enhanced information systems auditing capability. Inf. Softw. Technol. **190**, 107958 (2026). https://doi.org/10.1016/j.infsof.2025.107958
22. Kitchenham, B.: Procedures for performing systematic reviews. Technical report, Keele University (2004). Keele University Technical Report TR/SE-0401 and NICTA Technical Report 0400011T
23. Lake, K., et al.: Cybersecurity and privacy issues in extended reality health care applications: scoping review. JMIR XR Spat. Comput. **1**, e59409 (2024). https://doi.org/10.2196/59409
24. Machal, M.L.: Risks and benefits associated with the primary functions of artificial intelligence powered autoinjectors. Front. Med. Technol. **6**, 1331058 (2024). https://doi.org/10.3389/fmedt.2024.1331058
25. Malaivongs, S., Kiattisin, S., Chatjuthamard, P.: Cyber trust index: a framework for rating and improving cybersecurity performance. Appl. Sci. **12**(21), 11174 (2022). https://doi.org/10.3390/app122111174
26. Metin, B., Özhan, F.G., Wynn, M.: Digitalisation and cybersecurity: towards an operational framework. Electronics **13**(21), 4226 (2024). https://doi.org/10.3390/electronics13214226
27. Mizrak, F., Akkartal, G.R.: Prioritizing cybersecurity initiatives in aviation: a dematel-QSFS methodology. Heliyon **10**(16), e35487 (2024). https://doi.org/10.1016/j.heliyon.2024.e35487
28. Moreira, F.R., Da Silva Filho, D.A., Nze, G.D.A., De Sousa Junior, R.T., Nunes, R.R.: Evaluating the performance of NIST's framework cybersecurity controls through a constructivist multicriteria methodology. IEEE Access **9**, 129605–129618 (2021). https://doi.org/10.1109/ACCESS.2021.3113178
29. Mortágua, D., Zúquete, A., Salvador, P.: Enhancing 802.1x authentication with identity providers using eap-oauth and oauth 2.0. Comput. Netw. **244**, 110337 (2024).https://doi.org/10.1016/j.comnet.2024.110337
30. National Institute of Standards and Technology: Guide for conducting risk assessments. Technical report, NIST Special Publication 800-30 Revision 1, U.S. Department of Commerce (2012). https://doi.org/10.6028/NIST.SP.800-30r1
31. Sánchez, L.E., Santos-Olmo, A., Rosado, D.G., Blanco, C., Serrano, M.A., Mouratidis, H., Fernández-Medina, E.: MARISMA: a modern and context-aware framework for assessing and managing information cybersecurity risks. Comput. Stand. Interfaces **92**, 103935 (2025). https://doi.org/10.1016/j.csi.2024.103935
32. Sawangphol, W., Khurat, A., Niampradit, N.: SecSAGE: NIST cybersecurity framework visualization on SAGE2. ECTI Trans. Comput. Inf. Technol. **18**(3), 417–428 (2024). https://doi.org/10.37936/ecti-cit.2024183.256034

33. Shahzadi, A., et al.: Safeguarding the healthcare sector from ransomware attacks: Insights from a literature review. PeerJ Comput. Sci. **11**, e3073 (2025). https://doi.org/10.7717/peerj-cs.3073
34. Sheik, A.T., Maple, C., Epiphaniou, G., Dianati, M.: Securing cloud-assisted connected and autonomous vehicles: an in-depth threat analysis and risk assessment. Sensors **24**(1), 241 (2023). https://doi.org/10.3390/s24010241
35. Taherdoost, H.: Understanding cybersecurity frameworks and information security standards-a review and comprehensive overview. Electronics **11**(14), 2181 (2022). https://doi.org/10.3390/electronics11142181
36. U.S. Department of Justice: U.s. leads multi-national action against "gameover zeus" botnet and "cryptolocker" ransomware, charges botnet administrator (2014). https://www.justice.gov/archives/opa/pr/us-leads-multi-national-action-against-gameover-zeus-botnet-and-cryptolocker-ransomware
37. Wangen, G., Hallstensen, C., Snekkenes, E.: A framework for estimating information security risk assessment method completeness: core unified risk framework, curf. Int. J. Inf. Secur. **17**(6), 681–699 (2018). https://doi.org/10.1007/s10207-017-0382-0
38. Wohlin, C., Runeson, P., Höst, M., Ohlsson, M.C., Regnell, B., Wesslén, A.: Experimentation in Software Engineering. Springer (2012)

Towards Reliable Evaluation of Legal QA Systems Using LLM-as-a-Judge

Agris Šostaks[1(✉)], Sergejs Rikačovs[1], Artūrs Sproģis[1], Andris Hohbergs[1], and Uldis Lavrinovičs[2]

[1] Institute of Mathematics and Computer Science, University of Latvia, Riga, Latvia
{agris.sostaks,sergejs.rikacovs,arturs.sprogis,andris.hohbergs}@lumii.lv
[2] LETA, Latvian Information Agency, Riga, Latvia
uldis.lavrinovics@leta.lv

Abstract. Retrieval-Augmented Generation (RAG) systems based on large language models are increasingly used to answer legal questions by retrieving relevant legal texts and generating natural language responses. However, evaluating the quality of such systems remains a challenge. Legal answers often involve interpretation of statutory provisions, may have multiple valid formulations, and require references to legal sources, making traditional automatic metrics such as ROUGE or BERTScore insufficient. Human evaluation by legal experts is reliable, but slow and difficult to integrate into iterative system development.

In this paper, we explore the use of LLM-as-a-Judge as a practical approach for automatic evaluation of legal question answering systems. We study this problem in the context of a RAG-based legal QA system built on Latvian legislation and a data set of real legal consultation questions with expert-provided answers. We describe the iterative development of an evaluation framework, focusing on prompt design and evaluation criteria for judging legal answers. Our findings highlight key challenges and design considerations when applying LLM-based evaluation to domain-specific QA systems and provide guidance to build more reliable evaluation pipelines for legal AI.

Keywords: LLM-as-a-Judge · Legal QA · RAG

1 Introduction

Access to legal information is essential for both professionals and the general public. Legal practitioners, public institutions, and citizens need to interpret legislation and understand how legal norms apply to specific situations. Obtaining answers to legal questions requires searching through legal documents and consulting legal experts, or using publicly available legal consultation services. For example, the Latvian public information portal lvportals.lv hosts an e-consultation service where citizens can submit legal questions and receive written

E. Laurenzi et al. (Eds.): BIR 2026, LNBIP 601, pp. 209–224, 2027.
https://doi.org/10.1007/978-3-032-38498-0_14

answers from legal experts. Preparing a response may take up to 30 days, reflecting the effort required to analyze the situation and identify the applicable legal norms [12]. Similar services exist in other jurisdictions. In Germany, platforms such as Frag-einen-Anwalt.de enable users to submit legal questions online and receive written advice from practicing lawyers [3]. Providing high-quality legal advice remains a time-consuming and expertise-intensive process.

Recent advances in large language models (LLMs) have created new opportunities for automating legal question answering (Legal QA). LLM-based systems are capable of interpreting natural language queries and generating coherent responses, making them promising tools for improving access to legal information. Consequently, a growing body of research has explored the use of LLMs to answer legal questions and assist with legal reasoning tasks. Examples include benchmarks and systems designed to evaluate legal reasoning capabilities of language models, such as LegalBench [5], as well as domain-specific datasets and models for answering legal questions posed by laypeople [2]. Other work has investigated generative systems capable of producing long-form legal explanations grounded in statutory texts [11]. Surveys of the field highlight the increasing number of approaches that apply LLMs to legal tasks such as question answering, contract analysis, and legal decision prediction [1].

Despite recent progress, applying LLMs to legal question answering remains challenging. Legal texts are long, highly structured, and written in specialized language, while answering legal questions often requires interpreting relevant provisions and explaining their application to specific situations rather than retrieving simple facts. In addition, language models can produce hallucinated or unsupported statements, which is particularly problematic in legal contexts where accuracy and verifiability are essential [5,23].

One promising approach to address these issues is Retrieval-Augmented Generation (RAG) [7], where the system first retrieves relevant documents from a knowledge base and then model generates an answer using the retrieved context. RAG-based architectures have been increasingly adopted in legal applications [11] and other domain-specific legal QA systems that combine semantic retrieval with language model generation. However, building efficient RAG-based Legal QA systems introduces its own set of challenges. The quality of generated answers depends on multiple components, including document retrieval, context selection, and answer generation. Small changes in system configuration can significantly affect the final response. As a result, reliable evaluation becomes a critical component of system development. Traditional automatic metrics commonly used in natural language generation, such as ROUGE [10] or BLEU [17], are poorly suited for evaluating legal answers, as they fail to capture semantic correctness, legal grounding, or acceptable variation in phrasing. On the other hand, manual evaluation by legal experts provides reliable assessment but is time-consuming and difficult to integrate into iterative development cycles.

In this work, we address the challenge of evaluating answers produced by RAG-based legal question answering systems. We explore the use of the LLM-as-a-Judge paradigm as a practical approach for automatic evaluation of generated legal answers. In this approach, a language model (further referred as judge) evaluates a RAG systems outputs by comparing them with expert-provided reference answers according to a predefined evaluation rubric. We integrate this evaluation mechanism into the development workflow of a legal QA system. Our goal is not only to measure answer quality but also to support iterative system development, where automatic evaluation enables rapid comparison of system configurations and identification of problematic outputs.

The main contributions of this paper are **a methodology for integrating LLM-as-a-Judge into the iterative development workflow of legal QA systems, an experience report describing the iterative design and refinement of a domain-specific legal judge**, and **an experimental analysis of its behavior through large-scale automatic evaluation and qualitative validation**. Based on these experiments, we identify key considerations, strengths, and limitations of applying LLM-as-a-Judge evaluation in the legal domain.

The remainder of the paper is organized as follows. Section 2 briefly introduces the RAG-based legal QA system used as the case study throughout this work. Section 3 presents the proposed LLM-as-a-Judge evaluation framework, including related work, the evaluation methodology, and the iterative development of the judge. Section 4 describes the experimental methodology and presents both quantitative and qualitative evaluation results. Section 5 discusses the main limitations, methodological implications, and future research directions, while Sect. 6 concludes the paper.

2 Legal QA System Overview

Our Legal QA system follows the widely used RAG paradigm [7], in which relevant documents are first retrieved from a legal corpus and then used as context for answer generation by a large language model. Similar architectures have recently been applied in the legal domain, where language models generate answers grounded in statutory texts or legal document collections [2,11,16,22]. In this work we focus on the evaluation of generated answers. The system consists of several components (see Fig. 1): (1) legal document collection and preprocessing, (2) semantic indexing of legal texts, (3) document retrieval for user queries, and (4) answer generation using a large language model.

The system operates on a corpus of Latvian statutory documents obtained from the official legislation repository likumi.lv, which contains the normative acts currently in force in Latvia. During preprocessing, the documents are parsed and segmented into legally meaningful units such as articles or paragraphs. Each fragment is enriched with metadata describing the source document and article identifier, allowing the system to retrieve and reference specific legal provisions during answer generation. Each fragment is converted into a vector representation using the multilingual embedding model, which is also used to encode user queries. The resulting vectors are stored in a Weaviate vector database that enables semantic similarity search over the legal corpus. For each user question,

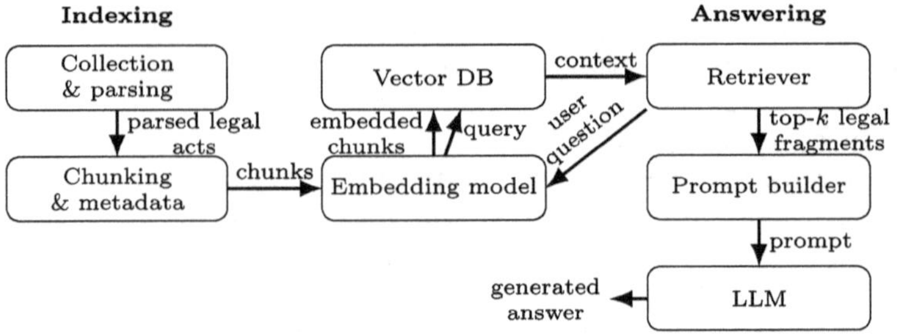

Fig. 1. Compact overview of the RAG-based legal QA system.

the system retrieves the top-k most relevant legal fragments and provides them as context to the language model, which generates a natural-language answer grounded in the retrieved legal provisions.

3 Evaluating Generated Legal Answers

Evaluating a retrieval-augmented legal QA system is itself a multi-stage problem. Earlier components, especially retrieval, can be assessed with standard information retrieval metrics while the effects of chunking and indexing are usually observed indirectly through retrieval quality. Since answer generation in RAG is conditioned on the retrieved context, retrieval errors directly affect the final answer [7,18]. In this paper, however, we focus on the final stage: evaluating the generated answer itself. In practice, generated answers are compared with expert reference answers that serve as a gold standard. Human evaluation is reliable but too costly for iterative development. We therefore explore the LLM-as-a-Judge paradigm, where a language model evaluates generated answers against predefined criteria and reference responses.

3.1 LLM-as-a-Judge in a Legal Domain

Recent work proposes the LLM-as-a-Judge paradigm as a scalable method for evaluating outputs of language models. In this approach, a language model acts as an evaluator or judge that assesses the quality of generated responses according to predefined criteria, focusing on semantic correctness, completeness, and relevance rather than surface-level similarity.

In a typical setup, the judge receives three elements: the candidate answer produced by the system, a reference answer representing the expected response, and an evaluation rubric defining the assessment criteria. These elements are combined in a structured prompt that instructs the judge to compare the candidate and reference answers and produce a score reflecting answer quality. In this work we focus on reference-based pointwise evaluation, where the judge evaluates a single generated answer against a reference answer and assigns a numerical score according to the rubric. However, the reliability of LLM judges remains difficult to verify, highlighting the need for carefully designed evaluation frameworks and analysis tools [4,13,23].

LLM-based evaluation has recently become increasingly common in legal AI benchmarks and RAG evaluation frameworks. Eval-RAG for Korean legal question answering evaluates generated answers directly against retrieved legal documents rather than against expert reference answers [20]. The approach aims to improve hallucination detection and achieves stronger correlation with human judgments than traditional automatic metrics. LexRAG applies an LLM-as-a-Judge framework for evaluating multi-turn legal consultation dialogues [8]. The judge compares generated responses against expert reference answers using several generic evaluation dimensions, including factuality, clarity, coherence, completeness, and user satisfaction. However, the reliability and behavior of the judge itself are not analyzed in detail.

LLM judges have also been studied in legal document recommendation tasks [19], where evaluations focus on dimensions such as relevance, correctness, hallucination risk, and overall quality. In contrast to many benchmark-oriented studies, this work explicitly investigates agreement between LLM judges and human experts using multiple inter-rater reliability metrics. Another related benchmark is PLawBench, which evaluates legal reasoning capabilities across several legal practice scenarios [21]. The benchmark uses expert-designed rubrics that decompose legal reasoning into fine-grained criteria, such as issue identification, legal rule application, and logical consistency. While this approach improves interpretability, designing detailed legal rubrics requires substantial expert effort and may be difficult to scale.

A broader overview of evaluation methodologies for legal language models is provided in recent survey work [6]. The survey highlights limitations of both traditional automatic metrics and LLM-as-a-Judge approaches, particularly for evaluating legal reasoning, and emphasizes the importance of expert-designed evaluation frameworks and fine-grained legal rubrics. Despite this growing body of work, relatively little attention has been paid to the engineering of practical evaluation pipelines for legal RAG systems, including rubric design, judge prompt engineering, diagnostic evaluation criteria, and tooling for systematic error analysis.

3.2 Evaluation Pipeline

Developing a RAG-based legal QA system is an iterative process: changes in chunking, embeddings, retrieval, or prompting may improve or degrade answer quality. To support systematic comparison of such configurations, we use an evaluation pipeline that integrates the RAG system with an automated LLM-as-a-Judge component (See Fig. 2). The Experiment UI runs test questions through the RAG system and forwards the generated answers to the judge for evaluation. Results are stored in the experiment database and analyzed in the UI. The analysis provides feedback to both developers, enabling continuous refinement of the QA system and the evaluation criteria.

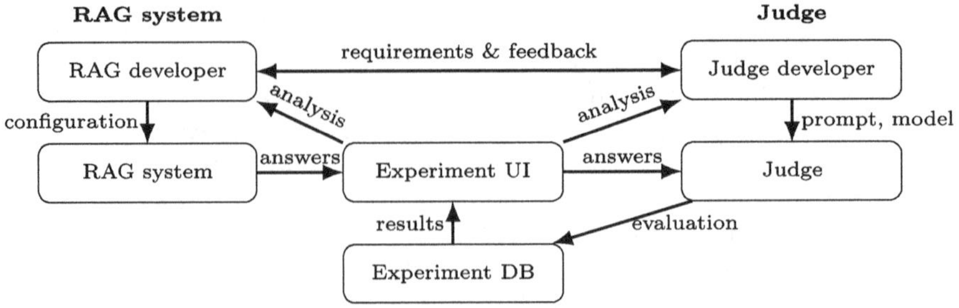

Fig. 2. Evaluation pipeline for iterative development of the RAG system and the judge.

Evaluation is performed on a dataset of legal question–answer pairs, where expert-written answers serve as reference responses. A selected test set is processed by the RAG system, which retrieves relevant legal context and generates new answers. Since these answers are not manually assessed in advance, repeated expert evaluation during development would be impractical. The generated answers are therefore evaluated automatically by the LLM. For each question, the LLM judge receives the user question, the generated answer, the expert reference answer, and the retrieved legal context. Using a structured prompt and predefined rubrics, it assigns criterion-level scores and short textual explanations. The evaluation results are stored in an experiment database and analyzed through the Experiment UI, which supports aggregate comparison across system configurations as well as inspection of individual cases. This enables a feedback loop in which both the RAG system and the judge are refined iteratively by adjusting system parameters, prompts, and evaluation criteria.

3.3 Datasets

Latvian Legislation Dataset. We constructed a corpus of legal documents from likumi.lv, the official repository of Latvian legislation [9]. These documents were automatically collected and processed in order to obtain a structured representation suitable for use in a RAG-based system. Each document was parsed into individual articles, which serve as the basic retrieval units for the QA system. In addition to the article text, the dataset contains metadata describing each legal act, including the document title, issuing authority, publication information, legal status, and thematic classification. The corpus contains 1,686 legal documents, including laws, regulations, and other normative acts referenced in the consultation dataset.

QA Dataset. The main evaluation dataset is derived from the lvportals.lv e-consultation platform, which contains authentic legal questions submitted by citizens and written answers prepared by legal experts. We also identified links to external legal sources cited in the answers and normalized references to likumi.lv documents. The resulting dataset contains 32,922 question–answer pairs covering the period from 2010 to 2024. The questions span a broad range of legal topics, including family law, taxation, inheritance, administrative procedures, and social protection. In total, the answers contain references to 1,699 distinct legal documents.

3.4 Iterative Development of the Judge Experience Report

Since no established evaluation benchmarks exist for the Latvian legal domain, the QA system and the evaluation methodology were developed simultaneously through several iterative refinements. The judge prompt defines the evaluator role, explicitly separates the evaluation inputs (question, generated answer, reference answer, and legal context), specifies the evaluation criteria for each rubric, and requires structured reasoning before scoring. To support automated analysis and reproducibility, the judge returns results in a predefined machine-readable output format. These principles are maintained through all iterations.

The initial version used four common QA criteria—correctness, faithfulness, completeness, and relevance—scored on a normalized 0–1 scale. In practice, this approach produced unstable and weakly interpretable results. The framework was then expanded into a larger rubric-based system with multiple evaluation dimensions capturing question coverage, consistency, context grounding, and practical usefulness. However, empirical analysis showed that several criteria overlapped or consistently received maximal scores, reducing their diagnostic value. To improve interpretability and reduce scoring ambiguity, the framework was gradually simplified and reformulated. The scoring scale was reduced from 1–10 to 1–4, rubric descriptions were rewritten as explicit evaluative statements, and scoring was transformed into binary sub-rubric decisions combined programmatically into final rubric scores. The final version introduces *hard*, *soft*, and *informative* sub-rubrics, explicit refusal handling, and few-shot prompting examples for more stable judge behavior. In addition, the evaluation process was migrated from English to Latvian to better match the target legal domain and simplify qualitative analysis.

Overall, the development process highlights an important methodological gap in current legal QA research: while benchmark results are commonly reported, the iterative engineering and calibration of evaluation frameworks themselves remain largely underexplored.

4 Experimental Evaluation

Our methodology consists of four stages. First, we construct an evaluation dataset from expert legal consultations by pairing each question with its expert answer and the corresponding legal provisions (gold context). Second, to isolate answer generation and judge behavior, **retrieval was not evaluated in these experiments**. Instead of executing the full RAG pipeline, the answering model received the gold legal context extracted from the expert answer, thereby simulating ideal retrieval conditions, allowing the experiment to evaluate answer generation independently of retrieval quality. Third, an LLM-as-a-Judge evaluates the generated answer against the expert answer using the proposed rubric-based evaluation framework. Finally, the automatically generated rubric scores are complemented by a qualitative manual evaluation of selected cases, enabling both large-scale quantitative analysis and validation of the proposed evaluation methodology. Generated answers were produced using the *gpt-oss-120b* model [14], primarily due to its local availability within our infrastructure, while *openai_ gpt-5-mini* [15] was used as the LLM-as-a-Judge evaluator.

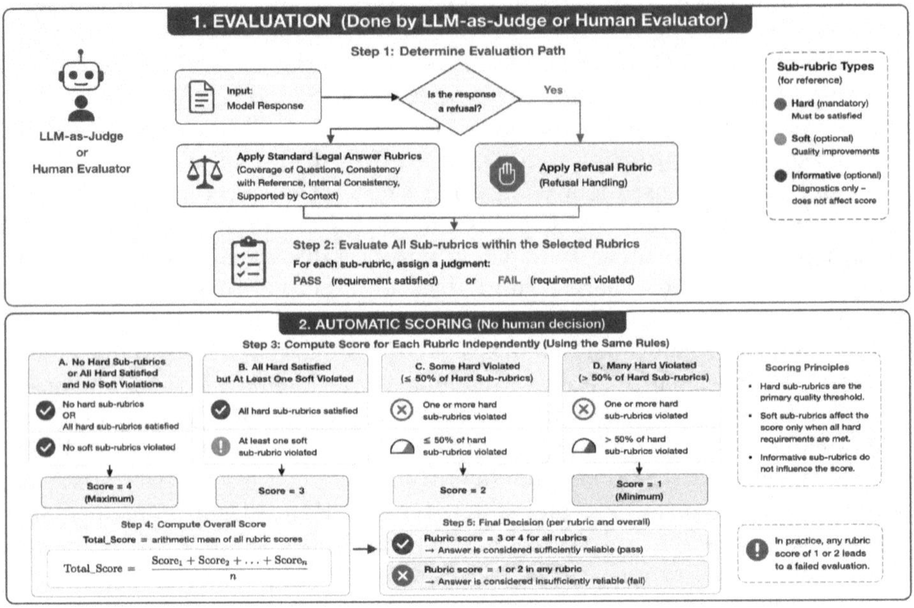

Fig. 3. Scoring procedure used by the LLM-as-a-Judge evaluator. Each response is first classified as either a refusal or a content-bearing answer, after which rubric scores are computed from hard, soft, and informative sub-rubrics.

4.1 Evaluation Rubrics and Scoring

The experiment was designed to evaluate answer quality, validate the revised rubric structure and the diagnostic capabilities of the proposed evaluation framework. In particular, the *no_ missing_ context_ in_ gold* sub-rubric was introduced to identify cases where the expert reference answer itself could not be fully justified using only the provided gold context. This made it possible to distinguish failures caused by incomplete or non-deterministic reference answers from failures originating in the evaluated RAG system itself. Table 1 summarizes the evaluation rubrics used by the LLM judge. Each rubric first defines the evaluated quality dimension together with its evaluation focus, followed by the corresponding sub-rubrics that specify the individual criteria assessed by the judge.

Table 1. Each rubric described with the evaluated quality dimension and its focus, and the corresponding sub-rubrics.

Coverage of Questions evaluates whether the answer addresses all parts of the user question and remains on topic. Correctness or depth are not the primary focus
answers_all_question (hard): covers all parts and sub-questions of the user query **no_unrelated_contents** (soft): remains focused on the user question and does not introduce unrelated content
Consistency with Reference evaluates how closely the SILVER answer aligns with the GOLD reference answer
no_missing_context_in_gold (informative): checks whether the reference answer is grounded in legal sources present in the provided gold context. This diagnostic sub-rubric helps identify reference answers that are impossible to use for evaluation, as the LLM is not allowed to incorporate outside knowledge **no_conflicting_conclusion** (hard): no contradiction with the reference answer. **no_practical_omissions** (hard): no practically important steps present in both the reference answer and reference context are omitted in the final answer
Internal Consistency evaluates whether the answer is logically coherent and internally consistent - doesn't introduce internal halucinations
internally_consistent (hard): the answer does not contain contradictory or logically inconsistent statements
Supported by Context evaluates how well the answer is grounded exclusively in the provided legal context
has_citations (hard): contains references to legal provisions present in the context **all_relevant_context_used** (hard): uses all important context information **correct_utilization_of_context** (hard): interprets legal provisions correctly **no_external_information_used** (hard): does not introduce legal claims outside the provided context **correct_formatting_of_references** (soft): references are correctly formatted and attached to newly introduced legal claims
Refusal Handling evaluates answers where the system does not substantially attempt to answer the user question and instead refuses, states lack of information, or claims that no safe conclusion can be made
refusal_because_missing_context: whether the refusal is justified because the context lacks sufficient information. **incorrect_refusal**: whether the refusal is unjustified despite sufficient information **refusal_other**: other refusal-related reasons in free-text form

The overall scoring procedure of the proposed evaluation framework is illustrated in Fig. 3.

The sub-rubric structure also enables partial diagnosis of system failures. Low scores in the *Coverage of Questions* and *Internal Consistency* rubrics are primarily associated with failures of the answer-generating LLM. Problems in the *Supported by Context* rubric are also generally attributable to the language model, except for *has citations*, which may additionally indicate retrieval failures in the RAG pipeline. In contrast, failures in the *Consistency with Reference* rubric may originate from several different sources. For example, *no missing context in gold* primarily functions as a data quality diagnostic, while failures in *no conflicting conclusion* and *no practical omissions* may result from deficiencies in retrieval, data quality, or answer generation.

4.2 Quantitative Results

The refusal analysis shows that refusals constitute a relatively small but non-negligible portion of the evaluated cases. Out of 1340 evaluated examples, 147 responses (10.97%) were classified as refusals. Among these, 86 cases (58.50% of refusals; 6.42% of all examples) were categorized as *refusal_because_missing_context*, indicating that the evaluator considered the available legal context insufficient to produce a reliable response. The remaining 61 cases (41.50% of refusals; 4.55% of all examples) were classified as *incorrect_refusal*, which means that the answering model refused to provide an answer despite sufficient information being available in the context. Overall, these results suggest that the refusal mechanism behaves conservatively, more frequently preferring refusal in uncertain situations rather than generating potentially unsupported legal conclusions.

The rubric-level evaluation results reveal that the majority of generated answers contain at least one critical quality issue according to the proposed evaluation framework. Out of all non-refusal cases, 1046 answers (87.68%) received a score of 2 or lower in at least one rubric, corresponding to 78.06% of all evaluated examples. The lowest scores were observed in the *ConsistencyWithReference* and *SupportedByContext* rubrics, indicating that the main weaknesses of the answering model are related to faithful legal reasoning and correct utilization of the provided legal context. In contrast, *CoverageOfQuestions* and *InternalConsistency* achieved substantially higher scores, suggesting that the model generally remains coherent and on-topic even when its legal reasoning is incomplete or incorrect. The aggregated rubric statistics are summarized in Table 2.

The sub-rubric analysis explains the rubric-level score distribution observed in Table 2. The relatively high scores in *CoverageOfQuestions* and *InternalConsistency* are consistent with the low failure rates of their corresponding sub-rubrics. The answering model almost always remained on topic and logically coherent, with *no_unrelated_content* failing in none of the evaluated cases and *internally_consistant* failing in only 8.21% of cases.

In contrast, the substantially lower scores of *SupportedByContext* and *ConsistencyWithReference* are directly reflected in the higher failure rates of their

Table 2. Aggregated rubric statistics for non-refusal cases.

Rubric	Mean	Median	Std. Dev.	≤2 (%)
CoverageOfQuestions	3.618	4.0	1.001	12.74
InternalConsistency	3.754	4.0	0.824	8.21
SupportedByContext	2.513	2.0	1.036	67.90
ConsistencyWithReference	2.137	2.0	1.131	76.11
Total_Score	3.005	3.0	0.604	–

semantic sub-rubrics shown in Fig. 4. Although the model almost always produced citations and generally formatted them correctly, failures were frequent in deeper legal reasoning tasks, particularly in *correct_utilization_of_context*, *all_relevant_context_used*, and *no_practical_omissions*. This indicates that the primary limitations of the answering model are not structural or linguistic, but rather related to complete and context-faithful legal reasoning.

The *no_missing_context_in_gold* sub-rubric should be interpreted separately from the other failure statistics because it primarily measures reference answer quality rather than answering model performance. The high failure rate of this sub-rubric indicates that a substantial portion of expert reference answers relied on implicit legal knowledge or information not fully derivable from the explicitly provided gold context. This result further justifies the inclusion of diagnostic sub-rubrics in the evaluation framework and demonstrates the importance of distinguishing dataset quality issues from actual RAG system failures.

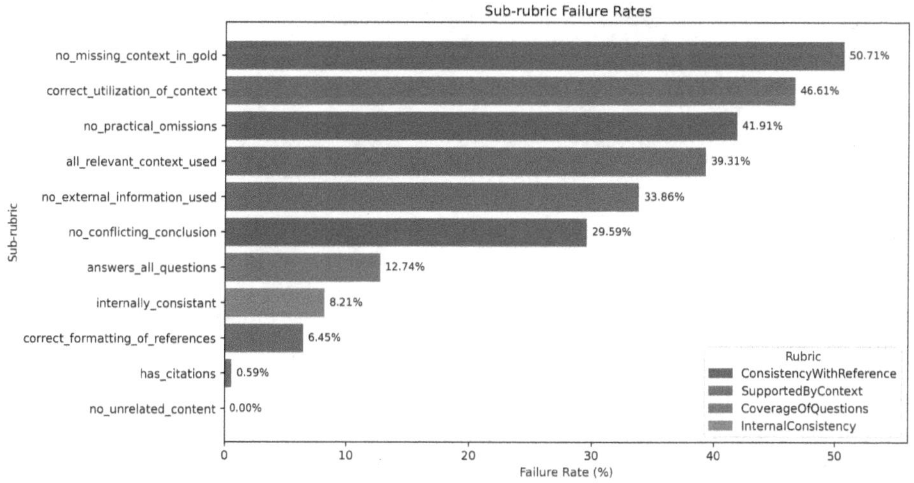

Fig. 4. Failure rates of individual sub-rubrics grouped by evaluation rubric. Colors indicate the corresponding parent rubric category.

Pear plausible, but the normative chain required to verify the claim remains incomplete. As a result, the rubric penalizes the answer not because it is logically incorrect but because its justification cannot be fully traced to the provided legal sources.

4.3 Qualitative Results

To assess the reliability of the LLM-as-a-Judge evaluator, we conducted a qualitative analysis using a blind manual review of sampled RAG outputs. Due to the large textual volume of each sample (question, lawyer answer, and legal context), the analysis was limited to 20 samples. The sampling strategy was designed to maximize rubric error diversity: each hard sub-rubric failure was represented by at least two samples, the diagnostic *no_missing_context_in_gold* rubric by at least three samples, and both justified and unjustified refusals were included. We additionally sampled at least two fully passing examples and biased the remaining selection toward samples containing a larger number of legal passages. The sampled subset broadly preserved the error distribution of the original dataset. To reduce reviewer bias, the dataset was shuffled and distributed across evaluators in a blind setup.

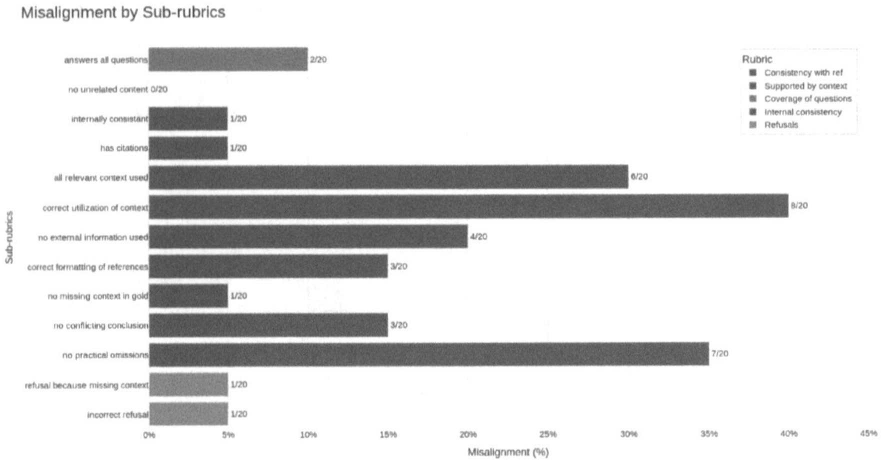

Fig. 5. Disagreement counts between manual and LLM-as-a-Judge evaluations grouped by rubric category.

Overlap between certain rubric failures was allowed, however, we intentionally favored samples with more isolated failures, as preliminary inspection revealed that the judge occasionally propagated a single underlying issue across multiple rubrics. For example, failures in *no_conflicting_conclusion* or *no_practical_omissions* rubrics were sometimes additionally labeled as *answers_all_questions* failures, despite the response still addressing the user query in some capacity. While such behavior has limited practical impact on overall acceptance decisions, it may inflate aggregate failure statistics for certain sub-rubrics.

Figure 5 shows the disagreement counts between manual and automated evaluations. Across all manually reviewed sub-rubric decisions, the judge agreed with human evaluation in 82.69% of cases with Cohen's $\kappa = 0.54$, indicating moderate agreement. The largest disagreement rates were observed for *correct_utilization_of_context*, *no_practical_omissions*, and *all_relevant_context_used*, which require detailed interpretation across multiple legal passages. In contrast, diagnostic rubrics such as *no_missing_context_in_gold* and *no_conflicting_conclusion* showed relatively low disagreement, suggesting that the evaluator is more reliable in detecting major factual inconsistencies and unsupported reference answers, which is really important. Most disagreements occurred because the LLM judge accepted answers that human evaluators considered insufficient, indicating a tendency toward more lenient evaluations. Manual inspection further indicated that many disagreements stemmed from ambiguous rubric boundaries rather than clear evaluator failures, particularly for *no_practical_omissions*. Overall, the qualitative analysis suggests that the proposed rubric design and LLM-as-a-Judge evaluator provide a sufficiently reliable proxy for large-scale evaluation, while also highlighting several rubric definitions that may benefit from refinement.

5 Discussion

Dataset limitations. A limitation of the *lvportals.lv* dataset is that expert answers do not always explicitly justify their conclusions using the provided legal context. They may rely on implicit legal knowledge, institutional practice, or external sources unavailable to the evaluated model. Consequently, disagreements between generated and reference answers do not necessarily indicate model failure. The diagnostic sub-rubric *no_missing_context_in_gold* was introduced specifically to identify such cases and separate dataset limitations from system errors.

Evaluator Reliability. Although the proposed LLM-as-a-Judge framework enables scalable evaluation, its reliability ultimately depends on agreement with human experts. Our qualitative analysis indicates that the evaluator is sufficiently reliable for comparative experiments, particularly for detecting major inconsistencies and unsupported reference answers. Most disagreements occurred in semantically complex rubrics requiring interpretation across multiple legal passages, suggesting that these rubric definitions and corresponding prompts warrant further refinement.

Prompt Design. The current judge evaluates all rubrics within a single prompt containing extensive legal context and detailed evaluation instructions. Such prompt complexity may contribute to disagreements in semantically demanding rubrics. Future work should investigate decomposing the evaluation into multiple specialized prompts or rubric-specific evaluators to improve robustness.

Diagnostic Value. Beyond producing aggregate benchmark scores, the proposed framework provides fine-grained diagnostic information through rubric and sub-rubric evaluations. Combined with judge explanations, these diagnostics help identify whether failures originate from incomplete reference answers, missing legal context, or shortcomings of the answering model, making the framework a practical tool for guiding iterative development of legal QA systems.

6 Conclusion

In this work we investigated the use of the LLM-as-a-Judge paradigm for evaluating answers of a RAG-based legal question answering system. We presented an evaluation pipeline that integrates automated answer generation, LLM-based judging, result storage, and interactive analysis into a unified framework that supports iterative system development. The study demonstrates how such a framework can be used to measure answer quality and guide the refinement of both the QA system and the evaluation methodology itself.

Are we at the point where such a judge can be confidently used in production? Most likely not yet. However, the results provide sufficient evidence that the approach is promising and worth pursuing further with direct involvement of legal experts, whose evaluations can be used to calibrate and align the judge's behavior. In addition, the evaluation framework itself has proven reusable beyond the legal QA setting and is currently being applied to other tasks, such as question answering over news archives.

Future work should focus on developing hybrid evaluation frameworks that combine large-scale automatic analysis with periodic expert-driven validation. Such frameworks should employ evaluation rubrics that remain lightweight and inexpensive to verify while still capturing legally important properties such as faithful legal grounding, correct interpretation of statutory provisions, and practical applicability of answers. The qualitative analysis also suggests that different legal question types require different evaluation strategies: fact-based questions grounded directly in statutory retrieval are substantially easier to evaluate automatically than open-ended or highly contextual legal reasoning tasks. Future systems could therefore incorporate question-type classification and adaptive evaluation workflows, combining fully automated evaluation for simpler cases with expert-in-the-loop assessment for ambiguous, high-risk, or contextually complex legal questions.

Acknowledgments. The research leading to these results has received funding from the research project "Competence Centre of Information and Communication Technologies for Digitalization" of the Recovery and Resilience Facility, contract No. 2.2.1.3.i.0/1 /24/A/CFLA/006 signed between IT Competence Centre and Central Finance and Contracts Agency Research No. 2.1 "Development of a large language model-based virtual assistant for retrieving answers from large volumes of text data".

Disclosure of Interests. The authors have no competing interests to declare that are relevant to the content of this article.

References

1. Ariai, F., Mackenzie, J., Demartini, G.: Natural language processing for the legal domain: a survey of tasks, datasets, models, and challenges. ACM Comput. Surv. **58**(6), 1–37 (2025)
2. Büttner, M., Habernal, I.: Answering legal questions from laymen in German civil law system. In: Proceedings of the 18th Conference of the European Chapter of the Association for Computational Linguistics (EACL), pp. 2015–2027 (2024)
3. Frag-einen-Anwalt.de: Frag-einen-Anwalt – Online Rechtsberatung. https://www.frag-einen-anwalt.de/. Accessed Mar 2026
4. Gu, J., Jiang, X., Shi, Z.: A survey on LLM-as-a-Judge. arXiv:2411.15594 (2025)
5. Guha, N., Nyarko, J., Ho, D.E.: LegalBench: a collaboratively built benchmark for measuring legal reasoning in large language models. arXiv:2308.11462 (2023)
6. Hu, Y., Liu, H., Wang, C.: Evaluation of large language models in legal applications: challenges, methods, and future directions. arXiv:2601.15267 (2026)
7. Lewis, P., Perez, E., Piktus, A.: Retrieval-augmented generation for knowledge-intensive NLP tasks. In: Advances in Neural Information Processing Systems (NeurIPS) (2020)
8. Li, H., Chen, Y., YiRan, H., et al.: LexRAG: benchmarking retrieval-augmented generation in multi-turn legal consultation conversation. In: Proceedings of the 48th International ACM SIGIR Conference on Research and Development in Information Retrieval (SIGIR), pp. 3606–3615 (2025)
9. VSIA Latvijas Vēstnesis: Likumi.lv – Latvijas Republikas tiesību akti. https://likumi.lv/. Accessed Mar 2026
10. Lin, C.Y.: ROUGE: a package for automatic evaluation of summaries. In: Text Summarization Branches Out, pp. 74–81 (2004)
11. Louis, A., Van Dijck, G., Spanakis, G.: Interpretable long-form legal question answering with retrieval-augmented large language models. In: Proceedings of the AAAI Conference on Artificial Intelligence, pp. 22266–22275 (2024)
12. LV portāls: E-konsultācijas. https://lvportals.lv/e-konsultacijas. Accessed Mar 2026
13. Muller, S., Loison, A., Omrani, B., Viaud, G.: Grouse: a benchmark to evaluate evaluators in grounded question answering. In: Proceedings of the 31st International Conference on Computational Linguistics (COLING), pp. 4510–4534 (2025)
14. Agarwal, S., et al.: gpt-oss-120b & gpt-oss20b model card. arXiv preprint arXiv:2508.10925 (2025)
15. OpenAI: GPT-5-mini language model. https://platform.openai.com. Accessed March 2026
16. Panchal, D.: LawPal: a retrieval-augmented generation based system for legal question answering. arXiv:2502.16573 (2025)
17. Papineni, K., Roukos, S., Ward, T., Zhu, W.J.: BLEU: a method for automatic evaluation of machine translation. In: Proceedings of the 40th Annual Meeting of the Association for Computational Linguistics (ACL) (2002)
18. Pipitone, V., Bouamor, H.: LegalBench-RAG: a benchmark for retrieval-augmented generation in the legal domain. arXiv:2404.XXXXX (2024)
19. Pradhan, A., Ortan, A., Verma, A., Seshadri, M.: LLM-as-a-Judge: rapid evaluation of legal document recommendation for retrieval-augmented generation. arXiv:2509.12382 (2025)
20. Ryu, C., Lee, S., Pang, S.: Retrieval-based evaluation for LLMs: a case study in Korean legal QA. In: Proceedings of the Natural Legal Language Processing Workshop, pp. 132–137 (2023)

21. Shi, Y., Liu, H., Hu, Y.: PLawBench: a rubric-based benchmark for evaluating LLMs in real-world legal practice. arXiv:2601.16669 (2026)
22. Wiratunga, N.: CBR-RAG: case-based reasoning for retrieval-augmented generation in legal question answering. arXiv:2404.04302 (2024)
23. Zheng, L., Chen, W.-L.: Judging LLM-as-a-judge with MT-bench and chatbot arena. In: Advances in Neural Information Processing Systems (NeurIPS) (2023)

The Low-Code/No-Code (LCNC) Solution for Identity Lifecycle Management Using Okta Workflows

Endija Darija Capkovska(✉)

Institute of Applied Computer Systems, Riga Technical University, Riga, Latvia
Endija-Darija.Capkovska@edu.rtu.lv

Abstract. Companies are increasingly turning to low-code/no-code (LCNC) platforms to automate identity lifecycle management (ILM) across heterogeneous enterprise environments, where provisioning, role transitions, and deprovisioning must operate across both integrated and manually managed application ecosystems. This paper presents the design, implementation, and evaluation of an LCNC-based ILM artefact built on Okta Workflows, following a Design Science Research methodology. The proposed solution is structured around five design principles, each grounded in established workflow pattern theory, dependability taxonomy, and IAM governance frameworks. Practitioner validation confirms that the artefact is consistent with enterprise IAM practice and accessible to administrators without software development expertise. The paper contributes a reusable reference design, an implementable artefact package, and a workflow-level evaluation framework for LCNC-based ILM – an area being underrepresented in both academic literature and published practitioner guidance.

Keywords: IAM · Automation · Identity Governance · Integration · Workflows · LCNC

1 Introduction

Increasingly, companies are using different software-as-a-service (SaaS) apps, cloud platforms, and hybrid information systems to support their main business processes. Identity and Access Management (IAM) is an important control tool in these situations because it must give employees access quickly, change it when their duties change, and take it away completely when they leave the company. If these identity lifecycle activities are delayed or not done correctly, it can lead to operational inefficiency, weak auditability, stale access, and accumulated privileges. Companies are expected to speed up the automation of their service processes, even though they have a shortage of engineers, and the systems are getting more and more complicated. In this context, low-code/no-code (LCNC) platforms have become important for implementing workflow-based automation through visual composition, reusable components, and integration through connectors. However, previous research has also pointed out ongoing problems with governance, maintainability, and platform limitations in LCNC-based solutions [1, 2].

E. Laurenzi et al. (Eds.): BIR 2026, LNBIP 601, pp. 225–238, 2027.
https://doi.org/10.1007/978-3-032-38498-0_15

These problems are especially important in Identity Lifecycle Management (ILM), where joiner, mover, and leaver (JML) processes must work across many systems, approval paths, and data sources. ILM execution in IAM is frequently hybrid; some applications can be provisioned centrally, while others require manual intervention [3–5]. In these situations, not having standardized orchestration and evidence generation makes it more likely that provisioning or deprovisioning will be incomplete and that accountability will be unclear. This paper examines the problem in an enterprise IAM environment with mixed lifecycle initiation and execution limits.

The problem is that there are no guidelines for a consistent, auditable, and practically reproducible way to use LCNC technology to automate identity lifecycle processes in an enterprise IAM environment. Although LCNC platforms are being used to automate workflows, there is not much information in the literature about how to use these platforms for workforce ILM by including process control, governance, and measurable evaluation. The solution proposed in this paper is anchored in three established bodies of knowledge: workflow pattern theory [6], dependability and fault tolerance taxonomy [7], and IAM governance control frameworks [5]. These provide the scientific basis from which the core design decisions are derived. The paper aims to build and test an ILM automation artefact that uses an LCNC platform. Specifically, Okta Workflows serves as the orchestration layer. The ILM automation artefact is developed in the specific context where the Okta platform is a mandatory part of the context (or a design constraint that enables not only the artefact development but also its evaluation).

The goal of this research is to create an LCNC solution for managing the identity lifecycle using Okta Workflows. This is expected to help make the JML process more consistent, easier to audit, and more effective in a heterogeneous IAM environment.

The main research question was formulated as follows:

"How can we design and test an LCNC solution based on Okta Workflows to make Identity Lifecycle Management more consistent, easier to audit, and more effective in a mixed enterprise IAM environment?". This question has the following sub-questions:

Sub-question 1: What are the operational, architectural, and governance issues that come up when the JML processes are carried out in the chosen business setting?

Sub-question 2: What design rules, control systems, and workflow structures does an LCNC-based ILM artefact need to support mixed initiation paths, hybrid execution, and governance-by-design?

Sub-question 3: How well does the designed artefact meet the specified functional and non-functional requirements and show that it is useful through workflow-level evaluation metrics and evidence-based validation?

The research follows the Design Science Research (DSR) approach because its main goal is not just to analyze the problem domain but also to build and evaluate a useful artefact.

The scientific value lies in addressing a gap that sits at the intersection of LCNC research, IAM lifecycle governance, and workflow-level assessment. The practical value is that it gives organizations that seek to improve lifecycle handling in partially integrated IAM landscapes a reference design and implementation method that they can use repeatedly.

The paper is structured as follows. The related work is briefly discussed in Sect. 2. Designed artifacts forming the solution are presented in Sect. 3. Section 4 discusses the implementation and evaluation of the solution. Section 5 concludes the paper.

2 Related Work and Contributions

This section demonstrates that enterprise IAM automation occupies a pivotal position at the intersection of (a) low-code/no-code workflow automation, (b) identity lifecycle governance, and (c) reliable API-driven integration. The literature shows that there are some gaps (G1-G4) when these issues need to be dealt with together in a practical, evaluable ILM solution, even though each area is well covered on its own.

G1 – There is not much research on LCNC for workforce ILM automation that focuses on artefacts. Low-code platforms are positioned as a major approach for enterprise development, yet research points to persistent challenges in maintainability, governance, and platform constraints [1, 2]. In IAM literature, lifecycle automation is often examined conceptually, with fewer studies offering a reproducible, workflow-level artefact aligned with design science standards [8, 9]. Drawing on Bock and Frank [1] and Luo et al. [2], the solution addresses maintainability through a configuration-driven access model and modular flow decomposition.

G2 – IAM performance measurement is increasingly recognized as important, but establishing what metrics mean and how they relate to IAM goals remains an open problem [10, 11]. Grounded in Baumer et al.'s [10] systematic review and Hummer et al.'s [11] expert survey, the solution operationalizes workflow-level KPI definitions – distinguishing orchestration latency from downstream propagation and manual task completion – as measurable success criteria rather than aspirational targets.

G3 – In real businesses, integrated and non-integrated applications coexist, and governance not built directly into the lifecycle workflow leads to inconsistent removals, privilege creep, and broken audit evidence [4, 5]. Drawing on NIST SP 800–53 [5] account management controls and SP 800–128 [4] configuration management requirements, the solution embeds approval enforcement, least-privilege sequencing, and a dual-log evidence model directly into the workflow structure.

G4 – Lifecycle automation is a distributed process that requires explicit strategies for failure. Drawing on Avizienis et al.'s [7] taxonomy of dependability and Garcia-Molina and Salem's [12] saga pattern for long-running transactions, the solution instantiates transaction-level recovery through retry-with-backoff, idempotency checks, and an intervention queue. IAM-specific implementations rarely expose or test these reliability patterns at the workflow level. This paper addresses the identified gaps by employing a design-science methodology for the construction and assessment of an artefact [8].

The identified gaps were treated using the following five design principles; (1) event-driven dual-trigger initiation (grounded in webhook-based integration practice), (2) group-mediated access control as the execution primitive (derived from directory-based provisioning patterns), (3) remove-before-add sequencing to prevent privilege accumulation (operationalizing least-privilege from NIST SP 800–53 [5]), (4) governance-by-design through embedded approvals and dual-log evidence generation (grounded in IAM control expectations [4, 5]), and (5) configuration-driven access mapping to enable maintainability without structural workflow changes (addressing LCNC maintainability limitations identified in [1, 2]).

The novelty lies not in any single foundation, but in jointly operationalizing all three – workflow patterns, dependability taxonomy, and IAM controls – into one evaluable artefact. Relative to full Identity Governance and Administration (IGA) platforms (e.g., SailPoint, Saviynt), which demand dedicated engineering and licensing investment, and custom-coded automation, which trades flexibility for maintenance cost, LCNC orchestration fits organizations without dedicated IAM engineering capacity and is a logical next step after fully manual IAM management.

From the identified gaps, the contributions of the paper are as follows: (C1) A workflow-based reference design for enterprise ILM automation in a mixed trigger and mixed integration environment; (C2) A reusable Okta Workflows artefact package; (C3) An evaluation framework combining requirements traceability with workflow-level KPIs; (C4) A governance mapping from lifecycle workflow control points to IAM control expectations; and (C5) A resilience-oriented workflow design using idempotency, retry, and remediation patterns.

3 Design Artefacts

To ensure the relevance of the proposed solution, the requirements were gathered in a real setting from an organization that works in the IT field. It is a platform-based corporation that heavily relies on SaaS tools (about 500) and identity-based access to internal systems. The company is sufficiently large to be called an enterprise, and it has about 2,500 workers and long-term contractors. The workforce is split up into different roles and teams, which leads to many applications and frequent changes to who can use them.

When it comes to IAM maturity, there is a centralized IAM capability that is only partially in place. For instance, there is a central identity layer and standard user accounts, but lifecycle operations (JML) are not fully automated from start to finish across all applications. This creates a mixed operating paradigm in which some systems are maintained from a central location, and others still rely on IT operations or application owners to process by hand.

The number of identity lifecycle changes can be impacted seasonally, such as when hiring peaks or when staffing changes are based on projects. The average number of JML events per month is about 50, which is the number used for planning and evaluation.

The present lifecycle process is a mix of centralized and decentralized activities, with a large amount of work being done through information technology service management (ITSM)-driven requests and manual execution across many platforms.

The as-is leaver process in Fig. 1 illustrates the governance risks in the as-is situation: account suspension depended on informal notification, and the time from the termination event to account suspension was unpredictable. This structural unpredictability is the primary risk that the proposed solution is designed to eliminate. While all three JML processes suffered from similar manual coordination problems, the leaver process is presented here as the representative as-is model because here the consequences of delay are most severe. Continued access after employment ends creates an immediate security exposure that cannot be corrected retroactively.

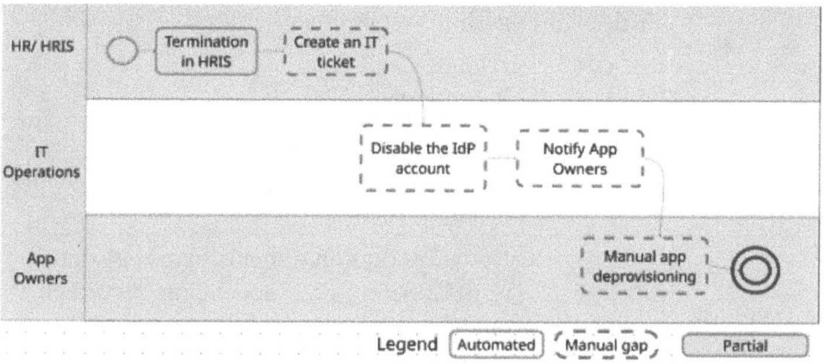

Fig. 1. Leaver (Deprovisioning) "as-is" BPMN-style model

The objectives were to design and validate an LCNC ILM solution built on Okta Workflows aimed at addressing the primary deficiencies identified. The paper takes a design-oriented approach, and the main contribution is an artefact (a workflow solution and operating instructions) that is shown to be useful and of high quality through structured evaluation, which is in line with design-science standards for making and testing artefacts [8].

According to the literature, success is defined as meeting functional coverage, quality attributes, and measurable outcomes that are in line with IAM goals and metrics practices [10]. The following success criteria will be used to evaluate the artefact:

SC1 – Functional coverage of joiner, mover, and leaver processing is demonstrated through traceable evaluation.

SC2 – Mixed-trigger initiation is supported for both human resources information systems (HRIS)-driven and ITSM-driven cases.

SC3 – Approval enforcement reflects system sensitivity and required approver roles.

SC4 – A minimum evidence set is generated and reviewable for each lifecycle transaction.

SC5 – Integrated targets are automated where possible, and non-integrated targets are handled through controlled manual tasks.

SC6 – The artefact demonstrates maintainability, observability, and operational readiness.

SC7 – Workflow-level KPIs are measurable and demonstrated in evaluation scenarios.

Requirements, both functional (FR) and non-functional (NFR), were obtained using workshops and semi-structured interviews and are written to fit the case organization's reality. The word "must" is used for mandatory requirements. All functional requirements are visible in Table 1 and in detail alongside non-functional requirements on GitHub [13].

Each of the five conceptual design principles mentioned in Sect. 2 is derived from an established scientific or normative foundation. The mapping in Table 2 makes this derivation explicit and distinguishes the solution from an ad hoc implementation choice.

The target architecture is meant to (1) support the organization's mixed-trigger reality, (2) centralize lifecycle execution where integrations exist, and (3) give non-integrated systems a controlled operational path while making sure that audit evidence is always the same.

Table 1. Functional requirement groups

ID	Requirement
FR1 – Joiner	Provision/activate identity and baseline + application access via HRIS- or ITSM-triggered events, with evidence recorded
FR2 – Mover	Update access on role/attribute change using remove-before-add sequencing; record all changes made
FR3 – Leaver	Disable identity immediately, revoke sessions, remove access (automated or manual), validate critical systems
FR4 – Access requests & approvals	Enforce configurable, logged approvals before any access change is executed
FR5 – Exceptions	Support contractor, VIP, and break-glass cases via explicit, auditable workflow states
FR6 – Audit reporting & evidence	Generate and export a traceable evidence package for every transaction

Table 2. Scientific foundation for design decisions

Scientific foundation	Design decision derived
Workflow patterns – Garcia - Molina & Salem [12]	Modular orchestrator, sub-flow decomposition, saga pattern transaction recovery from partial failures
Dependability taxonomy – Avizienis et al. [7]	Idempotency checks, retry with backoff and intervention queue to prevent silent identity state corruption
IAM metrics – Baumer et al. [10], Hummer et al. [11]	Workflow-level KPI definitions with orchestration latency, propagation time, and manual completion
NIST SP 800–53 [5], SP 800–128 [4]	Approval enforcement design, dual log evidence model, least privilege and configuration governance
DSR methodology – Hevner et al. [8]	Artefact construction cycle, structured evaluation framework, and reproducibility requirements

The target architecture (Fig. 2) comprises six logical components (by type, not vendor, except Okta):

- Source of authority – Cloud HRIS provides identity, date, and status data; emits JML events and scheduled triggers.

- Exception and governance layer – ITSM ticketing for outlier initiation, approval routing, and permanent evidence/task records.
- Identity platform – Okta IdP and Directory maintain the core identity profile; group and application assignments drive access management.
- Orchestration layer – Okta Workflows (LCNC).
- Target systems – Integrated apps via automated provisioning/deprovisioning; non-integrated apps via owner-executed ITSM tasks with completion confirmation.
- Evidence and reporting output – Structured export of lifecycle evidence and KPIs (ticket records, execution logs, periodic CSV/JSON summaries).

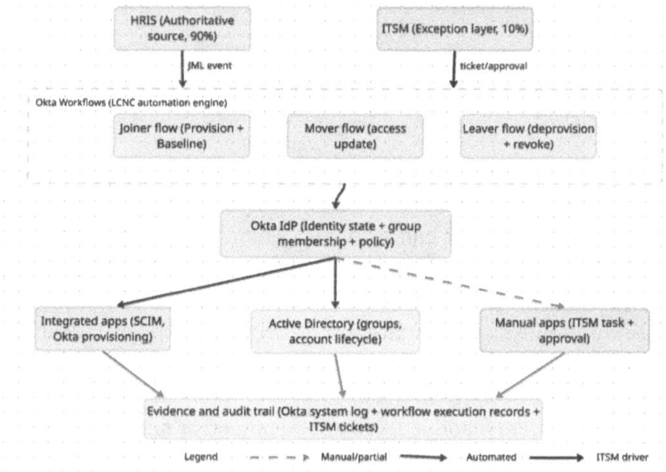

Fig. 2. Target ILM architecture ("to-be")

At a high abstraction level, JML flows follow the same architectural pattern – initiation from HRIS or ITSM, orchestration in Okta Workflows, central identity actions in Okta, routing to integrated or manual target execution, and production of evidence outputs. (Fig. 3).

Three integration patterns put into action the parts of the target architecture. SCIM 2.0 provisioning is used for cloud apps that are the system for cross-domain identity management (SCIM)-native. It allows for managing the lifecycle of accounts automatically through standardized API calls. Active Directory group-based provisioning handles apps that are connected to the directory. Changes to Okta group membership are shown through the AD connection. For applications that are not integrated, ITSM tickets are used to route tasks manually. This ensures that administrator activities are tracked with completion confirmations and audit trails. The Okta Workflows orchestration layer is where all three designs come together. It puts actions in order and makes a unified evidence record.

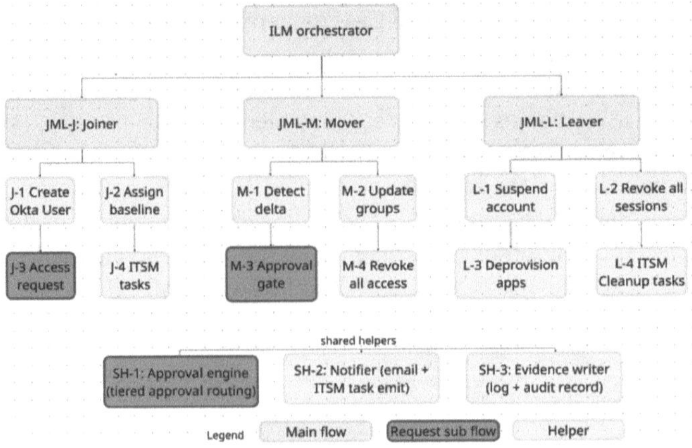

Fig. 3. Event and Control Flow Overview

The target architecture has a configuration layer that can be updated without having to redesign the whole workflow. This configuration layer allows for incremental maturity, which means that the organization can start with a small amount of mapping and slowly move toward more standardized role-based access.

Target architecture has operational controls to ensure that lifecycle execution is not "silent". Operational controls in the target architecture support traceability, exception visibility, and follow-up of incomplete transactions.

In essence, workflow design emphasizes (1) modular decomposition, (2) uniform processing for joiners, movers, and leavers, (3) strong error and exception handling, and (4) a configuration-driven access model that can change from today's mostly individualized access requests to more standardized mappings. The workflow solution is meant to coordinate identity lifecycle actions across the central identity platform and downstream apps in a mixed integration environment. Such an approach ensures that undocumented manual operator knowledge is not used. Instead, it defines states, outputs, and evidence so that lifecycle processing can be done the same way every time and checked.

The design breaks the solution down into main flows and shared sub-flows (reusable components) to make it easier to maintain and add new features. This structure works well for Okta Workflows, where it is possible to put separate flows into folders and use them as helpers.

A. Main flows (orchestrators):

- Joiner Orchestrator – input validation; identity creation/activation; baseline access; app access (central or manual task); evidence package.
- Mover Orchestrator – request/HRIS validation; remove-before-add access update; group/app/attribute changes; manual tasks as needed; evidence package.
- Leaver Orchestrator – immediate/scheduled timing; central disablement first; session/token revocation where supported; access removal (central/downstream); critical-system validation; evidence package.

B. Shared sub flows (building blocks that can be used again):

- Input validation/normalization – required attributes and formats (names, departments, usernames).
- Approval verification – confirms approval completion and approver metadata.
- Access mapping/decision engine - maps requests/attributes to access packages or manual-review paths.
- Group and assignment tasks – add/remove group memberships; assign/unassign applications (central path).
- Manual task generator – structured ITSM tasks with required evidence fields.
- Evidence recorder – standard record of fields, timestamps, and outcome.
- Error handler/retry coordinator – retry/backoff; routes to pending intervention when needed.
- Reporting/export builder – per-transaction and periodic summary formats.

This breakdown allows iterative development. The joiner and leaver can be added first (being the most important), and the mover logic and advanced exception handling can be added later. (Fig. 4).

The artefact is described as a deliverable package that includes its parts, how they are put together, and what makes a complete submission for both academic review and possible practical use. The artefact package delivers five categories of reusable contribution: workflow design specifications for all three JML orchestrators, configuration templates for access mapping and system classification, a step-by-step build guide enabling reconstruction in any compatible Okta tenant, a structured evaluation package including test cases and KPI definitions, and an operational runbook. Full contents are available at GitHub [13].

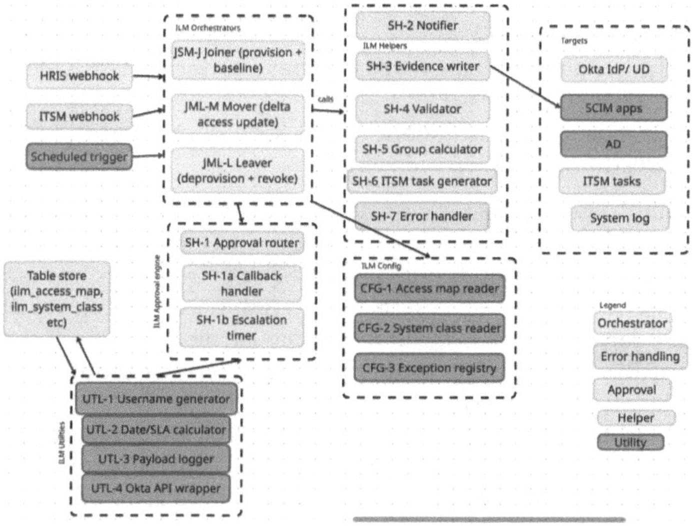

Fig. 4. Artefact Architecture Inside Okta Workflows

4 Implementation and Validation

Implementation and validation were performed using an Okta developer sandbox with synthetic data throughout, since production tenant access was unavailable during the research period; all workflow logic, configuration templates, and integration stubs were designed and tested in this environment. The resulting package is fully portable: flow definitions, configuration templates, and build instructions can be imported into any correctly configured Okta tenant without changing core logic. A three-tier development/test/production deployment model is recommended for production use; tenant prerequisites, API scopes, and Universal Directory configuration are documented in the GitHub prerequisites checklist [13].

The assessment follows the DSR evaluation framework. Consequently, the evaluation methodology integrates structured functional testing against scenarios (SCs), specified test cases, analytical examination of both functional and non-functional requirements, and simulated performance assessment using synthetic identity payloads at indicative volumes. All aforementioned means of evaluation are documented in GitHub [13]. The evaluation is not a field deployment study; it is a controlled result demonstration that the artefact meets its requirements, which is the eligible kind of proof for a DSR artefact at this stage of development [6, 8].

The evaluation is structured around five dimensions covering seven success criteria [13]:

- Functional validation – FR1-FR6 tested against defined test cases (SC1-SC5).
- Performance evaluation – timed scenario execution vs. SLA targets for time-to-provision/revoke (SC7).
- Reliability and failure mode evaluation – error handling, retry, and idempotency under simulated failures (SC6, NFR3).
- Security and governance evaluation – controls reviewed against NFR1, NFR2, NFR5-NFR7 (SC3, SC4, SC6).
- Stakeholder validation – practitioner feedback on design and results against the success criteria (SC6, overall usefulness).

The synthetic dataset used has 20 test identities for the following types of employees and situations: standard employee hires (joiner), contractor onboarding (joiner exception), department transfers (mover), title-only changes (mover, no delta expected), standard resignations (leaver), immediate terminations (leaver), and re-hires of accounts that were previously deprovisioned. In the development tier, the HTTP mock connector was used to copy HRIS webhook payloads. In the free-tier ServiceNow developer instance, ITSM interactions were simulated.

The requirements traceability matrix was established, which connects each FR and NFR to the test cases that show it was met, and the verdict. Full test case specifications and evaluation transcripts, alongside FRs and NFRs are available in the project repository in GitHub [13]. For instance, FR3.2 (central disablement on leaver execution) was verified by test case TC-LV-01, confirming disablement within the SLA window shown in Table 3. All requirements were satisfied except for one partial verdict for FR3.5 regarding license reclamation that depended on limitations of the sandbox environment.

Workflow execution history timestamps were used in the Okta developer console to measure performance across the main happy-path scenarios. The elapsed time between the webhook receipt event and the key identity action that made up the SLA endpoint was recorded as the relevant KPI for each scenario.

Table 3 shows that the automated path eliminates as-is variability: suspension happens during the flow's execution time, no matter what time of day or IT team availability. There were no rate-limiting events during the performance test runs, confirming that NFR4.2 (no execution before approval) is met at the expected operational scale. Per-scenario execution notes, sandbox variance analysis, and rate limit calculations are available at GitHub [13].

The reliability evaluation confirmed that none of the tested failure modes cause silent corruption of the identity state. Across four simulated failure scenarios – validation failure, API retry exhaustion, duplicate webhook delivery, and partial mover completion – the intervention queue surfaced all failures, all partial completions were recoverable without duplication, and the security-critical suspension action in the leaver flow completed independently of downstream API availability. Full reliability test case specifications and scenario transcripts are available at GitHub [13].

In addition to the structured technical evaluation, two practitioners with direct experience in enterprise IAM and identity automation were shown the artefact design, test results, and evidence outputs. The first practitioner is a senior IAM architect. The second practitioner is an IT specialist at a mid-sized tech company with experience in access governance processes based on ITSM. Both practitioners had previously contributed to requirements elicitation, which is acknowledged as a potential source of confirmation bias.

Table 3. Performance evaluation results by scenario

Scenario	SLA endpoint	Min	Max	Mean	SLA target	Result
Joiner - HRIS trigger, auto path	Account active + baseline groups assigned	9 s	41 s	18 s	15 min	Pass
Joiner - with approval (manager only)	Account active + all access assigned	4 min	62 min	-	Approval dependant	N/A
Joiner with a future date (pre provisioning)	Account activated on start date ± 5 min	-	-	On time (10/10)	Start date ± 5 min	Pass
Mover - HRIS trigger, non-empty delta, auto	All groups updated	11 s	38 s	22s	30 min	Pass
Mover - title only, no delta	Profile updated + closed	6 s	14 s	9 s	30 min	Pass

(*continued*)

Table 3. (*continued*)

Scenario	SLA endpoint	Min	Max	Mean	SLA target	Result
Leaver - same day, central suspension	Account suspended	4 s	12 s	7 s	5 min	Pass
Leaver - same day, full deprovisioning	All groups removed and deprovisioned	18 s	54 s	31 s	60 min	Pass
Leaver - future date, scheduled	Execution on end date ± 5 min	-	-	On time (10/10)	End date ± 5 min	Pass
Error - validation failure	Error record written, notification sent	3 s	8 s	5 s	2 min	Pass
Error - API retry, intervention	Intervention queue populated	34 s	71 s	48 s	5 min	Pass

Both practitioners agreed that the JML coverage solves the most common operational problems and that the functional scope was right for the environment described. The non-blocking asynchronous approval pattern (SH-1) was identified as a direct solution to the synchronous bottleneck failure mode common in approval-gated provisioning systems. The IAM architect confirmed that the ilm_tx_log and ilm_evidence_archive fields would likely meet the requirements of a typical IAM audit request and suggested adding full group membership state to leaver evidence records as a future improvement, recorded as a candidate for v1.1.0. Both practitioners independently confirmed that the artefact is accessible to IAM practitioners with system administration experience who are not software developers, directly supporting the argument for the practical utility of LCNC tooling in this domain. Both also independently identified the absence of a genuine SCIM integration test as the principal remaining limitation. Full structured feedback per success criterion from both practitioners is available at GitHub [13].

There are four limitations that, to some extent, hinder the drawing of conclusions from this evaluation. First, the sandbox environment meant there was no end-to-end observation of a live SCIM provisioning cycle. Group membership changes were confirmed as having reached the Okta SCIM engine, but downstream effects on target applications were not directly observable. The problem is with the evidence, not the design. Second, multi-tenant and high-concurrency behavior was not tested. The orchestrators are designed so that transactions do not share mutable state, making concurrent execution safe by design, but this was not validated under concurrent load. Third, practitioner validation was limited to two reviewers, both of whom contributed to requirements elicitation, introducing potential confirmation bias. A larger sample, including IAM governance and internal audit professionals, would provide stronger evidence of practical utility. Fourth, not every combination of FR5.1–4 exception types was tested. The break-glass and VIP scenarios were tested separately; their interaction with simultaneous mover or leaver events was not specifically covered. Before production deployment, each limitation maps to required evidence: a live SCIM pilot for the first, concurrency load testing for the second, an independent practitioner panel for the third, and combined exception-scenario testing for the fourth.

5 Conclusions

The solution proposed in this paper is a governance-by-design ILM orchestration model realized as an LCNC workflow artefact, built on the five design principles introduced in Sect. 2, each mapping directly to an identified literature gap. The proposed solution answers the main research question "How can we design and test an LCNC solution based on Okta Workflows to make Identity Lifecycle Management more consistent, easier to audit, and more effective in a mixed enterprise IAM environment?".

The three research sub-questions are addressed further. The as-is analysis identified mixed-trigger initiation and manual execution across non-integrated systems as the primary operational and governance problems. The conceptual solution and target architecture define the design rules and workflow structures that address these. The evaluation demonstrates that the artefact meets the specified requirements and performs within defined SLA targets.

The complete DSR cycle shows that this kind of solution is possible, can be put into action by non-programmers, and can be proven to work against a set of functional and non-functional requirements.

The as-is analysis of the case organization's JML processes clearly showed the issues where the proposed solution is useful. These issues are not exclusive to the case organization; they are indicative of the partially automated IAM landscape present among most mid-market and smaller enterprises.

Each detected problem maps to a specific architectural decision: webhook-driven initiation removes notification latency, group-mediated access constrains execution to reversible operations, remove-before-add sequencing prevents privilege creep, ITSM task generation extends governance to non-integrated systems, and the dual-log design (ilm_tx_log cross-referenced with the Okta System Log by transaction ID) yields unified, verifiable evidence for every lifecycle event.

These design choices meet their objectives: the leaver path suspends accounts in an average of 7 s (versus previously same-day to five days), and the joiner path reaches baseline access in 18 s (Table 3). Thirty-four of thirty-five requirements were passed; reliability testing showed no silent state corruption across five failure scenarios.

Three categories of contribution follow from this work. The reference architecture for LCNC-based ILM in mixed integration environments is the main contribution. The implementable artefact package, which includes flow specifications, configuration templates, a build guide, and an operational runbook, is the practical contribution. The evaluation framework is a methodological contribution that future work in this area can use and build on.

However, the evaluation took place in a sandbox environment, and the behavior of production deployment, especially when there are many activities performed at the same time and SCIM integrations are live, must be tested in a real business setting. The artefact possesses platform-agnostic features (config-driven mapping, dual-log evidence model, remove-before-add sequencing) and Okta-specific features (webhook connectors, Workflow cards), and, because of the latter, is not directly transferable to other platforms.

Future work will extend practitioner validation to an independent panel, including IAM governance and audit roles. For a mid-sized organization, LCNC tooling resides between an informal manual process and a full IGA platform and can be used as a path, not a destination. This paper offers reusable artefacts for this use case.

References

1. Bock, A.C., Frank, U.: Low-Code Platform. Bus. Inf. Syst. Eng. **63**(6), 733–740 (2021). https://doi.org/10.1007/s12599-021-00726-8
2. Luo, Y., Liang, P., Wang, C., Shahin, M., Zhan, J.: Characteristics and challenges of low-code development: the practitioners' perspective. In: Proceedings of the ACM/IEEE International Symposium on Empirical Software Engineering and Measurement (ESEM 2021), pp. 1–11. ACM, New York (2021). https://doi.org/10.1145/3475716.3475782
3. Hunt, P. (ed.), Grizzle, K., Ansari, M., Wahlstroem, E., Mortimore, C.: System for Cross-domain Identity Management: Protocol. RFC 7644. RFC Editor (2015). https://doi.org/10.17487/RFC7644
4. Johnson, A., Dempsey, K., Ross, R., Gupta, S., Bailey, D.: Guide for Security-Focused Configuration Management of Information Systems. NIST Special Publication 800–128. National Institute of Standards and Technology, Gaithersburg, MD (2011). https://doi.org/10.6028/NIST.SP.800-128
5. Joint Task Force: Security and Privacy Controls for Information Systems and Organizations. NIST Special Publication 800–53, Revision 5. National Institute of Standards and Technology, Gaithersburg, MD (2020). https://doi.org/10.6028/NIST.SP.800-53r5
6. van der Aalst, W.M.P., ter Hofstede, A.H.M., Kiepuszewski, B., Barros, A.P.: Workflow Patterns. Distributed and Parallel Databases 14, 5–51 (2003). https://doi.org/10.1023/A:1022883727209
7. Avizienis, A., Laprie, J.-C., Randell, B., Landwehr, C.: Basic concepts and taxonomy of dependable and secure computing. IEEE Trans. Dependable Secur. Comput. **1**(1), 11–33 (2004). https://doi.org/10.1109/TDSC.2004.2
8. Hevner, A.R., March, S.T., Park, J., Ram, S.: Design science in information systems research. MIS Q. **28**(1), 75–106 (2004). https://doi.org/10.2307/25148625
9. Gregor, S., Hevner, A.R.: Positioning and presenting design science research for maximum impact. MIS Q. **37**(2), 337–355 (2013). https://doi.org/10.25300/MISQ/2013/37.2.01
10. Baumer, T., Kern, S., Fuchs, L., Pernul, G.: Identity and access management metrics: a systematic review. ACM Comput. Surv. **58**(8), 213, 1–37 (2026). https://doi.org/10.1145/3788858
11. Hummer, M., Groll, S., Kunz, M., Fuchs, L., Pernul, G.: Measuring identity and access management performance – an expert survey on possible performance indicators. In: Proceedings of the 4th International Conference on Information Systems Security and Privacy (ICISSP 2018), pp. 233–240. SciTePress, Setúbal (2018).: https://doi.org/10.5220/0006557702330240
12. Garcia-Molina, H., Salem, K.: Sagas. In: Proceedings of the 1987 ACM SIGMOD International Conference on Management of Data, pp. 249–259. ACM, New York (1987).: https://doi.org/10.1145/38713.38742
13. Čapkovska, E.D.: IAM Research Outcomes. GitHub repository (2026), https://github.com/capkovska/thesisIAM/, Accessed 10 Jul 2026

AI-supported Data and Knowledge Management

Ontology-Guided Hybrid Intelligence for Diagnosing Underspecification in Reporting Standards

Ivars Blums[1(✉)] and Hans Weigand[2]

[1] SIA ODO, Riga, Latvia
ivars@odo.lv
[2] Tilburg University, Tilburg, The Netherlands
h.weigand@uvt.nl

Abstract. Business reporting standards such as International Financial Reporting Standards (IFRS) are high-impact business-rule artifacts whose clauses often compress evidence, institutional structure, recognition, measurement, and presentation into single surface labels. This creates underspecification that is difficult for both human readers and LLMs to diagnose consistently. We address this problem with OntoLER, a UFO/UFO-L/UFO-B-grounded layered relator architecture that separates L0 grounding facts, L1 Legal-Economic Relators, correlativity and reciprocity, L2 business-role overlays, L3 recognition overlays, L4 measurement overlays, and L5 representation surfaces. From this architecture, we derive constraint checkpoints T0–T7 and operationalize them in a staged analyst–LLM workflow with four roles: Epistemic Scoper, Ontologist, Diagnostician, and Repair Architect. These roles constrain LLM support for lexical screening and candidate reconstruction within a controlled hybrid-intelligence process with explicit re-entry rules and an audit trail. We illustrate the method on IFRS 16 sale-and-leaseback, and report bounded runs over selected full-IFRS fragments and a compact IFRS for SMEs stress test. The contribution is a traceable hybrid-intelligence architecture for diagnosing and guiding the repair of underspecification in complex business standards through conceptual modeling, semantic constraints, and controlled LLM assistance.

Keywords: Hybrid Intelligence · UFO-L · UFO-B · IFRS · COFRIS · OntoLER

1 Introduction

Reporting standards often compress several distinct commitments into one surface label. A single clause may mix grounding conditions, legal-economic relator structure, business-role classification, recognition under uncertainty, measurement treatment, and representation in a stated unit-of-account (UoA) context. As a result, clauses become harder to interpret consistently, compare across standards and cases, and test, automate, or repair. This layered compression is difficult to diagnose reliably by either human readers or large language models (LLMs) alone. A lease provides a concrete illustration: the

E. Laurenzi et al. (Eds.): BIR 2026, LNBIP 601, pp. 241–258, 2027.
https://doi.org/10.1007/978-3-032-38498-0_16

same reported label may refer at once to the leased building, the rental contract between the parties, the resulting right-of-use relation, its balance-sheet classification, and its later measurement. International Financial Reporting Standard (IFRS) 16 Leases [13] provides a further standard-level illustration. Its ongoing Post-Implementation Review (PIR) and related disclosure evidence suggest that some difficulties are structural, not merely implementation-related: an AI-assisted review of 2024 lease disclosures by 753 large global entities found sparse, largely boilerplate judgments and widespread collapsing of legally distinct lease changes into undifferentiated remeasurement language [15]. The AI used in the review could classify such disclosures, but not reconstruct the missing legal-economic relator, trigger, and phase structure.

We address this problem through an ontology-guided Hybrid Intelligence (HI) approach. Its semantic core is OntoLER, a UFO/UFO-L/UFO-B-grounded layered relator architecture that separates (L0) grounding facts and evidence, (L1) Legal-Economic Relators (LERs), Institutional Acts, correlativity and reciprocity, (L2) business-role and reporting-effect overlays, (L3) recognition under uncertainty overlays, (L4) measurement overlays, and (L5) representation surfaces. OntoLER serves here as an explicit unfolder and constraint set: it reconstructs what a reporting clause presupposes before classification, recognition, measurement, or representation. From this architecture, and from the ontological distinctions it makes explicit, we derive eight diagnostic checkpoints, T0–T7, that localize characteristic underspecification failures and guide minimal repairs. The checkpoint family is illustrated through IFRS clause examples for each constraint. IFRS 16 provides the motivating context, while sale-and-leaseback underspecification serves as the fuller focal analysis.

Operationally, OntoLER is used in a staged analyst–LLM workflow. LLMs support lexical screening, bounded reconstruction, and candidate LER typing, while the ontology, checkpoints, and re-entry rules govern diagnosis. The paper treats financial reporting as a demanding class of business standards requiring human expertise, conceptual models, and LLMs to cooperate under explicit semantic constraints.

Methodologically, the paper is framed as Design Science Research. The problem is layered underspecification in high-impact reporting standards. The artifact is the OntoLER diagnostic method: the UFO-grounded L0–L5 architecture, the T0–T7 checkpoints, and the staged analyst–LLM workflow. The artifact is demonstrated on IFRS 16 sale-and-leaseback and assessed through bounded runs over selected full-IFRS fragments and a compact IFRS for SMEs stress test. The evaluation focuses on whether the artifact produces traceable reconstructions, localizable diagnoses, and reviewable repair anchors over bounded reporting-standard artifacts.

This paper makes four contributions. First, it introduces OntoLER, a UFO/UFO-L/UFO-B-grounded L0–L5 ontology for reconstructing reporting-standard clauses across grounding facts, legal-economic relators, business-role overlays, recognition, measurement, and representation.

Second, it defines T0–T7 checkpoints that use the ontology as a partial oracle for analyst–LLM reconstruction, localizing underspecification across those layers.

Third, it provides reconstruction anchors and repair templates for standard-setters, implementers, auditors, and taxonomy designers.

Fourth, it contributes reviewable artifacts—worked cases, checkpoint tables, prompt protocols, run cards, and bounded LLM runs—showing how hybrid intelligence can be constrained and audited in this setting.

2 Foundations

Layered View. Financial reports provide information about the reporting entity's economic resources, obligations, and changes in them [2]. IFRS and related frameworks specify how transactions and other events affect the entity's rights and obligations, and how the resulting structures are classified, recognized, measured, and disclosed. OntoLER starts from this reporting task but asks what institutional and evidential structure must already be in place for such reporting to be coherent.

The IFRS Conceptual Framework (CF) [2] presupposes distinctions between the grounding basis of a reported item, its legal-economic structure, its business role, its recognition conditions, its measurement treatment, and its representation surface. OntoLER makes these distinctions explicit because institutional specifications cannot be adequately reconstructed when they are collapsed into a single surface label.

Following Mattessich's Onion Model of Reality [1], higher institutional layers depend on lower physical layers while exhibiting normative properties irreducible to them. Rights, obligations, permissions, and powers depend on grounding facts—agents, documents, and events—but are not identical to them. A lease agreement and the parties' existence may ground a lease reciprocity and later recognition of a right-of-use asset, but they do not by themselves specify the full LER structure, holder-change path, phase structure, measurement treatment, or disclosure representation.

A consequence of this layered view is that valuation is methodological rather than ontological [1]. The existence of a legal-economic relation does not depend on whether its expected value is positive, probable, or currently measurable. OntoLER therefore treats existence, recognition, measurement, and representation as distinct dimensions. Their conflation produces inter-layer failures when later overlays overwrite earlier structure, and intra-layer failures when an L1 legal-economic position is under-typed, asymmetrical, or internally inconsistent.

Ontological Grounding. OntoLER is grounded in the Unified Foundational Ontology (UFO) [3, 5]. UFO provides the distinctions needed to model endurants, roles, relators, events, and situations, and thus supports the separation between what persists and what happens to it. UFO's account of events and situations [6] is especially relevant because reporting standards concern not only enduring structures but also the events through which such structures are created, changed, or terminated.

OntoLER extends this basis through the Legal Core Ontology, UFO-L [4]. UFO-L provides the formal infrastructure for typing legal agents, legal positions, and legal relators, together with the structural relations needed to avoid orphaned, mistyped, or opposed positions. A legal position is not a monadic property of an isolated subject. In personam performance positions are reconstructed within relators mediated by the Entity and an Other Party; in rem object positions are object-grounded and hold with respect to Others. Hohfeld–Alexy correlativity is therefore explicit: claim-right and duty, permission and no-right, power and subjection, and immunity and disability are distinct positions rather than interchangeable senses of "right." In reporting practice, economic resources and obligations often bundle several such positions together. In OntoLER, the Legal Relator is specialized for economic context and is therefore termed a Legal-Economic Relator (LER).

OntoLER's broader orientation also has roots in Institutional Economics. Following Commons [7], it treats reciprocity broadly, not as market exchange only: standards may presuppose bargaining (economic exchange), managerial, or rationing relations. This is distinct from Hohfeldian correlativity inside a single LER. Correlativity concerns paired legal positions, such as claim–duty or power–subjection; reciprocity couples LERs, performances, compliance acts, allocations, or authority-governed positions. The reciprocity and exchange principles are active in REA [8], COEX [9], COFRIS [10], and OntoREA [11]; comparison work [12] documents how these ontologies differ in their treatment of rights as resources and lifecycle states. OntoLER extends this baseline by adding an explicit legal-relational layer and a cross-layer diagnostic architecture, making orphaned positions, modal incompatibilities, and trigger vacuums diagnosable rather than implicit.

Use of Hybrid Intelligence. For ontology-based diagnosis of standard documents, we adopt a Hybrid Intelligence approach. HI combines human and machine intelligence so that the combined system achieves outcomes neither side reliably produces alone [17]. The complementarity is specific: LLMs support lexical screening, bounded reconstruction, and candidate LER typing, but are less reliable at satisfying explicit constraints across layers, parties, reciprocity, triggers, and phases. The ontology and checkpoints are therefore primary; the LLM operates under their constraints. Recent work on IFRS IAS 37 problems [18], long-document inconsistency detection [19], hybrid AI systems for planning [20], and ontology-guided LLM assistance for conceptual modeling [21, 22] is close to our concern, but addresses different targets—schema engineering, document-level contradiction, or operational planning—rather than the layered structural compression of institutional standards.

3 OntoLER Architecture and IFRS Reconstruction

OntoLER is an ontology of institutional phenomena relevant to financial reporting. Its layered organization acts as an unfolder: it separates institutional and methodological distinctions that standards often collapse into a single reporting label. Formalized in OntoUML [5], its classes, stereotypes, examples, and constraints provide the controlled vocabulary for the reconstruction workflow. By requiring the LLM to map text to this schema, OntoLER constrains admissible reconstructions and reduces unconstrained inference. Figure 1, Fig. 2, Table 1, and Table 2 provide the semantic guardrails for the staged workflow in Sect. 4.

L0–L5 Stratification. Figure 1 distributes reporting reconstruction across one grounding layer and five institutional-reporting layers.

L0 records physical events, objects, agents, documents, and evidence, such as a leased building, a signed rental agreement, or a payment event.

L1 reconstructs the institutional core: Institutional Acts create, modify, or terminate Legal-Economic Relators (LERs), Reciprocity Relators, and Triggering Situations. This is the basis for T3: a reported lifecycle change should be reconstructable as the effect of an Institutional Act under an explicit Triggering Situation, not as an unexplained label change.

L2 attaches IFRS-facing Business Role overlays to LERs and Institutional Acts, including reporting-effect roles such as Income Statement Element and Balance Sheet Element. L3 adds Recognition Assessments, determining whether and how the reconstructed LER or Institutional Act enters reporting relevance.

L4 adds Measurement Assessments, attaching monetary Carrying Amounts through a Measurement Basis and Measurement Unit of Account.

L5 adds Representation surfaces: disclosures, presentation labels, taxonomy-facing anchors, and other reporting outputs that select, aggregate, or expose lower-layer reconstructions. Recognition, measurement, and representation Units of Account are modeled as selection situations over a bounded reporting surface. T7 tests whether this surface preserves the distinctions required by earlier checkpoints.

UoA choices do not replace prior Object/Event Specification or needed LER or Institutional Act delimitation, such as retained/transferred rights, fulfilled/unfulfilled portions, or lifecycle phase. This dependence order prevents later overlays from overwriting the legal-economic reality they presuppose.

L1 Institutional Core. Figure 2 zooms into OntoLER's L1 core. Its central construct is the simple or bundled Legal-Economic Relator (LER): a UFO-L Legal Relator specialized for economic contexts. The figure is not merely a taxonomy of labels; it encodes how legal positions, object-side positions, reciprocity, lifecycle phases, triggering situations, and institutional acts hang together. A lease provides the running example: object-side positions over the leased building, party-to-party use and payment obligations, their reciprocal coupling, and the acts that institute, manifest, reclassify, or fulfill them make the main L1 distinctions visible.

Within the LER, the first partition is by Hohfeld–Alexy legal-position subtype. An Entity may hold Rights—Claim-Right, Permission, Power, or Immunity—and Obligations correlative to the Rights of the Other Party: Duty, No-Right, Subjection, or Disability. In a lease, the lessor's right to receive payment is correlative to the lessee's duty to pay. T1 constrains the correct typing and compatibility of these positions.

A second distinction separates Performance LERs from Object LERs. Performance LERs are other-party-grounded: they concern relations between the Entity and a determinate Other Party, such as the obligation to pay rent and the corresponding right to receive payment. Object LERs are object-grounded: in the lease example, they concern the object-side position over the building, while holder-specific Holding LERs against them may change through transfer, grant, receipt, installation, delivery, or termination.

The Reciprocity Relator is composed of Performance LER components. In the lease example, one component concerns provision or grant of use, and the other concerns payment. The Object LER over the building is not itself a component of the Reciprocity Relator; it is the object-side position that a Performance LER may require, grant, or realize through a Holder Change. T2 therefore uses party-role cues to distinguish ordinary economic exchange, exchanges of objectified LERs, and cases that should instead be routed to managerial, rationing, or non-reciprocal analysis, as illustrated in Table 1. Further partitions distinguish Legal from Constructive LERs and Validated from Hypothetical LERs. Legal LERs arise through explicit legal or contractual form; Constructive LERs arise through conduct, reliance, established practice, statutory operation, or similar bases sufficient within the bounded context. Hypothetical LERs are provisional candidate LERs or proxies used before the evidence base is sufficient to validate them. Performance LERs are also partitioned by lifecycle phase: Executory, Conditional, Unconditional, and Fulfilled. Phase progression is competence-governed: fulfillment requires power and immunity (the competence for acceptation [12]) to enable contract-asset or receivable recognition [23]; the general necessity of competence-level positions for violable, consequential norms has since been established independently [24].

Object LERs have a two-level structure. An Object LER expresses a persistent in-rem position over an Underlying Object; a holder-specific, time-bracketed Holding LER bears the current holding position over that Object LER. A Holder Change terminates the prior Holding LER and instantiates a new one against the unchanged Object LER. The right-of-use case in Sect. 5 is reconstructed against this structure: the lessor's Holding LER over the leased asset persists, while a lessee Holding LER is created at lease commencement and terminates at lease end.

Figure 2 refines Institutional Act into three L1 act families used by the diagnostic core. Holder Changes create, terminate, or modify Holding LERs against an Object LER and may manifest Holder Change LERs within a Performance LER. Phase Changes move Performance LERs through Executory, Conditional, Unconditional, and Fulfilled phases when a Triggering Situation holds. Service Performances realize Performance

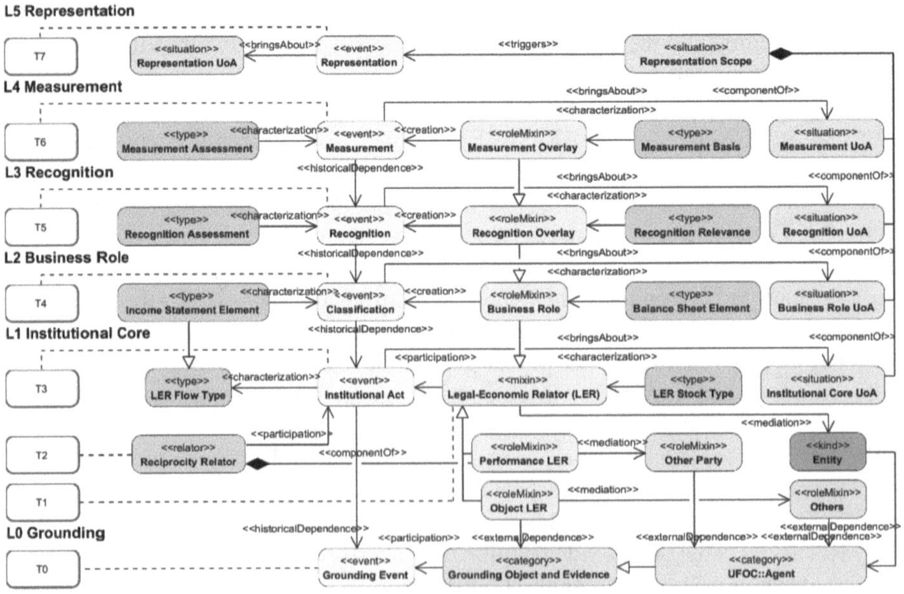

Fig. 1. Layered OntoLER architecture. Layer events produce scoped situations from institutional core to representation. L5 Representation depends on a Representation Scope selecting lower-layer Units of Account (UoAs). T0–T7 mark the reconstruction checkpoints.

LERs where no object-holder change is the primary manifestation path. Contract signing or commencement may institute the Reciprocity Relator and its Performance LER components; later Holder Change or Service Performance events may bring about Triggering Situations, which then trigger Phase Changes. T3 constrains any phase change whose constitutive trigger and institutional effect cannot be reconstructed.

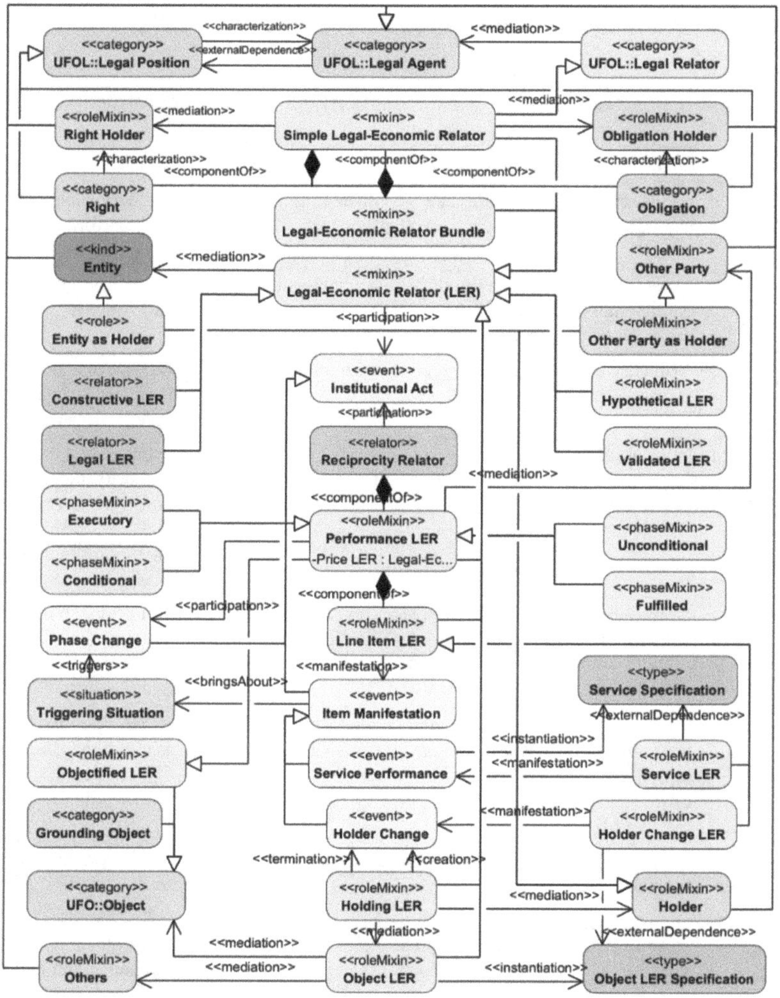

Fig. 2. Core OntoLER structure, lifecycle phases, reciprocity, and trigger discipline

T2 Reciprocity Typology. T2 does not ask merely whether reciprocity exists. It asks what kind of reciprocity, if any, is presupposed by the standard text. Party roles are useful routing cues because the same surface word—asset, liability, consideration, obligation, right, or transfer—can refer to different lower-layer structures. A customer contract, a financial instrument, a share-based payment, a tax levy, a government grant, a business combination, and a guarantee do not instantiate the same reciprocity pattern. Table 1 summarizes the cues used to route the reconstruction before applying the remaining checkpoints.

T0–T7 Checkpoints. Table 2 condenses OntoLER's main diagnostic checks for Construct Overload and Construct Deficit.

T0–T3 target the foundational reconstruction path: grounding, LER integrity, reciprocity, and trigger/lifecycle discipline.

Table 1. Selected party-role and reciprocity cues for T2 reconstruction.

Party Role	Object/Service	Leg Pattern	T2 Cue
Customer / supplier	goods, services, use rights	performance ↔ consideration	ordinary exchange; unfold both performance and price legs
Owner / investor / member	share, bond, claim, equity instrument	objectified LER ↔ consideration	exchanged object is itself a LER bundle
Lender / borrower / holder	cash claim, debt instrument	claim ↔ repayment or contingent duty	reconstruct correlative financial asset/liability before measurement
Employee / agent / service provider	labor, service, agency act, equity-linked entitlement	service/act ↔ wage, fee, benefit, or equity-linked right	exchange pattern; separate authority, deferred benefit, constructive obligation, and vesting/tax-withholding overlays
Government as grantor	grant, subsidy, public assistance	resource transfer subject to eligibility/compliance conditions	conditional public assistance; not customer-contract exchange
Tax authority	taxable profit, tax base, temporary difference, tax loss/credit	statutory imposition → burden; statutory entitlement → recovery	fiscal rationing; current tax is claim/duty, deferred tax is a construct
Buyer / supplier / finance provider	trade payable, financing facility	trade duty + financing intermediation	triadic structure; separate trade reciprocity from financing transformation
Parent / subsidiary / investee	control, group interest, reporting boundary	control acquisition/loss → reporting-boundary change	governance relation; not exchange, but may include consideration
Joint-control parties	shared activity, joint asset/entity	shared power + contributions, unanimous consent	distinguish joint control from mere participation or co-ownership
Acquirer / former owners / acquiree	business or control bundle	business/control bundle ↔ consideration	acquisition reciprocity; residual goodwill must not replace L1 reconstruction

(continued)

Table 1. (*continued*)

Party Role	Object/Service	Leg Pattern	T2 Cue
Guarantor / holder / debtor	financial guarantee	conditional duty triggered by debtor default	three-party LER; formal non-reciprocity may coexist with group-level substance
Public authority / concession operator	infrastructure right, concession asset/liability	grant of operating right ↔ build/operate/transfer obligation	public-infrastructure concession; distinct from an ordinary grant (no operating right transferred) and from ordinary exchange
Principal / agent (decision-maker)	delegated decision-making authority	power exercised for self ↔ power exercised for another	control-typing cue; an agent's own power does not count toward its own control assessment
Investor / associate (significant influence)	equity interest, board representation, policy participation	participation in policy decisions ↔ no control	weaker than Parent/subsidiary/investee; route by degree of power, not ownership percentage alone

T4–T6 evaluate later methodological overlays: Business Role attachment, Recognition Assessment, and Measurement Assessment, including whether the measured or impaired unit coincides with the recognized LER. T7 tests whether the reporting surface can express distinctions required by earlier checkpoints.

The checkpoints preserve methodological flexibility. Unit-of-Account choices, aggregation, monadic presentation, and residual valuation are not failures unless they overwrite or replace a required LER, Institutional Act, Triggering Situation, correlative structure, reciprocity component, or specification/delimitation criterion. L0, L1, and T0–T7 are domain-neutral; the L2–L5 overlays are IFRS-facing. Section 4 operationalizes this architecture as a staged analyst–LLM diagnostic and repair procedure.

Table 2. T0–T7 underspecification taxonomy and repair templates with example cases.

T	What is tested	Surface / failure	Minimal repair
T0 Substrate	Grounding activity, event, agent, object, and evidence basis are recoverable	IAS 37 levy trigger / disclosure: proxy timing, activity, or disclosure wording obscures the L0 grounding basis	State the grounding activity or event, parties, object, and evidence basis

(*continued*)

Table 2. (*continued*)

T	What is tested	Surface / failure	Minimal repair
T1 LER integrity	LER bearer, parties, powers, permissions, subjections, and immunities are typed, correlative, and compatible	IFRS 15 contract asset / receivable: a conditional right risks treatment as an unconditional claim-right / receivable	Distinguish the conditional right, unconditional claim-right, and route to unconditionality
T2 Reciprocity	Where reciprocity is presupposed, coupled Performance LER components are reconstructed rather than treated as a monadic item	IFRS 15 contract asset / liability / receivable: contract asset or liability risks monadic treatment; performance / consideration reciprocity is not unfolded	Reconstruct performance / consideration reciprocity before classifying the result as contract asset, liability, or receivable
T3 Lifecycle	Institutional Acts and lifecycle phase changes are tied to explicit Triggering Situations and institutional effects	IAS 37 levy constitutive activity: phase change or institution is stated through proxy wording without an explicit Triggering Situation and effect	State the Triggering Situation, Institutional Act, and resulting phase or institutional effect
T4 Role overlay	L2 roles depend on an identified L1 LER, LER Change Classification, or Institutional Act; they do not substitute for L1 typing	IFRS for SMEs §19 goodwill: goodwill residual may absorb unidentified L1 constructive content	Decompose the acquired bundle before assigning residual role or amount
T5 Recognition overlay	Recognition overlays an identified LER, LER change, or L2 role; timing, probability, or prudence does not constitute L1 existence	IFRS for SMEs §29 deferred tax: a deferred-tax item presents a current reporting item supported by probability and temporary-difference mechanics	Type as Hypothetical LER where appropriate; keep probability and recognition as L3 overlays

(*continued*)

Table 2. (*continued*)

T	What is tested	Surface / failure	Minimal repair
T6 Measurement overlay	L4 amount attachment follows LER / change identification and any required specification or delimitation criterion	IFRS 16 §100(a): leaseback gain or loss is attached before retained / transferred LER delimitation is explicit	State Holder Change Specification, Object LER Specification, and retained / transferred delimitation before attaching amount
T7 Representation	The reporting or taxonomy surface preserves reconstruction anchors needed to recover the standard's recognition, measurement, presentation, or disclosure logic	IFRS 16: lease taxonomy: the surface may not express the sale-and-leaseback retained / transferred portion distinction where it is required for reconstruction	Add or preserve sale-and-leaseback package / portion anchors in disclosure, taxonomy, documentation, or reconstruction tables; coarseness alone is not a failure

4 OntoLER Diagnostic and Repair Procedure

OntoLER is operated as a role-based HI procedure over a bounded standard artifact—a clause, worked example, disclosure requirement, or compact standard fragment—rather than over a whole standard at once. Four analytical episodes (Fig. 3) divide the work: Epistemic Scoper, Ontologist, Diagnostician, and Repair Architect. Their methodological purpose is to prevent evidence search, ontological reconstruction, diagnosis, and repair design from collapsing into a single opaque LLM answer.

In the reported runs, the LLM supported lexical screening, candidate boundary suggestions, provisional prose drafts, draft L0–L5 reconstructions, and preliminary checkpoint scorecards. The human analyst retained responsibility for source selection, scoping correction, acceptance or revision of typing, adjudication of ambiguity, final diagnosis, and repair anchoring. The workflow accepts no typing from labels alone: a candidate reconstruction is admissible only when the relevant commitment is present in the typed structure—relator, party, correlative position, reciprocity leg, triggering situation, manifestation path, phase, or representation scope.

The procedure has four episodes. The Epistemic Scoper fixes the bounded source artifact, institutional frame, reporting frame, admitted evidence, and aggregation risks; if the reconstruction object is too broad, the run returns to scoping before typing begins.

The Ontologist reconstructs the artifact in the dependence order fixed by OntoLER: L0 grounding; L1 LERs, correlatives, reciprocity legs, triggering situations, institutional acts, and effects; then L2 business-role, L3 recognition, L4 measurement, and L5 representation overlays.

The Diagnostician applies T0–T7 and records whether the defect is structural, overlay-related, or representational. The Repair Architect formulates the minimal useful repair as a reconstruction anchor for the relevant reader population.

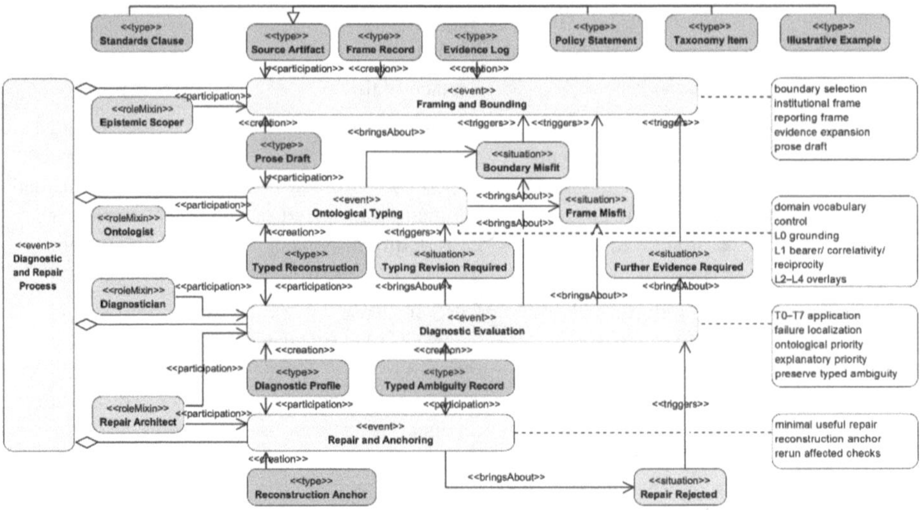

Fig. 3. OntoUML diagram of the staged Diagnostic and Repair Procedure

The checkpoints function as a partial oracle. Some failures are structurally checkable once the evidence and reconstruction are fixed: a reported reciprocal item without a second leg, a lifecycle change without a triggering situation, a measurement attached before the measured position is delimited, or a representation surface that loses anchors needed to recover lower-layer structure. Other outcomes remain expert-judgment cases and are recorded as such. The reported runs are therefore not a statistical validation of LLM performance, but evidence that the OntoLER-guided procedure yields traceable reconstructions, explicit checkpoint profiles, and reviewable repairs.

The evidence base used in Sect. 5 has two levels. First, analyst-validated parallel LLM runs were conducted on bounded IFRS fragments from PIR and revision contexts, including leases and leaseback, revenue, provisions and levies, financial instruments, and business-combination examples. Second, the 35 sections of IFRS for SMEs [16] served as a compact whole-corpus stress test, because that Standard covers most financial-reporting architecture in one manageable corpus. The runs are not claimed as a statistical validation of LLM performance. They are used to assess whether the OntoLER-guided procedure yields traceable reconstructions, explicit checkpoint failures, and reviewable repair suggestions. Recurring diagnostic patterns included reciprocity deficit, internal boundary split, residual-LER compression, dependence-order inversion, measurement-before-extent attachment, and representation-surface weakness. The OCL-style invariants, condensed run card, episode prompts, and IFRS-for-SMEs synthesis are available in the supplementary materials at odo.lv/cofris.

5 IFRS 16 Sale-and-Leaseback Diagnostic Run

Section 5 applies the procedure specified in Sect. 4 to IFRS 16 sale-and-leaseback accounting. The purpose is not to test LLM accuracy in isolation, nor to derive OntoLER from the case. The LER construct, the L0–L5 ordering, and checkpoints T0–T7 are motivated by the ontology and by recurring distinctions in IFRS texts. The diagnostic run tests a narrower methodological claim: whether an OntoLER-guided analyst–LLM procedure can produce a traceable reconstruction, an explicit diagnostic profile, and a reviewable repair anchor for a bounded standards artifact. The runs are not claimed as a statistical validation of LLM performance.

The case is useful because it is small enough to follow but structurally rich enough to expose the value of the procedure. A sale-and-leaseback involves two connected transactions: first, the entity transfers an underlying asset to another party; second, the entity leases back the right to use that asset. In OntoLER terms, the accounting labels presuppose rights and obligations, reciprocal party relations, holder changes over the underlying object, and later recognition, measurement, and representation overlays. The case also shows why the shared L1 lease reciprocity must be separated from asymmetric lessee / lessor reporting projections and from subsequent implementation and disclosure problems.

The bounded artifact consists of IFRS 16 §§99–103, the 2022 addition of §102A [14], and Examples 24–25. The diagnostic question is not whether IFRS 16 distinguishes the retained right from the transferred rights. It does. Paragraph 100(a) requires the seller-lessee to measure the right-of-use asset at the proportion of the previous carrying amount that relates to the right of use retained and to recognize only the gain or loss relating to the rights transferred to the buyer-lessor. The diagnostic question is more precise: does the standard state the antecedent, non-monetary criterion by which the retained and transferred rights are separated before monetary measurement is applied?

Scoping Correction. The first LLM-assisted run began from the broad expression "IFRS 16 leaseback." This produced a Boundary Misfit: the run treated leaseback as a topic rather than as a bounded clause family. It mixed the original sale-and-leaseback requirements, the 2022 amendment, illustrative examples, amendment rationale, and later measurement consequences into one reconstruction object.

The output was plausible but unstable. It read later accounting mechanics back into the original clause, as if IFRS 16 had already specified how to delimit the retained and transferred rights. This is precisely the type of failure the procedure is intended to detect. The problem was not that LLM failed to recognize familiar accounting terms. The problem was that it did not know which textual object it was reconstructing and which materials were only corroborating evidence.

The Scoper therefore narrowed the run as follows: the primary object was IFRS 16 §§99–103 and §102A, read with Illustrative Examples 24–25; secondary evidence consisted of amendment rationale and later practice material; and the diagnostic question was what right, obligation, transfer, or retained-use structure must exist before the standard attaches carrying amount, gain or loss, and subsequent measurement.

After this correction, the run stabilized. The issue was no longer a broad "leaseback ambiguity." It became a dependence-order problem: the standard attaches amounts to retained and transferred rights before it states the criterion by which those rights are delimited.

Typed Reconstruction. At L0, the grounding facts include the underlying asset, the sale agreement, the leaseback agreement, the parties, payment terms, fair value information, and facts relevant to the IFRS 15 sale test. These are evidential and transactional materials from which the accounting treatment is derived.

At L1, the entity's pre-existing position in the asset is reconstructed as a bundle of legal-economic rights over or concerning the underlying object, not as a simple asset label. The sale side comprises a transfer to the buyer-lessor and a right to consideration. The leaseback side comprises the buyer-lessor's obligation to provide use and the seller-lessee's obligation to make lease payments. The retained right of use is reconstructed as a holder-specific position of the seller-lessee over the leased asset, distinct from the rights transferred to the buyer-lessor. The accounting labels "right-of-use asset" and "lease liability" are therefore later reporting roles attached to this structure; they should not substitute for the prior reconstruction of what was transferred, what was retained, and by whom.

At L2, the reconstructed rights and obligations receive IFRS-facing roles such as right-of-use asset and lease liability. At L3, the standard determines recognition effects, including whether and when gain or loss is recognized. At L4, monetary measurement is applied through carrying amounts, present value mechanics, and gain / loss allocation. At L5, presentation, disclosure, and taxonomy-facing surfaces expose selected lower-layer distinctions but may fail to preserve the reconstruction anchors needed to recover retained / transferred rights, holder changes, and measurement dependencies.

The critical point is the ordering. The retained and transferred rights must be specified before monetary amounts are attached to them. Otherwise, the measurement rule is forced to do structural work that belongs earlier in the analysis.

Diagnostic Profile. The diagnosis is a dependence-order diagnosis, not a claim that IFRS 16 lacks accounting categories. IFRS 16 distinguishes the right of use retained from the rights transferred to the buyer-lessor, but it does not separately state the non-monetary delimitation criterion before applying the measurement mechanics. This matters because the distinction controls gain or loss recognition, later lease-liability mechanics, and the interpretation of subsequent changes. Where that prior delimitation remains implicit, preparers and review tools may report the monetary effect while losing the institutional event that produced it. The PIR evidence on boilerplate judgment disclosures and compressed "remeasurement" language is therefore not only an implementation observation. It is evidence of a T6/T7 vulnerability: T6 localizes the dependence-order problem, while T7 explains why the reporting surface can preserve labels and amounts while lacking the reconstruction anchors needed to recover the legal-economic distinction. Table 3 summarizes the diagnostic profile.

Why the 2022 Amendment Helps but Does Not Remove the Diagnosis. The 2022 amendment improves subsequent measurement by requiring the seller-lessee to determine lease payments so that no gain or loss is recognized in relation to the retained right. From an OntoLER perspective, however, this disciplines downstream recognition and measurement without supplying the prior non-monetary criterion for delimiting the retained and transferred rights at commencement. The T6 problem therefore remains: monetary allocation is applied to a distinction whose legal-economic extent is presupposed rather than explicitly reconstructed.

This is why the case is more than a local technical defect. When retained and transferred rights are not explicit, later "remeasurement" language may classify a numerical change without revealing whether it arose from a modification, reassessment, payment revision, lease-term change, scope change, or another legally distinct event. Standard-setting underspecification can therefore reappear as implementation difficulty, disclosure thinness, and automated-review weakness.

Minimal Repair and Reconstruction Anchor. The repair does not require replacing IFRS 16 sale-and-leaseback accounting. It requires an antecedent reconstruction step: identify the pre-existing right structure, the transfer to the buyer-lessor, the right of use retained or granted back to the seller-lessee, and the criterion for delimiting retained and transferred portions before attaching carrying amount, gain / loss allocation, and subsequent measurement.

The reconstruction anchor: before applying the sale-and-leaseback measurement rule, the retained right of use and the rights transferred to the buyer-lessor should be delimited by an explicit non-monetary specification of the underlying asset interest affected by the transaction. Monetary carrying amount, gain / loss allocation, and later remeasurement should be attached only after that delimitation. This preserves the existing IFRS 16 distinction while making the institutional event behind the accounting result representable.

Table 3. A scorecard for leaseback case. Status = PASS, WARN, or FAIL

Checkpoint	Status	Diagnosis	Minimal repair
T1 LER integrity	WARN	Rights, obligations, and parties are reachable but under-typed	State retained/transferred rights, parties, and correlatives explicitly
T2 Reciprocity	WARN	Sale and leaseback reciprocities are presupposed but compressed	Separate the sale reciprocity from the leaseback reciprocity
T4 Role overlay	WARN	The labels right-of-use asset and lease liability presuppose the retained-use and payment structure	Reconstruct retained-use right and payment obligation before attaching reporting roles
T5 Recognition overlay	WARN	Gain / loss recognition is controlled without resolving prior retained / transferred-right delimitation	Keep recognition consequences separate from retained/transferred-right specification
T6 Measurement overlay	FAIL	Amount is attached before retained/transferred-right delimitation is explicit	State the holder change, retained right, transferred rights, and delimitation criterion before measurement

(*continued*)

Table 3. (*continued*)

Checkpoint	Status	Diagnosis	Minimal repair
T7 Representation	WARN	Reporting and disclosure surfaces preserve labels and amounts but lack explicit reconstruction anchors for the retained/transferred-right distinction	Add representable retained/transferred-right anchors in disclosure, taxonomy, documentation, or reconstruction tables

6 Conclusion

This paper has presented OntoLER as a Design Science artifact for diagnosing underspecification in reporting standards: a UFO/UFO-L/UFO-B-grounded L0–L5 architecture, checkpoints T0–T7, and a staged analyst–LLM procedure that together make clause-level compression reconstructable, diagnosable, and minimally repairable.

Across lease accounting under IFRS 16, revenue, provisions, financial instruments, business combinations, sale-and-leaseback transactions, and a compact IFRS for SMEs stress test, the same failure recurs: labels stand in for ontology, and measurement or recognition work is performed before the L1 structure is specified. The runs also surfaced well-structured drafting patterns: contract before category, trigger before recognition, and component before measurement, showing that OntoLER diagnoses deficits while making good practice explicit. Evidence that natural-language labels dominate LLM type prediction in conceptual models [25] reinforces OntoLER's staged checks: candidate reconstructions are retained only after their path from source evidence through L0–L5 and T0–T7 is exposed and tested.

The hybrid-intelligence result is role-specific: LLMs proved useful when scoping, typing, diagnosis, and repair remained separated. OntoLER provides the semantic scaffold that constrains their outputs through dependence order, admissible distinctions, and explicit checkpoints.

The evaluation is analytical and case-based, not a statistical validation of LLM performance. Future work will extend validation to a fuller IFRS corpus, develop a reusable HI workbench that tests standards against shared checkpoints, and export reconstructions as RDF/OWL knowledge graphs linked to IFRS paragraphs and repair anchors—complementing, rather than replacing, OntoUML and the executable substrate [26].

References

1. Mattessich, R.: Reality and Accounting: Ontological Explorations in the Economic and Social Sciences (1st ed.). Routledge (2013). https://doi.org/10.4324/9780203798737
2. IASB. Conceptual Framework for Financial Reporting. IFRS Foundation (2018)

3. Guizzardi, G.: Ontological foundations for structural conceptual models. Ph.D. thesis, CTIT, Centre for Telematics and Information Technology, Enschede (2005)
4. Griffo, C., Almeida, J.P.A., Guizzardi, G., Nardi, J.C.: Service contract modeling in enterprise architecture: an ontology-based approach. Inf. Syst. **101**, 101454 (2021). https://doi.org/10.1016/j.is.2019.101454
5. Guizzardi, G., et al.: Endurant types in ontology-driven conceptual modeling: towards OntoUML 2.0. In: ER 2018, LNCS 11157, pp. 136–150. Springer, Cham (2018). https://doi.org/10.1007/978-3-030-00847-5_12
6. Almeida, J.P.A., Falbo, R.A., Guizzardi, G.: Events as entities in ontology-driven conceptual modeling. In: ER 2019, LNCS 11788, pp. 469–483. Springer, Cham (2019). https://doi.org/10.1007/978-3-030-33223-5_39
7. Commons, J.R.: Legal Foundations of Capitalism, ISBN 9781560007814, published Routledge (1995)
8. ISO/IEC 15944–4:2015. Information technology — Business operational view — Part 4: Business transaction scenarios — Accounting and economic ontology. https://www.iso.org/standard/67199.html
9. Amaral, G.C.M.: An Ontology Network in Finance and Economics — Money, Trust, Value, Risk and Economic Exchanges. LNBIP, vol. 532. Springer, Cham (2025). https://doi.org/10.1007/978-3-031-71082-7
10. Weigand, H., Blums, I., de Kruijff, J.: Shared ledger accounting — implementing the economic exchange pattern. Inf. Syst. **90**, 101437 (2020). https://doi.org/10.1016/j.is.2019.101437
11. Schwaiger, W.S.A., Nasufi, A., Kryvinska, N., Fischer-Pauzenberger, C., Dural, Ö.F.: The OntoREA© Accounting and Finance Model: Inclusion of Future Uncertainty. In: PoEM 2019, LNBIP 369, pp. 53–67. Springer, Cham (2019). https://doi.org/10.1007/978-3-030-35151-9_4
12. Blums, I., Weigand, H.: Consolidating economic exchange ontologies for financial reporting standard setting. Data Knowl. Eng. **145**, 102148 (2023). https://doi.org/10.1016/j.datak.2023.102148
13. IASB. IFRS 16 Leases. IFRS Foundation, London. Issued January 2016. https://www.ifrs.org/issued-standards/list-of-standards/ifrs-16-leases/
14. IASB. Lease Liability in a Sale and Leaseback (Amendments to IFRS 16). IFRS Foundation (2022). https://www.ifrs.org/projects/completed-projects/2022/lease-liability-in-a-sale-and-leaseback/
15. IASB. Post-implementation Review of IFRS 16 Leases: Request for Information (2025). IASB deliberations ongoing through 2026. https://www.ifrs.org/projects/work-plan/post-implementation-review-of-ifrs-16-leases/
16. International Accounting Standards Board (IASB). IFRS for SMEs Accounting Standard, Third Edition. IFRS Foundation, London (2025)
17. Akata, Z., et al.: A research agenda for hybrid intelligence: augmenting human intellect with collaborative, adaptive, responsible, and explainable artificial intelligence. Computer **53**(8), 18–28 (2020). https://doi.org/10.1109/MC.2020.2996587
18. Albuquerque, F., Gomes dos Santos, P.: Exploring ChatGPT's capabilities in solving accounting standards problems: the case of IAS 37. Cogent Educ. **11**(1), 2412492 (2024). https://doi.org/10.1080/2331186X.2024.2412492
19. Martin, A., Witschel, H.F., Stockhecke, M., Nydegger, P., Buga, K.: Discovering Inconsistencies in Documents with Long-Context LLMs. In: CAiSE 2025 Workshops, LNBIP 556, pp. 105–116. Springer, Cham (2025). https://doi.org/10.1007/978-3-031-94931-9_9
20. Spahic-Bogdanovic, M., et al.: iModuleBuddy — A Hybrid AI-Based Academic Planning System. Selected Papers of HybridAIMS 2025 and CAI 2025 (CAiSE 2025), CEUR-WS, Vol. 3996, pp. 21–29 (2025). https://ceur-ws.org/Vol-3996/paper-4.pdf

21. Laurenzi, E. et al.: An agile and ontology-based meta-modelling approach for the design and maintenance of enterprise knowledge graph schemas. enterprise modelling and information systems architectures. Int. J. Conceptual Model. EMISAJ 2024. https://emisa-journal.org/emisa/article/view/310
22. Coutinho, M.L., Almeida, J.P.A., Guizzardi, G.: LLM-Based Modeling Assistance for Textual Ontology-Driven Conceptual Modeling. In ER 2025 Companion Proceedings. CEUR Workshop Proc. **4099**, 338–342 (2025)
23. Blums, I., Weigand, H.: Hohfeldian refinement of exchange positions in COFRIS. In: Proc. VMBO 2025, University of Twente, Enschede (2025)
24. Mustafa, D.M., Lange, C., Guizzardi, G., Collarana, D., Quix, C., Decker, S.: What does ODRL mean? A cross-level ontological grounding of permissions, prohibitions, and duties in UFO-L. arXiv:2606.24344 (2026)
25. Ali, S.J., Zheng, Z., Bork, D.: Shortcut or Understanding? Diagnosing LLM Type Prediction in Conceptual Models. In: Fuentes, L., Plebani, P., Combi, C., Reijers, H. (eds.) Advanced Information Systems Engineering. CAiSE 2026. LNCS, vol. 16559, pp. 37–55. Springer, Cham (2026). https://doi.org/10.1007/978-3-032-28117-3_3
26. Blums, I., Weigand, H.: Refining Core Ontologies Through Executable Transformation. In: ER2025 Companion Proceedings: Industrial Track, ER Forum, CEUR-WS, Vol. 4099, pp. 101–112 (2025). https://ceur-ws.org/Vol-4099/forum_paper15.pdf

Model-Driven Knowledge Graphs for AI Sovereignty Through Enterprise Architecture: An Extension of the TEAM Toolkit

Andreea-Eva Adam and Robert Andrei Buchmann(✉)

OMILAB@UBB-FSEGA & Business Informatics Research Center, Faculty of Economics and Business Administration, Babeş-Bolyai University, 58-60 T. Mihali St, 400591 Cluj-Napoca, Romania

andreea.adam@stud.ubbcluj.ro, robert.buchmann@econ.ubbcluj.ro

Abstract. Sovereignty and accountability aspects in the usage of AI systems in distributed cloud infrastructures spread across multiple jurisdictions. From a governance point of view, it is increasingly important to get insight and traceability regarding how AI systems inter-dependencies, how they retrieve and process content across geographical and organizational boundaries. Existing architectural languages such as Archimate lack specific concepts to describe and enable traceability regarding these aspects.

This paper introduces an approach comprising domain-specific Archimate extensions and a knowledge graph treatment based on them, to enable sovereignty design decisions and traceability across Enterprise Architecture. The extended Archimate metamodel is realized in the ADOxx metamodeling platform on top of the TEAM toolkit - available in OMILAB's modeling ecosystem for TOGAF practitioners and experimentation. The modeling method is further augmented with the possibility of running SPARQL queries over multiple integrated Archimate viewpoints, thus leveraging the proposed extensions as semantic constructs capturing the specificity of AI sovereignty on architecture level.

Keywords: Knowledge Graphs · Archimate Extension · ADOxx · SPARQL · Digital Sovereignty · AI Governance · Enterprise Architecture

1 Introduction

Compared to traditional system behavior and deployment, Artificial Intelligence (AI) raises new architectural concerns - from how AI models are deployed to how they interoperate as enterprise system components [3]. As AI systems are increasingly deployed across entire enterprises, it is of strategic interest where exactly they are used, which infrastructure they depend on and how this propagates through organizational layers and national boundaries [17]. Scholars focusing on EU sovereignty indicate that organizations encounter cross-border dependencies and legal requirements, as systems are distributed across cloud providers and transnational infrastructure [5, 36].

Achieving AI sovereignty, more exactly being able to account for where an AI system runs, how it processes data, and to what dependencies an AI system and its data

E. Laurenzi et al. (Eds.): BIR 2026, LNBIP 601, pp. 259–275, 2027.
https://doi.org/10.1007/978-3-032-38498-0_17

are exposed, is particularly challenging for compliance and governance. As European legislation around data protection and AI accountability continues to evolve [18, 28], having components of an AI system distributed across multiple information systems and lacking a holistic traceable view makes it difficult to assess regulatory exposure or answer governance queries - a gap that model-based and knowledge graph approaches are well positioned to address [15, 30].

The General Data Protection Regulation (GDPR) creates a legal basis for data sovereignty by placing restrictions on data processing, storage, and transfer [40], while the EU AI Act introduces a risk-based regulatory framework emphasizing traceability [29]. However, these must be supported by the ability to answer questions such as "Where is this AI component running?", "Where is my data stored?" and "What dependencies exist outside the EU?" – we see these as *core governance queries that can be treated as competency questions for knowledge graphs*. The dependencies and constructs relevant to be captured in such knowledge graphs can be typically found in Enterprise Architecture (EA) models, where the physical deployment of an enterprise can be depicted in terms of its Technology and Physical architecture layers - physical devices, facilities, paths of access/distribution, locations etc. Standards such as Archimate [23] offer first class modeling constructs for these layers, but no explicit constructs for representing AI-specific assets - LLM hosting, training datasets, RAG dependencies among others. This requires extensions of EA standards, and for this purpose our work leverages open source work developed in the OMILAB Community of Practice[1] - namely the TOGAF-oriented TEAM toolkit [4] which was hereby extended with the help of the ADOxx metamodeling platform [2] and the ADOxx-to-RDF interoperability plug-in available in the ADOxx tooling ecosystem [31].

As a running example, to showcase feasibility in a Design Science [41] relevance sense, we build the paper around a fictional Enterprise Architecture investigation into the infrastructure and cross-border dependencies supporting AI Solutions Corp., a European IT company that operates a distributed cross-border AI Platform comprising several components: large language models (LLMs), knowledge graphs, and retrieval-augmented generation (RAG) pipelines, typical ingredients in modern AI systems [3, 24]. AI systems can be systematically described across the application, technology, and physical layers of Archimate. Additionally, we determine possible dependencies between AI system components through the lens of sovereignty. Consequently, we extend Archimate with new relationship types and component classifications to cover typical AI governance needs such as dataset replication, cross-layer containment, runtime retrieval, and training data dependencies.

The work follows Design Science Research (DSR) principles [41] and its development phase is operationalized through the AMME methodology [19, 20] - traditionally applied for DSML (domain-specific modeling language) engineering and tool development on the ADOxx metamodeling platform. This methodological framework is described in Sect. 3, after a survey of the literature on the aspects involved in this work. The proposed artifact and its competency evaluation are presented in Sect. 4. Conclusions are drawn at the end of the paper.

[1] https://omilab.org/

2 Related Works and Research Gap

2.1 Background on AI Sovereignty and Regulatory Frameworks

With the wide adoption of AI the idea of digital sovereignty, initially articulated in relation to Internet regulation and state control over digital infrastructure [11], has undergone substantial transformation. Floridi [16] argues that control over digital systems and data is a necessary condition for political and economic autonomy, offering an early formulation of digital sovereignty as a fundamental priority for the European Union. Beyond data ownership, AI sovereignty also refers to control over computation, model training procedures, infrastructure dependencies, and cross-border data flows [8, 34].

The GDPR created a legal basis for data sovereignty [40]. Based on this, the EU AI Act introduces a risk-based regulatory framework emphasizing accountability, transparency, and traceability of AI systems [14]. These legislative developments implicitly require organizations to comprehend and document the locations of AI systems' operations and the cross-jurisdictional data flows. The political and legal challenges of putting digital sovereignty into effect are further highlighted by Hulko et al. [17], who point out "conflicts between national preferences and institutional competences" at the EU level. Accountability and transparency are core design principles for responsible AI [34]. Data sovereignty entails also the possibility to determine decisions regarding the storage location of data and decisions regarding access to and governance of data [18]. From a critical political economy perspective, Mugge [27] contests a technologically driven interpretation of AI governance, pointing out that technology protectionism is not equivalent to effective governance. In a similar way, Nanni et al. [28] draw comparisons with Chinese AI governance and contest the notion that EU legal frameworks effectively provide individual data sovereignty.

Taylor et al. [38] suggest that controlling an AI system or service inherently requires the ability to control the relevant data pipelines, meaning that tracing the architectural distribution of training data flows is something that stakeholders should be able to request. Badawy [1] explores algorithmic sovereignty ideas beyond the traditional compliance framework for regulating generative AI models. Geopolitical perspectives [5, 10] place EU digital sovereignty initiatives within larger strategic autonomy goals and cybersecurity governance trends, highlighting the risks associated with cross-border dependencies of exactly the type that we intend to be able to model and navigate as part of EA. Taken as a whole, this body of work indicates that effective governance in dispersed AI contexts requires explicit architectural insight and traceability starting from the physical layer of enterprise architectures.

2.2 Enterprise Architecture Modeling and Archimate

Enterprise Architecture provides a structured method for characterizing complex organizational systems spanning several layers and stakeholder viewpoints. Early frameworks like Zachman's [42] introduced a taxonomy for organizing architectural artefacts, while TOGAF [39] formalized EA management into a lifecycle technique enabling business-IT alignment. The Open Group's Archimate [23] supports TOGAF with a standardized modeling language for representing EA across the Business, Application, and Technology layers, further expanded in recent versions to include a Physical layer encompassing locations, facilities, and equipment. AI systems introduce concerns on all architecting layers, but from a sovereignty perspective the Physical layer is particularly meaningful as it deals with geographical reachability and jurisdictions.

Prior studies have demonstrated EA applications for security risk management [25] and the modeling of digital ecosystems [33]. Bork et al. [4] investigated application in requirements engineering based on EA management; they also built artifacts such as TEAM - the TOGAF-oriented modeling tool that is the basis on which this work builds an extension with the help of the ADOxx metamodeling platform and RDF generation mechanisms initially designed for domain-specific enterprise modeling languages such as ComVantage [6], also adaptable in recent versions to any ADOxx metamodel through the generalized plugin available at [32]. Prior work has applied semantic techniques to integrate and query Archimate models alongside complementary modeling languages, showing that formal representation opens up analytical capabilities beyond what native Archimate tooling provides [7].

The architectural relevance of AI or data sovereignty means that languages like Archimate should be extended with explicit constructs to capture associated concerns. Current extensions do not address AI-specific architectural dependencies such as model training data flows, inference-time retrieval mechanisms, or dataset replication across jurisdictions, nor the sovereignty implications of component location.

2.3 Distributed AI Architectures and Dependency Modeling

Modern AI systems built on large language models are intrinsically distributed across three distinct stages: pre-training, domain-specific fine-tuning, and real-time inference. These stages frequently depend on different datasets, infrastructure components, and geographical locations. Lewis et al. [24] discussed retrieval-augmented generation (RAG) which emphasizes a crucial additional form of dependency: run-time retrieval from external knowledge sources, architecturally distinct from training-time data dependencies. Architectural analysis must therefore account for such dynamic, run-time connections created between AI models and external systems. Furthermore, Bommasani et al. [3] highlight that foundation models create intricate and frequently opaque dependency chains in which downstream applications inherit risks from upstream infrastructure and training data. Research on Internet governance and network infrastructure [12, 26] shows that data flows may cross numerous jurisdictions regardless of logical system boundaries. In the context of cloud sovereignty, Rone [35] demonstrates how maintaining sovereign cloud infrastructure at the European scale is made more difficult by fragmented institutional capabilities. Despite these intensively discussed concerns, formal modeling of such relationships within enterprise design frameworks that can facilitate cross-layer traceability has received little attention.

2.4 AI Classification and Component Governance

When aiming for effective AI governance it is important to make a clear distinction between parts of a system performing AI-related functionality and parts forming the supporting infrastructure. The EU AI Act defines AI systems primarily by their ability to process input, learn or adapt and produce output through the application of artificial intelligence. Sokol and Flach [37] argue that explainability and accountability in these systems can then be addressed by identifying the components actually performing the decision-making. Krafft et al. [22] identified a gap between how AI is defined from a policy perspective, and how it manifests itself within complex systems in practice. Badawy [1] extends this argument to generative AI, highlighting the necessity of governance techniques that can differentiate between algorithmic decision-making components and passive infrastructure, especially when generative models blur the line between tool and agent. Calzada [9] further argues that while some focus on distinguishing between end-user and ultimate beneficiary of the outcomes of AI, others frame the relevance of governance to how systems are embedded in organizations.

When viewed from the perspective of EA, this requires the ability to categorize between AI and non-AI elements of the infrastructure. Prior works on queryable architectural representations [7, 30] established that automated compliance verification can be performed, provided that a model includes metadata relevant to governance. However, no currently available techniques address the issue of AI sovereignty explicitly.

2.5 Research Gap

The literature survey of the previous sections indicates that AI sovereignty is a growing concern, especially in the European Union, but treated mostly at policy level and less with respect to EA practice. While Archimate offers a strong framework for multi-layer and multi-viewpoint system modeling, it does not have native constructs for the AI lifecycle and current enterprise design techniques do not account for the types of dependencies introduced by modern AI systems, such as training, runtime retrieval, replication, and physical containment. Earlier modeling languages also lack in this respect perhaps due to the popularity of virtualization in the age of Cloud and the blurring of physical boundaries, that now returns as a concern.

The identified gap is therefore the absence of a design-oriented approach facilitating sovereignty-focused analysis, AI-specific dependency representation, in the context of EA modeling, for which we propose the combination between Archimate-based DSMLs (with sovereignty as the "domain") and knowledge graphs (as traceability and reasoning enabler, potentially integrable with KG-driven AI systems).

3 Methodological Framework

This section describes our approach through the lens of a Design Science Research (DSR) cycle [32, 41], with the artifact development phase organized through the Agile Modeling Method Engineering (AMME) methodology [19, 20].

3.1 Problem Awareness and Solution Overview

Enterprise Architecture practice has well-proven methods to document systems at multiple levels of detail. Yet, organizations using distributed AI systems face the difficulty of answering basic governance questions about their systems, with challenges identified by Taylor et al. [38] and Broeders et al. [5]. European organizations whose AI systems have grown organically across diverse cloud environments and components are deployed wherever resources are available, with virtualization making less relevant the understanding or awareness of cross-border interdependence or physical location. The need for such awareness returns under current geopolitical circumstances, however, EA standards like Archimate lack native dependencies relevant for the AI lifecycle or sovereignty. The artifact developed here addresses this in the spirit of Design Science Research, i.e. by engineering a tooling-based treatment. Using the problem statement template proposed by Wieringa [41], the design problem is framed as follows:

(a) improve the possibilities of design & analysis of AI sovereignty in distributed enterprise AI systems (problem context); (b) by using a domain-specific modeling approach based on Archimate (artefact); (c) to enable sovereignty-oriented semantic traceability via graph queries (requirements); (d) to support AI governance decisions and jurisdictional risk management (stakeholder goals).

The proposed artefact can be viewed from two different perspectives: (a) as an extension to the Archimate language with new relationship types and component classification attributes; (b) as a domain-specific modeling language (DSML) for the AI sovereignty analysis domain, providing first-class domain concepts such as AI components, training datasets, knowledge graphs, physical locations and jurisdiction-crossing dependencies. Such a treatment can then support data management decisions, function migration planning, risk analysis regarding potential impacts, as well as documentation support for compliance reporting as required by legislation such as the EU AI Act, especially with respect to accountability and liability [29].

3.2 The AMME Tool Development Process

The Agile Modeling Method Engineering (AMME) methodology [19, 20] applies agile development principles to the engineering of diagrammatic modeling tools within a DSR cycle, aiming to produce and iteratively evolve DSMLs and associated tool support. Its five phases were implemented as follows:

Create phase: This is the phase focusing on "modeling method requirements" that motivate the engineering backlog. Based on the literature survey in earlier sections, we focus on several requirements: (a) cross-layer traceability to physical locations, grounded in the sovereignty visibility imperative articulated by Hummel et al. [18] and Taylor et al. [38]; (b) AI-specific dependency representation, since standard Archimate relationships (Assignment, Serving, Flow) do not capture training, retrieval, or replication semantics relevant to the AI lifecycle; and (c) EU AI Act compliance logic.

Design Phase: New constructs and connection types were added to the Archimate 3.0 metamodel, as derived from the motivating requirements. The focus was primarily on semantic distinctions (e.g. if an application component is AI-related or not, then specializing different subtypes of AI services or components) and on chains of dependencies on AI-specific resources (RAG knowledge bases, training datasets etc.). The design aspects are detailed in Sect. 4.

Formalize Phase: The ADOxx modeling constructs are reflected in a default set-theoretic formalism underlying the meta-metamodel of the platform [15]. Diagrams can be exported to RDF according to a metamodel-derived schema, following earlier work formalized through hypergraphs under the notion of Linked Open Models (diagrammatic enrichments of Linked Open Data) [6, 21]. This allows sovereignty queries to be expressed as SPARQL graph traversals over the knowledge graph, consistent with the large-scale graph querying architectures described by Noy et al. [30].

Develop Phase: This is the ADOxx tool development phase, using the platform capabilities to extend existing Archimate tooling available for ADOxx (TEAM [4]). ADOxx provides a metamodel designer, a notation designer, and the ADOScript scripting language [2]. Graph traversal across layer boundaries is supported by default in the ADOxx query engine (AQL), but to facilitate knowledge externalization and access from arbitrary clients an additional SPARQL-based interaction is enabled. The SPARQL queries discussed in Sect. 4.3 were written to express the governance competency questions defined for the AI sovereignty scenario, covering the specific traceability and jurisdictional analysis needs identified in the literature.

Deploy/Validate Phase: ADOxx enables tool distribution as a desktop application. Validation was limited to feasibility demonstration and competency question coverage, with several technical aspects left out of evaluation plans because they are inherited either from the underlying metamodeling platform (e.g. usability) or from the TEAM implementation (e.g. the graphical notation). The application scenario's sovereignty concerns addressed by the competency questions - infrastructure dependency, cross-border data flows, and regulatory responsibility - are derived from the literature survey on EU AI governance summarized in Sect. 2, to be expanded to concrete concerns of regional stakeholders in future DSR iterations of this work.

4 The Proposed Artifact

This section summarizes the design and realization of the extended Archimate modeling tool, its application to the AI Solutions Corp. Running example, and a competency evaluation confirming that all modeling requirements are met. ADOxx model files and exported RDF graphs are being maintained in the project repository[2].

4.1 Metamodel Extensions

The metamodel fragment in Fig. 1 illustrates the ADOxx additions to the legacy Archimate structures from Application and Technology/Physical layers. The extension is implemented by adding closed enumeration attributes for semantic differentiations and new types of Archimate connectors with dual behaviors - either as hyperlinks (ADOxx INTERREFs) that allow a modeler to navigate from one diagram into another by clicking an element, or as visible connectors within the same diagram.

Hyperlinks are intended to facilitate drill-down navigation - that is, clicking an element in a parent diagram opens a separate sub-diagram that reveals its internal structure - similarly to BPMN subprocess links but more generalizable to arbitrary Archimate viewpoints. The target of such a link is an INTERREF model: a named sub-diagram that any Archimate element can point into through containment, making it possible to hide complexity from the parent view and expose it on demand in a drill-down manner.

2 https://github.com/AndreeaEAdam/Archimate-AI-Sovereignty/blob/main/README.md.

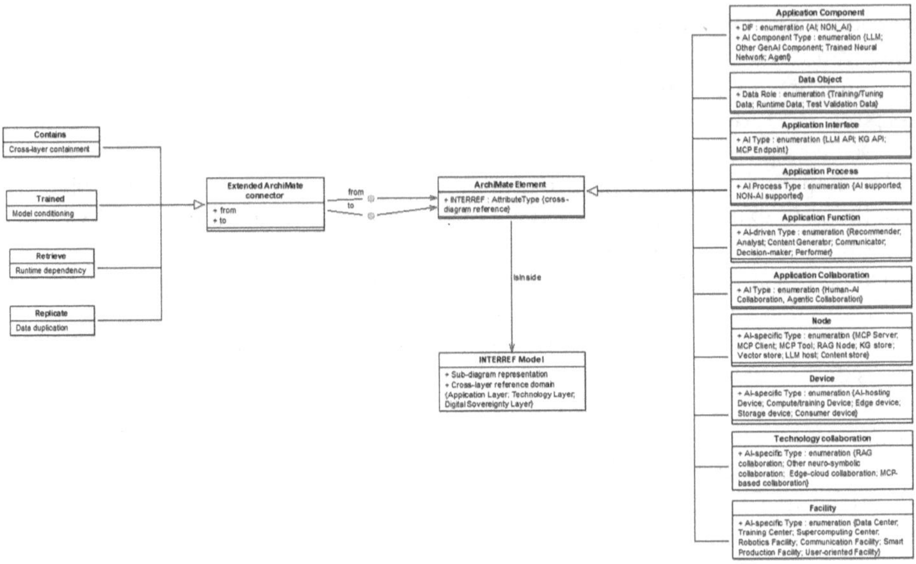

Fig. 1. Metamodel extensions for the Archimate AI sovereignty use case

The new Archimate connectors are by default relaxed to reflect permissive pairings encountered in real-world scenarios (e.g., a Facility contains a Node; a Data Object trains an Application Component). There are four relation types:

r_Contains: Directional wrapping, indicating that the target is either logically or physically included in the source. Used for infrastructure nesting (Facility → Device → Node) as a superproperty of Aggregation/Composition where their distinction is less relevant than the containment traceability from ownership/governance perspective.

r_Trained: Directional static dependence, indicating that a target AI model's parameters were influenced by the source dataset. Represents a static data dependence essential to training data traceability under EU AI Act Article 10 [14].

r_Retrieve: Directed runtime dependence, indicating that at inference time the source AI component actively queries the target knowledge base from outside its training resources. Consistent with the RAG retrieval pattern [25] and expressing on-demand querying and live operation.

r_Replicate: Directional data governance dependence, where the source is the original dataset and the target is a copy in a different jurisdiction. Critical for GDPR cross-border transfer evaluation under Article 46 [40]. Characterized by origin preservation, jurisdiction awareness, and sovereignty tracking.

The Application Component class has been extended with two new attributes, both visible in the ADOxx class definition. The first generic DIF is a binary flag set to either AI or NON_AI, used to determine whether a component falls within the EU AI Act's regulatory scope. All Application Components receive a yellow badge in the diagram; the badge label - "AI" or "NON_AI" - indicates the classification, allowing a reader to quickly distinguish regulated components from non-regulated ones at a glance without reading the full element description. Additional attributes visible in the metamodel add more in depth AI specificity and semantically richer distinctions to several constructs from the Application/Technology/Physical layers.

4.2 Running Example

The feasibility demonstration scenario involves AI Solutions Corp., a European IT firm offering enterprise clients hybrid RAG architectures, knowledge graph systems, and LLM-based chatbot services. An enterprise architect was engaged following a US cloud outage, with a client inquiry regarding data sovereignty compliance - a scenario of the type predicted by Mügge [27] and Nanni et al. [28] as a predictable consequence of underspecified EU AI governance. The investigation reveals five components distributed across five jurisdictions: an LLM running in Switzerland, which is outside the EU regulatory perimeter, meaning the LLM hosted there is not directly subject to the EU AI Act, which introduces an additional sovereignty consideration for the architecture, a knowledge graph hosted in Germany, a primary training dataset stored at an AWS facility in Alaska (USA), a backup dataset replicated to France, and an API Gateway deployed in Ireland. These components were functionally integrated but lacked a consistent architectural representation, making it difficult to identify cross-border connections, evaluate sovereignty risks, or answer impact analysis questions.

The Digital Sovereignty Layer (Fig. 2) captures physical locations represented by the orange rectangles, each represents one of the five jurisdictions (Switzerland; Germany; USA; France, Ireland). Components are placed inside the location element corresponding to their physical or legal deployment site, making cross border distribution visible at the first sight. INTERREF (hyperlink) drill-downs - hyperlinks that open dedicated sub-diagrams showing the internal structure of a complex element - are provided for the Technology Layer, Physical Layer, and Application Layer.

The four new relationship types introduced by the metamodel extension are each rendered in a distinct colour to separate them visually from standard Archimate connectors, which follow the default black notation. Specifically: r_Contains appears in pink; r_Trained in red with a white arrowhead; r_Retrieve in light pink with a green filled arrowhead, marking the retrieval dependency between LLM (SW) and Knowledge Graph (DE); and r_Replicate in red with a blue filled arrowhead. This colour coding allows a reader to identify sovereignty-relevant dependencies - physical containment, training lineage, retrieval chains, and replication events - without reading every connector label.

Several semantic patterns are encoded by the Digital Sovereignty Layer using the new connectors: *Training lineage*: Dataset → r_Trained → LLM (SW) and Training Dataset → r_Trained → LLM (US-A), establishing which AI model parameters were derived from which data sources; *RAG retrieval dependencies*: LLM (SW) → r_Retrieve → Knowledge Graph (DE) and LLM → r_Retrieve → KG, representing cognition during execution [25]; *Data replication*: Training Dataset → r_Replicate → Back-up Dataset, capturing the creation of a jurisdictionally distinct copy in France, relevant to GDPR Article 46 [40]; *Physical containment*: the r_Contains relationships link AI application components through devices, facilities, and locations, enabling SPARQL queries from any AI component to its host jurisdiction [22].

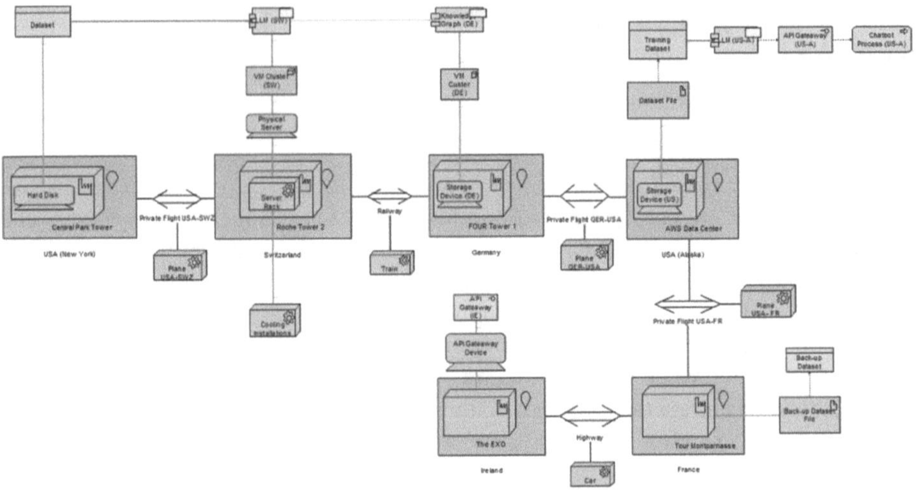

Fig. 2. Digital Sovereignty Layer diagram

Each of the following sub-diagrams is reached by following the INTERREF hyperlink embedded in the corresponding parent element. The *API Gateway INTER_REF* (Fig. 4) reveals the request pipeline: API Gateway (IE) → r_Flow → Chatbot Process (IE) → r_Triggering → LLM (IE); the *LLM_SW INTER_REF* shows the containerisation stack: VM Cluster (SW) → r_Composition → VM Instance → r_Assignment → Container Runtime → r_Association → LLM (SW); the *VM Cluster INTER_REF* exposes Kubernetes orchestration: Kubernetes Cluster → r_Composition → VM Instance 1 / VM Instance 2 → r_Association → Container Runtime (Docker); the *Training Dataset INTER_REF* shows the replication event: Training Dataset → r_Replicate → Back-up Dataset.

By applying the ADOxx-to-RDF plugin [31] - originating in an earlier domain-specific modeling method and its prescribed transformation patterns [6, 21] -, each diagram view becomes a unique named RDF graph accumulated in a Graphwise GraphDB repository[3]. Because ADOxx also exports INTERREF sub-diagrams, SPARQL queries can distinguish and drill-down to sub-diagrams, making it possible to run scoped queries that target only a specific granular aspect of the architecture decomposition (Fig. 3).

[3] HYPERLINK "https://graphwise.ai/" https://graphwise.ai/

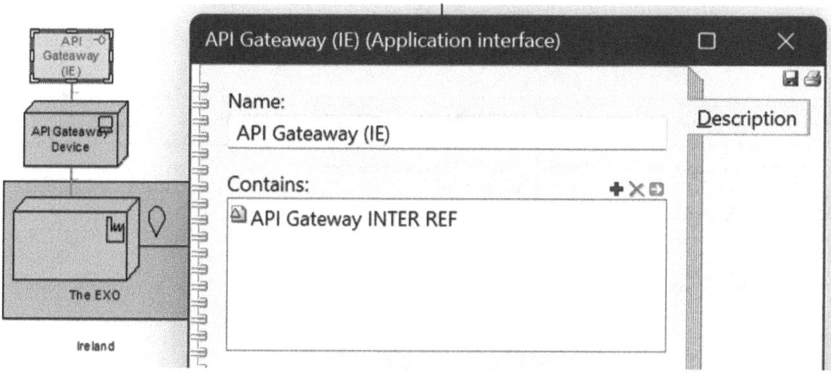

Fig. 3. Hyperlink example to detail the API Gateway

Fig. 4. Gateway INTERREF model example

4.3 Competency Evaluation

Evaluation-wise we are primarily interested in satisfying traceability and semantic patterns derived from the sovereignty analysis literature. Technical aspects of the diagrammatic tool are largely inherited - either from the underlying metamodeling platform (e.g. usability, scalability) or from the TEAM implementation that is extended here (e.g. the graphical notation, although quality of graphical extensions could be in the scope of our work). With the aid of the RDF transformation module, the model and metamodel are extracted from the modeling environment and converted into.trig files governed by a schema derived from the metamodel. These are hosted on a Graphwise GraphDB triplestore as named graphs where the SPARQL patterns exemplified below can then be executed by potential sovereignty analysis clients - and possibly by Graph RAG AI agents, an approach we experimented with in the past for BPMN only [13] but can be transferred also to DSMLs such as the one presented here. All SPARQL queries below can be further enriched with the AI-specific distinctions imposed on Archimate elements through the subtypes depicted in the metamodel in Fig. 1.

The competency evaluation showcases that the knowledge graph treatment enable query types specified and competency as derived from the literature: (a) *cross-layer traceability* - confirmed by the full relation chains (both visual and hyperlinks) spanning multiple diagrammatic views; (b) *AI-specific dependency representation* - confirmed by the training lineage and RAG dependency queries; and (c) *sovereignty-oriented classification* - confirmed by the data residency and cross-border transfer queries. These results demonstrate that Archimate extended with AI-specific constructs and transformed to RDF knowledge graphs can serve as a practical operational tool for AI sovereignty governance (Tables 1 and 2).

Table 1. SPARQL queries for AI component inventory and training data lineage

Competency Question	SPARQL Query (prefixes omitted)

Which application components are AI and which are NON_AI?
(EU AI Act scope identification)
	SELECT ?name ?classification
	WHERE {
	GRAPH ?g {
	?obj a :o_Application_component ;
	adoxx_mm:a_Name ?name ;
	:a_DIF ?classification .
	}
	FILTER(!CONTAINS(STR(?g), "INTER_REF"))
	}
	ORDER BY ?classification

What is the training data lineage for each AI model?
(EU AI Act Art. 10 traceability)
	SELECT ?datasetName ?modelName
	WHERE {
	GRAPH ?g {
	?ds adoxx_mm:a_Name ?datasetName ;
	:r_Trained ?m .
	?m adoxx_mm:a_Name ?modelName ;
	:a_DIF "AI" .
	}
	}

Where do LLMs get the data they are trained with?
(provenance risk)
	SELECT ?datasetName ?llmName
	WHERE {
	GRAPH ?g {
	?dataset adoxx_mm:a_Name ?datasetName ;
	:r_Trained ?llm .
	?llm adoxx_mm:a_Name ?llmName .
	}
	}

Which AI components retrieve from which Knowledge Graphs at runtime?
(RAG dependency map)
	SELECT ?llmName ?kgName
	WHERE {
	GRAPH ?g {
	?l adoxx_mm:a_Name ?llmName ;
	:a_DIF "AI" ;
	:r_Retrieve ?k .
	?k adoxx_mm:a_Name ?kgName .
	}}

Table 2. SPARQL queries for digital sovereignty and EU regulatory compliance

<table>
<tr><th>Competency Question</th><th>SPARQL Query (prefixes omitted)</th></tr>
<tr><td>Where are datasets physically stored and in which jurisdiction?
(GDPR data residency)</td><td>SELECT ?dataset ?storageDevice ?jurisdiction
WHERE {
GRAPH ?g {
?loc a :o_Location ;
adoxx_mm:a_Name ?jurisdiction ;
:r_Contains ?fac .
?fac a :o_Facility ; :r_Contains ?dev .
?dev a :o_Device ;
adoxx_mm:a_Name ?storageDevice ;
:r_Contains ?art .
?art adoxx_mm:a_Name ?dataset ; a ?artType .
FILTER(?artType IN (:o_Data_object, :o_Artifact))
}
}
ORDER BY ?jurisdiction</td></tr>
<tr><td>Which cross-border associations link EU and US locations?
(GDPR Art. 46 transfer detection)</td><td>SELECT DISTINCT ?routeName ?fromName ?toName
WHERE {
GRAPH ?g {
?route a :o_Distribution_network ;
adoxx_mm:a_Name ?routeName .
?assocIn a :r_Association ;
adoxx_mm:from ?fromObj ; adoxx_mm:to ?route .
?assocOut a :r_Association ;
adoxx_mm:from ?route ; adoxx_mm:to ?toObj .
?fromObj adoxx_mm:a_Name ?fromName .
?toObj adoxx_mm:a_Name ?toName .
FILTER((?fromName IN ("USA (Alaska)", "AWS Data Center")
&& ?toName IN ("Germany","Switzerland","Ireland","France"))
|| (?toName IN ("USA (Alaska)", "AWS Data Center")
&& ?fromName IN ("Germany","Switzerland","Ireland","France")))
}
}
ORDER BY ?routeName</td></tr>
<tr><td>List all INTERREF drill-down points: which diagram elements have sub-diagrams?
(structural navigation)</td><td>SELECT ?objectName ?interref
WHERE {
GRAPH ?g {
?obj adoxx_mm:a_Name ?objectName ;
:r_Contains ?interref .
FILTER(CONTAINS(STR(?interref), "INTER_REF"))
}
}</td></tr>
<tr><td>Full relation inventory across all diagrams: every from → relationType → to triple
(global dependency map)</td><td>SELECT ?graph ?fromName ?relType ?toName WHERE {
GRAPH ?graph {
{
?rel adoxx_mm:from ?from ; adoxx_mm:to ?to ; a ?relType .
FILTER(?relType NOT IN (adoxx_mm:r_Modeling_relation_a,
adoxx_mm:r_Modeling_relation_na))
} UNION {
?from ?relType ?to .
FILTER(?relType IN (:r_Flow, :r_Trained, :r_Retrieve,
:r_Replicate, :r_Composition,
:r_Assignment, :r_Realization))
}
?from adoxx_mm:a_Name ?fromName .
?to adoxx_mm:a_Name ?toName . }}</td></tr>
</table>

As a key limitation we indicate the overly relaxed metamodel that allows the new connectors to be applied to diverse constructs - this could be constrained by a SHACL validation while keeping the diagrammatic-oriented metamodel as relaxed as possible. A single running scenario was used to validate the modeling requirements; further iterations will need to demonstrate applicability in real case needs. Finally the knowledge graph treatment captures a point-in-time architectural snapshot but AI systems can be dynamic - models are retrained, datasets updated, infrastructure reconfigured - semantic queries address sovereignty issues relative to the model's current state rather than tracking changes over time. Architecture differentiators in relation to Archimate gaps (in migration models) thus become relevant and will be investigated in the future.

5 Conclusions and Future Work

This work shows that Enterprise Architecture modeling can serve as a useful instrument for AI sovereignty governance, helping to close the gap between the conceptual framing of digital sovereignty in the literature and operational requirements imposed by the EU AI Act and the GDPR. The proposed approach extends Archimate with an AI sovereignty modeling layer, realized in ADOxx the AMME methodology inside a Design Science Research cycle and complemented by a knowledge graph treatment that makes the resulting models queryable. Exemplary targeted cases are GDPR data residency (where are datasets stored?); GDPR Article 46 cross-border transfer detection (which associations link EU and US locations?); EU AI Act training data traceability (which datasets trained which AI models?); and RAG runtime dependency mapping (which AI models retrieve from which knowledge graphs at runtime?).

This is the initial DSR iteration of the project – the next iterations will evolve towards the recently launched Archimate 4.0 specification. We also consider the integration of SHACL validation rules as means to detect certain non-compliance situations. Finally, a key target is integration with GraphDB's Talk-To-Your-Graph feature[4] to facilitate natural language querying over diagrammatic designs, a model-driven Graph RAG integration pattern we're experimenting with in project-specific settings - for BPMN-based DSMLs [43], but equally applicable here.

6 Disclosure of Interests.

The authors have no competing interests to declare that are relevant to the content of this article.

Acknowledgments. This work was developed as part of the first author's master dissertation titled *Extending Archimate for AI Sovereignty: A Governance Framework for Multi-Jurisdictional AI Deployments* - by Andreea Eva-Adam, defended at Babeş-Bolyai University in 2026 under the supervision of Prof. Dr. Robert Andrei Buchmann.

The work extends the Archimate implementation of the TEAM OMILAB project available at https://www.omilab.org/activities/projects/details/?id=139. We are thankful to the TEAM authors and to OMILAB NPO for the shared resource.

[4] https://graphdb.ontotext.com/documentation/11.3/talk-to-graph.html.

References

1. Badawy, W.: Algorithmic sovereignty and democratic resilience: rethinking AI governance in the age of generative AI. AI Ethics **5**(5):4855–4862, https://doi.org/10.1007/s43681-025-00739-z (2025)
2. BOC GmbH, ADOxx Metamodeling Platform. https://www.adoxx.org, Accessed 26 June 2026
3. Bommasani, R. et al.: On the opportunities and risks of foundation models. arXiv:2108.07258. https://doi.org/10.48550/arXiv.2108.07258
4. Bork, D., et al.: Requirements engineering for model-based enterprise architecture management with archimate. In: Proceedings of EOMAS 2018, pp. 16–30. Springer, Cham (2018). https://doi.org/10.1007/978-3-030-00787-4_2
5. Broeders, D., Cristiano, F., Kaminska, M.: In search of digital sovereignty and strategic autonomy: normative power Europe to the test of its geopolitical ambitions. J. Common Market Stud. **61**(5):1261–1280 (2023). https://doi.org/10.1111/jcms.13462
6. Buchmann, R.A.: Modeling product-service systems for the Internet of Things: the ComVantage method. In: Domain-Specific Conceptual Modeling, pp. 417–437, Springer, Cham (2016). https://doi.org/10.1007/978-3-319-39417-6_19
7. Caetano, A., et al.: Representation and analysis of enterprise models with semantic techniques: an application to Archimate, e3value and business model canvas. Knowl. Inf. Syst. **50**, 315–346 (2017). https://doi.org/10.1007/s10115-016-0933-0
8. Calderaro, A., Blumfelde, S.: Artificial intelligence and EU security: the false promise of digital sovereignty. Eur. Secur. **31**(3), 415–434 (2022). https://doi.org/10.1080/09662839.2022.2101885
9. Calzada, I.: Artificial intelligence for social innovation: beyond the noise of algorithms and datafication. Sustainability **16**(19), 8638 (2024). https://doi.org/10.3390/su16198638
10. Carrapico, H., Farrand, B.: Cybersecurity trends in the European Union: regulatory mercantilism and the digitalisation of geopolitics. J. Common Mark. Stud. 62, 147–158 (2024). https://doi.org/10.1111/jcms.13654
11. Couture, S., Toupin, S.: What does the notion of "sovereignty" mean when referring to the digital? New Media Soc. **21**(10), 2305–2322 (2019). https://doi.org/10.1177/1461444819865984
12. Deibert, R.: The geopolitics of cyberspace after Snowden. Current History **114**(768), 9–15 (2015). https://doi.org/10.1525/curh.2015.114.768.9
13. Dolha, D.N., Buchmann, R.A.: Experimental assessments of retrieval-augmented conversational agents interpreting RDF-serialized BPMN models. In: Perspectives in Business Informatics Research. BIR 2025. Lecture Notes in Business Information Processing, vol. 562, pp. 286–304, Springer, Cham (2026). https://doi.org/10.1007/978-3-032-04375-7_18
14. European Commission, Proposal for a regulation laying down harmonised rules on Artificial Intelligence (Artificial Intelligence Act). https://eur-lex.europa.eu/legal-content/EN/TXT/?uri=celex:52021PC0206, Accessed 26 June 2026
15. Fill, H.G., Redmond, T., Karagiannis, D.: Formalizing metamodels with FDMM: The ADOxx case. In: Enterprise Information Systems, Lecture Notes in Business Information Processing 141, pp. 429–451, Springer Cham (2013). https://doi.org/10.1007/978-3-642-40654-6_26
16. Floridi, L.: The fight for digital sovereignty: what it is, and why it matters, especially for the EU. Philosop. Technol. **33**(3), 369–378 (2020). https://doi.org/10.1007/s13347-020-00423-6
17. Hulkó, G., Kalmán, J., Lapsánszky, A.: The politics of digital sovereignty and the European Union legislation: navigating crises. Front. Polit. Sci. **7**, 1548562 (2025). https://doi.org/10.3389/fpos.2025.1548562

18. Hummel, P., Braun, M., Tretter, M., Dabrock, P.: Data sovereignty: a review. Big Data Soc. **8**(1) (2021). https://doi.org/10.1177/2053951720982012
19. Karagiannis, D.: Conceptual modeling methods: the AMME agile engineering approach. In: Domain-Specific Conceptual Modeling, pp. 3–21. Springer Cham (2022). https://doi.org/10.1007/978-3-030-93547-4_1
20. Buchmann, R.A., Karagiannis, D.: Agile Modelling Method Engineering: Lessons Learned in the ComVantage Research Project. In: Ralyté, J., España, S., Pastor, Ó. (eds.) PoEM 2015. LNBIP, vol. 235, pp. 356–373. Springer, Cham (2015). https://doi.org/10.1007/978-3-319-25897-3_23
21. Karagiannis, D., Buchmann, R.A.: Extending linked open data with conceptual model information. Inf. Syst. **56**:174–197 (2016). https://doi.org/10.1016/j.is.2015.10.001
22. Krafft, P.M., et al.: An action-oriented AI policy toolkit for technology audits by and for communities. In: Proceedings of FAccT 2021, pp. 772–781, ACM (2021). https://doi.org/10.1145/3442188.3445938
23. The Open Group: Archimate 3.0 Specification. https://pubs.opengroup.org/architecture/Archimate3-doc/ , Accessed 26 June 2026
24. Lewis, P., et al.: Retrieval-augmented generation for knowledge-intensive NLP tasks. In: Advances in Neural Information Processing Systems, vol. 33, pp. 9459–9474 (2020). https://proceedings.neurips.cc/paper/2020/hash/6b493230205f780e1bc26945df7481e5-Abstract.html
25. Mayer, N., Aubert, J., Grandry, E., Feltus, C., Goettelmann, E., Wieringa, R.: An integrated conceptual model for information system security risk management supported by enterprise architecture management. Softw. Syst. Model. **18**, 2285–2312 (2019). https://doi.org/10.1007/s10270-018-0661-x
26. Mueller, M.L.: Will the Internet fragment? Sovereignty, globalization and cyberspace. Polity Press, Cambridge (2017)
27. Mügge, D.: EU AI sovereignty: for whom, to what end, and to whose benefit? Journal of Eur. Publ. Pol. **31**(8), 2200–2225 (2024). https://doi.org/10.1080/13501763.2024.2318475
28. Nanni, R., Bizzaro, P.G., Napolitano, M.: The false promise of individual digital sovereignty in Europe: Comparing AI and data regulations in China and the European Union. Pol. Internet **16**(4), 711–726 (2024). https://doi.org/10.1002/poi3.424
29. Novelli, C., Casolari, F., Rotolo, A., Taddeo, M., Floridi, L.: Taking AI risks seriously: a new assessment model for the AI Act. AI Soc. **39**, 2493–2497 (2024). https://doi.org/10.1007/s00146-023-01723-z
30. Noy, N., Gao, Y., Jain, A., Narayanan, A., Patterson, A., Taylor, J.: Industry-scale knowledge graphs: lessons and challenges. Commun. ACM **62**(8), 36–43 (2019). https://doi.org/10.1145/3331166
31. OMiLAB, Open Models Initiative Laboratory: ADOxx RDF Plugin. https://code.omilab.org/resources/adoxx-modules/rdf-transformation , Accessed 26 June 2026
32. Peffers, K., Tuunanen, T., Rothenberger, M.A., Chatterjee, S.: A Design Science research methodology for information systems research. J. Manag. Inf. Syst. **24**(3), 45–77 (2007). https://doi.org/10.2753/MIS0742-1222240302
33. Pittl, B., Bork, D.: Modeling digital enterprise ecosystems with Archimate: a mobility provision case study. In: Serviceology for Services. ICServ 2017. Lecture Notes in Computer Science, vol. 10371, pp. 178–189, Springer, Cham (2017). https://doi.org/10.1007/978-3-319-61240-9_17
34. Roberts, H.: Digital sovereignty and artificial intelligence: a normative approach. Ethics Inf. Technol. **26**, 70 (2024). https://doi.org/10.1007/s10676-024-09810-5
35. Rone, J.: 'The sovereign cloud' in Europe: diverging nation state preferences and disputed institutional competences in the context of limited technological capabilities. J. Eur. Publ. Pol. **31**(8), 2343–2369 (2024). https://doi.org/10.1080/13501763.2024.2348618

36. Sheikh, H.: European digital sovereignty: a layered approach. Digit. Soc. **1**, 25 (2022). https://doi.org/10.1007/s44206-022-00025-z
37. Sokol, K., Flach, P.: Explainability is in the mind of the beholder: establishing the foundations of explainable artificial intelligence. arXiv:2112.14466 (2021). https://doi.org/10.48550/arXiv.2112.14466
38. Taylor, L., de Souza, S. P., Martin, A., López-Solano, J.: Governing artificial intelligence means governing data: (re)setting the agenda for data justice. Dialogues Digit. Soc. **2**(1), 5–22 (2025). https://doi.org/10.1177/29768640241306800
39. The Open Group: TOGAF Standard, Version 9.2. The Open Group Standard, https://pubs.opengroup.org/architecture/togaf9-doc/arch/, Accessed 26 June 2026
40. Voigt, P., von dem Bussche, A.: The EU General Data Protection Regulation (GDPR): a practical guide. Springer, Cham (2017). https://doi.org/10.1007/978-3-319-57959-7
41. Wieringa, R.J.: Design Science methodology for information systems and software engineering. Springer, https://doi.org/10.1007/978-3-662-43839-8 (2014)
42. Zachman, J. A.: A framework for information systems architecture. IBM Syst. J. **26**(3), 276–292 (1987). https://doi.org/10.1147/sj.263.0276
43. Dolha, D.N., Osman, C.C., Chiş, A.: KM4ESG: BPMN and AI-powered knowledge management platform for ESG analysis and reporting. In: CAISE-RPE 2025, CEUR-WS, vol. 4050, (2025). https://ceur-ws.org/Vol-4050/paper01.pdf

Supporting Best Practices Propagation Within Fractal Organizations Using Large Language Models and Knowledge Graphs

Aritha Kumarasinghe(✉)

Institute of Applied Computer Systems, Riga Technical University, 6A Kipsalas Street, Riga 1048, Latvia
balasuriyage-aritha-dewnith.kumarasinghe@rtu.lv

Abstract. Decentralization of organizational structures can lead to the formation of silos, which limit the sharing of information (such as best practices) across organizational units. To potentially address this issue, this work considers the use of knowledge graphs and large language models combined with a fractal perspective on organization to support the propagation of best practices relating to the formulation of textual information. A novel system architecture is proposed to support the **P**ropagation of **B**est **P**ractices within **F**ractal **O**rganizations using **L**LMs and **K**Gs (PBP-FOLK). The proposed system architecture is implemented and demonstrated for the use case of developing and maintaining curriculum in universities. The results indicate improvements in the formulation of learning outcomes defined in curricula across 29 study courses belonging to a single study program.

Keywords: Fractal Information Systems · Best Practices · Knowledge Graphs · Large Language Models · Fractal Organizations · Knowledge Propagation

1 Introduction

The decentralization of organizations can lead to improved autonomy and adaptability within increasingly complex environments [1]. This complexity can lead to the formation of clusters/silos that limit the exchange of knowledge and information between organizational units [2]. A possible solution for improving the exchange of information across organizational units is the adoption of a fractal perspective of enterprises (referred to as fractal companies/organizations) which considers organizational units to have similar structures/aims across different hierarchical levels, resulting in self-similarity (the central characteristic of 'fractal' as a geometric concept) [3].

This self-similarity in terms of structure/aims can result in self-similarity of the functions and, in turn, the information structures of organizational units, which can be leveraged when developing information systems/architectures for fractal organizations [4–6]. Fractal-based information architecture offers a balance between stability and local adaptability by building a core ontology that defines the self-similar information

E. Laurenzi et al. (Eds.): BIR 2026, LNBIP 601, pp. 276–290, 2027.
https://doi.org/10.1007/978-3-032-38498-0_18

structure that is consistent across organizational units, which can then be freely adapted by local units based on the functions that are being carried out [4, 6]. Previous research has demonstrated how implementing a fractal-based information system led to increased collaboration between decentralized health care units by utilizing an observer component to monitor the changes in the data (patient records, examinations, diagnosis, treatments, etc.) utilized by a local unit and then reporting these changes to the information systems that are used by other units [5]. This monitoring and reporting of changes made led to the expansion of a global knowledge base (shared globally across organizational units) according to the functions that were carried out locally by each organizational unit [5]. This sharing/propagation of knowledge (as well as best practices) is a key benefit of utilizing a fractal perspective when developing information systems/architectures that enable flexible business processes as well as increased adaptability to changing environmental conditions [4, 5].

While previous research has demonstrated how a fractal perspective of information systems can facilitate the exchange of knowledge across the organizational units, the scope of identifying best practices is limited to the sharing of data records (as was the case in [5]) or the relying on manual knowledge propagation mechanisms where users have to monitor, share, and adopt best practices within an information system [7]. This presents a gap in the research relating to how the knowledge (best practices) produced during the functioning of fractal units can be identified and propagated without relying on fully manual processes.

The introduction of Large Language Models (LLMs) and the subsequent increased research interest in how they can be integrated with Knowledge Graphs (KGs) [8] present a possible solution to the reliance on manual processes for best practices identification and propagation within fractal organizations. LLMs represent a significant breakthrough in natural language processing that are capable of 'understanding' natural language without the need for training data based on the task performed [8]. KGs are formal representations of knowledge as nodes and edges, which can be used as a knowledge structure that can be read and altered by LLMs based on users' instructions (prompts) [8]. This synergy between the grounded knowledge representation of KGs and the natural language processing capabilities of LLMs represents a potential solution for the semi-automated identification and propagation of best practices between fractal units (organizational units that form a fractal organization). This can be achieved by representing the information produced/changed by fractal units as nodes within a KG and utilizing LLMs to analyze this information to identify the best practices that are represented in this information, which can then be shared across fractal units. It should be noted that this work focuses on best practices relating to the formulation of textual information, focusing on improving the wording, consistency of language use, and coherence. Whereas the author's previous work considered the propagation of best practices relating to how fractal-based LLM agents are structured [9], this work focuses on the identification and propagation of best practices based on the information produced by fractal agents.

Therefore, this work seeks to present a systems architecture that utilizes KGs to represent information within a fractal organization and to use LLMs to identify best practices relating to the formulation of textual information and to support the propagation of these best practices to other fractal units. By proposing such an architecture, this work seeks to answer the research question: *How can LLMs integrated with KGs support the semi-automated identification and propagation of best practices relating to the formulation of textual information across units within a fractal organization?* In order to demonstrate and validate this architecture, the development and maintenance (engineering) of curricula within a university is considered as a real-world use case, given that universities represent an organization that can face issues associated with silos [10], and since curricula have a fractal knowledge structure as demonstrated in [6] the elements of which can vary in quality based on the language used e.g., the use of action verbs when writing learning outcomes [11].

The remainder of the work is organized as follows. Section 2 presents the background of this research, introducing the concept of fractals and how it can be applied to organizations and the information systems that support them, as well as discussing LLMs and KGs. The subsequent Sect. 3 introduces the system architecture that utilizes LLMs and KGs for the propagation of best practices across fractal units. Section 4 demonstrates how the architecture can be implemented and utilized within the context of curriculum engineering at a university. Section 5 presents the evaluation of the implemented system for the reformulation of learning outcomes, based on metrics relating to action verb usage and semantic similarity. Section 6 presents the conclusion and possible directions for future research.

2 Background

This section presents concepts related to this research, with the first subsection presenting fractal organizations and the information systems that can be used to support them. The second subsection presents LLMs and KGs and the reasoning as to why they can be utilized in fractal information systems.

2.1 Fractal Organization and Information Systems

The concept of 'fractals' is rooted in geometry and is used to analyze complex patterns that have a recurring structure across different scales, resulting in parts of the system having the same structure as a whole (self-similarity) [11]. This concept was applied to organizations/companies, giving rise to the notion of a fractal company [3]. The fractal company applies the concept of fractals to organizations by representing them as proactive performing elements (units) referred to as fractals that have the main attributes/principles of (self) similarity, self-organization, self-optimization, and dynamism [3]. This allows fractals to organize themselves in order to achieve the goals of the organization and according to changes in their environment [3]. This makes fractal organizations particularly suitable for environments that require the ability to dynamically adapt (evolve) to changes in said environments, an example being manufacturing systems [13].

Based on the principles of fractal organizations, [14] presents an agent-based architecture for distributed fractal manufacturing systems, where the fractals conform to the structure of a Basic Fractal Unit (BFU). The BFU consists of five functional modules, namely (1) an observer responsible for monitoring the internal state of the fractal unit as well as conveying external information to the fractal unit, (2) an analyzer that evaluates different job/action plans and selects the most suitable, (3) a resolver/executer that makes decisions on the goals of the fractal-based on the selected action plan, (4) an organizer responsible for chaining the internal structure of the fractal unit, and (5) a reporter that sends internal results of the fractal to other fractals. The BFU structure ensures self-similarity within the fractal manufacturing system by making every fractal (unit) have a common structure while also being able to self-organize internal components based on the goal that is assigned. The application of fractal design principles to manufacturing systems has been demonstrated in several real-world cases, with the reported benefits being fast and flexible adaptation, production flexibility, and improved market alignment, etc. [13]. However, the systematic review presented in [13] also notes limitations within the context of fractal manufacturing systems with regard to digital and virtual requirements due to implementation complexity caused by a lack of technological development within the manufacturing domain.

Expanding on the theme of applying a fractal perspective to information systems, several works have discussed this topic [4–6]. The first of these presents a flexible information architecture for fractal information systems, considering educational institutions as an example of a system with fractal characteristics [4], where the pattern of educational institutions is replicated across different scales (department, institution, faculty, etc.) within the university. The presented information architecture is based on fractals to produce similar outputs from similar inputs using different internal procedures and structures [4]. This results in the information structures within the fractal having similar patterns based on a core ontology and core data structure [4]. By having the same core ontology and data structure across fractals, change propagation is possible through manual, semi-automatic, and automatic (through intelligent software) methods. Based on the flexible information architecture presented in [4], an information architecture is designed and implemented in [6]. This information architecture allows the user to manually define best practices in terms of new information element within the interface, which can then be shared with other fractals who can then adopt these best practices according to the information elements [6]. This information element sharing-based propagation of best practices is based on the results of [7], which defines a four-step procedure for changing business processes based on best practices (a single way of performing a task that is acknowledged as worthy of imitation across fractal units). The four steps within the best practices propagation procedure are as follows [7]: (1) Best practices identification: identifying a best practice that is used in a fractal unit; (2) Best practices acquisition planning: comparison of current processes and best practices; (3) Best practices acquisition cost estimation: estimation of the cost of changing the current process according to best practices; (4) Best practices acquisition: implementation of changes to the current process based on best practices.

In [7], an example case is considered relating to annual reports and discusses how an annual report template can be formulated by one fractal unit and then shared with other fractal units. While the exchange of information (e.g., templates) relating to best practices is facilitated using an information system, it is still reliant on manual processes to carry out the steps proposed in the best practices propagation procedure. Similarly, [5] presents a real-world implementation of a fractal information system for hospitals that consists of a BFU comprised of a controller module, analyzer and planner module, and executor module [5]. The fractals enable monitoring of new activities relating to patient care (controller module), accumulation of data relating to new activities (analyzer and planner module), and the sharing of data relating to new activities with other fractals (executor module) [5]. This sharing of data led to an increase in cooperation between hospitals based on survey and interview results [5]. Based on the results of [5–7], a previous work by the author applied a fractal perceptive to LLM-based multiagent systems and demonstrated how change propagation can occur by relaying information relating to how LLM-based agents are organized, and the benefits of doing so [9].

While these works [5–7] demonstrate how fractal information systems can be utilized to support the sharing of information relating to best practices and new activities, they are still reliant on manual processes for the identification, sharing, and adoption of best practices, or simply relay information about new activities and how they are organized (either by workers [5] of LLM-based agents [9]) across organizational units.

To further explore how a fractal perspective can be applied to information systems and the potential benefits of doing so, this work seeks to explore how the outputs generated by the fractal units within an organization can be analyzed to identify best practices and to propagate them to other units.

2.2 Large Language Models and Knowledge Graphs

LLMs are transformer-based models that are trained on vast amounts of textual data and are capable of performing various natural language processing tasks without having to be trained on task-specific data [8]. Their ability to 'understand' natural language has been utilized in previous research to generate evidence-based recommendations within the context of healthcare [15]. The consistency of the recommendations generated, when compared to existing guidelines, ranged from 50% to 91.7%. Similarly, [16] presents Quicker, an application that uses LLMs to synthesize clinical evidence and provide recommendations, with the evaluation results demonstrating how LLM-based pipelines can be used to support the synthesis of evidence and generate recommendations that have alignment scores comparable to those of attending physicians. These two studies provide evidence on how LLMs can be used to synthesize large amounts of information and generate recommendations within the high-risk domain of health care [15, 16]. The application of LLMs discussed in this paper is of lower risk since it is related to identifying best practices related to linguistic and structural aspects within textual artifacts.

Focusing on business contexts, [17] utilized LLMs within a large multinational company to extract process knowledge from heterogeneous enterprise content and used LLMs to generate responses to queries relating to these business processes. The results of evaluating the answers generated for 29 queries concluded that 28 of the answers generated by the solution were satisfactory [17]. This work demonstrates how LLMs can be combined with external data sources (enterprise content) to extract process knowledge and to provide answers to user queries based on this knowledge. While this and other studies demonstrate how LLMs can be used to extract process knowledge and provide responses to user queries based on this knowledge, the research discussed in this paper focuses more on the outputs of business processes and on using LLMs to identify best practices based on these outputs.

While LLMs are capable of carrying out natural language processing, they can still require external knowledge to carry out these tasks [8]. To address this issue, KGs can be used as a formal representation of knowledge, where nodes represent real-world entities, and edges represent the relationships between these entities [8]. By allowing LLMs to retrieve required knowledge from KGs, LLMs may benefit from reduced hallucinations, enhanced coherence, and higher accuracy [8]. Beyond simple LLM tasks, KGs have also been used in LLM-based agent systems by acting as a representation of the environment in which the LLM-based agents interact [8].

Additionally, LLMs can be used to address the static nature of KGs by leveraging their natural language generation capabilities to generate/update the knowledge contained within the KG [8]. In our work, KGs will serve as a formal representation of the textual information that can be retrieved and altered based on user queries. Using a KG provides the additional benefit relating to fractal information systems since they can directly utilize ontologies (e.g., the core ontology relating to the problem domain [4, 6]) as a schema where the ontology represents classes, and the KG represents instances of those classes [17]. An LLM can be used to identify what parts of the schema (classes and class properties) should be used. This approach is similar to the schema-aware approach proposed in [19].

Previous research has applied KGs within fractal contexts, especially [20], which utilizes KGs to represent self-similar knowledge structures in terms of how nodes and edges are organized. This work applies fractality to KGs in terms of the internal structure of the nodes (attributes), where the same node attributes are present across different levels. Given this similarity in how information is structured within nodes, the process, in terms of prompt knowledge retrieval and propagation, can be applied when utilizing LLMs for the identification and propagation of best practices related to the formulation of textual information. Therefore, the current research introduces the concept of a fractal attribute KG, which has the characteristic of the same attribute appearing across nodes at different hierarchical levels.

3 A System Architecture to Support the Propagation of Best Practices Within Fractal Organizations Using LLMs and KGs

As discussed in Sect. 2.1, fractal systems are composed of fractals that are structured based on BFU. Based on the BFU, presented in [5] and [14], which carry out the functions relating to the observation of fractal units and the execution of fractal-related tasks, the current research defines a BFU consisting of an LLM-based observer and executor modules. The observer is responsible for analyzing the textual data within a node of a KG and identifying the best practices related to how the text is formulated. Given the self-similarity in the attributes of the nodes (e.g., attribute 1.a and attribute 1.1.a shown in Fig. 1 are the same attribute across nodes but with specific values), the prompt and information retrieval from the KG can be utilized by all fractal units, thereby making the LLM-based best practices identification process less complex.

However, this also means that the prompts and the information that will be needed for the identification of best practices must be implemented by all fractal units. To address this issue, the software architecture consists of a single LLM-based fractal planner that

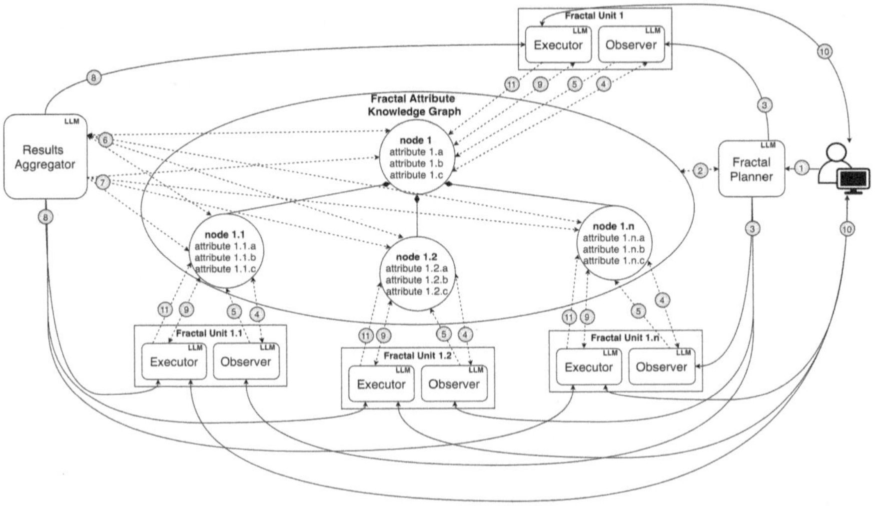

Fig. 1. Model representing PBP-FOLK and the interactions between the user, KG, and LLMs

is responsible for defining what prompt and what textual information (node attributes) need to be used by the fractal units. The fractal planner retrieves the current schema of the KG (which defines the types of nodes, edges, and node attributes) using relevant graph database queries (e.g., using Neo4j's CALL apoc.meta.schema) and specifies a prompt, relevant node(s), and node properties based on the request made by the user. These prompts and specific nodes/properties are then utilized by the observer agents to identify best practices. Once an observer module within a fractal unit has identified best practices represented in the textual information stored in a node, it writes the identified best practices to the same node. This results in each node containing information relating to the best practices that it has inferred from the observer module based on the current textual information that it contains.

The propagation of best practices requires that those practices, identified in each fractal unit, be shared with other units. To accomplish this, an LLM-based Results Aggregator is used to analyze all the best practices identified by the fractal units to synthesize a complete list of best practices that can be implemented for the formulation of specific textual information.

This aggregated list of best practices is then written to all the nodes within the KG, which are queried by the LLM-based executor. The executor then reformulates the textual information stored in its specific node based on the aggregated list of best practices. Before changes are made to the information stored in the KG, the user is shown the changes made (reformulated textual information), which can then be accepted or rejected. If accepted, the textual information stored in the KG is updated.

A model representing the proposed system's architecture for propagating best practices in fractal organizations using LLMs and KGs (PBP-FOLK) is presented in Fig. 1.

The corresponding steps defined to address the four-step procedure for the propagation of best practices introduced in [7] are presented in Table 1.

Table 1. List of steps for supporting the propagation of best practices for the formulation of textual information using LLMs and KGs.

Task No. (see. Fig. 1)	Corresponding Best Practices Propagation Step [7]	Description
1	Best practices identification	User initiates a request (prompt) for discovering/propagating best practices related to text formulation
2	Best practices identification	Fractal planner queries KG to identify relevant node attributes that must be analyzed to identify best practices
3	Best practices identification	Planner defines the prompt and node attributes that should be used to identify text formulation best practices
4	Best practices identification	Observer queries KG node attributes related to identifying text formulation best practices
5	Best practices identification	Observer executes the prompt to identify best practices and saves the identified best practices to the relevant node
6	Best practices identification	Results aggregator analyzes all the best practices saved in the nodes
7	Best practices identification	The Results Aggregator saves best practices related to text formulation for all KG nodes
8	Best practices acquisition	The Results Aggregator defines a prompt to be used by executors to define new textual information based on best practices
9	Best practices acquisition	Executor queries the best practices' current information stored in the KG nodes and executes a prompt to define new textual information based on best practices
10	Best practices' acquisition cost estimation	The system presents to the user new textual information formulated based on best practices identified, and the user decides whether to accept the best practices
11	Best practices acquisition	Saves new textual information in the KG node

4 Implementation and Demonstration of PBP-FOLK in the Context of Curriculum Engineering

A central aspect relating to the implementation of PBP-FOLK is the fractal attribute KG. Therefore, constructing this KG was the first task that was accomplished to implement PBP-FOLK within the context of curriculum engineering. First, a review of the current representations of curriculum information was conducted, which in the current case were represented as PDF documents describing the study programs and study courses offered by the university. The documents relating to the study programs define the program title, identification code, type of study program, language, abstract, aim, learning outcomes, etc. of the study program. The documents relating to the courses describe the course title, identification code, language of instruction, abstract, goals and objectives of the course in terms of competences and skills, and learning outcomes, etc. The attributes listed demonstrate how the same attributes (e.g., abstract and learning outcomes) co-occur at different curriculum organization levels.

These attributes represent the fractal structure in which information is organized within the curriculum engineering process. Based on this information structure, two types of nodes (ontological classes) were defined for the curriculum KG to represent study programs (:StudyProgram) and study courses (:StudyCourse), and a single type of edge (consists_of) was defined between the:StudyProgram and:StudyCourse nodes based on the courses that are taught in a given program. In terms of node properties/attributes, both node types consist of Title, Identification Code, Abstract, Aims, and LearningOutcomes. This ensures that the same information structure is present in all nodes within the curriculum KG.

Based on the above-discussed structure, a curriculum KG was constructed in an Neo4j graph database to represent a single study program and the underlying 29 study courses taught within that study program. To ensure transparency and the reproducibility of this research, an export of the curriculum KG is made available on a GitHub repository [21], which can be imported into Neo4j.

To implement the PBP-FOLK, which can be used to identify and propagate best practices represented in the information represented in the curriculum KG, a Python script was defined. The script implements PBP-FOLK, consisting of an LLM-based planner, observer, results aggregator, and executor modules being implemented using OpenAI's GPT-5.4-mini (temperature = 0.1) in order to provide a balance between speed, performance, and cost. In addition, the Python script implements a Streamlit-based user interface (UI), which allows the user to input prompts (Task No. 1 in Table 1) into the PBP-FOLK implementation. Once the query is inputted, the UI (Fig. 2, 3 and 4) allows the user to see the outputs of individual modules, in addition to allowing the user to select which outputs are generated by the executors of each fractal unit.

To demonstrate the implementation of PBP-FOLK and its UI (Fig. 2, 3 and 4), this research considers the improvement of learning outcomes, which are statements that specify what learners are supposed to demonstrate in terms of understanding and what knowledge they should be able to apply. The query intended to improve the learning outcomes defined in the curriculum represented in the KG is '*Identify and propagate best practices for writing learning outcomes*'.

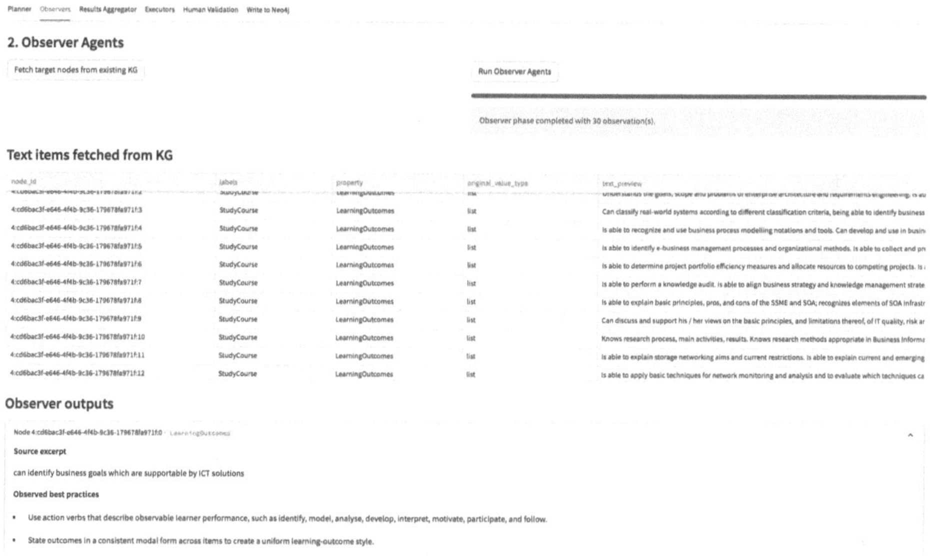

Fig. 2. Observer modules related interface of PBP-FOLK implementation.

As expected, the LLM-based planner module correctly identifies the LearningOutcomes node properties/attributes of the node types StudyProgram and StudyCourse, which define the learning outcomes of a study course/program. The identification of relevant node types and properties is accomplished using the apoc.meta.schema() Neo4j (Cypher) query, which means that this implementation of PBP-FOLK can be used with any KG.

Once the LLM-based planner identifies relevant properties and a prompt for the observer module based on the user query, individual LLM instances are used to execute said prompt on each of the nodes within the KG that have the identified property. This results in the identification of best practices based on the textual information contained in each node, a segment of which is shown at the bottom of Fig. 2.

Once all the observer modules for each fractal unit have written the best practices identified to the respective nodes, the Results aggregator analyzes all these best practices to formulate a single list of best practices which in this case consists of 12 best practices relating to the formulation of learning outcomes (see Fig. 3). Special attention should be drawn to the 11th best practice shown in Fig. 3 which states that learning outcomes should cover "understanding, application, analysis, evaluation, design, and communication". The first four of these aspects draw parallels to Bloom's taxonomy of educational objectives [22], which consists of remembering, understanding, applying, analyzing, evaluating, and creating, even though none of the best practices identified for the 29 course and 1 program learning outcomes relate directly to this taxonomy.

Based on this list of 12 best practices, the executors reformulated all 30 of the learning objectives, with the before and after of two courses being represented in Fig. 4. For each of these reformulations, the users can accept or decline them as they see fit, thereby ensuring human validation as opposed to fully automated changes of curricula.

Overall, the learning outcomes formulated by the executor modules are more consistent (all stating the "is able to") across the two courses and more granular in the case of the first course.

Fig. 3. Results Aggregator module related interface of the PBP-FOLK implementation showing a list of 12 identified best practices for formulating learning outcomes within curricula.

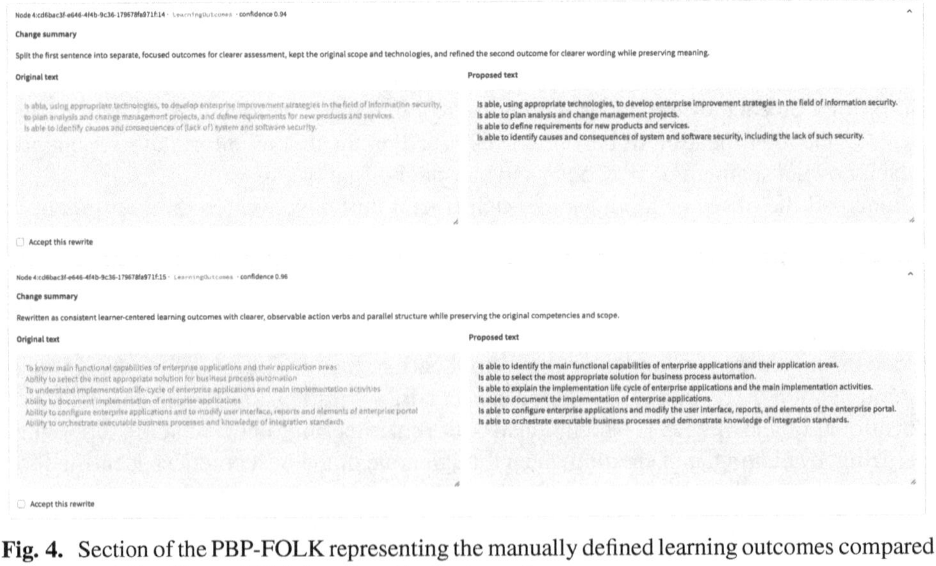

Fig. 4. Section of the PBP-FOLK representing the manually defined learning outcomes compared with those defined by an LLM, based on the best practices.

5 Evaluation of PBP-FOLK for Supporting Learning Outcome Formulation

To evaluate the ability of PBP-FOLK to support the reformulation of learning outcomes, a comparison of the learning outcomes before (the original written by the lecturers) and after reformulation (rewritten by the executor agent based on the identified best practices) was done.

To compare learning outcomes pre- and post-reformulation, metrics were related to the writing learning outcomes based on Bloom's taxonomy and the associated action verbs that should be and should not be used [11, 23]. The analysis conducted in [23] presents a list of action verbs related to each level of Bloom's taxonomy, which should be used when writing learning outcomes, and a list of action verbs that should be avoided while formulating learning outcomes. Therefore, the total number of action verbs in the formulated learning outcomes that are from the list of action verbs that should be used (defined as recommended action verb count in Table 2), e.g., rate, create, and analyze [23], as well as the number of action verbs used from the list of action verbs that should be avoided (defined as discouraged action verb count in Table 2), e.g., appreciate, know, aware, when formulating the learning outcomes is counted.

Additionally, according to the guidelines defined in [11], one learning outcome should have one action verb, with the metric of the number of atomic learning outcomes being presented in Table 2. It should be noted that neither the guidelines presented in [11] nor the action verbs presented in [23] were explicitly included in the prompts; therefore, this evaluation indicates how the best practices identified can coincide with the best practices identified in the literature.

To address the non-deterministic nature of LLMs [24], the same prompt presented in Sect. 4 (*'Identify and propagate best practices for writing learning outcomes'*) was executed 10 separate times with the same input KG. The mean execution results across all study programs/courses and the subsequent mean of these results across the 10 runs are shown in Table 2. The results of the planner module for the ten runs selected the correct node property of LearingOutcomes in nine out of ten iterations, but in the fourth iteration, it also selected the Aims property; hence there is a variation in the inputs considered before reformulation caused by that single run.

Table 2. Action verb-based evaluation of learning outcomes before and after reformulation using PBP-FOLK.

	recommended action verb count (mean ± standard deviation over ten iterations)	discouraged action verb count (mean ± standard deviation for ten iterations)	atomic learning outcomes defined (mean ± standard deviation over ten iterations)
Before	112.50 ± 23.72	48.60 ± 8.22	59.40 ± 1.26
After	120.50 ± 24.08	42.40 ± 9.75	63.60 ± 8.30

These results indicate that using PBP-FOLK increased the usage of recommended action verbs by an average of 8.0 action verbs across the ten runs and reduced the usage of discouraged action verbs by 6.2 across the ten runs. This indicates that the proposed solution can support the improvement of the quality of learning outcomes.

While the previous three metrics were used to evaluate changes in terms of action verbs of reformulating learning outcomes, the evaluation also had to ensure that the reformulated learning outcomes kept their original meaning. To evaluate this, the semantic similarity (cosine similarity) between the learning outcomes before and after reformulation was measured. Semantic similarity was calculated using an embeddings model (which in this case was OpenAI's text-embedding-3-large) to generate embeddings to represent the learning outcomes defined for a single study course/program either before or after reformulation. Then the cosine similarity between the embedding representing the learning outcomes before reformulation and the embeddings representing the learning outcomes after reformulation is calculated. The mean cosine similarity across all study courses/programs for the ten runs was 0.89 ± 0.06.

These results indicate that the reformulated learning outcomes retained most of the semantic content of the learning outcomes before reformulation, and the change in the usage of action verbs indicates that there is an improvement in the usage of action verbs that are recommended to be used and a decrease in the usage of action verbs that should be avoided. This indicates that the reformulation does improve the quality of the formulation of learning outcomes defined without altering the original meaning of manually written learning outcomes.

6 Conclusion and Future Work

This work seeks to address the identification and propagation of best practices within fractal organizations using LLMs and KGs by proposing a system architecture (PBP-FOLK). This architecture defines a BFU consisting of an LLM-based observer module and executor module, in addition to a planner and results aggregator module. By doing so, it supports the identification and propagation of best practices within fractal organizations using a Fractal Attribute KG to represent information and using the planner module to identify which node properties (attributes) within the KG are needed to execute the best practice propagation-related queries defined by the user (e.g., '*Identify and propagate best practices for writing learning outcomes*'). Based on the identified nodes' properties and the prompts defined by the planner modules, observer modules execute these prompts on individual nodes within the KG to identify the best practices represented in the textual information stored in each node. These identified best practices are aggregated and propagated to the executor instances (by the results aggregator modules), which are responsible for reformulating the textual information based on these best practices. Finally, the user can specify whether to accept or reject the reformulated text, thereby ensuring human validation of the LLM outputs.

PBP-FOLK is implemented using a Python script in combination with a curriculum KG (both of which are publicly available on GitHub [21]) to improve the formulation of curricula at a university. The aforementioned scenario was used for identifying and propagating best practices related to the formulation of learning outcomes, where the implementation synthesized a list of 12 best practices that can be used when writing learning outcomes. The demonstration results indicate an improvement in consistency and structure of learning outcomes defined across 29 study courses taught in a single study program.

To evaluate the proposed solution the task of reformulating learning outcomes was considered, with evaluation metrics relating to the usage of action verbs and semantic similarity being defined. The results indicate that the learning outcomes reformulated by the PBP-FOLK had an improvement in the action verbs used both in terms of the verbs that are recommended and those that should be avoided (as defined in [23]). Additionally, the near 0.9 cosine similarity between the learning outcomes before and after reformulation indicates that most of the original semantic content was preserved during the reformulation process.

While this initial demonstration and evaluation of the utility of PBP-FOLK within the context of curriculum engineering provides evidence of how it can be used for the propagation of best practices related to the formulation of text, it does not represent conclusive experimental results. Therefore, future research can seek to implement PBP-FOLK within a real-world setting and to gather feedback from curriculum developers on how it can be used to support the propagation of best practices.

References

1. Helmrich, A., et al.: Centralization and decentralization for resilient infrastructure and complexity. Environ. Res. Infrastruct. Sustain. **1**(2), 021001 (2021)
2. Bento, F., Tagliabue, M., Lorenzo, F.: Organizational silos: A scoping review informed by a behavioral perspective on systems and networks. Societies **10**(3), 56 (2020)
3. Warnecke, H.J.: Fractal company. Acta Mechanica Slovaca **13**(3), 6–13 (2009)
4. Kirikova, M.: Towards flexible information architecture for fractal information systems. In: 2009 International Conference on Information, Process, and Knowledge Management, pp. 135–140. IEEE (2009)
5. Ahmed, N.S.: A fractal-based model to improve cooperation among physicians in distributed healthcare information systems. University of Malaya, Malaysia (2013)
6. Grabis, J., Kirikova, M., Vanags, J.: Information architecture of fractal information systems. In: International Conference on Enterprise Information Systems, vol. 1, pp. 150–155. SCITEPRESS (2009)
7. Stecjuka, J., Makna, J., Kirikova, M.: Best practices oriented business process operation and design. In: Proceedings of the 9th Workshop on Business Process Modeling, Development and Support: Business Process Life-Cycle—Design, Deployment, Operation and Evaluation, BPMDS 2008, pp. 16–17. Montpellier, France (2008)
8. Cai, L., Yu, C., Kang, Y., Fu, Y., Zhang, H., Zhao, Y.: Practices, opportunities and challenges in the fusion of knowledge graphs and large language models. Front. Comput. Sci. **7**, 1590632 (2025)
9. Kumarasinghe, A., Kirikova, M.: Towards a fractal-based system architecture for LLM-based multiagent systems. In: International Baltic Conference on Digital Business and Intelligent Systems, pp. 37–51. Springer, Cham (2026)
10. Mhlongo, P.M.: Breaking silos to foster knowledge sharing in universities: A systems thinking perspective. In: European Conference on Knowledge Management, vol. 1, pp. 644–651. Academic Conferences International Limited (2025)
11. Dang, T.M.T., Pham, T.Q.: Alignment between course learning outcomes and assessments: An analysis within linguistic programs at a university in Vietnam. Int. J. TESOL & Educ. **4**(2), 31–45 (2024)

12. Frischer, R., Singh, M.P., Porcaro, C., Namazi, H.: Fractal theory: A comprehensive review of applications across engineering disciplines. Fractals **33**(7), 1–18 (2025)
13. Peralta, M.E., Soltero, V.M.: Analysis of fractal manufacturing systems framework towards Industry 4.0. J. Manuf. Syst. **57**, 46–60 (2020)
14. Ryu, K., Jung, M.: Agent-based fractal architecture and modelling for developing distributed manufacturing systems. Int. J. Prod. Res. **41**(17), 4233–4255 (2003)
15. Zhao, W., et al.: From evidence to recommendations with large language models: A feasibility study. J. Evid. Based Med. **18**(3), e70067 (2025)
16. Li, D., et al.: Streamlining evidence-based clinical recommendations with large language models. npj Digit. Med. (2025)
17. Franzoi, S., Delwaulle, M., Dyong, J., Schaffner, J., Burger, M., vom Brocke, J.: Using large language models to generate process knowledge from enterprise content. In: International Conference on Business Process Management, pp. 247–258. Springer, Cham (2024)
18. Dou, J., Qin, J., Jin, Z., Li, Z.: Knowledge graph based on domain ontology and natural language processing technology for Chinese intangible cultural heritage. J. Vis. Lang. Comput. **48**, 19–28 (2018)
19. Kumarasinghe, A., Kirikova, M.: Multi-step schema-aware RAG for ArchiMate model-based answering of natural language queries. In: International Conference on Advanced Information Systems Engineering, pp. 347–358. Springer, Cham (2026)
20. Amouzouvi, K., et al.: SimE: A knowledge graph embedding model to encode self-similar structures through algebraic and geometric transformations. IEEE Access (2025)
21. PBP-FOLK GitHub repository, https://github.com/ArithaRTU/PBP-FOLK, Accessed 18 May 2026
22. Krathwohl, D.R.: A revision of Bloom's taxonomy: An overview. Theory Pract. **41**(4), 212–218 (2002)
23. Newton, P.M., Da Silva, A., Peters, L.G.: A pragmatic master list of action verbs for Bloom's taxonomy. Front. Educ. **5**, 107. Frontiers Media SA (2020)
24. Atil, B., et al.: Non-determinism of "deterministic" LLM settings. arXiv preprint arXiv:2408.04667 (2024)

A Knowledge Management Method for Frascati-Compatible R&D Conceptualization in Multi-project Software Engineering Organizations

Alisher Kosimov(✉)

Riga Technical University, Riga, Latvia
alisher.kosimov@edu.rtu.lv

Abstract. Software engineering organizations claiming benefits under national R&D tax incentive schemes built on the OECD Frascati Manual face structural barriers in producing acceptable evidence. Software work is intangible, novel and routine components share the same codebase, operational documentation is rarely written for evidential purposes, and consultant interpretive knowledge is largely tacit. Claim quality therefore depends heavily on individual consultant experience. This paper presents a six-step concept-mapping method, designed within a Design Science Research framework, that addresses these barriers. The method is grounded in Nonaka and Takeuchi's externalization concept and in Novak and Gowin's concept-mapping methodology. It produces structured evidence packages through a fixed sequence of steps and five supporting artifacts: a Legal Concept Map, a Software Engineering Knowledge Map, an Activity Classification Table, an Employee-Activity Linkage Table, and an Epistemic Drilling Protocol. All artifacts are realized as tables in standard office software. The method is applied to two contrasting national schemes – the Irish R&D Tax Credit and the Swedish Forskningsavdrag – through anonymous project scenario analysis and assessed through a structured expert practitioner evaluation. Initial validation indicates that the method produces complete and reproducible evidence structures for both schemes, with scheme differences absorbed primarily by the Legal Concept Map. The expert evaluation (n = 4), while confirming the method's component-level credibility, constitutes a thin evidential basis; strengthening this validation is a priority for future research. The contribution is a transferable method that reduces, but does not eliminate, the dependence of claim quality on individual consultant experience.

Keywords: R&D Tax Incentives · Frascati Manual · Knowledge Management · Concept Mapping · Software Engineering · Tacit Knowledge · Design Science Research

E. Laurenzi et al. (Eds.): BIR 2026, LNBIP 601, pp. 291–306, 2027.
https://doi.org/10.1007/978-3-032-38498-0_19

1 Introduction

Problem Context. Deciding whether a specific organizational activity counts as Research and Development is not straightforward. The OECD Frascati Manual, last revised in 2015, provides the internationally accepted framework for the R&D definition through the criteria of novelty, creativity, uncertainty, systematic progression, and transferability [1]. Many governments have built national R&D tax incentive schemes on top of these criteria, offering financial benefits to organizations that can demonstrate eligible activity. When Frascati criteria are translated into national law, however, interpretive differences appear [2]. Legislators refine, separate, or reframe the Manual's concepts to fit their own legal and fiscal context, creating ambiguity for both claimants and tax authorities.

The Frascati Manual is an OECD measurement guideline rather than a binding legal instrument. It defines R&D through five criteria that an activity must satisfy simultaneously:

- **Novelty** – the activity must aim at new findings, covering incremental advances beyond the documented knowledge base [1].
- **Creativity** – the activity must be based on original, non-obvious concepts not derivable by routine application of existing methods [1].
- **Uncertainty** – the outcome must be uncertain at the outset in the epistemic sense: it cannot be predetermined whether the technical or scientific objective is achievable, or by what method. This is not commercial or financial risk, but specifically scientific or technical uncertainty about feasibility [1].
- **Systematic progression** – the activity must be conducted according to a plan, with findings at each stage informing subsequent steps [1].
- **Transferability** – results must be documented well enough for independent reconstruction of the inquiry process [1].

These criteria were developed with laboratory-based scientific inquiry in mind. In software engineering, the challenge is fundamentally different. Software development produces intangible artifacts; novel and routine components sit together in the same codebase and the same sprint. The transferability criterion sits in deep tension with how software engineering documentation actually works – documentation is written for operational purposes, not as a log of epistemic progress [4]. As a result, the knowledge that would form R&D evidence often exists only as tacit knowledge, held by individual engineers but not present in any formal record [5, 6].

A further structural problem makes this worse. Organizations that want R&D tax incentives usually engage specialist consultants to prepare claims. In practice, claim quality depends heavily on the individual consultant's accumulated understanding of how Frascati criteria map onto software engineering activities under a given national scheme. This understanding is largely tacit – acquired through repeated case exposure and rarely formalized into a method that another consultant could pick up and follow [5, 7]. The result is significant variability in claim quality across consultants and cases, even within the same scheme [3].

Contribution Preview. This paper presents a six-step concept-mapping method that addresses the four structural barriers identified above. The method enables specialist consultants to: (1) decompose national R&D tax criteria into observable indicators through a Legal Concept Map; (2) surface both explicit and tacit engineering knowledge through a structured SE Knowledge Map and an Epistemic Drilling Protocol; (3) classify software engineering activities against legal criteria at the activity level; (4) link qualifying activities to individual employees; and (5) assemble a submission-ready evidence package verified against the terminal evidence requirements of the applicable scheme. All artifacts are realized as structured tables in standard office software. The method is grounded in Nonaka and Takeuchi's [5] concept of knowledge externalization and in Novak and Gowin's [9] concept-mapping methodology, and is constructed and validated within the Design Science Research paradigm [11, 12].

Research Questions and Paper Structure. This paper presents a Knowledge Management based concept-mapping method that enables specialist consultants to systematically classify software engineering activities against Frascati-compatible R&D criteria and produce national-standards-aligned documentation. Three research questions structure the work: RQ1 – What are the structural barriers that prevent software engineering organizations from producing Frascati-compatible R&D evidence within national tax incentive regimes? RQ2 – How can a knowledge-management-based concept-mapping method enable consultants to systematically classify software engineering activities against Frascati-compatible criteria? RQ3 – To what extent does the proposed method demonstrate validity and generalizability across contrasting national R&D tax regimes?

Section 2 reviews the relevant background. Section 3 sets out the research method. Section 4 characterizes the structural barriers. Section 5 presents the proposed method with its concrete artifacts. Section 6 reports the validation. Section 7 discusses the contribution, limitations, and directions for future work.

2 Background and Related Work

Knowledge Management Theory. Nonaka and Takeuchi's SECI model [5] treats knowledge creation as a continuous conversion between tacit and explicit forms. Of the four conversion modes – socialization, externalization, combination, and internalization – externalization is most relevant here: the conversion of tacit knowledge into explicit, communicable form through structured representations. Polanyi's original formulation – "we can know more than we can tell" [6] – captures the essential character of tacit knowledge: it is embedded in practice, judgment, and experience, and resists propositional articulation.

Tsoukas [8] challenged the SECI model by arguing that all knowing has a tacit dimension and that there is no clean act of externalization. The position taken in this paper is the moderate one: the method does not claim to convert tacit knowledge into explicit knowledge in a one-to-one mapping. It reduces the dependence of claim quality on tacit expertise by creating explicit, transferable scaffolding around the consultant's interpretive work – movement in the direction of externalization, not its completion.

Cook and Brown [15] distinguished between knowledge-as-possession and knowledge-as-practice; the method addresses both through the SE Knowledge Map categorization and the process-behavior questions in the Epistemic Drilling Protocol, respectively.

Concept Mapping. Novak and Gowin [9] developed concept mapping as a tool for representing the structure of knowledge through nodes (concepts) and labelled links (relationships). In this paper, concept mapping is applied not as a graphical artifact but as a structural commitment: the intellectual structure of a concept map – nodes for criteria, linking phrases for evidence relationships – is preserved in the column architecture of the Legal Concept Map and the Activity Classification Table. The use of concept mapping for knowledge elicitation has been validated in contexts where domain experts hold complex knowledge that they find difficult to articulate [16].

Frascati Interpretation and R&D Tax Research. The Frascati Manual acquires legal force only through incorporation into national legislation, and this process always introduces interpretive divergence. Legislators must translate abstract measurement criteria into justiciable standards – a process involving choices about emphasis, borderline treatment, and the balance between encouraging R&D and controlling fiscal cost. The OECD has acknowledged the specific difficulty of applying Frascati to software development [10]. The Swedish government's SOU 2025:3 [2] documents that approximately 80–90% of audited claims in some periods resulted in changes by the tax authority – a quantitative anchor for the qualitative observation that claim quality varies widely.

Software Engineering Documentation. Agile practices intensify the documentation gap. The Agile Manifesto's preference for working software over comprehensive documentation [17] has shaped practices where project knowledge is maintained through stand-ups, retrospectives, and informal communication rather than formal records. Aranda and Venolia [18] found that significant contextual knowledge in software projects existed only in engineers' memories and was rarely captured in formal documentation.

Research Gap. No prior work, to the author's knowledge, has combined knowledge management theory, R&D tax law, and software engineering documentation analysis in service of a structured, practitioner-deployable method for Frascati-compatible R&D conceptualization in software engineering organizations. This cross-domain synthesis is the primary scholarly contribution.

3 Research Method

The study uses the Design Science Research (DSR) paradigm [11, 12]. DSR is distinguished by its emphasis on the creation and evaluation of purposeful artifacts, producing knowledge through the act of building. The paradigm is well-established in Information Systems and Knowledge Management.

Hevner's three-cycle model [12] structures the study. The Relevance Cycle provides the problem definition and artifact requirements, drawn from systematic observation of claim preparation processes across multiple client engagements in a Big Four professional services firm (2024–2026). The Rigor Cycle anchors the design in Nonaka and

Takeuchi [5] and Novak and Gowin [9]. The Design Cycle iterates between construction and evaluation.

Six artifact requirements (R1–R6) were derived from the Relevance Cycle: R1 – consistency through criterion decomposition; R2 – engineering grounding (elicitation of tacit and explicit knowledge); R3 – transferability across regimes without redesign; R4 – auditability of employee-activity linkage; R5 – operational feasibility within standard office software; R6 – scheme-independence at the procedural level, with national variation absorbed into the Legal Concept Map.

The artifact is classified, following March and Smith [13], as a method with embedded constructs and instantiations. Validation is performed through two complementary instruments: anonymous project scenario analysis under two contrasting national schemes and a structured anonymous expert practitioner evaluation (see Sect. 6). The scenarios are abstracted from patterns observed across multiple real engagements, with all identifying details removed. The label "anonymous" rather than "hypothetical" is used deliberately, because the scenarios are abstracted from real cases rather than invented from scratch.

4 Structural Barriers to Frascati-Compatible Evidence

Four interlocking structural barriers are identified. Three are well recognized in practice; the fourth – person-dependency – is the most direct justification for the method.

Classification Challenge. Software engineering entangles qualifying and non-qualifying work within a single project, sprint, and sometimes a single feature. A team developing a novel ML pipeline may simultaneously perform unambiguously qualifying R&D (a new model architecture), clearly non-qualifying work (API integration using documented procedures), and boundary work (adapting an established algorithm to a domain where its applicability was uncertain).

Of the five Frascati criteria, uncertainty presents the most acute challenge. Software engineers are trained to reduce uncertainty and characteristically describe their work in terms that minimize its uncertain character, even when genuine Frascati uncertainty was present. A team that spent months determining whether a particular algorithmic approach could achieve acceptable performance will typically describe that work as "performance optimization." This is the _*retrospective uncertainty problem*_ [14]: once a technical problem has been resolved, the uncertainty that existed during its investigation becomes psychologically invisible.

Documentation and Evidence Gap. Software engineering documentation is produced for operational purposes – understanding, maintaining, and extending a codebase. Operational documentation describes what was built and how it works, not why specific technical choices were made, what alternatives were considered and rejected, or what was unknown at each stage of the work. In a typical engagement, the client's Jira backlogs are clean and user stories are well written, but they follow the standard structure "As a user, I would like X, So that Y", which describes a future application state, not the inquiry process that led there.

Multi-project Structural Complication. In multi-project organizations, employees split their time across qualifying and non-qualifying work in patterns that change week by week. Attribution must be at the activity level within projects, not at the project level. This is particularly acute for the Swedish Forskningsavdrag, where employee-level attribution is the primary evidential requirement.

Person-Dependency of Consultant Knowledge. Experienced consultants develop sophisticated understanding of how Frascati criteria map onto software engineering activities – pattern recognition, calibrated interrogation techniques, and judgment about boundary cases. This knowledge exists almost exclusively in tacit form. The author's own professional practice illustrates this: on more than one occasion, the author's initial eligibility judgment diverged from a senior consultant's judgment – not because of a difference of legal opinion, but because the senior asked behavioral questions about iteration and pivots while the author asked direct questions about uncertainty. The senior's questions surfaced qualifying signals; the direct questions did not.

These four barriers form a dependency chain. Classification cannot proceed until criteria have been made explicit. Evidence cannot be assembled until classification has separated qualifying from non-qualifying activity. Attribution cannot be performed until activities have been classified and evidenced. This dependency chain forces the six-step sequence described in Sect. 5.

5 The Proposed Method

5.1 Method Overview

The method comprises six sequential steps organized across two functional phases. Steps 1 and 2 form the Qualification Phase. Steps 3 through 6 form the Evidence Construction Phase. The two-phase structure reflects a practical observation: a substantial proportion of consultant time is spent assessing whether to take on a claim at all. Separating qualification from evidence construction allows early termination for non-qualifying projects.

Five artifacts support the method. Two are method components (constructed once, reused): the Legal Concept Map and the Epistemic Drilling Protocol. Three are method templates (structurally fixed, populated per engagement): the SE Knowledge Map, the Activity Classification Table, and the Employee-Activity Linkage Table. Components carry the scientific commitments of the method; templates carry case-specific content.

5.2 The Six-Step Method

Table 1 summarizes the six steps procedure.

Table 1. Six-step concept-mapping method: structural overview.

Step	Name	Description	Output
1	Regime Instantiation	Decompose the applicable national R&D tax law into a Legal Concept Map by mapping each statutory criterion onto the corresponding Frascati criterion and identifying the terminal evidence requirement for each node	Completed Legal Concept Map for the regime (reusable across clients)
2	Project-Level Qualification	Apply the Legal Concept Map as a real-time listening filter during kick-off. Classify the project as Qualifying/Partially Qualifying/Non-Qualifying and identify candidate R&D threads	Project qualification decision and list of candidate R&D threads
3	Knowledge Elicitation	For each candidate thread, collect explicit SE knowledge and reconstruct tacit knowledge using the Epistemic Drilling Protocol. Apply the Retrospective Uncertainty Reversal technique where direct uncertainty reports are absent	Populated SE Knowledge Map per candidate activity
4	Activity-Level Classification	Map elicited knowledge onto the Legal Concept Map at the activity level. Classify each activity as Qualifying (Q), Boundary (B), or Non-Qualifying (N). Record the rationale for every B decision	Completed Activity Classification Table
5	Employee-Activity Linkage	For each Q or B activity, identify the employees who performed it, the time period, and the proportion of working time attributable to the activity	Completed Employee-Activity Linkage Table

(continued)

Table 1. (*continued*)

Step	Name	Description	Output
6	Evidence Package Assembly	Compile Steps 3–5 into a structured evidence package. Use the Legal Concept Map from Step 1 as a completeness checklist – every terminal evidence requirement must be addressed before submission	Submission-ready evidence package matched to regime requirements

5.3 Concrete Artifacts

This subsection presents the key artifacts in concrete form.

Legal Concept Map. Grounded in Novak and Gowin's [9] concept-mapping methodology applied to a legal-criteria domain, the Legal Concept Map addresses the interpretive divergence between Frascati and national law. It is a structured table that decomposes the scheme's statutory R&D criteria into their Frascati equivalents and identifies the terminal evidence requirement for each. It is constructed once per scheme by the method designer and reused across all client engagements. Construction follows a four-step procedure: statutory decomposition, Frascati alignment, indicator identification, and terminal evidence specification. Table 2 presents the instantiation for the Swedish Forskningsavdrag.

Table 2. Legal Concept Map: Swedish Forskningsavdrag (illustrative instantiation).

Frascati Criterion	Swedish Law Criterion	Interpretive Standard	Terminal Evidence Requirement
Novelty	FoU ska avse ny kunskap	Work must advance knowledge beyond what is publicly known	Evidence that the problem was not solvable by existing documented solutions
Uncertainty	Vetenskaplig eller teknisk osäkerhet	Scientific or technical uncertainty must exist at the project outset	Documentation of unknowns at project start; iterative problem-solving records; abandoned or revised approaches
Systematic Progression	Systematiskt bedriven	Work must follow a planned, methodical process	Project plan or equivalent; sprint/iteration structure; evidence of findings informing subsequent steps

(*continued*)

Table 2. *(continued)*

Frascati Criterion	Swedish Law Criterion	Interpretive Standard	Terminal Evidence Requirement
Transferability	Dokumenterad process	Process documented for independent reconstruction	Technical reports, architectural records, or equivalent artifacts
(Non-Frascati)	Kommersiellt syfte	Activity must serve the claimant's commercial operations	Documentation linking R&D activity to a commercial product or service
(Non-Frascati)	Kvalificerat arbete	Work performed by personnel with relevant qualifications	CVs, position descriptions, or equivalent records

SE Knowledge Map. Grounded in Nonaka and Takeuchi's [5] tacit/explicit distinction and Polanyi's [6] concept of tacit knowledge, the SE Knowledge Map addresses the operational rather than evidential character of software engineering documentation. It organizes available evidence into four categories extended along a recoverability dimension. The template structure is fixed by the method designer and populated per engagement at Step 3. Table 3 presents the map structure.

Table 3. SE Knowledge Map: evidence categories and Frascati addressability.

Knowledge Category	Typical SE Artifacts	Frascati Criterion Addressed
Explicit – Structured	Project plans, sprint backlogs, ADRs, issue-tracker tickets, test reports, code review records	Systematic progression; evidence of planned inquiry
Explicit – Unstructured	Commit messages, PR descriptions, internal wikis, Slack/Teams threads, email chains, informal technical notes	Uncertainty (iterative signals); novelty (problem framing); requires interpretation
Tacit – Reconstructable	Engineer recall of abandoned approaches, failure points, pivots, and unresolved problems – surfaced through structured elicitation	Uncertainty (primary source); novelty where no prior solution was known to the team
Tacit – Irrecoverable	Knowledge lost due to staff turnover, undocumented decisions, or elapsed time beyond reliable recall	Evidence gap – flag for consultant risk assessment

Recognizing irrecoverable tacit knowledge as a distinct category allows the method to treat it as a flagged evidence gap requiring risk assessment, rather than as missing information to be elicited.

Activity Classification Table. Derived from the Frascati five-criterion test operationalized as observable indicators, this artifact addresses the entanglement of qualifying and non-qualifying work within software engineering projects. Classification is performed at the activity level. Each activity is classified as Qualifying (Q), Boundary (B), or Non-Qualifying (N), with explicit written justification required for boundary decisions. Table 4 shows the template.

Table 4. Activity Classification Table (template).

Activity Description	Evidence Collected	Novelty Assessment	Uncertainty Assessment	Systematic Progression	Classification (Q/B/N)
[Specific SE activity]	[Explicit docs + elicited tacit knowledge]	[Yes/Partial/No + justification]	[Yes/Partial/No + justification]	[Yes/Partial/No + justification]	Q/B/N

Employee-Activity Linkage Table. Addressing multi-project allocation and employee-attribution defensibility, employee linkage can only be performed reliably after activities have been classified. Table 5 shows the template.

Table 5. Employee-Activity Linkage Table (template).

Employee Name/Role	Qualifying Activity	Period (Start – End)	FTE/Time %	Evidence Reference
[Name, Job Title]	[Activity ID from Classification Table]	[YYYY-MM-DD – YYYY-MM-DD]	[e.g. 0.4 FTE/40%]	[Timesheets, sprint records, HR data]

The relative weight of this step differs between schemes. In the Swedish Forskningsavdrag, employee-activity linkage is the primary evidence requirement and the claim unit is the individual employee's qualifying activities. In the Irish R&D Tax Credit, employee linkage serves a secondary function supporting FTE calculation, and the claim unit is the qualifying project with its challenge narrative. These structural differences – project-level versus employee-level, challenge narrative versus time attribution – are absorbed entirely by the Legal Concept Map and the weighting of Step 5, with no modification to the core six-step procedure.

5.4 The Epistemic Drilling Protocol

Grounded in structured elicitation methodology [16] and the hindsight-bias literature [14], the Epistemic Drilling Protocol is the key elicitation instrument embedded in Step 3. It is a fixed method component that addresses person-dependency and the retrospective invisibility of uncertainty: once an engineering team has solved a technical problem, the solution tends to feel obvious in hindsight. This phenomenon, documented in cognitive science as the hindsight bias [14], causes engineering teams to underreport qualifying uncertainty when asked directly. Table 6 presents the full protocol.

Table 6. Epistemic Drilling Protocol: question patterns by Frascati criterion.

Frascati Criterion	Question Pattern	What a Qualifying Answer Looks Like
Novelty	"Before starting this work, was there an existing solution, library, or documented approach you could have adopted?"/"Why was the off-the-shelf option insufficient?"	Team describes a technical gap not addressable by existing tools or known methods
Uncertainty (direct)	"At the start of this activity, did you know whether your approach would work?"/"Were there competing approaches you considered?"	Team describes genuine unknowns about feasibility, performance, or correctness at the outset
Uncertainty (retrospective reversal)	"Walk me through what you tried first – and what happened next."/"Was there a point where you had to change approach?"/"What would you have done differently knowing what you know now?"	Iterative process narrative, pivots, or abandoned approaches – behavioral signatures of uncertainty even when the team does not self-report it
Systematic Progression	"How did the team decide what to try next after an approach failed?"/"Was there a plan or framework guiding the investigation?"	Team describes a structured inquiry process – findings informing subsequent steps
Transferability	"Where would I find a record of how this problem was investigated?"/"If a new engineer joined today, what documentation exists about how this was solved?"	Team points to ADRs, retrospectives, technical reports, or equivalent records

The protocol addresses retrospectively erased uncertainty by replacing direct uncertainty questions with process-behavior questions that reconstruct uncertainty indirectly. Back-and-forth iteration, approach pivots, and abandoned solutions are behavioral signatures of uncertainty visible in the process record even when the team does not label them as such.

6 Validation

The method was validated through two complementary instruments: anonymous project scenario analysis under two contrasting national schemes and a structured expert practitioner evaluation.

6.1 Scenario a – Mixed R&D and Routine Work, Irish R&D Tax Credit

Scenario Description. A medium-sized software engineering company (approximately 80 employees) develops a cloud-based financial analytics platform. During the claim period, three parallel workstreams were active: (1) a novel real-time anomaly detection engine using a hybrid machine learning approach not previously documented in the literature; (2) integration with third-party data providers using standard API protocols; (3) a UI layer using an established front-end framework. The internal project manager described all three as a single "R&D project." The scenario is abstracted from patterns observed across multiple real engagements, with all identifying details removed.

Validation. The Legal Concept Map for the Irish scheme was applied as a listening filter at kick-off (Step 2), immediately separating Workstream 1 as the sole candidate R&D thread from two non-qualifying workstreams. During knowledge elicitation (Step 3), the technical lead initially described the work as "standard ML development." Application of the Retrospective Uncertainty Reversal technique surfaced a substantially different narrative: the team had attempted a purely statistical approach that failed after three months, pivoted to a hybrid ML architecture, encountered a second failure mode related to data sparsity, and developed a novel data augmentation technique to resolve it. Activity-level classification (Step 4) confirmed Workstream 1 as Qualifying across novelty, uncertainty, systematic progression, and transferability. Employee-activity linkage (Step 5) identified four engineers with reconstructed FTE allocations. Evidence package assembly (Step 6) verified completeness against all terminal evidence requirements of the Irish scheme.

The scenario demonstrates two outcomes: completeness (every terminal evidence requirement addressed) and reproducibility (the same evidence structure can in principle be reconstructed by a different consultant following the same procedure). Without the method, a less experienced consultant might either include all three workstreams – producing a legally vulnerable claim – or exclude the anomaly detection workstream on the basis of the technical lead's initial framing, leaving a genuinely qualifying claim on the table.

6.2 Scenario B – Novel Algorithm with Incomplete Documentation, Swedish Forskningsavdrag

Scenario Description. A smaller firm (approximately 25 employees) specializing in spatial data for autonomous vehicles developed a novel sensor fusion algorithm for adverse weather conditions – a problem documented in the academic literature as unsolved. The company operated with informal Agile practices, minimal documentation, no structured time-tracking, and two of six contributing engineers had since left the organization. The scenario is abstracted from patterns observed across multiple real engagements, with all identifying details removed.

Validation. Knowledge elicitation (Step 3) categorized the departed engineers' contributions as irrecoverable tacit knowledge and flagged them for risk assessment. For the remaining four engineers, the Epistemic Drilling Protocol surfaced detailed narratives of approaches tested, failure modes encountered, and solutions developed. Employee-activity linkage (Step 5) – the primary evidential requirement under the Swedish scheme – mapped four of the six engineers to qualifying activities; the two former employees were assessed as insufficiently evidenced for inclusion. Evidence package assembly (Step 6) included an explicit evidence-narrative explaining the documentation gap.

The scenario demonstrates the method's capacity to navigate documentation gaps while maintaining claim defensibility. Scheme-specific calibration – driven by Skatteverket's stricter employee-level attribution requirement – was achieved through the Swedish Legal Concept Map and the weighting of Step 5, with no modification to the core six-step procedure.

6.3 Expert Practitioner Evaluation

Four practitioners completed the evaluation. All met the minimum experience threshold of five years. Scheme exposure is skewed: three respondents reported Irish experience, one reported Swedish and additional Nordic and U.S. experience.

Problem Confirmation. The documentation gap (Q7) received the strongest endorsement, with a median of 4.5 and no respondent below the neutral midpoint.

Per-Requirement Evaluation. Table 7 summarizes the findings.

Table 7. Per-requirement Likert responses (n = 4).

Item	Requirement	Median
Q12	R1 – Consistency through criterion decomposition	3.5
Q13	R2 – Engineering grounding via SE Knowledge Map	4.0
Q14	R3 – Transferability through explicit bridging	4.0
Q15	R4 – Auditability of employee-activity linkage	4.0
Q16	R5 – Operational feasibility of Epistemic Drilling	4.0
Q17	R6 – Scheme-independence	3.0
Q18	Method takes significantly more time	3.5
Q19	Worth it even if more time	3.0

No requirement was rejected. R2 (engineering grounding) and R5 (operational feasibility) attracted the most uniform support. R6 (scheme-independence) is the weakest, with a strongly negative rating from the single Swedish-experienced respondent.

Substantive Expert Criticisms. Three criticisms emerged from open-text responses: (1) the method lacks an explicit state-of-the-art assessment step, risking classifications that fail an industry-novelty test; (2) the Swedish Forskningsavdrag includes non-Frascati legislative requirements and requires month-by-month rather than retrospective assessment; (3) tooling and automation are not addressed, though the table-based design preserves the option.

Adoption Gap. A separate item asked respondents how likely they were to adopt parts of the method in their own practice (median 1.5/5: two "very unlikely," one neutral, one "somewhat unlikely"). Notably, the respondent whose profile most closely matched the target practitioner rated every per-requirement item positively and agreed the method was worth its added time, yet still rated adoption as unlikely. Per-requirement endorsement without adoption intent is the most informative single pattern in the dataset, and points to causes external to the method's design – organizational inertia, unfamiliarity with a new workflow, or the difficulty of internalizing a tacit-knowledge-heavy method from a brief written questionnaire rather than hands-on use.

Limitations of this Evaluation Component. Four respondents is below the lower bound at which Likert-scale findings can be reported with confidence. The Likert results are reported with this caveat and are not promoted to load-bearing evidence; the open-text findings carry the substantive weight. Cross-regime portability rests disproportionately on a single Swedish-experienced respondent. This limitation is acknowledged as the most significant methodological weakness of the present study and is discussed further in Sect. 7.

7 Discussion, Limitations, and Future Work

Theoretical Contribution. The method externalizes legal-criteria structure and software engineering knowledge simultaneously inside a single transferable artifact. The externalization context differs from the organizational settings in which the SECI model was originally developed: the challenge here is triangular – converting knowledge distributed across a client's engineering team into evidence acceptable to a third-party administrative authority. This triangular externalization problem (consultant, client, authority) has not been previously examined in the knowledge management literature. The framing avoids the strong claim challenged by Tsoukas [8]; the method does not claim to convert tacit knowledge into explicit form, but produces structured scaffolding that reduces dependence on individual consultant experience. This adoption gap is itself consistent with the paper's central claim: if experienced practitioners cannot fully internalize the method from a self-contained brief, that is direct evidence of how deeply embedded the consulting expertise is that the method aims to externalize. For practitioners, the Retrospective Uncertainty Reversal technique addresses a specific, well-recognized elicitation challenge for which no prior structured solution existed. Additionally, the study demonstrates that the analytical structure of Novak and Gowin's [9] concept mapping can be preserved in table form without loss of analytical power when deployment constraints preclude graphical representation.

Limitations. Five limitations are acknowledged, listed in order of significance. (1) The expert evaluation sample is small (n = 4) and scheme-skewed toward Irish experience; four respondents is below the threshold at which Likert-scale findings can be reported with confidence, and cross-regime portability rests disproportionately on a single Swedish-experienced respondent. (2) The scenarios are author-constructed abstractions from real engagements, not independent live cases. (3) Demonstrated transferability is two-regime, not n-regime; transferability claims should be read as preliminary indications. (4) The method does not include an explicit state-of-the-art assessment step. (5) The method operates retrospectively, whereas the Swedish scheme requires month-by-month assessment – a concurrent-capture variant would be more powerful but more invasive.

Future Work. Six directions follow: (1) expand the expert evaluation across multiple national schemes with interview-based follow-up; (2) validate against live claim outcomes through a longitudinal study tracking rejection and audit survival rates; (3) extend the Legal Concept Map to additional schemes (UK, France, Australia); (4) develop a concurrent assessment variant for jurisdictions requiring real-time eligibility tracking; (5) explore AI-assisted evidence assembly from elicited transcripts; (6) examine how upstream SE documentation practices could be adjusted to make qualifying evidence directly observable in operational artifacts.

References

1. OECD: Frascati manual 2015: guidelines for collecting and reporting data on research and experimental development. OECD Publishing, Paris (2015)
2. SOU 2025:3: Swedish Government Official Report on R&D tax incentives. Statens offentliga utredningar (2025)
3. Skatteverket: Investigative report on Forskningsavdrag. Swedish Tax Agency, Stockholm (2025)
4. Lethbridge, T.C., Singer, J., Forward, A.: How software engineers use documentation: the state of the practice. IEEE Softw. **20**(6), 35–39 (2003)
5. Nonaka, I., Takeuchi, H.: The Knowledge-Creating Company. Oxford University Press, New York (1995)
6. Polanyi, M.: The Tacit Dimension. Routledge & Kegan Paul, London (1966)
7. Hansen, M.T., Nohria, N., Tierney, T.: What's your strategy for managing knowledge? Harv. Bus. Rev. **77**(2), 106–116 (1999)
8. Tsoukas, H.: Do we really understand tacit knowledge? In: Easterby-Smith, M., Lyles, M.A. (eds.) The Blackwell Handbook of Organizational Learning and Knowledge Management, pp. 410–427. Blackwell, Oxford (2003)
9. Novak, J.D., Gowin, D.B.: Learning How to Learn. Cambridge University Press, Cambridge (1984)
10. OECD: Implications of Software Development for R&D Measurement. OECD Science, Technology and Industry Working Papers. OECD Publishing, Paris (2025). https://doi.org/10.1787/fba501fc-en
11. Bichler, M.: Design science in information systems research. Wirtschaftsinformatik **48**(2), 133–135 (2006). https://doi.org/10.1007/s11576-006-0028-8
12. Hevner, A.R.: A three cycle view of design science research. Scand. J. Inf. Syst. **19**(2), 87–92 (2007)
13. March, S.T., Smith, G.F.: Design and natural science research on information technology. Decis. Support. Syst. **15**(4), 251–266 (1995)

14. Fischhoff, B.: Hindsight $\neq$ foresight: the effect of outcome knowledge on judgment under uncertainty. J. Exp. Psychol.: Hum. Percept. Perform. **1**(3), 288–299 (1975)
15. Cook, S.D.N., Brown, J.S.: Bridging epistemologies: the generative dance between organizational knowledge and organizational knowing. Organ. Sci. **10**(4), 381–400 (1999)
16. Coffey, J.W., Hoffman, R.R., Cañas, A.J., Ford, K.M.: A concept map-based knowledge modeling approach to expert knowledge sharing. In: Proceedings of the IASTED International Conference on Information and Knowledge Sharing (IKS 2003), pp. 212–217. Acta Press (2003)
17. Beck, K., Beedle, M., van Bennekum, A., et al.: Manifesto for Agile software development. Agile Alliance (2001). https://agilemanifesto.org
18. Aranda, J., Venolia, G.: The secret life of bugs: going past the errors and omissions in software repositories. In: Proceedings of the 31st International Conference on Software Engineering (ICSE 2009), pp. 298–308. IEEE Computer Society (2009)

Experiments with Template-Based SPARQL Generation from Natural Language Questions

Andrei Chis(✉), Ana-Maria Ghiran, and Robert Andrei Buchmann

Babeş-Bolyai University, Cluj Napoca, Romania
{andrei.chis,anamaria.ghiran,robert.buchmann}@econ.ubbcluj.ro

Abstract. This paper reports on experimentation with SPARQL query templates in combination with a Zero-Shot Chain-of-Thought prompting approach to automatically generate queries from natural language inputs. Two experimental workflows were deployed for comparisons: one leveraging SPARQL templates to guide query construction, and another relying solely on Large Language Models provided with the ontology and natural language input. This dual approach enables a comparative evaluation of the advantages and limitations of template-based versus free-form SPARQL query generation. Motivated by the growing interest in translating natural language into SPARQL for enterprise knowledge graphs management, this study examines the effectiveness and challenges of these methods. The findings provide valuable insights into optimizing prompt design and workflow configuration for enhanced semantic query generation, offering a foundation for further developments in automated knowledge graph interaction.

Keywords: Knowledge Graphs · Large Language Models · SPARQL · RDF

1 Introduction

Interaction with Enterprise Knowledge Graphs through formal languages like SPARQL has been challenging for knowledge managers lacking RDF expertise [1], and this possibly caused delays in the general uptake of Semantic Web technologies. Generative AI now shows promising mechanisms for generating such queries [2] and democratizing knowledge graph access, however its capabilities must be assessed to inform prompting strategies and interaction workflows – there is an on-going preoccupation reporting such assessments for different large language model (LLM) versions [3–5].

During recent years knowledge graphs have been moving from experimentation artifacts to full-scale operational solutions demonstrating industrial viability. They proved their effectiveness in integrating heterogeneous data sources [6], capturing domain knowledge from graphical modeling languages [7], enabling reasoning over complex enterprise models [8], supporting sophisticated recommendation engines [9], facilitating threat analysis [10] etc.

More recently, the rise of retrieval-augmented generation (RAG) architectures [11] has transformed how enterprises approach private information access through LLMs – i.e. non-technical users can address questions in natural language without any intermediaries for translating their business requirements into specialized queries [12]. In

E. Laurenzi et al. (Eds.): BIR 2026, LNBIP 601, pp. 307–322, 2027.
https://doi.org/10.1007/978-3-032-38498-0_20

RAG systems, a retrieval component first extracts relevant knowledge from a structured or unstructured repository then employs the LLM to generate natural language answers based on that retrieved context - this enables an enhanced quality of LLM-generated responses by providing more factual responses, anchored in specific contexts with domain-specific purposes rather than relying solely on training data.

GraphRAG [13] is a family of RAG approaches that leverage structured context in the form of knowledge graphs [14]. In a typical GraphRAG scenario, one or more knowledge graphs are accessed through different endpoints which can be queried through a dedicated mechanism or querying language - e.g. SPARQL [15] for RDF knowledge graphs. The quality of the retrieved data directly influences the results returned by an LLM. For enterprise environments where organizational knowledge resides in RDF repositories, conventional vector-based retrieval often fails to extract relevant relational data leading to poor or even wrong contexts for response generation. For this, SPARQL-based retrieval is a standard way to ground generative AI responses. SPARQL syntax is expressive but at the same time it can become extremely complex, requiring familiarity with the RDF ecosystem or graph patterns. LLMs can be employed not only to generate responses but also to enhance this retrieval step itself - by leveraging their ability to interpret user intent, extract entities and relationships, LLMs can assist in dynamically constructing SPARQL queries. This task can be further enhanced when the model is guided by some templates. Conceiving a series of query templates with placeholders for values and entities supports the query generation task as the LLM only needs to fill the placeholder based on the input received in the user questions.

This paper presents a comparative experiment which highlights the key advantages in using templates for generating SPARQL queries rather than fully relying on LLMs in the process. The experiment employs RAGAS (Retrieval Augmented Generation Assessment) [16] for evaluating the retrieval and the generation part in each case.

The rest of the paper is structured as follows: Sect. 2 discusses the problem scope and research objectives, Sect. 3 presents several related works and some background. Section 4 offers a detailed view on the experimental design and set-up, while Sect. 5 analyses the obtained results. Section 6 concludes the paper.

2 Problem Scope and Research Objectives

LLMs can be employed to generate SPARQL or Cypher queries from natural language user inputs [17, 18], democratizing in this way the access to graph-structured domain-specific knowledge. As a result, enterprises can achieve a higher degree of neuro-symbolic AI integration flows in organizational operations [19].

However, this approach has certain drawbacks as LLMs can hallucinate in the process of transforming natural language into SPARQL, leading to incorrect queries, or queries which fail to retrieve any sort of relevant data. In enterprise settings which involve monetary operations or regulatory compliance, failures in querying data can have severe consequences.

Considering such shortcomings, this paper investigates the use of SPARQL query templates as a base for LLMs in the process of generating queries, rather than relying strictly on their capability to generate syntactically correct queries even when the LLM operates within the context of a known ontology and can ground its query construction into a correct semantic structure.

The intuition is that in the template-based approach, the generated SPARQL queries adhere to a predefined structure and are guaranteed to be syntactically correct. The downside is that if the question is less frequent or highly complex, the generated SPARQL query might not fit pre-existing templates. The free formulation approach provides greater flexibility and the potential to handle unseen query structures. However, it is susceptible to errors and structural inconsistencies impacting the accuracy and trustworthiness of results.

The primary objective of this research is to systematically evaluate and compare the performance, robustness and generalizability of two distinct LLM-assisted SPARQL query generation approaches. We used RAGAS Framework [16] for this with a small adaptation, as RAGAS was primarily designed to evaluate RAG pipelines for which the answer is provided into natural language. Specifically, we aimed to:

- Perform a comparative analysis of retrieval effectiveness and precision
- Assess the generative integrity and factual grounding
- Assess the query flexibility vs. imposed constraints

In the following section we contextualized our research by reviewing related works in LLM- assisted Knowledge Graph Question Answering.

3 Related Works

Pereira et al. [20] performed a systematic review over various methods on question answering over semantic data knowledge bases and classified them according to four different types: semantic parsing pipelines, information extraction solutions, subgraph matching, template-based queries.

In the semantic parsing pipelines, first, the question is processed to identify entities, part-of speech tagging etc. followed by entity linking, query generation, execution of the query and answer generation. The query generation step posed some challenges as usually there was a mismatch between the user's vocabulary on one hand and the vocabulary used on the dataset of interest [20]. Adopting popular terminologies (such as DBpedia or Wikidata) was proposed by Ruseti et al. [21] who generated the SPARQL query by using the most probable interpretation of a directed acyclic graph, with vertices and edges corresponding to identified entities and their dependencies in the formulated question. Zafar et al. [22] proposed to use the set of identified entities and relationships and generate walks on the knowledge graph by using close relations (i.e.one-hop adjacent relations).

While in semantic parsing pipelines the question was translated into a logical form before generating the SPARQL query, in information extraction solutions the focus is on applying deep neural networks for tasks like entity linking or relation detection. Panchbhai et al. [23] use sequence-to-sequence models to transform long utterances into complex SPARQL queries.

The subgraph matching is seen as an alternative way to the semantic parsing: executing a formal query is equivalent to finding a subgraph. Instead of converting the question into a formal query, the KBQA system directly identifies the corresponding subgraph that represents the question's meaning: e.g. Hu et al. [24] constructed the subgraph corresponding to the user question called semantic query graph by disambiguating the question to match the existing graph structure.

In template-based queries, a template represents a type of query that can be instantiated at run-time having the natural language question mapped to a suitable template. To achieve this mapping, various techniques can be employed: e.g. Formica et al. [25] used machine learning techniques. Their work considered various classification techniques such as Gradient-Boosted Decision Trees, Naïve Bayes and Support Vector Machines to identify the most suitable query template from a set of predefined templates. In our approach we delegate the task of finding the appropriate template to an LLM. This enables a more flexible and scalable solution which does not require retraining and can generalize across different domains.

Translating natural language questions into formal query languages (e.g. SPARQL or Cypher) using LLMs has seen an increased attention as a practical means of using LLMs' capabilities in processing natural language and generating structured output.

The work of Avila et al. [26] introduced Auto-KGQAGPT, an autonomous framework used to question answering on KGs using LLMs. The framework generates SPARQL queries translating users' natural language questions by making use of some KG fragments as context. The output of the SPARQL query against the KG is subsequently used to generate the natural language response.

Another approach is represented by the work done in [27] which proposes a novel LLM-based SPARQL generation model. This approach verifies multiple candidate entities and relations in order to produce multiple SPARQL queries for a single question to boost the chances of finding the correct answer.

Another interesting approach is presented in [5] where the authors provide the LLM with an RDF subgraph containing the relevant facts and an example of a correct SPARQL query. This enriched input context is intended to guide the model toward producing more accurate and semantically grounded query formulation.

Our approach leverages the knowledge graph TBOX (to be referred as "ontology") rather than subgraph fragments since ontologies tend to be relatively static after a knowledge graph is created.

4 Experimental Design and Setup

The experiment was performed using a series of specialized tools and environments, namely an Azure cloud deployment of an OpenAI GPT 4o model, GraphDB [28] for knowledge graph storage and Python as a scripting language for interoperability.

A knowledge graph was created to model fictional companies, organizations, and people connected by various relationships and an ontology was defined to map classes and relationships. Figure 1 shows an excerpt of the instances' graph, including ontology-level classes (e.g., schema:Person) required to illustrate typing relationships in GraphRAG workflows. The ontology draws on well-known RDF vocabularies like RDF Schema 1.1 [29] and Schema.org [30], using terms such as rdfs:Class, rdfs:Property, schema:Corporation, schema:Person, schema:name, schema:address, schema:numberOfEmployees, schema:worksFor, schema:jobTitle, xsd:string, and xsd:integer. A custom class,:BusinessSector, was added to indicate industries in which companies operate. Several new properties, listed in Table 1, capture the ecosystem's relationships.

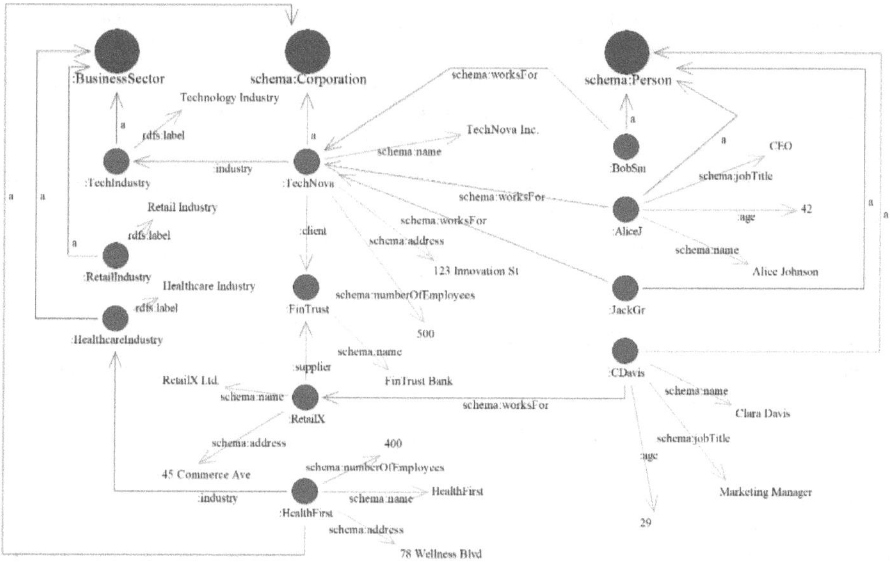

Fig. 1. Knowledge Graph exemplar, graphically realized in GraphXX (https://github.com/andreichis97/GRAPHxx)

Table 1. Ontology properties

Property	Description	Domain	Range
:businessRelation	Acts as a generic superproperty for the various types of business relations below	Not explicit	Not explicit
:industry	Links to the industry in which a specific company operates	schema:Corporation	:BusinessSector
:age	Shows the age of a person	schema:Person	xsd:integer
:client	Indicates that one company is the client of another	schema:Corporation	schema:Corporation
:supplier	Indicates that one company supplies goods/services to another	schema:Corporation	schema:Corporation
:rival	Indicates competition between two companies	schema:Corporation	schema:Corporation
:partner	Indicates a business partnership between two companies	schema:Corporation	schema:Corporation

Two different GraphRAG workflows were implemented, one of them relying on SPARQL template patterns and the knowledge graph ontology, while the second one had access only to the knowledge graph ontology.

We will first describe the first workflow, which uses the SPARQL query templates to guide the generation process.

The template patterns were defined as dictionaries in Python. They were organized and stored in two different dictionaries to separate the semantic description (how the template is described conceptually) from syntactic structures (the actual SPARQL query skeletons). This design promotes flexibility and easier matching during query generation.

The first dictionary provides a human-readable and domain-oriented description of what each SPARQL template does. It contains (a) ID, which is a unique identifier used in matching the corresponding SPARQL pattern in the second dictionary, (b) a template description – expressed in RDF jargon and (c) a domain-specific example – showing how the template can be applied within a specific use case. This helps the LLM identify what kind of query structure fits the user's intent, acting as a semantic catalog of available query types.

The second dictionary stores the actual query patterns in SPARQL syntax, generalized with placeholders (e.g. @node, @predicate) that the LLM will fill in. It contains (a) ID, which is identical to those used in the first dictionary (for linking) and (b) the SPARQL pattern – which is the corresponding SPARQL query structure. This dictionary provides the syntactic constraints needed to ensure that the LLM generates a valid SPARQL query.

The ID field acts essentially as a foreign key between the two dictionaries: when the LLM identifies a template description that matches the user's intent (from the first dictionary), it will retrieve the corresponding SPARQL query skeleton (from the second dictionary). A consolidated view of the two dictionaries, showing the correspondence between template semantics and SPARQL structures is illustrated in Table 2.

Figure 2 presents an overview of the two GraphRAG querying workflows.

The upper one leveraged SPARQL templates, alongside an ontology, in order to generate queries, while the lower one didn't have access to templates, relying strictly on LLMs capacity to generate SPARQL queries based on a given user prompt and an ontology. The functions are described in the following:

- A **pattern choice function** provides the OpenAI GPT-4o model the list of templates descriptions and the user prompt, asking the model to return the id of the most suitable template for responding to the given user prompt. The sys prompt in this case instructs the AI model to perform a Chain of Thought (CoT) [31] process in analyzing inputs, falling in the category of level 4 prompts, as defined in the TELeR taxonomy [32];
- The **GPT model interaction** is also enhanced by using structured outputs [33] leveraging pydantic classes. These classes are dynamically transformed into JSON structures at run-time, providing the model with explicit constraints on the type of output it should provide;
- A **SPARQL query generation function** takes as input the user prompt, the identified Template's description, the SPARQL pattern of the template and the knowledge graph ontology aiming to generate a SPARQL query in which placeholders are replaced by actual user prompt data. In the end, the function returns the SPARQL query which

Table 2. Template descriptions and SPARQL patterns

ID	Template description	Example	SPARQL pattern
1	For the resource @node, knowing that it has a data property @predicate, return the value(s) of that data property	Return the salary of:Jane	SELECT ?val WHERE {@node @predicate ?val.}
2	For the value @value, knowing that it occurs as value of the data property @predicate, return the subject)(s) for which @predicate has the value @value	Return those having a salary of 4000	SELECT ?s WHERE {?s @predicate @value.}
3	For the resources @node1 and @node2, return the object property(ies) by which they are directly connected, regardless of the direction of the object property	By which relationship are:Jane and:John connected?	SELECT ?prop WHERE { {@node1 ?prop @node2.} UNION {@node2 ?prop @node1.}}
4	For the resource @node, return all properties of it together with their values, regardless if they are literals or objects	What attributes and relationships does:Jane have?	SELECT ?prop ?val WHERE {@node ?prop ?val.}
5	For the resource @x, return all triples that involve that resource, regardless of the position it has in the triple	Return all statements that involve:Jane	SELECT ?sub ?prop ?val WHERE {?sub ?prop ?val. FILTER (@x = ?sub || @x = ?prop || @x = ?val)}
6	For the resource @node, return all nodes related to it through the object property @relationship, regardless of the direction of the object property	Return all relatives of:Jane	SELECT ?ent WHERE { @node @relationship |^ @relationship ?ent.}
7	For the resource @node, is there a property @predicate available, regardless of its value?	Does:Jane have a salary declared in the graph, re-gardless of its value?	ASK WHERE { @node @predicate ?val}

is then used in the following step. The sys prompt for this interaction was built as a Zero-Shot CoT prompt which falls again in the level 4 of the TELeR taxonomy [32]. These characteristics were applied to all the system prompts used throughout this experiment.

The second workflow explores an LLM-only configuration, in which the model constructs the SPARQL queries solely based on the ontology and the user input, without the support of template patterns. In this case, the system prompt is slightly modified so that no template or description is provided to the AI model.

- **The SPARQL query processing function** takes as input the generated SPARQL query and sends it to the knowledge graph repository, receiving a JSON structure from the endpoint which is then decoded to extract the results;
- **The SPARQL query results conversion function** takes as input the decoded JSON structure for the response and transforms the response from JSON to natural language

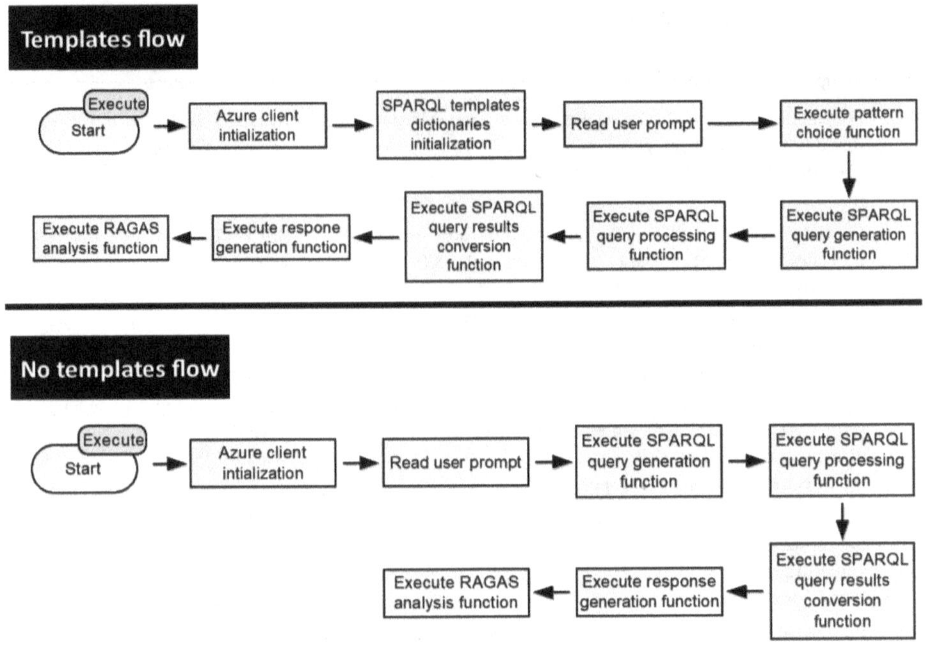

Fig. 2. GraphRAG workflows

text. This step could be omitted in a workflow which doesn't use RAGAS, but in our implementation, as the retrieved context is analyzed with RAGAS as part of the experiment metrics it was necessary to have it in natural language form;

- **The response generation function** takes as input the natural language context and the user prompt, analyzing them with the OpenAI LLM to generate a suitable response. According to Ontotext [13], our approach leverages knowledge graphs as content stores, extracting relevant chunks of information, but also following a "Graph as Database" scenario because the natural language question is mapped to a graph query leveraging GPT-4o;
- **The RAGAS analysis function** takes as input the natural language transformed contexts and the responses, having access to a list of questions and ground truths. It then analyzes the faithfulness, answer relevancy, context recall and context precision in each case.

The functions in the second workflow were defined in the same manner, using the same sys prompts as in the first workflow, the only difference being the absence of the SPARQL templates and the pattern choice function.

5 Results and Interpretations

The GraphRAG workflows were analyzed with the help of RAGAS Framework [16], relying specifically on 4 metrics:

- **Faithfulness:** Measures how factually consistent a response is with the retrieved context; (i.e. the goal of faithfulness is to ensure the response is grounded in the retrieved context and the LLM did not hallucinate); to compute this metric, Retrieved context and Response are compared; a score close to 0 for this metric means that most/all answer was a hallucination, while a score close to 1 means perfect faithfulness or most/all parts of the answer are supported and verifiable by the retrieved context;
- **Answer Relevancy:** Assesses how to-the-point and relevant the generated answer is to the given prompt; (i.e. it checks if the answer makes sense for the question); to compute this metric the Prompt and the Response are compared; the higher the metric (close to 1) means the answer is the most direct, concise, containing zero extraneous information (i.e. does not include irrelevant details);
- **Context Recall:** Measures how many of the relevant documents (or pieces of information) were successfully retrieved; (i.e. the extent to which the retrieved context covers all the information needed to derive the correct answer); to compute this metric, the Ground Truth and the Retrieved Context are compared; a value close to 1 means the context is complete and contains all the necessary facts to fully answer the question;
- **Context Precision:** Measures the proportion of relevant chunks in the retrieved contexts (i.e. ensure the retrieved documents are all necessary for an LLM to answer the question); to compute this metric the Prompt and the Retrieved Context are compared; perfect precision or a value close to 1 means the retrieved context contains only information relevant to the prompt.

Faithfulness and Answer Relevancy are used to analyze the generation component of the GraphRAG workflows, while Context Recall and Context Precision are used to analyze the retrieval component. Under the hood, RAGAS employs LLMs to conduct the evaluation. The obtained results are presented after running each workflow 5 times followed by data aggregation.

Table 3 presents the user prompts which were used to query the knowledge graph alongside the ground truths used to validate LLM response in each case.

Table 3. User prompts and ground truths

ID	User prompt	Ground truth
1	Return the number of employees of:TechNova	TechNova Inc. Has 500 employees
2	Return the people who are 29 years old	Clara Davis is 29 years old
3	What is the relationship between:TechNova and:FinTrust?	TechNova Inc. is a client of FinTrust Bank
4	What attributes and relationships does:AliceJ have?	Alice Johnson is 42 years old. She is the CEO of TechNova Inc
5	Return all statements that involve:HealthFirst	HealthFirst is a corporation in the healthcare industry. HealthFirst is located at 78 Wellness Blvd, Berlin, Germany. HealthFirst has 400 employees. HealthFirst is a partner of FinTrust Bank. HealthFirst is a client of AutoMotiveTech. Eva Wilson works at HealthFirst as the Medical Director. Isabel Foster works at HealthFirst as the Head of R&D
6	Return all the employees of:TechNova declared in the graph	The employees are Alice Johnson who works as a CEO, Bob Smith who works as a Software Engineer and Jack Green who works as a CTO
7	Does:RetailX have an address declared in the graph, regardless of its value?	Yes

Table 4 presents the obtained contexts in the GraphRAG workflows and the generated responses in each case. The generated responses represented a core element in the analysis process using RAGAS.

Table 4. Retrieved context and generated responses

ID	Retrieved context from Template-based workflow	Response from Template-based workflow	Retrieved context from No templates workflow	Response from No templates workflow
1	The entity relevant to your query is TechNova Inc., which is a corporation located at 123 Innovation St, Silicon Valley, USA. TechNova Inc. has 500 employees	500 employees	The entity relevant to your query is Tech-Nova, which has a total of 500 employees	500 employees
2	The entity relevant to your query is CDavis, who is 29 years old	CDavis	The entity relevant to your query is CDavis, who is 29 years old	CDavis

(*continued*)

Table 4. (*continued*)

ID	Retrieved context from Template-based workflow	Response from Template-based workflow	Retrieved context from No templates workflow	Response from No templates workflow
3	The entity relevant to your query is:TechNova, which is related to:FinTrust through the relationship of being a client	:TechNova is a client of:FinTrust	The entity relevant to your query is:TechNova, but there is no recorded relationship with:FinTrust in the provided data	There is no recorded relationship between:TechNova and:FinTrust in the provided data
4	The entity relevant to your query is Alice Johnson, who is identified as a Person. Alice Johnson works for TechNova and holds the job title of CEO. Additionally, Alice Johnson is 42 years old	Alice Johnson is a Person, works for TechNova, holds the job title of CEO, and is 42 years old	The entity relevant to your query is Alice Johnson, who is identified as a Person. Alice Johnson works for TechNova and holds the job title of CEO. Additionally, Alice Johnson is 42 years old	Alice Johnson is a Person, works for Tech-Nova, holds the job title of CEO, and is 42 years old
5	The entity relevant to your query is HealthFirst, which is a Corporation. HealthFirst is located at 78 Wellness Blvd, Berlin, Germany, and employs 400 people. It operates within the Healthcare Industry. HealthFirst has a business relationship with AutoMotiveTech, serving as both a client and a supplier. Additionally, HealthFirst is a partner of FinTrust. Employees such as Eva Wilson and Isabel Foster work for HealthFirst	1. HealthFirst is a Corporation 2. HealthFirst is located at 78 Wellness Blvd, Berlin, Germany 3. HealthFirst employs 400 people 4. HealthFirst operates within the Healthcare Industry 5. HealthFirst has a business relationship with AutoMotiveTech, serving as both a client and a supplier 6. HealthFirst is a partner of FinTrust 7. Employees such as Eva Wilson and Isabel Foster work for HealthFirst	The entity relevant to your query is Health-First, which is a Corporation. HealthFirst is located at 78 Wellness Blvd, Berlin, Germany, and employs 400 people. It operates within the Healthcare Industry. HealthFirst has a business relationship with AutoMotiveTech, serving as both a client and a supplier. Additionally, HealthFirst is partnered with FinTrust. Employees such as Eva Wilson and Isabel Foster work for HealthFirst	1. HealthFirst is a Corporation 2. HealthFirst is located at 78 Wellness Blvd, Berlin, Germany 3. HealthFirst employs 400 people 4. HealthFirst operates within the Healthcare Industry 5. HealthFirst has a business relationship with AutoMotiveTech, serving as both a client and a supplier 6. HealthFirst is partnered with FinTrust 7. Employees such as Eva Wilson and Isabel Foster work for HealthFirst

(*continued*)

Tables 5 and 6 present the scores obtained by employing the RAGAS assessment metrics in the experiment.

Table 4. (*continued*)

ID	Retrieved context from Template-based workflow	Response from Template-based workflow	Retrieved context from No templates workflow	Response from No templates workflow
6	The entities relevant to your query are AliceJ, BobSm, and JackGr, who are employees of TechNova as declared in the graph	AliceJ, BobSm, JackGr	The entities relevant to your query are the employees of TechNova. They include Alice Johnson, who holds the position of CEO, Bob Smith, who works as a Software Engineer, and Jack Green, who serves as the CTO	Alice Johnson, Bob Smith, Jack Green
7	The entity relevant to your query is:RetailX, which does have an address declared in the graph	Yes,:RetailX does have an address declared in the graph	The entity relevant to your query is:RetailX, which does have an address declared in the graph	Yes,:RetailX does have an address declared in the graph

Table 5. RAGAS aggregated metrics of the templates workflow

ID	Context Precision	Context Recall	Faithfulness	Answer Relevancy
Q1	1	1	1	0.838
Q2	1	1	1	0.599
Q3	1	1	0.6	0.929
Q4	1	0.9	1	0.805
Q5	1	0.714	1	0.804
Q6	1	0	1	0.713
Q7	1	1	1	0.954

Regarding Context Precision, the workflow leveraging template-based SPARQL queries successfully selected relevant pieces of context in all cases, while the workflow without templates didn't manage to retrieve any relevant context in the case of Q3. The query generated by the LLM fails to check the relationship in both ways. This shortcoming can be particularly problematic in situations in which knowledge graphs are used to represent networks of relationships between different entities. Moreover, the ontology and the knowledge graphs used over the course of this experiment were relatively lightweight, but in the case of complex knowledge graphs structures with extensive ontologies, there is an increased risk of failure to identify relevant context.

On the Context Recall side both approaches achieve full recall on most questions, but two particularly notable differences emerge: Q3 has perfect recall (1) with templates, but zero recall without. Q6 is behaving in the exact opposite manner. This sort of behavior

Table 6. RAGAS aggregated metrics of the no templates workflow

ID	Context Precision	Context Recall	Faithfulness	Answer Relevancy
Q1	1	1	1	0.837
Q2	1	0.8	1	0.442
Q3	0	0	1	0.762
Q4	1	0.9	1	0.809
Q5	1	0.714	1	0.804
Q6	1	1	1	0.719
Q7	1	1	1	0.954

suggests that template strategies can introduce constraints in queries which might be helpful in some cases, but they might also filter out relevant context in others.

The aggregated Faithfulness is uniformly high in both cases. There is again a divergence in the case of Q3, where the template-based approach provided a not fully faithful response (0.6), whereas the no-templates workflow offered much more faithfulness. This can be regarded in the same context as the earlier observation, highlighting the fact that templates can obtain high precision recall but ending up with less faithful final answers. A situation like this can happen when the system retrieves the correct context but fails to incorporate it in its final answer.

Regarding the aggregated Answer relevancy metric, both approaches offered good results in the case of Q1, Q4, Q5, Q6 and Q7, with close values in the 0.8–0.95 range. In the case of Q2, the template-based approach yielded a significantly higher relevancy score of 0.599, than 0.442 in the case of no-templates approach. For Q3, the relevancy score was again significantly higher (0.929 vs. 0.762) in the template-based approach, indicating that even the final faithfulness was partially off – the answer was deemed to be more aligned with the user question.

The slight reduction in the Answer Relevancy suggests the assessment framework has penalized the response for lacking fluency or full containment.

Overall, the results point out three important aspects:

- Using SPARQL templates is not uniformly better. Instead, it appears beneficial for certain query types (often those that match well with the structure of the template) but may restrict relevant retrieval or hamper the final generation if the question does not align neatly with a template;
- Templates might improve consistency in certain structured queries but can also over-constrain other queries, highlighting the need to tune templates or combine them with a fallback strategy;
- Retrieving the right context does not automatically guarantee the final answer will be perfectly faithful, because the LLM's synthesis step can introduce inaccuracies or omissions.

6 Conclusions and Future Work

LLM-assisted SPARQL query generation has the potential to transform enterprise data access as any non-technical user (e.g. business analysts, managers etc.) can instantly query complex Enterprise Knowledge Graphs, which are increasingly used to model business processes, systems, organizational assets. They can use natural language questions instead of technical SPARQL syntax and this is essential in critical tasks for maximizing the enterprise value or compliance requirements. Activities such as cause analysis, dependency tracking across IT systems, governance checks, risks assessments which require a high level holistic view, typically are performed by enterprise executives and most of the times were hard to express into technical jargon.

Considering this context, the paper at hand presents a comparative analysis of how using query templates can enhance LLM-based generation of SPARQL queries, thus improving automated GraphRAG workflows. Results highlight that SPARQL templates can significantly boost retrieval performance for some questions (e.g., Q3) and improve the alignment between user intent and final output (e.g., Q2's relevancy). However, they do not guarantee perfect outcomes. Templates risk "locking" queries into a particular pattern, sometimes leading to missed context (as with Q6) or unexpected drops in faithfulness (Q3). On the other hand, the absence of templates can allow more flexibility but risks a total miss in retrieval (Q3: zero context precision/recall). Our experiments used relatively simple and homogeneous RDF knowledge graphs.

Future work will include moving to more realistic and challenging data sources. For more complex and varied knowledge graphs, Zero-Shot prompting might not suffice. Few-Shot CoT prompting aims to enhance the reasoning quality by combining Few-Shot Learning (including a small number of high-quality examples in the prompt) and Chain-of-Thought (instructing the LLMs to articulate its reasoning steps before generating the final SPARQL code). Our future investigations also aim to implement a multi-stage LLM process, i.e. implementing a self-correction loop.

Disclosure of Interests. The authors have no competing interests to declare that are relevant to the content of this article.

References

1. Warren, P., Mulholland, P.: A comparison of the cognitive difficulties posed by SPARQL query constructs. In: Proceedings of EKAW 2020. LNAI, vol. 12387, pp. 3–19. Springer (2020). https://doi.org/10.1007/978-3-030-61244-3_1
2. Rony, M.R.A.H., Kumar, U., Teucher, R., Kovriguina, L., Lehmann, J.: SGPT: a generative approach for SPARQL query generation from natural language questions. IEEE Access **10**, 70712–70723 (2022). https://doi.org/10.1109/ACCESS.2022.3188714
3. Chen, Y., Kokar, M.M., Moskal, J.J.: SPARQL query generator (SQG). J. Data Semant. **10**(3), 291–307 (2021). https://doi.org/10.1007/s13740-021-00133-y
4. Chen, Y.H., Lu, E.J.L., Lin, Y.Y.: Efficient SPARQL queries generator for question answering systems. IEEE Access **10**, 99850–99860 (2022). https://doi.org/10.1109/ACCESS.2022.3206794

5. Kovriguina, L., Teucher, R., Radyush, D., Mouromtsev, D.: SPARQLGEN: one-shot prompt-based approach for SPARQL query generation. In: Proceedings of SEMANTICS 2023, vol. 3526. CEUR-WS (2023). https://ceur-ws.org/Vol-3526/paper-08.pdf
6. Buchmann, R.A., Ghiran, A.M.: Knowledge graphs as a scholarly data fabric: a data silo transformation pipeline with visualization semantics. In: Proceedings of POEM 2024, LNBIP, vol. 538, pp. 157–172. Springer (2024). https://doi.org/10.1007/978-3-031-77908-4_10
7. Bachhofner, S., Kiesling, E., Revoredo, K., Waibel, P., Polleres, A.: Automated process knowledge graph construction from BPMN models. In: Proceedings of DEXA 2022. LNCS vol. 13426, pp. 32–47. Springer (2022). https://doi.org/10.1007/978-3-031-12423-5_3
8. Smajevic, M., Hacks, S., Bork, D.: Using knowledge graphs to detect enterprise architecture smells. In: Proceedings of POEM 2021. LNBIP vol. 432, pp. 48–63. Springer (2021). https://doi.org/10.1007/978-3-030-91279-6_4
9. Ghiran, A.M., Chis, A., Florea, A., Buchmann, R.A.: Enhanced movie reservation system–a hybrid approach using knowledge graphs and generative AI. Inf. Discov. Deliv. (2025). https://doi.org/10.1108/IDD-09-2024-0141
10. Chiş, A., Stoica, O.I., Ghiran, A.M., Buchmann, R.A.: A knowledge graph approach to cyber threat mitigation derived from data flow diagrams. In: Proceedings of IEEE AQTR 2024, pp. 1–6. IEEE (2024). https://doi.org/10.1109/AQTR61889.2024.10554074
11. Lewis, P., et al.: Retrieval-augmented generation for knowledge-intensive NLP tasks. In: Proceedings of NIPS 2020 - Advances in Neural Information Processing Systems 33, article 793, pp. 9459–9474. Curran Associates (2020). https://proceedings.neurips.cc/paper/2020/file/6b493230205f780e1bc26945df7481e5-Paper.pdf
12. Nemtoc, T.C.,Ghiran, A.M.: Natural language querying of invoice data using RAG and GraphRAG: leveraging LLMs for financial document insights. In: Proceedings of CAISE 2025 Workshops. LNBIP, vol. 556, pp. 69–80. Springer (2025). https://doi.org/10.1007/978-3-031-94931-9_6
13. Graphwise. What is GraphRAG (n.d.). https://graphwise.ai/fundamentals/what-is-graph-rag//. Accessed 21 June 2026
14. Ji, S., Pan, S., Cambria, E., Marttinen, P., Yu, P.S.: A survey on knowledge graphs: representation, acquisition, and applications. IEEE Trans. Neural Netw. Learn. Syst. **33**(2), 494–514 (2022). https://doi.org/10.1109/TNNLS.2021.3070843
15. W3C. SPARQL 1.1 query language (2013). https://www.w3.org/TR/sparql11-query/. Accessed 21 June 2026
16. VibrantLabs. RAGAs Framework Documentation (2025). https://docs.ragas.io/en/stable/. Accessed 21 June 2026
17. Zahera, H.M., Ali, M., Sherif, M.A., Moussallem, D., Ngonga Ngomo, A.-C.: Generating SPARQL from natural language using chain-of-thoughts prompting. In: Proceedings of SEMANTICS 2024, pp. 353–368. IOS Press (2023). https://doi.org/10.3233/SSW240028
18. Vollmers, D., Srivastava, N., Zahera, H.M., Moussalem, D., Ngonga Ngomo, A.-C. UniQ-Gen: Unified query generation across multiple knowledge graphs. In: Knowledge Engineering and Knowledge Management, Proceedings of EKAW 2024. LNCS, vol. 15370, pp. 162–177. Springer (2024). https://doi.org/10.1007/978-3-031-77792-9_11
19. Ngonga Ngomo, A.-C., Bühmann, L., Unger, C., Lehmann, J., Gerber, D.: Sorry, I don't speak SPARQL: translating SPARQL queries into natural language. In: Proceedings of WWW 2013, pp. 977–988. ACM Press (2013). https://doi.org/10.1145/2488388.2488473
20. Pereira, A., Trifan, A., Lopes, R.P., Oliveira, J.L.: Systematic review of question answering over knowledge bases. IET Softw. **16**(1), 1–13 (2022). https://doi.org/10.1049/sfw2.12028
21. Ruseti, S., Mirea, A., Rebedea, T., Trausan-Matu, S.: QAnswer-enhanced entity matching for question answering over Linked Data. In: Working Notes of CLEF 2015, vol. 1391, pp. 28–35. CEUR-WS (2015). https://ceur-ws.org/Vol-1391/99-CR.pdf

22. Zafar, H., Napolitano, G., Lehmann, J.: Formal query generation for question answering over knowledge bases. In: Proceedings of ESWC 2018. LNCS, vol. 10843, pp. 714–728. Springer (2018). https://doi.org/10.1007/978-3-319-93417-4_46
23. Panchbhai, A., Soru, T., Marx, E.: Exploring sequence-to-sequence models for SPARQL pattern composition. In: Proceedings of KGSWC 2020. CCIS, vol. 1232, pp. 158–165. Springer, Cham (2020). https://doi.org/10.1007/978-3-030-65384-2_12
24. Hu, S., Zou, L., Yu, J.X., Wang, H., Zhao, D.: Answering natural language questions by subgraph matching over knowledge graphs. IEEE Trans. Knowl. Data Eng. **30**(5), 824–837 (2017). https://doi.org/10.1109/TKDE.2017.2766634
25. Formica, A., Mele, I., Taglino, F.: A template-based approach for question answering over knowledge bases. Knowl. Inf. Syst. **66**, 453–479 (2024). https://doi.org/10.1007/s10115-023-01966-8
26. Avila, C.V.S., Vidal, V.M.P., Franco, W., Casanova, M.A.: Experiments with text-to-SPARQL based on ChatGPT. In: Proceedings of IEEE ICSC 2024, pp. 277–284. IEEE (2024). https://doi.org/10.1109/ICSC59802.2024.00050
27. Yang, S., Teng, M., Dong, X., Bo, F.: LLM-based SPARQL generation with selected schema from large scale knowledge base. In: Proceedings of CCKS 2023. CCIS, vol. 1923, pp. 304–316. Springer (2023). https://doi.org/10.1007/978-981-99-7224-1_24
28. Graphwise. GraphDB semantic graph database (2026). https://graphwise.ai/components/graphdb/. Accessed 21 June 2026
29. W3C. RDF 1.1 concepts and abstract syntax (2014). https://www.w3.org/TR/rdf11-concepts/. Accessed 21 June 2026
30. Schema.org Community Group. Schema.org (2026). https://schema.org/. Accessed 21 June 2026
31. Wei, J., et al.: Chain-of-thought prompting elicits reasoning in large language models. In: Proceedings of NIPS 2022, Article 1800, pp. 24824–24837. Curran Associates (2022). https://proceedings.neurips.cc/paper_files/paper/2022/file/9d5609613524ecf4f15af0f7b31abca4-Paper-Conference.pdf
32. Karmaker, S. K., Feng, D.: TELeR: a general taxonomy of LLM prompts for benchmarking complex tasks. In: Proceedings of EMNLP 2023, pp. 14197–14203. ACL Anthology (2023). https://doi.org/10.18653/v1/2023.findings-emnlp.946
33. OpenAI, Inc. Structured model outputs (2026). https://developers.openai.com/api/docs/guides/structured-outputs?api-mode=chat. Accessed 21 June 2026

Alignment, Interoperability, and Openness

On the Claimed Benefits of Enterprise Architecture Management

Paul Walder[1], Marianne Schnellmann[1(✉)], and Henderik A. Proper[1,2]

[1] TU Wien, Vienna, Austria
marianne.schnellmann@tuwien.ac.at
[2] HU University of Applied Sciences, Utrecht, The Netherlands

Abstract. In a world facing increasing organisational complexity and accelerated digital transformation, Enterprise Architecture Management (EAM) is frequently cited as a key enabler of strategic change, operational alignment, and IT optimisation. However, the claimed benefits of (doing) EAM vary across literature sources, while industry perspectives and insight into their realisation in practice remain limited. We conducted a multivocal literature review, selecting relevant publications from both academia and industry based on predefined criteria and classified the benefits as IT- or business-related. The analysis identified a variety of value dimensions that make these benefits explicit, ranging from cost reduction and risk mitigation to strategic alignment, innovation enablement, and improved decision-making. In addition, the paper highlights drivers, such as artefact quality, governance, and tooling, that contribute to realising the benefits of EAM, as well as challenges for EA value measurement, including attribution, intangibility, and time horizons. This study provides a structured analytical frame that encourages and guides targeted interviews with practitioners, enabling deeper insights into EAM benefits and the conditions under which they emerge.

Keywords: Enterprise Architecture Management · EAM · Benefits of EA

1 Introduction

In an era defined by rapid technological change, Enterprise Architecture Management (EAM) has become a key discipline for guiding organisations through increasingly complex transformation initiatives [32]. Organisations are challenged to deliver shareholder value while simultaneously meeting evolving policy, compliance, and mission goals [32]. In this context, EAM is frequently positioned as a discipline for guiding transformation by increasing transparency, structuring decision-making, and steering the evolution of enterprise-wide capabilities. As described in prior work [23], Enterprise Architecture (EA) is not limited to descriptive representations, but also encompasses informing and governing aspects that enable the deliberate evolution of an enterprise.

E. Laurenzi et al. (Eds.): BIR 2026, LNBIP 601, pp. 325–342, 2027.
https://doi.org/10.1007/978-3-032-38498-0_21

Nevertheless, despite more than three decades of discussion and practice, the value of EA remains difficult to assess consistently [35]. Reported benefits are heterogeneous across sources and are often articulated as high-level value propositions rather than as empirically verified outcomes. This lack of comparability complicates both the accumulation of scholarly evidence and practitioners' efforts to justify, prioritise and guide EA initiatives. Moreover, research syntheses still predominantly focus on academic publications, while the systematic integration of industry-oriented sources remains less common. Yet industry publications provide practice-driven accounts [11] of reported benefit claims and value propositions, and shape prevailing organisational narratives about what EA is expected to deliver. What remains less explicit is how benefit claims from academic literature and practice-oriented industry publications can be consolidated, compared, and interpreted within a shared EA value discourse. Their inclusion, however, requires caution. Such publications are not peer-reviewed and may reflect commercial interests, particularly when produced by vendors or consultancies. Therefore, this study treats industry publications as sources of *claimed* or *reported* benefits, not as direct evidence that these benefits are necessarily realised in practice. By combining academic and industry-oriented literature, the goal is not to validate causal EA impact, but to provide a structured synthesis of the benefit claims that currently inform both research and practice.

In this paper, we build on the foundations laid in [44] and focus on *doing* EA, understood as the active and purposeful practice of creating, modelling, and managing architectural representations to steer transformation from an as-is state to a to-be state. To provide a structured interpretation of value claims beyond unconnected benefit lists, we employ three recurring roles of EA [15]: an *informative* role that increases transparency and supports decision-making, an *instructive* role that translates direction into actionable guidance across abstraction levels, and a *regulative* role that constrains and governs design through principles, standards, and compliance mechanisms. This lens provides a structured way to organise benefit statements and to articulate the assumed mechanisms through which EA is expected to contribute to value creation.
This paper therefore answers the following research question:

RQ: What are the claimed benefits of 'Doing' Enterprise Architecture in academic and industry-oriented literature?
In addition, drawing on the reviewed literature, we address two sub-questions:

SQ1: What are drivers for EA benefit realisation?
SQ2: What are challenges and propositions for EA value measurement?
We use the term *claimed* deliberately, since the reviewed sources differ in evidential strength and not all reported benefits are empirically demonstrated.

This paper contributes (1) a structured synthesis of EA benefit claims organised into IT-related and business-related value dimensions, (2) a role-based interpretation (informative, instructive, and regulative) that links benefit narratives to recurring mechanisms, and (3) a synthesis of reported drivers of benefit realisation and recurring challenges in measuring EA value. The contribution is therefore not the discovery of entirely new benefit types, but the consolidation, classification, and interpretation of dispersed EA value claims across academic and practitioner-oriented sources.

Drawing on 11 academic and 13 industry publications, we synthesise seven dimensions of EA value, identify measurement challenges, and provide an analytical perspective on how recurring drivers and the informative, instructive, and regulative roles of EA interact in realising these benefits. The remainder of this paper is organised as follows. Section 2 discusses the background and related work. Section 3 describes the applied research design and method. Section 4 presents the identified value propositions and benefit claims. Section 5 discusses the findings in relation to the research questions. Finally, Sect. 6 outlines future work and concludes the paper.

2 Background and Related Work

The concepts of *Value* and *Value Proposition* play a central role in understanding the contribution of EA to organisations. However, the notion of *value* is inherently context-dependent and, in the EA discourse, frequently invoked without being defined explicitly [33]. This lack of conceptual clarity creates ambiguity, particularly when value is to be assessed or measured in concrete terms. More generally, value is not an intrinsic property of objects, but is attributed based on the experiences and effects they enable [31]. For the purpose of this study, we adopt a *use value* perspective: EA value is understood not as something inherent in architectural artefacts or practices, but as a situationally ascribed quality that emerges when architectural actions align with and advance organisational goals. This ontological lens enables a more nuanced discussion of EA's contribution and supports goal- and context-specific accounts of how, when, and for whom this value is realised [31].

Importance of Understanding EA Value for Organisations – A clear understanding of EA value is central to the paper's relevance. Following Gong and Janssen [13], its importance can be summarised in two main reasons. First, understanding value is necessary to assess the returns of EA initiatives and better anticipate associated risks. Second, articulated benefits help align different stakeholders by making their value expectations explicit. EA initiatives and the use of EA in transformation programmes typically require substantial investments. To build a compelling business case, organisations therefore need a credible rationale for return on investment, which in turn depends on clearly articulated benefits. According to [13], practitioners often struggle to justify EA budgets, and initiatives may fail to secure funding when value is not convincingly evidenced. By articulating the value propositions of EA more clearly, organisations can more effectively assess the potential return on investment and build stronger, evidence-based arguments for funding EA initiatives. Beyond investment justification, EA is inherently cross-functional and involves stakeholders from diverse backgrounds, including architects, software engineers, and business stakeholders. Because EA can generate value along multiple dimensions, a shared understanding of what EA delivers is crucial for alignment and sustained commitment. Creating awareness of these value dimensions supports a shared vision and helps maintain stakeholder buy-in, which is often a prerequisite for the long-term success of EA efforts [13].

Related Work – While existing review papers synthesise EA value and benefits (e.g., [1,5,7,13,41]), our work builds on this foundation by consolidating and classifying reported benefits into value dimensions, complemented by the structured inclusion of industry publications that have so far been under-represented in review research, thereby providing a basis for further analytical and empirical work. This classification makes value discussions more comparable by linking benefit statements to a consistent set of dimensions. Finally, it creates a foundation for practitioner-focused studies by indicating where deeper probing is required to understand benefit realisation, its enabling conditions, and the contexts in which value materialises over time.

3 Research Method

We conducted a multivocal literature review (MLR), which extends structured literature review approaches by explicitly including grey literature [10]. The review protocol was adapted from Kitchenham and Charters [19] and complemented by MLR-specific guidance [10,18,20]. The study is structured into three phases: planning, conducting, and reporting the review.

Planning – To synthesise the vast body of EA literature on value claims across academia and industry, this review focuses on identifying and structuring the value claims associated with *doing* EA. In line with its multivocal design, we considered both peer-reviewed academic literature and selected grey literature, including white papers, case studies, position papers, and practitioner-oriented reports. Grey literature was included because it provides insight into how EA value is framed, communicated, and justified in practice. However, it was treated as a source of reported benefit claims rather than as direct empirical evidence of realised benefits.

To search for potentially relevant studies, we used the bibliographic sources: Scopus, Web of Science, SpringerLink, IEEE Xplore, and ScienceDirect. The search string reflects the two core concepts of this study: *Enterprise Architecture* and *Value add.* Including IT Governance extends the search to studies that discuss EA in a governance context. James Getter [12] characterises EA as a foundational component of IT Governance, which operationalises governance through EA principles and artefacts. Since the terms are often used interchangeably, querying both reduces the risk of missing literature that situates EA within governance frameworks or frames governance initiatives as architectural efforts [12]. Consequently, we combined the keywords into the following search string:

```
("Enterprise Architecture" OR "EA" OR "IT Governance" OR "IT-Governance")
AND
("value" OR "benefit" OR "strength" OR "advantage")
```

Conducting – Given the very high number of results returned by an initial Scopus query using *article title, abstract, and keywords* (TITLE-ABS-KEY; over 20,000 hits), we narrowed the search strategy to a *article title* search only. After conducting this search in Q2 2025, we screened the retrieved literature using predefined inclusion (IC) and exclusion (EC) criteria. We included (IC1) publications that explicitly highlight benefits and value claims associated with *doing* EA, and (IC2) academic sources published as peer-reviewed papers, studies, or books. Because formal peer review is uncommon in industry, we additionally considered (IC3) practitioner sources if they were formally published (e.g., white papers, case studies, or position papers) by organisations, consultancies, or vendors with recognised engagement in EA practice. We excluded publications that (EC1) focused primarily on the advantages of specific EA frameworks, tools, or practices rather than EA value more generally, (EC2) were secondary/tertiary studies, (EC3) were not written in English, or (EC4) were published before 2000.

Across the five academic databases, the title search yielded 591 records (Scopus: 173; Web of Science: 73; SpringerLink: 19; IEEE Xplore: 25; ScienceDirect: 301). After deleting duplicates and screening for inclusion and exclusion criteria, 117 unique papers remained for full-text assessment. To reduce the risk of missing relevant academic sources due to the title-only search strategy, we conducted backward and forward snowballing. This process, together with the subsequent full-text review, resulted in 11 academic publications being included in the review.

To broaden coverage of industry-oriented literature, we complemented the database search with a targeted grey literature search. We focused on key EA stakeholders, as these actors often maintain knowledge repositories, such as formally published reports, that explicitly articulate value propositions of *doing* EA. To identify influential technology vendors, we used the Gartner Magic Quadrant for EA tools [25] as an external selection criterion and selected publications from vendors positioned in the Leaders quadrant, such as SAP LeanIX, Ardoq, Bizzdesign, and BOC Group. In addition, we included selected consultancies with recognised engagement in digital transformation and EA practice to capture practice-oriented value claims closely tied to transformation initiatives. Trustworthiness was considered indirectly through grey literature quality and relevance checks, while industry sources were treated as reported benefit claims rather than empirical evidence of realised benefits. We considered whether a publication was publicly available, clearly attributable to an identifiable organisation, explicitly focused on EA or EAM, sufficiently detailed to extract concrete benefit claims, and relevant to the research question. We also considered the publication type, such as white paper, case study, position paper, report, or practitioner article. Industry publications were excluded if they were purely promotional, product-specific, lacked a broader EA value discussion, were insufficiently detailed, or were not clearly attributable. In total, 13 industry publications were included to capture explicit, practice-oriented EA value propositions.

The coding was performed by the first author. In a first step, relevant benefit statements were extracted from the included publications. In a second step, these statements were assigned initial descriptive codes that captured the type of claimed benefit, such as cost reduction, complexity management, risk reduction, quality improvement, strategic alignment, innovation enablement, decision-making, or governance. In a third step, related codes were grouped into higher-level value dimensions and assigned to either an IT-related or business-related perspective. Where applicable, claims were also interpreted in relation to the informative, instructive, and regulative roles of EA. The coding process was iterative. Identified statements, assigned codes, and emerging categories were discussed among the co-authors to challenge interpretations, clarify category boundaries, and reduce the risk of intra-observer inconsistencies. Instead of conducting independent double coding and formally assessing inter-observer agreement, exchanges among the co-authors were used as a quality-control mechanism to strengthen the analytical consistency of the study. Ambiguous assignments were discussed until a shared interpretation was reached. This process increased transparency in the synthesis while acknowledging that the coding remains interpretive in nature and that no formal inter-observer agreement was calculated.

Reporting – The selected literature proposes a variety of ways to structure and categorise EA value claims. For example, Shanks et al. [37] distinguish between *project benefits* and *organisational benefits*, thereby separating value claims at different levels of abstraction: a project-level view emphasising improvements to IS platforms and project delivery, and an organisational view capturing strategic outcomes such as increased agility and enterprise-wide value. In contrast, Jusuf and Kurnia [17] propose a more fine-grained classification into *operational, managerial, strategic, IT infrastructure, and organisational* categories. Based on a critical examination of these approaches, we adopt a categorisation aligned with Op 't Land et al. [23] and Shanks et al. [37], consolidating value claims into two overarching categories in line with [30]:
IT-related benefits: encompassing claims about cost and time efficiencies, complexity reduction, governance support, and technical risk mitigation.
Business-related benefits: covering strategic alignment, organisational agility, innovation enablement, value creation, and other outcome-oriented advantages.

Within each of these two high-level perspectives, we further decomposed the identified value claims into more granular subcategories. The resulting categories were used to structure the synthesis and to compare how EA benefits are discussed across academic and industry-oriented sources. The categorisation does not claim to represent a universal or empirically validated classification of EA value. Rather, it provides an analytical structure suited to the purpose of this review and a basis for subsequent empirical validation.

4 Identified Value Propositions

This section presents the core findings of the literature analysis by synthesising reported value claims associated with *doing* EA. We structure the claims using a dual perspective that distinguishes between IT-related and business-oriented value dimensions. This distinction reflects the domains in which the value is typically realised and captures the multifaceted nature of EA's contribution across organisational layers. Building on our definition of *doing* EA as an active effort to design, manage, and govern enterprise structures, we outline how these activities translate into both tangible and intangible outcomes. Finally, we relate the identified value dimensions to EA's informative, instructive, and regulative roles to provide a coherent account across IT and business contexts.

4.1 IT Perspective

The first bucket of identified values comprises IT-related benefits (see Table 1), including improved IT delivery, cost optimisation, and reduced complexity. Although closely linked to broader business outcomes, we distinguish these benefits to highlight advantages specific to EA work and IT functions. Below, we briefly discuss the key publications rather than all sources listed in Table 1.

Table 1. Identified IT-related benefits

Value Dimensions	Academic Papers	Industry Papers
Cost Reduction		
Accelerate delivery & reduce project duration	[3, 8, 9, 17, 23, 24, 34, 41]	[6, 27, 40]
Enhance project management effectiveness	[37]	[39]
Optimise costs and cost-management	[9, 17, 22, 29, 34, 41]	[2, 6, 14, 26–28, 39, 40, 43]
Reduce maintenance & support costs	[41]	[14, 21, 39, 40, 43]
Improve return on investments	[3, 29]	[27, 40, 43]
Complexity Management		
Reduce organisational complexity	[8, 9]	[27]
Reduce project complexity & overhead	[8, 17, 22, 24, 29, 34]	[4, 6, 14, 21, 27, 28, 36, 43]
Facilitate the integration of processes & systems	[3, 8, 9, 29, 34]	[14, 32, 36, 43]
Risk Management		
Identify & reduce project risk	[3, 8, 9, 22, 24, 34, 41]	[27, 43]
Reduce IT compliance risk	[23, 34]	[2, 14, 27, 32, 36]
Reduce dependency- and change risk	[29, 41]	[4, 40]
Improve security management	[17, 23]	[6, 28, 36, 43]
Quality Improvement		
Standardise & drive consistency	[3, 8, 17, 22, 24, 29, 34, 41]	[21, 28, 36, 40]
Enhance IT platform functionality	[9, 17, 29, 34, 37]	[27, 36, 43]
Increase IT asset reuse & mitigate duplication	[3, 8, 9, 17, 22, 23, 29, 41]	[4, 14, 21, 27, 40]
Enhance interoperability	[3, 17, 22, 34, 41]	[43]

Cost Reduction – It is one of the most frequently reported EA advantages, largely driven by improved time efficiency in IT-enabled transformation projects. As project cost is strongly influenced by labour and duration, EA contributes by reducing redundant work, improving process effectiveness, and standardising development practices, which shortens delivery cycles and accelerates platform design and development [8,17]. EA can also accelerate project initiation by supporting up-front scoping and early decision-making through coherent enterprise models [8]. Many value claims explicitly link EA to increased transparency and reduced complexity, enabling earlier and more robust decisions that lower rework and coordination overhead [24]. In the longer-term, maintenance and support costs may decline through classified and reusable assets and improved reliability and availability [40,41]. Overall, EA realises savings through an *instructive* role (planning guidance, standards, principles) and an *informative* role (timely insight that supports cost management).

Complexity Management – EA is repeatedly associated with reduced organisational and project complexity by offering modular representations of the enterprise (e.g., functions and aspect areas) that improve visibility and control [8,9]. This benefit is closely tied to standardisation and rationalisation, which streamline the application and technology landscape and reduce the number of platforms and frameworks in use [22,24]. The effect is particularly relevant under transformation pressure, where urgency is associated with technical debt and legacy complexity [4]. EA helps by making dependencies (e.g., point-to-point interfaces) explicit and by structuring processes, information, and applications into coherent building blocks [4]. While enterprise-wide roll-outs are often difficult in practice, EA is argued to facilitate integration via reusable components and standardised interfaces, improving scalability across silos [3,29]. Overall, complexity reduction is realised through EA's *informative* role (visibility into dependencies and structures) and *instructive* role (standards and guidance that enable rationalisation and modularisation).

Risk Management – Risk reduction is commonly attributed to EA's holistic view of platforms, services, and interdependencies, enabling earlier risk identification, better-informed project selection, and sounder design choices before implementation [3,8,9,27]. At programme level, EA can support dependency-aware sequencing and planning, lowering risk in coupled initiatives [41]. Regulatory and compliance demands further motivate EA, as top-down transparency over IT assets and information supports responses to oversight while limiting disruption [32]. EA is also positioned as enabling compliance-by-design and facilitating assessment through shareable solution architectures, mapping data flows is described as an initial step towards effective IT compliance [2,32,36]. Security is less emphasised overall, but is framed around understanding interdependencies and embedding security by design within architectural governance [6,23,28]. Overall, risk management is realised through EA's *informative* role (transparency into dependencies and exposure), its *regulative* role (standards and compliance enforcement), and, where applicable, its *instructive* role (design guidance and patterns).

Quality Improvement – Quality improvements are primarily linked to standardisation and reuse. Standardised principles and artefacts (notably interface standards) accelerate initiation, simplify integration, and strengthen interoperability across the IT landscape [3,22,41]. EA can also reduce ad-hoc procurement decisions by narrowing viable solution options through architectural guidance, supporting faster and more consistent selection and execution [41]. Moreover, transparency in heterogeneous landscapes helps identify existing solutions, avoid duplication, and justify replacement or retirement decisions. Together with reuse, this contributes to more reliable delivery outcomes [21,23,41]. Overall, this dimension reflects EA's *instructive* role (standards and principles) and *informative* role (landscape visibility) and is closely related to cost reduction and complexity management.

4.2 Business Perspective

This perspective primarily reflects the *regulative* and *informative* roles of EA, positioning EA as a strategic enabler for high-level decision-making and organisational planning. In contrast to the more *instructive* and solution-oriented focus of the Sect. 4.1, it emphasises EA's ability to steer the organisation through strategic transparency and guidance. At the enterprise design level, EA provides frameworks and decision-relevant insights that support the value dimensions in Table 2. Below, we briefly discuss the key publications, again, not necessarily discussing all listed sources.

Table 2. Identified business-related benefits

Value Dimensions	Academic Papers	Industry Papers
Strategy & Innovation		
Provide Transparency & Enterprise Overview	[3, 8, 9, 22–24]	[4, 27, 28, 36, 43]
Identify change requirements & foster innovation	[3, 17, 24, 29, 34]	[4, 14, 21, 27, 28, 32]
Drive business growth	[17, 29, 34]	[2, 14, 27]
Increase customer centricity & value	[3, 17, 29, 34, 37]	[4, 27, 28, 36]
Decision Making & Agility		
Increase agility & situational awareness	[3, 8, 9, 17, 22, 24, 29, 34, 37, 41]	[4, 14, 21, 26–28, 36, 43]
Support better investment & solution-selection decisions	[17, 22, 29, 41]	[43]
Provide prioritised guidance	[3, 17, 22, 29, 41]	[2, 21, 28, 36]
Improve decision quality	[17, 23, 29, 34, 37, 41]	[4, 14, 26, 39]
Alignment & Governance		
Align business strategy & IT	[3, 8, 9, 17, 22–24, 29, 34, 37]	[4, 14, 21, 26–28, 32, 36, 43]
Foster collaboration & shared knowledge	[3, 9, 17, 22, 24, 29, 34]	[2, 6, 14, 28, 32, 36, 39, 40]
Enable governance standards	[3, 9, 17, 23, 29, 34]	[4, 6, 26, 32, 36, 40]

Strategy and Innovation – Prior research emphasises EA's *informative* role as a foundation for strategy formation. By providing a holistic, multilayered view of the enterprise (people, processes, roles, goals, and policies), EA creates a consistent understanding of organisational assets and interdependencies [23]. This enterprise-wide perspective supports coherent strategy making and reduces the risk of fragmented, locally optimised decisions [8,40]. From an innovation management standpoint, EA increases transparency about how the organisation is structured and where complexity accumulates, helping leaders identify where change is required and anticipate downstream effects of initiatives [3,24]. When closely linked to corporate strategy, EA can leverage near-complete knowledge of the IT landscape and business data to detect structural gaps, recurring issues, and opportunities for IT and business innovation [21]. Moreover, EA supports growth by translating strategy into implementable roadmaps through explicit *as-is* and *to-be* models and transformation paths [40]. It can also improve decision transparency regarding financial implications and investment outcomes and enable scenario modelling and proof-of-value without disrupting live systems [2,3]. Finally, EA is linked to stronger customer centricity by deepening customer knowledge and supporting the translation of customer needs into concrete IT solutions and improved service experiences [4,29,37].

Decision-Making and Agility – A second major benefit cluster concerns agility and decision-making. Organisational agility is commonly defined as the capability to sense environmental change and respond quickly and effectively, including adapting products and services, adopting new technologies, and reacting to shifts in customer behaviour or markets [37]. EA contributes primarily through transparency: by making dependencies, constraints, and change impacts visible, EA supports rapid adjustment and organisational resilience [24,28]. This effect is often operationalised through decoupling and modularisation of information systems, enabling applications to be reconfigured or replaced with minimal disruption and supporting integration efforts such as acquisitions or divestitures while maintaining enterprise-wide standards [42]. The literature also frames EA as a decision-support instrument in contexts where decision-makers face information overload and insufficient data for evaluating options [2]. By documenting systems, principles, and the *as-is* state, EA provides reliable facts that underpin decision processes and improve predictability. In addition, EA practitioners support stakeholders by disseminating reusable practices and architectural reasoning beyond individual artefacts [40,41]. Moreover, EA can strengthen procurement and sourcing decisions by assessing the impact of new solutions and clarifying build-versus-buy or outsourcing choices [23]. Activities such as opportunity assessment and business capability modelling structure early-stage evaluation, increase benefit-to-cost transparency, mitigate implementation risks, and align investment programmes with capability priorities and maturity targets [22]. Overall, these benefits reflect EA's *informative* role (decision-relevant transparency) and its *instructive/regulative* contributions (architectural guidance and governance that preserve coherence under change).

Alignment and Governance – Alignment and governance are among the most frequently cited EA value dimensions and are repeatedly reported as key reasons organisations invest in EA [41]. Alignment refers to the degree to which information systems support strategic and operational business objectives [41]. In digitisation-driven transformation, EA can address the historical separation between business and IT by adopting an organisation-wide perspective on requirements and digitised processes, enabling information systems to support business needs more effectively [4,17,41]. This helps detect project-level misalignment early, reduce waste, and sustain a shared future vision and integrated change planning across business and IT stakeholders [23]. Communication and collaboration benefits emerge through mechanisms such as capability mapping (as a shared language across domains) and through the active engagement, mentoring, and coordination roles of enterprise architects across portfolios and ecosystems [6,22,24]. Governance effects are closely tied to standardisation, cost control, and interoperability across the IT landscape [22]. Overall, this value dimension reflects EA's *regulative*, *instructive*, and *informative* roles in aligning governance, implementation, and decision-making [41].

5 Discussion

Value Dimensions of *Doing* Enterprise Architecture – Distinguishing between IT and business perspectives provides a useful structure for discussing EA value claims. However, our synthesis indicates that these perspectives and their sub-dimensions cannot be clearly separated in practice. Rather than producing isolated benefits, EA contributes through interconnected effects that reinforce one another and unfold across organisational layers.

For instance, modular structures that enable efficient scaling can also support experimentation and foster innovation, potentially leading to new offerings and growth. Similarly, transparency created through architectural artefacts can improve decision quality and cost optimisation while clarifying dependencies and reducing maintenance effort. Standardisation may reduce complexity and enable higher-level abstraction, strengthening enterprise-wide oversight and supporting change, risk management, governance, and strategic alignment. As a result, the boundaries between value dimensions often blur, and observed outcomes frequently reflect combined mechanisms rather than single, independent effects.

This interdependence also applies to EA's roles. As discussed in Sect. 1, EA operates through informative, instructive, and regulative roles whose value typically emerges from their interplay. Regulative steering depends on informative transparency about artefacts and dependencies and becomes actionable through instructive mechanisms such as principles and standards. Conversely, informative transparency relies on purposeful abstraction tailored to decision needs, which, in turn, informs the development of regulatory and instructional elements. Consequently, initiatives that target one value dimension often generate secondary effects in others – creating positive synergies, but also complicating the attribution of realised business value to any single EA characteristic or role.

Drivers of Benefits Realisation. Synthesising the reviewed literature, we group drivers of EA benefit realisation into four categories, in line with [17].

Product Quality – High-quality EA artefacts are repeatedly described as a prerequisite for benefit realisation. Accurate *as-is* representations provide a reliable baseline for decision-making, while coherent *to-be* models support long-term planning and investment [24]. Roadmaps with intermediate milestones are further argued to improve stakeholder alignment and enable incremental value delivery [24]. Beyond these graphical outputs, the rigour of EA's conceptual and strategic grounding plays a critical role. Frameworks underpinned by sound business rationale and methodological consistency yield artefacts that stakeholders trust and adopt [29]. Overall, the literature links benefit realisation to the combination of precise current-state insight, well-defined future visions, and strategically grounded EA artefacts – capturing the product-related driver of EA benefits [17].

Infrastructure Quality – The literature suggests that EA success is enabled by clear implementation goals and a shared understanding of EA's purpose across business and IT stakeholders [17]. Robust governance mechanisms and supportive infrastructure underpin the reliable delivery of EA services. Conformance assessments and standardised documentation templates are reported to improve consistency and traceability across projects, while incentive structures (including sanctions) reinforce adherence to architectural guidelines [8,38]. Clear decision-making accountabilities further align EA objectives with organisational priorities [6,24]. Technical infrastructure and tool support (e.g., repositories and modelling environments) facilitate efficient EA service delivery and collaboration [6,17,24]. Capgemini Invent argues that principles and objectives should guide tool configuration and use, and that a capable EA team is required to leverage tooling effectively [6]. Adequate funding and resourcing are likewise highlighted as prerequisites for achieving EA goals [6]. Finally, a mature technical environment – characterised by a well-organised IT landscape and continuous platform improvement – is argued to amplify EA's impact [16,29].

Service Delivery Quality – Several sources emphasise that benefit realisation depends on how effectively EA services are delivered and communicated to stakeholders [8,38]. Knowledge exchange between architects and business stakeholders, as well as early project engagement (e.g., project start architectures), embeds architectural guidance into implementation work and can increase conformance [8,38]. Communication capabilities that educate and engage stakeholders are argued to increase perceived usefulness, while decision-support and compliance-validation mechanisms help decision-makers navigate trade-offs [4,24]. Integrating EA services with project execution is further highlighted as necessary to translate recommendations into concrete change and to keep services relevant to evolving business needs [29]. Finally, approaches to measuring success are frequently mentioned as important for sustaining benefits over time.

Organisational Embedding – The organisational context is repeatedly discussed as a key condition for whether EA practices are adopted and sustained. Linking EA activities to business objectives and communicating their relevance across the enterprise are argued to foster alignment and buy-in [8,38]. Practitioner sources and empirical studies note that architects' involvement in strategic discussions, stakeholder empowerment, and top-management support enable EA to influence decision-making and resource allocation [4,6,24,29]. Addressing social and political dynamics, raising awareness, and developing internal competencies through training are also associated with reducing resistance and increasing organisational maturity in EA capabilities [24,27,29]. Finally, embedding EA into existing processes and strategic planning is argued to sustain and evolve EA benefits over time [16,27]. In this sense, organisational embedding institutionalises EA's *informative*, *instructive*, and *regulative* roles by making them part of everyday decision-making and delivery practices.

Overall, EA benefits appear to be realised through the interplay of these four categories, particularly when they are aligned with business objectives and supported by suitable governance, tools, processes, and stakeholder engagement [17]. Despite limited empirical validation, this categorisation offers a structured perspective for understanding how diverse factors collectively enable the translation of EA initiatives into tangible organisational value.

EA Value Measurement – Organisations typically require reliable, often monetary, evidence to justify initiatives and investments. Accordingly, EA should be assessed using measurable, goal-aligned metrics, even though attributing observable organisational improvements to specific EA activities in a traceable and widely accepted way remains challenging [33].

Challenges – A central challenge concerns *attribution*. Many EA effects are indirect (e.g., governance, reduced risk, improved decision quality) and unfold through multiple intermediate steps, complicating causal links between EA work and financial outcomes [33]. Relatedly, EA involves substantial *intangible* costs and benefits. Although practitioner sources propose applying ROI-oriented metrics – for instance, the company Strategy& suggests cost/income ratios and cost-saving targets to quantify cost reduction effects [27] – several authors caution that purely financial measurement often requires deep contextual knowledge and may still fail to capture holistic value [33]. This difficulty is illustrated by interview evidence where preventing undesirable investment is clearly beneficial, yet assigning a precise monetary value is contested or impractical [41].

A further challenge is the *time horizon* of EA value. Organisational pressure often demands short-term evidence, whereas EA impacts may materialise predominantly over longer horizons [33]. Empirical work on stakeholder perspectives indicates a strong tendency towards long-term benefit realisation and reports limited perceived measurability for many value drivers [34]. Such time-lags complicate demonstrating quick wins and increase the risk that EA value is underestimated when assessed only within short reporting cycles.

Propositions and Measurement Approaches – To address intangibility and attribution, the literature proposes complementing financial metrics with operational and performance indicators. Examples include time-to-market as a proxy for agility and innovation [27], process and product quality measures to track quality-related effects [29], and before–after portfolio analyses (e.g., number of technologies or interfaces) to capture reductions in complexity and increases in standardisation [29]. Customer-centric outcomes can be collected via surveys and combined with basic counts such as new channels or services [27,29]. Practitioner accounts further suggest stakeholder-based scoring (e.g., surveys on the perceived value of architectural deliverables and EA input to projects) as a pragmatic way to capture decision and governance contributions [27].

Beyond selecting metrics, several sources argue for making the assumed value logic explicit. Rodrigues and Amaral [33] discuss that commonly used approaches such as the Balanced Scorecard are helpful but not sufficient for EA-specific value assessment, and propose a *value tree* approach. A value tree links operational metrics to higher-level value drivers and, ultimately, to shareholder value and financial outcomes. It focuses on a small set of key drivers that are both impactful and decomposable, enabling different abstraction levels aligned with stakeholder perspectives and supporting transparent metric definition and reporting [33].

Overall, the literature suggests that EA value measurement benefits from hybrid designs: traditional financial metrics where direct cost effects exist, complemented by operational, quality, and stakeholder-oriented indicators to capture indirect and long-term contributions [27,33]. Value-driver models such as value trees provide a coherent structure for connecting short-term indicators to long-term outcomes, while empirical validation of these measurement relationships remains limited and warrants further study [34].

6 Conclusion and Future Work

The analysis indicates that the value of *doing* EA is multifaceted and emerges from the interplay of EA's informative, instructive, and regulative roles. On the IT side, the literature most consistently links EA to cost and complexity reduction, risk mitigation, and quality improvements, often enabled through transparency, standardisation, and architectural reuse. On the business side, EA is primarily framed as a strategic capability supporting strategic alignment, informed decision-making, organisational agility, and innovation enablement.

Overall, these value claims are best understood as mutually reinforcing rather than isolated effects. Academic and industry sources frame them differently, while their often indirect, intangible, and difficult-to-attribute nature limits the extent to which reported claims can be empirically measured.

From a research perspective, this study provides a structured basis for future empirical work on EA value by consolidating dispersed benefit claims from academic and industry-oriented literature into a coherent set of value dimensions. These dimensions can inform the development of interview guides, survey instruments, and coding schemes for practitioner-oriented studies.

Future work should empirically validate and contextualise the identified value dimensions through practitioner-focused studies, particularly semi-structured expert interviews and complementary case research. Such work should examine how these benefits are experienced across stakeholder roles and organisational contexts, how they interact over time, and how EA capability maturity and governance arrangements shape benefit realisation. Furthermore, the distinction between claimed benefits and empirically demonstrated outcomes highlights the need to investigate how, when, and under which organisational conditions EA benefits are actually realised. This can help bridge the gap between literature-based claims and organisational impact, ultimately supporting more informed decisions about when, why, and how to invest in *doing* EA.

References

1. Ahlemann, F., Legner, C., Lux, J.: A resource-based perspective of value generation through enterprise architecture management. Inf. Manag. **58**(1), 103266 (2021). https://doi.org/10.1016/j.im.2020.103266
2. Ardoq: 7 Key Benefits of Enterprise Architecture That Can Change Your Organization (2024). https://www.ardoq.com/knowledge-hub/benefits-of-enterprise-architecture. Accessed 29 May 2025
3. Bachoo, A.: Enterprise architecture practices to achieve business value. In: Proper, H.A., Strecker, S., Huemer, C. (eds.) 20th IEEE Conference on Business Informatics, CBI 2018, Vienna, Austria, July 11-14, 2018 – Research Papers, vol. 1, pp. 1–9, IEEE Computer Society, Washington DC, USA (2018). ISBN 978-1-5386-7016-3, https://doi.org/10.1109/CBI.2018.00010
4. Bossert, O., Manwani, S.: Enterprise Architecture and Digital Leaders: A Survey Report Based on Research with McKinsey & Company and Henley Business School. Survey report, Association of Enterprise Architects (2021). https://assets.henley.ac.uk/v3/fileUploads/Enterprise-Architecture-and-Digital-Leaders.pdf. Accessed 29 May 2025
5. Boucharas, V., van Steenbergen, M., Jansen, S., Brinkkemper, S.: The contribution of enterprise architecture to the achievement of organizational goals: a review of the evidence. In: Proper, H.A., Lankhorst, M.M., Schönherr, M., Barjis, J., Overbeek, S.J. (eds.) Trends in Enterprise Architecture Research – 5th International Workshop, TEAR 2010, Delft, The Netherlands, 12 November 2010. Proceedings, LNBIP, vol. 70, pp. 1–15, Springer, Berlin, Germany (2010). ISBN 978-3-642-16819-2, ISSN 1865-1356, https://doi.org/10.1007/978-3-642-16819-2_1
6. Capgemini Invent: Digital Architecture Study 2024: How EAM Creates Business Value in Different Organizational Types. Technical report, Capgemini, Utrecht, The Netherlands (2024). https://www.capgemini.com/de-de/wp-content/uploads/sites/8/2024/11/Digital-Architecture-Study-2024_vF.pdf. Accessed 29 May 2025
7. Denzel, J., Jung, J.: A literature study on benefits provided by enterprise architecture management. Enterp. Archit. Prof. J. 1–14 (2022)
8. Foorthuis, R., van Steenbergen, M., Brinkkemper, S., Bruls, W.: A theory building study of enterprise architecture practices and benefits. CoRR (2020a). https://doi.org/10.48550/arXiv.2008.08112
9. Foorthuis, R., van Steenbergen, M., Mushkudiani, N., Bruls, W., Brinkkemper, S., Bos, R.: On course, But not there yet: enterprise architecture conformance and benefits in systems development. CoRR (2020b). https://doi.org/10.48550/arXiv.2008.11026
10. Garousi, V., Felderer, M., Mäntylä, M.V.: Guidelines for including grey literature and conducting multivocal literature reviews in software engineering. IST **106**, 101–121 (2019). ISSN 0950-5849, https://doi.org/10.1016/j.infsof.2018.09.006
11. Garousi, V., Felderer, M., Mäntylä, M.V., Rainer, A.: Benefitting from the Grey Literature in Software Engineering Research, pp. 385–413. Springer, Cham (2020). ISBN 978-3-030-32489-6, https://doi.org/10.1007/978-3-030-32489-6_14
12. Getter, J.R.: Enterprise architecture and it governance: a risk-based approach. In: 2007 40th Annual Hawaii International Conference on System Sciences (HICSS'07), p. 220 (2007). https://doi.org/10.1109/HICSS.2007.210
13. Gong, Y., Janssen, M.: The value of and myths about enterprise architecture. Int. J. Inf. Manag. **46**, 1–9 (2019). https://doi.org/10.1016/J.IJINFOMGT.2018.11.006

14. Graves, T.: Real Enterprise Architecture: Beyond IT to the Whole Enterprise. Tetradian Books, Colchester, England, UK (2008)
15. Greefhorst, D., Proper, H.A.: Architecture Principles - The Cornerstones of Enterprise Architecture, The Enterprise Engineering Series, vol. 4. Springer, Berlin, Germany (2011). ISBN 978-3-642-20279-7, https://doi.org/10.1007/978-3-642-20279-7
16. Härting, R.C., Reichstein, C., Sandkuhl, K.: Determinants to benefit from enterprise architecture management – a research model. In: Abramowicz, W., Paschke, A. (eds.) Business Information Systems Workshops – BIS 2018 International Workshops, Berlin, Germany, July 18-20, 2018, Revised Papers, LNBIP, vol. 339, pp. 101–111, Springer, Berlin (2019). https://doi.org/10.1007/978-3-030-04849-5_9, ISBN 978-3-030-04849-5, ISSN 1865-1356
17. Jusuf, M.B., Kurnia, S.: Understanding the benefits and success factors of enterprise architecture. In: Bui, T. (ed.) 50th Hawaii International Conference on System Sciences, HICSS 2017, Hilton Waikoloa Village, Hawaii, USA, 4–7 January 2017, pp. 1–10, ScholarSpace/AIS Electronic Library (AISeL), Washington DC, USA (2017). https://doi.org/10125/41755
18. Kamei, F., et al.: Grey literature in software engineering: a critical review. IST **138**, 106609 (2021). https://doi.org/10.1016/j.infsof.2021.106609
19. Kitchenham, B., Charters, S.: Guidelines for performing systematic literature reviews in software engineering. Tech. Rep. EBSE 2007-001, Keele University and Durham University Joint Report (2007). http://www.dur.ac.uk/ebse/resources/Systematic-reviews-5-8.pdf. Accessed 20 Dec 2007
20. Kitchenham, B.A., Madeyski, L., Budgen, D.: How should software engineering secondary studies include grey material? IEEE TSE **49**(2), 872–882 (2023). https://doi.org/10.1109/TSE.2022.3165938
21. Könnecke, L., Kaiser, S., Doemer, D.F.: Why effectively managing enterprise architecture is key to transformation. Technical report, Arthur D. Little (2023). https://www.adlittle.com/en/insights/viewpoints/why-effectively-managing-enterprise-architecture-key-transformation. Accessed 29 May 2025
22. Kurnia, S., Kotusev, S., Taylor, P., Dilnutt, R.: Artifacts, activities, benefits and blockers: exploring enterprise architecture practice in depth, pp. 1–10 (2017). https://doi.org/10125/64429
23. Op 't Land, M., Proper, H.A., Waage, M., Cloo, J., Steghuis, C.: Enterprise Architecture – Creating Value by Informed Governance. The Enterprise Engineering Series, Springer, Cham (2009). ISBN 978-3-540-85232-2, https://doi.org/10.1007/978-3-540-85232-2
24. Lange, M., Mendling, J., Recker, J.: A comprehensive ea benefit realization model-an exploratory study. In: 45th Hawaii International Conference on System Sciences, pp. 4230–4239 (2012). https://doi.org/10.1109/HICSS.2012.50
25. LeanIX: Gartner Magic Quadrant for Enterprise Architecture Tools (2024). https://www.leanix.net/en/download/gartner-magic-quadrant-for-enterprise-architecture-tools-2024. Accessed 29 May 2025
26. LeanIX: Value of Enterprise Architecture (2025). https://www.leanix.net/en/wiki/ea/value-of-enterprise-architecture. Accessed 29 May 2025
27. Makhoul, R., et al.: Building Value through Enterprise Architecture: A Global Study. Research report, Strategy & (formerly Booz & Company) (2009). https://www.strategyand.pwc.com/gx/en/insights/archive/building-value-through-enterprise-architecture/strategyand-building-value-through-enterprise-architecture.pdf. Accessed 29 May 2025

28. Moser, C.: The Role of Enterprise Architecture in Business Transformation (2025). https://www.adoit-community.com/blog/enterprise-architecture-in-business-transformation. Accessed 29 May 2025
29. Niemi, E.I., Pekkola, S.: The benefits of enterprise architecture in organizational transformation. BISE **62**(6), 585–597 (2020). https://doi.org/10.1007/S12599-019-00605-3
30. Nogueira, J.M., Romero, D., Espadas, J., Molina, A.: Leveraging the zachman framework implementation using action - research methodology - a case study: aligning the enterprise architecture and the business goals. Enterp. Inf. Syst. **7**(1), 100–132 (2013). https://doi.org/10.1080/17517575.2012.678387
31. Prince Sales, T., Baião, F., Guizzardi, G., Almeida, J.P.A., Guarino, N., Mylopoulos, J.: The common ontology of value and risk. In: Trujillo, J.C., et al. (eds.) Conceptual Modeling – 37th International Conference, ER 2018, Xi'an, China, 22–25 October 2018, Proceedings, LNCS, vol. 11157, pp. 121–135, Springer, Berlin, Germany (2018). ISBN 978-3-030-00847-5, ISSN 1611-3349, https://doi.org/10.1007/978-3-030-00847-5_11
32. Reed, N.: The evolution of Enterprise Architecture in business transformation (2024). https://www.bizzdesign.com/blog/the-evolution-of-enterprise-architecture-in-business-transformation. Accessed 29 May 2025
33. Rodrigues, L.S., Amaral, L.: Issues in enterprise architecture value. J. Enterp. Archit. **6**(4), 27–32 (2010)
34. Rodrigues, L.S., Amaral, L.: Stakeholders perspectives on time horizon and quantification of enterprise architectures benefits/value drivers. In: 2nd IBIMA Conference: 15–16 November 2018, Seville, Spain, pp. 5958–5967 (2018)
35. Santos, W.F., Ribeiro, M.G., Santos, S.C., Junior, I.H.D.F., Rodrigues, C.M.D.O.: The state-of-the-art of enterprise architecture its definitions, contexts, frameworks, benefits, and challenges: a systematic mapping of literature. In: 2020 15th Iberian Conference on Information Systems and Technologies (CISTI), pp. 1–6 (2020). https://doi.org/10.23919/CISTI49556.2020.9140808
36. SAP: Explaining the Value of Enterprise Architecture (2024). https://learning.sap.com/courses/becoming-an-sap-btp-solution-architect/explaining-the-value-of-enterprise-architecture. Accessed 29 May 2025
37. Shanks, G.G., Gloet, M., Someh, I.A., Frampton, K., Tamm, T.: Achieving benefits with enterprise architecture. J. Strateg. Inf. Syst. **27**(2), 139–156 (2018). https://doi.org/10.1016/J.JSIS.2018.03.001
38. van Steenbergen, M., Foorthuis, R., Mushkudiani, N., Bruls, W., Brinkkemper, S., Bos, R.: Achieving enterprise architecture benefits: What makes the difference? In: 2011 IEEE 15th International Enterprise Distributed Object Computing Conference Workshops, pp. 350–359 (2011). https://doi.org/10.1109/EDOCW.2011.36
39. Stovers, R., Ruijter, J.d., Wagter, R.: GEA Enterprise Architecture in Practice: Better Performance by Managing Coherence. Dialoog, Zaltbommel, The Netherlands (2021). ISBN 978-94-6126-477-0
40. Sullivan, S.: From Inception to Implementation: Delivering Business Value Through Enterprise Architecture. Tech. Rep. G507-1006-00, IBM Rational Software, IBM Corporation, Somers, New York, USA (2004). https://public.dhe.ibm.com/software/rational/web/whitepapers/G507-1006-00_EntArch4.pdf. Accessed 29 May 2025
41. Tamm, T., Seddon, P.B., Shanks, G.G.: How enterprise architecture leads to organisational benefits. Int. J. Inf. Manag. **67**, 102554 (2022). https://doi.org/10.1016/J.IJINFOMGT.2022.102554

42. Tamm, T., Seddon, P.B., Shanks, G.G., Reynolds, P.: How does enterprise architecture add value to organisations? CAIS **28**, 10 (2011). https://doi.org/10.17705/1CAIS.02810
43. The Open Group: TOGAF Standard, Version 9.2 (2018). https://pubs.opengroup.org/architecture/togaf9-doc/arch/. Accessed 17 May 2025
44. Walder, P.: Value claims of doing Enterprise Architecture - A literature analysis, Vienna, Austria (2025). https://doi.org/10.5281/zenodo.20053847. Bachelor's thesis

Effects of Digital Transformation on the Enterprise Architecture of SMEs

Benjamin Nast[1(✉)], Nikola Ivanovic[1], Sebastian Dannehl[1], Ansgar Kock[1], Gideon Seidel[1], and Kurt Sandkuhl[1,2]

[1] University of Rostock, Rostock, Germany
{Benjamin.Nast,Nikola.Ivanovic,Sebastian.Dannehl, Ansgar.Kock,Gideon.Seidel,Kurt.Sandkuhl}@uni-rostock.de
[2] Jönköping University, Jönköping, Sweden

Abstract. Digitalization is leading to fundamental changes in organizational structures, processes, IT infrastructure, and business models. These changes are intensified by technology trends and evolving customer needs, presenting enterprises with enormous challenges. The successful adoption of new technologies and the implementation of new customer requirements necessitate a comprehensive digital strategy. Enterprise architecture management (EAM) is considered a promising approach for this. However, there is a lack of existing work examining the effects of digital transformation on multiple layers of the enterprise architecture (EA) and their inter-layer relationships. Small and medium-sized enterprises (SMEs) require particular support in this regard, as EAM is not well established in these, and often no (comprehensive) EA exists. In this paper, we examine the effects of digital transformation on the EA of an SME using two real-world case studies. We modeled the EA before and after implementing a digital twin (DT) for heating, ventilation, and air conditioning (HVAC) facilities, as well as a digitized warehouse management process. By comparing multiple layers, we analyze the extent and nature of the effects in this SME. The case studies show that EAs can serve as a suitable instrument for investigating the effects of digital transformation. Furthermore, the adaptability of TOGAF for effective use in SMEs was demonstrated.

Keywords: Enterprise Architecture · Digital Transformation · SME · Digital Twin · Internet of Things · Warehouse Management · TOGAF

1 Introduction

In today's rapidly evolving economic landscape, digital transformation has become a strategic necessity for organizations seeking to sustain their market position and competitiveness [41]. It goes far beyond mere technological adoption and fundamentally reshapes core operations of enterprises, organizational structures, and business models [4,21]. These technological advancements present

E. Laurenzi et al. (Eds.): BIR 2026, LNBIP 601, pp. 343–360, 2027.
https://doi.org/10.1007/978-3-032-38498-0_22

profound opportunities to co-create value with customers and discover novel service-oriented business pathways [5,9].

However, managing such comprehensive, organization-wide transformations remains highly complex, as they deeply affect how enterprises operate, interact, and deliver value [41]. Enterprise architecture management (EAM) is increasingly used by organizations to manage and navigate these complex changes [20,25]. EAM serves as a critical instrument for modeling, aligning, and understanding the complex interactions between business strategies and IT infrastructures [1,20]. Despite the established value of EAM in structuring organizational change, existing literature does not focus on the holistic effects of digital transformation on enterprise architectures (EAs) [16]. While prior work often focuses on isolated layers or on a high architectural level (cf. Sect. 2.3), there remains a gap in detailed comparative analyses of EA concepts across multiple layers before and after digital transformation initiatives. In particular, empirical studies that capture the shift from the current to the future state in real-world enterprises are largely lacking. Consequently, practitioners and researchers lack reference models to understand which architectural elements, such as roles, application services, or technological nodes, are typically modified, integrated, or removed during digital transformation. Another aspect is that EAM is not well established in small and medium-sized enterprises (SMEs) and thus requires special attention [40,43].

To address this gap, this paper investigates the effects of digital transformation through an exploratory, qualitative case study approach [44]. We examine two distinct projects of an SME operating in the heating, ventilation, and air conditioning (HVAC) sector. The first case study concerns the implementation of a digital twin (DT) for predictive maintenance and introduces an innovative energy contracting business model. The second case study is about the digitization of the warehouse management process. We systematically analyze structural changes across the business, application and data, technological, and motivational layers by mapping and comparing the EAs in both cases *Before* and *After* the digital transformation. The research question (RQ) guiding our work is: *What are the effects of digital transformation on the EA in SMEs?*

The paper is structured as follows: Sect. 2 provides an overview of digital transformation, EAM, and related work. The research approach applied is described in Sect. 3. Section 4 presents two case studies followed by an analysis in Sect. 5. Section 6 summarizes findings and provides an outlook on future work.

2 Background

2.1 Digital Transformation

Digital transformation is an important topic in information systems research [26] and practice [9]. It can be described as the adoption of innovative digital technologies, e.g., DTs, big data, and artificial intelligence, to digitalize the organization's operations and business model [21]. An organization-wide transformation program is needed because it affects not only the products and services enterprises offer but also how they operate [41].

Digital transformation can be defined as the efforts for transferring information, processes, products, or services into a form that is more digitized [5] and software-intensive [33]. As a result, these are expected to be more flexible and scalable, and usually service-oriented [8]. There exist different technology-driven (internal or external) approaches that structure digital transformation into viewpoints, phases, or maturity levels [20]. These focus on changing existing elements of an EA [39] or integrating new ones.

Digital products and services provide new forms of smart connected functionalities and offer great opportunities for new business solutions [5]. They support the co-creation of value with customers and stakeholders, including third-party developer networks, in different ways [33]. It is possible to provide ongoing feedback [8]. Usage data that can yield new insights and inform the development of new services can be collected continuously via the internet [34].

2.2 Enterprise Architecture Management

An EA can be used to model, align, and understand the interactions between IT and business. It supports well-adjusted, strategically oriented decision-making for both digital business and digital technologies [25]. EA is primarily described using a formal model that captures the key architectural components of an enterprise and their relationships [1]. The goal of EAM is to provide a structured approach to developing and maintaining EAs aligned with an enterprise's strategic objectives [20]. EAM includes planning, transformation, and monitoring activities, and establishes guidelines, architecture principles, and governance mechanisms to achieve transformation goals [20,35]. It is nowadays an established discipline in large companies and has been the subject of extensive research. Wißotzki and Sandkuhl [42] presented a literature review outlining commonly explored areas, including implementation strategies [20], EAM components [6], and processes and guiding principles [31].

As defined by standards such as TOGAF [39] and ArchiMate [38], a large set of views is used in EAM to manage and document the alignment of business and IT [35]. While TOGAF includes guidelines for developing viewpoints, techniques, and reference models, it does not provide a formal modeling language [15]. For this reason, ArchiMate is used alongside TOGAF because it provides a formal modeling language and graphical notation that cover the diverse elements of EAs [38]. TOGAF contains four architectural layers, which are also found in other frameworks: **Business Architecture** defines the business strategy, governance, organization, and key business processes. **Data Architecture** describes the structure of logical and physical data elements and data management resources in the organization. **Application Architecture** defines a blueprint for the application system deployed individually and its relationship to the organization's core business processes. **Technology Architecture** describes the software and hardware functions needed to support the development of business, data, and application services. This includes IT infrastructure, middleware, networks, communications, processing, and standards.

While the adoption and benefits of EAM have already been demonstrated in large companies, the situation is different for smaller organizations [40,43], due to their overall maturity and the complexity of current approaches relative to available human resources [3]. However, a study by Alm and Wißotzki [2] found that it can be applied effectively in SMEs, particularly in dynamic environments or during growth, if a longer company "lifetime" is targeted. They also point out that, according to the TOGAF documentation [39], all parts of the framework form a coherent whole, while also referring to adaptability. So it may make sense within SMEs to implement only a portion of it to handle the complexity of such a framework that is hard to handle for users [7]. Current research already confirms that EA adoption in SMEs is possible and can be useful (e.g., [11,30]).

2.3 Related Work on Effects of Digital Transformation on EAs

There is extensive research on the effects of digital transformation on EAs. In [19], for example, an approach for systematically identifying and adapting EA elements affected by the implementation of Industry 4.0 technologies is proposed. The aim is to help organizations maintain their performance, alignment, and competitiveness despite digital transformation. Using TOGAF as an example, they demonstrate the direct impacts of a transformation and how these impacts can be tracked to identify all elements of EA models that should be adjusted following the introduction of an Industry 4.0 component within an organization.

Pohl et al. [28] conduct a literature review of existing work on integrating data science projects into EAs. They aim to provide an overview of data science integration to enhance architectural frameworks. The results show that existing research in this field either takes a high-level perspective, thereby neglecting essential details (e.g., [10,12]), or focuses solely on the business architecture level (e.g., [36,37]). The authors therefore propose a framework that links the various architectural layers with relevant data science methods. The aim is to establish a common understanding of how data science can be effectively integrated into the overall EA to ensure both strategic and operational elements are aligned.

Ilin et al. [13] investigate how emerging technologies transform the structure and operation of modern production enterprises. Their study shows how these factors impact EA focus, technological infrastructure, and organizational processes. A metamodel is presented that integrates findings on the potential evolution of a digitally transformed enterprise. Kochetkova and Shiryaeva [18] analyzed EAs of diary enterprises, revealing insufficient support and compliance with business and IT goals. Based on this, they propose an EA that supports these aspects and enables the integration of new technologies in such companies. The key findings of these studies, namely, that new technologies necessitate additional EA elements (e.g., new services or products), that roles are changing, and some elements are to be removed (often due to process automation), are very similar. Pittl and Bork [27] confirm these findings and highlight that, in this context, new roles are often added to maintain the newly implemented technologies, and that the total number of traditional roles may decrease.

One paper was found examining detailed effects across multiple architectural layers [32]. EAs are compared before and after the digitization of existing products and services. For each layer, the authors compared the elements (identical, new, modified, or removed) and assessed how well the identified changes could be integrated. Their results illustrate that digital transformation can mean more than just an extension of existing EAs; it often gives rise to a distinct area of digital architecture with its own processes, platforms, and organizational forms.

3 Research Approach

We began our research by reviewing existing literature on the effects of digital transformation on EA (cf. Sect. 2.3). While we identified several relevant papers, we observed that there is little work comparing EAs before and after digital transformation. Thus, we decided to adopt a qualitative case study approach to investigate real-world cases and better understand the challenges, barriers, and potential integration paths. A qualitative case study is a research approach that explores a phenomenon within its context using multiple data sources [44]. This ensures that the subject under consideration is explored not from a single perspective but from multiple perspectives, allowing multiple facets of the phenomenon to be revealed and understood. According to Yin [44], the case studies described in this work can be classified as exploratory, i.e., we explore the phenomenon of digital transformation and its effects on the EA in its real-world setting of the case study enterprise. We decided to address the topic from architectural and management perspectives, with the case study as the focus.

Our investigation comprises two case studies in the same SME operating in the HVAC sector. For each case study, we first modeled the SMEs' current EA (*Before*) and *After* the digital transformation, focusing solely on the relevant elements across the business, application and data, technology, and motivational layers. We conducted semi-structured interviews with two employees in two separate sessions (*Before* and *After*), each of whom was actively involved in both case studies in their respective roles. Subsequently, the corresponding EA models were created, reviewed, and refined in consultation with them. To prepare the qualitative data collection, interview guides were developed following [17]. Four separate interview guides were created: one each for *Before* and *After* for both digital transformations. The structure of all interview guides strictly followed the selected ArchiMate layers (cf. Fig. 1) to ensure systematic data collection.

4 Case Studies on Effects of Digital Transformation

The first case study concerns the implementation of a DT for HVAC facilities (see Sect. 4.2); the second concerns the digitization of the warehouse management process (see Sect. 4.3). The case study enterprise, in which both case studies were conducted, is introduced in Sect. 4.1. Given the specific situation in SMEs (cf. Sect. 2.2), we selected a subset of the ArchiMate metamodel based on the *Layered View*, including only elements relevant to the case studies (cf. Fig. 1).

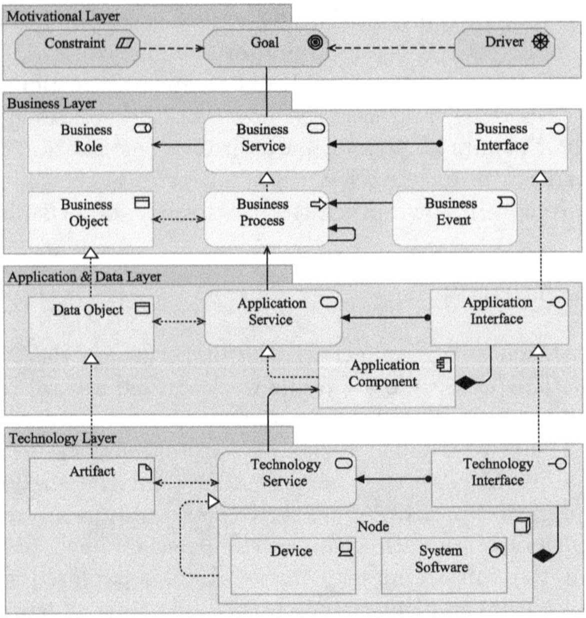

Fig. 1. Subset of the ArchiMate metamodel used in the case studies.

4.1 Case Study Enterprise

The case study enterprise was founded over 30 years ago and has an annual turnover of about 15 million euros. The SME operates in several fields, including air conditioning, refrigeration, electrical engineering, cleanroom technology, and maintenance and service. It offers comprehensive services, including development, engineering, administrative tasks, and in-house production and installation of sophisticated building systems. Through various research and development projects, it has built in-depth technical expertise, enabling it to implement complex solutions in ventilation, air conditioning, and fluid dynamics.

Current research projects include pressure and volume flow control in HVAC facilities, IT tools for situational maintenance support, and the development of a compact controller for HVAC facilities in cleanrooms. These projects underscore the enterprises' high technological standards and innovation potential.

4.2 Case Study A: Implementing a Digital Twin for HVAC Facilities

Case study A focuses on the development and implementation of a DT for HVAC facilities. Further information about the overall project [14,23] and the modeling tool developed to support the creation of the DTs [24] can be found in our previous publications. The physical state of these facilities could not be monitored remotely. Consequently, system anomalies, inefficiencies, and component failures were only detected during routine on-site inspections or when customers actively reported service disruptions. This often led to increased operational costs, unpredictable downtimes, and delayed response times.

To address these problems, the DT introduces continuous, real-time state monitoring. Standardized measurement cases are installed in the facilities to collect vital sensor data, which is then stored centrally for calculating supplementary performance metrics. Through a dedicated WebGUI, staff from the research and development department can analyze the aggregated data and generate automated internal and customer reports. This continuous analytical capability allows for the detection of emerging defects and the prediction of upcoming maintenance needs. By enabling predictive maintenance, the enterprise can proactively contact customers and resolve issues before a system failure occurs.

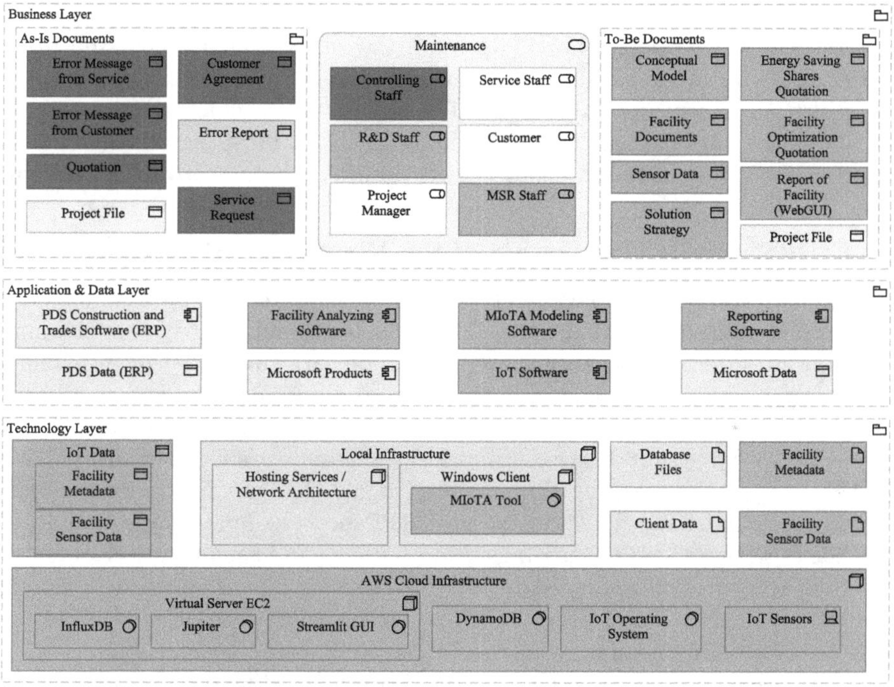

Fig. 2. High-level view of the EA for the digital twin case study.

Beyond optimizing maintenance operations, the DT data enables the introduction of innovative, service-oriented business models, such as energy contracting. By analyzing long-term facility performance, underperforming or poorly dimensioned components that, if replaced, would yield substantial energy savings can be identified. To mitigate financial risks and capital constraints that often prevent customers from investing in these upgrades, offers are made to replace components at no upfront cost. The standardized measurement case remains installed at the customer's facility for the entire duration of the contracting agreement to accurately calculate and verify these savings. This continuous presence allows tracking of actual system utilization, load factors (such as building occupancy), and other external variables, dynamically simulating what the energy consumption would have been with the legacy components under identical operating conditions. The precise financial savings are calculated by comparing the simulated baseline with the actual consumption of the new equipment, using current market energy prices, to refinance the initial investment.

Figure 2 shows a high-level view of the created EA elements relevant in this case study. The complete EA models for both case studies are available in our repository [22]; Tables 1 and 2 show the numbers of elements and relationships per layer. The different colors indicate whether they are identical (standard ArchiMate color), modified (orange), new (green), or removed (red) in the EAs *Before* and *After* implementation. It becomes clear that many business objects are being removed because the DT changes the way errors are detected in the facilities. On the other hand, many new ones are being added as conceptual models of the systems are created for DT configuration, which requires certain data about the facilities and their components. The most significant changes stem from the newly required cloud infrastructure and the software it contains.

4.3 Case Study B: Digitization of the Warehouse Management

The current warehouse management process is characterized by manual workflows and fragmented communication. The cycle begins when project or site managers request materials. Because these requisitions are submitted inconsistently, ranging from ERP entries and emails to verbal or phone requests, purchasing staff must frequently manually create and complete requisitions before placing orders. Once ordered, goods are delivered to the main warehouse, inspected, and stored. However, the tracking remains inefficient. Delivery notes are manually forwarded to purchasing for entry in the ERP, and consumables are withdrawn by installers without system postings. Maintenance and repair materials for the service department are managed in separate service files. Due to delayed and outdated documentation of goods receipts, missing parts are often only noticed during final assembly, leading to project delays.

An analysis across departments revealed several systemic issues that hinder process efficiency and prevent effective KPI measurement. The ERP material catalog is poorly maintained and contains over three million duplicate or unstandardized entries. Due to unstructured storage locations and a lack of standardized item names, warehouse staff maintains independent Excel sheets rather than using the ERP system's built-in services. Customer service requests are often routed to project managers rather than to the service department. Consequently, critical information is lost or delayed, disrupting the internal information chain. Installers, site managers, and executives bypass the purchasing department to place direct orders, leading to duplicate orders and a lack of transparency. Delivery notes often remain on-site for too long or are lost, preventing timely invoice verification and resulting in missed early-payment discounts.

The digitized warehouse management standardizes workflows within a single ERP system environment, reducing complexity and establishing a reliable information chain. Ordering authority is restricted exclusively to purchasing staff to prevent duplicate orders and ensure transparency. Manual Excel files are eliminated. The warehouse staff now manages inventory digitally via a mobile application (ERP app) that automatically updates stock levels via barcode scans upon delivery. The integrated ticket system ensures that customer inquiries are routed directly to the service department, preventing communication gaps. Return notifications, invoice generation, and cost settlements are automated within the ERP system, ensuring that all employees create a unified documentation.

Figure 3 shows a high-level view of the relevant EA elements and their changes in the warehouse case study. At first glance, only a few changes to the EA appear to be needed. While the figure shows, for example, that separate inventory lists and inconsistent customer inquiries are eliminated and that paper invoices are converted to electronic invoices, the most significant changes are not immediately apparent. These changes are particularly evident in the processes. Through automation (particularly the creation and forwarding of documents), many processes are eliminated, and a few new ones are added (e.g., due to the new ability to order and deliver goods directly to the construction site).

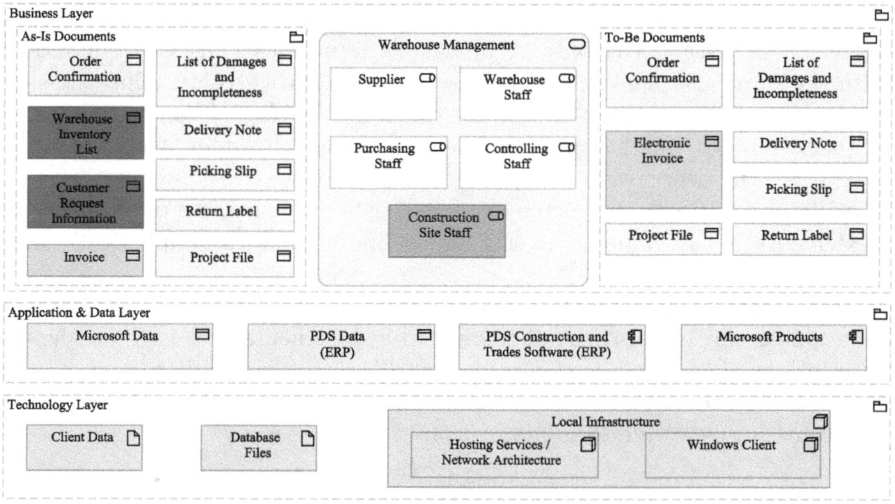

Fig. 3. High-level view of the EA for the warehouse management case study.

5 Analysis of the Case Studies

The idea behind analyzing the case studies is to compare the EAs of the case study enterprise *Before* and *After* the digital transformation by calculating the percentage change in the elements and counting the number of relationships. Based on this, we assess the effects to provide support for other SMEs undergoing similar digital transformation projects. Section 5.1 introduces the approach, followed by the actual analysis in the case studies in Sect. 5.2 and 5.3.

5.1 Approach for the Analysis

The analysis approach is based on [32]; we additionally include the motivational layer and relationships. To determine the percentage change, we compare the EA models *Before* and *After* the digital transformation. A model of an EA contains elements that are instances of the ArchiMate metamodel. These elements have identifiers, attributes (e.g., name or description), and sometimes relationships to other elements or refinements in the model. For the analysis, we grouped the elements and relationships in the different layers and provided the total numbers (*Before*/*After*) in Tables 1 and 2. The percentage change was determined manually for both case studies by comparing the models.

Step One of determining the change was to identify for each element of *After* the related or corresponding element of *Before*, if existing. *Step Two* was to determine the percentage change. According to [32], we also distinguished four different categories of elements of *Before* and *After*:

- **Identical Element:** An element exists in both EAs and has the same manifestation in both. Examples: A process is represented in both EA models with the same activities in the same sequence; a data structure has the same concepts and attributes. Note: Solely checking the description of an element in the EA model might not be sufficient, as the implementation can differ even when the description is identical.
- **Modified Element:** The same element exists in both EA models, but their implementation is different, or the name differs while the implementation is similar.
- **New Element:** An element of *After* does not exist in *Before*. Note: Elements that appear new might turn out to be modified elements because their element descriptions change, while the implementation remains similar.
- **Removed Element:** An element of *Before* no longer exists in *After* because it became obsolete due to digitalization.

We calculated the percentage of identical, modified, and new elements by dividing their number in *After* by the total number of group elements in *After*. For removed elements, we divided by the total number of group elements in the *Before* model. These percentage values show the proportion of the *After* that is new compared to the *Before*, the proportion that has been modified and is operated in parallel in both the *Before* and the *After* (i.e., the original and modified versions), and the proportion that is actually in use in both EA models.

In addition to calculating the percentage change for the element groups, we also count the number of relationships per layer and inter-layer relationships, assess the effort required to integrate new or modified elements or remove them from the current EA, and interpret possible changes in the number of relationships. In this context, integration means adding, removing, or changing the model elements (e.g., extending existing systems for digitized processes or services) and adapting new elements to the policies established for *Before*, if necessary. This assessment was conducted with the two employees who helped develop the EA models and actively supported the digital transformation efforts. When evaluating the effort of integration, we distinguish between: *ok* (no effort or problems), *low* (moderate effort or problems), and *high* (high effort or problems).

5.2 Correlation in Case Study A

A comparison of the EAs clearly shows that the number of elements increases at a similar rate across the business, application and data, and technology layers. The business layer exhibits the largest and most profound changes. Although many elements are removed and many new ones are added in the processes, the integration effort is classified as low. This is primarily because the DT enables continuous facility monitoring and eliminates many manual maintenance steps. A different picture emerges for roles and objects (high effort). The newly added role, R&D Staff, is now the focus and is assigned new tasks that did not previously exist in the enterprise. The contracting service is also new, requires a high degree of reliability in calculations, and therefore poses a major challenge.

At the application and data layer, integration challenges are evident for the data and service elements. When creating new DT applications, a significant amount of data, such as information on installed components and sensors, must be collected to ensure the calculations work properly. Currently, this data stems from various sources and is stored both digitally and in various physical locations.

The challenges of deploying, for example, the new services, then become apparent at the technology layer. In the case study enterprise, a new cloud infrastructure was set up on AWS to host a time-series database, a facility metadata database, the new WebGUI, and other instances required for data analysis and report generation. Since the case study enterprise is an SME and does not primarily deal with such technologies, most of these new elements have never been present before and require significant new knowledge and expertise.

Notably, hardly any elements are modified; rather, they are removed, and new ones are added. This is primarily because maintenance is being fundamentally transformed by new technologies, processes are being eliminated, and, particularly due to the new contracting offerings, entirely new processes and elements required for them are being introduced. It is also evident that, while most changes in the business layer occur within the elements, integration there is assessed as requiring relatively little effort. In the technology layer, the changes are minor in terms of the number of elements, but they are comprehensive, affect many other elements, and are novel, making them difficult to integrate. The EAs reveal the classic pattern of a process-driven restructuring. The business workflows (business processes and objects) are being fundamentally redesigned. To support these new processes, services, components, and system software, they are being introduced in a targeted manner across the underlying layers, while the existing infrastructure (e.g., nodes, devices) is largely reused as a stable foundation.

At the motivational layer, goals that have been achieved (e.g., increasing transparency or creating new opportunities for energy inspection) or constraints that have been overcome (e.g., media breaks) disappear. Drivers, such as laws and standards, remain the same. One new constraint is that employees must be trained on the new applications and systems.

The total number of relationships increases in all layers (except motivational), with the largest increase in the business layer. While this can be attributed to the added elements, the rise in inter-layer relationships also reflects an increasing degree of interconnection of the elements, resulting in a high integration effort.

Table 1. Comparison results across layers for the digital twin

Enterprise Architecture		**Correlation**				**Integration**
Layer	**Element**	**Identical**	**Modified**	**New**	**Removed**	
Business Architecture (30/42)	Role	60%	0%	40%	25%	high
	Object	27%	0%	73%	50%	high
	Process	18%	6%	76%	67%	low
	Event	0%	0%	100%	0%	ok
	Interface	63%	0%	37%	0%	low
	No. Relationships	*Before*: 52		*After*: 77		low
Application and Data Architecture (28/42)	Data	67%	0%	33%	0%	high
	Service	64%	0%	36%	13%	high
	Component	69%	0%	31%	0%	low
	Access Interface	56%	0%	44%	0%	ok
	No. Relationships	*Before*: 38		*After*: 50		low
Technology Architecture (20/33)	Node	60%	0%	40%	0%	high
	System Software	40%	0%	60%	0%	low
	Device	86%	0%	14%	0%	low
	Artifact	67%	0%	33%	0%	ok
	Interface	50%	0%	50%	0%	ok
	No. Relationships	*Before:* 25		*After:* 37		low
Motivational Architecture (17/14)	Goal	86%	0%	14%	25%	low
	Driver	100%	0%	0%	0%	—
	Constraint	0%	0%	100%	100%	low
	No. Relationships	*Before:* 16		*After:* 13		low
No. Inter-layer Relationships		*Before:* 34		*After:* 63		high

5.3 Correlation in Case Study B

In the business layer of the warehouse management EA, the number of existing processes has been drastically reduced, while many new ones have been added. The ERP systems' warehouse service used in the digitized process ensures that all inventory changes occur automatically in one place and that most documents are also generated automatically and forwarded digitally. As a result, many processes and objects disappear from this layer. The additional standardization of the process also means there is now only one way to initiate a procurement.

No elements are deleted in the application and data, and technology layers. A few are added, and in the technology layer, element groups have changes in the *Before* and *After* states. Consequently, integration in these layers is very straightforward. This can be attributed to the fact that a significant portion of warehouse management digitization is supported by a component of enterprises' existing ERP systems that was not previously purchased commercially.

Table 2. Comparison results across layers for the warehouse management

Enterprise Architecture		**Correlation**				**Integration**
Layer	**Element**	**Identical**	**Modified**	**New**	**Removed**	
Business Architecture (50/45)	Role	80%	0%	20%	0%	ok
	Object	86%	14%	0%	22%	ok
	Process	64%	12%	24%	67%	low
	Event	100%	0%	0%	67%	ok
	Interface	83%	0%	17%	0%	low
	No. Relationships	*Before:* 114		*After:* 88		ok
Application and Data Architecture (28/31)	Data	100%	0%	0%	0%	—
	Service	87%	0%	13%	0%	low
	Component	89%	0%	11%	0%	ok
	Access Interface	83%	0%	17%	0%	ok
	No. Relationships	*Before:* 39		*After:* 42		ok
Technology Architecture (20/21)	Node	100%	0%	0%	0%	—
	System Software	100%	0%	0%	0%	—
	Device	86%	0%	14%	0%	low
	Artifact	100%	0%	0%	0%	—
	Interface	100%	0%	0%	0%	—
	No. Relationships	*Before:* 25		*After:* 26		ok
Motivational Architecture (14/13)	Goal	86%	0%	14%	14%	low
	Driver	100%	0%	0%	0%	—
	Constraint	0%	0%	100%	100%	low
	No. Relationships	*Before:* 13		*After:* 12		ok
No. Inter-layer Relationships		*Before:* 36		*After:* 36		low

Although few to no changes are noticeable in many element groups, the transformation does require some effort. This applies to the complete transfer of the current inventory and a review of existing items. In addition, because some areas or roles involve fundamentally new processes, some employees need to be made aware of the changes, as they are accustomed to the non-standardized processes that existed before digitization. Part of it is also visible at the motivational layer. While goals, such as transparency and efficiency in the overall process, disappear, a new goal to train the employees appears, as well as a new constraint that employees lack technical expertise, hindering the digitalization.

While the number of relationships decreases in the business layer, it remains largely stable in the other layers, as does the number of inter-layer relationships. The decreasing numbers lead to reduced interconnectivity, for example, because new objects are automatically created and edited in the processes.

6 Conclusion

6.1 Summary of Findings

The case studies showed that EAs can be a suitable instrument for investigating the effects of digital transformation. In contrast to related work, our approach for comparing the EAs *Before* and *After* the digital transformation focuses on multiple layers and their inter-layer relationships. Furthermore, we demonstrated the adaptability of TOGAF for SMEs by focusing our modeling solely on the layers and elements of the ArchiMate metamodel that were relevant to the case studies (cf. Fig. 1). Since the organizational context should always be acknowledged when introducing new technology [29], the effects of the identified changes on other areas and layers in the EA should be considered. While this is easily implementable in enterprises with an existing comprehensive EA, we recommend that enterprises without an EA create one that at least includes the dependencies on other areas in the organization.

The analysis revealed that digital transformation can lead to significant changes across all layers of the EA in SMEs, depending heavily on the strategic objective. While case study A is based on significant expansions at all layers as well as the introduction of novel paradigms (e.g., IoT sensors or cloud hosting) and thus involves high integration effort, case study B is characterized by standardization and automation, which significantly reduces elements at the business layer while keeping the application and data and technology layers largely stable. These findings confirm general conclusions of related studies (cf. Sect. 2.3) that while new technologies eliminate elements in EAs, they also introduce new ones.

6.2 Limitations and Future Work

The main limitation of our study is that only two case studies from one SME are considered. Since our work aims to provide SMEs with guidelines on the expected effects before they undertake a digital transformation, further case studies including additional SMEs and domains are needed to improve generalizability and allow for more specific guidance for different cases. However, our experience across various projects, particularly in creating the EAs for this study, has shown that it is difficult to find SMEs willing to participate. Many SMEs lack a (comprehensive) EA, and creating one is very time-consuming, making it difficult to find motivated partners. However, after conducting further case studies, it is conceivable that high-level guidelines could be developed to account for general implications, regardless of SME type, domain, or specific use case.

Another limitation is that the distribution of the number of elements and relationships is not immediately clear, and the quantitative analysis assumes that the EAs accurately reflect reality and include all relevant elements at an appropriate level of detail. Since the EAs were created specifically for the analysis conducted in this study, this risk was minimized.

Acknowledgment. The authors have no competing interests to declare that are relevant to the content of this article.

References

1. Ahlemann, F., Stettiner, E., Messerschmidt, M., Legner, C.: Strategic Enterprise Architecture Management: Challenges, Best Practices, and Future Developments. Springer, Cham (2012). https://doi.org/10.1007/978-3-642-24223-6
2. Alm, R., Wißotzki, M.: TOGAF adaption for small and medium enterprises. In: Abramowicz, W. (ed.) Business Information Systems Workshops. BIS 2013. LNBIP, vol. 160, pp. 112–123. Springer, Berlin, Heidelberg (2013). https://doi.org/10.1007/978-3-642-41687-3_12
3. Bhagwat, R., Sharma, M.K.: Information system architecture: a framework for a cluster of small-and medium-sized enterprises (SMEs). Prod. Plan. Control **18**(4), 283–296 (2007)
4. Bharadwaj, A., El Sawy, O.A., Pavlou, P.A., Venkatraman, N.V.: Digital business strategy: toward a next generation of insights (2013)
5. Brynjolfsson, E.: The Second Machine Age: Work, Progress, and Prosperity in A Time of Brilliant Technologies, vol. 336. WW Norton & Company, New York (2014)
6. Buckl, S., Dierl, T., Matthes, F., Schweda, C.M.: Building blocks for enterprise architecture management solutions. In: Harmsen, F., Proper, E., Schalkwijk, F., Barjis, J., Overbeek, S. (eds.) Practice-Driven Research on Enterprise Transformation. PRET 2010. LNBIP, vol. 69, pp. 17–46. Springer, Berlin, Heidelberg (2010). https://doi.org/10.1007/978-3-642-16770-6_2
7. Dube, M.R., Dixit, S.K.: Comprehensive measurement framework for enterprise architectures. Int. J. Comput. Sci. Inf. Technol. (IJCSIT) **3**(4), 71–92 (2011)
8. El-Sheikh, E., Zimmermann, A., Jain, L.C.: Emerging Trends in the Evolution of Service-Oriented and Enterprise Architectures. Springer, Cham (2016). https://doi.org/10.1007/978-3-319-40564-3
9. Fitzgerald, M., Kruschwitz, N., Bonnet, D., Welch, M.: Embracing digital technology: a new strategic imperative. MIT Sloan Manag. Rev. **55**(2) (2014)

10. Geerdink, B.: A reference architecture for big data solutions-introducing a model to perform predictive analytics using big data technology. Int. J. Big Data Intell. **2**(4), 236–249 (2015)
11. Griesch, L., Rittelmeyer, J., Sandkuhl, K.: Towards AI as a service for small and medium-sized enterprises (SME). In: Almeida, J.P.A., Kaczmarek-Heß, M., Koschmider, A., Proper, H.A. (eds.) The Practice of Enterprise Modeling. PoEM 2023. LNBIP, vol. 497, pp. 37–53. Springer, Cham (2024). https://doi.org/10.1007/978-3-031-48583-1_3
12. Husen, J.H., Washizaki, H., Yoshioka, N., Tun, H.T., Fukazawa, Y., Takeuchi, H.: Metamodel-based multi-view modeling framework for machine learning systems, pp. 194–201. MODELSWARD (2023)
13. Ilin, I., Levina, A., Borremans, A., Kalyazina, S.: Enterprise architecture modeling in digital transformation era. In: Murgul, V., Pukhkal, V. (eds.) International Scientific Conference Energy Management of Municipal Facilities and Sustainable Energy Technologies EMMFT 2019. EMMFT 2019. AISC, vol. 1259, pp. 124–142 . Springer, Cham (2021). https://doi.org/10.1007/978-3-030-57453-6_11
14. Ivanovic, N., Nast, B., Reiz, A., Sandkuhl, K.: Technologies for a diagnostic technique for HVAC systems using IoT and cloud-based architecture. In: International Interdisciplinary PhD Workshop, IIPhDW (2023) for HVAC systems using IoT and cloud-based architecture. In: International Interdisciplinary PhD Workshop, IIPhDW (2023)
15. Jonkers, H., Proper, E., Turner, M.: TOGAF 9 and ArchiMate 1.0. White Paper. The Open Group (2009) The Open Group (2009)
16. Kaidalova, J., Sandkuhl, K., Seigerroth, U.: Challenges in integrating product-it into enterprise architecture-a case study. Procedia Comput. Sci. **121**, 525–533 (2017)
17. Kallus, K.W.: Erstellung von Fragebogen, vol. 4465, UTB (2016)
18. Kochetkova, O., Shiryaeva, E.: Perspective architecture of dairy farming enterprises, using modern digital technologies for sustainable development. In: IOP Conference Series: Earth and Environmental Science. vol. 965 (1), p. 012062. IOP Publishing (2022)
19. Kornyshova, E., Barrios, J.: Industry 4.0 impact propagation on enterprise architecture models. Procedia Comput. Sci. **176**, 2497–2506 (2020)
20. Lankhorst, M.: Enterprise Architecture at Work: Modelling, Communication, and Analysis. Springer, Cham (2013). https://doi.org/10.1007/978-3-662-53933-0
21. Matt, C., Hess, T., Benlian, A.: Digital transformation strategies. Bus. Inf. Syst. Eng. **57**(5), 339–343 (2015)
22. Nast, B., Ivanovic, N., Dannehl, S., Kock, A., Seidel, G., Sandkuhl, K.: Dataset for Effects of Digital Transformation on the Enterprise Architecture of SMEs (2026). https://doi.org/10.5281/zenodo.20155567
23. Nast, B., Reiz, A., Ivanovic, N., Sandkuhl, K.: A modeling approach supporting digital twin engineering: optimizing the energy consumption of air conditioning facilities. In: 2023 ACM/IEEE International Conference on Model Driven Engineering Languages and Systems Companion (MODELS-C), pp. 479–483. IEEE (2023)
24. Nast, B., Sandkuhl, K.: MODTWIN: a method for model-driven engineering of digital twins for SMEs. In: Fill, H.G., Wautelet, Y., Ralyté, J., Zdravkovic, J. (eds.) The Practice of Enterprise Modeling. PoEM 2025. LNBIP, vol. 570, pp. 65–82. Springer, Cham (2026). https://doi.org/10.1007/978-3-032-12063-2_5
25. Niemi, E., Pekkola, S.: Using enterprise architecture artefacts in an organisation. Enterp. Inf. Syst. **11**(3), 313–338 (2017)

26. Piccinini, E., Gregory, R.W., Kolbe, L.M.: Changes in the producer-consumer relationship-towards digital transformation. Wirtschaftsinformatik Proceedings (2015)
27. Pittl, B., Bork, D.: Modeling digital enterprise ecosystems with archimate: a mobility provision case study. In: Hara, Y., Karagiannis, D. (eds.) Serviceology for Services. ICServ 2017. LNCS, vol 10371. Springer, Cham (2017). https://doi.org/10.1007/978-3-319-61240-9_17
28. Pohl, M., Haertel, C., Staegemann, D., Turowski, K.: Integration of data science projects in enterprise architecture modeling. In: Gianola, A., Guizzardi, R., Borbinha, J., Mira da Silva, M., Barateiro, J. (eds.) Enterprise Design, Operations, and Computing. EDOC 2025. LNCS, vol. 16213, pp. 40–58. Springer, Cham (2026). https://doi.org/10.1007/978-3-032-15140-7_3
29. Sandkuhl, K.: Putting ai into context-method support for the introduction of artificial intelligence into organizations. In: IEEE 21st Conference on Business Informatics (CBI), vol. 1, pp. 157–164. IEEE (2019)
30. Sandkuhl, K., Rittelmeyer, J.D.: Use of EA models in organizational AI solution development. In: Aveiro, D., Proper, H.A., Guerreiro, S., de Vries, M. (eds.) Advances in Enterprise Engineering XV. EEWC 2021. LNCS, vol. 441. Springer, Cham (2022). https://doi.org/10.1007/978-3-031-11520-2_10
31. Sandkuhl, K., Simon, D., Wißotzki, M., Starke, C.: The nature and a process for development of enterprise architecture principles. In: Abramowicz, W. (eds.) Business Information Systems. BIS 2015. LNCS, vol. 208, pp. 260–272. Springer, Cham (2015). https://doi.org/10.1007/978-3-319-19027-3_21
32. Sandkuhl, K., Wißotzki, M., Schmidt, R., Zimmermann, A.: On the effect of digitalization of products and services on enterprise architectures. In: ISD 2019 Proceedings (2019)
33. Schmidt, R., Möhring, M., Härting, RC., Reichstein, C., Neumaier, P., Jozinović, P. Industry 4.0 - potentials for creating smart products: empirical research results. In: Abramowicz, W. (ed.) Business Information Systems. BIS 2015. LNCS, vol. 208, pp. 16–27. Springer, Cham (2015). https://doi.org/10.1007/978-3-319-19027-3_2
34. Schmidt, R., Zimmermann, A., Möhring, M., Nurcan, S., Keller, B., Bär, F.: Digitization – perspectives for conceptualization. In: Celesti, A., Leitner, P. (eds.) Advances in Service-Oriented and Cloud Computing. ESOCC 2015. CCIS, vol. 567, pp. 263–275. Springer, Cham (2016). https://doi.org/10.1007/978-3-319-33313-7_20
35. Simon, D., Fischbach, K., Schoder, D.: Enterprise architecture management and its role in corporate strategic management. IseB **12**(1), 5–42 (2014)
36. Takeuchi, H., Husen, J.H., Tun, H.T., Washizaki, H., Yoshioka, N.: Enterprise architecture-based metamodel for machine learning projects and its management. Futur. Gener. Comput. Syst. **161**, 135–145 (2024)
37. Takeuchi, H., Ichitsuka, A., Iino, T., Ishikawa, S., Saito, K.: Assessment method for identifying business activities to be replaced by AI technologies. Procedia Comput. Sci. **192**, 1601–1610 (2021)
38. The Open Group: ArchiMate®3.2 Specification. https://publications.opengroup.org/c226
39. The Open Group Standard: The TOGAF® Standard, Version 9.2 (2024). https://pubs.opengroup.org/architecture/togaf9-doc/arch/
40. Timm, F., Wißotzki, M., Köpp, C., Sandkuhl, K.: Current state of enterprise architecture management in SME utilities. In: INFORMATIK 2015, pp. 895–907. Gesellschaft für Informatik eV (2015)

41. Vial, G.: Understanding digital transformation: a review and a research agenda. Manag. Digit. Transformation 13–66 (2021)
42. Wißotzki, M., Sandkuhl, K.: Elements and characteristics of enterprise architecture capabilities. In: Matulevičius, R., Dumas, M. (eds.) Perspectives in Business Informatics Research. BIR 2015. LNBIP, vol. 229, pp. 82–96. Springer, Cham (2015). https://doi.org/10.1007/978-3-319-21915-8_6
43. Wißotzki, M., Timm, F., Sonnenberger, A.: A survey on enterprise architecture management in small and medium enterprises. In: International Conference on Enterprise Information Systems, vol. 2, pp. 213–220. SciTePress (2015)
44. Yin, R.K.: Case Study Research: Design and Methods, vol. 5. Sage, London (2009)

Towards a Challenge-Aware Approach for Choosing Requirements Management Methods

Linards Rezevskis(✉) and Marite Kirikova

Institute of Applied Computer Systems, Riga Technical University, Kipsalas iela 6A, Riga 1048, Latvia

linards.rezevskis@edu.rtu.lv, marite.kirikova@rtu.lv

Abstract. As with any process, the processes regarding requirements engineering also encounter both internal and external challenges that must be tackled if the project for which the requirements are being defined, gathered, and managed is to be successful. For these challenges, solutions must be found and utilized so that projects can move forward. Also, best practices must be implemented to minimize the possibility that these challenges will occur in the future within any part of the process. While many requirements engineering methods and tools are available, there is a lack of guidelines regarding which methods and tools to choose for meeting specific project challenges. This paper proposes an extendable approach for selecting requirements management methods and tools based on encountered requirements engineering challenges and the project context. The use of the approach helps benefit from the reported experience in requirements engineering,

Keywords: Requirements Engineering · Requirements Management · Requirements Engineering Challenges · Method Selection · Tool Selection

1 Introduction

Requirements management is considered a part of requirements engineering in which requirements are elicited, prioritized, documented, altered, and analyzed throughout the lifecycle of a project. It is referred to as an ongoing process as long as the project itself is ongoing [1, 2].

As with any process, the processes regarding requirements engineering also encounter both internal and external challenges that must be tackled if the project for which the requirements are defined, gathered, and managed is to be successful [3]. For these challenges, solutions must be found and used to move projects forward. Moreover, best practices must be implemented to minimize the possibility that the challenges will recur in the future within the requirements engineering process.

It must also be considered that requirements management might differ based on the already existing digital environment in which the project will reside. Increasingly more IT projects are being restricted by already existing legacy systems [4], which

E. Laurenzi et al. (Eds.): BIR 2026, LNBIP 601, pp. 361–373, 2027.
https://doi.org/10.1007/978-3-032-38498-0_23

provide another angle of consideration when defining requirements. Additionally, the quality of the requirements has been shown to influence the desired outcomes of projects. Having poorly described requirements can potentially induce extra costs and delays within software project timelines [5]. Moreover, unclear requirements and excessive changes to already defined requirements can cause IT projects to fail [6].

Bearing this in mind, it can be inferred that requirements management is an integral part of IT-related project success. This means that selecting the correct methods for requirements management is important for anyone trying to realize a software or IT project. Many methods can be used in practice for the elicitation, reviewing, representation, and estimation of requirements [7], but rarely can a single method fit any project in need of it, as the context does matter here as well [8, 9].

But how can one know which methods are the ones that can fit their specific project's needs and should be used for the project? Various best practices and methods are reported in the literature, which in turn makes it even more difficult to understand which of these methods are appropriate for a project, as there are not many guides in selecting the most appropriate ones, considering the project context. Also, practitioners must be vigilant of any challenges that may occur within requirements management, so as not to impact their project's desired outcome negatively. There is an apparent gap in challenge-driven method selection approaches. This remains a relevant topic as investments in IT and software-related project areas are increasing [10], which in turn can indicate the continuous need for successful requirements management.

The goal of this paper is to develop a challenge-driven approach for selecting requirements management methods. This approach aims to be applicable in contexts where there are different variables that a practitioner must consider.

The paper is organized according to the research steps methodologically taken to achieve the stated goal. Section 2 identifies challenges and success factors/best practices of requirements management from the related work. Section 3 establishes the linkages between the challenges and success factors/best practices and methods of requirements management. Section 4 discusses the validation of the established linkages. Section 5 demonstrates the context-aware requirements management method selection via the interface of a simple prototype and demonstrates how the gaps, identified by linkages in Sect. 3, could be closed by new methods for requirements management. Section 6 briefly concludes the paper.

2 Challenges, Best Practices, and Methods of Requirements Management

A review of "challenges", "success factors", and "best practices" in requirements engineering-related sources was performed to identify reported requirements management challenges, success factors, and best practices. The results of this review are amalgamated in Table 1, where 6 types of challenges (C1–C6) are shown. Throughout the sources, it has become apparent that the context of a project must also be considered to meet the challenges, and different context variables can point to the sources from which some of the identified challenges can stem. The following context variables (V1–V5) were identified:

- V1: current project fit/alignment with existing legacy systems [4],
- V2: project scale and methodology (potential source for C1) [11],
- V3: cultural and language differences caused by geographical distribution of colleagues and stakeholders (potential source for C2) [12, 13],
- V4: structural organization of teams within a project (potential source for C4) [14],
- V5: selected tool fit/alignment with current processes (potential source for C5) [15].

Table 1. Identified types of challenges in requirements management

#	Challenge type	Number of sources	Studies
C1	Poorly defined requirements management process	4	[11, 14–16]
C2	Communication and relationship building with stakeholders	4	[13, 14, 16, 17]
C3	Difficulties in updating already created requirements	3	[11, 14, 17]
C4	Lack of quality in the created requirements	3	[11, 14, 18]
C5	Correct tool choice and usage	2	[11, 15]
C6	Lack of understanding of the overall value being delivered to the project	1	[11]

To meet the challenges, researchers have conducted various studies to find practices that help to overcome the challenges in a particular domain and improve requirements management processes with eventual positive consequences. As proposed by [19], there are many different practices, but not all of them correlate with wide success. Moreover, as suggested by [15], employees must be willing to change and adapt. This suggests that best practice and method adoption success is also dependent on the contextual environment of the organization in terms of the willingness of people to accept change in ways of working.

To provide an opportunity to map challenges to the appropriate success factors and best practices, success factors (or best practices) were identified in the related work and amalgamated in Table 2. Altogether, 13 success factors (F1–F13) were identified and will be further discussed in the paper.

Once the success factors were identified, the methods that supported them were searched for and mapped to the factors. For instance, Recurring meetings, Workshops, Interviews, and Informal spontaneous communication were mapped to the F1 (communication with stakeholders). On the other hand, the challenges were linked to the success factors, providing an indirect linkage from challenges to the requirements management methods, as explained in Sect. 3.

Table 2. Identified success factors and best practices in requirements management

Factor #	Success factor/best practice	Count of studies	Studies
F1	Communication with stakeholders	5	[15, 19–22]
F2	Prioritization and Re-prioritization based on expected value, resources, and risk	4	[14, 21, 23, 24]
F3	Well-defined requirements governance	3	[14, 22, 24]
F4	Avoidance of excessive, incomplete, and hard-to-read documentation	2	[14, 21]
F5	Usage of user stories	2	[17, 21]
F6	Usage of standardized templates	2	[22]
F7	Validation of requirements	2	[21, 23]
F8	Metrics and KPIs as a preemptive requirement for quality issue detection	1	[18]
F9	Dividing larger user stories into smaller ones	1	[17]
F10	Usage of scenarios and business cases	1	[19]
F11	Competence of the person working with the requirements	1	[22]
F12	Identification and usage of relevant requirement sources	1	[23]
F13	Unified product vision between Customer and Developers	1	[14]

3 Linking Challenges, Success Factors, and Methods

As mentioned above, the success factors and best practices were linked to the methods that were mentioned as contributing to success. All methods were numbered by the factors represented in Table 2 and organized into groups and subgroups. For instance, the methods, supporting factor (success factor/best practice) F2, would be numbered as *M2.x.y*, where the first number corresponds to the factor number and is equal to the method group number, the *x* corresponds to the method subgroup within a group, and the *y* corresponds to the method number in the subgroup. In case there are no subgroups, the *x* was omitted. The main focus of the research represented in this paper is on the relationship between the challenges and the requirements management methods. Therefore, the linkages between the challenges and the success factors/best practices were established. This linkage gives an opportunity to indirectly relate the challenge to the method that can meet it. The result of establishing the linkages is represented in Fig. 1.

Challenge type	Link Nr.	Success Factors and Best Practice Groups	Identified Methods
C1: Poorly defined requirements management process	L1.1	F1	**M1.1.1** Daily Team Alignments, **M1.1.2** Sprint Reviews, **M1.2** Workshops, **M1.3.1** Unstructured Interviews, **M1.3.2** Structured Interviews
	L1.2	F2	**M2.1** AHP, **M2.2** HCV + Macbeth, **M2.3** TOPSIS, **M2.4** Priority Grouping, **M2.4.1** MoSCoW, **M2.5** Hundred Dollars, **M2.6** Bubble Sorting
	L1.3	F3 and F12	**M3.2** – Defined and context-flexible elicitation process
	L1.4	F4	**M4.3** Working in pairs when writing documents
	L1.5	F7	**M7.1** Formal Validation, M7.2 Acceptance Criteria, **M7.3** Informal validation
	L1.6	F11	N/a
C2: Communication and relationship building with stakeholders	L2.1	F1	**M1.1.1** Daily Team Alignments, **M1.1.2** Sprint Reviews, **M1.2** Workshops, **M1.3.1** Unstructured Interviews, **M1.3.2** Structured Interviews, **M1.4.** Informal Spontaneous Communication
	L2.2	F11	N/a
	L2.3	F13	N/a
C3: Difficulties in updating already created requirements	L3.1	F3	**M3.1.1** Traceability Matrices
	L3.2	F4	**M4.1** "Just Enough Upfront", **M4.2** Light but sufficient documentation,
	L3.3	F4	**M4.3** Working in pairs when writing documentation, **M4.4** ISO/IEC/IEEE 29148 standard suggestion on what requirements should contain
	L3.4	F6	**M6.1** EARS Template, **M6.2** MASTeR Template,
C4: Lack of quality in the created requirements	L4.1	F5	**M5.1** Collaboration with different stakeholders when writing user stories, **M5.2** Use of a standardized user story model
	L4.2	F3 and F9	M3.1.1 Traceability Matrices
	L4.3	F6	M6.1 EARS Template, **M6.2** MASTeR Template
	L4.4	F7	M7.1 Formal Validation, **M7.2** Acceptance Criteria, **M7.3** Informal validation
	L4.5	F8	N/a
	L4.6	F10	N/a
	L4.7	F11	N/a
	L4.8	F12	N/a
C5: Correct tool choice and usage	N/a	**Not found**	**No methods found**
C6: Lack of understanding of the overall value being delivered to the project	N/a	**Not found**	**No methods found**

Fig.1. Linkages for the first version of the method selection approach

The link was created if there was a source that pointed to the success factor or practice as being useful for meeting a particular challenge. The detailed description of the reasons for establishing a particular link is outside the scope of this paper.

Figure 1, to some extent, can already serve as a means for challenge-aware requirements management method selection. However, respecting a measure of subjectivity and not a large number of sources for each lineage, the linkages were put to the practitioner evaluation, which is briefly discussed in the next section.

4 Expert Evaluation of the Linkages

The evaluation was performed by 8 experts (P1–P8) – participants in the evaluation procedure, being business analysts or in similar positions with work experience from 3 to 10 years in the global shipping and banking industries. The profile of the participants was established by 5 variables characterizing the project context, namely, V1 – necessity to deal with a legacy system, V2 – project scale and methodology, V3 – team cultural differences and distribution, V4 – team dependencies, and V5 – current tool fit with processes.

The participant profiles are shown in Table 3.

Table 3. Interview participant profiles

#	V1 (Legacy systems)	V2 (Proj. Scale and method-gy)	V3(Cultural and language differences, distributed teams)	V4 (Team organization)	V5 (Current tool fit with processes)
P1	Yes	Small - medium/Hybrid	Some differences/team in two locations	Single team/does not rely on other teams	No fragmentation, good fit
P2	Yes	Large/Hybrid	Some differences/team in multiple locations	Global team, with smaller siloed sub-teams	High fragmentation/poor fit
P3	Yes	Large/Hybrid	Some differences/team in multiple locations	Global team, with smaller siloed sub-teams	Fragmented/medium fit
P4	Yes	Large/Hybrid	Large differences/team in multiple locations	Global team, with smaller siloed sub-teams	Some fragmentation/good fit
P5	Yes	Large/Hybrid	Some differences/team in multiple locations	Global team, with smaller siloed sub-teams	Severe fragmentation/poor fit
P6	Yes	Large/Hybrid	Some differences/team in the two locations	Department decomposed into sub-teams with their own projects	No fragmentation/good fit
P7	Yes	Large/Hybrid	Large differences/team in a single location	Global team, with smaller siloed sub-teams	High Fragmentation/poor fit

(continued)

Table 3. (*continued*)

#	V1 (Legacy systems)	V2 (Proj. Scale and method-gy)	V3(Cultural and language differences, distributed teams)	V4 (Team organization)	V5 (Current tool fit with processes)
P8	Yes	Large/Agile	No differences/single location	Large departments with multiple sub-teams	No fragmentation/good fit

The validation of the links was performed through one or two-cycle interviews, depending on the results of the first cycle. The links were classified based on whether the validation was received within the first-tier open-ended question (spontaneously) or within one of the second-tier directed questions aimed at validating specific links. Links can be classified as spontaneous, direct, or direct conditional (validated by second-tier additional questions), contradictory, or with no feedback. Links are classified as *direct conditional* whenever an expert agrees with it, but adds a condition that has to be observed. *Spontaneous* is considered a stronger form of validation, since the expert has mentioned this link on their own, without hearing the more direct questions first. *A contradictory* type of link signifies that the expert has had an opposite opinion. *No feedback* indicates that the link was not validated or contradicted, either because the interviewee did not have an opinion on it, or the question was not asked due to time constraints or the conversation flow of the interview. Challenge types C5 and C6 did not have any proposed links on Fig. 1. Therefore, the experts were asked whether they could think of any mitigating factors, practices, or methods that could address these challenge types. The answers obtained were used to create new links for these challenge groups.

The responses were collected for each challenge type separately; an example of responses regarding Challenge type 2 (Communication and relationship building with stakeholders) is shown in Fig. 2.

Nr. Link	**L2.1** F1, M1.1.1, M1.1.2, M1.2, M1.3.1, M1.3.2, M1.4.	**L2.2** F11	**L2.3** F13
P1	Direct	Direct	Direct
P2	Direct Conditional	Direct	No Feedback
P3	Direct Conditional	Direct	Direct Conditional
P4	**Spontaneous**	Direct	Direct
P5	Direct Conditional	Direct Conditional	Direct
P6	Direct	Direct	Direct Conditional
P7	Direct Conditional	Direct	Direct
P8	**Spontaneous**	Direct	Contradicts

Fig. 2. Summary of C2 link validation

5 Challenge-Aware Method Selection and Creation of a New Method

Based on the initial linkage establishment results discussed in Sect. 3 and expert evaluations, *the approach for requirements management method selection was established.* The approach is demonstrated by a prototype of a simple IT solution that utilizes established linkages. The tool is easy to use as it requires just two steps from the user: (1) select the challenge and (2) choose the methods via available links.

The outlook of the prototype of the tool supporting the proposed approach is presented in Fig. 3.

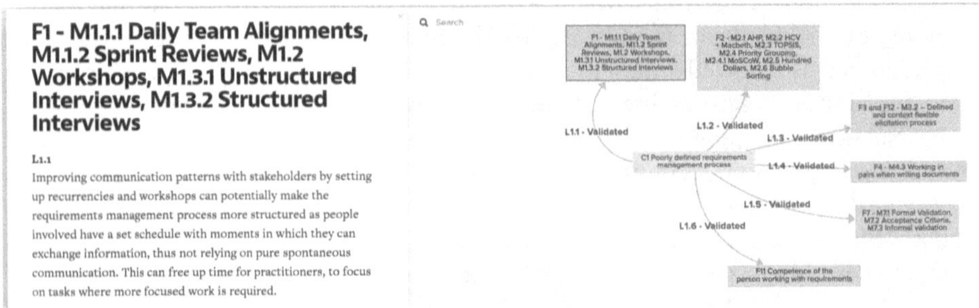

Fig. 3. Method selection interface

The approach is intended to be made resilient to the changes in the requirements management practices so that new challenges, linkages, and methods can be introduced, and the obsolete ones can be erased.

While this is only the initial version of the approach, it is based on expert-validated knowledge derived from scientific literature. It can be used by practitioners as well as requirements engineering and IT systems development students.

Nevertheless, the approach, in its implemented version, should be further validated to see what extensions and changes would be needed to make it handy for practitioners.

For instance, there was no linkage available for the challenge of using appropriate requirements management tools. The proposed approach of challenge-aware method selection can be extrapolated to the tools.

For selecting the requirements management tools, we have developed *a new method* that uses a prompt template for generative AI-based search of requirements management tools. The proposed prompt template can be adapted to search for requirements management tools based on the current context, the challenges that are encountered, and the desired practices and methods that the tool should facilitate.

The results generated by the prompt will be evaluated against the requirements management tool recommendations from the literature. This method was chosen because tools evolve and new tools are introduced to the market, and a static tool comparison might not be relevant as time moves forward.

In terms of selecting requirements management tools, [25] proposes to use an approach in which the practitioner first considers their own context and challenges as factors when selecting the appropriate tool for them. Similar logic was used when associating best practices and methods with challenges. The same approach was taken for the design of the prompt template, where practitioners shall insert their own context variables and challenges that they face within the prompt to search for the requirements management tools that best fit their situation.

The method respects that, currently, AI-based search is rising in popularity in professional contexts, as more practitioners in the IT industry are relying on generative AI to perform research-based tasks on specific topics [26]. Moreover, when performing search tasks, ChatGPT users were more likely to select the best available option based on a search with predefined criteria when compared to Google search engine users [27]. This indicates that the usage of generative AI, such as ChatGPT, can allow for an accurate selection of the best available options based on the criteria given.

Accurate prompting of generative AI is also shown to produce more accurate and context-sensitive results [28]. Therefore, to craft the prompt template that is to be used for selecting requirements management tools, concepts stemming from prompt engineering are combined with aspects defined from the research performed for requirements management method selection.

For the generative AI to perform any action, a directive has to be included in the prompt that states what actions the AI tool should perform [29]. In the context of the prompt for requirements management tool selection, the directive would be to "search for requirements management tools".

Furthermore, additional information should also be included in the prompt for the generative AI to be able to perform the directive [29]. This additional information should come in the form of context, which can specify conditions that the AI has to respect to grant a response [30]. In terms of the prompt template, the context would be the challenges faced and the context variables of the practitioner. This also aligns with the above-mentioned proposal [25] for selecting requirements management tools.

Miller [30] suggests that the desired output of the answer should also be specified to ensure that the response fulfils the goal of the prompt for the practitioner. For the proposed prompt template, the output can be defined by the practitioner based on their needs. The specifications for the output could contain the reasoning for the selection of the tool, a limit on how many tools are listed, the format in which the tools are presented in the answer, and output criteria.

Additionally, to gain insight into how the generative AI came up with its answer, chain-of-thought prompting can be used. Chain-of-thought prompting forces the AI to show its reasoning in a step-by-step process within the provided answer [30]. This can be useful for practitioners to see where the searches of the tools occurred and what the progressive reasoning was for including specific tools in the final output answer. To perform chain-of-thought prompting, the practitioner should prompt the AI to commence "step-by-step thinking" when providing output answers [30].

Based on the reviewed literature and the above-mentioned generative AI usage tendencies, the prompt template, shown in Fig. 4, was defined for practitioners to deploy when conducting searches for requirements management tools.

In the first block of the prompt, the practitioner is expected to fill in his contextual information (as discussed in Sect. 2 and shown in Fig. 1) in terms of whether they are working with legacy systems (V1), the project scale and methodology (V2), if they have geographically distributed teams and if they face cultural and language barriers (V3), how the teams in the project are structured (V4) and current tool fit with processes (V5). Then they are expected to only list the types of challenges they face currently; all challenge types are not to be listed unless encountered. For each challenge type, a brief description is to be provided for additional context. This description can be equal to the one used in Fig. 2. In the "Desired Output" block, the practitioner can define how many tools they wish to retrieve in the output answer.

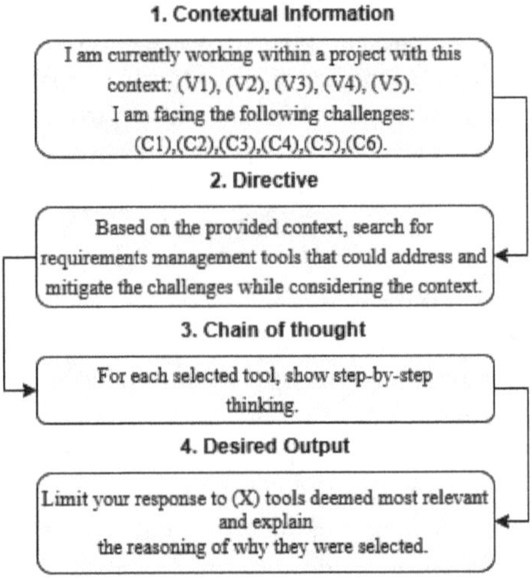

Fig. 4. Prompt template for prompting requirements management tool search

To test the prompt template, it was populated and inserted into 2 generative AI models: ChatGPT, created by OpenAI, and Gemini, created by Google. Both tools are amongst the most widely available and used generative AI tools globally [31]. Both generative AI tools provided a modified version of Azure DevOps as a fitting option to address the challenges and context for the profile of expert P5, thus showing potential for inclusion of this generative AI-based method in the approach for challenge-aware selection for requirements management.

6 Conclusion

The paper introduces a challenge-aware approach for requirements management method selection. The approach is based on the state of the art in requirements management as of 2025. It establishes a linkage between the challenges, success factors/best practices, and methods for their achievement. The linkages are first derived from literature and then validated by practitioners. Based on the validated linkages, the online tool's prototype is created that can help to choose the methods that can help to meet the challenges.

The paper contributes the original linkage between the challenges and the success factors or best practices related to the requirements management methods. The linkage approach proved useful not only for method selection but also for identifying the gaps in the spectrum of available methods. The first attempt to close one of such gaps was made by using generative AI by providing a prompt based on the variables used and the challenge types used in the accomplishment of the linkage. The prompt template might be seen as a method for selecting context- and challenge-compatible requirements management tools. The details on the mappings, expert evaluation, and toll prototype are available in [32].

The proposed approach for challenge-aware requirements management method selection is only initially validated. The mutual relationships of challenges or the possibility of extracting a group of methods corresponding to the group of challenges are not investigated.

Further work is needed to make the approach even more effective and to ensure the resilience of the tool that supports the context-aware approach for selecting requirements management methods, in terms of its automatic maintenance and change management.

References

1. Khan, M.N.A., Khalid, M., Ulhaq, S.: Review of requirements management issues in software development. Int. J. Mod. Educ. Comput. Sci. (IJMECS) **5**(1), 21–27 (2013). https://doi.org/10.5815/ijmecs.2013.01.03
2. Heath, F.: Managing Software Requirements the Agile Way. Packt Publishing, Birmingham (2020)
3. Mello, O.C., Fontoura, L.M.: Challenges in requirements engineering and its solutions: a systematic review. In: Proceedings of the 24th International Conference on Enterprise Information Systems, pp. 70–77 (2022). https://doi.org/10.5220/0011079000003179
4. Hopkins, R., Jenkins, K.: Eating the IT Elephant: Moving from Greenfield Development to Brownfield. IBM Press (2008)
5. Kamata, M.I., Tamai, T.: How does requirements quality relate to project success or failure? In: 15th IEEE International Requirements Engineering Conference (RE 2007), pp. 69–78. IEEE, Delhi (2007). https://doi.org/10.1109/RE.2007.31
6. Schmidt, J.: Mitigating risk of failure in information technology projects: causes and mechanisms. Proj. Leadersh. Soc. **4** (2023). https://doi.org/10.1016/j.plas.2023.100097
7. Laplante, P.A., Kassab, M.: Requirements Engineering for Software and Systems, 4th edn. Auerbach Publications, Boca Raton (2022)
8. Ozkaya, M., Kardas, G., Kose, M.A.: An analysis of the features of requirements engineering tools. Systems **11**(12), 1–32 (2023). https://doi.org/10.3390/systems11120576
9. Nadeem, M.A., Lee, S.U.-J., Younus, M.U.: A comparison of recent requirements gathering and management tools in requirements engineering for IoT-enabled sustainable cities. Sustainability **14**(4), 1–18 (2022). https://doi.org/10.3390/su14042427
10. Gartner: Gartner forecasts worldwide IT spending to grow 10.8% in 2026, totaling $6.15 trillion (2026)
11. Kasauli, R., Knauss, E., Horkoff, J., Liebel, G., Gomes de Oliveira Neto, F.: Requirements engineering challenges and practices in large scale agile system development. J. Syst. Softw. **172**, 1–26 (2021). https://doi.org/10.1016/j.jss.2020.110851
12. Damian, D., Zowghi, D.: Requirements engineering challenges in multi-site software development organizations. Requirements Eng. **8**, 149–160 (2003). https://doi.org/10.1007/s00766-003-0173-1

13. Damian, D.: Stakeholders in global requirements engineering: lessons learned from practice. IEEE Softw. **24**(2), 21–27 (2007). https://doi.org/10.1109/MS.2007.55
14. Hoy, Z., Xu, M.: Agile software requirements engineering challenges-solutions—a conceptual framework from systematic literature review. Information **14**(6) (2023). https://doi.org/10.3390/info14060322
15. Kauppinen, M., Vartiainen, M., Kontio, J., Kujala, S., Sulonen, R.: Implementing requirements engineering processes throughout organizations: success factors and challenges. Inf. Softw. Technol. **46**(14), 937–953 (2004). https://doi.org/10.1016/j.infsof.2004.04.002
16. Mahaju, S., Carver, J.C., Bradshaw, G.L.: Human error management in requirements engineering: should we fix people, the process or the environment. Inf. Softw. Technol. **160** (2023). https://doi.org/10.1016/j.infsof.2023.107223
17. Sporsem, T., Dingsøyr, T., Stol, K.J.: User stories as boundary objects in agile requirements engineering: a theoretical literature review. J. Syst. Softw. **233** (2025). https://doi.org/10.1016/j.jss.2025.112693
18. Gentili, E., Falessi, D.: Practitioners' perceptions on requirements smells. Inf. Softw. Technol. **187** (2025). https://doi.org/10.1016/j.infsof.2025.107823
19. Fricker, S., Grau, R., Zwingli, A.: Requirements engineering: best practices. In: Fricker, S., Thümmler, C., Gavras, A. (eds.) Requirements Engineering for Digital Health, pp. 25–46. Springer, Cham (2015)
20. Malcher, P., Viana, D., Antonio, P.O., Pereira dos Santos, R.: Towards an understanding of requirements management in software ecosystems. Inf. Softw. Technol. **180**(6), 1–19 (2025). https://doi.org/10.1016/j.infsof.2025.107672
21. Inayat, I., Salim, S.S., Marczak, S., Daneva, M., Shamshirband, S.: A systematic literature review on agile requirements engineering practices and challenges. Comput. Hum. Behav. **51**, 915–929 (2015). https://doi.org/10.1016/j.chb.2014.10.046
22. Attanayaka, B., Nawinna, D., Manathunga, K., Abeygunawardhana, P.K.W.: Success factors of requirement elicitation in the field of software engineering. In: 4th International Conference on Advancements in Computing (ICAC), pp. 240–245. IEEE, Colombo (2022). https://doi.org/10.1109/ICAC57685.2022.10025166
23. Khalid, S., et al.: Ensuring quality in software requirements engineering process: a comparative study. Egypt. Inform. J. **31**, 1–15 (2025). https://doi.org/10.1016/j.eij.2025.100754
24. Wawak, S.: Enhancing project quality through effective requirements management. Int. J. Qual. Res. **19**(1), 151–168 (2024)
25. Goetel, O., Mäder, P.: How to select a requirements management tool: initial steps. In: 17th IEEE International Requirements Engineering Conference (RE 2009), pp. 365–367. IEEE Computer Society, Atlanta (2009)
26. OpenAI: ChatGPT usage and adoption patterns at work (2026). ChatGPT usage and adoption patterns at work | OpenAI. Accessed 11 May 2026
27. Kaiser, C., Kaiser, J., Schaller, R., Schneider, S.: A new era of online search? A large-scale study of user behavior and personal preferences during practical search tasks with generative AI versus traditional search engines. In: CHI EA 2025: Extended Abstracts of the CHI Conference on Human Factors in Computing Systems, pp. 1–7. Yokohama (2025). https://doi.org/10.1145/3706599.3720123
28. Korzynski, P., Mazurek, G., Krzypkowska, P., Kurasinski, A.: Artificial intelligence prompt engineering as a new digital competence: analysis of generative AI technologies such as ChatGPT. Entrep. Bus. Econ. Rev. **11**(3), 25–37 (2023). https://doi.org/10.15678/EBER.2023.110302
29. Schulhoff, S., Ilie, M., Balepur, N., Kahadze, K. et al.: The prompt report: a systematic survey of prompt engineering techniques (2024). https://doi.org/10.48550/arXiv.2406.06608
30. Miller, M.: AI Prompt Engineering Absolute Beginners Guide, 1st edn. Addison-Wesley Professional, Hoboken (2025)

31. Liu, Y., Huang, H., Wang, H.: Who on earth is using generative AI? Global trends and shifts in 2025. World Bank Group (2025). https://doi.org/10.1596/1813-9450-11231
32. Rezevskis, L.: Approach for selecting requirements management methods and tools. Master's thesis, Riga Technical University (2026)

Evaluating LLM-Generated Conceptual Models: A Theoretical Approach for Formalizing the Calculation of Metrics on the Meta Level

Iva Vasic(✉), Benedikt Reitemeyer, and Hans-Georg Fill

University of Fribourg, Research Group Digitalization and Information Systems, 1700 Fribourg, Switzerland
{iva.vasic,benedikt.reitemeyer,hans-georg.fill}@unifr.ch

Abstract. The generation of conceptual models using large language models (LLMs) for supporting information systems engineering is today being widely discussed. However, since each conceptual model is expressed in a specific modeling language, the evaluation approaches are often domain-dependent. In addition, previous approaches often do not fully disclose how the evaluated model elements are obtained before calculating the metrics. In this paper we thus propose a formal framework for calculating evaluation metrics on a meta level. The goal is to provide a first solid basis for the automated and thus scalable evaluation of AI-generated models. We revert to the FDMM formalism to ensure a sound formalization for modeling languages and their instantiation. We then employ two key steps in our evaluation procedure: (i) mapping of the baseline and LLM-generated models to the generic FDMM constructs, (ii) evaluation of LLM-generated models against a baseline by comparing their FDMM representations. This allows for the consistent calculation of evaluation metrics for various modeling languages using common metrics such as precision, recall, and $F1$ score. We demonstrate the application of the framework by applying the formalization to enterprise architecture models with ArchiMate and knowledge graphs in the cultural heritage domain. Finally, we compare the framework against other methodological approaches and highlight points for further extensions.

Keywords: Conceptual Model · Large Language Model · Evaluation

1 Introduction

In the field of information systems engineering it is largely undisputed that conceptual models play an important role for the development of software and data-intensive systems [29,31]. This stretches today from the support of human understanding and communication [29,32], to the automated processing using algorithms, e.g. in model-driven engineering [8], for analytics and simulations, or

E. Laurenzi et al. (Eds.): BIR 2026, LNBIP 601, pp. 374–390, 2027.
https://doi.org/10.1007/978-3-032-38498-0_24

via formal reasoning [6,17]. Thereby, the creation of models has been traditionally accomplished manually with the help of software-based modeling tools. Due to the large effort required for creating models, several proposals have been made to apply natural language processing (NLP) techniques to this task in order to automate the generation of models from textual descriptions, e.g. [1,2,36]. Most recently, the availability of large language models (LLMs) has considerably boosted the quality of such generations and the effects of this technology are being increasingly studied [18,19,42].

However, there are still several open issues regarding the use of AI for modeling, one major challenge being the quality of AI output. The quality of models thereby includes physical, empirical, syntactic, semantic, pragmatic, social and deontic quality [26]. According to Krogstie, physical quality pertains to the availability of a model, i.e. that it is persistent and available for further processing. Syntactic quality relates to *syntactic completeness*, i.e. that only constructs of the syntax of the language are used, and *semantic quality* relates to the valid and complete correspondence between a model and its domain. In previous approaches, it was common to compare AI output to human-curated baselines or to some ground truth [42], whereby mostly syntactic and semantic quality were considered [12]. Similar to previous approaches in model extraction through natural language processing [4], also LLM-based model creation approaches are evaluated using metrics from information retrieval such as precision, recall, and F1 scores [42].

The evaluation of the correctness of generated models is a non-trivial task and would typically require a human expert to assess potential differences in naming and structure that are still considered correct. However, in order to automate the evaluation of generated models as required for large scale experiments, an exact, machine-processable evaluation procedure is necessary. Previously, this has been approached for example using simple matching, the use of semantic schemata or even LLMs themselves [12,43]. In addition, evaluations were specifically adapted to single modeling languages, such as class diagrams, use case diagrams, process or entity-relationship models, cf. [37].

For providing a formal basis for such evaluations that is applicable to multiple modeling languages, we thus propose in the following a generic, formal evaluation framework for arbitrary types of conceptual models. The goal of this framework is to enable the automated and thus scalable evaluation of LLM outputs using common metrics to ensure evaluations beyond human judgments. In this paper we will therefore focus first on *physical* and *syntactic* quality as *pre-requisites for other aspects of quality such as empirical, semantic and pragmatic quality* [26]. In addition we will consider attribute similarity for checking the existence of correct attribute values, including labels and reference attributes. We do not consider at this stage aspects of behavioral semantics nor semantic similarity of attributes but rather aim at the syntactic comparison to some ground truth.

For guiding the development of the framework we derived three research questions:

- **RQ1**: How can conceptual models based on different modeling languages be formally represented in a unified way for enabling the application of standard metrics for comparisons?
- **RQ2**: How can such formally represented conceptual models that are either generated by AI or by humans be quantitatively compared to baseline representations using an algorithmic approach?
- **RQ3**: What are the benefits of such an approach in comparison to previous approaches?

As shown in Fig. 1, the approach is comprised of four main parts: the generation of models using CMAG prompting [20] and with the resulting output $\mathrm{OUT}_{\mathrm{llm}}$; the filtering of this output through the validation of the syntax and removal of incorrect outputs; the mapping to the formal framework based on the FDMM formalism, which includes a meta model and instance model mapping of the filtered output and the baseline model $\mathrm{OUT}_{\mathrm{base}}$; and finally the evaluation of the mapped outputs.

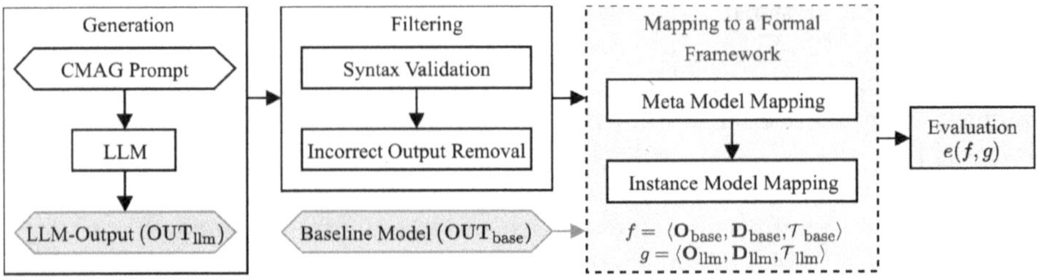

Fig. 1. Overview of our formal framework for evaluating LLM-generated conceptual models.

The remainder of the paper is structured as follows: Sect. 2 will outline related approaches for the evaluation of LLM-generated models. Section 3 will introduce the foundations necessary for our approach in terms of the FDMM formalism and the CMAG prompt structure. Section 4 presents our framework, followed by two application examples in Sect. 5 that exemplify the framework usage for formalizing enterprise architecture models and knowledge graphs. Section 6 discusses the approach and its comparison to previous approaches. Section 7 concludes the paper with an outlook on future work.

2 Related Work on Evaluating LLM-Generated Models

Since LLMs demonstrate impressive capabilities in generating conceptual models, evaluation approaches have likewise evolved. From the existing literature on evaluating generated models, frequently identified methods include the manual verification by experts, the comparison of the LLM output to some ground truth dataset, and evaluation using LLMs themselves.

As LLM-generated output has not yet reached fully reliable outcomes, human experts remain essential in the evaluation process. For software modeling with UML class diagrams, Shehata et al. [40] evaluate GPT-generated models by involving experts who compare the models to ground truth diagrams. Automated domain modeling with LLMs has also been tested on UML class diagram generation and evaluated by experts in [11], highlighting the challenge to reach consensus among human modelers. In the work of De Bari et al. [14], both students and LLMs were employed to generate UML diagrams based on several modeling exercises, whose solutions were then compared and checked against syntactic, semantic, and pragmatic errors by a human expert. Cámara et al. [13] observed various flaws in ChatGPT-generated software models by evaluating the output themselves manually.

In the work of [35], LLM-generated class, attribute, and association generators are evaluated by manually assigning matching scores across various strictness criteria, i.e., beyond strict matching like in our workflow, after which the statistical analysis was reported for each level of strictness. In a similar idea to ours, that is, primarily mapping to a formal framework before evaluation, Lo et al. [28] leveraged knowledge graphs to map ontologies and measure their similarity with the ground truth. They tested semantic and structural similarity in a fuzzy manner, which gives different results than strict matching, by using edges and subgraphs as evaluation elements.

As LLMs advance, they have emerged as tools for evaluation themselves [45], as presented by Calamo et al. [10] for assessing generated UML class diagrams against the human-generated dataset. Huang et al. [23] used a fine-tuned LLM to evaluate the factual correctness of knowledge graph triples. Precision, recall, and $F1$ score metrics were employed by Silva et al. [41] to evaluate the Tree-of-Thoughts prompting technique for UML class diagram generation, comparing it against a reference solution using an LLM-based evaluation. However, Ibáñez et al. [24] found that LLMs are unreliable in evaluating UML class diagram designs compared to expert evaluation performance, due to the inability to interpret semantics and evaluative reasoning. On the other hand, the findings of Tsaneva et al. [43] indicate that the inclusion of LLMs in the knowledge graph evaluation process increases the precision while negatively affecting the recall and consequently the $F1$ score. Moreover, the hybrid approach, where human involvement complements the LLM evaluator, demonstrated the best overall outcome.

Despite these previous efforts, a formal framework for evaluations against a baseline of models of arbitrary type has not yet been proposed. We thus present in the following a solution approach based on the FDMM formalism for laying the basis for automated and scalable evaluations.

3 Foundations on Formalizing Conceptual Models

In this chapter we will describe the foundations required for our approach. This will include a brief characterization of the core parts of FDMM and the CMAG prompt structure. FDMM (Formalism for Describing Metamodels and Models) was developed to provide an exact description of meta models and their instantiation to models using only set theory and first-order logic [21]. Its original intention was to formalize modeling languages in ADOxx, which is widely used in domain-specific conceptual modeling. It has been applied e.g. to process modeling [25,39], service modeling [5], or rule modeling [34]. For the scope of this paper we will use it for describing meta models and models on a common, technology-independent level.

According to FDMM, meta models $\mathbf{MM}$ are used for deriving model instances $\mathbf{mt}$. A meta-model is a tuple $\mathbf{MM} = \langle \mathbf{MT}, \preceq, \text{domain}, \text{range}, \text{card} \rangle$ where $\mathbf{MT}$ is the set of model types and $\mathbf{MT}_i$ is a tuple $\mathbf{MT}_i = \langle \mathbf{O}_i^T, \mathbf{D}_i^T, \mathbf{A}_i \rangle$, which consists of a set of object types $\mathbf{O}_i^T$, a set of data types $\mathbf{D}_i^T$, and a set of attributes $\mathbf{A}_i$.

The attributes $\mathbf{A}_i$ will also be used for expressing relations between object types through references. This will be used for realizing attributes that point to other object types as well as for describing the start and end of edges, which are described as object types as well. The object types, data types, and attributes are part of their respective total sets, i.e. $\mathbf{O}^T = \bigcup_j \mathbf{O}_j^T, \mathbf{D}^T = \bigcup \mathbf{D}_i^T, \mathbf{A} = \bigcup \mathbf{A}_i$. The $\preceq$ operator describes an ordering on the set of object types $\mathbf{O}^T$, in the sense that $o_1^t \preceq o_2^t$ states that the object type o_1^t is a subtype of the object type o_2^t and inherits its attributes.

FDMM defines functions for attaching attributes to object types, for defining the range of attribute values, and for the number of attribute values per object type instance. The domain function maps attributes to the power set of all object types, i.e. domain : $\mathbf{A} \rightarrow \mathcal{P}(\bigcup_j \mathbf{O}_j^T)$. It will constrain what objects an attribute can map in the model instances and is thus used to attach attributes to a particular set of object types. The range function maps an attribute to the power set of all pairs of object types and model types, all data types, and all model types, i.e. range : $\mathbf{A} \rightarrow \mathcal{P}\left(\bigcup_j (\mathbf{O}_j^T \times \{\mathbf{MT}_j\}) \cup \mathbf{D}^T \cup \mathbf{MT}\right)$. On the level of the model instances, the range function will later constrain what values an attribute can have. For the definition of a meta model it serves to describe the type of an attribute. We can distinguish three cases that may be combined: *i.* where the attribute points to an instance of an object type that is contained in a particular model type $(\mathbf{O}_j^T \times \{\mathbf{MT}_j\}$; *ii.* where the attribute points to an instance of a datatype $\mathbf{D}^T$, or *iii.* where the attribute points to an instance of a model type $\mathbf{MT}$. With the card function it can be specified how many instances of object types, data types, or model types an attribute of a particular object type may have, i.e. card : $O^T \times \mathbf{A} \rightarrow \mathcal{P}(\mathbb{N} \times (\mathbb{N} \cup \{\infty\}))$. FDMM defines several correctness criteria for meta models, which we will omit here for brevity and which the interested reader may find in the original source [21].

Next, we describe how FDMM defines the instantiation of meta models to models. For this purpose, FDMM maps model types, object types, and data types to model instances, objects, and data values. In addition, so-called *triples* are defined that assign values of attributes to objects. The instantiation of a metamodel $\mathbf{MM}$ is a tuple $\langle \mu_{\mathbf{mt}}, \mu_{\mathbf{O}}, \mu_{\mathbf{D}}, \mathcal{T}, \beta \rangle$. $\mu_{\mathbf{mt}}$, $\mu_{\mathbf{O}}$, and $\mu_{\mathbf{D}}$ are functions that map from the elements in the meta model to instances.

The function $\mu_{\mathbf{mt}} : \mathbf{MT} \rightarrow \mathcal{P}(\mathbf{mt})$ maps model types to the power set of model instances. The function $\mu_{\mathbf{O}} : \bigcup_j \left(\mathbf{O}_j^T \times \{\mathbf{MT}_j\}\right) \rightarrow \mathcal{P}(\mathbf{O})$ stands for the mapping of object types of a specific model type to the power set of object instances where the set of all object instances is $\mathbf{O} = \bigcup_j \mu_{\mathbf{O}}(\mathbf{O}_j^T \times \{\mathbf{MT}_j\})$. For brevity we omit here the specification of abstract object type, which can be specified in FDMM and that is not to be instantiated directly. The function $\mu_{\mathbf{D}} : \mathbf{D}^T \rightarrow \mathcal{P}(\mathbf{D})$ maps data types to the power set of data objects. Further constraints on data types are not contained in FDMM itself. Rather, it is left to the user to add them if necessary or otherwise refer to commonly known data types such as integer numbers or strings.

Finally, triples $\mathcal{T} \subseteq \mathbf{O} \times \mathbf{A} \times (\mathbf{D} \cup \mathbf{O} \cup \mathbf{mt})$ are used to describe the contents of model instances. They combine object instances and their attributes with instances of data types, other object instances, or model instances. The triples are then assigned to concrete model instances via the map $\beta : \mathbf{mt} \rightarrow \mathcal{P}(\mathcal{T})$.

3.1 CMAG Prompt Structure

The CMAG (Conceptual Model Augmented Generative Artificial Intelligence) framework positions conceptual models as interfaces to large language models during the prompting and the generation phase [20]. It proposes a prompt structure based on the following elements: a *few shot context* for informing the LLM about the modeling language, a *task framing* to reference the modeling language, the actual *task content* for describing the intended answer of the LLM, and the *output description* that refers again to the modeling language. As LLMs can adapt their responses through few-shot prompting, they may be guided with information about a meta^2 model, metamodel and sample instances in the few shot context. Alternatively, the task framing and the output description may reference a modeling language that the LLM has already been trained on. The result of this prompt structure is that LLMs can be forced to create models for a given task content. For example, instead of producing the description of the steps of a business process for some service in textual form, the LLM can be thus forced to create a model in BPMN notation. Similarly, other schemata for modeling languages can be defined specifically for CMAG prompts or existing languages re-used. As a consequence, users can more easily assess an LLM's output and conduct modifications in the created models, which can be sent back to the LLM for further processing, e.g. in agentic workflows [16].

Thus, the expected output from an LLM after using the CMAG prompt is a model instance ($\mathrm{OUT}_{\mathrm{llm}}$) that tends to exhibit higher accuracy than the output obtained from an unstructured regular prompt to an LLM.

4 Formal Evaluation Framework Based on FDMM

Following our schematic workflow in Fig. 1, we advance now with the presentation of the two main blocks for the evaluation after the generation of $\mathrm{OUT}_{\mathrm{llm}}$: the filtering of the raw LLM-generated output, the mapping to FDMM and the formal definition of evaluation metrics.

4.1 Filtering LLM-Generated Output

Considering that the LLM output is inherently unstructured and represented in a raw format, its filtering becomes an important pre-processing step to discard undesired outputs before the formal evaluation. Hence, we perform a strict filtering on syntactically incorrect instances. More precisely, if any part of the generated output is syntactically incorrect, the entire output instance is discarded. The filtering is thereby accomplished using modeling language specific validation standards since there is no universal tool for evaluating the syntactical accuracy of arbitrary model instances. For instance, we used an RDF validator for RDF instances, which focuses on structural correctness, whereas the validator we use for ArchiMate models additionally performs some semantic checks. This can be considered a limitation of the approach since it needs to be adapted to each language individually once. However, once the syntactically erroneous instances are discarded, the workflow can proceed to mapping LLM-generated output $\mathrm{OUT}_{\mathrm{llm}}$ to FDMM.

4.2 Mapping to FDMM and Formal Definition of Evaluation Metrics

Our assumption is that every conceptual model can be mapped to FDMM constructs, as the formalism provides a sufficiently general framework to represent diverse domain-specific languages. The mapping of a modeling language to FDMM needs to be defined once and can subsequently be used for an arbitrary number of model instances based on this language, thereby ensuring the scalability of the approach.

A formal evaluation step is defined as $e(f, g)$, where f is a result of mapping any baseline model ($\mathrm{OUT}_{\mathrm{base}}$) to FDMM, such that $f = \langle \mathbf{O}_{\mathrm{base}}, \mathbf{D}_{\mathrm{base}}, \mathcal{T}_{\mathrm{base}} \rangle$, and g is a result of mapping any LLM output ($\mathrm{OUT}_{\mathrm{llm}}$) to FDMM, such that $g = \langle \mathbf{O}_{\mathrm{llm}}, \mathbf{D}_{\mathrm{llm}}, \mathcal{T}_{\mathrm{llm}} \rangle$. The general function e represents any evaluation metric instantiated by the list of specific measures, such as lexical and semantic included in [9]. In this study, only a few of them are used for representation. We use subscripts "base" and "llm" to denote the baseline and LLM-generated elements. Considering any meta model $\mathbf{MM}$ and its model types $\mathbf{MT}_i = \langle \mathbf{O}_i^T, \mathbf{D}_i^T, \mathbf{A}_i \rangle$, the evaluation sets—LLM-generated object type instances $\mathbf{O}_{\mathrm{llm}}$, data type instances $\mathbf{D}_{\mathrm{llm}}$, and triples $\mathcal{T}_{\mathrm{llm}}$—are being compared to their respective baseline counterparts $\mathbf{O}_{\mathrm{base}}$, $\mathbf{D}_{\mathrm{base}}$, and $\mathcal{T}_{\mathrm{base}}$.

Next, we introduce an FDMM-based formal foundation of the evaluation framework, which serves for calculating metrics commonly used in the literature. We define $S_{\mathbf{O}}$, $S_{\mathbf{D}}$, and $S_{\mathcal{T}}$, each providing insights into whether the expected FDMM elements are generated. Given the baseline and LLM-generated sets of elements, we can write a simple matching score expression: $S_{\mathbf{O}} = |\mathbf{O}_{\mathrm{base}} \cap \mathbf{O}_{\mathrm{llm}}|$, $S_{\mathbf{D}} = |\mathbf{D}_{\mathrm{base}} \cap \mathbf{D}_{\mathrm{llm}}|$, $S_{\mathcal{T}} = |\mathcal{T}_{\mathrm{base}} \cap \mathcal{T}_{\mathrm{llm}}|$.

However, the comparison is not always straightforward since LLMs occasionally generate additional, unexpected elements. Furthermore, the quantity of generated elements might fall below that in the baseline sets, additionally prompting for extending the evaluation strategy. Therefore, we introduced a new evaluation criterion, which respectively shows whether there exist additional or missing set elements in the LLM-generated output. Accordingly, symbols $(+)$, $(-)$, and Δ are assigned to the score S to respectively denote missing elements, extra generated elements, and their difference. We denote a general scoring function $S_{(\cdot)}$ where the subscript denotes one of the sets $\mathbf{O}$, $\mathbf{D}$, or $\mathcal{T}$. We can now generalize the expressions for $S_{\mathbf{O}}$, $S_{\mathbf{D}}$, and $\mathcal{T}$ into $S_{(\cdot)} = |(\cdot)_{\text{base}} \cap (\cdot)_{\text{llm}}|$, where $(\cdot) \in \{\mathbf{O}, \mathbf{D}, \mathcal{T}\}$. Similarly, for any baseline and LLM-generated sets, and considering the defined notation $(\cdot)$ previously, we introduce: $S^{-}_{(\cdot)} = |(\cdot)_{\text{base}} \setminus (\cdot)_{\text{llm}}|$, $S^{+}_{(\cdot)} = |(\cdot)_{\text{llm}} \setminus (\cdot)_{\text{base}}|$, and $S^{\Delta}_{(\cdot)} = S^{+}_{(\cdot)} - S^{-}_{(\cdot)}$, where $S^{-}_{(\cdot)}$ denotes the number of missing elements in LLM-generated sets and $S^{+}_{(\cdot)}$ denotes the number of extra elements in the LLM-generated sets and $S^{\Delta}_{(\cdot)}$ refers to the final difference between missing and extra counts in the generated sets. The sign of $S^{\Delta}_{(\cdot)}$ indicates the balance between extra and missing elements, such that $S^{\Delta}_{(\cdot)} > 0$, $S^{\Delta}_{(\cdot)} = 0$, $S^{\Delta}_{(\cdot)} < 0$, if it holds $S^{+} > S^{-}$, $S^{+} = S^{-}$, $S^{+} < S^{-}$, respectively.

Guided by the evaluation metrics in the literature, our approach enables the formal formulation of standard metrics for models of any type[1], such as precision, recall, and F_1-score. For simplicity, our metric considers strict matching rules although it could be extended to the semantic precision and recall similarly to proposed research by Euzenat [15]. The evaluation function $e(f, g)$ introduced earlier is formally expressed in a general way as follows:

$$p_{(\cdot)} = \frac{S_{(\cdot)}}{|(\cdot)_{\text{llm}}|}, \quad r_{(\cdot)} = \frac{S_{(\cdot)}}{|(\cdot)_{\text{base}}|}, \quad F_{1(\cdot)} = \frac{2p_{(\cdot)}r_{(\cdot)}}{p_{(\cdot)} + r_{(\cdot)}} \quad ; \tag{1}$$

where p and r stand for precision and recall. For a collection of K evaluated models, indexed by $k = 1, \ldots, K$, the aggregated statistics of these metrics (Eq. 1) can be expressed through the mean and standard deviation. The empirical evaluation that can accordingly be derived is presented in the following section.

5 Demonstration of Application

For demonstrating the application of our approach, we apply the mapping step to FDMM to two modeling languages from very separate domains. First to the ArchiMate modeling language and second to knowledge graphs[2]

[1] Note that recall and F_1-score are calculated in terms of the baseline set instance $(\cdot)_{\text{base}}$ rather than the world set relevant elements. The inclusion of the world set of relevant values would demand extending the baseline in order to further classify the extra LLM-generated instance. This is envisaged for future work.

[2] Code and supplementary material can be found online at: https://doi.org/10.5281/zenodo.21263688.

5.1 Enterprise Architecture Models in ArchiMate

ArchiMate [33] is an open and independent modeling language for enterprise architecture that provides instruments to describe, analyze, and visualize relationships among business domains used by many large organizations [27]. The elaborations in the following are based on Open Group's ArchiMate version 3.2 [33] and the concrete realization of ArchiMate in PlantUML, which we found to work well in LLM-based settings.

As can be seen in Fig. 2, mapping PlantUML and ArchiMate to FDMM is accomplished through the definition of a meta model composed of one model type $\mathbf{MM} = \{\mathbf{MT}_{\mathrm{AM}}\}$ where $\mathbf{MT}_{\mathrm{AM}} = \langle \mathbf{O}^T_{\mathrm{AM}}, \mathbf{D}^T_{\mathrm{AM}}, \mathbf{A}_{\mathrm{AM}} \rangle$. Then we assume $\mathbf{O}^T_{\mathrm{AM}} =$ {Category, ElementType, Element, RelationType, Relation}, $\mathbf{D}^T_{\mathrm{AM}} =$ {string}, and finally $\mathbf{A}_{\mathrm{AM}} =$ {relationName, description, hasRelationType, hasCategory, hasElementType, identifier, label, fromElement, toElement, elementName, fromElementType, toElementType, categorization, categoryName}.

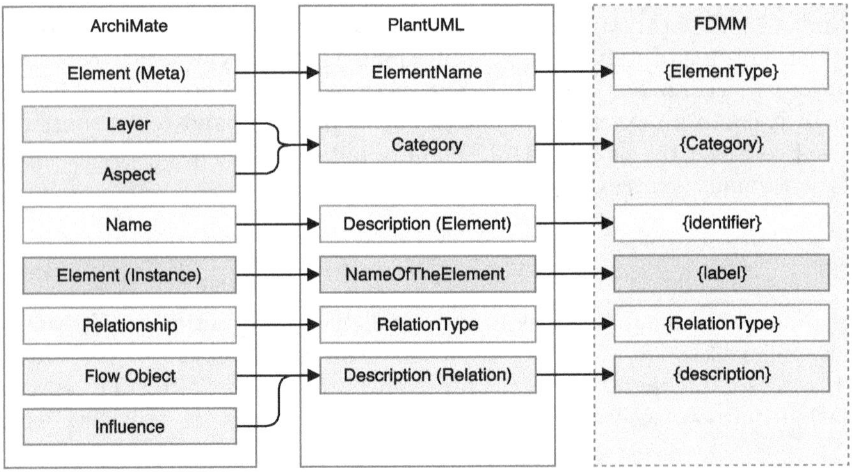

Fig. 2. Mapping between ArchiMate and PlantUML for formalization in FDMM.

A concrete model can then be instantiated as $\mu_{\mathbf{mt}}(\mathbf{MT}_{\mathrm{AM}}) = \{\mathbf{mt}_{\mathrm{am}_1}\}$ along with some object types instances $\mu_{\mathbf{O}}(\text{Category}, \mathbf{MT}_{\mathrm{AM}}) = \{\mathit{Business}\}$, $\mu_{\mathbf{O}}(\text{Element}, \mathbf{MT}_{\mathrm{AM}}) = \{\mathit{Underwrite}\}$, $\mu_{\mathbf{O}}(\text{ElemenType}, \mathbf{MT}_{\mathrm{am}}) = \{\mathit{Process}\}$ and data type instances $\mu_{\mathbf{D}}(\text{string}) = \{\mathit{underwrite}, \mathit{UnderwriteRisk}\}$. Finally, we describe triples of the model instance, ($\mathit{Process}$ categorization $\mathit{Business}$) $\in \beta(\mathbf{mt}_{\mathrm{am}_1})$ or ($\mathit{Underwrite}$ label "$\mathit{UnderwriteRisk}$") $\in \beta(\mathbf{mt}_{\mathrm{am}_1})$.

The filtering step was executed using the PlantUML web editor. In the subsequent phase, only models that were deemed valid were transferred to FDMM. The majority of invalidations were attributed to prefixes and suffixes surrounding the PlantUML code or the inclusion of non-existent elements, such as "Business Domain". Through this mapping we can show that ArchiMate models in PlantUML notation can be successfully mapped to FDMM, thus providing the basis for calculating the comparison metrics.

5.2 Knowledge Graphs in Cultural Heritage

The second demonstration refers to the generation of knowledge graphs in the domain of cultural heritage, similar to the work of Vasic et al. [44]. Knowledge graphs represent formal structures of information systems where entities (also known as nodes and vertices) and semantic relationships are connected as a graph [22]. Two entities and their mutual relationships form a triple, often represented in RDF format as subject, predicate, and object [30]. The Getty Collection was chosen as a reference dataset in this study, and it is organized through the Linked Art model [38] built upon Linked Open Data standards and serialized in RDF-compatible JSON-LD format.

Since certain parts of the Getty Collection URIs are entirely specific to the internal organization of the museum, we intentionally do not consider them in their full format, as our objective is not to evaluate LLM output against these specific identifiers. Instead, we simplify them by introducing a custom prefix *concept* and mapping the Getty-specific one to it. For example, we introduced concept:object, concept:material, and others listed in the supplementary material. Moreover, since our generation and evaluation algorithm processes one painting at a time, there is no possibility that one concept overlaps with another contained in the rest of the artworks.

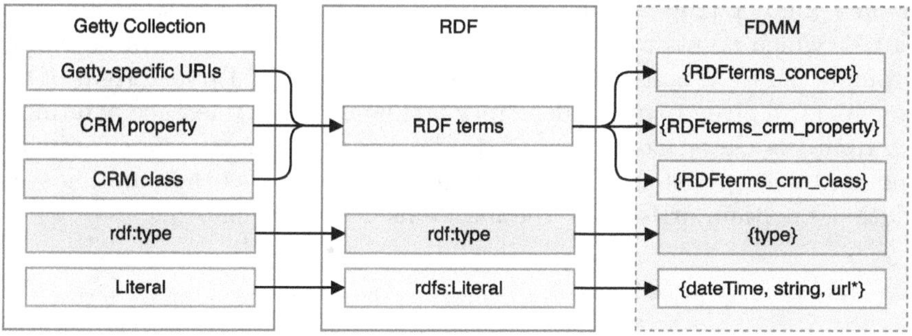

Fig. 3. Mapping Getty collection knowledge graphs elements to FDMM through RDF. (*) denotes elements that exist in the model but are excluded from the generation or the evaluation.

Next, we describe the mapping process of the baseline model $\mathrm{OUT}_{\mathrm{base}}$ and the resulting tuples $\langle \mathbf{O}_{\mathrm{base}}, \mathbf{D}_{\mathrm{base}}, \mathcal{T}_{\mathrm{base}} \rangle$. A meta model is defined involving one model type, $\mathbf{MM} = \{\mathbf{MT}_{\mathrm{GC}}\}$, for which the subscript is assigned according to the Getty Collection and CIDOC-CRM ontology, and where $\mathbf{MT}_{\mathrm{GC}} = \langle \mathbf{O}^{T}_{\mathrm{GC}}, \mathbf{D}^{T}_{\mathrm{GC}}, \mathbf{A}_{\mathrm{GC}} \rangle$. Then we define object types, data types, and attributes, respectively, as follows: $\mathbf{O}^{T}_{\mathrm{GC}} = \{$RDFterms_concept, RDFterms_crm_property, RDFterms_crm_class$\}$, $\mathbf{D}^{T}_{\mathrm{GC}} = \{$dateType, dateTime, url$\}$, and $\mathbf{A}_{\mathrm{GC}} = \{$type, has_concept, has_property, literal, identifier$\}$. Note that we introduced *identifier* as an attribute construct that links the RDFterms_concept to the original Getty identifiers[3]. Its role serves to complete our mapping but is excluded from evaluation, as it is meant to map back the previously mentioned *concepts* to the Getty URI. Figure 3 presents the mapping of the Getty Collection concepts to FDMM, with alignment to the RDF concepts.

In the model instantiation phase, we may assume $\mu_{\mathbf{O}}(concept,\ \mathbf{MT}_{\mathrm{GC}}) = \{concept : material\}$ and $\mu_{\mathbf{O}}(RDFterms\_crm\_property,\ \mathbf{MT}_{\mathrm{GC}}) = \{crm : P190\_has\_symbolic\_content\}$ as object type instances. We further assume one data type instance as $\mu_{\mathbf{D}}(string, \mathbf{MT}_{\mathrm{GC}}) = \{'Oil\ on\ canvas'\}$. Finally, we may write triples out of these elements to express the material used for a painting: (concept:material *has_property* crm:P190_has_symbolic_content) $\in \beta(\mathbf{mt}_{gc})$ and (crm:P190_has_symbolic_content *literal* 'Oil on canvas') $\in \beta(\mathbf{mt}_{gc})$. The filtering step was performed using an open-source tool[4].

5.3 Demonstration of the Calculation of Metrics

For demonstrating the calculation of the evaluation metrics introduced in 4.2, we show in the following only first results for generating 20 knowledge graphs for paintings in the cultural heritage domain to give an impression how results can be generated. We used Gemma3:12b, GPT-oss-120b, and Gemini-2.5-pro models. The CMAG prompt structure was used to force model creation for a given task content [20]. At first, a CMAG context reference was provided to each LLM, which points to the Getty Collection and CIDOC-CRM ontology. In the prompt, the LLM is requested to generate a model in Turtle format of triple statements for a given painting description. The included reference painting was chosen from the Getty Collection[5]. Additionally, the context reference includes the required concepts that will be evaluated after, such as the painting's place and date of creation, artist, and the materials used, among others.

Table 1. Illustrative evaluation scores for the knowledge graph use case.

LLM	$S_{\mathbf{O}_{\mathrm{GC}}}$	$S^-_{\mathbf{O}_{\mathrm{GC}}}$	$S^+_{\mathbf{O}_{\mathrm{GC}}}$	$S^\Delta_{\mathbf{O}_{\mathrm{GC}}}$	$S_{\mathbf{D}_{\mathrm{GC}}}$	$S^-_{\mathbf{D}_{\mathrm{GC}}}$	$S^+_{\mathbf{D}_{\mathrm{GC}}}$	$S^\Delta_{\mathbf{D}_{\mathrm{GC}}}$	$S_{T_{\mathrm{GC}}}$	$S^-_{T_{\mathrm{GC}}}$	$S^+_{T_{\mathrm{GC}}}$	$S^\Delta_{T_{\mathrm{GC}}}$
Gemini	440	8	17	9	**119**	9	18	9	794	26	77	51
Gemma	446	2	14	12	118	10	21	11	**808**	12	71	59
GPT	**447**	1	13	12	110	18	29	11	801	19	79	60

The model in CMAG terms includes an example for a few-shot prompt. Finally, a pattern is included, representing a painting description, based on which

[3] An example of the original Getty identifier is https://data.getty.edu/museum/collection/object/e79dc10c-da13-481a-8e81-4b30474d6778.

[4] Available at: [https://github.com/IDLabResearch/TurtleValidator], accessed: 14.11.2025.

[5] *Portrait of a Woman*, available at: [https://www.getty.edu/art/collection/object/114T8J], accessed 05.11.2025.

the KG should be derived. The filtering step was then performed using an open-source tool[4], which reported that all LLM-generated graphs complied with the Turtle syntax. Therefore, 20 knowledge graphs, each related to a specific painting, were considered for evaluation. The summary of missing and extra LLM-generated elements, and their respective differences, are represented in Table 1 as well as the calculation of first results of precision, recall, and F1 score in Table 2. Note that these results are only for verifying the feasibility of the calculations due to limitations of space here. For a sound evaluation, a larger number of LLMs as well as variations on the number of runs and parameter settings would need to be included in addition. We reported the descriptive statistics across the 20 paintings, however, no statistical significance tests were performed because it is currently beyond the scope of the study to measure the differences in performance across LLMs. Therefore, with such illustrative analysis, we cannot conclude on whether the observed differences across LLMs are statistically significant.

Table 2. Illustrative statistical results for the knowledge graph use case: Precision, recall, and F_1-score are reported as mean $(\bar{\cdot})$ ± standard deviation (σ) across the K generated models ($K = 20$).

	precision (%)		
	$\mathbf{O}_{\mathrm{GC}}^{T}$	$\mathbf{D}_{\mathrm{GC}}^{T}$	$\mathcal{T}$
Gemini	96.30 ± 4.06	**87.14 ± 13.83**	91.25 ± 8.48
Gemma	96.95 ± 2.86	84.64 ± 12.75	**91.91 ± 6.08**
GPT	**97.17 ± 2.13**	79.16 ± 14.96	91.02 ± 6.19
	recall (%)		
	$\mathbf{O}_{\mathrm{GC}}^{T}$	$\mathbf{D}_{\mathrm{GC}}^{T}$	$\mathcal{T}$
Gemini	98.22 ± 3.65	**92.86 ± 12.09**	96.81 ± 5.88
Gemma	99.54 ± 1.40	92.14 ± 13.23	**98.52 ± 2.20**
GPT	**99.78 ± 0.97**	85.71 ± 13.88	97.67 ± 2.21
	F1 Score (%)		
	$\mathbf{O}_{\mathrm{GC}}^{T}$	$\mathbf{D}_{\mathrm{GC}}^{T}$	$\mathcal{T}$
Gemini	97.23 ± 3.51	**89.61 ± 12.05**	93.84 ± 6.63
Gemma	98.22 ± 1.99	88.10 ± 12.49	**95.02 ± 3.76**
GPT	**98.45 ± 1.26**	82.14 ± 14.01	94.15 ± 3.86

6 Discussion and Guidelines for Applying the Framework

With our approach we could show how an evaluation of LLM-generated conceptual models can be addressed in a modeling language agnostic way, thereby answering RQ1 and RQ2. For answering RQ3, we present in Table 3 a comparison of our approach against previous approaches. The comparison focuses only on the evaluation step rather than the methods for the generation of conceptual models, pre-processing, or post-processing.

We distinguish between purely *Automatic* and *Human in the Loop* where at least some step is conducted manually. In the column *Modeling Language Independent* we assess whether an approach is designed as independent of a particular modeling language. Although some approaches use generic constructs, e.g. for describing domain models, this has so far not been the case.

Another advantage of our approach is that we formally express the evaluation artifacts in terms of FDMM, while most other approaches do not present this information, which may limit the applicability when evaluating other types of models. The column *Formal Representation* indicates that the evaluated elements are formally represented, either in mathematical terms, through an implementation, or using models themselves.

Table 3. Comparison of techniques and metrics used for evaluating LLM-generated conceptual models across studies in the literature. The reported values for our approach are reported in the last column. NS - Not Specified

Article	*Automatic/ Human in the Loop*	*Code Available*	*Output Format(s)*	*Evaluation Metrics*	*Modeling Language Independent*	*Evaluation Artefacts*	*Formal Representation*
[7]	A	✓	Custom	Mean, Standard Deviation, Significance, Precision, Recall, F0.5 Score, F1 Score, F2 Score	✗	Classes, Associations	✗
[40]	H	✗	PlantUML	Average structure rating	✗	Classes, Attributes, Relationships	✗
[11]	H	✓	Custom	Precision, Recall, F1 Score	✗	Classes, Attributes, Relationships	✗
[3]	NS	✓	Custom	F1 Score	✗	Custom DSL	✗
[10]	A	✓	PlantUML	Precision, Recall, F1 score	✗	Classes, Associations, Attributes (Name, Cardinality)	✗
[35]	H	✓	JSON	Precision, Recall, F1 Score	✗	Classes, Attributes, Associations	✓
[41]	A	✓	PlantUML	Precision, Recall, F1 Score	✗	Classes, Attributes, Relationships, Association Classes	✓
[44]	H	✓	JSON	Agreement rate	✗	CIDOC-CRM class Value	✗
Ours	H	✓	Turtle, PlantUML	Precision, Recall, F1 Score	✓	$\mathbf{O}^T$, $\mathbf{D}^T$, $\mathcal{T}$	✓

6.1 Guidelines for Applying the Framework

For applying our framework we derived the following guidelines to ensure its correct and efficient usage. First, potential users need to familiarize themselves with the FDMM formalism and how to map modeling languages to it. Potential sources include previous contributions to this topic, e.g. [5,25,34,39]. Second, the mapping of a modeling language to FDMM requires high familiarity with the modeling language to guarantee a correct mapping. Ideally, the creators of the modeling language or senior users are involved in this step. Finally, the setup of the automated pipeline includes the choice of a suitable tool for checking the syntactical correctness of generated models. This depends on the used modeling language. It is preferable to use official validation tools for this step if available or to use at least well-documented formats such as PlantUML or Mermaid that can be well processed by current AI models.

6.2 Limitations

In contrast to other approaches, our approach is the only one that has been applied to multiple modeling languages. However, this comes at the cost of having to map first the language constructs to FDMM. At the moment this has to be performed manually, however, it does not affect scalability in terms of the number of evaluated model instances later. Further, our approach so far mainly considers the syntactic quality of models. However, we consider it as a sound basis for adding the evaluation of semantics in the future.

7 Conclusion

This paper introduced a formal framework based on the FDMM formalism for evaluating LLM-generated models on a meta level, by formally describing the contents of metamodels and their instantiation to models on the level of syntax. The evaluation was presented as a function of comparison of LLM-generated and baseline model tuples formed from FDMM constructs. The strength of our approach lies in its ability to generalize across different domains, compared to other approaches which, to our knowledge, focus on a single domain.

One limitation of our approach stems from the manual effort involved in the mapping process and from relying primarily on syntactical similarity in the comparison phase. Future work will extend the approach towards including additional semantic measures such as reproducible semantic evaluations and providing further support, e.g. for automating the mapping to FDMM.

Acknowledgment. This work was financially supported by the Smart Living Lab, a joint project funded by the University of Fribourg, EPFL, and HEIA-FR.

References

1. van der Aa, H., Carmona, J., Leopold, H., Mendling, J., Padró, L.: Challenges and opportunities of applying natural language processing in business process management. In: International Conference on Computational Linguistics, pp. 2791–2801. Association for Computational Linguistics (2018)
2. Arora, C., Sabetzadeh, M., Briand, L., Zimmer, F.: Extracting domain models from natural-language requirements: approach and industrial evaluation. In: Proceedings of the ACM/IEEE 19th International Conference on Model Driven Engineering Languages and Systems, MODELS '16, pp. 250–260. ACM, New York, (2016)
3. Arulmohan, S., Meurs, M.J., Mosser, S.: Extracting domain models from textual requirements in the era of large language models. In: 2023 ACM/IEEE MODELS-C, pp. 580–587 (2023)
4. Bellan, P., Dragoni, M., Ghidini, C., Aa, H.V.D., Ponzetto, S.P.: Process extraction from text: benchmarking the state of the art and paving the way for future challenges. arXiv (2023). https://doi.org/10.48550/arXiv.2110.03754
5. Boucher, X., Medini, K., Fill, H.-G.: Product-service-system modeling method. In: Domain-Specific Conceptual Modeling, pp. 455–482. Springer, Cham (2016). https://doi.org/10.1007/978-3-319-39417-6_21
6. Braga, B.F.B., Almeida, J.P.A., Guizzardi, G., Benevides, A.B.: Transforming OntoUML into alloy: towards conceptual model validation using a lightweight formal method. Innovations Syst. Softw. Eng. **6**(1), 55–63 (2010)
7. Bragilovski, M., van Can, A.T., Dalpiaz, F., Sturm, A.: Leveraging machines to derive domain models from user stories. Requir. Eng. **30**(2), 241–262 (2025)
8. Brambilla, M., Cabot, J., Wimmer, M.: Model-driven software engineering in practice, second edition. Synth. Lect. Softw. Eng. **3**(1), 1–207 (2017)
9. Bulygin, L.: Combining lexical and semantic similarity measures with machine learning approach for ontology matching problem. In: Kalinichenko, L.A., Manolopoulos, Y., Stupnikov, S.A., Skvortsov, N.A., Sukhomlin, V. (eds.) Selected Papers of the XX International Conference on Data Analytics and Management in Data Intensive Domains (DAMDID/RCDL 2018), Moscow, Russia, 9–12 October 2018. CEUR Workshop Proceedings, vol. 2277, pp. 245–249. CEUR-WS.org (2018). https://ceur-ws.org/Vol-2277/paper42.pdf
10. Calamo, M., Mecella, M., Snoeck, M.: Assessing the suitability of large language models in generating UML class diagrams as conceptual models. In: Enterprise. Business-Process and Information Systems Modeling, pp. 211–226. Springer, Cham (2025). https://doi.org/10.1007/978-3-031-95397-2_13
11. Chen, K., et al.: Automated domain modeling with large language models: a comparative study. In: 2023 ACM/IEEE MODELS, pp. 162–172. IEEE (2023)
12. Cámara, J., Burgueño, L., Troya, J.: Towards standardized benchmarks of LLMs in software modeling tasks: a conceptual framework. Softw. Syst. Model. **23**(6), 1309–1318 (2024)
13. Cámara, J., Troya, J., Burgueño, L., Vallecillo, A.: On the assessment of generative AI in modeling tasks: an experience report with ChatGPT and UML. Softw. Syst. Model. **22**(3), 781–793 (2023)
14. De Bari, D., Garaccione, G., Coppola, R., Torchiano, M., Ardito, L.: Evaluating large language models in exercises of UML class diagram modeling. In: ACM/IEEE International Symposium on Empirical Software Engineering and Measurement, ESEM '24, pp. 393–399. ACM, New York (2024)

15. Euzenat, J.: Semantic precision and recall for ontology alignment evaluation. In: Proceedings of the 20th International Joint Conference on Artifical Intelligence, IJCAI'07, pp. 348–353. Morgan Kaufmann Publishers Inc, San Francisco (2007)
16. Fettke, P., Fill, H.G., Köpke, J.: LLM, LAM, LxM agent: from talking to acting machines: insights from the perspective of conceptual modeling. Enterp. Model. Inf. Syst. Arch. (EMISAJ) - Int. J. Concept. Model. **20** (2025). https://doi.org/10.18417/emisa.20.3
17. Fill, H.G.: Semantic annotations of enterprise models for supporting the evolution of model-driven organizations. Enterp. Model. Inf. Syst. Arch. (EMISAJ) - Int. J. Concept. Model. **13**, (5),1–25 (2018)
18. Fill, H.G., Fettke, P., Köpke, J.: Conceptual modeling and large language models: impressions from first experiments with ChatGPT. Enterp. Model. Inf. Syst. Archit. Int. J. Concept. Model **18**, 3 (2023). https://doi.org/10.18417/EMISA.18.3
19. Fill, H.G., Horkoff, J., Fettke, P., Köpke, J.: Generative AI and conceptual modeling. Bus. Inf. Syst. Eng. **68**(1), 1–5 (2026). https://doi.org/10.1007/s12599-025-00978-8
20. Fill, H.G., et al.: CMAG: a framework for conceptual model augmented generative artificial intelligence. In: Companion Proceedings of the 43rd International Conference on Conceptual Modeling, pp. 56–69. CEUR-WS.org (2024). https://ceur-ws.org/Vol-3849/forum5.pdf
21. Fill, H.G., Redmond, T., Karagiannis, D.: FDMM: a formalism for describing ADOxx meta models and models. In: ICEIS 2012, pp. 133–144. SciTePress (2012)
22. Gutierrez, C., Sequeda, J.F.: Knowledge graphs. Commun. ACM **64**(3), 96–104 (2021). https://doi.org/10.1145/3418294
23. Huang, H., Chen, C., Sheng, Z., Li, Y., Zhang, W.: Can LLMs be good graph judge for knowledge graph construction? In: Proceedings of the 2025 Conference on Empirical Methods in Natural Language Processing, pp. 10940–10959. ACL, Suzhou (2025)
24. Ibáñez, M.B., Barrón-Estrada, M.L., Zatarain-Cabada, R.: Can multimodal large language models grade like an expert? A study on UML class diagram assessment accuracy. Comput. Appl. Eng. Educ. **33**(5), e70080 (2025)
25. Johannsen, F., Fill, H.G.: Meta modeling for business process improvement. Bus. Inf. Syst. Eng. **59**(4), 251–275 (2017). https://doi.org/10.1007/s12599-017-0477-1
26. Krogstie, J.: Quality of business process models. In: Quality in Business Process Modeling, pp. 53–102. Springer, Cham (2016). https://doi.org/10.1007/978-3-319-42512-2_2
27. Lankhorst, M., et al.: Enterprise Architecture at Work: Modelling, Communication and Analysis, 3 edn. Springer, Heidelberg (2013).https://doi.org/10.1007/978-3-642-29651-2
28. Lo, A., et al.: End-to-End ontology learning with large language models. In: Tomczak, J.M., Zhang, C. (eds.) Adv. Neural Inf. Process. Syst. (2024)
29. Mayr, H.C., Thalheim, B.: The triptych of conceptual modeling. Softw. Syst. Model. **20**(1), 7–24 (2021)
30. McBride, B.: The resource description framework (RDF) and its vocabulary description language RDFS. In: Staab, S., Studer, R. (eds.) Handbook on Ontologies, pp. 51–65. Springer, Heidelberg (2004). https://doi.org/10.1007/978-3-540-24750-0_3
31. Michael, J., Bork, D., Wimmer, M., Mayr, H.C.: Quo Vadis modeling? Softw. Syst. Model. **23**(1), 7–28 (2024)

32. Mylopoulos, J.: Conceptual modelling and Telos. In: Conceptual Modelling, Databases, and CASE: An Integrated View of Information System Development, pp. 49–68. John Wiley & Sons, Chichester (1992)
33. The Open Group: ArchiMate® Specification, Version 3.2 (2021). https://publications.opengroup.org/c20c, document Number C20C
34. Pittl, B., Fill, H.G.: A visual modeling approach for the Semantic Web Rule Language. Semantic Web **11**(2), 361–389 (2020). https://doi.org/10.3233/SW-180340
35. Prokop, D., Stenchlák, Škoda, P., Klímek, J., Nečaský, M.: Enhancing domain modeling with pre-trained large language models: an automated assistant for domain modelers. In: Conceptual Modeling, pp. 235–253. Springer, Cham (2025). https://doi.org/10.1007/978-3-031-75872-0_13
36. Pérez-Soler, S., Guerra, E., de Lara, J.: Flexible modelling using conversational agents. In: 2019 ACM/IEEE 22nd International Conference on Model Driven Engineering Languages and Systems Companion (MODELS-C), pp. 478–482 (2019)
37. Reinhartz-Berger, I., Ali, S.J., Bork, D.: Leveraging LLMs for domain modeling: the impact of granularity and strategy on quality. In: Advanced Information Systems Engineering, pp. 3–19. Springer, Cham (2025). https://doi.org/10.1007/978-3-031-94569-4_1
38. Sanderson, R.: Implementing linked art in a multi-modal database for cross-collection discovery. Open Libr. Human. **10**(2) (2024). https://doi.org/10.16995/olh.15407
39. Schoknecht, A., Vetter, A., Fill, H.-G., Oberweis, A.: Using the horus method for succeeding in business process engineering projects. In: Domain-Specific Conceptual Modeling, pp. 127–147. Springer, Cham (2016). https://doi.org/10.1007/978-3-319-39417-6_6
40. Shehata, M., Lepore, B., Cummings, H., Parra, E.: Creating UML class diagrams with general-purpose LLMs. In: IEEE VISSOFT, pp. 157–158 (2024)
41. Silva, J., Ma, Q., Cabot, J., Kelsen, P., Proper, H.A.: Application of the tree-of-thoughts framework to LLM-enabled domain modeling. In: Conceptual Modeling, pp. 94–111. Springer, Cham (2025). https://doi.org/10.1007/978-3-031-75872-0_6
42. Storey, V.C., et al.: Large language models for conceptual modeling: assessment and application potential. Data Knowl. Eng. **160**, 102480 (2025)
43. Tsaneva, S., Dessì, D., Osborne, F., Sabou, M.: Knowledge graph validation by integrating LLMs and human-in-the-loop. Inf. Process. Manag. **62**(5), 104145 (2025)
44. Vasic, I., Fill, H.G., Quattrini, R., Pierdicca, R.: Knowledge graphs vs. large language models: Competitors or partners in supporting virtual museums. ACM J. Comput. Cult. Herit **18**(4) (2025). https://doi.org/10.1145/3756016
45. Zheng, L., et al.: Judging LLM-as-a-judge with MT-bench and Chatbot Arena. In: Neurips, NIPS '23, pp. 46595–46623. Curran Associates Inc., Red Hook (2023)

Smart Systems and Application Areas

Configurations and Extension Points in Predictive Maintenance Business Models

Matthias Pohl[1(✉)], Christian Haertel[2], Daniel Staegemann[2], and Klaus Turowski[2]

[1] German Aerospace Center (DLR) - Institute of Data Science, Jena, Germany
matthias.pohl@dlr.de
[2] Otto von Guericke University, Magdeburg, Germany
{christian.haertel,daniel.staegemann,klaus.turowski}@ovgu.de

Abstract. Predictive maintenance (PdM) has matured technically, but there remains debate over how firms configure and monetize it commercially. Drawing on prior work that synthesized the literature into an integrative business model framework, this study tests its configurational predictions against empirical evidence. A corpus of 116 case descriptions from a German-language industrial services portal covering the DACH region was coded with dimensions spanning provider type, delivery archetype, revenue model, value-capture locus, and the stages of the PdM data-to-value pipeline. A cluster analysis on the categorical matrix yielded seven empirical archetypes that delineate a static configurational space populated by industry. The findings reposition the framework from a normative articulation of possible configurations toward a corpus-grounded characterization of which cells are commercially populated and which extension paths appear tractable.

Keywords: Predictive Maintenance · Business Model · Case Study · Business Model Evolution

1 Introduction

Industrial maintenance has become a focal site of digital transformation in manufacturing, energy, transport, and process industries. Connected sensors, edge computing, and machine-learning models are routinely deployed to monitor equipment condition and to forecast remaining useful life, with predictive maintenance (PdM) representing the most prominent commercial expression of this shift [1–3]. Industry adoption is driven by a combination of converging factors. The falling cost of industrial sensing and connectivity [4,5], the rapid maturation of cloud-based analytics platforms [6,7], the application of artificial intelligence to condition data [8–10], and the growing pressure to extract additional commercial value from installed industrial assets through servitization [11,12] play a pivotal role in enhancing operational efficiencies [13,14]. At the same time, the

E. Laurenzi et al. (Eds.): BIR 2026, LNBIP 601, pp. 393–412, 2027.
https://doi.org/10.1007/978-3-032-38498-0_25

literature on operations and business models has recognized PdM as a unique case where the configuration of the product being sold, the method of delivery, and the pricing strategy vary more significantly than the underlying technology would imply [15–17]. The technical viability of PdM is, to a first approximation, no longer in doubt. The commercial configuration through which firms monetize it remains an active object of inquiry. In a prior study, we synthesized the peer-reviewed corpus at the intersection of PdM and business model research into an integrative framework [18]. The framework characterizes PdM along the data-to-value pipeline, spanning sensor-based data acquisition to insight delivery, and monetization [1,4,5,8]. Further, the business model landscape is organized around three configurational dimensions, a provider-side taxonomy [15], a delivery-side typology [16,17,19,20], and revenue-model categories [15,21,22]. While the framework articulates a theoretically meaningful design space, it does so based on a structured literature review, which comes with well-known limitations. As a result, it delineates the possible configurations within the design space rather than the actual configurations utilized in industry [23–25]. Additionally, it largely overlooks the issue of archetype transitions, specifically, the paths along which a firm can shift from one configuration to another, the triggers and enablers of such transitions, and the failure modes that may hinder them [11,17]. This study addresses these issues by assembling and analyzing a corpus of PdM and adjacent maintenance-digitalization case descriptions drawn from a German-language industrial services portal. Each case is characterized across approximately twenty-five dimensions, with verbatim evidence retained for auditability. Further, a cluster analysis is applied to the coded matrix to derive empirical archetypes, configurations of the design space that recur in observed deployments, and contrast them with the conceptual archetypes proposed by the framework. This logic has been argued for industrial business models more generally [26–28] and is particularly pertinent to PdM, where the configurational diversity is high [15,16] and the diffusion path between configurations remains underspecified [17]. We pursue this research agenda through the explicit research questions:

RQ: Which configurations of business model archetypes are empirically observed in the industry, and which configurations the framework specifies are absent? Which structurally adjacent archetype pairs suggest tractable points for extension in business model reconfiguration?

The remainder of the paper is structured as follows. Section 2 develops the framework dimensions in the depth required for the empirical analysis and motivates the coding scheme. Section 3 describes the corpus, the coding procedure, and the clustering methodology. Section 4 reports the descriptive coding results and the cluster analysis on both the strict-PdM subset and the full corpus. Sect. 5 discusses the empirical archetypes, the configurational cells, and the implications for business model transformation. Sect. 6 concludes with a research agenda addressing the open questions on archetype transitions.

2 Background

The conceptual scaffolding for this study is drawn from our prior synthesis of the PdM business model literature [18]. For the case-study analysis to follow, these elements need to be developed in the depth required to ground the coding scheme and the cluster-analytic interpretation, the data-to-value pipeline (Sect. 2.1), and the business model archetype framework (Sect. 2.2).

2.1 The PdM Data-to-Value Pipeline

The literature converges on a five-stage operational architecture for this transformation, together with feedback loops that close the pipeline back onto its upstream stages. The pipeline originates at the asset layer, where instrumentation captures operational signals that proxy for equipment health (**Stage 1**). Typical monitored parameters with the choice and density of instrumentation determining the upper bound on what subsequent stages can infer [5,8,29]. Two acquisition strategies coexist in practice. The first equips new equipment with PdM-ready sensing at the design stage [5,30], and the second retrofits installed assets that were not originally instrumented for condition monitoring [4,29]. Acquired data must be moved from the asset to the location at which it is processed (**Stage 2**). Cloud-based transmission centralizes raw or pre-aggregated data in remote storage and computation infrastructure, optimizing for analytical depth and cross-asset learning at the cost of bandwidth and latency [6,31,32]. Edge processing performs analytic operations at or near the asset itself, focusing on minimizing latency, bandwidth efficiency, and operational continuity under intermittent connectivity [4,33]. Hybrid architectures combine the two, performing time-sensitive inference at the edge and aggregate analysis in the cloud [6,7,34]. **Stage 3** converts curated data into operational intelligence. The literature distinguishes a maturity gradient running from descriptive monitoring (e.g., raw data visualization and threshold alarms) through diagnostic analysis (e.g., anomaly detection, root-cause inference) and predictive modeling (e.g., failure-time or remaining-useful-life forecasts) toward prescriptive systems that recommend or automate the next action [3,8,9,35]. Generated intelligence creates value only when it reaches the actor. **Stage 4** covers the channel and the cognitive interface through which insights are delivered. Dashboards designed for operations teams, alerting systems for maintenance schedulers, work-order integration into computerized maintenance management systems (CMMS) or enterprise resource planning (ERP) systems, mobile notifications for field technicians, and innovative approaches like augmented-reality overlays for on-site repair guidance are commonly utilized [31,36–38]. The terminal stage converts delivered insight into economic value, with two principal pathways (**Stage 5**). Internal monetization (utilization) captures value within the operating organization through cost reductions, energy savings, lifetime extension of capital assets, or risk reduction [34,39]. External monetization converts data and insights into offerings sold to third parties, typically through PMaaS subscriptions, joint offerings within asset-performance-management networks, or data products consumed by complementary actors such as insurers, lenders, or fleet operators [20,21,40,41]. Furthermore, two feedback loops are documented, as the pipeline is not unidirectional. Failure events observed downstream are labeled and used to retrain upstream analytics models, with the result that prediction quality improves as the installed base grows (**Model Refinement**) [8,42,43]. In addition, insights derived downstream redirect upstream data strategy. For instance, the discovery that a particular sensor signature predicts a class of failures motivates retrofitting of additional instrumentation across the fleet (**Data Strategy Redesign**) [36,44].

2.2 Business Model Archetypes

The pipeline serves as the operational backbone of PdM, while the business model framework represents the commercial superstructure constructed upon it. This framework is configurational, as it delineates a limited number of dimensions along which providers make significant design choices, treating each combination of these choices as a potential archetype. The most-cited **classification of PdM providers** identifies six archetypes [15]. The archetypes differ in the layers of the information stack the provider operates on, the deployment channels the provider uses, and the payment models the provider employs. Hardware development providers manufacture the sensors, gateways, and physical instrumentation required for Stage 1 data acquisition. Their revenue is dominantly transactional, one-time sales, and their deployment channel is physical [4,15]. Software and analytics providers specialize in the algorithms that execute Stages 3 and 4, typically deployed via cloud platforms with subscription or project-based payment [8,15,23]. Consulting providers operate without proprietary technology, instead advising on PdM design, integration, and process change. Their revenue is project-based, and their deployment is on-site [15,24]. Platform providers combine cloud-based application platforms with forecasting capabilities and integration services, typically employing hybrid time-based and usage-based payment models and serving manufacturing customers [7,15,45,46]. Information managers function at the data-handling and infrastructure levels, thereby establishing the foundational layer upon which other stakeholders can develop PdM offerings. Their role is more that of facilitators of the ecosystem than of direct providers of customer-facing solutions. [15,47]. All-in-one providers span the full stack, typically with hybrid payment models and both physical and cloud deployment channels [5,15,27,38]. The **delivery-side typology** integrates partially overlapping servitization pathways describing governance of the data-to-value chain [17], commercialization strategies describing how PdM is bundled with existing offerings [28], and market-mechanism archetypes describing the commercial framework through which PdM is delivered [16,19,40]. In summary, Product-attached PdM serves as a supplement to an existing equipment transaction. The provider (e.g., an OEM) offers condition monitoring or failure forecasting as an add-on to machinery sales, either cloud-hosted alongside the product or installed locally alongside retrofit sensing [11,28,39]. Standalone PMaaS delivers PdM as an independent cloud-based service decoupled from any specific equipment transaction. The provider, typically a specialist analytics firm, offers standardized, modular PdM capabilities that customers can adopt without the in-house expertise required to build them themselves [20,40,48]. Outcome-based availability service shifts the contractual object from PdM itself to a guaranteed performance level. The provider commits to a specified asset availability or output level and internalizes the maintenance risk of meeting it [16,19,41]. Usage-embedded PdM integrates PdM into pay-per-use or equipment-as-a-service offerings, in which the consumption signal also drives the maintenance schedule and commercial billing simultaneously [21,39]. Platform orchestration refers to configurations in which the provider operates a multi-actor platform that coordinates ecosystem contributions from third-party application developers, integrators, and sensor vendors into a coherent offering [7,45,46]. **Revenue models** in PdM are typically categorized into five non-exclusive types, one-time sales, time-based subscriptions, project-based fees, usage-based payments, and explicit hybrids combining two or more of the above [15,21]. The framework identifies primary technology clusters that constitute the necessary infrastructure for PdM business models. IoT and sensor systems enable Stage 1 acquisition and are the most frequently cited enabling technology in the literature [5,32,49]. Cloud and edge computing support Stages 2 and 3 and define the trade-off space between latency, bandwidth, and analytical depth [4,6,31]. Machine learning and artificial intelligence operate primarily at Stage 3 and have moved from research demonstration to deployment over the past decade [8,10,23,30,50]. Digital-twin technology supports Stages 3 and 4 by providing system-level models against which observed data can be interpreted, although the gap between conceptual prominence and empirical deployment is wider for digital twins than for the other three clusters [43,51]. A frequently underexamined infrastructure layer is the data-integration middleware that connects heterogeneous equipment, sensors, and enterprise systems into a unified analytical platform [7,24,28].

3 Methodology

The research design is a case-survey or multiple-case analysis [52–54] in which a set of business cases is examined through a shared analytical lens to generate generalizable inferences. Compared to an in-depth single-case study [53,55], the case-survey design trades depth for breadth and is therefore appropriate when the research question concerns the distribution of configurational choices across a population of empirical instances rather than the dynamics of any single deployment [52]. The design has been applied to business model research previously [56,57]. The corpus consists of 116 case descriptions published on a German-language industrial services portal that aggregates PdM, condition monitoring, and adjacent maintenance digitalization deployments from German, Austrian, and Swiss industrial firms[1]. Cases are written predominantly from the perspective of the solution providers and follow a loose template. Corpus-level limitations

[1] https://iotusecase.com.

at the outset have to be acknowledged, consistent with the case-survey literature [52]. Cases describing failed deployments or unfavorable outcomes are systematically absent [23,54]. Therefore, the analysis is best understood as a taxonomy validation on a vendor-sourced corpus rather than as an outcome evaluation. Further, the corpus is geographically and linguistically bounded to the DACH region, which is a strong PdM market [16,24] but is not representative of the global distribution of PdM business models. The coding scheme was developed through a hybrid deductive-inductive approach [58,59]. Deductive codes were seeded from the framework dimensions summarized in Sect. 2, business model archetypes, and the pipeline-stage dimensions [4,6,15–17]. Inductive codes were admitted for themes the framework did not anticipate. These were captured initially as free-text residuals and reviewed for promotion to dimensional codes after the pilot phase of 20 cases [60,61]. The codebook was iteratively refined following the cycle recommended for case-survey work [52]. The final coding scheme spans approximately twenty-five dimensions across record metadata, scoping flags, provider- and delivery-side dimensions, value-side dimensions (value proposition, monetization pathway, outcome metrics, sustainability claim), pipeline dimensions mapped one-to-one to the five framework stages, enabling-technology dimensions, and implementation-context dimensions [59]. For each non-trivial categorical decision, a verbatim quotation from the case text is retained, as this is a standard auditability device in qualitative content analysis [60–62] and supports the post-hoc verification described.

The descriptive analysis begins with a frequency analysis of each categorical dimension to identify the distribution of values within the corpus. Further, cross-tabulation was applied to selected dimension pairs to surface joint distributions and configurational asymmetries [63,64]. Finally, a graphical visualization of the configurational space was constructed using parallel sets diagrams [65], displaying flows across multiple ordinal or nominal dimensions simultaneously. The clustering procedure aims to derive empirical archetypes, recurrent configurational patterns observed from the per-case coded matrix [63,64,66]. The clustering is applied along the five configurational dimensions most central to the framework. Because all five dimensions are categorical, distance metrics and clustering algorithms developed for numerical data are not directly applicable [67,68]. Therefore, K-modes clustering is used [67], which generalizes the K-means algorithm to categorical data by replacing the Euclidean distance with a simple-matching dissimilarity measure (Hamming distance) and the cluster centroid with the cluster mode. Furthermore, Ward linkage is utilized on a representation of the categorical data, which approximates a Euclidean treatment [69]. The number of clusters was selected through the elbow heuristic [70], the average silhouette coefficient [71] computed with the Hamming metric, which provides a model-selection signal for categorical clustering [72], and the interpretability of the cluster profiles [64,66]. Cluster labels were assigned through a staged process consistent with established typology-development guidance [59,63,66].

4 Case Study Analysis

4.1 Exploratory Analysis

This section reports descriptive findings on the 116 coded cases prior to the cluster-analytic interpretation. Figure 1 arranges the five business model dimensions of the framework as parallel categorical axes connected by bands proportional to case counts [65]. The diagram reads from left to right as a configurational pathway through the design space proposed by the framework [15–17], and the color anchor on the leftmost axis allows tracking the share of analytically advanced cases through subsequent dimensions. The configurational diagram reveals several patterns consistent with conjectures in the prior literature. The All-in-One provider category dominates the corpus (49%), with platform providers and hardware-development providers occupying the second and third positions, respectively. The consulting category, which the literature has long flagged as an unstable middle position [11,12], is represented by only three cases. Less expected is the empirical absence of the Information Manager archetype from the cluster of cases, although the archetype is theoretically articulated in the framework and adjacent IoT-business model work [15,45,47]. On the delivery side, the dominance of Product-Attached configurations and Standalone PMaaS configurations reproduces the pattern documented in earlier industrial-services research [16,20,39,40]. The flow from delivery to revenue model shows that subscription pricing dominates among Standalone PMaaS and Platform Orchestration cases, whereas Product-Attached configurations split roughly evenly. Value capture in turn concentrates at the platform and acquisition layers.

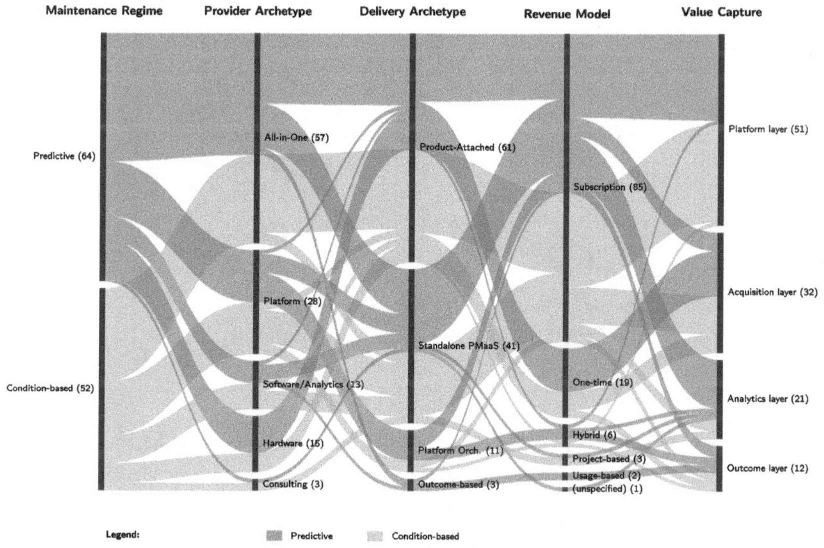

Fig. 1. Overview of the Descriptive Results on Business Model Archetypes.

In Fig. 2, the five pipeline-stage dimensions of the framework are presented as connected axes, with bands colored by the maturity of deployed analytics. In combination with the business model diagram, this view describes the operational substrate underneath the commercial configurations. The presence of two coexisting data acquisition strategies, factory instrumentation for new equipment and retrofit instrumentation for installed assets, is consistent with the dual-strategy account given in the technical literature [4,5,29,30]. Further, the layout shows that the hybrid-edge-cloud architecture is overrepresented among predictive-mechanism cases relative to its share of the corpus, while pure cloud is more strongly associated with diagnostic and descriptive maturity, a pattern that mirrors the architectural trade-off literature [4,6,31,34]. While analytics maturity, insight delivery, and monetization stages are consistent with literature, the color-grouped stacking makes a configurational asymmetry visible that has been hypothesized but seldom quantified in the literature [34,39]. Predictive-mechanism cases are overrepresented in external-service monetization, whereas diagnostic-mechanism cases are more evenly distributed between internal and external monetization pathways. The implication, consistent with arguments in the servitization literature [11,12,16], is that the commercial externalization of PdM intelligence into a service offering is more strongly enabled by the depth of the analytics layer than by the choice of acquisition strategy or transmission architecture.

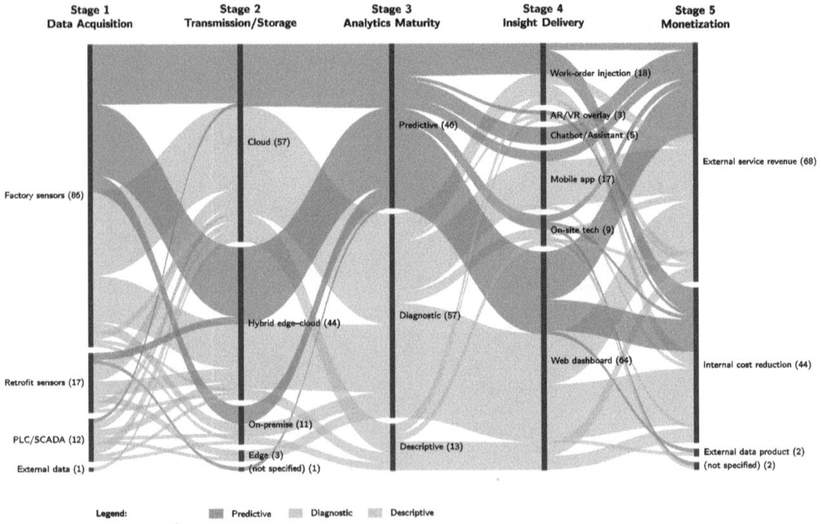

Fig. 2. Overview of the Descriptive Results on PdM Data-to-Value Pipeline.

The enabling-technology distribution closely follows the clusters identified in the framework synthesis [8,15,36,43] but reveals important asymmetries. IoT and sensor infrastructure are near-universal across the corpus (96.6%), confirming its status as the necessary foundation of PdM business models [32,36,49].

Cloud computing appears in 84.5% of cases and edge computing in 30.2%, with the relative weights consistent with the trade-off discussion in the architectural literature [4,6,7,31]. Machine learning and artificial intelligence are reported in only 33.6% of cases overall, which is notably lower than the share of cases that invoke PdM in their marketing language and is therefore one of the empirical anchors of the marketing-versus-mechanism gap. Data-integration middleware is reported in 44.8% of cases, which is below the share that the conceptual literature treats as foundational [7,24,28], and consistent with the observation that data-integration infrastructure is often present but undocumented in case narratives focused on customer-facing functionality [7,42]. Therefore, the overall enabling-technology distribution is characterized by a stable hardware-and-cloud foundation present in nearly all cases, a substantial but heterogeneously deployed analytics layer that strongly differentiates the strict-PdM subset, and a long tail of higher-maturity technologies whose rhetorical visibility far exceeds their empirical deployment.

Implementation barriers are reported less frequently than anticipated by the prevailing academic literature. This observation aligns with the vendor-curation bias identified in case narratives authored from the perspective of solution providers [23,54]. Approximately a quarter of the corpus (26.7%) reports no barriers, which is notable given the widely recognized complexities associated with industrial PdM deployments [7,24,28]. Among the reported barriers, integration with legacy systems is the most frequent concern (28.4%). This pattern aligns with the identification of legacy heterogeneity as the principal obstacle to industrial-IoT diffusion [7,27,28,38]. Data quality and data volume issues are mentioned in 23.3% of cases [5,8,23,42], and data-standards interoperability concerns appear in 20.7%, reflecting the recurring observation that industrial-protocol heterogeneity remains a constraint despite the availability of OPC UA, MQTT and related standards [7,31,45]. A skills gap is reported in 12.9% of cases, a share that under-represents the magnitude of the workforce concern [9,11,24,73], and security and privacy barriers appear in 9.5% of cases, concentrated in deployments touching critical infrastructure [6,32,33]. Further, the academic literature on PdM adoption identifies difficulty in cost justification as a substantial constraint on uptake [23,27,74,75]. Its near-absence from the case narratives is a clear indication of the vendor-curation bias and should not be read as evidence that PdM adoption decisions are commercially uncontested in the broader market.

4.2 Cluster Analysis

The cluster analysis is designed to derive empirical archetypes [63,64,66] from the per-case coded matrix. The first archetype recovered from clustering scopes is the **Smart Component Vendor**. This archetype is the most cleanly delineated. Every case in the cluster is configured as a hardware-development provider, delivers PdM as a product-attached service, embeds pricing in the equipment capital expenditure, and captures value at the acquisition layer of the pipeline. The deployed mechanisms are predominantly predictive, with a minority using descriptive instrumentation, consistent with the documented evolution of smart-component offerings from straightforward sensing toward embedded analytics [4,5,8,23]. The second archetype is the **Standalone PMaaS Analytics Service**. The cluster represents the empirical realization of the standalone-service-delivery archetype [16,20,40,48]. Cases in the cluster are typically delivered as cloud-based subscription services in which, predominantly predictive, the analytics layer is the locus of value capture. The revenue model is time-based, with pricing per monitored asset, while provider configurations within the cluster are mixed [15,23,50]. The third archetype is the **Bundled CapEx Solution (Diagnostic)** , which is the single largest cluster in the corpus and represents the configurational space in which all-in-one providers deliver an integrated maintenance-digitalization solution as part of a capital purchase, and value capture at the acquisition layer of the equipment transaction. The cluster is predominantly characterized by diagnostic-mechanism cases, reflecting the broad installed base of condition-monitoring deployments that operate at threshold-based or rule-based maturity without reaching the predictive level [23,24,28]. The fourth archetype is the **Predictive Integrated Solution Bundle**. The cluster is structurally similar to the Bundled CapEx Solution cluster but is differentiated by the deployed mechanism and by the value-capture locus. The revenue model is uniformly time-based, suggesting that the analytics extension to a product-attached integration carries a subscription overlay onto the original capital purchase [15,21,34]. The fifth archetype is the **Industrial IoT Platform Orchestrator** that comprises platform-provider cases delivering PdM through a platform-orchestration configuration or through a standalone-service configuration anchored on a platform [7,15,45]. Value capture is located in the platform layer, the predictive mechanism, and time-based subscription revenue. The sixth archetype is the **Platform/PMaaS Service (Diagnostic)**. This is the diagnostic-mechanism counterpart to the previous two predictive archetypes and represents the case configurations that are not identified as Industrial IoT Platform Orchestrator at the strict-PdM scope. The cluster represents the lower-maturity stratum of the platform/PMaaS service market, in which the commercial form mirrors the higher-maturity Industrial IoT Platform Orchestrator archetype, but the analytics layer has not yet been instantiated at predictive depth [23,24,42]. The seventh and smallest archetype is the **Outcome-Oriented Service Provider**. The cluster comprises all-in-one provider cases in which value capture sits at the outcome layer of the pipeline. Two cases are delivered as outcome-based availability services [16,19,41], and two are delivered as product-attached configurations in which the commercial logic is anchored to a guaranteed outcome rather than to the equipment transaction itself. Revenue models include usage-based and time-based pricing in equal proportion. The empirical scarcity of the cluster reproduces the longstanding observation that outcome-based business models are extensively discussed in the conceptual literature but rarely instantiated in the documented case base [16,23,41,57]. The seven-cluster typology delineates the dimensions of the design space empirically represented in vendor-published case studies. Furthermore, through negative inference, it highlights the cells that, while conceptually coherent within the established framework, are conspicuously absent from the documented case base (Table 1).

Table 1. Overview of the Empirical Archetypes from the Cluster Analysis

Cluster	n	PdM	Provider	Delivery	Value capture	Mechanism	Revenue (dom.)
Smart Component Vendor	12	75%	hardware-development (100%)	product-attached (100%)	acquisition (100%)	predictive (58%) descriptive (25%)	one-time (75%)
Standalone PMaaS Analytics Service	26	88%	all-in-one (58%) software/analyt. (23%)	standalone PMaaS (73%)	analytics (69%)	predictive (77%)	time-based (88%)
Bundled CapEx Solution (Diagnostic)	31	23%	all-in-one (84%)	product-attached (100%)	acquisition (65%) platform (19%) outcome (16%)	diagnostic (81%)	time-based (65%) one-time (35%)
Predictive Integrated Solution Bundle	9	67%	all-in-one (78%) software/analyt. (22%)	product-attached (100%)	platform (100%)	predictive (67%) descriptive (33%)	time-based (100%)
Industrial IoT Platform Orchestrator	8	100%	platform-provider (100%)	platform orch. (75%) standalone PMaaS (25%)	platform (88%)	predictive (62%) diagnostic (38%)	time-based (100%)
Platform/PMaaS Service (Diagnostic)	26	0%	platform-prov. (58%) sw/analyt. (19%) all-in-one (19%)	standalone PMaaS (77%)	platform (88%)	diagnostic (77%) descriptive (19%)	time-based (92%)
Outcome-Oriented Service Provider	4	100%	all-in-one (100%)	outcome-based (50%) product-attached (50%)	outcome (75%) platform (25%)	predictive (50%) diagnostic (50%)	usage-based (50%) time-based (50%)

5 Business Model Evolution

Business model evolution has been studied as a distinct theoretical object from business model design over the past two decades [57, 76–78]. The literature converges on the view that the business model of a firm is not a static configuration chosen at founding but a configurational artifact that is reshaped over time through deliberate experimentation, trial-and-error learning, and adaptive response to environmental shifts [79–82]. The strategic question of how a firm transitions from one configuration to another has received less analytical attention in the business model literature than the question of which configurations can be theoretically distinguished. This is partly due to the challenges in specifying evolutionary paths without empirical evidence. [57, 64, 77]. The seven derived empirical archetypes provide substantial evidence for the PdM design space, enabling clear exploration of transition paths within the framework. Each archetype represents a distinct configurational destination that the corpus demonstrates to be empirically occupied. Furthermore, each pair of adjacent archetypes allows for a transition trajectory, the feasibility of which depends on the dimensions along which the two archetypes differ. The following discussion expands on this perspective by interpreting the empirical archetype landscape as a map of viable business model configurations and by pinpointing the structural extension points. The most prominent extension point in the empirical landscape concerns the analytics-maturity dimension of the pipeline. The typology comprises two pairs of structurally adjacent archetypes that differ solely along this dimension. The Bundled CapEx Solution at the diagnostic maturity level and the Predictive Integrated Solution Bundle at the predictive maturity level share the same provider, delivery, and value-capture configurations, with the analytics layer serving as the primary point of distinction. Similarly, the diagnostic-stratum Platform/PMaaS Service and the Industrial IoT Platform Orchestrator occupy a comparable configurational position on the platform side of the framework, differentiated mainly by the depth of their analytics mechanisms. The empirical distribution indicates that the analytics-maturity gradient is the most accessible transition pathway for firms already engaged in an established maintenance-digitalization business model, as the upgrade requires no restructuring of the commercial form, value-capture locus, or customer-segment configuration, but instead focuses on enhancing the analytics layer [8,17,23,44]. Another extension point, structurally orthogonal to the analytics-maturity gradient, concerns the shift from product-attached delivery configurations to standalone service configurations. The empirical landscape distinguishes the Bundled CapEx Solution and the Predictive Integrated Solution Bundle on the product-attached side from the Standalone PMaaS Analytics Service on the service-decoupled side, with the principal structural differences being the delivery archetype, the dominant revenue model, and the value-capture locus. The transition from product-attached to standalone PMaaS corresponds to the servitization pathway that has been identified as the dominant strategic move in industrial-equipment markets [83–86]. The transition is structurally more demanding than the analytics-maturity extension because it requires not only the deepening of the analytics layer but also the decoupling of the commercial transaction from the physical equipment, the development of a per-asset-monitored pricing infrastructure, the construction of a customer-relationship governance model suited to recurring rather than transactional engagements, and a reorientation of revenue recognition and channel architecture [85,87,88]. Further, a transition opportunity connects the Standalone PMaaS Analytics Service to the Industrial IoT Platform Orchestrator. The two archetypes share the time-based revenue model and the subscription pricing basis, but differ in the delivery archetype and in the breadth of the value-network governance the provider undertakes. The transition involves the extension of a single-provider service offering into a multi-actor platform that admits third-party application developers, integrators, and component vendors, and is therefore structurally equivalent to the platform-ecosystem move that platform-economics and industrial-platforms identify as a distinctive strategic decision rather than an extension of an existing service offering [7,30,41,45,46]. An alternative structure extension concerns the shift from any predominantly transactional or subscription configuration to the Outcome-Oriented Service Provider configuration. The empirical scarcity of the outcome-oriented cluster and the longstanding observation in the literature that outcome-based business models are extensively conceptualized but rarely instantiated [16,19,23,41,57] jointly indicate that this transition is the most demanding of the extension paths the empirical landscape admits. The structural requirements include not only the analytics-maturity depth necessary to predict failures with sufficient reliability to underwrite an availability guarantee. It also demands the contractual infrastructure required to attribute outcomes to provider action, the financial capacity to internalize the maintenance risk that the customer transfers to the provider, and frequently an insurance or risk-sharing arrangement with a third party to absorb tail outcomes [16,21,41]. In addition, distinctively visible in the empirical landscape but undertheorized in the conceptual models, an extension is related to the trajectory of the Smart Component Vendor archetype. The cluster is delimited and strongly characterized by a one-time revenue model and capex-embedded pricing. The knowledge base on smart-product development and industrial servitization describes a strategic temptation for component vendors to extend their embedded-intelligence offerings into either a recurring data-service offering or participation in a downstream platform ecosystem [11,12,42,85]. Another extension point operates along the monetization axis of the data-to-value pipeline. The trajectory concerns the move by which a firm first develops a maintenance-digitalization capability for the internal optimization of its own operations and subsequently externalizes that capability as a productized offering to third-party customers. The Stage-5 distinction between internal monetization (e.g., cost reduction of internal processes) and external monetization (e.g., revenue generated by selling data or insights) is treated in the framework as a primary axis of the pipeline [23,27,34]. The pivot is structurally distinct from the analytics maturity and the servitization extension because it preserves the archetype identity while transforming the revenue source. An additional extension option operates at the level of multi-actor value-network composition, in which the configurational identity of an offering is jointly produced by a coalition of firms rather than by any one of them in isolation. The findings on asset-performance-management offerings, industrial ecosystems, and platform value-networks identify joint configurations of this kind as a distinctive empirical category that the conventional provider-by-delivery cross-classification undercaptures [7,41,89–91].

The extension points described above identify a set of feasible transition trajectories that the empirical archetype landscape admits and a set of trajectories that the design space describes as conceptually well-formed (see Fig. 3). The analytics-maturity extension and the servitization extension are the two most well-researched transition paths. These paths are structurally less demanding than platform-orchestration and outcome-oriented extensions and allow for incremental staging through pilot deployments and the accumulation of capabilities, which dynamic-capability research identifies as the primary mechanism for successfully changing business models [80,81,87,92,93].

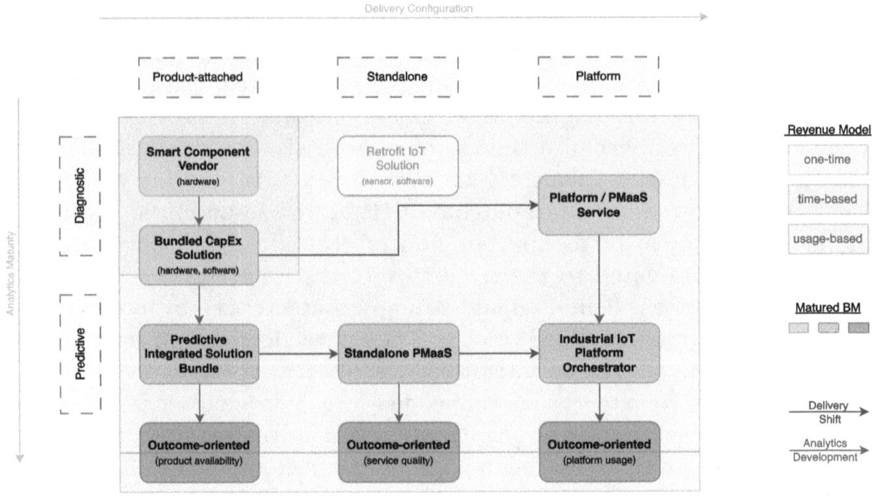

Fig. 3. Overview of configuration and extension points in PdM business models.

6 Discussion

The study set out to test the configurational predictions of an integrative framework for PdM business models [15,18] against an empirical case base drawn from a German-language industrial services portal. It turns out that the empirical configurational landscape is materially sparser than the combinatorial space suggests. Only seven cells of the theoretical design space are robustly populated and display configurational coherence. The Information Manager provider archetype is empirically absent from the corpus despite its inclusion in the most-cited vendor-sample taxonomy [15], and the Usage-Embedded delivery archetype is empirically absent despite extensive conceptual treatment in the work on usage-focused business models [16,39]. A substantive finding is the documented gap between the analytics maturity providers market, as described in their narratives, and the analytics mechanisms the cases actually deploy. In summary, the findings carry several practical implications for the actors operating in the PdM market. For solution providers, the seven empirical archetypes constitute a map of destination configurations toward which transformation can be plausibly directed, and the extension points identify the transition pathways that the empirical landscape and the broader community jointly suggest are most feasible from a given starting position [11,12,77,80,81]. The study is bounded by limitations that condition the interpretation of its findings. The corpus consists of vendor-curated case narratives, and the systematic absence of failure cases, customer-perspective accounts, and contractually sensitive material from such corpora is a well-documented property of the source type [23,52,54]. The findings open several directions for future research. The most consequential is a longitudinal extension of the case-survey design that would directly observe archetype transitions over time, identify the triggers and enablers of transitions, and distinguish successful from unsuccessful transitions in the manner the dynamic-capability and business model evolution research have argued is necessary for substantive theoretical progress [76,80,81,92,93]. The empirical evidence developed in this study repositions the conceptual framework from a normative articulation of the theoretically distinguishable configurations in the PdM business model design space toward a corpus-grounded characterization of which configurations are commercially populated and which extension paths between them appear empirically tractable.

References

1. Wang, Y., Wu, M., Li, X., Xie, L., Chen, Z.: A survey on graph neural networks for remaining useful life prediction: methodologies, evaluation and future trends. Mech. Syst. Signal Process. **229** (2025)
2. March, S.T., Scudder, G.D.: Predictive maintenance: strategic use of IT in manufacturing organizations. Inf. Syst. Front. **21**(2), 327–341 (2019)
3. Gautam, S., Noureddine, R., Solvang, W.D.: Machine learning and IIoT application for predictive maintenance. Lect. Notes Electr. Eng. **994**, 257–265 (2023)
4. Mangels, T., Murarasu, A., Oden, F., Fishkin, A., Becker, D.: Efficient analysis at edge. In: ICPE 2017 - Companion of the 2017 ACM/SPEC International Conference on Performance Engineering, pp. 85–90. ACM (2017)
5. Hoffmann, M.W., et al.: Integration of novel sensors and machine learning for predictive maintenance in medium voltage switchgear to enable the energy and mobility revolutions. Sensors (Switzerland) **20**(7) (2020)
6. Wang, J., Zhang, L., Duan, L., Gao, R.X.: A new paradigm of cloud-based predictive maintenance for intelligent manufacturing. J. Intell. Manuf. **28**(5), 1125–1137 (2017)
7. Donnelly, J., et al.: Enabling the smart factory – a digital platform concept for standardized data integration. In: Proceedings of the Conference on Production Systems and Logistics, TIB, pp. 234–243 (2021)
8. Bott, A., Liu, B., Puchta, A., Fleischer, J.: Machine learning-driven rul prediction and uncertainty quantification for ball screw drives in a cloud-ready maintenance framework. J. Mach. Eng. **24**(3), 17–31 (2024)
9. Espina-Romero, L., et al.: Challenges and opportunities in the implementation of AI in manufacturing: a bibliometric analysis. Science **6**(4) (2024)
10. Franki, V., Majnarić, D., Višković, A.: A comprehensive review of artificial intelligence (AI) companies in the power sector. Energies **16**(3) (2023)
11. Tewari, A.: Servitization in the Era of Industry 4.0 – a realist review to identify enablers of servitization for business-to-business models in the manufacturing industry globally (2020)
12. Bartwal, S., Kumar, R.: Servitization 4.0 for circular economy: a review study of use cases for resource-wise manufacturing. Int. J. Adv. Manuf. Technol. (2025)
13. Haertel, C., et al.: Methodological case study approach for detecting business model enablers in copycat ventures. Int. J. Organ. Collect. Intell. (IJOCI) **11**(4), 35–54 (2021)

14. Pohl, M., Haertel, C., Turowski, K.: Value creation from data science applications- a literature review. In: International Conference on Business Informatics Research, pp. 327–338. Springer, Heidelberg (2023). https://doi.org/10.1007/978-3-031-43126-5_23
15. Passlick, J., Dreyer, S., Olivotti, D., Grützner, L., Eilers, D., Breitner, M.H.: Predictive maintenance as an internet of things enabled business model: a taxonomy. Electron. Mark. **31**(1), 67–87 (2021)
16. Olivotti, D., Dreyer, S., Kölsch, P., Herder, C., Breitner, M., Aurich, J.: Realizing availability-oriented business models in the capital goods industry. Procedia CIRP **73**, 297–303 (2018)
17. Li, J., Milisavljevic-Syed, J., Salonitis, K.: Predictive maintenance servitisation pathways. IFAC-PapersOnLine. Number **8**, 329–334 (2024)
18. Pohl, M., Haertel, C., Staegemann, D., Turowski, K.: The business model landscape of predictive maintenance scenarios. In: International Conference on Smart Business Technologies. Springer, Heidelberg (2026)
19. Paaranan, S., Andrej, K., Jorg, S.: Technical realisation of availability-oriented business models for potato harvesters by using aMR sensors. In: Proceedings of IEEE Sensors, Institute of Electrical and Electronics Engineers Inc. (2018)
20. Chit, T.W., Toro, C., Lim, H.C., Muthu, R.: Scalable remote cloud data center for vessel equipment predictive maintenance service-as-a-product (SaaP). Procedia Comput. Sci. **225**, 2826–2834 (2023)
21. Lehmann, B., Jacobs, G., Habermehl, C., Gentz, C., Neumann, S.: Using Data from Agricultural and Construction Machinery profitably: Analysis of Current Monetisation Mechanisms and Recommendations for the Future. Springer, Heidelberg (2023). https://doi.org/10.1007/978-3-662-66509-1_25
22. Osako, L.F., Matsubayashi, M.O., Takey, S.M., Cauchick-Miguel, P.A., Zancul, E.: Cost evaluation challenges for Internet of Things (IoT) based Product/Service-Systems (PSS). Procedia CIRP **84**, 302–306 (2019)
23. Cassoli, B.B., Hoffmann, F., Metternich, J.: Comparison of AI-based business models in manufacturing: case studies on predictive maintenance. In: Proceedings of the Conference on Production Systems and Logistics, TIB, pp. 637–647 (2021)
24. Olivan, P., Hutschek, U., Rummel, S.: Predictive Maintenance - Voraussetzungen und Potenziale Richtlinien für die Industriepraxis, um den technologischen Ansatz und das übergeordnete Geschäftsmodell zu bestimmen. ZWF Zeitschrift fuer Wirtschaftlichen Fabrikbetrieb **116**(10), 667–672 (2021)
25. Basingab, M., Rose, C., Rabelo, L., Gutiérrez, E., Nagadi, K., Jung, W.I.: Business modeling based on internet of things: a case study of predictive maintenance software using ABS model. In: ACM ICPS. ACM (2017)
26. Arnold, C., Kiel, D., Voigt, K.I.: Innovative business models for the industrial internet of things. Berg Huettenmaenn Monatsh (2017)
27. Bock, M., Wiener, M., Gronau, R., Martin, A.: Industry 4.0 enabling smart air: digital transformation at kaeser compressors. In: Management for Professionals Part F518, pp. 101–117 (2019)
28. Burggräf, P., et al.: Adaptive remanufacturing for lifecycle optimization of connected production resources - a literature review. Procedia CIRP **90**, 61–66 (2020)
29. Lüttenberg, H., Bartelheimer, C., Beverungen, D.: Designing predictive maintenance for agricultural machines. In: 26th ECIS, AIS (2018)
30. Cui, J., Wan, Q., Shin, S.: Human-AI integration and sound-vibration technology-driven enterprise digital transformation: the mediating role of technological innovation. Sound Vib. **59**(1) (2025)

31. Brandtner, P., Mayrboeck, R., Zimmermann, R.: Data-driven digital services in the automotive industry: implementation in practice, success factors, and future potential. In: Proceedings of the 13th International Conference on E-Business, Management and Economics, pp. 185–191. ACM, New York (2022)
32. Gupta, S.K., Yadav, S.K., Soni, S.K.: Exploring the power of big data for IoT: a comprehensive review. In: ICICAT. IEEE Inc. (2023)
33. Berge, J.: Digital transformation and IIoT for Oil and gas production. In: Proceedings of the Annual Offshore Technology Conference, Offshore Technology Conference, pp. 1204–1213 (2018)
34. Berndt, S., Geismar, L.: Erfolgsgrößen datengetriebener geschäftsmodelle - wie sich datengetriebene geschäftsmodelle in der produzierenden industrie erfolgsgetrieben steuern lassen. ZWF Zeitschrift fuer Wirtschaftlichen Fabrikbetrieb **116**(5), 289–293 (2021)
35. Rahman, H., D'Cruze, R.S., Ahmed, M.U., Sohlberg, R., Sakao, T., Funk, P.: Artificial intelligence-based life cycle engineering in industrial production: a systematic literature review. IEEE ACCESS **10**, 133001–133015 (2022)
36. Hoffmann, F., Brockhaus, B., Metternich, J., Weigold, M.: Predictive maintenance for protective covers – from business model to application; [Vom geschäftsmodell zur anwendung predictive maintenance für schutzabdeckungen]. WT Werkstattstechnik **110**(7–8), 496–500 (2020)
37. Tsakalerou, M., Nurmaganbetov, D., Beltenov, N.: Aircraft maintenance 4.0 in an era of disruptions. Procedia Comput. Sci.**200**, 121–131 (2022)
38. Slama, D.: Predictive Maintenance for Hydraulic Components. Springer, Heidelberg (2023)
39. Bressanelli, G., Adrodegari, F., Perona, M., Saccani, N.: Exploring how usage-focused business models enable circular economy through digital technologies. Sustainability (Switzerland) **10**(3) (2018)
40. Zoll, M., Jack, D., Vogt, M.W.: Evaluation of predictive-maintenance-as-a-service business models in the internet of things. In: IEEE ICE/ITMC - Proceedings. IEEE Inc. (2018)
41. Räikkönen, M., Saari, L., Valkokari, K., Rantala, A., Kortelainen, H.: Creating value and business benefits from joint offerings of asset performance management tools in the capital-intensive industries. In: Lecture Notes in Mechanical Engineering, pp. 126–136 (2022)
42. Wiesner, S., Egbert, L., Zitnikov, A.: Using operational data to represent machine components health and derive data-driven services. In: IFIP Advances in Information and Communication Technology, vol. 664, pp. 294–301 (2022)
43. Rosen, K.M., Pattipati, K.R.: Operating Digital Twins Within an Enterprise Process, vol. 2. Springer, Heidelberg (2023)
44. McLoughlin, S., Puvvala, A., Connolly, N., Maccani, G., Donnellan, B.: Embedding service logic into business model design: the case of predictive maintenance for industry 4.0. In: International Conference on Information Systems, ICIS 2022. Association for Information Systems (2022)
45. Nast, B., Sandkuhl, K.: Meta-model and tool support for the organizational aspects of internet-of-things development methods: organizational aspects of IoT development methods. In: Proceedings of the 3rd AISS. ACM, New York (2022)
46. Zeydan, E., Blanco, L., Barrachina-Munoz, S., Rezazadeh, F., Vettori, L., Mangues, J.: A Marketplace solution for distributed network management and orchestration of slices. In: 19th CNSM. IEEE Inc. (2023)
47. Gupta, T., Verma, R., Dhanda, N.: Applications of Internet of Things (IoT) Technologies in the Fields of Business and Healthcare. CRC Press, Boca Raton (2024)

48. Parker, K.: SaaS will revolutionize predictive maintenance in motor-driven systems. Plant Eng. (2020)
49. Basingab, M.: Investigating the adoption of Internet of Things technology using agent-based simulation. In: Proceedings of the International Conference on Industrial Engineering and Operations Management. IEOM Society (2019)
50. Kolhe, K., Somatkar, A.A., Bhandarkar, M.S., Kotangale, K.B., Ayane, S.S., Shirke, S.I.: Applications and challenges of machine learning techniques for smart manufacturing in industry 4.0. In: 7th ICCUBEA. IEEE Inc. (2023)
51. Shi, T., Ompusunggu, A.P.: Shaping extended product design and development with predictive maintenance capability for digital servitisation. Procedia CIRP **128**, 716–721 (2024)
52. Larsson, R.: Case survey methodology: quantitative analysis of patterns across case studies. Acad. Manag. J. **36**(6), 1515–1546 (1993)
53. Yin, R.K.: Case Study Research and Applications, vol. 6. Sage, Thousand Oaks (2018)
54. Eisenhardt, K.M., Graebner, M.E.: Theory building from cases: opportunities and challenges. Acad. Manag. J. **50**(1), 25–32 (2007)
55. Eisenhardt, K.M.: Building theories from case study research. Acad. Manag. Rev. **14**(4), 532–550 (1989)
56. Lambert, S.: The importance of classification to business model research. J. Bus. Models **3**(1) (2015)
57. Massa, L., Tucci, C.L., Afuah, A.: A critical assessment of business model research. Acad. Manag. Ann. **11**(1), 73–104 (2017)
58. Fereday, J., Muir-Cochrane, E.: Demonstrating rigor using thematic analysis: a hybrid approach of inductive and deductive coding and theme development. Int J Qual Methods **5**(1), 80–92 (2006)
59. Hsieh, H.F., Shannon, S.E.: Three approaches to qualitative content analysis. Qual. Health Res. **15**(9), 1277–1288 (2005)
60. Saldaña, J.: The coding manual for qualitative researchers (2021)
61. Mayring, P.: Qualitative content analysis: theoretical foundation, basic procedures and software solution, (2014)
62. Krippendorff, K.: Content Analysis: An Introduction to its Methodology. Sage Publications, Thousands Oaks (2018)
63. Bailey, K.D.: Typologies and Taxonomies: An Introduction to Classification Techniques, vol. 12. Sage, Thousands Oaks (1994)
64. Doty, D.H., Glick, W.H.: Typologies as a unique form of theory building: toward improved understanding and modeling. Acad. Manag. Rev. **19**(2), 230–251 (1994)
65. Bendix, F., Kosara, R., Hauser, H.: Parallel sets: visual analysis of categorical data. In: IEEE Symposium on Information Visualization, 2005. INFOVIS 2005, pp. 133–140. IEEE (2005)
66. Nickerson, R.C., Varshney, U., Muntermann, J.: A method for taxonomy development and its application in information systems. Eur. J. Inf. Syst. **22**(3), 336–359 (2013)
67. Huang, Z.: Extensions to the k-means algorithm for clustering large data sets with categorical values. Data Min. Knowl. Disc. **2**(3), 283–304 (1998)
68. Kaufman, L., Rousseeuw, P.J.: Finding Groups in Data: An Introduction to Cluster Analysis. John Wiley & Sons, Hoboken (2009)
69. Ward, J.H., Jr.: Hierarchical grouping to optimize an objective function. J. Am. Stat. Assoc. **58**(301), 236–244 (1963)
70. Thorndike, R.L.: Who belongs in the family? Psychometrika **18**(4), 267–276 (1953)

71. Rousseeuw, P.J.: Silhouettes: a graphical aid to the interpretation and validation of cluster analysis. J. Comput. Appl. Math. **20**, 53–65 (1987)
72. Hennig, C.: Cluster-wise assessment of cluster stability. Comput. Stat. Data Anal. **52**(1), 258–271 (2007)
73. Su, Z.: The impact of artificial intelligence on IoT application technology talent demand. In: Proceedings of the 2nd DEAI, pp. 1753–1758. ACM (2025)
74. Omar, Y.M., Minoufekr, M., Plapper, P.: Business analytics in manufacturing: current trends, challenges and pathway to market leadership. Oper. Res. Perspect. **6** (2019)
75. Okokpujie, I.P., Tartibu, L.K.: Study of the economic viability of internet of things (IoTs) in additive and advanced manufacturing: a comprehensive review. Prog. Addit. Manuf. **10**(5), 3175–3194 (2025)
76. Demil, B., Lecocq, X.: Business model evolution: in search of dynamic consistency. Long Range Plan. **43**(2–3), 227–246 (2010)
77. Foss, N.J., Saebi, T.: Fifteen years of research on business model innovation: how far have we come, and where should we go? J. Manag. **43**(1), 200–227 (2017)
78. Cavalcante, S., Kesting, P., Ulhøi, J.: Business model dynamics and innovation:(re) establishing the missing linkages. Manag. Decis. **49**(8), 1327–1342 (2011)
79. Sosna, M., Trevinyo-Rodríguez, R.N., Velamuri, S.R.: Business model innovation through trial-and-error learning: the naturhouse case. Long Range Plan. **43**(2–3), 383–407 (2010)
80. Achtenhagen, L., Melin, L., Naldi, L.: Dynamics of business models-strategizing, critical capabilities and activities for sustained value creation. Long Range Plan. **46**(6), 427–442 (2013)
81. Saebi, T., Lien, L., Foss, N.J.: What drives business model adaptation? The impact of opportunities, threats and strategic orientation. Long Range Plan. **50**(5), 567–581 (2017)
82. McGrath, R.G.: Business models: a discovery driven approach. Long Range Plan. **43**(2–3), 247–261 (2010)
83. Vandermerwe, S., Rada, J.: Servitization of business: adding value by adding services. Eur. Manag. J. **6**(4), 314–324 (1988)
84. Baines, T.S., Lightfoot, H.W., Benedettini, O., Kay, J.M.: The servitization of manufacturing: a review of literature and reflection on future challenges. J. Manuf. Technol. Manag. **20**(5), 547–567 (2009)
85. Kohtamäki, M., Parida, V., Patel, P.C., Gebauer, H.: The relationship between digitalization and servitization: the role of servitization in capturing the financial potential of digitalization. Technol. Forecast. Soc. Chang. **151** (2020)
86. Visnjic, I., Wiengarten, F., Neely, A.: Only the brave: product innovation, service business model innovation, and their impact on performance. J. Prod. Innov. Manag. **33**(1), 36–52 (2016)
87. Kindström, D., Kowalkowski, C., Sandberg, E.: Enabling service innovation: a dynamic capabilities approach. J. Bus. Res. **66**(8) (2013)
88. Storbacka, K.: A solution business model: capabilities and management practices for integrated solutions. Ind. Mark. Manag. **40**(5), 699–711 (2011)
89. Pagani, M.: Digital business strategy and value creation: framing the dynamic cycle of control points1. MIS Q. **37**(2), 617–632 (2013)
90. Adner, R.: Ecosystem as structure: an actionable construct for strategy. J. Manag. **43**(1), 39–58 (2017)

91. Frow, P., Nenonen, S., Payne, A., Storbacka, K.: Managing co-creation design: a strategic approach to innovation. Br. J. Manag. **26**(3) (2015)
92. Teece, D.J., Pisano, G., Shuen, A.: Dynamic capabilities and strategic management. Strateg. Manag. J. **18**(7), 509–533 (1997)
93. Helfat, C.E., Peteraf, M.A.: The dynamic resource-based view: capability lifecycles. Strateg. Manag. J. **24**(10), 997–1010 (2003)

A Meta-model for Integrated Management of Quality and Risk in Organizational Change

Athanasios Tsolakis(✉) and Georgios Koutsopoulos

Department of Computer and Systems Sciences, Stockholm University, Borgarfjordsgatan 12, Kista, 16407 Stockholm, Sweden
tsolakis.thanos@outlook.com, georgios@dsv.su.se

Abstract. Organizational change initiatives often introduce significant uncertainty and operational risk, requiring coordinated governance mechanisms to ensure quality and mitigate emerging threats. In practice, however, Quality Control, Quality Assurance, and Risk Management are frequently implemented as separate organizational practices, resulting in fragmented governance and limited traceability between operational observations and corrective interventions. This paper proposes a meta-model for a method supporting integrated quality and risk governance in organizational change. The meta-model introduces domain control points as a unifying abstraction that embeds governance mechanisms within organizational processes. Control points are triggered by process stages and enable coordinated quality verification, risk evaluation, issue escalation, and corrective action management. The artifact was developed using Design Science Research, with requirements derived from a systematic literature review. The meta-model was evaluated via scenario-based analysis and expert walkthroughs demonstrating both reactive governance responses to quality failures and proactive detection of emerging risks. The results indicate that the proposed approach supports traceable and coordinated governance of organizational change processes.

Keywords: Method · Meta-model · Domain-specific · Quality Assurance · Quality Control · Risk Management · Design Science Research

1 Introduction

Achieving organizational excellence has long depended on the ability to sustain high standards of quality, ensuring that deliverables consistently fulfil stakeholder needs. As industries have advanced technologically, the reliance on systematic methodologies, in particular, Quality Control (QC), Quality Assurance (QA), and Risk Management (RM), has become central to maintaining operational efficacy and competitive advantage. The necessity for these tools is most apparent during periods of organizational change, which often introduce significant variability and uncertainty into established processes [1, 2].

To preserve stability during such transitions, organizations must employ structured approaches that minimize performance fluctuations [3, 4]. In this dynamic landscape, Information Systems (IS) and Information Technology (IT) serve as critical enablers,

E. Laurenzi et al. (Eds.): BIR 2026, LNBIP 601, pp. 413–428, 2027.
https://doi.org/10.1007/978-3-032-38498-0_26

providing the digital infrastructure required for real-time data capture, performance monitoring, and informed strategic decision-making [5, 6].

While the fundamentals of quality management are well-established, maintaining these standards is not a static endeavor. Processes of transformation, ranging from digital shifts to structural reorganizations, introduce layers of complexity and disruption that can undermine an organization's stability. A primary challenge is that current quality and risk tools often operate in functional silos [1, 3, 4]. This fragmentation makes it difficult for organizations to ensure high standards when faced with the rising complexity of modern technologies and market demands [1, 2, 7].

Existing frameworks such as ISO 9001:2015, COSO ERM, and Capability Maturity Model Integration (CMMI) provide valuable but often isolated guidance, failing to fully integrate the domains of QC, QA, and RM into a single, cohesive architecture [1, 2, 8–11]. This gap is particularly significant for the IS field, as the absence of integrated models limits the effectiveness of digital tools in supporting quality governance during change [1, 11–13]. Developing a framework that leverages IS/IT capabilities to monitor performance and assess risks is therefore a strategic necessity for ensuring sustained organizational quality during transformation [6].

Conceptual modeling (CM) approaches provide an opportunity to address this necessity by formalizing governance structures and their relationships to organizational processes. By representing quality and risk constructs within a unified modeling framework, organizations can improve coordination between governance mechanisms and support tool-assisted operationalization of governance practices.

This paper proposes a domain-specific method meta-model for integrated quality and risk governance in organizational change. The meta-model unifies QC, QA, and RM mechanisms through the concept of Domain Control Points, which represent governance mechanisms included within change processes. Control points are triggered by process stages and initiate governance activities such as quality verification, risk assessment, issue escalation, and corrective activities. The meta-model further includes supporting concepts for governance coordination, including issue management, escalation rules, and compliance traceability. The suggested meta-model was developed using a Design Science Research (DSR) approach and evaluated through scenario-based analysis derived from organizational change situations. The evaluation demonstrates how the meta-model supports both reactive governance responses to operational failures and proactive detection of emerging risks.

The aim of this paper is *to propose a meta-model for a domain-specific method, integrating QC, QA, and RM within organizational change processes* via the introduction of Domain Control Points as a unifying abstraction enabling coordinated governance activities across quality and risk domains.

The rest of the paper is structured as follows. Section 2 discusses related work on quality management, risk governance, and CM approaches supporting organizational change. Section 3 presents the research methodology. Sections 4 and 5 introduce the systematically derived requirements and the proposed method meta-model, respectively. Section 6 describes the evaluation scenarios used to assess the artifact and the results of the evaluation. Section 7 discusses implications and limitations, and Sect. 8 provides concluding remarks.

2 Background and Literature Review

2.1 Defining Key Concepts

Quality: Definition, Evolution, and Theoretical Foundations. Quality is a foundational concept in business and manufacturing, ensuring that products and services reliably meet stakeholder expectations [4, 14, 15]. Historically, quality was rooted in artisanal craftsmanship, where individual skill defined the value of goods. The Industrial Revolution necessitated a shift toward systematic QC and mass-production efficiency. In the 20th century, statistical methods and QA processes, such as statistical process control and design of experiments, were introduced to reduce variability and enhance stability [2, 15].

Modern quality management has evolved toward systems thinking, which links design, production, and feedback loops into a holistic framework. Established models like ISO 9001:2015, Total Quality Management (TQM), and CMMI have refined business processes but are often criticised for assuming stable environments and lacking the adaptability required during disruptive change [7, 14, 16]. Today, quality is viewed as a strategic imperative that integrates process optimization with technological advancement and risk governance [6, 12].

RM: Principles, Importance, and Applications. RM emerged as a formal strategic discipline in the late 20th century [5, 17]. It focuses on identifying, analyzing, and mitigating threats to an organization's objectives. Traditional RM often relies on compliance-based rules, which may be insufficient for navigating complex strategic or external risks [1, 5].

Key methodologies include Failure Modes and Effects Analysis (FMEA) and SWOT analysis, with strategies ranging from risk avoidance and mitigation to transfer and acceptance [5, 18]. The development of IS has further revolutionized the field, enabling the use of data-driven analytics and enterprise platforms to monitor and respond to risks in real-time during periods of organizational volatility [13].

Change Management: Origins, Principles and Contemporary Perspectives. Change management is the structured process of transitioning an organization from its current state to a desired future state. Early frameworks, such as Lewin's three-step model and Kotter's eight-step process, established foundational principles like stakeholder engagement and leadership alignment [19]. However, these linear models are often critiqued for failing to account for the iterative feedback loops and emergent resistance common in modern environments [20].

Contemporary perspectives advocate for agility and cultural readiness, viewing change as an institutional norm rather than a one-time event [21]. Despite the availability of sophisticated models, approximately 70% of change initiatives fail due to leadership flaws or poor design [3]. This underscores the necessity of integrating change processes with quality and risk governance to ensure stability and successful execution [5].

Information Systems and Information Technology: Definitions, Development, and Organizational Impact. IS describes socio-technical structures that combine people, data, and workflows to support organizational decision-making [22]. In contrast, IT refers to the hardware, software, and infrastructure that facilitate these systems [16].

IS/IT has evolved from centralized mainframe systems in the 1960s to decentralized personal computing and, eventually, integrated cloud-based enterprise platforms [23]. In modern organizations, IS/IT serves as a critical enabler for operational agility and process monitoring [24]. Deep integration between an organization's Quality Management System (QMS) and IS allows for real-time performance tracking and compliance enforcement [25]. However, challenges such as "information islands," user resistance, and outdated legacy infrastructure often hinder the successful implementation of these digital tools [26].

Conceptual Modeling: Foundations, Purpose, and Role in IS Research. Conceptual modeling is the formal activity of abstracting aspects of the physical or social world to facilitate communication and understanding [27, 28]. By using standardized notations like the Unified Modeling Language (UML) [29], models provide a platform-independent representation of complex systems [30]. In the context of IS development, these models serve as a link between system design and requirements gathering, clarifying functionality before implementation [31].

Within IS research, conceptual modeling is an essential tool for organizing investigation and visualizing system structures [32]. In this paper, it provides the framework for unifying QC, QA, and RM into a single, cohesive architecture, helping to clarify dependencies and guide the development of integrated organizational strategies.

2.2 Measuring Quality and Stability in Organizations

Assessing an organization's performance during change requires a combination of quality and stability metrics. Quality is typically measured through Key Performance Indicators (KPIs) such as return rates, first-pass yield, and compliance with ISO 9001:2015 standards. These metrics provide quantifiable data on product reliability and customer trust [2, 15, 33].

Prior research on quality governance mechanisms emphasizes the importance of monitoring, escalation, and corrective action processes in managing organizational performance and addressing emerging issues. These mechanisms enable organizations to respond to deviations from expected outcomes and ensure that governance decisions are traceable and accountable.

Stability is evaluated through operational factors like on-time project delivery, employee retention, and psychological safety, which measures an employee's comfort in speaking up without fear of repercussion [34, 35]. Furthermore, Deming's Plan-Do-Check-Act (PDCA) cycle remains central to modern monitoring, encouraging organizations to use iterative feedback for continuous process refinement [4].

3 Methodology

This paper utilizes DSR as the core methodological framework to develop a method meta-model that integrates QC, QA, and RM within IS. The method is specifically tailored for organizations undergoing strategic or structural transitions, where maintaining process integrity and mitigating risks are paramount. DSR is particularly effective in this context as it bridges the gap between theoretical knowledge and practical application through the iterative construction and evaluation of purposeful artifacts [36]. This research follows five primary activities: problem explication, requirements elicitation, artifact development, demonstration, and evaluation [36].

Problem Explication. The paper is driven by the persistent fragmentation of quality and risk practices during complex organizational shifts. While standards like ISO 9001, COSO, and CMMI offer valuable guidance, they often operate in isolation and lack the interoperability needed for dynamic, emergent change [37]. To validate this gap, a Systematic Literature Review (SLR) [38] was conducted to identify recurring integration failures and synthesize principles for a more adaptive model.

Requirements Elicitation. Requirements [39] for the method were systematically derived via the SLR and supplemented by industry standards and seminal works. Following the guidelines of Kitchenham and Charters [38], the SLR was divided into three phases: planning, conducting, and reporting [38]. Academic databases including Scopus, Web of Science, and Google Scholar were used to identify relevant publications. Search strings combined keywords related to quality management, RM, organizational change, and governance mechanisms. The search process initially identified a large set of candidate publications, which were then filtered through inclusion and exclusion criteria focusing on relevance to governance coordination, QA practices, and RM integration.

Artifact Development. The artifact is a meta-model for a method designed to unify QC, QA, and RM in IS environments, with a specific focus on organizational change. It was constructed by synthesizing the requirements and mapping them to the meta-model's classes. The meta-model incorporates foundational principles from recognized standards to ensure academic and practical rigor [36]. The meta-model was specified using a UML class diagram [29] and implemented within the Astah modeling environment. This implementation supported validation of the structural consistency of the model and demonstrated its suitability for potential tool-supported operationalization.

Artifact Demonstration and Evaluation. The demonstration phase illustrates the framework's feasibility through real-life scenario-based cases from a Swedish organization. Due to logistical constraints, this was conducted as a structured walkthrough using real, anonymized organizational data. Two evaluation scenarios were developed based on governance situations discussed in the literature and practical organizational contexts. The development involved mapping quality and risk elements to transformation milestones to prove the model's capacity for traceability and monitoring [36]. The scenario-based evaluation was selected to assess whether the suggested meta-model can support realistic governance situations encountered during organizational change processes. The evaluation was formative and ex ante [36], aiming to determine if the model fulfills its defined requirements. Eight senior domain experts in the fields of systems engineering, quality and risk management, and change management participated in semi-structured interviews and walkthroughs. During these sessions, participants examined how the meta-model constructs could represent governance actions occurring in the scenarios. Feedback from the walkthrough sessions was used to assess whether the model supports (i) integration of QC, QA, and RM mechanisms, (ii) traceability between operational observations and governance actions, (iii) escalation and corrective intervention processes, and (iv) governance monitoring and compliance documentation. The evaluation criteria were grounded in the Framework for Evaluation in Design Science (FEDS) [40] and the Technology Acceptance Model (TAM) [41], focusing on Perceived Usefulness and Perceived Ease of Use. The collected data were analyzed using deductive thematic analysis [42].

4 Elicited Requirements

The requirements for the proposed method and its meta-model were systematically derived through a synthesis of the SLR and comparative analysis of existing frameworks, including ISO 9001, COSO ERM, and CMMI. The analysis identified recurring limitations in current governance approaches, particularly the fragmentation of QC, QA, and RM, the lack of process-embedded governance mechanisms, and limited traceability between operational observations and governance actions.

Based on these findings, a set of requirements was formulated to guide the development of the meta-model. The requirements define the capabilities needed to support integrated governance of quality and risk during organizational change. To ensure transparency in the design process, Table 1 presents a traceability chain linking the identified problems in the literature to the systematically elicited requirements and example corresponding meta-model constructs. The resulting requirements are defined as follows:

R1. The Method Should Support the Integration of QC, QA, and RM Mechanisms within a Unified Conceptual Structure. As discussed in Sect. 2, QC, QA, and RM are often implemented through separate organizational processes and tools. This separation may hinder the coordination of governance responses when operational issues arise. An integrated modeling approach should therefore represent these mechanisms within a shared conceptual structure that allows governance activities to interact. This requirement motivated the introduction of Domain Control Points in the proposed meta-model, which provide a unified abstraction for representing governance mechanisms across quality and risk domains.

R2. The Method Should Embed Governance Mechanisms within Organizational Processes, Enabling Their Activation During Process Execution. Quality and risk governance is most effective when monitoring mechanisms operate directly within operational workflows. However, existing governance approaches often rely on periodic reviews or external audits rather than continuous process-embedded monitoring. To address this limitation, the modeling approach should support mechanisms that are triggered by specific stages of organizational processes, allowing governance actions to be activated when relevant activities occur. This requirement is reflected in the proposed meta-model through the association between Process Stages and Domain Control Points, where process stages trigger governance mechanisms during execution.

R3. The Method Should Support Explicit Representation of Operational Issues Detected During Governance Activities. Operational observations such as quality failures, deviations from expected performance, or emerging risk indicators must be represented in a way that allows governance mechanisms to respond to them. Without explicit representation of such events, it becomes difficult to maintain traceability between operational observations and governance responses. The modeling method should therefore include constructs representing detected issues, which serve as governance events requiring evaluation and potential escalation.

R4. The Method Should Include Mechanisms for Structured Escalation and Corrective Intervention. When operational issues or risks are detected, organizations must determine how governance responses should be coordinated. This may involve escalation procedures, decision-making processes, and the initiation of corrective actions. Existing governance frameworks often define such mechanisms procedurally but do not explicitly represent them within modeling structures. The modeling approach should therefore support constructs representing escalation rules, escalation actions, and corrective activities, enabling the representation of governance response workflows.

R5. The Method Should Represent Organizational Actors, Roles, and Responsibilities Associated with Governance Activities. Quality and risk governance involve multiple organizational stakeholders who are responsible for monitoring, decision-making, and intervention. Modeling approaches supporting governance must therefore represent the relationships between governance activities and the actors responsible for executing them. This requirement ensures that governance actions can be linked to specific organizational roles and responsibilities.

R6. The Method Should Support Traceability Between Governance Actions and Compliance Artifacts. Organizations often need to demonstrate that governance decisions and corrective interventions comply not only with internal policies but also with external regulatory requirements. This requires mechanisms that document governance actions and link them to compliance references and audit records. The modeling method should support constructs representing audit trails, compliance references, and governance monitoring mechanisms, enabling traceable governance documentation.

Table 1. Requirements for the domain-specific modeling method, mapped to SLR findings and example concepts in the meta-model.

SLR Findings	Requirement	Example meta-model concept
Fragmentation among QC, QA, and RM practices	R1	Domain Control Point
Lack of process-embedded governance	R2	Association between Process Stage and Domain Control Point
Limited representation of operational issues	R3	Issue
Weak or implicit escalation mechanisms	R4	Escalation Rule, Escalation Action, Corrective Activity
Unclear organizational responsibility structures	R5	Actor, Role, Organizational Unit
Lack of traceability and compliance documentation	R6	Audit Trail, Compliance Reference

5 The Meta-Model

The meta-model was designed to satisfy the elicited requirements and provides a structure that integrates QC, QA, and RM mechanisms within organizational processes. The central concept of the meta-model is the Domain Control Point, which represents a governance mechanism embedded within organizational change processes. Control points are triggered during the execution of process stages and enable coordinated governance activities such as quality verification, risk assessment, issue escalation, and corrective activities. Figure 1 presents the meta-model. It defines constructs supporting governance integration, organizational responsibility structures, escalation mechanisms, and compliance traceability. The design of the meta-model is directly guided by the requirements and their corresponding constructs (Table 1), ensuring traceability between identified governance challenges and the proposed modeling solution.

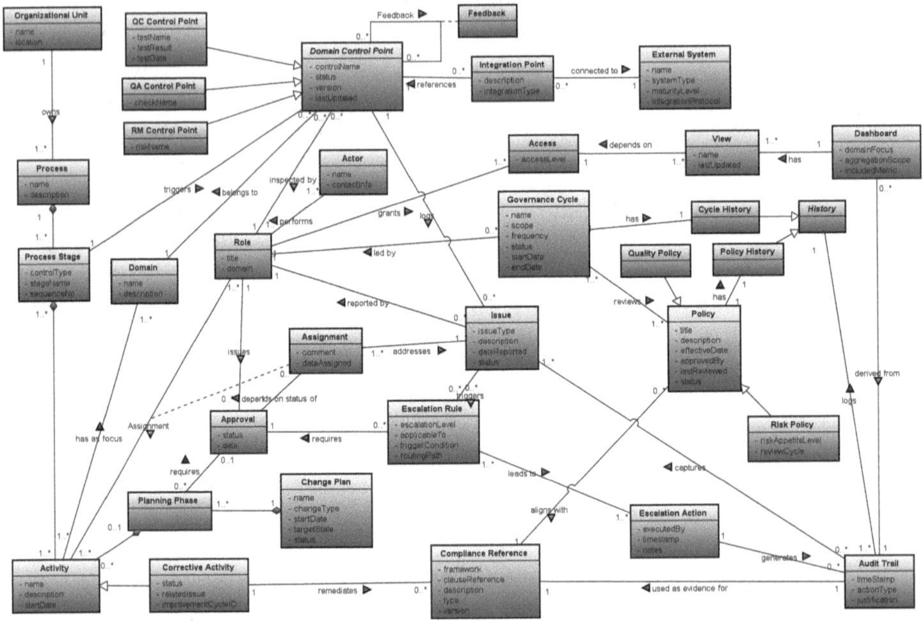

Fig. 1. The method meta-model for integrated management of quality and risk.

From a modeling perspective, the meta-model integrates governance mechanisms with organizational processes through a set of interconnected modeling constructs. The design of the meta-model was guided by the requirements derived from the literature review. First, the model must support integration of quality and risk governance mechanisms (R1). This requirement motivated the introduction of the Domain Control Point abstraction, which provides a unified representation for governance mechanisms across QC, QA, and RM domains. Second, governance mechanisms must be embedded within organizational processes (R2). To support this capability, the meta-model connects control points directly to process stages, allowing governance mechanisms to be triggered during the execution of change activities. Third, the method must support representation of governance events and responses (R3 and R4). This requirement is addressed through constructs representing issues, escalation rules, escalation actions, and corrective activities, which allow governance responses to be explicitly represented. Finally, the model must support organizational accountability and governance traceability (R5 and R6). To achieve this, the meta-model includes constructs representing organizational roles, actors, policies, audit trails, and compliance references, enabling traceability between governance decisions and compliance documentation.

The main concept introduced by the meta-model is the Domain Control Point, which represents a governance mechanism responsible for monitoring and evaluating operational activities within organizational processes. Domain Control Points provide a unified abstraction for integrating QC, QA, and RM mechanisms. The model distinguishes among three specialized control point types (i) QC Control Points, which perform operational verification activities such as testing and inspection, (ii) QA Control Points, which evaluate compliance with organizational policies and process standards, and (iii) RM Control Points, which perform risk identification and risk evaluation activities. By representing these governance mechanisms through a shared abstraction, the meta-model enables coordinated governance activities across quality and risk domains. When a control point detects an operational deviation or potential risk, the observation is represented as an Issue. Issues serve as governance events that may trigger escalation procedures or corrective interventions. The meta-model therefore includes constructs representing escalation rules and escalation actions, which define how governance responses are coordinated. When required, escalation mechanisms may initiate corrective activities that address detected issues and mitigate associated risks.

To support process-embedded governance, the meta-model integrates control points directly with organizational process structures. Organizational change activities are represented through processes and process stages, which define the operational steps involved in change initiatives. Each process stage may trigger one or more Domain Control Points, activating governance mechanisms relevant to the activities performed in that stage. This relationship allows governance mechanisms to operate directly within operational workflows, enabling monitoring and evaluation during the execution of organizational change processes. By embedding governance mechanisms within process stages, the model supports both reactive governance responses to detected failures and proactive monitoring of emerging risks.

Effective governance requires clear representation of the organizational actors responsible for governance activities. The meta-model therefore includes constructs representing organizational units, roles, actors, and assignments, which define the responsibility structures associated with governance mechanisms. In addition to responsibility structures, the model supports traceability of governance actions through constructs representing compliance artifacts. Governance actions may be associated with policies, compliance references, and audit trails, enabling organizations to document governance decisions and demonstrate compliance with internal or external requirements. To support governance monitoring, the meta-model also includes constructs representing dashboards, views, and historical records, which enable analysis and visualization of governance activities and outcomes. Together, these constructs enable traceability between operational observations, governance decisions, corrective interventions, and compliance documentation.

From a procedural perspective, the model is founded on the Domain Control Point superclass, which is specialized into QA Control Point, QC Control Point, and RM Control Point. This inheritance ensures a shared control logic while maintaining domain-specific data such as test results for QC or risk status for RM.

Controls are mapped to specific lifecycle junctures through the Process Stage class that triggers them. This allows for the dynamic assignment of quality and risk functions to specific Organizational Units, Roles and Actors.

The Issue class captures deviations and incidents, which are then processed via Escalation Rules. All actions are recorded in an Audit Trail tagged with the specific phase of the improvement cycle.

This iterative quality loop will serve as the operational core of the method, providing a dynamic feedback system that can bridge the gaps found in static, siloed standards. While the logic of the loop is rooted in the widely accepted PDCA principle, the phases are specifically tailored to align with the method's structure:

- Define: Focuses on planning quality goals, assigning specific responsibilities to Actors, and establishing measurable metrics.
- Execute: Involves the active operationalization of QA, QC, and RM through interlinked processes and system-wide activities.
- Monitor: Represents the data-capture phase, where results from inspections, audits, and control points are systematically recorded.
- Optimize: Triggers improvements, corrective actions, and escalations to refine the model's overall effectiveness based on monitored data.

Unlike legacy frameworks, such as ISO 9001 or CMMI, which experts often critique as being reactive or offering "static guidelines"—the quality loop provides a dynamic control and feedback mechanism. The core differentiation lies in how the model moves beyond documentation to active system behavior.

In traditional models, feedback loops are often manual or functionally disjointed. The loop addresses this limitation by establishing a "closed-loop feedback system" where every domain is aware of what happens in the others. For example, a failure at a QC point does not merely exist as a test result; it is linked to an RM alert and an Issue, ensuring that operational events propagate upward to policy-level improvements in real-time.

The quality loop aims to achieve temporal and causal traceability by embedding lifecycle logic directly into the method's architecture. By linking these phases to specific Actors, Organizational Units, and External Systems, the meta-model provides a sequence of "who performs what action and how information moves," which is essential for maintaining stability during complex transformations.

6 Meta-model Evaluation

The proposed meta-model was evaluated using a scenario-based approach combined with expert walkthrough sessions. The evaluation aims to assess whether the meta-model fulfills the requirements defined in Sect. 4 and supports realistic governance situations during organizational change.

The meta-model was evaluated using eight senior domain experts across two distinct complementary scenarios. The first scenario represents a reactive governance situation in which an operational quality failure triggers governance responses. The second scenario represents a proactive governance situation in which monitoring mechanisms detect emerging risks before operational failures occur. Both scenarios were instantiated using the meta-model, producing models in the form of UML class diagrams. Due to page limitations, the instantiations of the meta-model have not been included in this paper, and only a brief summary of the second scenario is included.

Scenario 1 – NPI Failure (Reactive Cycle). The first evaluation scenario represents a reactive governance situation occurring during a new product introduction process. In this scenario, a product undergoing thermal testing during a product validation stage exhibits an unexpected overheating condition. Within the proposed meta-model, the testing activity is associated with a QC Control Point triggered during the relevant process stage. The QC control point detects the failure and generates an Issue representing the detected deviation. The issue is subsequently evaluated through an RM Control Point, which assesses the risk associated with the overheating condition. The evaluation identifies a potential design risk related to supplier material properties. Based on this evaluation, the issue triggers an escalation process, activating escalation rules that determine the appropriate governance response. As a result, a corrective activity is initiated to address the identified risk, including supplier material requalification. The corrective intervention is documented through audit trail and compliance constructs, enabling traceability between the detected issue, the governance decision, and the corrective intervention. The scenario demonstrates how the meta-model supports coordination between QC detection, RM evaluation, escalation procedures, and corrective intervention processes.

Scenario 2 – Predictive Risk/Soft Thresholds (Proactive Capability). It showcased the model's potential ability to detect "soft thresholds" – statistical drifts in device telemetry (e.g., a 4% thermal drift) that are unusual but remain below formal warning limits. The RM system would treat this as a predictive risk, allowing for early human intervention before a formal quality failure occurred.

Evaluation Procedure. The evaluation was conducted through artifact walkthrough sessions with domain experts experienced in quality governance and organizational change management. during these sessions, participants examined the proposed meta-model and analyzed how the modeling constructs could represent governance activities occurring in the evaluation scenarios.

Participants were provided with descriptions of the scenarios and asked to map the events and governance actions described in the scenarios to elements of the proposed meta-model. The walkthrough sessions focused on evaluating whether the meta-model constructs could represent (i) detection of quality deviations or emerging risks, (ii) escalation procedures and governance decisions, (iii) corrective interventions, (iv) documentation of governance outcomes.

Main Findings. The collected feedback was analyzed thematically and structured according to TAM [41]. The main findings follow. experts noted a high conceptual fit, particularly for large organizations. while the underlying logic was praised as "crystal clear", the visual architecture was deemed too complex for non-expert users. The model effectively clarified lines of accountability, showing "who should do what and when".. It was seen as a potentially powerful tool to break functional silos, though it remains dependent on human skill for high-stakes interpretations. The closed-loop design was praised for showing potential in improving ownership, though experts warned against over-reliance on automated systems. Further evaluation highlighted a critical need for ai integration ("agentic AI") to detect "hidden problems" like faulty hardware registers that escape traditional metrics. According to the interviewees, the quality loop transforms the framework from a passive reference into a "blueprint designed to manage the high-risk nature of digital transformation". Expert evaluation confirmed that this structured traceability makes the cycle of learning "very natural" and could significantly enhance an organization's capacity to proactively detect underperformance.

The evaluation feedback indicates that the proposed meta-model has the potential to support the representation of governance activities across both reactive and proactive governance situations. Initially, the scenarios show that the Domain Control Point abstraction enables integration of QC, QA, and RM mechanisms within a unified governance structure. Control points triggered during process execution provide a common mechanism for monitoring operational activities and initiating governance responses. Additionally, the meta-model enables traceability between operational observations and governance decisions through the explicit representation of issues, escalation mechanisms, corrective activities, and compliance artifacts. Finally, the scenarios demonstrate that governance responses can be represented as coordinated processes involving multiple organizational actors and governance mechanisms. Overall, the evaluation indicates that the proposed meta-model has the potential to support integrated governance of organizational change processes by enabling coordinated monitoring, escalation, and corrective intervention mechanisms across quality and RM domains.

7 Discussion

The results presented in this paper demonstrate the potential of CM approaches to support integrated governance of quality and risk mechanisms during organizational change processes. The proposed method meta-model introduces a modeling structure that connects QC, QA, and RM mechanisms through a shared abstraction based on Domain Control Points. By embedding governance mechanisms within organizational processes, the model enables monitoring, escalation, and corrective activities.

A key contribution of the proposed approach lies in the integration of quality and risk governance mechanisms within a unified modeling structure. Prior research typically addresses quality management and RM as separate governance domains, often supported by different organizational practices and tools. The proposed meta-model demonstrates how these mechanisms can be represented within a common modeling framework, enabling coordinated governance responses when operational deviations or emerging risks are detected.

Another contribution of the meta-model concerns the explicit representation of governance events and responses. The modeling constructs representing issues, escalation mechanisms, and corrective activities enable traceability between operational observations and governance decisions. This traceability is particularly important in organizational change contexts, where deviations from expected outcomes must be analyzed and addressed in a systematic manner. A noteworthy fact is that terms like "management", "governance", and "control" are semantically overlapping to a degree, they have all been used to reflect the misalignment in the existing terminology in the literature.

The evaluation scenarios illustrate how the proposed meta-model can support both reactive and proactive governance mechanisms. The first scenario demonstrated how quality failures detected during product introduction can trigger coordinated governance responses involving risk evaluation and corrective intervention. The second scenario illustrated how monitoring mechanisms embedded within operational processes can identify emerging risks before they develop into operational failures. Together, these scenarios highlight the potential of the proposed modeling approach to support governance mechanisms that operate across multiple stages of organizational change processes.

The development process highlighted a significant terminological misalignment between quality and risk domains, such as the divergent taxonomies used in ISO 9001 and CMMI. Furthermore, procedural interoperability was hindered by existing functional silos that interrupt process flow, making cross-domain integration difficult.

Technological constraints also emerged, as legacy systems often act as "information islands" that lack the modularity required for unified dashboards. Finally, maintaining contextual relevance is challenging because different organizational units often have misaligned internal policies regarding metrics and naming conventions.

Despite these contributions, several limitations should be acknowledged. First, the evaluation presented in this paper relies on scenario-based analysis and expert walkthroughs, which provide qualitative insights into the applicability of the meta-model but do not constitute large-scale empirical validation. Future research could extend the evaluation through case studies or pilot implementations in organizational environments where integrated quality and risk governance mechanisms are required.

Second, the proposed meta-model focuses primarily on the conceptual modeling of governance mechanisms, rather than on the implementation of operational governance tools. Although the meta-model was implemented in a modeling environment to verify structural consistency, further research could explore how the modeling approach can be integrated into CM platforms or governance management systems.

Finally, the scope of the proposed meta-model focuses on governance mechanisms related to quality and risk management within organizational change contexts. Additional research may investigate how the modeling approach could be extended to incorporate other governance domains, such as security governance, regulatory compliance, or sustainability management.

Overall, the results suggest that CM approaches can play an important role in supporting integrated governance mechanisms for complex organizational change processes. By representing governance structures and their relationships to organizational processes, modeling approaches such as the one proposed in this paper may help organizations improve coordination between operational monitoring, risk evaluation, and governance decision-making.

8 Conclusions

This paper proposed a method meta-model for integrated quality and risk governance in organizational change. The meta-model introduces the concept of Domain Control Points, which provide a unified abstraction for representing governance mechanisms embedded within organizational processes. By linking control points to process stages, the proposed modeling approach enables coordinated monitoring, issue detection, escalation, and corrective intervention activities across quality and risk management domains. The proposed meta-model was evaluated through scenario-based analysis and expert walkthrough sessions, demonstrating how the modeling constructs support both reactive governance responses to operational failures and proactive detection of emerging risks. The results suggest that CM approaches can support improved coordination between quality and risk governance mechanisms in organizational change processes. Future research may extend this work through empirical case studies and the development of tool-supported implementations that operationalize the proposed meta-model in organizational governance environments.

Disclosure of Interests. The authors have no competing interests to declare that are relevant to the content of this article.

References

1. Kaplan, R.S., Mikes, A.: Managing risks: a new framework. Presented at the (2020)
2. Juran, J.M., Godfrey, A.B.: Juran's Quality Handbook. McGraw Hill, New York (1999)
3. By, R.T.: Organisational change management: a critical review. J. Chang. Manag. **5**, 369–380 (2005)
4. Deming, W.E.: Out of the Crisis. The MIT Press, Cambridge (2018)
5. Aven, T.: Risk assessment and risk management: review of recent advances on their foundation. Eur. J. Oper. Res. **253**, 1–13 (2016)
6. Siu Mane David Lai Wai, L., Keshwar Seebaluck, A., Teeroovengadum, V.: Impact of information technology on quality management dimensions and its implications. Eur. Bus. Rev. **23**, 592–608 (2011)
7. Dahlgaard, J.J., Khanji, G.K., Kristensen, K.: Fundamentals of Total Quality Management. Taylor & Francis, Hoboken (2007)
8. Fourie, H., Ackermann, C.: The impact of COSO control components on internal control effectiveness: an internal audit perspective. J. Econ. Financ. Sci. **6**, 495–518 (2013). https://doi.org/10.4102/jef.v6i2.272
9. Huang, J., You, J.-X., Liu, H.-C., Song, M.-S.: Failure mode and effect analysis improvement: a systematic literature review and future research agenda. Reliab. Eng. Syst. Saf. **199**, 106885 (2020)
10. Fariz, A.A., Raharjo, T., Genia, V.: ISO 9001:2015 and capability maturity model integration 3.0 in software development project. IJCS **12** (2023)
11. Ponsignon, F., Kleinhans, S., Bressolles, G.: The contribution of quality management to an organisation's digital transformation: a qualitative study. Total Qual. Manag. Bus. Excell. **30**, S17–S34 (2019)
12. Hemmatfar, M., Salehi, M., Bayat, M.: Competitive advantages and strategic information systems. IJBM **5**, 158 (2010). https://doi.org/10.5539/ijbm.v5n7p158

13. Taherdoost, H.: A review on risk management in information systems: risk policy, control fraud detection. Electronics **10**, 3065 (2021)
14. Feigenbaum, A.V.: Total Quality Control. McGraw-Hill, New York (1988)
15. Montgomery, D.C.: Introduction to Statistical Quality Control. Wiley, Hoboken (2013)
16. Attaran, M.: Information technology and business-process redesign. Bus. Process. Manag. J. **9**, 440–458 (2003)
17. Haimes, Y.Y.: Risk Modeling, Assessment, and Management. Wiley, Hoboken (2009)
18. Department of Defense: Military Standard Procedures for Performing a Failure Mode, Effects and Criticality Analysis (1980)
19. Burnes, B.: Kurt Lewin and the planned approach to change: a re-appraisal. J. Manage. Stud. **41**, 977–1002 (2004)
20. Armenakis, A.A., Bedeian, A.G.: Organizational change: a review of theory and research in the 1990s. J. Manag. **25**, 293–315 (1999)
21. Ford, J., Ford, L., Polin, B.: Leadership in the implementation of change: functions, sources, and requisite variety. J. Chang. Manag. **21**, 87–119 (2021). https://doi.org/10.1080/14697017.2021.1861697
22. Alter, S.: Defining information systems as work systems: implications for the IS field. Eur. J. Inf. Syst. **17**, 448–469 (2008)
23. Anderson, R.: Evolution of information technology. In: Management, Information Systems and Computers, pp. 144–167. Macmillan Education, UK (1986)
24. Zheng, Y.: Do information systems today play a strategic role in business? J. Soft. Comput. Decis. Anal. **2**, 65–70 (2024)
25. Cunha, P.R., de Figueiredo, A.D.: Quality management systems and information systems: getting more than the sum of the parts (2005)
26. Gonçalves, N., Sapateiro, C.: Aspects for information systems implementation: challenges and impacts. A higher education institution experience. Tékhne – Rev. Estudos Politécnicos 225–241 (2008)
27. Brodie, M.L., Mylopoulos, J., Schmidt, J.W. (eds.): On Conceptual Modelling: Perspectives from Artificial Intelligence, Databases, and Programming Languages. Springer, New York (1984)
28. Karagiannis, D., Lee, M., Hinkelmann, K., Utz, W. (eds.): Domain-Specific Conceptual Modeling: Concepts, Methods and ADOxx Tools. Springer, Cham (2022)
29. Object Management Group (OMG): OMG® Unified Modeling Language® (2017). https://www.omg.org/spec/UML/2.5.1/PDF
30. Wand, Y., Weber, R.: An ontological model of an information system. IIEEE Trans. Softw. Eng. **16**, 1282–1292 (1990). https://doi.org/10.1109/32.60316
31. Olivé, A.: Conceptual Modeling of Information Systems. Springer, Berlin (2007)
32. Wand, Y., Weber, R.: Research commentary: information systems and conceptual modeling—a research agenda. ISR. **13**, 363–376 (2002)
33. International Organization for Standardization: Occupational health and safety management systems–requirements with guidance for use (2018). https://www.iso.org/standard/63787.html
34. Gallup: State of the Global Workplace Report (2021)
35. Schaufeli, W.B., Bakker, A.B.: Job demands, job resources, and their relationship with burnout and engagement: a multi-sample study. J. Organ. Behav. **25**, 293–315 (2004). https://doi.org/10.1002/job.248
36. Johannesson, P., Perjons, E.: An Introduction to Design Science. Springer (2014)
37. Olechowski, A., Oehmen, J., Seering, W., Ben-Daya, M.: The professionalization of risk management: What role can the ISO 31000 risk management principles play? Int. J. Proj. Manage. **34**, 1568–1578 (2016)

38. Kitchenham, B., Charters, S.: Guidelines for performing systematic literature reviews in software engineering. Software Engineering Group, School of Computer Science and Mathematics, Keele University and Department of Computer Science, University of Durham, Durham, UK and Keele, Staffs ST5 5BG, UK (2007)
39. Pohl, K.: Requirements Engineering: Fundamentals, Principles, and Techniques. Springer, Heidelberg (2010)
40. Venable, J., Pries-Heje, J., Baskerville, R.: FEDS: a framework for evaluation in design science research. EJIS. **25**, 77–89 (2016)
41. Davis, F.D.: Perceived usefulness, perceived ease of use, and user acceptance of information technology. MIS Q. **13**, 319 (1989)
42. Braun, V., Clarke, V.: Using thematic analysis in psychology. Qual. Res. Psychol. **3**, 77–101 (2006)

The Dual Identity Dilemma: A Multi-Level Framework for Understanding Platform-Dependent Entrepreneurship

Johan Lubbe and Hanlie Smuts(✉)

Department of Informatics, University of Pretoria, Pretoria 0083, South Africa
{johan.lubbe,hanlie.smuts}@up.ac.za

Abstract. Entrepreneurship has fundamentally been transformed by the platform economy. However, this transformation carries a paradox that remains undertheorized: the same platforms that empower individual entrepreneurs simultaneously constrain them through asymmetric governance structures designed to extract value whilst simultaneously locking in their users. This concept paper advances a multi-level framework to address this paradox, through combining three analytical levels into an integrated explanation of platform-dependent entrepreneurship. The dual identity dilemma emerges as the core theoretical puzzle – how do platform-dependent entrepreneurs maintain legal autonomy whilst being operationally dependent on the platform and its governance? This paper makes three contributions. First, it adapts the established concept of the dual identity dilemma to platform-dependent entrepreneurship, defines it as the tension between legal independence and operational platform dependence that is operationalised with four observable markers, and embeds it within a process model of platform dependence. Second, it positions the dilemma as the psychological mechanism driving entrepreneurial behaviour across the Platform Dependency Lifecycle. Third, it identifies adult platforms as an illustrative extreme case where the dilemma is most observable and where innovations diffuse to mainstream platforms. The framework provides a roadmap for empirical investigation and offers actionable insights for platform-dependant entrepreneurs, platform designers and policymakers.

Keywords: Platform-dependent entrepreneurship (PDE) · Dual identity dilemma · platform dependency · platform ecosystems · platform governance

1 Background and Motivation

The emergence of ecosystems are enabling platform entrepreneurship, a distinctive organizational form, based on modularity, which allows interdependent firms to independently co-ordinate with each other, without a full hierarchical structure [1]. Consequently, modular coordination has fundamentally changed how individual entrepreneurs access infrastructure, markets and customers necessary for value creation. The entrepreneur's stock can either physically be trapped (Amazon's Fulfilment by Amazon) where switching cost are extremely high, or the platform could allow low switching costs (Airbnb

E. Laurenzi et al. (Eds.): BIR 2026, LNBIP 601, pp. 429–446, 2027.
https://doi.org/10.1007/978-3-032-38498-0_27

through calendar sharing) [2, 3]. This economic trap relies on switching costs to create locked-in customers, monetize a loyal base, and make it hard for competitors to enter the market [4].

Existing research has predominantly focussed on how platforms operate, govern and control their ecosystems [5, 6]. Less attention has been paid on how entrepreneurs respond to these asymmetric power relationships [3, 5]. This study focusses on a critical shift in perspective: examining the innovations, strategies and tactics used by platform-dependent entrepreneurs (PDEs) to adapt, navigate and transform platform dependencies for better long-term sustainability [3, 5]. The central puzzle we address is this: how do PDEs maintain their self-conception as independent business owners whilst being operationally dependent on platform governance?

The term "dual identity dilemma" has been used across multiple disciplines – from philosophy and psychology to cultural and organisational studies to describe the psychological tension arising from navigating incompatible identities [7–9]. This established concept is applied in a novel domain, platform-dependent entrepreneurship. While prior work has examined identity tensions in cultural and organisational contexts, no study has theorised how PDEs experience and navigate the tension between their structural independence and operational dependence. This paper extends the concept by operationalising it with four observable markers, embedding it within a process model of platform dependence and linking it to platform governance mechanisms.

The dual identity dilemma is defined as a construct where the legally and economically independent structural identity stands in tension with the platform-governed, operationally dependent relational identity [5]. Importantly, this tension is not merely a cognitive inconvenience but a structural condition mediated by platform business informatics (e.g., API structures, algorithmic sorting parameters, and payment routing protocols) that shapes behaviour, resource allocation and business viability. The dilemma exhibits in four observable architecturally reactive ways: strategic self-presentation (using the entrepreneur persona to mask platform dependence); oscillating between platform compliance and resistance; identity fragmentation (managing a unified brand across diverse platforms); and narrative reconciliation (aligning conflicting identities to stay motivated) [10].

This paper is structured as follows. Section 2 reviews the literature. Section 3 introduces the Platform Dependency Lifecycle as an organising framework and positions the dual identity dilemma as the psychological mechanism driving stage transitions. Section 4 presents four testable propositions. Section 5 outlines the research design and methodology. Section 6 discusses data collection methods. Section 7 outlines data analysis. Section 8 introduces an illustrative case, adult platforms as innovation laboratories. Section 9 ends with contributions, limitations, and future research directions.

This paper is the first of two companion papers and focusses on the dual identity dilemma as the psychological mechanism driving platform dependence. The companion paper [11] develops the platform dependency lifecycle in full as a process model. Together, the two papers provide a comprehensive theoretical framework for understanding platform-dependent entrepreneurship.

2 Literature Review

This review followed a structured approach to ensure traceability. We searched Scopus, Web of Science and Google Scholar using combinations of: ("platform-dependent entrepreneur" OR "platform complementor") AND ("identity" OR "algorithmic governance" OR "switching cost*"). The search was limited to peer-reviewed outputs from 2015–2025. We supplemented this with backward citation tracing from seminal works [3, 5, 12, 13]. Of the 142 unique records, those with direct relevance to platform governance, dependency mechanisms or entrepreneurial identity were retained. This section synthesizes this corpus.

2.1 Platform Ecosystems, Governance and Political Economy

Institutional Voids and Platform Power. Platforms gain power in weakly regulated markets by providing parallel services internalised within their digital architecture. A "grey area" or void is defined as the absence or failure of institutions to support efficient market transactions [14]. Critically, platforms intentionally create and maintain new strategic voids, forming the structural antecedent of the dual identity dilemma.

Institutional isomorphism manifests through, coercive mimetic and normative forces [15]. Governance becomes homogenised when an industry matures, reinforcing manufactured uncertainty, and limiting diversity of PDE strategies. Manufactured uncertainty is reinforced through platform governance practices that tend to become isomorphic for a specific industry [16]. Extended institutional theory classifies voids as formal (weak government institutions or weakly enforced laws) or informal (failed societal norms) [17]. Thus, platforms do not merely fill voids, but actively navigate, maintain and produce regulatory ambiguity to entrench power and extract value.

Foundational Theories of the Firm and Governance. Transaction cost economics [18] explains why PDEs become locked in: asset specificity makes investments are so specialised that the parties become vulnerable to opportunism [19]. When switching costs are strategically created through asset specificity, economic lock-in exacerbates and the investments made within the platform can only be deployed with a significant loss [4] allowing platforms to act opportunistically.

Agency theory explains the incentive misalignments [20]. Platforms control the algorithm and have information asymmetry, allowing monitoring through algorithmic surveillance, while PDEs adopt MIDAS safeguards [3]. Organisational control through market, bureaucratic and clan mechanisms [21] are seamlessly blended by platforms to create manufactured uncertainty. Therefore, from an agency perspective, platforms use near-zero-cost algorithmic surveillance to enforce behaviour rules. Where outcomes are harder to predict, outcome-based rewards [6] offload risk onto the PDEs, forcing anticipatory compliance as a survival tactic [22].

While rent extraction [23, 24] and algorithmic weaponisation [25] further entrench this power, we treat these as operational tactics of platform governance (meso-level) rather than as distinct foundational theories.

2.2 Algorithms as Governance and Manufactured Uncertainty

Manufactured uncertainty is a governance mechanism designed to keep PDEs compliant and reactive. Algorithmic bureaucracy replaces human managers with rule-based systems [26]. This feature maximises profit and fragments collective action [27].

Uber drivers experience information asymmetries and soft control through surge pricing and ratings [28]. The "socio-technical architecture of digital labour", defines how platforms and human actors interact [29]. Workers use "qualculation" [30], trial-and-error [31], and the "visibility game" [32] to challenge boundaries and platform rules. Anticipatory compliance or "pacifying the algorithm" causes extra labour to avoid algorithmic punishment [22]. Kafkaesque uncertainty [5] and "fantasmatic attachment", the irrational affective bonds with algorithms, disarms resistance [33].

2.3 Platform-Dependent Entrepreneurship.

PDEs have business interests tied to platforms they cannot control [5]. The paradox of the dual identity dilemma emerges when operational dependence on platform governance clashes with legal independence, causing PDEs to operate in "grey zones". Dependency is dynamic and increases over the platform lifecycle [34]. Platforms are best understood as "meta-organisations" [35] or "private regulators" [36]. Manufactured uncertainty is the tension between complementor autonomy and platform integrity [37].

The dual identity dilemma captures the tension between the legally and economically independent structural identity and the platform-governed, operationally dependent relational identity [5]. This construct is distinct from related concepts. Table 1 differentiates the dual identity dilemma from the autonomy paradox, algorithmic control, platform dependency and complementor lock-in.

Table 1. Defining the dual identity dilemma and differentiating it from related constructs

Concept	Definition	Distinction
Dual identity dilemma (general concept)	The psychological tension arising from navigating incompatible identities (philosophy, psychology, cultural studies) [7–9]	Broad concept, applies across multiple domains
Dual identity dilemma (this paper)	The tension between the legally independent structural identity and the platform-governed operationally dependent relational identity in PDEs [5]	Context-specific application, adapted to platform-dependent entrepreneurship; operationalised with four markers; embedded in the Platform Dependency Lifecycle
Autonomy paradox [38]	The tension between increased connectivity and reduced autonomy enabled by mobile technology	The autonomy paradox focusses on technology affordances; the dual identity dilemma focusses on platform governance as the source of constraint

(*continued*)

Table 1. *(continued)*

Concept	Definition	Distinction
Algorithmic control [26]	The use of algorithms to direct, evaluate, and sanction workers	Algorithmic control describes the governance mechanism; the dual identity dilemma describes the psychological experience of that control
Platform dependency [5]	The structural condition of being locked into a platform	Platform dependency describes the structural condition; the dual identity dilemma describes the psychological tension arising from that condition
Complementor lock-in [2]	The economic condition of being unable to exit without loss	Lock-in describes economic constraints; the dual identity dilemma adds the identity dimension of reconciling independence with dependence

2.4 Entrepreneurial Responses to Platform Dependency

The MIDAS framework [3] comprises: Monitoring (M) - tracking algorithm changes, competitor moves and policy updates [31]; Insuring (I) - income diversification and multi-homing [2]; Dependency-creating (D) – creating portable assets (email lists, contact lists and direct relationships); Attachment-creating (A) - community building and branding [39]; Shifting (S) - platform migration [40]. Metrics include scraping forums (M), Herfindahl-Hirschman Index to quantify income concentration (I) [41], transferrable assets comparison (D), audience retention rate (A), and verified migration events (S) [3, 42].

"Digital irritation" [43], the sensemaking cycle [44], anticipatory compliance [22], algorithmic gossip [45, 46], "playing the visibility game" [32] and "visibility labour" [39] are key coping tactics.

Reactive tactics include visibility hacks [47], strategic invisibility [48], and shadow-banning workarounds [49]. Online forums turn individual acts into how-to instructions [50].

2.5 The Moderating Role of Switching Costs

Lock-in is driven by complementors affiliating with dominant platforms and two-sided network effects create winner-takes-all markets [2]. Switching costs are classified as procedural (time and energy), financial (loss of platform specific assets) and relational (emotional drain of losing community) [12]. MIDAS safeguards mitigate these costs: Monitoring reduces procedural, insuring offsets financial, attachment-creating builds portable assets. Reputation non-transferability is the primary lock-in mechanism [40], creating a psychological dependency when the PDE internalises the platform's logic [51] and the "Sword of Damocles" effect [40]. Cross platform dependency by design forces uncompensated visibility labour [52].

Switching Cost Type	M: Monitoring	I: Insuring	D: Dependency-creating	A: Attachment-creating	S: Shifting
PROCEDURAL Time, effort, learning curve	PRIMARY Continuously track algorithm change, policy updates and rule shifts	SECONDARY Adopt professional indemnity or cyber insurance to mitigate economic risk during transition	HIGH BARRIER Requires building proprietary technical assets deeply embedded in the platform.	SECONDARY Establish direct relational links with technical support staff to reduce hassle	PRIMARY Standardise internal workflows to facilitate fast switch between alternative platforms
FINANCIAL Sunk costs, lost benefits	SECONDARY Monitor unilateral fee changes and payment terms to detect any exploitation	PRIMARY Purchase business interruption insurance against revenue loss from sudden suspension	PRIMARY Offer specialised niche products that generate high commissions making the platform dependent on you	SECONDARY Negotiate favourable ex ante contractual terms or fee waivers via partnership managers	PRIMARY Implement multi-homing and direct sales to diversify income away from single platform
RELATIONAL Community, reputation, identity	SECONDARY Track platform brand sentiment and community mood to detect identity dissonance	SECONDARY Use liability insurance to cover costs from platform-related reputational damage	SECONDARY Build a unique "anchor brand" presence that draws specific users making you vital to the ecosystem	PRIMARY Foster deep relational capital and norms of reciprocity with platform stakeholders (managers)	PRIMARY Develop off-platform backups (email lists, Discord communities etc.) to preserve audience identity

Fig. 1. The MIDAS strategic switching cost matrix (adapted from [3, 12])

The switching cost matrix presented in Fig. 1, represents how the different types of switching costs shape the optimal selection of MIDAS safeguards, - with Proposition 1 predicting that financial costs drive insuring and shifting, whilst relational costs drive attachment-creating.

3 Theoretical Framework: The Platform Dependency Lifecycle and the Dual Identity Dilemma.

The central contribution of this paper is to position the dual identity dilemma as the psychological mechanism that drives entrepreneurial behaviour across the platform dependency lifecycle (PDL). Whilst prior research has documented identity tensions in platform work [5, 10, 38], no study has proposed a process model that traces how platform dependence, and the accompanying identity tension evolves over time. Rather than introducing the dual identity dilemma as a new psychological construct, this study adapts an established concept to the context of platform-dependent entrepreneurship, operationalising it through observable markers and embedding it within a temporal process model that links identity work to platform governance and switching costs.

The platform dependency lifecycle consists of six stages [11] that synthesise recurring dependency patterns reported across the platform governance and platform-dependent literature into a temporal analytical model. The lifecycle is intended as an analytical framework rather than a deterministic sequence, recognising that entrepreneurs may revisit, overlap or skip stages depending on context. Table 2 presents the stages, their descriptions, autonomy status and primary mechanisms.

Table 2. The platform dependency lifecycle

Stage	Description	Autonomy Status	Primary Mechanism
Opportunity	Platform lowers barriers, enables market entry	High autonomy	Institutional void filling
Growth	Entrepreneur invests, builds audience, optimises to satisfy algorithm	Declining autonomy	Asset specificity increases
Dependence	Income concentration, reputation lock-in, anticipatory compliance	Low autonomy	Switching costs crystallise
Entrenchment	Internalisation of platform logic, psychological colonisation	Minimal autonomy	Identity fragmentation
Resistance	MIDAS safeguards, collective action, migration attempts	Reclaiming autonomy	Strategic responses
Capture or exit	Successful migration or permanent lock-in	Resolved or terminated	Switching cost outcome

The dual identity dilemma is the most observable during the dependence and entrenchment stages. In the dependence stage, PDEs recognise that their income is concentrated and exit options are limited. In the entrenchment stage, they internalise platform logic and their identities become fragmented – the tension between their self-conception as independent entrepreneurs and their operational dependence becomes unbearable. This dilemma drives the transition to the resistance stage, where PDEs attempt to reclaim autonomy through MIDAS safeguards, collective action or platform migration.

The dual identity dilemma intensifies through the four observable markers as PDEs progress through the lifecycle. In the Dependence stage, PDEs begin to feel the tension between their self-conception as independent entrepreneurs and the operational reality which manifests as strategic self-preservation, where an entrepreneur persona is used to mask platform control. As the PDEs move into the Entrenchment stage, the tension becomes unbearable when the oscillation between platform compliance and "under the radar" autonomy starts to consume emotional and cognitive resources. Identity fragmentation occurs when a unified brand must be managed across diverse platforms and narrative reconciliation becomes an ongoing struggle to align the different conflicting identities [10]. When the costs of maintaining the fragmented identities exceeds the cost of resistance, PDEs are driven to reclaim autonomy through MIDAS safeguards, collective action or migration. The dilemma thus acts as a psychological tension that, when sufficiently intense, triggers a behavioural change.

This multi-level temporal framework (Fig. 2), shows the proposed stages of the dilemma as PDEs progresses through the platform dependency lifecycle (Table 2). The horizontal time axis depicts the platform maturity cycle: emergence → consolidation → dependency → adaptation. The three vertical layers depict the macro, meso and micro layers with vertical causal flow between layers with Table 3 detailing the mechanisms at each layer. The macro layer represents the institutional environment, moving from institutional voids that enable platform entry to institutional isomorphism that creates a structural PDE dependency. The meso layer represents platform governance that evolves from regulation to weaponised governance to control and punish PDEs. The micro layer represents the PDE response, moving from narrative identity work, to MIDAS safeguards, for reduced dependency and long-term resilience.

Table 3. The three levels of the platform dependency lifecycle framework.

Level	Mechanism	Contribution to the Dilemma
Macro-level	Institutional voids, platform capitalism, lock-in dynamics, institutional isomorphism, manufactured uncertainty and power asymmetry	Creates manufactured uncertainty and structural dependence [5, 14–19, 53]
Meso-level	Platform regulation, algorithmic management, value (rent) extraction, and weaponised governance	Creates asset-specific lock-in through algorithmic surveillance, opaque rule enforcement, and value appropriation [20, 24–28, 36]
Micro-level	Narrative identity work, algorithmic coping, resistance and organising, switching costs, and MIDAS safeguards	Navigates the dilemma through strategic responses, identity negotiation, and collective action [3, 10, 12, 22, 39, 40, 48, 54, 55]

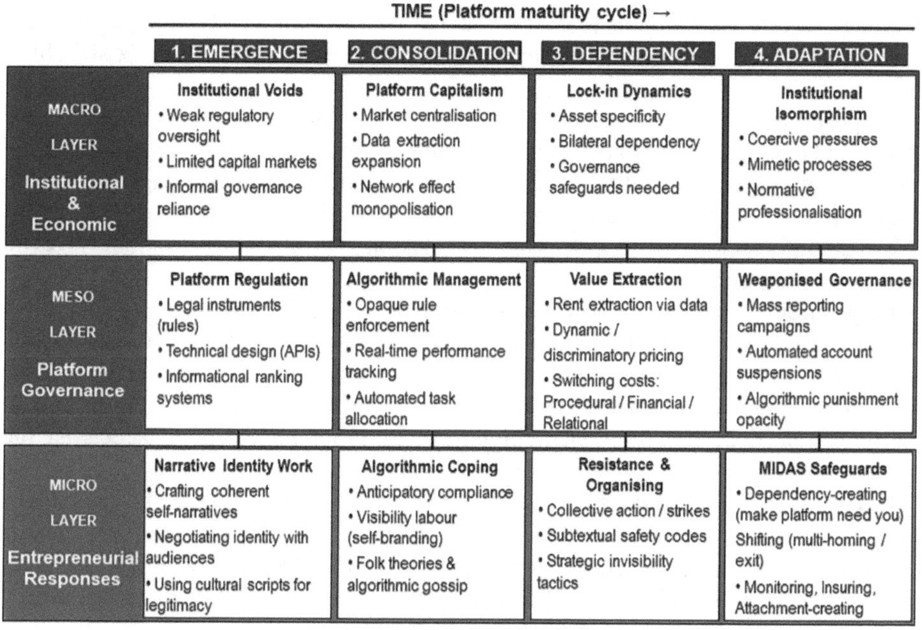

Fig. 2. A multi-level framework for platform-dependent entrepreneurship

The dual identity dilemma is not merely a cognitive inconvenience, but forms a structural condition that shapes behaviour, resource allocation and business viability. Whereas platform dependency describes the structural relationship between entrepreneurs and digital platforms, the dual identity dilemma explains how that dependency is experienced, interpreted and negotiated by entrepreneurs throughout the platform dependency lifecycle. It is operationalised through four strategic markers - strategic self-preservation, that oscillates between compliance and resistance, identity fragmentation and narrative reconciliation. These markers provide empirical indicators for investigating the dilemma that intensifies in the dependence and entrenchment stages of the platform dependency lifecycle and drives the transition to resistance.

Prior research has observed analogous lifecycle transitions in YouTube creators, identifying three phases, hobby-level engagement, full-time job and independence [56]. The work however did not theorise the entrenchment stage where the internalisation of platform logic and identity fragmentation precede resistance. The present study extends this work by adding granularity to the middle stages and linking stage transitions to switching costs, identity dissonance and platform shocks.

4 Testable Propositions

Based on the Platform Dependency Lifecycle organising framework and its complementary theoretical lenses, we propose four testable propositions.

Proposition 1 (Switching Cost Sequencing): PDEs facing primarily financial switching costs will adopt MIDAS insuring safeguards (e.g., income diversification, multi-homing) earlier than those facing relational stitching costs, who will prioritise MIDAS attachment-creating safeguards (e.g., community building, portable branding). This predicts that the timing of the growth-to-dependence transition is moderated by the switching cost type.

Proposition 2 (Stigma as an Accelerant): PDEs in high-stigma sectors will move through the opportunity and growth stages faster than mainstream PDEs, reaching the entrenchment stage earlier. Some safeguards developed in the resistance stage will diffuse to mainstream platforms as stigma barriers reduce over time. This tests the extreme case logic: if stigma accelerates lifecycle progression, adult platform practices should precede mainstream adoption.

Proposition 3 (Collective Resistance Efficiency): The effectiveness of collective resistance as a trigger for the entrenchment-to-resistance transition is moderated by switching cost type. PDEs with high relational switching costs will show reduced likelihood of sustained collective action due to reputational damage, delaying the transition to resistance, whereas PDEs with high financial switching costs will accelerate the transition to resistance.

Proposition 4 (Narrative as Resilience): PDEs who reframe platform dependency as a strategic choice (rather than a structural constraint) will have higher self-efficacy during the entrenchment stage, greater adoption of MIDAS safeguards and a higher likelihood of transitioning to exit rather than capture. Those who internalise dependency as inevitable are more likely to transition to capture.

5 Research Design Protocol: An Empirical Agenda

The framework developed in this paper is conceptual and serves as a methodological blueprint for subsequent Information Systems research. This section outlines the structural protocol designed to operationalise and validate the framework's propositions.

5.1 Research Philosophy

To map these dynamics, a critical realist philosophy is adopted [57–59], which acknowledges that a real world exists independently of our perceptions while recognising that our knowledge of it is always socially mediated and fallible. The dual-identity dilemma, switching costs and the platform dependency lifecycle are treated as real casual mechanisms that generate effects regardless of whether an individual PDE articulates them. Critical realism divides reality into three overlapping domains, as shown in Table 4, and measuring these mechanisms is only possible through transitive knowledge obtained from interviews, Reddit posts, and how these texts are interpreted.

Table 4. Critical realism divides reality into three overlapping domains [57]

Domain	Definition	Used in the study
Real	Underlying mechanisms may be unobserved	Inferred through process tracing

(continued)

Table 4. (*continued*)

Domain	Definition	Used in the study
Actual	Events generated by mechanisms	Detected through scraping and event study
Empirical	Human experience, interpretation, narrative	Accessed through interviews and thematic analysis

Using computational analysis to perform keyword classification through subreddit scraping cannot measure the dual identity dilemma directly, but identifies observable patterns consistent with an underlying mechanism at work. The computational pattern provides the when and where to look with interviews providing the how and why.

5.2 Research Strategy

A multiple case study design is employed, where each PDE serves as a case within the interview component and each platform (such as Twitch, YouTube, OnlyFans, Fansly, Uber) serves as a case within the digital trace component. A cross-case comparison enables identification of platform-specific dependency mechanisms, strategy differences across switching-cost environments, and diffusion patterns.

The study adopts a hybrid longitudinal design; a fully longitudinal study for the digital trace component (Reddit archive data spanning 2013–2025 as available) and a single-wave cross-sectional study for the interview component, supplemented by retrospective timeline mapping and tenure-based comparative analysis. This hybrid approach is justified as the research questions primarily focus on aggregate discourse patterns and platform-level temporal shifts, rather than individual identity trajectories over time.

6 Data Collection

Participants are recruited through purposive sampling from platform specific subreddits, followed by snowball sampling. Inclusion criteria are: active on the platform > 6 months, deriving at least 20% of income from platform activity, aged > 18 years, and fluent in English. The target sample size is 20–30 participants.

Across sectional proxy for longitudinal change is established by sorting participants into three tenure groups: novice (6–18 months), intermediate (19–48 months) and veteran (>48 months). This stratification enables comparative analytics across tenure groups as a proxy for developmental patterns.

The semi-structured interviews are used to cover: platform joining motivations, platform changes encountered, coping strategies (inclusive of MIDAS safeguards), identity self-description, stigma experiences and future plans. A digital timeline template is shared 48 h prior to the interview to reconstruct chronological trajectories [60, 61].

The blueprint specifies that digital trace data be extracted from public subreddits (such as r/Twitch, r/PartneredYoutube, r/Onlyfansadvice, r/Onlyfansgirls, r/Fanslyadvice, r/UberEATS, r/Uberdrivers) using the Reddit Arctic dump archive.

An iterative, AI-assisted time-segmented keyword thesaurus classification program is defined to detect technical and socio-technical PDE discourse at scale. The proposed protocol operationalises a two-layer exclusion filter and platform-specific filters, utilising a specialised ModernBERT classifier architecturally fine-tuned to score MIDAS classifications against architectural platform shifts.

7 Data Analysis

Thematic analysis [62] is conducted using Braun and Clarke's six-phase approach. Coding begins deductively from the MIDAS framework and identity themes, with inductive codes added as patterns emerge.

Process tracing [63] is employed to identify causal mechanisms linking platform events to changes in narrative identities and strategy adoption [64]. Table 5 shows the analysis methods used to test the four propositions.

Table 5. The alignment of propositions, analytical methods and data sources

Proposition	Analysis method	Data source
Proposition 1	Event study and Mann-Whitney U test	Reddit digital trace
Proposition 2	Kaplan-Meier survival analysis and log-rank test	Reddit and policy archives
Proposition 3	Chi-square and logistic regression and process tracing	Reddit and interviews
Proposition 4	Thematic analysis and narrative analysis and process tracing	Interviews and follow-up

The trustworthiness criteria include credibility (member checking), transferability (thick description), dependability (audit trail) and confirmability (reflexivity journal).

8 Adult Platforms as Innovation Laboratories: An Illustrative Case

The dual identity dilemma is most observable in high-stigma sectors where conventional exit options are removed, and accelerates movement through the lifecycle stages. This section presents adult platforms as an illustrative extreme case [55, 65, 66] used to examine platform dependency under conditions of unusually high stigma and platform dependency, rather than to suggest that the observed mechanisms are unique to adult-content platforms.

Platforms in the adult services industry have operated in the grey margins of the digital economy for decades and yet remain remarkably unexplored [51, 55, 66]. However, this neglect is not merely an empirical gap, but a theoretical loss, as these platforms operate under extreme constraints of stigma, payment processing exclusion and regularity ambiguity that forces innovation. Critical insight can be gained from the informal economy through the exploration these grey margins - activities illegal according to formal institutions, yet deemed legitimate by specific social circles [64].

Recent research suggests that these platforms have acted as innovation pioneers, developing monetization models (e.g., subscription, tipping, pay-per-view and algorithmic management), later adopted by mainstream platforms such as YouTube, Twitch and Patreon [51, 52]. Thus, the pattern of innovation diffusion from stigmatised sectors to mainstream platforms suggests that adult platforms may function as an innovation laboratory in which dependency-driven responses become particularly visible and may, under appropriate boundary conditions, diffuse to mainstream platform ecosystems [51, 67, 68].

Three boundary conditions must be met in order to apply these findings correctly: reputation and followers must create an audience-based dependency rather than physical inventory to provide the lock-in mechanism, there must be algorithmic opacity with hidden or changing rules governing the operating environment and the PDE must have a dual identity: an independent legal identity but be bound operationally to the platform rules. This environment is in alignment with the gig creator economy on platforms such as Twitch, OnlyFans or TikTok, but not with asset heavy environments such as Amazon FBA. Exploitation dynamics only come into effect in mature markets when platform power has already become consolidated and not in emerging markets where platforms are greenfield market enablers (Milone et al., 2025).

9 Contributions, Limitations, and Future Research

9.1 Theoretical Contributions

Prior PDE research has treated identity tensions as a background condition or a by-product of economic lock-in [5, 34]. Our distinctive contribution moves identity from background to the primary mechanism. Unlike static accounts of this occurrence, we operationalise the dilemma via four observable markers, making it empirically traceable, we embed it within a six-stage lifecycle that specifies when and why the dilemma intensifies to trigger resistance and specify stigma as a sixth barrier in Rogers' diffusion model, with explicit boundary conditions. This parsimonious integration that uses agency and institutional theory to explain the lifecycle engine is the primary novel synthesis.

Secondly, this paper positions the dual-identity dilemma as the psychological mechanism driving entrepreneurial behaviour across the platform dependency lifecycle, providing a process model that explains how platform dependence and identity tension evolves over time.

Thirdly, this paper identifies stigma as the sixth barrier to technology adoption, extending diffusion of innovations theory [69] to explain how innovations from stigmatised sectors migrate to mainstream platforms.

9.2 Practical and Social Contributions

The framework provides actionable insights for PDEs through a switching cost decision matrix, multi-homing threshold guide and a brand-asset portability checklist. Platform designers and policy makers can use the framework to reduce harmful lock-in, and distinguish between strategic and pathological dependency. The framework also reduces stigma-driven research neglect by highlighting adult platforms as innovation laboratories.

9.3 Limitations and Future Research Directions

This framework is conceptual and requires empirical testing of the four propositions via longitudinal qualitative methods and comparative case study analysis. Boundary conditions apply: audience-based dependency (not physical inventory), algorithmic opacity, and dual identity (legal independence but operational dependence). This framework applies to the gig creator economy (Twitch, OnlyFans or TikTok) but not with asset heavy environments (Amazon FBA). Exploitation dynamics only apply to mature markets, not emerging greenfield enablers [70].

Future research directions: (1) prospective or retrospective tracking of PDE narratives over extended periods; (2) comparative studies across platform types; (3) large-N survey research to test switching-cost sequencing; (4) cross-geographic studies of how institutional voids moderate platform relationships.

9.4 Concluding Remarks

This concept paper has provided a multi-level theoretical framework to understand how PDEs navigate the dual identity dilemma – the tension between their self-conception as independent business owners and operational dependence on platform governance. This framework explains how macro-level forces translate into meso-level governance and micro-level responses by integrating extended institutional theory, agency theory and identity work literature. Switching costs acts as a moderating mechanism, with the specific type of switching cost predicting which safeguards PDEs adopt.

Furthermore, the framework positions the dual-identity dilemma as the psychological mechanism driving entrepreneurial behaviour across the platform dependency lifecycle and provides a process model that explains how platform dependence and identity tension evolve over time.

Furthermore, the framework addresses how high-stigma sectors function as innovation laboratories, where practices are pioneered and eventually diffuse through relative advantage, observability and reduced stigma barriers – with stigma operating as a sixth barrier in Roger's diffusion model.

As the gig economy makes platform dependence a central feature of entrepreneurship, understanding how entrepreneurs survive and thrive within these ecosystems has become imperative. This framework forms a foundation for understanding, while propositions provide a roadmap for empirical work. The dual identity dilemma is a lived reality for millions of PDEs, and explaining how they navigate it to build sustainable business, is the contribution this framework provides.

Disclosure of Interests. Both authors A and B have no competing interests to declare that are relevant to the context of this article.

References

1. Jacobides, M.G., Cennamo, C., Gawer, A.: Towards a theory of ecosystems. Strateg. Manag. J. **39**, 2255–2276 (2018). https://doi.org/10.1002/smj.2904

2. Zhu, F., Liu, Q.: Competing with complementors: an empirical look at Amazon.com. Strateg. Manage. J. **39**, 2618–2642 (2018) https://doi.org/10.1002/smj.2932
3. Verbeke, A., Yuan, W.: Defying the unfortunate destiny of platform complementors: managerial guidelines for adopting effective safeguards. Strateg. Manage. Rev. (2025).https://doi.org/10.1177/25151789251314984
4. Klemperer, P.: The competitiveness of markets with switching costs. RAND J. Econ. 138–150 (1987). https://doi.org/10.2307/2555540
5. Cutolo, D., Kenney, M.: Platform-dependent entrepreneurs: power asymmetries, risks, and strategies in the platform economy. Acad. Manag. Perspect. **35**, 584–605 (2021). https://doi.org/10.5465/amp.2019.0103
6. Vallas, S., Schor, J.B.: What do platforms do? Understanding the gig economy. Ann. Rev. Sociol. **46**, 273–294 (2020). https://doi.org/10.1146/annurev-soc-121919-054857
7. Krauth, S., Fladerer, M.P., Hehnen, M.M., Frey, D.: A matter of mindset? A multi-study exploration of agency-communion tensions and emerging mindsets among female (and male) leaders. J. Manage. Sci. Rep. **3**, 297–323 (2025). https://doi.org/10.1177/27550311251357944
8. Chiang, Y.-F., Tsai, C.-T., Peng, J.C., Lin, S.-Y.: Dual-path effects of the relationship between multiple identities and employee innovative behavior: the moderating role of the situational aesthetic. Technium Soc. Sci. J. **48**, 231–251 (2023). https://doi.org/10.47577/tssj.v48i1.9551
9. Blazejewski, S.: Betwixt or beyond the lines of conflict? Biculturalism as situated identity in multinational corporations. Crit. Perspect. Int. Bus. **8**, 111–135 (2012). https://doi.org/10.1108/17422041211230703
10. Radu-Lefebvre, M., Lefebvre, V., Crosina, E., Hytti, U.: Entrepreneurial identity: a review and research agenda. Entrep. Theory Pract. **45**, 1550–1590 (2021). https://doi.org/10.1177/10422587211013795
11. Lubbe, J., Smuts, H.: The platform dependency lifecycle: A process model of entrepreneurial evolution in platform ecosystems. University of Pretoria (2026)
12. Burnham, T.A., Frels, J.K., Mahajan, V.: Consumer switching costs: a typology, antecedents, and consequences. J. Acad. Mark. Sci. **31**, 109–126 (2003). https://doi.org/10.1177/0092070302250897
13. Parker, G.G., Van Alstyne, M.W.: Two-sided network effects: a theory of information product design. Manage. Sci. **51**, 1494–1504 (2005). https://doi.org/10.1287/mnsc.1050.0400
14. Khanna, T., Palepu, K.: Why focused strategies may be wrong for emerging markets. Harv. Bus. Rev. **75**, 41–51 (1997)
15. DiMaggio, P.J., Powell, W.W.: The iron cage revisited: institutional isomorphism and collective rationality in organizational fields. Am. Sociol. Rev. **48**, 147–160 (1983). https://doi.org/10.2307/2095101
16. Steiner, A., Jack, S., Farmer, J., Steinerowska-Streb, I.: Are they really a new species? Exploring the emergence of social entrepreneurs through Giddens's structuration theory. Bus. Soc. **61**, 1919–1961 (2022). https://doi.org/10.1177/00076503211053014
17. Webb, J.W., Khoury, T.A., Hitt, M.A.: The influence of formal and informal institutional voids on entrepreneurship. Entrep. Theory Pract. **44**, 504–526 (2020). https://doi.org/10.1177/1042258719830310
18. Coase, R.H.: The nature of the firm (1937). The nature of the firm: origins, evolution, and development, 18–33 (1993). https://doi.org/10.1111/j.1468-0335.1937.tb00002.x
19. Williamson, O.E.: The economic institutions of capitalism. The political economy reader: Markets as institutions **27** (1985)
20. Eisenhardt, K.M.: Agency theory: an assessment and review. Acad. Manag. Rev. **14**, 57–74 (1989). https://doi.org/10.2307/258191
21. Ouchi, W.G.: A conceptual framework for the design of organizational control mechanisms. Manage. Sci. **25**, 833–848 (1979). https://doi.org/10.1287/mnsc.25.9.833

22. Bucher, E.L., Schou, P.K., Waldkirch, M.: Pacifying the algorithm–anticipatory compliance in the face of algorithmic management in the gig economy. Organization **28**, 44–67 (2021). https://doi.org/10.1177/1350508420961531
23. Nedzhvetskaya, N.: Brave new (Digital) world: translating knowledge into collective action-Shoshana Zuboff, the age of surveillance capitalism: the fight for a human future at the new frontier of power (New York, Public Affairs, 2019). Eur. J. Sociol./Arch. Européennes de Sociologie **60**, 528–533 (2019). https://doi.org/10.1017/S0003975619000444
24. Khan, L.M.: Amazon's antitrust paradox. Yale Law J. **126**, 710 (2016)
25. Meisner, C.: The weaponization of platform governance: mass reporting and algorithmic punishments in the creator economy. Policy Internet **15**, 466–477 (2023). https://doi.org/10.1002/poi3.359
26. Kellogg, K.C., Valentine, M.A., Christin, A.: Algorithms at work: the new contested terrain of control. Acad. Manag. Ann. **14**, 366–410 (2020). https://doi.org/10.5465/annals.2018.0174
27. Wood, A.J., Graham, M., Lehdonvirta, V., Hjorth, I.: Good gig, bad gig: autonomy and algorithmic control in the global gig economy. Work Employ Soc. **33**, 56–75 (2019). https://doi.org/10.1177/0950017018785616
28. Rosenblat, A., Stark, L.: Algorithmic labor and information asymmetries: a case study of Uber's drivers. Int. J. Commun. **10**, 27 (2016). https://doi.org/10.5210/fm.v21i1.6340
29. Postigo, H.: The socio-technical architecture of digital labor: converting play into YouTube money. New Media Soc. **18**, 332–349 (2016). https://doi.org/10.1177/1461444814541527
30. Shapiro, A.: Between autonomy and control: strategies of arbitrage in the "on-demand" economy. New Media Soc. **20**, 2954–2971 (2018). https://doi.org/10.1177/1461444817738236
31. Jhaver, S., Karpfen, Y., Antin, J.: Algorithmic anxiety and coping strategies of Airbnb hosts. In: Proceedings of the 2018 CHI Conference on Human Factors in Computing Systems, pp. 1–12. ACM, New York (2018). https://doi.org/10.1145/3173574.3173995
32. Cotter, K.: Playing the visibility game: How digital influencers and algorithms negotiate influence on Instagram. New Media Soc. **21**, 895–913 (2019). https://doi.org/10.1177/1461444818815684
33. Pignot, E.: Who is pulling the strings in the platform economy? Accounting for the dark and unexpected sides of algorithmic control. Organization **30**, 140–167 (2023). https://doi.org/10.1177/1350508420974523
34. Rietveld, J., Eggers, J.: Demand heterogeneity in platform markets: implications for complementors. Organ. Sci. **29**, 304–322 (2018). https://doi.org/10.1287/orsc.2017.1183
35. Gawer, A., Harracá, M.: Inconsistent platform governance and social contagion of misconduct in digital ecosystems: a complementors perspective. Res. Policy **54**, 105300 (2025). https://doi.org/10.1016/j.respol.2025.105300
36. Boudreau, K.J., Hagiu, A.: Platform rules: multi-sided platforms as regulators. Platforms, Markets Innovation **1**, 163–191 (2009)
37. Tiwana, A., Konsynski, B., Bush, A.A.: Research commentary—platform evolution: coevolution of platform architecture, governance, and environmental dynamics. Inf. Syst. Res. **21**, 675–687 (2010). https://doi.org/10.1287/isre.1100.0323
38. Mazmanian, M., Orlikowski, W.J., Yates, J.: The autonomy paradox: the implications of mobile email devices for knowledge professionals. Organ. Sci. **24**, 1337–1357 (2013). https://doi.org/10.1287/orsc.1120.0806
39. Abidin, C.: Visibility labour: engaging with Influencers' fashion brands and #OOTD advertorial campaigns on Instagram. Media Int. Australia **161**, 86–100 (2016). https://doi.org/10.1177/1329878X16665177
40. Curchod, C., Patriotta, G., Cohen, L., Neysen, N.: Working for an algorithm: power asymmetries and agency in online work settings. Adm. Sci. Q. **65**, 644–676 (2020). https://doi.org/10.1177/0001839219867024

41. Chikoto, G.L., Ling, Q., Neely, D.G.: The adoption and use of the Hirschman–Herfindahl index in nonprofit research: does revenue diversification measurement matter? Voluntas: Int. J. Voluntary Nonprofit Organ. **27**, 1425–1447 (2016). https://doi.org/10.1007/s11266-015-9562-6
42. Yu, S., Sekiguchi, T.: Platform-dependent entrepreneurship: a systematic review. Admin. Sci. **14**, 326 (2024). https://doi.org/10.3390/admsci14120326
43. Ytre-Arne, B., Moe, H.: Folk theories of algorithms: understanding digital irritation. Media Cult. Soc. **43**, 807–824 (2021). https://doi.org/10.1177/0163443720972314
44. Zhao, J., Syed, T.A.: Making sense of algorithms: Workers' coping strategies for algorithmic management on digital platforms. Technol. Forecast. Soc. Chang. **223**, 124443 (2026). https://doi.org/10.1016/j.techfore.2025.124443
45. Bishop, S.: Managing visibility on YouTube through algorithmic gossip. New Media Soc. **21**, 2589–2606 (2019). https://doi.org/10.1177/1461444819854731
46. Cao, G., Wen, Z., Liu, P.: Algorithmic Gossiping: sharing and non-sharing that evolve algorithmic imaginaries to folk theories. Inf. Res. Int. Electron. J. **30**, 664–672 (2025). https://doi.org/10.47989/ir30CoLIS51922
47. Duffy, B.E., Meisner, C.: Platform governance at the margins: Social media creators' experiences with algorithmic (in)visibility. Media Cult. Soc. **45**, 285–304 (2023). https://doi.org/10.1177/01634437221111923
48. Stegeman, H.M., Are, C., Poell, T.: Strategic invisibility: How creators manage the risks and constraints of online hyper (in) visibility. Soc. Media+ Soc. **10**, 20563051241244674 (2024) https://doi.org/10.1177/20563051241244674
49. Kojah, S.A., Zhang, B.Z., Are, C., Delmonaco, D., Haimson, O.L.: "Dialing it back:" Shadowbanning, invisible digital labor, and how marginalized content creators attempt to mitigate the impacts of opaque platform governance. Proc. ACM Hum. Comput. Interact. **9**, 1–22 (2025). https://doi.org/10.1145/3701191
50. McDaid, E., Free, C.: Stories of resistance: The role of online forums in response to Uber's algorithmic management. Crit. Perspect. Account. **101**, 102790 (2025). https://doi.org/10.1016/j.cpa.2025.102790
51. Gorissen, S.: Content creation and gig-work in the platform economy: what contemporary sex work can teach us about the futures of digital labor. Inf. Soc. **40**, 309–328 (2024). https://doi.org/10.1080/01972243.2024.2381481
52. Di Cicco, M., Beraldo, D.: Sex work as cross-platform self-branding. Challenges and strategies of OnlyFans' content creators in a precarious ecosystem. Platforms Soc. **2**, 29768624251359797 (2025) https://doi.org/10.1177/29768624251359797
53. Srnicek, N.: The challenges of platform capitalism: understanding the logic of a new business model. Juncture **23**, 254–257 (2017). https://doi.org/10.1111/newe.12023
54. Ibarra, H., Barbulescu, R.: Identity as narrative: Prevalence, effectiveness, and consequences of narrative identity work in macro work role transitions. Acad. Manag. Rev. **35**, 135–154 (2010). https://doi.org/10.5465/amr.2010.45577925
55. Hardy, K., Barbagallo, C.: Hustling the platform: capitalist experiments and resistance in the digital sex industry. South Atlantic Q. **120**, 533–551 (2021). https://doi.org/10.1215/00382876-9154898
56. Gastaldi, L., Appio, F.P., Trabucchi, D., Buganza, T., Corso, M.: From mutualism to commensalism: assessing the evolving relationship between complementors and digital platforms. Inf. Syst. J. **34**, 1217–1263 (2024). https://doi.org/10.1111/isj.12491
57. Bhaskar, R.: A Realist Theory of Science. Routledge (2013)
58. Archer, M., Bhaskar, R., Collier, A., Lawson, T., Norrie, A.: Critical Realism: Essential Readings. Routledge (2013)
59. Fleetwood, S.: Ontology in organization and management studies: a critical realist perspective. Organization **12**, 197–222 (2005). https://doi.org/10.1177/1350508405051188

60. Langley, A.: Strategies for theorizing from process data. Acad. Manag. Rev. **24**, 691–710 (1999). https://doi.org/10.5465/amr.1999.2553248
61. van Dun, D.H., Wijnmaalen, J.R., Wilderom, C.P.: Mapping team dynamics through retrospective team events analysis. Int J Qual Methods **21**, 16094069221120744 (2022). https://doi.org/10.1177/16094069221120745
62. Braun, V., Clarke, V.: Using thematic analysis in psychology. Qual. Res. Psychol. **3**, 77–101 (2006). https://doi.org/10.1191/1478088706qp063oa
63. George, A.L., Bennett, A.: Process tracing and historical explanation. Case Stud. Theory Dev. Soc. Sci. **206** (2005)
64. Webb, J.W., Tihanyi, L., Ireland, R.D., Sirmon, D.G.: You say illegal, I say legitimate: entrepreneurship in the informal economy. Acad. Manag. Rev. **34**, 492–510 (2009). https://doi.org/10.5465/AMR.2009.40632826
65. Easterbrook-Smith, G.: OnlyFans as gig-economy work: a nexus of precarity and stigma. Porn Studies **10**, 252–267 (2023). https://doi.org/10.1080/23268743.2022.2096682
66. Van Doorn, N., Velthuis, O.: A Good Hustle: the moral economy of market competition in adult webcam modeling. J. Cult. Econ. **11**, 177–192 (2018). https://doi.org/10.1080/17530350.2018.1446183
67. Jokubauskaitė, E., Peeters, S.: Visibility in the shadows: tips in mainstream versus alternative streaming on Chaturbate. New Media Soc. **28**, 2360–2382 (2025). https://doi.org/10.1177/14614448251336422
68. Schuchmann, S.: Elites of the Whorearchy—OnlyFans creators' power, identity and sex work stigma negotiation. Gend. Work Organ. **32**, 2308–2321 (2025). https://doi.org/10.1111/gwao.70010
69. Rogers, E.: Diffusion of Innovations 5th. Free press (2003)
70. Milone, F.L., Paolucci, E., Raguseo, E.: Do digital platforms create entrepreneurial opportunities? Evidence from marginal areas. Strateg. Entrep. J. (2025). https://doi.org/10.1002/sej.1542

Modelling Professional Experience for Career-Aware Academic Planning: A Weighted Occupation Profile Approach

Maja Spahic-Bogdanovic[1,2](✉) and Knut Hinkelmann[1,2]

[1] University of Applied Sciences and Arts Northwestern Switzerland FHNW, Olten, Switzerland
{maja.spahic,knut.hinkelmann}@fhnw.ch
[2] University of Camerino (UNICAM), Camerino, MC, Italy

Abstract. Professional experience can shape course relevance for post-graduate students, especially in flexible programmes where many study while working. Academic planning systems rarely treat work history as a structured input. When considered, it is often reduced to free-text job titles or flat role lists that ignore duration, recency, employment intensity, employment type, and overlap. This paper presents JobRanking, a deterministic method that takes job episodes assigned to ESCO occupations, computes monthly full-time-equivalent contributions from employment intensity and type, caps overlapping exposure, applies duration and configurable recency weighting, and normalises the result into an explainable occupation profile. The profile provides a professional-background signal for downstream occupation–course scoring. Controlled profile variants verify design-conformant behaviour for recency, overlap handling, intensity, employment type, and boundedness.

Keywords: Professional experience modelling · Academic planning · Educational decision support · Career-aware planning

1 Introduction

Flexible higher education gives students more choice over which courses to take, when to take them, and how to sequence them across a study path. Flexibility is commonly realised through part-time, online, blended, and modular formats [3,6,7]. It also includes pace, deadlines, assessment schedules, and curricular choice within a programme [9,24,25]. This creates autonomy, but it also makes course selection and study planning more demanding. In elective-rich curricula, students must compose a coherent trajectory from many possible courses, while course catalogues often provide only limited search, filtering, and comparison support [24,25]. In postgraduate education, this planning problem is closely connected to professional experience. Many students enter master's programmes with prior work experience, which can influence their perceived employability and academic decision-making [4]. Many also study while working and therefore

E. Laurenzi et al. (Eds.): BIR 2026, LNBIP 601, pp. 447–463, 2027.
https://doi.org/10.1007/978-3-032-38498-0_28

plan under constraints of time, workload, and income stability [1,8,17,22]. For these students, course planning is not only a question of interest or programme compliance. It also involves judging how courses relate to existing professional experience, future career direction, and practical constraints. Existing academic planning and course recommendation systems address parts of this problem. Some systems focus on feasibility and programme rules, others on personalised recommendations, and others on long-term study planning [16,21,23,26]. However, professional experience is rarely treated as a structured planning input. Work history is often ignored, represented as free text, or reduced to a flat list of job titles. Such representations are too weak as a professional-background signal for course prioritisation because they do not distinguish between short and long experience, recent and older experience, different employment intensities, employment types, or overlapping work periods. JobRanking was introduced in earlier work as one component of the iModuleBuddy academic planning system [27]. The present article develops this component further by focusing on the work-experience modelling problem itself. JobRanking takes job episodes that have already been assigned to ESCO occupations. ESCO is a European multilingual classification of skills, competences, qualifications, and occupations that provides stable occupation identifiers [10]. The assigned episodes are then transformed into a weighted occupation profile that accounts for duration, employment percentage, employment type, overlapping work periods, and a configurable recency component. This paper therefore addresses the following research question: *RQ: How can heterogeneous professional work histories be transformed into a transparent occupation-level profile that can serve as an input to career-aware academic planning?*

The contribution is a deterministic modelling method for transforming a person's professional history into a structured, explainable, occupation-level profile. JobRanking focuses on the professional-background side of the planning problem. It provides a weighted occupation vector that can be combined with an occupation–course similarity layer and other planning criteria such as career goals, preferences, workload, and institutional constraints.

The article proceeds as follows. Section 2 discusses professional experience in academic planning and course selection. Section 3 explains the research strategy. Section 4 presents the design objectives and occupation representation. Section 5 introduces JobRanking, its downstream use in course scoring, and reports the analytical verification of its design-conformance properties. Section 6 discusses the contribution, limitations, future work, and conclusion.

2 Professional Experience in Academic Planning and Course Selection

Digital support for course selection can be examined from two sides. One side concerns the systems that support planning, comparison, and recommendation. The other concerns the factors students actually use when deciding which courses to take. Both perspectives help explain why professional experience remains challenging to incorporate into career-aware academic planning.

2.1 Educational Planning, Decision Support, and Recommendation

Academic planning systems usually focus on structural feasibility. They commonly model programme rules, prerequisites, semester availability, credit requirements, and sequencing constraints. This is visible in long-term curriculum planning and course-scheduling approaches, where the central problem is to generate valid paths through a curriculum [21,26]. More recent planning work also considers temporal effects such as prerequisite order, knowledge decay, and long-term feasibility across several terms [16]. These approaches are useful for constructing valid study paths, but they mainly represent the student through academic state and planning constraints. Educational decision support systems (DSSs) and recommender systems (RSs) extend this view by adding comparison and personalisation. Some systems recommend courses based on academic performance, prior enrolments, interests, preferences, or predicted success. Others include broader student characteristics or allow students to compare several possible options [23]. Course recommender systems also use content, collaborative signals, or semantic similarity to suggest relevant courses [15,28]. These systems improve course discovery, but they often focus on what the student has studied, what the student prefers, or what similar students selected. Career-related information appears in some systems, but it is often handled at a broad level. Some approaches include career goals, labour-market relevance, or competency alignment as recommendation signals, for example, through career-driven course planning or competency-based course–career matching [5,30,31]. This is relevant for career-aware planning, but career goals and professional background are not the same. Career goals describe where a student wants to go. Professional background describes what the student has already done.

2.2 Factors Influencing Course Selection

Research on course selection shows that students rarely rely on one criterion. Interest in the topic and perceived usefulness often shape the initial attraction of a course [2,29]. Students also consider expected workload and perceived difficulty, because course choice involves an assessment of effort, risk, and available study capacity [12,18]. Timetable fit is another important factor, especially when students need to coordinate study with work or other obligations [20]. In addition, students use social and contextual information, such as peer advice, lecturer reputation, and informal knowledge about course organisation, to reduce uncertainty before enrolment [18,20]. In flexible and elective-rich programmes, these factors interact across several semesters. A course may be attractive in content but difficult to take because of workload, timetable clashes, or its effect on later study options. Long-term planning is therefore not only a matter of choosing individually appealing courses. It also requires students to consider sequencing, feasibility, and how one course choice affects later options [16,21]. The student population in higher education is also changing. Many students combine higher education with paid work, which affects the time and energy they can allocate to study [8,22]. More recent studies also show that working while studying remains a common condition across higher-education contexts [1,17]. At postgraduate level, students may also enter a programme with prior work experience, which can influence how they understand employability and how they approach academic decisions [4]. These conditions make professional experience relevant for course selection. Students may use courses to deepen existing expertise, broaden their profile, or prepare for a new professional direction. Professional experience is therefore different from a simple preference. It consists of job episodes, occupational areas, employment intensity, duration, recency, and sometimes overlapping roles. A planning system that wants to use professional background, therefore, needs more than a field for job titles. At the same time, mapping reported job titles to a standard occupation framework is itself a modelling step. Job titles are ambiguous, organisation-specific, and language-dependent. An occupation-based approach should therefore make this mapping explicit and treat it as a potential source of uncertainty.

2.3 Synthesis of the Gap

The reviewed approaches support feasibility, comparison, and personalisation, but rarely treat professional experience as a structured planning input. The specific gap is the absence of a mechanism that transforms heterogeneous work histories into a transparent occupation-level professional-background signal while accounting for duration, recency, employment intensity, employment type, and overlap. JobRanking addresses this modelling step. It does not replace course recommendation or multi-semester planning. Instead, its weighted occupation profile can be combined with occupation–course similarity and other criteria in downstream course prioritisation.

3 Research Strategy

JobRanking was developed using a Design Science Research (DSR) strategy. DSR is suitable when the aim is to address a practical problem by constructing and evaluating an artefact, while also deriving knowledge from the design process [13,32]. The research process follows the main DSR phases of awareness, suggestion, development, evaluation, and conclusion. The awareness phase identified the problem of a weakly represented professional background in academic planning and course selection support. The suggestion phase translated this problem into the idea of modelling work experience as a structured occupation-level profile. The development phase formalised and implemented the JobRanking method. The evaluation phase employed an analytical design-conformance check using controlled examples to assess whether the method behaves consistently with its formal specification under relevant input conditions. This evaluation verifies the internal behaviour of JobRanking as a modelling component. The conclusion phase reflects on the method's contribution, limitations, and future use in career-aware academic planning. The following section outlines the design objectives for JobRanking and introduces the occupation representation used in the method.

4 Design Objectives and Occupation Representation

The literature gap identified above shows the need for a method that can transform work history into a usable planning signal. The design of such a method depends on two elements: the application context in which professional experience becomes relevant for course selection, and the occupation representation that makes different job episodes comparable.

4.1 Application Context

The application context is the MSc Business Information Systems (MSc BIS) programme at the University of Applied Sciences and Arts Northwestern Switzerland (FHNW). The programme combines flexible study conditions with a broad elective portfolio. Programme administrative data collected for this study show that the average entry age of students enrolled in the MSc BIS programme was about 29.6 years, and roughly 70% were between 25 and 33 years old. In addition, an analysis of 464 LinkedIn student profiles indicates that the student demographic primarily comprises early- to mid-career professionals. Students study while working or enter the programme with an average of about five years of professional experience. This makes professional background a relevant input for course prioritisation. Workshop and survey insights from the programme further showed that some students prefer courses that build on their existing expertise, while others use electives to move into a new area or avoid repetition.

4.2 Design Objectives

The application context shows why professional experience has to be represented more carefully than through job titles alone. MSc BIS students often bring several years of work experience, but this experience differs in occupational area, duration, recency, employment intensity, and employment type. A professional-experience modelling method, therefore, needs a profile representation that preserves these differences and remains understandable for later use in educational decision support. The resulting profile can subsequently be combined with occupation–course similarity in a downstream course-prioritisation pipeline. The design objectives for JobRanking follow from this context and from the literature gap identified in Sect. 2. Table 1 summarises these objectives and illustrates the intended scope of JobRanking.

JobRanking uses ESCO as the occupation representation layer because job titles vary across organisations and cannot be reliably aggregated. ESCO provides stable occupation identifiers within a European classification of occupations, skills, competences, and knowledge [10]. In JobRanking, the ESCO occupation URI is the aggregation key, while the occupation label keeps the output readable. ESCO defines what is being weighted, and JobRanking defines how strongly each occupation is weighted. In JobRanking, o_i denotes the ESCO occupation assigned to job episode j_i. This assignment is an upstream modelling step, for example through guided ESCO search, manual confirmation, or a documented title-to-ESCO mapping procedure.

Table 1. Design objectives for JobRanking

ID	Objective	Rationale
DO1	Occupation-level profile	Professional experience should be represented through stable occupational categories so that several work episodes can be aggregated and compared.
DO2	Episode-level input	Individual job episodes should be preserved before aggregation because students may report several roles with different durations, employment types, and employment percentages.
DO3	Duration sensitivity	Longer exposure to an occupational area should usually contribute more strongly than short exposure.
DO4	Recency sensitivity	Recent experience should receive more weight than older experience, while older experience should not disappear abruptly.
DO5	Employment intensity and type sensitivity	Employment percentage should capture employment intensity, while employment type should allow configurable differentiation between forms of work such as regular employment, internship, trainee, and other.
DO6	Overlap handling	Overlapping job episodes should be handled explicitly to prevent parallel roles from inflating professional exposure without bounds.
DO7	Bounded output	The resulting occupation weights should remain within a defined range to ensure consistent use in downstream course scoring.
DO8	Explainable profile	The output should show which occupational areas are represented and why they receive stronger or weaker weights.

5 The JobRanking Method

JobRanking transforms a student's work history into an occupation-level weight profile. The input is a set of job episodes. Each episode contains an ESCO occupation, a start month, an optional end month, an employment type, and an employment percentage. The output consists of raw occupation weights and a separately normalised occupation vector. These values represent the relative strength of professional exposure to each occupation and can serve as input to downstream course prioritisation.

5.1 Algorithm Overview and Method Explanation

Algorithm 1 gives the compact version of JobRanking. The method first validates and normalises job episodes, then aggregates professional exposure at the occupation-month level, applies duration and recency weighting, and finally returns raw and normalised occupation weights. The method assumes that each job episode has already been assigned to an ESCO occupation.

JobRanking begins with job episodes, because students may report several roles, and these roles can differ in occupational area, duration, employment intensity, and employment type. A job episode is defined as

$$j_i = (o_i, s_i, e_i, \tau_i, p_i) \tag{1}$$

Algorithm 1. JobRanking

Require: Work episodes $\mathcal{J}$ with assigned ESCO occupations, configuration parameters, reference month t_{now}
Ensure: Raw occupation weights $w(o)$ and normalised weights $\hat{w}(o)$
Initialise $F(o, m) \leftarrow 0$ for all occupation–month pairs
for each episode $j_i \in \mathcal{J}$ **do**
    Validate assigned ESCO occupation o_i
    Validate start month s_i
    Resolve end month e_i ▷ missing or invalid end dates are treated as ongoing
    Clip future end dates to t_{now}
    Resolve employment type τ_i
    Resolve employment percentage $p_i \in [0, 100]$
    if strict mode and p_i was inferred and τ_i is not full-time **then**
        Raise validation error
    end if
    $q_i \leftarrow (p_i/100)\, k_{\tau_i}$ ▷ monthly FTE contribution
    Store source episode metadata for traceability
    for each month $m \in [s_i, e_i]$ **do**
        $F(o_i, m) \leftarrow \min\{c, F(o_i, m) + q_i\}$
    end for
end for
for each occupation o with any activity **do**
    $\text{fteMonths}(o) \leftarrow \sum_m F(o, m)$
    $l(o) \leftarrow \max\{m \mid F(o, m) > 0\}$
    $\Delta(o) \leftarrow t_{\text{now}} - l(o)$ ▷ $l(o)$ is the last active month of o
    $r(o) \leftarrow R(\Delta(o))$ ▷ normalised and clamped recency score
    $d(o) \leftarrow 1 - \exp(-\text{fteMonths}(o)/\sigma)$
    if combination mode is product **then**
        $w(o) \leftarrow d(o)\, r(o)$
    else
        $(\lambda_d, \lambda_r) \leftarrow$ internally normalised duration/recency weights
        $w(o) \leftarrow \lambda_d d(o) + \lambda_r r(o)$
    end if
end for
if $\sum_{o'} w(o') > 0$ **then**
    $\hat{w}(o) \leftarrow \dfrac{w(o)}{\sum_{o'} w(o')}$ for all occupations o
else
    $\hat{w}(o) \leftarrow 0$ for all occupations o
end if
return occupation table with raw `experience_weight`, normalised vector `vector_normalised_l1`, warnings, source-episode traces, and configuration snapshot

where o_i is the ESCO occupation, s_i is the start month, e_i is the end month, τ_i is the employment type, and p_i is the employment percentage. The occupation o_i denotes the ESCO occupation assigned to the job episode before JobRanking is applied. JobRanking then uses the selected ESCO occupation URI as the aggregation key. Temporal data are handled at month granularity. If the end date is missing or invalid, the episode is treated as ongoing and the reference month t_{now} is used. If the end date lies in the future, it is clipped to t_{now}. Invalid or missing start dates are handled according to the selected validation mode.

The employment percentage is read from the job episode or inferred from configurable defaults. In strict mode, inferred percentages are only accepted automatically for full-time jobs. For non-full-time jobs, strict mode raises a validation error when the percentage is missing and would have to be inferred. This avoids silently assigning a default percentage to part-time, internship, trainee, or other employment episodes when stricter data quality is required.

The employment type is converted into a configurable type factor k_{τ_i}. Employment type is included because work episodes can differ in responsibility, autonomy, learning setting, and workplace exposure. Internship and work-integrated learning research shows that such experiences can support employability, but they are also structured learning experiences and should not be automatically treated as identical to regular employment [11,14,19]. JobRanking therefore treats employment type as a configurable factor, not as a fixed theoretical constant. In the default configuration used in this paper, full-time and part-time employment use the same type factor. This does not mean that part-time work is treated as equally intensive as full-time work, as lower intensity is represented separately through the employment percentage p_i. The monthly contribution of a job episode is computed as

$$q_i = \frac{p_i}{100} k_{\tau_i} \tag{2}$$

The value q_i can be interpreted as the monthly full-time-equivalent contribution of the episode. The method then aggregates exposure month by month. For each occupation o and month m, all active job episodes mapped to o contribute to the monthly exposure value $F(o, m)$. The value is capped by a maximum monthly contribution:

$$F(o, m) = \min\left(c, \sum_{i:o_i=o,\, m\in[s_i,e_i]} q_i\right) \tag{3}$$

This cap prevents overlapping work episodes from inflating professional exposure without bounds. If a student reports two parallel jobs mapped to the same occupation, the method does not automatically count the same month twice. It limits the monthly contribution according to the configured cap. The accumulated full-time-equivalent exposure for an occupation is

$$\text{fteMonths}(o) = \sum_m F(o, m). \tag{4}$$

This value is transformed into a bounded duration score:

$$d(o) = 1 - \exp\left(-\frac{\text{fteMonths}(o)}{\sigma}\right) \tag{5}$$

The parameter σ controls how quickly the duration effect saturates. This prevents very long work histories from dominating the profile entirely. Recency is modelled separately. Let $l(o)$ denote the last active month for occupation o. The elapsed time since the last active month is

$$\Delta(o) = t_{\text{now}} - l(o) \tag{6}$$

The recency score is computed with a normalised and clamped decay function:

$$r(o) = R(\Delta(o)), \qquad r(o) \in [0, 1] \tag{7}$$

In the default configuration, R is implemented as:

$$\delta(\Delta) = \text{clip}\left(\frac{e^{\Delta/s} + \beta}{\gamma}, 0, 1\right), \qquad R(\Delta) = 1 - \text{clip}\left(\frac{\delta(\Delta) - \delta(0)}{1 - \delta(0)}, 0, 1\right) \tag{8}$$

where $\text{clip}(x, 0, 1)$ bounds x to the interval $[0, 1]$. The use of a recency component is inspired by temporal decay models in long-term planning contexts [16]. In JobRanking, however, the decay function is used as a configurable modelling choice for occupational exposure, not as an empirical claim about the decay of learned knowledge. Recent experience receives a higher value, while older experience is reduced gradually according to the selected parameter configuration. Duration and recency are then combined into a raw occupation weight. In the default product mode, the weight is

$$w(o) = d(o)\, r(o) \tag{9}$$

A weighted-sum mode is also available. Let $\omega_d \geq 0$ and $\omega_r \geq 0$ denote the configured duration and recency weights. If $\omega_d + \omega_r > 0$, these values are internally normalised as

$$\lambda_d = \frac{\omega_d}{\omega_d + \omega_r}, \qquad \lambda_r = \frac{\omega_r}{\omega_d + \omega_r}. \tag{10}$$

If both configured weights are zero, the implementation falls back to the configured default weighting. The raw occupation weight is then computed as

$$w(o) = \lambda_d d(o) + \lambda_r r(o). \tag{11}$$

The raw weights are normalised as

$$\hat{w}(o) = \frac{w(o)}{\sum_{o'} w(o')}. \tag{12}$$

If $\sum_{o'} w(o') = 0$, all normalised weights are set to zero. Keeping raw and normalised values separate is useful because the raw value shows the strength of exposure after duration and recency weighting, while the normalised vector shows the relative distribution of the student's professional background across occupations. The normalised vector is the value later used when JobRanking is combined with occupation–course similarity in downstream course scoring.

5.2 Worked Example

This example illustrates how JobRanking transforms job episodes into occupation-level experience weights. It uses the default configuration shown in Table 2 and assumes the reference month $t_{\text{now}} = 2026\text{-}04$.

Table 2. Default configuration used in the worked example

Parameter	Value	Meaning
c	1.0	Maximum monthly occupation contribution
σ	36	Duration saturation parameter
s	24	Recency stability parameter
β	5	Recency offset parameter
γ	100	Recency scale parameter

Table 3. Example job episodes with overlapping periods and different employment types

Job	Occupation	Type	Percentage used	Start	End
J1	Data Analyst	full-time	100	2024-01	2024-12
J2	Data Analyst	part-time	50	2024-07	2025-06
J3	Business Analyst	trainee	100	2025-01	2025-06
J4	Business Analyst	internship	100	2025-04	2025-09
J5	Product Manager	other	100	2023-10	2024-03

If p_i is missing, configurable defaults are used: $\{\text{full-time} : 100, \text{part-time} : 50, \text{internship} : 100, \text{trainee} : 100, \text{other} : 100\}$. The default type factors are $\{\text{full-time} : 1.0, \text{part-time} : 1.0, \text{internship} : 0.7, \text{trainee} : 0.85, \text{other} : 0.6\}$. Table 3 shows the input episodes. The percentage column shows the value used after applying the defaults.

Using Eq. (2), the monthly contributions are $q_{J1} = 1.00$, $q_{J2} = 0.50$, $q_{J3} = 0.85$, $q_{J4} = 0.70$, and $q_{J5} = 0.60$. The occupation-month aggregation applies the overlap cap from Eq. (3). For Data Analyst, J1 is active from 2024-01 to 2024-12, and J2 is active from 2024-07 to 2025-06.

The monthly exposure is therefore:

- 2024-01 to 2024-06: only J1, giving $6 \times 1.00 = 6.00$;
- 2024-07 to 2024-12: J1 and J2 overlap, giving 1.50, capped to 1.00, hence $6 \times 1.00 = 6.00$;
- 2025-01 to 2025-06: only J2, giving $6 \times 0.50 = 3.00$.

Thus, fteMonths(Data Analyst) = 15.00.

For Business Analyst, J3 and J4 overlap between 2025-04 and 2025-06:

- 2025-01 to 2025-03: only J3, giving $3 \times 0.85 = 2.55$;
- 2025-04 to 2025-06: J3 and J4 overlap, giving 1.55, capped to 1.00, hence $3 \times 1.00 = 3.00$;
- 2025-07 to 2025-09: only J4, giving $3 \times 0.70 = 2.10$.

Thus, fteMonths(Business Analyst) = 7.65.

For Product Manager, only J5 is active, giving fteMonths(Product Manager) $= 6 \times 0.60 = 3.60$. With $\sigma = 36$, Eq. (5) gives the following duration scores: $d(\text{Data Analyst}) \approx 0.3408$, $d(\text{Business Analyst}) \approx 0.1914$, $d(\text{Product Manager}) \approx 0.0952$. The last active months are 2025-06 for Data Analyst, 2025-09 for Business Analyst, and 2024-03 for Product Manager. With $t_{\text{now}} = $ 2026-04, the elapsed months are: $\Delta(\text{Data Analyst}) = 10$, $\Delta(\text{Business Analyst}) = 7$, $\Delta(\text{Product Manager}) = 25$.

Using the default recency configuration from Eq. (8), the approximate recency scores are: $r(\text{Data Analyst}) \approx 0.9945$, $r(\text{Business Analyst}) \approx 0.9964$, $r(\text{Product Manager}) \approx 0.9805$.

These values show that the default recency configuration is conservative for recent work episodes. Within the recent range covered by this example, recency has only a small differentiating effect, and the ranking is mainly driven by duration, employment intensity, employment type, and overlap handling. The recency component becomes more visible for older episodes. With the same parameter configuration, $R(24) \approx 0.9817$, $R(60) \approx 0.8810$, $R(84) \approx 0.6583$, and $R(108) \approx 0.0530$. Thus, the default parameters do not abruptly discount recent work experience, but they substantially reduce the contribution of occupations that have not been active for several years. In the default product mode from Eq. (9), the raw occupation weights are: $w(\text{Data Analyst}) \approx 0.3389$, $w(\text{Business Analyst}) \approx 0.1907$, $w(\text{Product Manager}) \approx 0.0933$. The raw ranking is therefore: Data Analyst > Business Analyst > Product Manager. For the normalised vector, let $W = \sum_o w(o) = 0.6229$. Using Eq. (12), the normalised values are: $\hat{w}(\text{Data Analyst}) \approx 0.5440$, $\hat{w}(\text{Business Analyst}) \approx 0.3062$, $\hat{w}(\text{Product Manager}) \approx 0.1498$.

The example shows the role of each part of the method. The overlap cap prevents parallel roles from inflating the same occupation. Duration captures cumulative exposure with diminishing returns. Employment percentage and employment type determine the monthly FTE contribution. Recency keeps the signal temporally sensitive, but the default configuration treats recent work experience conservatively. The final normalised vector provides a transparent occupation-level professional-background profile for downstream course scoring.

5.3 Use in Career-Aware Academic Planning

JobRanking is designed as an input to educational decision support. It produces a weighted professional-background profile that can be combined with occupation–course similarity in a downstream course-scoring pipeline. In the iModuleBuddy instantiation [27], the similarity between an occupation o and a course c is implemented as a hybrid occupation–course similarity score. For each course, a course text bundle is derived from selected course-description and ontology fields. For each ESCO occupation, an occupation text bundle is derived from the ESCO occupation representation and its associated information. The similarity layer then combines lexical and semantic similarity:

$$\text{sim}(o, c) = S_{\text{hyb}}(o, c) = \lambda_{\text{tfidf}} S_{\text{tfidf}}(o, c) + \lambda_{\text{emb}} S_{\text{emb}}(o, c), \tag{13}$$

where $S_{\text{tfidf}}(o, c)$ denotes TF-IDF-based lexical similarity, $S_{\text{emb}}(o, c)$ denotes embedding-based semantic similarity, and the configurable weights are set to $\lambda_{\text{tfidf}} = 0.2$ and $\lambda_{\text{emb}} = 0.8$ in the current iModuleBuddy configuration. The experience-based course score for user u and course c is then computed as

$$S_{\text{exp}}(u, c) = \sum_{o \in O_u^{pb}} \hat{w}_{JR}(u, o)\, S_{\text{hyb}}(o, c), \tag{14}$$

where O_u^{pb} is the set of occupations derived from the user's professional background and $\hat{w}_{JR}(u, o)$ is the L1-normalised JobRanking weight of occupation o. The formula gives more influence to courses that are similar to occupations with stronger professional-experience weights. The resulting score is an intermediate professional-background signal. It can be used to prioritise courses aligned with the student's prior experience. In a planning system, this signal can be combined downstream with career-goal alignment, preferences, workload indicators, and institutional constraints. The distinction between professional background and career goals is important. Career goals describe a future direction, whereas professional background describes accumulated prior exposure. They can overlap, but they do not have the same meaning. JobRanking supports the professional-background side by making prior experience computable without merging it with future aspirations. The method also supports explanation. For each course score, the system can retain the strongest occupation-level contributors:

$$\phi(u, o, c) = \hat{w}_{JR}(u, o)\, S_{\text{hyb}}(o, c). \tag{15}$$

These contribution values can be shown to users or advisors to explain why a course is considered relevant to a student's background. They also make clear whether a course score is driven by one dominant occupation or by several weaker occupation–course matches.

5.4 Analytical Verification

The analytical verification focuses on the internal behaviour of JobRanking as a professional-experience modelling component. It checks whether the implementation behaves consistently with the formal specification under controlled input variations. Controlled synthetic profiles derived from one baseline profile are used to isolate the effects of individual input dimensions. ESCO occupations remain fixed, while dates, employment percentages, employment types, and overlap conditions are varied. All scenarios are specified relative to the reference month t_{now}. Five design-conformance properties are checked: monotonic recency behaviour, overlap handling without double counting, proportional FTE scaling, employment-type differentiation, and boundedness of intermediate and final weights. These tests mainly operationalise DO4–DO7 from Table 1. DO3 follows analytically from Eq. (5): for $\sigma > 0$, $d(o)$ is strictly increasing in fteMonths(o). DO1 and DO2 are satisfied structurally by the occupation-level output and episode-level input representation. DO8 is supported by traceable occupation-level contribution values, but perceived explainability is not empirically evaluated in this paper. Table 4 summarises the results.

Table 4. Analytical verification results for JobRanking

Property	Test and result	Interpretation
Monotonic recency (DO4)	Identical duration and intensity with different elapsed times since last activity. Raw weights decreased from 0.234072 at 0 months to 0.232456 at 12 months and 0.229793 at 24 months.	Weights are non-increasing as elapsed time increases; in the tested scenario they decrease monotonically.
Overlap handling (DO6)	Two 60% part-time jobs with and without overlap. Sequential employment produced 14.4 FTE months. Overlapping employment produced 13.2 FTE months after monthly capping.	Overlapping jobs are aggregated correctly and capped at the occupation-month level.
FTE scaling (DO5)	Identical dates with 50% and 100% employment. The 50% case produced 6.0 FTE months and raw weight 0.153518. The 100% case produced 12.0 FTE months and raw weight 0.283469.	Employment percentage scales FTE months proportionally and affects the raw weight as expected.
Employment type (DO5)	Identical dates and 100% employment with different employment types. Raw weights were 0.283469 for full-time and part-time, 0.246731 for trainee, 0.208110 for internship, and 0.181269 for other.	The ordering matches the configured employment-type factors. Part-time has the same default type factor as full-time; lower intensity is represented through the employment percentage.
Boundedness (DO7)	Extreme cases with very long ongoing employment and very old employment. Long ongoing employment produced a duration-strength value and a raw weight of 0.976482. Very old employment produced a recency score and a raw weight of 0.0.	Duration saturation and recency decay remain within the intended [0, 1] interval.

The results show that JobRanking behaves consistently with the tested design-conformance properties. Recency changes in the expected direction, overlapping jobs do not create double counting beyond the monthly cap, employment percentage affects FTE months proportionally, employment-type factors are reflected in the output, and all tested weights remain bounded. The recency test confirms monotonic behaviour, but it does not by itself establish that the default recency parameters are empirically optimal. The small numerical differences in the 0–24 month scenario reflect the conservative default configuration. This configuration avoids abruptly discounting recent work experience and makes recency effects more visible for substantially older episodes. The verification also illustrates why a flat representation would be weaker. If all occupations were weighted equally, the model would ignore whether a role was recent, long-lasting, full-time, part-time, or overlapping with another role. If duration alone were used, older roles could dominate even when they are no longer central to the student's current professional profile. JobRanking provides a transparent middle ground, as it remains deterministic and inspectable while representing the temporal and intensity-related structure of work histories.

6 Discussion and Conclusion

JobRanking contributes a deterministic and explainable method for transforming heterogeneous job episodes into a weighted ESCO-based occupation profile. By retaining duration, recency, employment intensity, employment type, and overlap, it preserves information that is lost in free-text job titles or flat role lists. JobRanking is not a complete course recommender; its output is a professional-background signal for downstream occupation–course scoring. Keeping this signal separate from future-oriented career goals allows planning systems to distinguish courses that build on prior experience from those that support a professional transition. Each occupation weight remains traceable to its source episodes and configuration choices. Employment-type factors, duration saturation, the monthly overlap cap, and recency parameters are therefore explicit and adaptable, but they are not universal or empirically calibrated constants. The analytical verification shows that JobRanking behaves consistently with its formal specification under controlled input variations. It provides evidence of design conformance, not of the external utility of downstream course scoring.

Several limitations remain. First, the result depends on the correctness of the upstream mapping from job episodes to ESCO occupations. Second, JobRanking models occupational exposure and not demonstrated competence. Third, its configurable factors cannot fully capture actual tasks, responsibility, or workplace quality. The output should therefore be interpreted as a planning signal instead of evidence of competence. Guided ESCO search, advisor confirmation, and richer episode descriptions could reduce these limitations.

Future work should compare JobRanking with simpler baselines, including flat occupation lists, duration-only weighting, and job-title matching; calibrate its parameters using real student profiles; and compare its outputs with student and advisor judgements. Longer-term studies should examine whether experience-based course scores relate to enrolment choices, perceived relevance, satisfaction, or learning and career outcomes. Overall, JobRanking offers a transparent bridge from professional histories to downstream course scoring while leaving the final decision with students and advisors.

References

1. Antoniadou, M., Crowder, M., Cunningham, E.: Parallel Lives: Exploring the Experiences of Students who Work. Work-Life Inclusion: Broadening Perspectives Across the Life-Course (November), 27–40 (2024). https://doi.org/10.1108/978-1-80382-219-820241003
2. Babad, E., Tayeb, A.: Experimental analysis of students' course selection. Br. J. Educ. Psychol. **73**(3), 373–393 (2003). https://doi.org/10.1348/000709903322275894
3. Barua, L., Lockee, B.B.: A review of strategies to incorporate flexibility in higher education course designs. Discov. Educ. **3**(1), 127 (2024). https://doi.org/10.1007/s44217-024-00213-8
4. Bennett, D., Knight, E., Li, I.: The impact of pre-entry work experience on university students' perceived employability. J. Furth. High. Educ. **47**(8), 1140–1154 (2023). https://doi.org/10.1080/0309877X.2023.2220286
5. Beutling, N., Spahic-Bogdanovic, M.: Personalised course recommender: linking learning objectives and career goals through competencies. In: AAAI Symposium, vol. 3, pp. 72–81. (2024). https://doi.org/10.1609/aaaiss.v3i1.31185
6. Brink, S., Carlsson, C.J., Enelund, M., Georgsson, F., Keller, E., Lyng, R., McCartan, C.: Curriculum agility: responsive organization, dynamic content, and flexible education. In: 2021 IEEE Frontiers in Education Conference (FIE), pp. 1–5, IEEE (2021). https://doi.org/10.1109/FIE49875.2021.9637287
7. Butcher, J., Rose-Adams, J.: Part-time learners in open and distance learning: revisiting the critical importance of choice, flexibility and employability. Open Learn. J. Open, Distance e-Learn. **30**(2), 127–137 (2015). https://doi.org/10.1080/02680513.2015.1055719
8. Callender, C.: The impact of term-time employment on higher education students' academic attainment and achievement. J. Educ. Policy **23**(4), 359–377 (2008). https://doi.org/10.1080/02680930801924490
9. El Galad, A., Betts, D.H., Campbell, N.: Flexible learning dimensions in higher education: aligning students' and educators' perspectives for more inclusive practices. Front. Educ. **9**(April), 1–13 (2024). https://doi.org/10.3389/feduc.2024.1347432
10. European Commission: ESCO Strategic framework: Vision, mission, position statement, added value and guiding principles. Technical report, European Commission (2017). https://ec.europa.eu/esco/portal/document/en/89a2ca9a-bc79-4b95-a33b-cf36ae1ac6db
11. Gault, J., Leach, E., Duey, M.: Effects of business internships on job marketability: the employers' perspective. Educ. Training **52**(1), 76–88 (2010). https://doi.org/10.1108/00400911011017690
12. Hedges, M.R., Pacheco, G.A., Webber, D.J.: What determines students' choices of elective modules? Int. Rev. Econ. Educ. **17**, 39–54 (2014). https://doi.org/10.1016/j.iree.2014.05.003

13. Hevner, A.R., March, S.T., Park, J., Ram, S.: Design science in information systems research. MIS Q. **28**(1), 75–106 (2004). https://doi.org/10.2307/25148625
14. Jackson, D.: Employability skill development in work-integrated learning: barriers and best practice. Stud. High. Educ. **40**(2), 350–367 (2015). https://doi.org/10.1080/03075079.2013.842221
15. Koutrika, G., Ikeda, R., Bercovitz, B., Garcia-Molina, H.: Flexible recommendations over rich data. In: RecSys, pp. 203–210. ACM, New York, NY, USA (2008). https://doi.org/10.1145/1454008.1454041
16. Lebis, A., Humeau, J., Fleury, A., Lucas, F., Vermeulen, M.: Fully individualized curriculum with decaying knowledge, a new hard problem: investigation and recommendations. Int. J. Artif. Intell. Educ. **34**(3), 1102–1137 (2024). https://doi.org/10.1007/s40593-023-00376-9
17. Lessky, F., Unger, M.: Working long hours while studying: a higher risk for First-in-Family students and students of particular fields of study? Eur. J. High. Educ. **13**(3), 347–366 (2023). https://doi.org/10.1080/21568235.2022.2047084
18. Ma, B., Lu, M., Taniguchi, Y., Konomi, S.: Investigating course choice motivations in university environments. Smart Learn. Environ. **8**(1), 31 (2021). https://doi.org/10.1186/s40561-021-00177-4
19. Maertz, C.P., Jr., Stoeberl, P.A., Marks, J.: Building successful internships: lessons from the research for interns, schools, and employers. Career Dev. Int. **19**(1), 123–142 (2014). https://doi.org/10.1108/CDI-03-2013-0025
20. Méndez, G.G., Mendoza, P.: Students' Habits, Strategies, and Decisive Factors Around Course Selection. Lecture Notes in Networks and Systems, vol. 799, pp. 249–258 (2024). https://doi.org/10.1007/978-3-031-45642-8_25
21. Mohamed, A.: A decision support model for long-term course planning. Decis. Support Syst. **74**, 33–45 (2015). https://doi.org/10.1016/j.dss.2015.03.002
22. Moreau, M., Leathwood, C.: Balancing paid work and studies: working (-class) students in higher education. Stud. High. Educ. **31**(1), 23–42 (2006). https://doi.org/10.1080/03075070500340135
23. Ospankulov, E., Abdigapbarova, U., Rakhimzhanova, L., Issabayeva, D., Nazarbekova, K., Issabayeva, Z.: Using the digital platform in personalized student learning. In: ICFET, pp. 23–28, ACM, New York (2022). https://doi.org/10.1145/3545862.3545895
24. van Rossen, S., et al.: Design ideas for recommender systems in flexible education: how algorithmic affordances may address ethical concerns. In: Bramwell-Dicks, A., Evans, A., Winckler, M., Petrie, H., Abdelnour-Nocera, J. (eds.) Design for Equality and Justice. INTERACT 2023, pp. 205–213, Springer, cham (2024),https://doi.org/10.1007/978-3-031-61698-3_19
25. van Rossen, S., Kluijtmans, E., van Brussel, S., van Harsel, M., Smarius, J., van der Stappen, E.: Recommender systems for students in flexible education: an exploration of benefits and risks. In: Bramwell-Dicks, A., Evans, A., Winckler, M., Petrie, H., Abdelnour-Nocera, J. (eds.) INTERACT 2023, pp. 196–204. Springer, Cham (2024). https://doi.org/10.1007/978-3-031-61698-3_18
26. Shakhsi-Niaei, M., Abuei-Mehrizi, H.: An optimization-based decision support system for students' personalized long-term course planning. Comput. Appl. Eng. Educ. **28**(5), 1247–1264 (2020), https://doi.org/10.1002/cae.22299
27. Spahic-Bogdanovic, M., Witschel, H.F., Porumboiu, D., Rosati, P., Hierro Canchari, P.J.P., Kostic, M.: iModuleBuddy - a hybrid AI-based academic planning system. In: Grabis, J., et al (eds.) HybridAIMS, vol. 3996, pp. 21–29, CEUR Workshop Proceedings (2025). https://ceur-ws.org/Vol-3996/paper-4.pdf

28. Tan, X., Shen, R.: Personalized course generation based on layered recommendation systems. In: Popescu, E., Lau, R.W.H., Pata, K., Leung, H., Laanpere, M. (eds.) ICWL 2014. LNCS, vol. 8613, pp. 166–172. Springer, Cham (2014). https://doi.org/10.1007/978-3-319-09635-3_18
29. Ting, D.H., Lee, C.K.C.: Understanding students' choice of electives and its implications. Stud. High. Educ. **37**(3), 309–325 (2012). https://doi.org/10.1080/03075079.2010.512383
30. Tomy, S., Pardede, E.: Course map: a career-driven course planning tool. In: Gervasi, O., et al. (eds.) ICCSA 2018. LNCS, vol. 10961, pp. 185–198. Springer, Cham (2018). https://doi.org/10.1007/978-3-319-95165-2_13
31. Tomy, S., Pardede, E.: Map my career: career planning tool to improve student satisfaction. IEEE Access **7**, 132950–132965 (2019). https://doi.org/10.1109/ACCESS.2019.2940986
32. Vaishnavi, V.K., Kuechler, W.J.: Design Science Research Methods and Patterns. Auerbach Publications, 1 edn. (2007). https://doi.org/10.1201/9781420059335

Short Papers

Investigating Developer Productivity Enhancement Through SAP Joule for Developers: A Case Study Evaluation

Maryke Schoeman[1], Charl Scholtz[1], Hanlie Smuts[2(✉)], Paul Louw[1], and Danie Smit[1]

[1] Automotive Industry, Pretoria 0181, South Africa
[2] University of Pretoria, Hatfield, Pretoria 0083, South Africa
hanlie.smuts@up.ac.za

Abstract. As artificial intelligence (AI) continues to transform software development practices, enterprise organizations are increasingly adopting AI-powered tools to enhance developer productivity. This paper presents a case study evaluation of SAP *Joule for Developers*, an AI-powered assistant designed specifically for SAP development environments. Through a controlled A/B crossover study involving SAP developers, the authors evaluated the impact of *Joule* across three key dimensions: developer sentiment, productivity metrics (throughput and cycle time), and code quality. The findings reveal that the majority of participants reported improved productivity. These results are particularly noteworthy, given that measurements were taken against an already AI-augmented baseline using established tools like *GitHub Copilot*. Using the enterprise systems engineering (ESE) profiler framework, the paper contextualizes these findings within the complexity of introducing emerging AI technology into established development environments. The study contributes empirical evidence of the efficacy of AI tools in specialized enterprise development contexts and provides insights for organizations considering AI adoption in their development workflows.

Keywords: SAP *Joule* · Developer Productivity · AI-Powered Development Tools · Enterprise Systems Engineering · Code Quality

1 Introduction

SAP has long been synonymous with enterprise resource planning (ERP) software used by organizations to streamline core business processes. As development complexity continues to grow and evolve, the need for more intelligent development tools becomes increasingly apparent. SAP has introduced *Joule*, an artificial intelligence (AI) powered assistant to enhance the productivity of SAP developers [1]. It forms part of the broader SAP AI strategy designed to support developers by accelerating tasks and providing contextual assistance. *Joule* is an enterprise AI copilot with a product set that includes components, such as *Joule*, *Joule Agents*, *Joule Studio*, and role-specific offerings for developers and consultants, all designed to embed AI across core business functions and workflows [1].

E. Laurenzi et al. (Eds.): BIR 2026, LNBIP 601, pp. 467–477, 2027.
https://doi.org/10.1007/978-3-032-38498-0_29

The introduction of AI-powered development tools represents a significant shift in how software is created and maintained. While general-purpose AI coding assistants (ACATs) like *GitHub Copilot* have demonstrated measurable benefits across various programming contexts, specialized tools tailored to specific enterprise platforms remain less studied [2]. SAP *Joule* represents just such a specialized tool designed to address the unique challenges in SAP development environments, including complex module structures, proprietary frameworks, and intricate business logic requirements.

Therefore, the research question this study addressed is: "*In what ways does SAP* Joule for Developers *contribute to developer productivity enhancement within software development teams?*" By understanding how the AI-driven capabilities of *Joule for Developers* streamline workflows, reduce cognitive load, support decision-making, and accelerate routine development tasks, the study aimed to reveal the specific mechanisms through which the tool influences team efficiency, code quality, and overall delivery performance.

The paper is structured as follows: Sect. 2 provides background to the study; Sect. 3 details the research methodology, and Sect. 4 provides the findings. Section 5 presents the discussion, and Sect. 6 concludes the paper.

2 Background

Enterprise systems have long been recognized as powerful drivers of organization-level productivity. These systems enhance operational efficiency across the organization by automating routine tasks, integrating fragmented processes, and streamlining information flows.

2.1 The Enterprise Systems Engineering (ESE) Profiler

An enterprise is a complex, adaptive socio-technical system designed to create stakeholder value. It comprises an organisation (or network of organisations) and its transactional environment, which interact and evolve to achieve a shared mission [3–5]. Technological systems within enterprises have become increasingly complex, giving rise to key disciplines, such as enterprise architecture (EA) and enterprise engineering (EE). These approaches have converged into enterprise systems engineering (ESE), which applies systems engineering principles to the enterprise as a whole, including its environment and product systems [5, 6].

Software engineering productivity refers to the efficiency with which developers deliver and evolve software, typically measured as the ratio of outputs to inputs [7]. Research has shown that productivity is multidimensional, shaped not only by technical tools but also by human, process, and organizational factors [8]. Studies have further indicated that focusing solely on technical metrics is insufficient; effective productivity improvement requires considering context, practices, and communication [9]. Recent evidence highlights the growing impact of AI-assisted development tools in enterprise environments, demonstrating notable gains in efficiency, reduced cycle times, and increased code output. These findings suggest that modern tooling, practices, and organizational alignment, typically embedded within enterprise systems engineering, are crucial in enhancing developer productivity [10].

The idea of defining the problem context across multiple dimensions forms the foundation of the Enterprise Systems Engineering (ESE) Profiler presented in Table 1. The ESE Profiler is designed as a self-assessment tool to help systems engineers and program managers better understand the nature and context of a given project. It also forms the basis for a situational model, supporting the selection and adaptation of processes, tools, and techniques best suited to the specific problem and its context [11].

Table 1. The Enterprise Systems Engineering Profiler (Authors derived table from [11])

Context	Dimension	Level 1 (centre ring)	Level 2	Level 3 (outer ring)
System Context	Desired Outcome	Improve existing capability	Change existing capability	Build fundamentally new capability
	System Behaviour	Known system behaviour	System behaviour fairly predictable	System behaviour will evolve
Strategic Context	Mission Environment	Stable mission	Mission evolves slowly	Mission very fluid, ad-hoc
	Scope of Effort	Single function	Single enterprise	Extended enterprise
Implementation Context	Scale of Effort	Single user	Similar users	Many different users
	Acquisition Environment	Single program, single system	Single program, multiple systems	Multiple programs, multiple systems
Stakeholder Context	Stakeholder Involvement	Stakeholders concur	Agree in principle; some not involved	Multiple equities; distrust
	Stakeholder Relationship	Relationships stable	New relationships	Resistance to changing relationships

Measuring software developer productivity has long been a challenge in software engineering research and practice. Traditional metrics, such as lines of code written or number of commits made, have proven inadequate, as they fail to capture the multifaceted nature of software development work [12]. Modern frameworks recognize that productivity encompasses not only output velocity but also code quality, developer well-being, and a sustainable work pace [13]. The SPACE framework (satisfaction and well-being, performance, activity, communication and collaboration, efficiency and flow) provides a comprehensive approach to measuring developer productivity by acknowledging multiple dimensions of work. This study focuses on three key constructs of this framework:

Developer Satisfaction (the S in SPACE), Performance through Throughput and Cycle-Time Metrics (the P in SPACE), and Efficiency through Code-Quality Measures (the E in SPACE) [14]. We applied the ESE Profiler to contextualize the complexity of introducing a new generative AI tool into an established engineering environment. The ESE framework provides a structured approach to understanding the interplay between System Context, Mission Environment, Strategic Context, and Stakeholder Context, all of which influence the adoption and effectiveness of new development tools [11].

2.2 Productivity Through AI Tools

AI has become an essential enabler of modern software development, with capabilities spanning code completion, debugging, and solution brainstorming. AI coding assistant tools (ACATs) like *GitHub Copilot* have demonstrated meaningful productivity improvements, with studies showing reduced task completion times and increased code output [2]. However, the effectiveness of these tools can vary significantly based on the development context, programming language, and specific task types [15]. Scholars investigated task types from multiple perspectives, such as a focus on software engineering education introducing ACATs to evaluate the performance of code generation tools in introductory programming contexts [16–18], Another focus of enquiry is based on software developer performance highlighting qualitative studies assessing develop perceptions when engaging with ACATs, ACAT's performance compared to software developers and engineers, and ACATs' impact on development tasks [2, 19, 20].

SAP *Joule for Developers* builds on these focus areas by integrating AI capabilities directly into the SAP development environment, providing a tailored support ecosystem that understands SAP-specific frameworks, patterns, and best practices. The specialized focus of this tool distinguishes it from general-purpose ACATs and positions it to address unique challenges in enterprise system development.

2.3 Case Study Environment

This study was conducted within an automotive industry organization characterized by a fast-paced development environment and high technology adoption rates. The organization maintains a mature SAP development infrastructure with established processes and tooling. Developers in this environment regularly work with complex business logic, integration requirements, and stringent quality standards typical of enterprise automotive systems.

The development teams already utilize ACATs, including *GitHub Copilot* and other internal AI assistants, establishing a sophisticated baseline for productivity comparison. This context is significant because it means that the observed improvements from SAP *Joule for Developers* represent additive value on top of an already enhanced development workflow, rather than improvements over traditional, non-AI-assisted development practices. Organizational commitment to continuous improvement and willingness to evaluate emerging technologies provided an ideal setting for assessing the effectiveness of the pre-release version of SAP *Joule for Developers* in a realistic, high-performance development environment [21].

3 Research Methodology

The research leading to this paper aimed to investigate how SAP *Joule for Developers* contributed to enhancing developer productivity within software development teams. This objective was achieved through a case study research strategy, with data collected via a controlled experiment, employing A/B testing [22]. A/B testing is a method for comparing two software variants, denoted as Variant A and Variant B, by evaluating the merits of the variants through exposure to system end-users [23].

Our study adopted a controlled empirical evaluation as guided by the evaluation philosophy of Vaithilingam et. al. [24] and Maragheh and Deldjoo [25]. In the case study organization, we had access to 33 ABAP developers from multiple departments in the IT hub to participate in the case study. In addition, due to business requirements and demand on work outputs, the case organization approved two timeboxes of 180 min each per group. Therefore, Group A (17 developers × 180 min) yielded 3,060 min of active coding under condition A and the same number of minutes under condition B, while Group B (16 developers × 180 min) yielded 2,880 min of active coding for each of their conditions. During these active coding timeboxes, developers were not distracted by meetings, emails, and coffee breaks typical of a normal multi-week A/B test. Our experiment design therefore evaluated the immediate, high-focus onboarding and short-term velocity impact of SAP *Joule for Developers* within a controlled 180-min sprint. While it does not capture long-term codebase maintenance or habit formation, it successfully isolates tool-assisted speed and accuracy across 5,940 min of uninterrupted engineering data for timeboxes 1 and 2. The sample of 33 ABAP developers' levels of expertise were classified as either beginner (B), intermediate (I), or expert (E) based on their roles in the case study organization and years of experience. These developers were then divided into two groups, Group A and Group B. To ensure that we balance the level of expertise between the two groups, the cumulative level of expertise was determined by assigning weights to each level: B = 1, I = 2, and E = 3, and calculating the sum of the average weighted score per group. Group A (17 developers) reported 43 as a cumulative level of expertise and Group B (16 developers) a cumulative level of 41.

The ESE Profiler informed the content design of the experiment. The *business perspective* guided the task selection that required an understanding of business processes rather than isolated coding exercises, while the *information perspective* included tasks involving enterprise data models, core data services views, database access and data integrity. The *application perspective* focus on software developer activities such as coding, debugging, refactoring and testing. Lastly, the *technology perspective* ensured inclusion of task using the actual SAP development environment. Table 3 presents the analysis of the measurements, utilizing ESE Profiler (see Sect. 2.1) to contextualize the complexity of introducing a new generative AI tool into an established engineering environment.

The evaluation of SAP *Joule for Developers* yielded quantitative and qualitative data across three primary dimensions: developer sentiment, productivity, and code quality. The developer sentiment data were obtained through a questionnaire on perceived productivity, quality, and overall usefulness. The productivity measurements identified as relevant for this study included throughput (how many tasks were completed within the timebox) and cycle time (how long tasks took from start to finish). In addition, the

Table 3. Measurement analysis

Measurement	ESE Profiler Mapping	Data Collection Tool
Developer Sentiment	Stakeholder Context – Stakeholder Relationship	Microsoft Forms
Throughput	Strategic Context – Desired Outcome	SAP Development Workbench – Change Logs
Cycle Time	Strategic Context – Desired Outcome	SAP Development Workbench – Change Logs
Code Quality	Strategic Context – Desired Outcome	SAP Development Workbench

study determined code quality by conducting a quality assurance (QA) review of random samples of completed work. The productivity measurements were collected within two 180-min timeboxes over two days by using a controlled and structured A/B test with a crossover design:

- On Day 1, Group A used their standard toolset, such as *GitHub Copilot* and other internal AI assistants. Group B used SAP *Joule for Developers* only (no other AI tools).
- On Day 2, the groups swapped tool access. Group A used SAP *Joule for Developers* only, while Group B worked with their standard tools. Both groups received a fresh set of everyday ABAP tasks.

Seeing that Group A consisted of one more participant, the throughput measurements were analyzed at a participant level, from where the average was determined using the following formula:

$$Average\ Throughput\ of\ Group\ (x)\ on\ Day\ (y) = \frac{\sum_{i=1}^{n} Average\ Throughput\ of\ Participant\ (i)\ in\ Group\ (x)\ on\ Day\ (y)}{n}$$

As mentioned, cycle time was set at 180 min for both groups each day, with all participants beginning and ending at the same predetermined time. In addition, because Group B had a slightly lower cumulative level of expertise, the throughput and cycle time data from Group A were multiplied by a factor of 0.95 to equalize the findings between the respective groups and enable fair comparisons. The factor was calculated from the level of expertise stated in Table 2, as follows:

$$Factor = \frac{41}{43} = 0.95$$

The design above compares SAP *Joule for Developers* to how developers currently work and also allows each group to act as both "test" and "control" over the two days. This approach allows the IT hub to compare the performance of these groups individually and with each other to assess how SAP *Joule for Developers* affects their work.

4 Findings

We discuss the quantitative and qualitative findings in this section. Although the case study organization supported the empirical study, organizational confidentiality policies did not permit the publication of internal operational statistics. Consequently, only aggregated and anonymized findings are reported to protect organizational interests while preserving the integrity of the research.

4.1 Productivity Metrics

The analysis of the productivity metrics yielded the following observations:

- **Productivity**: The quantitative data collected through the A/B crossover design corroborates the sentiment regarding productivity.
- **Throughput**: There was an observable increase in the number of use cases delivered when participants utilized SAP *Joule for Developers* compared to the control group. This metric indicates that the tool effectively helped increase the volume of work delivered within the time constraints of the challenge.
- **Cycle Time**: Similarly, the overall cycle time, measuring the duration from start to finish of a task, was lower during the *Joule*-augmented sessions. This reduction in time-to-completion aligns with the self-reported productivity improvements from the sentiment survey.

4.2 Developer Sentiment

Querying developers directly was an efficient way to gauge their sentiments [14]. A Likert-scale survey posed this statement to participating developers: "As a developer, my job satisfaction has increased or will increase due to the use of SAP *Joule for Developers.*" Developers could select between "Strongly Agree," "Agree," "Neither Agree nor Disagree," "Disagree," and "Strongly Disagree." As part of software professional practices, the impact of software products on social and personal life must be considered, as well as their influence on personal well-being and societal harmony [26]. Therefore, developer satisfaction is not only an important Stakeholder Context measurement within the ESE Profiler, specifically regarding Stakeholder Relationships and Involvement, but also because of the potential impact of generative AI, including SAP *Joule for Developers*, on people. The developers in this study expressed that the use of SAP *Joule* did not affect their job satisfaction. This opinion should be viewed through the lens of the System Context of the ESE Profiler. The System Behavior tool is currently evolving, as it is at an earlier stage of maturity than the established toolsets developers typically use. A second statement posed in the Likert-scale survey was: "*Joule for Developers* improved my overall productivity during the SAP *Joule* Developer Challenge." The response here was markedly more positive. The results indicated that the majority of respondents felt that SAP *Joule for Developers* improved their overall productivity.

4.3 Reflection

These productivity findings are particularly significant when viewed through the System and Mission Environment contexts of the ESE Profiler. As highlighted in the case study documentation, high fluidity and evolving system behaviour characterized the environment due to four key factors:

- **Novelty**: For most participants, this was their first exposure to *Joule*. Therefore, the results include the friction of a learning curve, indicating a fluid rather than a stable Mission Environment.
- **Constraint**: *Joule* currently runs only in *Eclipse*, whereas many developers utilize *GitHub Copilot* in their standard workflows. This factor introduces a specific System Context constraint regarding tool accessibility.
- **Baseline**: Efficiency uplift was observed in addition to an already AI-augmented baseline, consisting of *GitHub Copilot* and other more mature internal AI tools. The study did not compare *Joule* against "no AI" but rather demonstrated additive value to an existing high-performance toolset.
- **Maturity**: *Joule* is a relatively "infant" technology compared to the "toddler" maturity of *GitHub Copilot*. It is also important to note that ABAP developers in enterprise environments may exhibit comparatively lower AI maturity than full-stack developers, who typically operate in more AI tool-diverse ecosystem. However, observing a measurable efficiency improvement at this early stage signals a strong potential trajectory as the tool matures within the System Context.
- **Quality**: Crucially, the increase in velocity detailed above did not come at the expense of stability. Code quality remained constant throughout the challenge. This finding is significant. Typically, an increase in throughput without a corresponding maturity in processes and people can lead to technical debt. The delivery of more work with stable quality suggests that the Desired Outcome of "Improving existing capability," per the ESE Profiler, is being met, even at this early stage of adoption.

5 Discussion and Contribution

This study contributes to the growing body of literature examining the impact of AI tools on software development productivity, with particular focus on specialized enterprise contexts. Several key insights emerged from the findings:

Additive Value in AI-augmented Environments: SAP *Joule for Developers* demonstrated measurable improvements even when evaluated against an already AI-enhanced baseline. This outcome suggests that specialized, domain-specific AI tools can provide value beyond general-purpose coding assistants. The complementary nature of these tools indicates that organizations should consider multi-tool strategies rather than assuming a single AI assistant will address all development needs.

The Satisfaction/Productivity Gap: Organizations introducing AI development tools should manage expectations appropriately. While productivity benefits may materialize relatively quickly, satisfaction and emotional attachment to new tools may develop more gradually. Training programs, community building, and patience during adoption periods may be necessary to realize the full benefits of AI tool investments.

Quality Maintenance During Productivity Gains: Maintaining code quality while achieving productivity improvements possibly represents the most important practical finding of this study. This result disproves common concerns that AI coding assistants might create technical debt or reduce code quality in pursuit of speed. For enterprise organizations considering AI tool adoption, this finding offers reassurance that productivity gains do not necessarily entail quality compromises. However, the finding should be interpreted with appropriate caution. In addition, AI tool productivity gains should be accompanied by a corresponding growth in processes and individuals' maturity, considering a sociotechnical approach.

6 Conclusion

SAP *Joule* represents a significant step toward AI-augmented software development within the SAP ecosystem. This study provides empirical evidence that specialized AI development tools can enhance developer productivity through contextual assistance and seamless integration with enterprise development environments. By demonstrating measurable improvements in throughput and cycle time while maintaining code quality, the findings support strategic SAP goals of enabling faster, more efficient business process customization and system development.

The research reveals several important insights. First, specialized AI tools can add value, even in environments already using general-purpose coding assistants, suggesting that multi-tool strategies could be optimal for complex enterprise development contexts. Second, the divergence between perceptions of productivity and improvements in job satisfaction highlights the multifaceted nature of tool adoption, which indicates that functional benefits might materialize before emotional or affective benefits. Third, maintaining code quality during productivity improvements addresses a critical concern about AI-assisted development and provides reassurance to organizations considering investing in such tools.

This study had several significant limitations. First, the evaluation period was relatively short, capturing initial adoption experiences but not long-term usage patterns or sustained productivity changes. Second, the study was conducted within a single organization in the automotive industry; hence, generalization to other sectors, organizational sizes, or development contexts requires careful consideration. Moreover, although the crossover design was methodologically sound, all participants experienced both conditions, which potentially introduced carryover effects that the analysis might not have fully captured. The self-selected nature of challenge participation could also have introduced selection bias toward developers who were more open to new tools.

As AI-assisted development continues to evolve, ongoing research is essential to understand how these tools can be most effectively deployed to enhance both developer productivity and well-being in enterprise contexts. Furthermore, although tools, such as SAP *Joule for Developers*, demonstrate clear value in enhancing developer productivity, the transition from initial adoption to mature, integrated use remains underexplored. Thus, future research should extend to understanding what defines AI maturity in enterprise environments, viewed through a sociotechnical lens.

References

1. SAP. Joule Assistants (2026). https://www.sap.com/products/artificial-intelligence/ai-assistant.html. Accessed Mar 2026
2. Smit, D., Smuts, H., Louw, P., Pielmeier, J., Eidelloth, C.: The impact of GitHub Copilot on developer productivity from a software engineering body of knowledge perspective. In: AMCIS. 2024, AIS: Salt Lake City, Utah. https://aisel.aisnet.org/amcis2024/ai_aa/ai_aa/10
3. Giachetti, R.E.: Design of Enterprise Systems: Theory, Architecture, and Methods. Boca Raton, CRC Press, Taylor and Francis Group (2010)
4. McCaughin, K.L., DeRosa, J.K.: Stakeholder analysis to shape the enterprise. In: Minai, A., Braha, D., Bar-Yam, Y., (eds.) Unifying Themes in Complex Systems: Proceedings of the Sixth International Conference on Complex Systems, pp. 548–555. Springer, Berlin
5. Hoogervorst, J.A.P.: Enterprise Governance and Enterprise Engineering. The Enterprise Engineering Series, ed. J.L.G. Dietz, E. Proper, and J. Tribolet. Diemen: Springer, Heidelberg (2009)
6. Martin, J.N.: The Great Transition: Using the Seven Principles of Enterprise Engineering to Align People, Technology and Strategy. AMACOM, New York (1995)
7. Sadowski, C., Zimmermann, T.: Rethinking Productivity in Software Engineering. Springer, Heidelberg (2019)
8. Smuts, S., Smuts, H.: Society 5.0 and the future of work skills for software engineers and developers. In: Gerber, A., Hinkelmann, K., (eds.) Society 5.0, EPiC Series in Computing, pp. 169–182. Olten, Switzerland (2022). https://doi.org/10.29007/9kzd
9. Razzaq, A., Buckley, J., Lai, Q., Yu, T., Botterweck, G.: A systematic literature review on the influence of enhanced developer experience on developers' productivity: factors, practices, and recommendations. ACM Comput. Surv. **57**(1), 1–46 (2024)
10. Akdur, D.: Analysis of software engineering skills gap in the industry. ACM Trans. Comput. Educ. **23**(1), 1–28 (2022)
11. DeRosa, J., Grisogono, A.-M., Ryan, A., Norman, D.: A Research Agenda for the Engineering of Complex Systems, pp. 1–8 (2008)
12. Storey, M.-A., Zimmermann, T., Bird, C., Czerwonka, J., Murphy, B., Kalliamvakou, E.: Towards a theory of software developer job satisfaction and perceived productivity. IEEE Trans. Softw. Eng. **47**(10), 2125–2142 (2019)
13. Murphy-Hill, E., et al.: What predicts software developers' productivity? IEEE Trans. Softw. Eng. **47**(3), 582–594 (2019)
14. Forsgren, N., Storey, M.-A., Maddila, C., Zimmermann, T., Houck, B., Butler, J.: The SPACE of developer productivity. Commun. ACM **64**(6), 46–53 (2021)
15. Long, X., Tan, X., Zhu, Y., Jiang, J., Zhang, L.: Understanding and enhancing CS students' interaction experience with AI coding assistant tools. ACM Trans. Softw. Eng. Methodol. (2025)
16. Denny, P., Kumar, V., Giacaman, N.: Conversing with copilot: Exploring prompt engineering for solving cs1 problems using natural language. In Proceedings of the 54th ACM Technical Symposium on Computer Science Education V. 1 (2023)
17. Finnie-Ansley, J., Denny, P., Becker, B.A., Luxton-Reilly, A., Prather, J.: The robots are coming: Exploring the implications of openai codex on introductory programming. In: Proceedings of the 24th Australasian Computing Education Conference (2022)
18. Savelka, J., Agarwal, A., Bogart, C., Song, Y., Sakr, M.: Can generative pre-trained transformers (GPT) pass assessments in higher education programming courses? In: Proceedings of the 2023 Conference on Innovation and Technology in Computer Science Education V. 1 (2023)

19. Dakhel, A.M., Majdinasab, V., Nikanjam, A., Khomh, F., Desmarais, M.C., Jiang, Z.M.J.: Github copilot AI pair programmer: asset or liability? J. Syst. Softw. **203**, 111734 (2023)
20. Nascimento, N., Alencar, P., Cowan, D.: Comparing software developers with chatgpt: An empirical investigation. arXiv preprint arXiv:2305.11837 (2023)
21. ARC Advisory Group, Industrial digital transformation top 25, in ARC Special Report (2022). www.arcweb.com
22. Yin, R.K.: Case Study Research: Design and Methods, vol. 5. Sage (2009)
23. Quin, F., Weyns, D., Galster, M., Silva, C.C.: A/B testing: a systematic literature review. J. Syst. Softw. **211**, 112011 (2024). https://doi.org/10.1016/j.jss.2024.112011
24. Vaithilingam, P., Zhang, T., Glassman, E.L.: Expectation vs. experience: evaluating the usability of code generation tools powered by large language models. In Chi conference on Human Factors in Computing Systems Extended Abstracts (2022)
25. Maragheh, R.Y., Deldjoo, Y.: The future is agentic: Definitions, perspectives, and open challenges of multi-agent recommender systems. arXiv preprint arXiv:2507.02097 (2025)
26. Washizaki, H.: Guide to the software engineering body of knowledge. IEEE Comput. Soc. **4** (2024)

Cyber Resilience in the Age of Digital Sovereignty: A Comparative Analysis of Assessment Frameworks for Sovereign Cloud Environments

Renate Strazdina(✉)

Institute of Applied Computer Systems, Riga Technical University, Riga, Latvia
renate.strazdina@outlook.lv

Abstract. This paper investigates the convergence of cyber resilience and digital sovereignty in cloud-dependent environments, with particular emphasis on the European regulatory landscape. As reliance on public and hybrid cloud services intensifies, concerns over data protection, jurisdictional exposure and strategic dependency transform cyber resilience from a predominantly technical concern into a broader governance and policy challenge. The paper traces the co-evolution of digital sovereignty and cyber resilience in European policy and scholarship and examines how it reshapes contemporary interpretations of cyber resilience. Using a qualitative, document-based comparative method, the study derives eight digital-sovereignty dimensions from EU legislation and peer-reviewed taxonomies and evaluates five widely adopted frameworks - NIST CSF 2.0, ISO 22301, CERT-RMM, COBIT 2019 and the MITRE Cyber Resiliency Engineering Framework/NIST SP 800-160 Vol. 2 - against them through transparent deductive coding. While the frameworks cover continuity, governance, assurance and third-party risk well, they systematically under-represent sovereignty-specific dimensions including jurisdictional control, portability and exit readiness, rights-aligned data governance and strategic autonomy. The paper concludes that existing frameworks require sovereignty-aware adaptation rather than wholesale replacement, and identifies an integrated assessment model as the principal direction for future work.

Keywords: Digital sovereignty · Cyber resilience · Cloud computing · EU regulation · Assessment frameworks

1 Introduction

Over the past decade, cloud computing has become the dominant service-delivery paradigm and a foundational enabler of industrial digitalisation [31, 40]. Society's reliance on continuously available cloud services has elevated cyber resilience - the capacity to withstand disruptions and rapidly recover - from a desirable property to a precondition for organisational continuity [2, 8]. In Europe this shift is now embedded in binding regulation: NIS2 [12] and DORA [3] impose risk-management, continuity and

E. Laurenzi et al. (Eds.): BIR 2026, LNBIP 601, pp. 478–486, 2027.
https://doi.org/10.1007/978-3-032-38498-0_30

third-party-oversight duties, the Cyber Resilience Act [20] adds security-by-design, and the Data Act [17] introduces cloud-switching rights and a restriction on non-EU governmental access to data. In parallel, digital sovereignty has matured into a multi-faceted policy objective, yet no prevailing model reconciles regulatory effectiveness with the pace of technological change [22, 33].

The relationship between the two agendas is best understood as co-evolutionary rather than hierarchical: each has developed in tandem with the other. Cyber resilience supplies the operational capabilities - anticipation, continuity, recovery and adaptation - on which sovereign control of critical services depends, while sovereignty supplies the jurisdictional and strategic conditions under which they can be exercised. In the European setting, sovereignty is becoming a constitutive dimension of resilience: an organisation that can technically recover a service but cannot guarantee the jurisdiction under which its data is processed is, in regulatory terms, only partially resilient.

Existing cyber-resilience assessment frameworks have not, however, been systematically evaluated against digital-sovereignty requirements; a Scopus search combining "cyber resilience" with "sovereignty" returns fewer than a dozen peer-reviewed contributions. This paper addresses that gap by evaluating five frameworks chosen to span distinct families of the resilience-and-governance landscape - NIST CSF 2.0, ISO 22301, CERT-RMM, COBIT 2019 and the MITRE Cyber Resiliency Engineering Framework (CREF) / NIST SP 800-160 Vol. 2 (characterised in Sect. 4). Governance frameworks are deliberately included, because digital sovereignty is itself substantially a governance problem and their exclusion would bias the analysis against the dimensions under examination.

The study addresses two research questions. **RQ1:** how have digital sovereignty and cyber resilience evolved in European policy and scholarship, and how does this evolution reshape the understanding of cyber resilience for cloud-dependent services? **RQ2:** to what extent do the five frameworks reflect the key elements of digital sovereignty articulated in recent EU instruments?

The remainder of the paper is organised as follows. Section 2 describes the methodology; Sect. 3 reviews the literature and establishes the eight sovereignty dimensions; Sect. 4 presents the comparative analysis; Sect. 5 discusses the findings; and Sect. 6 concludes with directions for future research.

2 Methodology

2.1 Research Design

The study adopts a qualitative, document-based comparative analysis combining two evidence streams kept methodologically distinct: a systematic review of peer-reviewed scholarship, used to trace the conceptual evolution of the two concepts and to derive the assessment dimensions (RQ1); and a direct documentary analysis of primary sources - EU legal instruments, ENISA outputs and official framework documentation - used to ground the dimensions and to evaluate framework coverage (RQ2).

2.2 Systematic Literature Review

The review followed the inclusion criteria of Fratini et al. [22]: English-language, peer-reviewed contributions, with a small number of seminal pre-2013 works for lineage and an extension to 2026 for recent regulation. Searches in Scopus and Google Scholar combined the terms "digital sovereignty", "cyber sovereignty", "data sovereignty", "technology sovereignty", "cyber resilience" and "sovereign cloud"; the exact Scopus strings and resulting counts are reported below. Records were screened in two stages - title/abstract, then full text - retaining a contribution only if it addressed (i) the conceptualisation or measurement of digital sovereignty, (ii) cyber-resilience theory or frameworks, or (iii) their intersection in cloud-dependent settings.

To characterise the trajectory quantitatively, six Scopus sub-corpora were harvested on 27 May 2026 (English-language records). Writing S for the phrase set *("digital sovereignty" OR "data sovereignty" OR "cyber sovereignty" OR "technology sovereignty")*, the queries and counts were: digital sovereignty, *TITLE-ABS-KEY("digital sovereignty")*, n = 731; sovereignty, *TITLE ("sovereignty")*, n = 453; sovereignty-extended, *TITLE-ABS-KEY("data sovereignty" OR "cyber sovereignty" OR "technology sovereignty")*, n = 581; sovereignty-and-resilience, *TITLE-ABS-KEY (S AND "resilience")*, n = 191; sovereignty-and-cyber-resilience, *TITLE-ABS-KEY (S AND "cyber resilience")*, n = 10; and cyber-resilience-and-sovereign, *TITLE-ABS-KEY ("cyber resilience" AND sovereign*)*, n = 3. The identical quoted phrases were run in Google Scholar (no field operators) to cross-check coverage. The small size of the last two corpora is itself a finding: the intersection, though salient in regulation, is markedly under-represented in the literature.

2.3 Rationale for Combining Review and Policy Analysis

Because RQ2 is framed around EU instruments, the use of a Scopus and Google Scholar review warrants justification. The review is not used to retrieve or interpret the regulation itself: EU legislation, ENISA guidance and framework documentation are read directly, at source, as primary documents. The bibliometric review serves a complementary purpose - mapping the scholarly conceptualisation over time, identifying the taxonomies from which the dimensions are synthesised, and evidencing the scarcity of work at the intersection. Triangulating the two mitigates the limitations of either approach used alone.

2.4 Deductive Coding and Rating

For RQ2 the official documentation of the five frameworks was coded against the eight dimensions, and each framework-dimension pair was rated on a four-level scale - High (dedicated, explicit coverage), Medium (partial or indirect), Low-Medium (possible with tailoring) and Low (minimal or absent) - with the rating justified by reference to specific provisions of the documentation. The complete coding scheme and the per-pair justifications is not provided in the paper due to page limitations, but it demonstrates that the ratings are auditable rather than asserted. The coding was performed by a single researcher; the absence of an inter-coder reliability check is acknowledged as a limitation, and multi-coder validation is identified as future work.

3 Literature Review

3.1 The Evolution of Digital Sovereignty

Westphalian sovereignty is defined by "territoriality and the exclusion of external actors from domestic authority structures" [28]. Cyberspace destabilises this paradigm, as digital governance has emerged through multi-stakeholder cooperation and transnational norms rather than treaties [29]. Couture and Toupin [6] trace how "sovereignty" migrated to data-, rights- and platform-centred meanings, while Pohle and Thiel [33] show it to be a discursive construct mobilised differently by states, firms and civil society. Synthesising 271 articles, Fratini et al. [22] identify four models - rights-based, market-oriented, centralisation and state-based - and conclude that none reconciles comprehensive regulation with responsiveness to innovation. Catalytic events such as the Snowden revelations and COVID-19 accelerated sovereignty measures across jurisdictions [35].

Within Europe, Floridi [21] and Roberts et al. [34] ground sovereignty in rights-based normativity, and Moerel and Timmers [30] operationalise its legal dimensions. The EU has codified these positions across horizontal resilience rules - NIS2 [12], DORA [3], the CRA [20], the CER Directive [13], the Cybersecurity Act [14] and the AI Act [19] - and sovereignty rules - the Data Act [17], the Data Governance Act [15], eIDAS 2.0 [18] and the Chips Act [16] - within the targets of the 2030 Digital Decade [11]. National schemes diverge [35]: France's SecNumCloud is the most stringent benchmark for jurisdictional immunity, Germany's BSI C5 a widely adopted but lighter attestation. These respond to extraterritorial reach - the US CLOUD Act [39] and FISA Section 702 can compel disclosure by US-headquartered providers, held disproportionate in Schrems II [5] - and Gomes et al. [24] show that major hyperscaler "sovereign cloud" offerings remain subject to US jurisdiction. AI sovereignty [7] is an accelerating frontier and a candidate ninth dimension.

3.2 The Eight Digital-Sovereignty Dimensions

Eight dimensions are derived as the analytical lens for RQ2, each anchored in identifiable sources: (1) *continuity and resilience of essential services* (NIS2 and DORA duties; [2, 8]); (2) *governance and accountability* (NIS2 management-body accountability); (3) *third-party and supply-chain ICT risk oversight* (DORA; [37]); (4) *assurance, auditability and certification readiness* (Cybersecurity Act; EUCC/EUCS); (5) *rights-aligned data protection* (GDPR; [25]); (6) *jurisdictional control and exposure management* (Data Act Art. 32; Schrems II; [24]); (7) *portability, interoperability and exit readiness* (Data Act cloud-switching); and (8) *strategic autonomy and dependency reduction* ([9]; Chips Act; Digital Decade). These dimensions were synthesised by triangulating two evidence streams. The systematic review traced the conceptual evolution of digital sovereignty (RQ1) and supplied the peer-reviewed taxonomies from which the candidate dimensions were distilled: the four models identified by Fratini et al. [22] - furnished the conceptual map, while individual studies sharpened specific dimensions, Hummel et al. [25] disambiguating data sovereignty to anchor dimension 5 and Edler et al. [9] distinguishing technology sovereignty from autarky to anchor dimension 8. This scholarly reading was then triangulated against a direct documentary analysis of

EU instruments - so that each dimension is anchored simultaneously in a regulatory obligation and a scholarly construct; dimensions 6 and 7 in particular were derived as responses to the structural legal asymmetry that Gomes et al. [24] identify between European requirements and the jurisdiction of hyperscale providers. A candidate dimension was retained only where regulation and scholarship converged.

3.3 Cyber Resilience: Theory and Frameworks

Resilience entered cybersecurity from ecology, where Holling reframed it as the persistence of systems under disturbance [8]. Bjorck et al. [2] define cyber resilience as "the ability to continuously deliver the intended outcome despite adverse cyber events", and Dupont [8] argues that the predict-and-protect paradigm is inadequate because vulnerability cannot be eliminated. Annarelli et al. [1] show framework choice to be context-dependent, Galaitsi et al. [23] separate resilience from robustness, redundancy and risk, and Seid et al. [37] find one-size-fits-all approaches inadequate. The argument is structural: a sovereignty-aware evaluation that extends this context-dependence [1, 38] to a further factor - the jurisdictional regime - is a justified contribution rather than a duplication.

4 Comparative Analysis of the Frameworks

This section evaluates the five frameworks against the eight dimensions, applying the rating of Sect. 2.4. Each dimension is assessed uniformly; the resulting coverage pattern - not any prior labelling - is the finding. The frameworks span distinct families: NIST CSF 2.0 [32] (security functions, including Govern), ISO 22301 [26] (certifiable business continuity), CERT-RMM [4] (operational-resilience maturity), COBIT 2019 [27] (enterprise IT governance) and MITRE CREF / NIST SP 800-160 Vol. 2 [36] (resilience engineering). Table 1 reports the ratings.

Coverage of the first four dimensions is generally strong. Continuity (D1) is most comprehensively addressed - NIST CSF 2.0, ISO 22301, CERT-RMM and CREF rate High, only COBIT 2019 Medium. Governance (D2) is High for COBIT 2019, ISO 22301, CERT-RMM and NIST CSF 2.0 (Govern function) and Medium for CREF. Third-party risk (D3) is High only for CERT-RMM, whose "External Dependencies Management" is a named process area [37], the others Medium. Assurance and certification (D4) is High for ISO 22301, CERT-RMM and COBIT 2019, but Medium for NIST CSF 2.0 and CREF, neither tied to an EU scheme such as EUCS or EUCC.

Table 1. Qualitative ratings of five frameworks against the eight digital-sovereignty dimensions (H = High, M = Medium, LM = Low–Medium, L = Low)

Sovereignty dimension	NIST CSF 2.0	ISO 22301	CERT-RMM	COBIT 2019	CREF / SP 800–160
1. Continuity and resilience	H	H	H	M	H
2. Governance and accountability	H	H	H	H	M
3. Third-party / supply-chain risk	M	M	H	M	M
4. Assurance and certification	M	H	H	H	M
5. Rights-aligned data protection	LM	LM	LM	M	LM
6. Jurisdictional control	L	L	M	M	M
7. Portability and exit readiness	L	M	M	LM	M
8. Strategic autonomy	LM	L	M	M	M

Coverage of the remaining dimensions is markedly weaker. Rights-aligned data protection (D5) receives no High rating - four frameworks rate Low–Medium and COBIT 2019 Medium. Jurisdictional control (D6) is least covered: NIST CSF 2.0 and ISO 22301 rate Low, the others Medium, none providing standardised sovereignty guidance. Portability and exit readiness (D7) is weak - NIST CSF 2.0 Low, COBIT 2019 Low–Medium, the others Medium. Strategic autonomy (D8) follows the same pattern - ISO 22301 Low, NIST CSF 2.0 Low–Medium, the rest Medium.

Read across the five frameworks, the pattern is consistent and constitutes the principal finding of RQ2: dimensions 1–4 are covered well, frequently at High, whereas the sovereignty-specific dimensions 5–8 are systematically under-addressed even where the former are comprehensive. None was designed with jurisdictional control, exit readiness or strategic autonomy as a central concern. This misalignment creates a critical blind spot for organisations that must satisfy resilience obligations under NIS2, DORA and the CRA while also meeting sovereignty expectations under the Data Act, the EUCS and schemes such as SecNumCloud.

5 Discussion

Three observations follow. First, the blind spot is not random: the under-addressed dimensions each concern an organisation's relationship to an external legal or strategic order - the jurisdiction to which its data is exposed, the providers it depends on, and its capacity to exit them - rather than the internal management of disruption the frameworks were built to govern. They under-perform on sovereignty because it introduces a class of concern outside their original design intent, extending the context-dependence thesis of Annarelli et al. [1] to the jurisdictional regime as a further contextual factor.

Second, the finding has practical consequences. An organisation may score High on continuity and governance yet remain exposed on jurisdiction and portability - satisfying the letter of NIS2 or DORA but unprepared for the Data Act and national certification schemes - and because the frameworks do not surface these dimensions, the exposure stays invisible to assessments built on them. The recommendation is adaptation, not replacement: retain the resilience constructs the frameworks cover well and add the sovereignty-specific dimensions as explicit, measurable extensions. Limitations apply: the analysis is documentary, capturing design rather than implementation; the ratings involve interpretive judgement without an inter-coder reliability check; and the dimensions reflect the EU context.

6 Conclusions and Future Research

This paper evaluated five established frameworks against eight digital-sovereignty dimensions derived from EU regulation and peer-reviewed taxonomies. The frameworks, largely designed before sovereignty-driven regulation consolidated, emphasise operational robustness over jurisdictional control, strategic autonomy and provider independence, leaving the sovereignty-specific dimensions weakly operationalised or implicit. Under NIS2, DORA and the Data Act this creates practical assessment and compliance challenges, underlining the need to adapt existing frameworks through sovereignty-aligned criteria rather than replace them.

Future work follows three directions: an integrated assessment model that retains the strongest resilience constructs and adds the missing sovereignty extensions on a maturity scale anchored to the EU Cloud Sovereignty Framework [10]; empirical validation through interviews, case studies and multi-coder coding; and a prospective ninth dimension for AI sovereignty [7].

References

1. Annarelli, A., Nonino, F., Palombi, G.: Understanding the management of cyber resilient systems. Comput. Ind. Eng. **149**, 106829 (2020). https://doi.org/10.1016/j.cie.2020.106829
2. Bjorck, F., Henkel, M., Stirna, J., Zdravkovic, J.: Cyber resilience - fundamentals for a definition. In: Advances in Intelligent Systems and Computing, vol. 353, pp. 311–316 (2015). https://doi.org/10.1007/978-3-319-16486-1_31
3. Buttigieg, C.P., Zimmermann, B.B.: The digital operational resilience act: challenges and some reflections on the adequacy of Europe's architecture for financial supervision. ERA Forum **25**, 11–28 (2024). https://doi.org/10.1007/s12027-024-00793-w

4. Caralli, R., Allen, J., White, D.: CERT Resilience Management Model: A Maturity Model for Managing Operational Resilience. Carnegie Mellon University, Software Engineering Institute (2016)
5. Court of Justice of the European Union: Data Protection Commissioner v. Facebook Ireland and Schrems, Case C-311/18 (Schrems II) (2020)
6. Couture, S., Toupin, S.: What does the notion of "sovereignty" mean when referring to the digital? New Media Soc. **21**(10), 2305–2322 (2019). https://doi.org/10.1177/1461444819865984
7. Dale, R.: Sovereign AI in 2025. Nat. Lang. Process. **31**(5) (2025)
8. Dupont, B.: The cyber-resilience of financial institutions: significance and applicability. J. Cybersecur. **5**(1), tyz013 (2019). https://doi.org/10.1093/cybsec/tyz013
9. Edler, J., Blind, K., Kroll, H., Schubert, T.: Technology sovereignty as an emerging frame for innovation policy. Res. Policy **52**(6), 104765 (2023). https://doi.org/10.1016/j.respol.2023.104765
10. European Commission, Directorate-General for Digital Services: The EU Cloud Sovereignty Framework (2026)
11. European Parliament and Council of the EU: Decision (EU) 2022/2481 establishing the 2030 Policy Programme "Path to the Digital Decade" (2022)
12. European Parliament and Council of the EU: Directive (EU) 2022/2555 (NIS2) on measures for a high common level of cybersecurity across the Union (2022)
13. European Parliament and Council of the EU: Directive (EU) 2022/2557 (CER) on the resilience of critical entities (2022)
14. European Parliament and Council of the EU: Regulation (EU) 2019/881 (Cybersecurity Act) (2019)
15. European Parliament and Council of the EU: Regulation (EU) 2022/868 (Data Governance Act) (2022)
16. European Parliament and Council of the EU: Regulation (EU) 2023/1781 (Chips Act) (2023)
17. European Parliament and Council of the EU: Regulation (EU) 2023/2854 (Data Act), incl. Chapter VI and Article 32 (2023)
18. European Parliament and Council of the EU: Regulation (EU) 2024/1183 (eIDAS 2.0) (2024)
19. European Parliament and Council of the EU: Regulation (EU) 2024/1689 (AI Act) (2024)
20. European Parliament and Council of the EU: Regulation (EU) 2024/2847 (Cyber Resilience Act, CRA) (2024)
21. Floridi, L.: The fight for digital sovereignty: what it is, and why it matters, especially for the EU. Philos. Technol. **33**(3), 369–378 (2020). https://doi.org/10.1007/s13347-020-00423-6
22. Fratini, S., Hine, E., Novelli, C., Roberts, H., Floridi, L.: Digital sovereignty: a descriptive analysis and a critical evaluation of existing models. Digital Soc. **3**, 59 (2024). https://doi.org/10.1007/s44206-024-00146-7
23. Galaitsi, S.E., Keisler, J.M., Trump, B.D., Linkov, I.: The need to reconcile concepts that characterize systems facing threats. Risk Anal. **41**(1), 3–15 (2021). https://doi.org/10.1111/risa.13577
24. Gomes, A.F., Okano-Heijmans, M., van den Wijngaard, J.: 'Sovereign clouds': a non-answer to Europe's concerns. In: From Common Worries to Digital Commons, pp. 9–11. Clingendael Institute (2026)
25. Hummel, P., Braun, M., Tretter, M., Dabrock, P.: Data sovereignty: a review. Big Data Soc. **8**(1) (2021). https://doi.org/10.1177/2053951720982012
26. International Organization for Standardization: ISO 22301:2019 - Security and resilience: Business continuity management systems - Requirements (2019)
27. ISACA: COBIT 2019 Framework: Introduction and Methodology (2018)
28. Krasner, S.D., Baquero, M.M.: Sovereignty: organized hypocrisy. New York University J. Int. Law Politics, 221–224 (1999)

29. Küçükuncular, A.: Addressing ethical challenges in cyberspace governance: recommendations for the digital sovereignty era. Digital Soc. **5**, 3 (2026). https://doi.org/10.1007/s44206-025-00241-3
30. Moerel, L., Timmers, P.: Reflections on Digital Sovereignty. EU Cyber Direct (2021)
31. Mušić, D., Hribar, J., Fortuna, C.: Digital transformation with a lightweight on-premise PaaS. Futur. Gener. Comput. Syst. **160**, 619–629 (2024). https://doi.org/10.1016/j.future.2024.06.026
32. National Institute of Standards and Technology: The NIST Cybersecurity Framework (CSF) 2.0 (NIST CSWP 29) (2024). https://doi.org/10.6028/NIST.CSWP.29
33. Pohle, J., Thiel, T.: Digital sovereignty. Internet Policy Rev. **9**(4) (2020). https://doi.org/10.14763/2020.4.1532
34. Roberts, H., Cowls, J., Casolari, F., Morley, J., Taddeo, M., Floridi, L.: Safeguarding European values with digital sovereignty. Internet Policy Rev. **10**(3) (2021). https://doi.org/10.14763/2021.3.1575
35. Rone, J.: 'The sovereign cloud' in Europe: diverging nation-state preferences and disputed institutional competences in the context of limited technological capabilities. J. Eur. Publ. Policy **31**(8), 2343–2369 (2024). https://doi.org/10.1080/13501763.2024.2348618
36. Ross, R., Pillitteri, V., Graubart, R., Bodeau, D., McQuaid, R.: Developing cyber-resilient systems: a systems security engineering approach (NIST SP 800-160 Vol. 2 Rev. 1) (2021). https://doi.org/10.6028/NIST.SP.800-160v2r1
37. Seid, E., Ilter, D., Blix, F., Popov, O.: Cyber supply chain resilience: analyzing ISO, NIST and NIS2 frameworks for mitigating third-party risks. Procedia Comput. Sci. **263**, 591–599 (2025). https://doi.org/10.1016/j.procs.2025.07.071
38. Sepulveda-Estay, D.A., Sahay, R., Barfod, M.B., Jensen, C.D.: A systematic review of cyber-resilience assessment frameworks. Comput. Secur. **97**, 101996 (2020). https://doi.org/10.1016/j.cose.2020.101996
39. US Congress: Clarifying Lawful Overseas Use of Data Act (CLOUD Act), Pub. L. 115–141, Div. V (2018)
40. Welsh, T., Benkhelifa, E.: On resilience in cloud computing: a survey of techniques across the cloud domain. ACM Comput. Surv. **53**(3), 59 (2020). https://doi.org/10.1145/3388922

Consumer Apps as Support for Increased Sustainability: An Investigation in Food Retailing

Sebastian Dannehl[1] and Kurt Sandkuhl[1,2(✉)]

[1] Institute of Computer Science, University of Rostock, Albert-Einstein-Street 22, 18057 Rostock, Germany
kurt.sandkuhl@uni-rostock.de, kurt.sandkuhl@ju.se
[2] School of Engineering, Jönköping University, Jönköping, Sweden

Abstract. International initiatives to establish sustainability have been important drivers of a societal and industrial transition towards sustainable business models (SBM). Using food retailing as an example, the paper investigates whether companies actively use consumer apps to support SBM and whether consumers perceive these apps as supporting their sustainability ambitions. One part of the research addresses the extent to which the consumer apps reflect the objectives of food retailers when it comes to increasing sustainability. Another part of the work takes the customer perspective, i.e., how much the consumers are supported in sustainable lifestyle. The functions and information in mobile apps that support consumers and the consumer perception are investigated. The paper aims to contribute to research by analyzing the sustainability-related content and functionality offered, the perception of the consumers, and the improvement potential.

Keywords: Consumer app · sustainability · food retailing

1 Introduction

International initiatives to establish sustainability, like the United Nations' sustainability goals [1] and the related regulations, have been important drivers of a societal and industrial transition towards more sustainable production and sustainable business models (SBM) [2]. SBM can help embed sustainability into business processes and serve as a driver of competitive advantage [3]. A central framework for sustainable development is the 2030 Agenda; its Sustainable Development Goals (SDGs) [1] comprise 17 goals and 169 sub-goals addressing environmental, economic, and social sustainability dimensions [4]. Sustainability reporting has become an instrument for transparency and accountability [5]. Another major trend is digital transformation, which is affecting all aspects of business [6], including customer-related processes. In this context, consumer apps have emerged as one of the key links to customers, establishing a self-service technology (SST) [7] in the retailer–customer relationships for activities such as information seeking, price scanning, and actual purchases [8]. In the context of SBM, consumer apps

E. Laurenzi et al. (Eds.): BIR 2026, LNBIP 601, pp. 487–493, 2027.
https://doi.org/10.1007/978-3-032-38498-0_31

are a bi-directional interface between company and consumer: Companies can use apps to motivate a shift in the consumer's behavior towards more sustainable product selection or product delivery. For a consumer striving for a more sustainable lifestyle, apps form an instrument for informed product or service selection. However, there is a lack of research (see Sect. 2) on the role of consumer apps in increasing sustainability, which motivates this paper.

Using food retailing as an example, our research question is whether companies actively use consumer apps to support SBM and whether consumers perceive these apps as supporting their sustainability ambitions. The food retail sector plays a particularly important role in sustainable development due to its economic significance and influence on supply chains and consumer behaviour. In relation to the SDGs, food production and food retail are directly and indirectly linked to all 17 sustainability goals. While retailers have significant influence over product offerings and shape sustainability directly within stores [9], consumer preferences also affect which products are included in retail assortments. We selected food retailing as an application area because the food industry is one of the largest industry sectors worldwide and continues to grow substantially (see [10]). Most data for our investigation was collected in the German market, as the market penetration of consumer apps is relatively high [11].

One part of our research addresses the extent to which the consumer apps reflect the objectives of food retailers (in functionalities or content) when it comes to increasing sustainability as documented in the retailers' sustainability reports. Another part of our work investigates, how much the consumers perceive that they are supported in sustainable lifestyle. Both parts are combined in the research question: *What sustainability-related offerings do consumer apps in food retail provide, and how are these perceived from the customer perspective?* The paper aims to contribute to research by analyzing the sustainability-related content and functionality offered, the perception of the consumers, and the improvement potential.

2 Literature Analysis on Consumer Apps and Sustainability

Related work on consumer apps in the context of sustainability in food retail was identified by a structured literature review (SLR) according to Kitchenham [12]. The research question for the SLR was: RQ-SLR: "What is the state of research on consumer apps to support sustainability in food retailing?". The literature sources included in the search were IEEE Xplore, Scopus, and AISeL. The search string was based on the main keywords in RQ-SLR: (TITLE-ABS-KEY ("consumer app" OR "mobile app") AND TITLE-ABS-KEY (sustain*) AND TITLE-ABS-KEY (retail*)). We excluded papers that did not address consumers, but used mobile apps for other purposes (e.g., in supply chains or medical contexts). The search returned 36 hits in Scopus; these hits included the 3 hits in IEEE Xplore and one in AISeL. Among the 36 hits were several proceedings volumes, papers addressing technical functionality or implementation details of mobile apps, and apps outside the food area (e.g., in fashion and health care). These papers were excluded. 5 papers were found relevant for RQ-SLR: Lewis et al. [13] present the design of a mobile app intended to engage community members in improving access to healthy foods in under-resourced urban areas. Stevens et al. [14] explore how shopping and consumption data generated through Internet-of-Things (IoT) enabled environments can support the design of sustainable consumer applications. Jagatheesan et al. [15] introduce an IoT-based system that supports personalized shopping and automated inventory management. Head et al. [16] investigate the environmental impacts of protein-rich foods by developing extensive life cycle assessment models. Tavill [17] examines the growing industry focus on food waste and discusses the economic, ethical, and environmental drivers behind it. In conclusion, none of the identified papers study the sustainability of consumer apps in food retailing.

3 Research Methodology

To answer the research questions presented in the introduction, an exploratory research design was applied. The study examined 14 food retail companies with strong market dominance in the German grocery retail sector. First, the companies' consumer apps were analyzed for sustainability-related functions and content. Subsequently, the apps were reviewed over a 6-week period to identify newly added sustainability-related functions and information. Existing and new content was assigned to the sustainability categories for food retail (see 4). In addition, sustainability reports on the companies' websites were examined. The sustainability efforts were also assigned to the developed sustainability categories to investigate whether the sustainability efforts in the reports were reflected in the content and functions of the companies' apps. Furthermore, an online survey was conducted to examine customer perceptions of sustainability in food retail apps. Responses from 74 individuals were included in the analysis. The survey consisted of 23 questions, including 18 closed-ended questions, four partially closed questions with optional text input, and one open-ended question. Seven of the closed-ended questions used a five-point ordinal scale to quantitatively measure customer attitudes (1 = lowest level of agreement; 5 = highest level). The survey followed a deductive approach based on "if–then" hypotheses as foundation of the questionnaire:

- If sustainability/sustainable products are promoted more strongly in apps, customers will pay more attention to sustainability/buy more sustainable products.
- If apps provide sustainability-related features, customers will use the consumer apps of specific retailers more frequently.
- If food retailers present sustainability-related topics in their consumer apps, customers will perceive this positively, depending on age.

Following the survey, a qualitative expert interview was conducted with a customer loyalty trainer responsible for Rewe Group's app, again based on "if–then" hypotheses:

- If food retailers implement sustainability-related functions and information in their consumer apps, these are based on criteria from sustainability reports.
- If sustainability/sustainable products are promoted more strongly in apps, customers will pay more attention to sustainability/buy more sustainable products.
- If food retailers present sustainability-related topics in their consumer apps, customers will perceive this positively, depending on age.
- If food retailers use their consumer apps and cooperate with other apps, they do so to support the implementation of sustainability goals.

The survey questions were evaluated based on frequency distributions. The statements from expert interview were analyzed using inductive category formation following Mayring's qualitative content analysis approach [18].

4 Results

Consumer app functionalities, and user and expert perceptions were classified into six categories derived from Keller et al. [19] and related to the food retail value chain: producer, retailer, and consumer. For the producer perspective, the categories included labor, working, and supply conditions (LWS) and product, raw material, and assortment selection (SOR). At the retailer level, the categories were SOR, resource and operations management (ROM), employee management and development (EMD), and pricing strategies (PR). For the consumer perspective, the category information provision and communication (INF) was applied.

4.1 Analysis of Sustainability Reports of Large Food Retail Companies

The strategic sustainability objectives of companies were analyzed based on published sustainability reports. The examined companies included Aldi, Edeka, Schwarz Group (including Lidl and Kaufland), Rewe Group (including Penny and Rewe), Rossmann, Norma, Globus, dm-drogerie markt, and Markant / Famila.

All investigated companies stated that they implement sustainability measures across the entire supply chain. The categories SOR, LWS, ROM, and INF were addressed in all sustainability reports, whereas PR was only considered by five of the fourteen companies. All companies addressed environmental, economic, and social sustainability and aimed to cover the entire supply chain. The results indicate that all companies regard sustainability as a strategic corporate objective and have defined implementation measures, which should also be reflected in their consumer apps.

4.2 Analysis of Consumer App Content and Functions

In the SOR category, the apps mainly featured labels and promotions for organic private-label products. This corresponds to the consumer focus on product sustainability when purchasing food products. In the ROM category, app functionality is very limited, mostly to the provision of digital advertising brochures and digital receipts aimed at reducing paper waste. This feature was already implemented in six of the fourteen analyzed apps and, according to the customer survey, was used by 44.3% of respondents.

Coupons for sustainable products were primarily used to support the category product, raw material, and assortment selection, including regional products. Several apps also provided information regarding sustainable packaging concepts.

Frequently implemented functions in the apps in the LWS category included product scanners, and in PR category sustainability-related pricing incentives, discount coupons for organic private-label products, and information regarding product origin and cooperation with sustainable producers. All apps provided digital access to current offers and advertising brochures. The companies used their apps as communication channels for presenting sustainability initiatives.

4.3 User Perception

Of the 74 respondents, 17.6% were between 18–24 years old, 17.6% between 25–34, 33.8% between 35–44, 10.8% between 45–54, and 20.3% were 55 years or older. In total, 55.4% identified as female and 44.6% as male. The app users in our sample primarily value product quality and a reasonable price-performance ratio when purchasing food products. In comparison, sustainability was considered less important. However, nearly three-quarters of respondents regarded sustainable packaging and the reduction of food waste as particularly important sustainability aspects. The respondents paid special attention to sustainability in the categories of fruit and vegetables (82.4%), meat (81.1%), and eggs (71.6%), whereas sustainability considerations for beverages were less important (23%). It also seems that "Ecologically produced seasonal regional products" have a particularly strong impact on sustainability. 66.2% of survey participants considered the origin and regionality of sustainable food products to be very important.

In general, sustainability-related functions and information in the apps were perceived as moderately important. At the same time, the current implementation of sustainable app functions was evaluated rather critically, with many respondents rating it as average or below average. Features most frequently recognized by users included the labeling of organic/ecological products and digital sales slips aimed at reducing paper waste. The results also showed that respondents wished for a broader range of sustainable products and more sustainability-related information. More than 50% of participants considered additional sustainability information to be important or very important. Respondents requested additional information related to product origin, farming, and production conditions. Furthermore, sustainable packaging and the reduction of food waste were identified as especially important issues.

The majority of respondents preferred sustainability-related information directly on the product. In this context, consumers have a great interest in nutrition-related topics and personalization. As for general app functions and information, customers expressed stronger interest in personalized functions and content, in-store navigation services, and additional product information through the apps while shopping. Thus, consumer apps in food retail offer considerable potential to further promote sustainability-related topics through this digital interface while simultaneously addressing user needs.

4.4 Expert Perspective

The interview did not provide evidence that consumer apps are important for the strategic objectives described in sustainability reports. According to the expert, Rewe primarily uses its app to reduce resource consumption and to influence purchasing behavior through sustainability-related pricing. It was confirmed that all app functions and content, including sustainability-related features, are continuously monitored and analyzed. A clear trend toward increased purchases of organic products due to app-based coupons was also confirmed. The expert stated that customers generally respond positively to sustainability-related app content, depending on age group. At present, the company's sustainability focus in the app mainly concerns reducing paper waste and promoting sustainable products through temporary discount campaigns and coupons.

5 Conclusions and Future Work

The study showed that consumer apps provide a highly differentiated range of sustainability-related functions and information. Depending on the company, sustainability is addressed to varying degrees and implemented differently across individual apps. However, no comprehensive direct relationship could be established between the sustainability measures presented in the published sustainability reports and the content provided within the apps. None of the analyzed apps covered the entire spectrum of sustainability categories. Through their consumer apps, companies primarily implemented measures related to production and supply chains as well as their own business operations. This finding was also supported by the expert interview, which emphasized a focus on resource- and consumer-behavior-related sustainability measures.

The limited range of sustainability-related functions and content corresponded with customer perceptions. Users evaluated the current implementation of sustainable functions as average to poor and expressed a desire for a broader range of sustainable products within the apps. Despite increasing interest in sustainability-related information and rising revenues, particularly within the organic product segment, sustainability was not considered a necessary criterion for app usage by current and potential users. These findings suggest that sustainable app content and features are primarily aligned with user preferences and companies' economic interests.

In conclusion, the research question—"What sustainability-related offerings do consumer apps in food retail provide, and how are these perceived from the customer perspective?"—can be answered as follows: Due to its role as an intermediary between food manufacturers and consumers, the food retail sector contributes significantly to sustainable development. However, this responsibility is only addressed to a limited extent through the sustainability-related offerings provided in consumer apps. The technical characteristics of smartphone apps create both opportunities and challenges for companies regarding user interaction and engagement. Because of the focus on consumer preferences and potential economic risks, sustainability implementation within consumer apps is not being fully advanced. Customers also perceive this limited offering. At the same time, they demonstrate only moderate interest in sustainability-related content and mainly demand selected functions and information. Additional sustainability-related content would therefore only partially influence purchasing behavior and increase app usage.

This study has several limitations. It focuses exclusively on Germany, limiting the international applicability of the findings. The sustainability report and consumer app analyses covered only the highest-revenue food retailers and examined apps over a limited period, reducing completeness. The online survey was constrained by time, resulting in a small sample size, few responses, and a short data collection period, which limited the reliability, validity, and robustness of the results. In addition, survey responses were based on subjective perceptions and may have been influenced by external factors. Finally, only one expert interview was conducted, limiting generalizability.

References

1. United Nations, Department of Economic and Social Affairs: Sustainable Development Goals. The 17 Goals. https://sdgs.un.org/goals
2. Schaltegger, S., Hansen, E.G., Lüdeke-Freund, F.: Business models for sustainability: origins, present research, and future avenues. Organ. Environ. **29**, 3–10 (2016)
3. Bocken, N.M.P., Short, S.W., Rana, P., Evans, S.: A literature and practice review to develop sustainable business model archetypes. J. Clean. Prod. **65**, 42–56 (2014)
4. Carlsen, L., Bruggemann, R.: The 17 United Nations' sustainable development goals: a status by 2020. Int. J. Sustain. Dev. World **29**, 219–229 (2022)
5. Dienes, D., Sassen, R., Fischer, J.: What are the drivers of sustainability reporting? A systematic review. Sustainabil. Account. Manag. Policy J. **7**, 154–189 (2016)
6. Schwertner, K.: Digital transformation of business. Trakia J. Sci. **15**, 388–393 (2017)
7. Robertson, N., McDonald, H., Leckie, C., McQuilken, L.: Examining customer evaluations across different self-service technologies. J. Serv. Mark. **30**, 88–102 (2016)
8. Newman, C.L., Wachter, K., White, A.: Bricks or clicks? Understanding consumer usage of retail mobile apps. J. Serv. Mark. **32**, 211–222 (2017)
9. Claro, D.P., Neto, S.A.L., de Oliveira Claro, P.B.: Sustainability drivers in food retail. J. Retail. Consum. Serv. **20**, 365–371 (2013)
10. Statista: Market Insights - Food, worldwide (2024)
11. Statista: Mobile Apps. Statista Dossier (2024)
12. Kitchenham, B., Brereton, P.: A systematic review of systematic review process research in software engineering. Inf. Softw. Technol. **55**, 2049–2075 (2013)
13. Lewis, E.C., et al.: Design of a mobile app interface that engages community members in a food system pilot study. Nutrients **16** (2024). https://doi.org/10.3390/nu16111723
14. Stevens, G., Bossauer, P., Neifer, T., Hanschke, S.: Using shopping data to design sustainable consumer apps. In: 5th IFIP Conference on Sustainable Internet and ICT for Sustainability, SustainIT 2017 (2018). https://doi.org/10.23919/SustainIT.2017.8379810
15. Jagatheesan, M., Karthick, R., Yokesh, V.G., Dineshkumar, P., Saravanan, K., Geetha, K.: Intelligent grocery management system using IoT for personalized shopping and inventory management. In: International Conference on Advanced Computing Technologies, ICoACT 2025 (2025). https://doi.org/10.1109/ICoACT63339.2025.11005200
16. Head, M., Sevenster, M., Odegard, I., Krutwagen, B., Croezen, H., Bergsma, G.: Life cycle impacts of protein-rich foods: creating robust yet extensive life cycle models for use in a consumer app. J. Clean. Prod. **73**, 165–174 (2014). https://doi.org/10.1016/j.jclepro.2013.11.026
17. Tavill, G.: Industry challenges and approaches to food waste. Physiol. Behav. **223** (2020). https://doi.org/10.1016/j.physbeh.2020.112993
18. Mayring, P.: Qualitative content analysis: theoretical background and procedures. In: Approaches to Qualitative Research in Mathematics Education: Examples of Methodology and Methods, pp. 365–380. Springer, Heidelberg (2014)
19. Keller, O., Sager, R., Schader, C., Jungmichel, N., Teriete, M.: Wie nachhaltig sind die deutschen Supermärkte? - Systematische Bewertung der acht umsatzstärksten Unternehmen des Lebensmitteleinzelhandels in Deutschland aus Umweltsicht. In: Umweltbundesamt (ed.) Texte, pp. 1–166 (2022)

A Method for Defining and Tracking Objectives of Research Projects

Jānis Grabis(✉)

Information Technology, Riga Technical University, Zunda Krastmala 10, Riga, Latvia
grabis@rtu.lv

Abstract. Funding agencies provide funding for research and innovations projects, and their specific application goals and requirements are defined in the call for projects. This paper suggests that goal modeling supplemented with natural language processing could aid project ideation to ensure better alignment with funding objectives and requirements. Additionally, the goal model provides a specification for designing the project performance management systems, which serves for the lifetime of the project consortium and provides shareable data for further processing. The objective of the paper is to outline a method for designing project performance management systems with emphasis on research and innovation projects requiring alignment with goals and requirements set by funding agencies. The natural language processing is used to match the goal model to call requirements.

Keywords: Performance management · Goal modeling · LLM

1 Introduction

Funding agencies provide funding for research and innovations projects, and their specific application goals and requirements are defined in the call for proposals. These requirements can be expressed as short statements or extensive program documents also containing external references to various national, corporate and international strategic planning documents. Success of project applications significantly depends on alignment of the proposed project to the call objectives. There is also a strong emphasis on achieving measurable objectives in many research and development projects. The project team must formulate suitable objectives, provide appropriate ways of measuring these objectives (often expressed as performance indicators) and establish a performance monitoring system once the project is approved and goes into execution. The performance monitoring system is an information system for management, monitoring and analyzing performance indicators to ensure fulfillment of the objectives [1]. It is often a part of organization's strategic management and core systems. Research and innovation projects on the other hand are usually temporal and distributed, and their project performance management systems (PPMS) are established in

E. Laurenzi et al. (Eds.): BIR 2026, LNBIP 601, pp. 494–501, 2027.
https://doi.org/10.1007/978-3-032-38498-0_32

an ad hoc manner [2,3]. Information systems engineering methods should be used ensure efficient and systematic performance management in research and innovation projects.

Goal modeling is an established approach in information systems development [4]. It is a natural choice for design of performance management systems though there are few actual application examples. This paper suggests that goal modeling should be considered as an aid in the project ideation proposal writing phase to ensure better alignment with funding objectives and requirements. Additionally, the goal model (GM) provides a specification for designing PPMS, which serves for the life-time of the project consortium and provides shareable data for further analysis.

The objective of the paper is to outline a method for designing PPMS with emphasis on research and innovation projects requiring alignment with goals and requirements set by funding agencies. The method is based on goal modeling, which specifies the projects objectives and performance indicators. The specification is translated into an API specification for the PPMS what serves as the basis for implementation. The natural language processing is used to match the GM to the call requirements. A specialized large language model is trained for these purposes.

The rest of the paper is organized as follows. The modeling method is introduced in Sect. 2. Sections 3 elaborated the large language model for matching projects to calls. A demonstration example is provided Sect. 4. Section 5 briefly reviews the related work, and Sect. 6 concludes.

2 Modeling Method

The modeling method allows a project management team to identify suitable project calls and to setup the PPMS. The potential uses cases are: 1) A team has formulated project objectives and searches for a project call suitable for their intentions; 2) the initial project application was not successful and the team searches for a suitable call for a follow-up submission; 3) the call requires alignment with external strategic documents such as UN Sustainable Development Goals and 4) the project should be aligned with organizational strategy, particularly, in the case of portfolio management for internal projects.

The overall modeling process is shown in Fig. 1: 1) the project team discusses the project idea, sets the project goal and describes specific objectives informally; 2) the GM is created to refine the objectives and to specify them in a structured manner; 3) the GM is evaluated against project calls published by a funding agency or strategic planning documents. It is provided as an input to a specifically trained large language model (LLM). LLM suggests matching calls (Sect. 3); 4) performance indicators measuring the goals are added to the GM; 5) an OpenAPI specification of the performance management system is generated by transforming the GM. It is used to generate client side and server side of the project performance management system; 6) the client side is implemented as a project performance management dashboard and the server side is implemented to retrieve performance data from the relevant data sources; and 7) deploy and operate the PPMS.

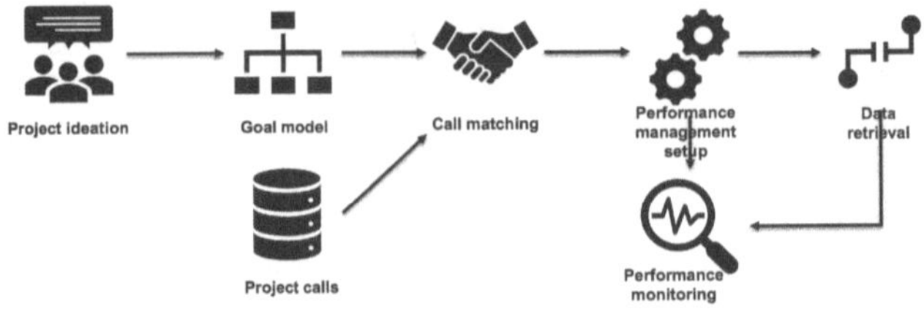

Fig. 1. The overall process of development of the PPMS.

The call matching model can operate with textual descriptions of the goal and the objectives. It is argued that the GM for the project is useful as a visualized collaboration and communication tool among members of the project team as well as with other stakeholders.

3 Matching Model

A machine learning model is used to match project objectives to calls. It is a classification model returning a matching score, which is used to rank calls corresponding to the envisioned project. A data set is prepared by extracting abstracts of accepted projects and their associated call information from the Cordis database (https://data.europa.eu/data/datasets/cordisref-data for Horizon 2020 and Horizon programmes). The call description contains: 1) call code and title, 2) expected outcomes and deliverables, 3) objective and 4) scope. The call description often includes specific aims and requirements towards proposal, e.g., involvement of small and medium enterprises.

The dataset is split into the training set and the test set according to the 80/20 principle. The training data set is used to train the classification model for the following problem. Given a set of project abstracts $A = \{a_1, a_2, \ldots, a_n\}$, a set of funding calls $C = \{c_1, c_2, \ldots, c_m\}$, and a set of evaluation outcomes $O = \{\text{Granted}, \text{Not granted}\}$, a text classification function $f : A \rightarrow C \times O$ is defined to jointly predict the funding call and the evaluation outcome for each project abstract. Specifically, for each abstract $a_i \in A$, the function produces $f(a_i) = (c_j, o_k)$, where $c_j \in C$ denotes the assigned funding call and $o_k \in O$ represents the corresponding evaluation outcome. The classification functions is defined using a model based on the BERT classifier [8]. The training process is iterated until no further significant accuracy improvements are achieved. The model trained is used to match a proposed project with the current calls. The proposed project is described using its GM. The GM is converted into a textual description using an LLM. The classification model compares the project's textual description with the current calls. That yields a ranked list of calls suited to the proposed project. The project team selects one of the top ranked calls.

The training data set includes 1077 different call codes, and the total of 17114 items are used in the training process split equally according to application outcome, i.e., accepted proposals as listed in the database and reject proposals approximated by abstracts of scientific articles related to the theme of the call. There are on average 7.9 accepted proposal per call code and title. The BERT project classifier is used and trained over three epochs. High overall accuracy has been achieved as indicated by F1-score and other performance metric being around 0.9.

4 Application Example

The application of the proposed method is demonstrated using an example of preparing a project proposal on management of resilient ICT supply chains. The GM is elaborated, the Horizon database is searched for appropriate calls, and the performance management system is designed to monitor the project delivery if the proposal is successful. The example is derived from an actual Horizon project application.

The overall goal of the project was to develop and manage resilient ICT supply chains (Fig. 2). They concern the complete scope of a typical research and innovation project and include elaboration of new innovative methods for addressing the aforementioned problem, evaluation of the methods in collaboration with end-users (e.g., commercial companies) and dissemination and exploitation of the project results. Suitable KPI are also identified. A dashboard is a centerpiece of PPMS 3. It is generated according to the project GM. Procedures for calculation of KPI values are implemented using reusable components and generative AI.

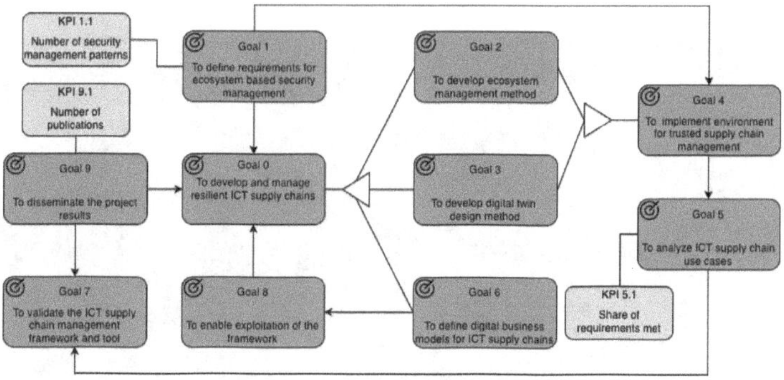

Fig. 2. A sample GM for the resilient ICT supply chain project proposal with selected KPIs.

A set of current project calls were identified in the Cordis database. The calls for 2026 and 2026 in all thematic areas under Pilar 2 were considered. The project abstract was generated using LLM from the GM, and it was matched to the published calls. The matching tool is available at https://callintel.iti.onl [9]. Table 1 shows the top 3 matching calls as well as some calls with a low matching score for illustration. The best matching call HORIZON-CL3-2026-02-CS-ECCC-01 indeed is well-aligned with the GM. The call has Secured hardware systems over trusted Chips and Software Supply Chain security as focus areas, and the project proposal is well-aligned with the second focus area. On the other hand, although the HORIZON-CL3-2026-01-SSRI-04 call addresses secure communications and ecosystems, it focuses on the technical layer is less concerned with method development, supply chains and digital twins. As the results, the matching score is low.

Table 1. Matching Horizon calls (maximum score is 10)

Call ID	Title	Score
HORIZON-CL3-2026-02-CS-ECCC-01	Approaches and tools for security in software and hardware d...	8.67
HORIZON-CL5-2026-10-D6-06	Increasing competitiveness and resilience of multimodal frei...	7.67
HORIZON-CL3-2027-02-CS-ECCC-02	Secure Computing Continuum (IoT, Edge, Cloud, Data spaces)	7.67
HORIZON-CL3-2026-01-SSRI-04	Development of ecosystem and next-generation capabilities fo...	4
HORIZON-CL4-2026-SPACE-03-31	Digital enablers and building-blocks for Earth Observation a...	1

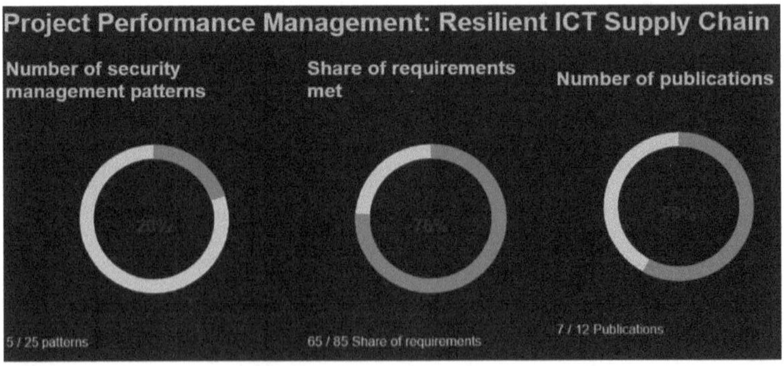

Fig. 3. Dashboard of project KPIs.

5 Related Work

Goal modeling techniques are suitable for design of performance management systems [5]. MetricM [6] is elaborated on the basis of the Multi-perspective enterprise modeling (MEMO) method. It represents associations among KPI and their measurement systems such as ERP systems. The capability driven development [7] method explicates associations among goals and KPI during the information system design phases and supports generation of monitoring and adaptation tools for measuring and controlling KPI during the execution phase. Model-based approaches also have been used to extract measures and KPI to develop business analytics [10] and as a result a data warehouse is built to support strategic decision-making. Reusable components of the performance management system can be built on the basis of common knowledge represented in performance management ontologies [11]. A KPIOWL semantic approach is proposed to formally conceptualize a KPI selection model for enriching Business Intelligence solutions [12]. KPI are also defined for specific project areas. For example, Van de Ven et al. [13] has elaborated the catalog of KPI for business models. This research also relates to the problem of project selection and project portfolio management. Duarte et al. [15] suggests that operations management approaches should be applied in project selection. Multi-criteria decision-making techniques are often employed for project prioritization and selection (see [16] for a recent review). LLM help to account for strategic and other textual factors in project selection [18]. Natural language processing models are finding their way in enterprise modeling and related challenges [17]. Barn et al. [20] points out that generative models are helpful in development and analysis of enterprise models. The generative models are rapidly finding many applications across the project management life-cycle, for instance, definition of the project scope and project planing [19].

6 Conclusion

The paper combines goal modeling, API driven development and LLM to develop the PPMS. The method addresses performance management concerns across the project life-cycle starting with project ideation till implementation and operation of the performance management system. The goal modeling and API driven development channel generative artificial intelligence towards a predictable result. LLM provide opportunities for finding suitable calls for project proposals in variety of sources. The system is not restricted to European Commission funded projects. Additional, funding agencies can be added to the call pipeline. The usage of the performance management system facilities communication among the project partners and reporting to funding body and other stakeholders. The further evaluation of the method envisions its deployment in actual research project to gather feedback for further elaboration.

Disclosure of Interests. The authors have no competing interests to declare that are relevant to the content of this article.

References

1. Grosswiele, L., Röglinger, M., Friedl, B.: A decision framework for the consolidation of performance measurement systems. Decis. Support Syst. **54**, 1016–1029 (2013)
2. Wedekind, G.K., Philbin, S.P.: Research and Grant Management: The Role of the Project Management Office (PMO) in a European Research Consortium Context. J. Res. Adm. **49**(1), 43–62 (2018)
3. Stjerne, I.S., Söderlund, J., Minbaeva, D.: Crossing times: Temporal boundary-spanning practices in interorganizational projects. Int. J. Proj. Manag. **37**(2), 347–365 (2019)
4. Giorgini, P., Mylopoulos, J., Sebastiani, R.: Goal-oriented requirements analysis and reasoning in the Tropos methodology. Eng. Appl. Artif. Intell. **18**(2), 159–171 (2005). https://doi.org/10.1016/j.engappai.2004.11.017
5. Horkoff, J., Yu, E.: Interactive goal model analysis for early requirements engineering. Requirements Eng. **21**, 29–61 (2016)
6. Strecker, S., Frank, U., Heise, D., et al.: MetricM: a modeling method in support of the reflective design and use of performance measurement systems. Inf Syst E-Bus Manag. **10**, 241–276 (2012)
7. Grabis, J., Zdravkovic, J., Stirna, J.: Overview of Capability-Driven Development Methodology. In: Sandkuhl, K., Stirna, J. (eds.) Capability Management in Digital Enterprises. Springer, Cham (2018)
8. Matisons, R.: The Development of an Adapted Language Model for the Identification and Verification of Project Calls, Master Thesis. Riga Technical University (2024)
9. Kampars, J., Find the right EU calls — and a clear strategy to pursue them. https://callintel.iti.onl (2026)
10. Maté, A., Trujillo, J., Mylopoulos, J.: Specification and derivation of key performance indicators for business analytics: A semantic approach. Data Knowl. Eng. **108**, pp. 30–49 (2017)
11. Livieri, B., Di Cagno, P., Bochicchio, M.: A Bibliometric Analysis and Review on Performance Modeling Literature. Complex Syst. Inf. Model. Q. **2**, 56–71 (2015). https://doi.org/10.7250/csimq.2015-2.05
12. Del Mar Roldán-García, M., García-Nieto, J., Maté, A., Trujillo, J., Aldana-Montes, J.F.: Ontology-driven approach for KPI meta-modelling, selection and reasoning. Int. J. Inf. Manage. **58** (2021). https://doi.org/10.1016/j.ijinfomgt.2019.10.003.
13. van de Ven, M., Lara Machado, P., Athanasopoulou, A. et al. Key performance indicators for business models: a systematic review and catalog. Inf. Syst. E-Bus Manag. **21**, 753–794 (2023)
14. Gilsing, R., Wilbik, A., Grefen, P., et al.: Defining business model key performance indicators using intentional linguistic summaries. Softw. Syst. Model. **20**, 965–996 (2021)
15. Duarte, R., Deschamps, F., de Lima, E.P., Pepino, A., Clavijo, R.M.G.: Performance management systems for project management offices: A case-based study. Procedia Manuf. **39**, 923–931 (2019). https://doi.org/10.1016/j.promfg.2020.01.397
16. Kandakoglu, M., Walther, G., Ben Amor, S.: The use of multi-criteria decision-making methods in project portfolio selection: a literature review and future research directions. Ann. Oper. Res. **332**, 807–830 (2024)

17. Antons, D., Grünwald, E., Cichy, P., Salge, T.O.: The application of text mining methods in innovation research: current state, evolution patterns, and development priorities. R D Manag. **50**(3), 329–351 (2020)
18. Saiz, M., Calvet, L.: Combining LLMs and Simheuristics: An Application to the Project Portfolio Selection Problem. In: Juan, A.A., Faulin, J., Lopez-Lopez, D. (eds) Decision Sciences. DSA ISC 2024. Lecture Notes in Computer Science, vol. 14778. Springer, Cham (2025). https://doi.org/10.1007/978-3-031-78238-1-1
19. Nikiforova, O., Bobkovs, R., MiÄijūne, M.K., Babris, K., Pastor, O., Grabis, J.: MAPS-AI – A Tool for AI-Assisted Model-Driven Generation of IT Project Plan and Scope. In: Scanniello, G., Lenarduzzi, V., Romano, S., Vegas, S., Francese, R. (eds.) Product-Focused Software Process Improvement. PROFES 2025. Lecture Notes in Computer Science, vol 16361. Springer, Cham (2026). https://doi.org/10.1007/978-3-032-12089-2-34
20. Barn, B.S., Barat, S., Sandkuhl, K.: Adaptation of Enterprise Modeling Methods for Large Language Models. In: Almeida, J.P.A., Kaczmarek-Heß, M., Koschmider, A., Proper, H.A. (eds.) The Practice of Enterprise Modeling. PoEM 2023. Lecture Notes in Business Information Processing, vol. 497, Springer, Cham (2024). https://doi.org/10.1007/978-3-031-48583-1_1

AI-Based Data Analytics in Public Administration: A Conceptual Model of Organizational Constraints

Edgars Cirulis(✉) and Kaspars Osis

Vidzeme University of Applied Sciences, Terbatas Street 10, Valmiera, Latvia
{edgars.cirulis,kaspars.osis}@va.lv

Abstract. The increasing integration of AI-based data analytics in public administration is significantly transforming organizational decision-making, knowledge management, and public service delivery. Despite the growing adoption of such solutions, public administrations continue to face multiple constraining factors affecting their successful implementation and use, while a comprehensive identification and systematization of these constraints remain limited in existing research. Based on a scoping review of 28 studies, supplemented with inductive coding and conceptual synthesis, 16 constraining factors are identified and conceptually organized into four dimensions. The findings indicate that successful AI adoption in public administration depends not only on technological capability but also on organizational readiness, workforce capability development, governance maturity, and societal legitimacy. The proposed Conceptual Model of Constraining Factors (CMCF) organizes and relates these constraints, providing a conceptual basis for assessing implementation readiness and supporting future empirical validation.

Keywords: Artificial intelligence · Data analytics · Public administration · Constraining factors · Conceptual model · Organizational transformation

1 Introduction

Public administrations are increasingly integrating AI-based data analytics to enhance evidence-based decision-making, organizational knowledge management, and public service delivery. However, successful AI integration extends beyond technology deployment and requires organizational transformation, including governance, workforce capabilities, institutional readiness, and societal legitimacy.

Although existing studies have identified barriers and enablers of AI adoption across organizational contexts, research providing an integrated conceptual organization of constraining factors affecting AI-based data analytics implementation and use in public administration remains limited. The identified constraining factors should not be interpreted as orthogonal categories. Several factors

E. Laurenzi et al. (Eds.): BIR 2026, LNBIP 601, pp. 502–510, 2027.
https://doi.org/10.1007/978-3-032-38498-0_33

conceptually overlap and may influence one another during AI implementation. Conceptually overlapping statements are assigned to the constraining factor that best reflected their primary importance in the context of the original study.

To address the gap, the study investigates the following research questions: 1) What are the main constraining factors for implementation and use of AI-based data analytics solutions in public administration? 2) How do these constraining factors interrelate?

Based on a scoping review and inductive conceptual synthesis, this study identifies constraining factors and organizes them into dimensions. This contributes to understanding AI-supported organizational transformation in public administration by integrating technological, administrative, social, and economic perspectives into a unified conceptual structure.

2 Related Work

AI is increasingly being adopted in public administration to enhance decision-making, knowledge management, and public service delivery [23]. AI-based data analytics supports evidence-based decision-making and organizational knowledge management, enabling more effective public governance [27].

Despite these opportunities, the implementation and use of AI-based data analytics in public administration are still constrained by technological, organizational, ethical, and governance-related challenges. The use of AI in public administration raises concerns related to fairness, transparency, privacy, and human rights [21].

Current discussions on AI often emphasize the technology itself while overlooking the broader systems within which it operates. Consequently, fairness and explainability are frequently treated as technological properties, even though they are also shaped by the sociotechnical systems in which AI technologies are implemented [15]. Further research is required to investigate and evaluate the impact of technological, organizational, and environmental contextual variables, as well as absorptive capacity, on the adoption of AI [21]. This study addresses this gap by identifying and conceptually organizing the main constraining factors affecting the implementation and use of AI-based data analytics in public administration.

3 Research Methodology

A scoping review following the PRISMA-ScR guidelines [35] [28] is conducted to identify factors constraining the implementation and use of AI-based data analytics in public administration. Evidence is synthesized from interdisciplinary literature retrieved from Scopus and Web of Science. The literature search targets journal articles and conference papers. Search queries combine keywords related to AI, data analytics, implementation, public administration, decision-making, and organizational constraints. Records are screened using predefined inclusion and exclusion criteria. Studies unrelated to AI-based data analytics in public administration, purely technical studies, and single case studies without conceptual contributions are excluded. Nineteen studies are identified through the database search, while nine additional studies are obtained through backward and forward citation tracking and continuous monitoring of newly published literature during the review period. The same eligibility criteria are applied to all studies, resulting in a final dataset of 28 publications.

The selected studies are analyzed using inductive coding and conceptual synthesis. Explicit statements describing constraining factors are coded, iteratively compared, merged into conceptually equivalent factors, and grouped into higher-level dimensions based on their conceptual similarity and dominant organizational role. This process results in the proposed CMCF.

4 Results

The scoping review identifies 156 references to organizational constraints in 28 scientific articles. Through inductive coding and conceptual synthesis, these references are consolidated into 16 constraining factors forming the basis of the CMCF.

4.1 Identification of the Constraining Factors

The identified constraining factors are derived from the reviewed studies through inductive coding and conceptual synthesis. Due to space limitations, the complete coding table and illustrative coding examples are not included in this paper. The reported constraining factors and their conceptual synthesis are summarized in Fig. 1 and the proposed CMCF.

Figure 1 represents a summary of the recurrence of each constraining factor as identified in the literature.

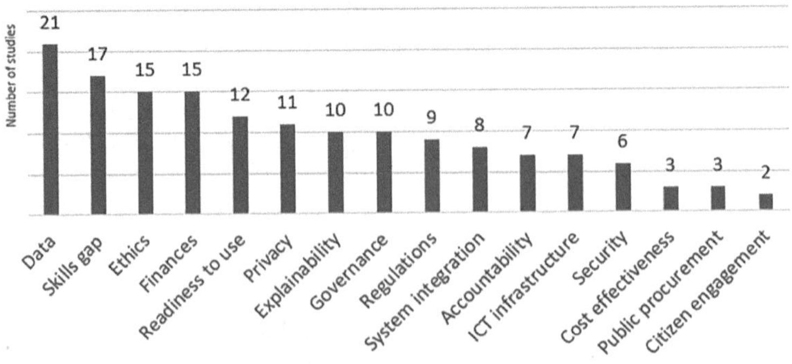

Fig. 1. Frequency of constraining factors identified across the reviewed studies.

Among the most frequently cited constraints are data, skills gap, ethical considerations, and funding availability, as noted in over half of the 28 analyzed articles. These four factors can be considered general constraints in the implementation and use of AI-based solutions in public administration. Other factors, such as readiness to use, privacy, explainability, governance, regulations, system integration, accountability, ICT infrastructure, and security, are widely discussed in the scientific literature. However, the focus on these factors depends on the perspective from which the implementation and use of AI-based solutions in public administration are analyzed. The dominance of data-related and skills-related constraints suggests that AI adoption in public administration depends not only on technological maturity but also on organizational capability.

4.2 Constraining Factor Dimensions

The identified constraining factors are categorized into four dimensions recognized in previous studies: technical, administrative, social, and economic. These dimensions respectively represent the technological capability, organizational capacity, societal legitimacy, and economic feasibility of AI implementation and use. Data availability emerges as the most significant technical constraint, while the skills gap is recognized as the most critical administrative constraint. Ethical considerations are deemed the foremost social constraint, and funding availability is highlighted as the primary economic constraint. Table 1 presents the distribution of constraining factors across various dimensions.

Table 1. Conceptual distribution of constraining factors across CMCF dimensions

Constraining factor	Technical	Administrative	Social	Economic
Data	X			
Skills gap		X	X	
Ethics			X	
Finances				X
Readiness to use		X	X	
Privacy		X	X	
Explainability	X		X	
Governance		X		
Regulations		X	X	
System integration	X			
Accountability		X	X	
ICT infrastructure	X			
Security	X	X		
Cost effectiveness				X
Public procurement		X		
Citizen engagement			X	

Several constraining factors span multiple dimensions. They were assigned according to their dominant conceptual role while acknowledging their cross-dimensional nature.

4.3 Conceptual Model of Constraining Factors

The model organizes the identified dimensions into two complementary perspectives: implementation feasibility and legitimate and accepted use. Although conceptually distinct, the dimensions interact and collectively influence AI integration without implying causal relationships.

Figure 2 presents the proposed Conceptual Model of Constraining Factors (CMCF).

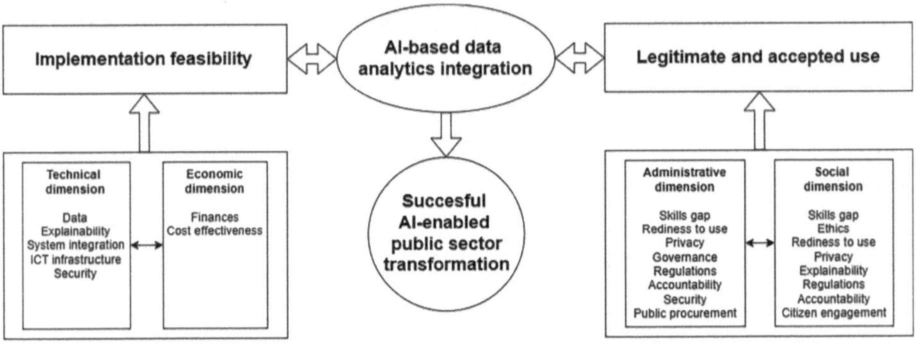

Fig. 2. Conceptual Model of Constraining Factors (CMCF).

Although conceptually distinct, several constraining factors interact and can simultaneously affect the adoption and use of artificial intelligence. The model does not assume causal relationships between dimensions but highlights their complementary influence on AI integration.

5 Discussions

The proposed CMCF organizes and relates constraining factors into a sociotechnical representation of AI adoption in public administration. Unlike previous studies focusing on individual barriers, it integrates technological, administrative, social, and economic constraints without assuming causal relationships.

Although the four dimensions emerge inductively from the reviewed studies, final conceptual organization aligns with the sociotechnical systems perspective (Kudina and van de Poel, 2024), which views AI adoption as the outcome of interactions between technological, organizational, and social elements rather than purely technological change. The persistent emphasis on skills-related constraints indicates that the effective integration of AI in public administration is contingent not only upon technological infrastructure but also on the transformation of the workforce and the enhancement of organizational learning capabilities.

The proposed CMCF integrates generic organizational constraints common to AI adoption across sectors with public-administration-specific constraints that arise from the institutional, regulatory, and societal context of digital government. These constraining factors include, for example, public procurement, regulations, and citizen engagement.

The primary scientific contribution of this study is the development of the CMCF, integrating technological, administrative, social, and economic constraints into a unified conceptual model. Unlike previous studies focusing on isolated barriers, the model conceptualizes AI implementation in public administration as a sociotechnical organizational transformation process. From a practical perspective, CMCF can aid in AI implementation planning and execution by conducting future implementation readiness assessments, thereby serving as a readiness assessment framework for AI adoption in public administration.

This study has several limitations that must be considered when reviewing and interpreting the findings. The review focused on interdisciplinary studies indexed in Scopus and Web of Science and therefore may not cover all relevant publications. Although the number of analysed studies is insufficient for drawing definitive and generalizable conclusions, it is appropriate for exploratory conceptual synthesis. Although the same eligibility criteria are applied throughout the review, the inclusion of supplementary studies identified through manual search procedures may introduce some selection bias. Further empirical validation and refinement of the CMCF are needed as the identified set of constraining factors should be regarded as a preliminary conceptual synthesis. The coding and synthesis are performed by a single researcher, which introduces the possibility of subjective interpretation. However, future studies could strengthen reliability through independent multi-coder validation.

6 Conclusion

This study identifies and conceptually organizes 16 constraining factors affecting the implementation and use of AI-based data analytics solutions in public administration and organizes them into four interconnected dimensions and two complementary implementation perspectives. The proposed CMCF contributes to understanding AI-supported organizational transformation by integrating technological, administrative, social, and economic perspectives into a unified conceptual structure. The findings indicate that successful AI adoption in public administration depends not only on technological factors but also on institutional adaptation, workforce capability development, societal legitimacy, and economic sustainability. From a practical perspective, CMCF may support public-sector digital transformation initiatives by providing a structured conceptual model for understanding organizational constraints that may inform future implementation readiness assessments. Future research should empirically validate the proposed

CMCF and evaluate its applicability across different public administration contexts.

Acknowledgment. The authors used the Paperpal writing assistance platform [30] for grammar, translation, and paraphrasing and Zotero [36] for reference management.

References

1. Ahatsi, E., Olanrewaju, O.A.: Resilience in humanitarian supply chains: addressing artificial intelligence and big data hurdles across borders. Eng. Rep. **7**(7) (2025). https://doi.org/10.1002/eng2.70310
2. Alrawahna, A. S., Alzghoul, A., Awad, H.: The impact of artificial intelligence on public sector decision-making: benefits, challenges, and policy implications. Int. Rev. Manag. Mark. **15**(5), 125–138 (2025). https://doi.org/10.32479/irmm.19419
3. Amariles, D. R., Troussel, A. C., Hamdani, R.E.: Compliance Generation for Privacy Documents under GDPR: A Roadmap for Implementing Automation and Machine Learning (2020). https://doi.org/10.48550/arXiv.2012.12718
4. Amoush, M., Khwaileh, K., AlKhasawneh, F.: Intellectualization of administrative law: challenges and prospects for the implementation of artificial intelligence in public administration. Veredas do Direito *22*(3) (2025). https://doi.org/10.18623/rvd.v22.n3.3406
5. Bagirov, M.: Industrial economy and artificial intelligence: real situation and development directions. Revista Universidad y Sociedad **17**(5) (2025)
6. Bamashmous, M.: The role of artificial intelligence in transforming dental public health: current applications, ethical considerations, and future directions. Open Dent. J. **19**, (2025). https://doi.org/10.2174/0118742106363413250211053942
7. Bassi, C.A., David-Planas, J., Souza, S.N., de Souza, L.S.: Data-Driven Culture Requires Overcoming Data Governance and Data Literacy Challenges. In Coenen, F., et al. (eds.) International Joint Conference on Knowledge Discovery, Knowledge Engineering and Knowledge Management, IC3K - Proceedings, Vol. 2, pp. 349–356. Science and Technology Publications, Lda (2025). https://doi.org/10.5220/0013670200004000
8. Camacho, J.M., Couce-Vieira, A., Arroyo, D., Insua, D.R.: A Cybersecurity Risk Analysis Framework for Systems with Artificial Intelligence Component (2024). https://doi.org/10.48550/arXiv.2401.01630
9. Chao, K., Sarker, M., Ali, I., Firdaus, R., Azman, A., Shaed, M.: Big data-driven public health policy making: Potential for the healthcare industry. Heliyon *9*(9) (2023). https://doi.org/10.1016/j.heliyon.2023.e19681
10. Da Bormida, M.: The big data world: benefits, threats and ethical challenges. In O'Mathuna, D., Iphofen, R. (eds.) Ethical Issues Covert Secur. Surveill. Res. **8**, 71–91 (2022). https://doi.org/10.1108/S2398-601820210000008007
11. Del-Rey-Puech, P., Payne, R., Saund, J., McKee, M.: Mind the (widening) gap: Why public health must engage with AI now. Public Health **250** (2026). https://doi.org/10.1016/j.puhe.2025.106047
12. Goktas, P., Grzybowski, A.: Shaping the future of healthcare: ethical clinical challenges and pathways to trustworthy AI. J. Clin. Med. **14**(5) (2025). https://doi.org/10.3390/jcm14051605

13. Joshi, S., Sharma, M., Das, R., Rosak-Szyrocka, J., Zywiolek, J., Muduli, K.P.M.: Modeling conceptual framework for implementing barriers of ai in public healthcare for improving operational excellence: experiences from developing countries. Sustainability 14 (2022). https://doi.org/10.3390/su141811698
14. Kolkman, D., Bex, F., Narayan, N., van der Put, M.: Justitia ex machina: The impact of an AI system on legal decision-making and discretionary authority. Big Data Soc. **11**(2) (2024). https://doi.org/10.1177/20539517241255101
15. Kudina, O., van de Poel, I.: A sociotechnical system perspective on AI. Mind. Mach. **34**(3), 21 (2024). https://doi.org/10.1007/s11023-024-09680-2
16. Kulothungan, V., Gupta, D.: Towards Adaptive AI Governance: Comparative Insights from the U.S., EU, and Asia (2025). https://doi.org/10.48550/arXiv.2504.00652
17. Kuppler, M., Kern, C., Bach, R.L., Kreuter, F.: From fair predictions to just decisions? Conceptualizing algorithmic fairness and distributive justice in the context of data-driven decision-making. Front. Sociol. **7**, 883999 (2022). https://doi.org/10.3389/fsoc.2022.883999
18. Lei, Y., Duan, Y., Song, M.: Technical implementation framework of AI governance policies for cross-modal privacy protection. In: Gao, H., Wang, X., Iqbal, M., Yin, Y., Yin, J., Gu, N. (eds.) Lect. Notes Inst. Comput. Sci. Soc. Informatics Telecommun. Eng., Vol. 350, pp. 431–443). Springer Science and Business Media Deutschland GmbH (2021). https://doi.org/10.1007/978-3-030-67540-0_27
19. Li, L., Haley, L., Boyd, A., Bernstam, E.: Technical/algorithm, stakeholder, and society (TASS) barriers to the application of artificial intelligence in medicine: A systematic review. J. Biomed. Inform. **147** (2023). https://doi.org/10.1016/j.jbi.2023.104531
20. Loi, M., Spielkamp, M.: Towards accountability in the use of artificial intelligence for public administrations. In: Proceedings of the 2021 AAAI/ACM Conference on AI, Ethics, and Society, pp. 757–766 (2021). https://doi.org/10.1145/3461702.3462631
21. Madan, R., Ashok, M.: AI adoption and diffusion in public administration: A systematic literature review and future research agenda. Gov. Inf. Q. **40**(1), 101774 (2023). https://doi.org/10.1016/j.giq.2022.101774
22. Malawani, A.: Artificial intelligence in public administration: Opportunities, challenges, and ethical considerations. Otoritas-J. ILMU Pemerintahan **15**(1), 205–221 (2025). https://doi.org/10.26618/ojip.v15i1.17387
23. Matias-Pereira, J.: Artificial Intelligence Adoption in Public Administration: Evolution, Challenges and Global Perspectives. Int. J. Econ. Financ. **17**(9), p36 (2025). https://doi.org/10.5539/ijef.v17n9p36
24. McDermid, J.A., Jia, Y., Porter, Z., Habli, I.: Artificial intelligence explainability: The technical and ethical dimensions. Philosop. Trans. Royal Soc. A Math. Phys. Eng. Sci. **379**(2207), 20200363 (2021). https://doi.org/10.1098/rsta.2020.0363
25. Mellouli, S., Janssen, M., Ojo, A.: Introduction to the issue on artificial intelligence in the public sector: risks and benefits of AI for governments. Digit. Govern. Res. Pract. **5**(1) (2024). https://doi.org/10.1145/3636550
26. Mushkani, R., Berard, H., Cohen, A., Koeski, S.: The Right to AI (2025). https://doi.org/10.48550/arXiv.2501.17899
27. OECD. A data-driven public sector: Enabling the strategic use of data for productive, inclusive and trustworthy governance (OECD Working Papers on Public Governance No. 33) (2019). https://doi.org/10.1787/09ab162c-en
28. Page, M.J., et al.: The PRISMA 2020 statement: An updated guideline for reporting systematic reviews. BMJ **372**, n7 (2021). https://doi.org/10.1136/bmj.n71

29. Panteli, D., et al.: Artificial intelligence in public health: Promises, challenges, and an agenda for policy makers and public health institutions. Lancet Publ. Health **10**(5), e428–e432 (2025). https://doi.org/10.1016/S2468-2667(25)00036-2
30. Paperpal (n.d.). AI-powered academic writing support tool. https://paperpal.com/
31. Pencheva, I., Esteve, M., Mikhaylov, S.J.: Big Data and AI – A transformational shift for government: So, what next for research? Public Policy Adm. **35**(1), 24–44 (2020). https://doi.org/10.1177/0952076718780537
32. Rakšnys, A.V., Gudelis, D., Guogis, A.: The uses of artificial intelligence in the public sector: challenges and prospects. Public Policy Adm. **24**(3), 467–477 (2025). https://doi.org/10.5755/j01.ppaa.24.3.39489
33. Rožman, M., Tominc, P., Milfelner, B.: Maximizing employee engagement through artificial intelligent organizational culture in the context of leadership and training of employees: Testing linear and non-linear relationships. Cogent Bus. Manag. **10**(2), 2248732 (2023). https://doi.org/10.1080/23311975.2023.2248732
34. Savelka, J., et al.: AI technicians: developing rapid occupational training methods for a competitive ai workforce. In: Proceedings of the 56th ACM Technical Symposium on Computer Science Education V, Vol. 1, pp. 1029–1035 (2025). https://doi.org/10.1145/3641554.3701935
35. Tricco, A.C., et al.: A scoping review on the conduct and reporting of scoping reviews. BMC Med. Res. Methodol. **16**(1), 15 (2016). https://doi.org/10.1186/s12874-016-0116-4
36. Zotero (n.d.). Zotero reference management software. https://www.zotero.org/

Business Process Analysis and Re-engineering by Synthetic Expert Panel and Human Expert Collaboration

Tarmo Koppel(✉) and Tanel Tammet

Tallinn University of Technology, Ehitajate Tee 5, 19086 Tallinn, Estonia
correspondence@koppel.ee

Abstract. This study presents a synthetic expert panel employing four large language models as synthetic experts for business process automation assessment. The framework implements a six-stage pipeline: process decomposition, multi-model solution generation, cross-model evaluation, optimal solution selection through voting mechanisms, process optimization, and documentation generation. Empirical validation with 140 business professionals across diverse domains demonstrated the framework's practical applicability across three successive model generations. The framework proved most effective for production-related fields ($M = 4.41$) and marketing & sales processes ($M = 4.28$), while administrative workflows showed the greatest variability. At the activity level, Anthropic's models produced the highest-rated automation suggestions, and Sonnet 4.6 was the highest-rated model overall ($M = 4.46$), though newer model versions did not consistently outperform predecessors across all providers. The synthetic expert panel approach reduces single-model biases and provides a systematic, scalable methodology for AI-driven process transformation in business information systems.

Keywords: Business process automation · expert panel · voting · large language models · process transformation

1 Introduction

The digital transformation of business processes has accelerated with LLM development. Cross-industry surveys show LLMs are used across customer service, fraud detection, risk management, recommendation systems, predictive maintenance, personalized training, healthcare, and other workflows [1–3].

Organizations struggle to systematically evaluate which processes suit AI automation and determine optimal AI solutions for specific activities. Traditional single-model assessments or human expert panels often produce biased or limited solutions, failing to address real-world workflow complexity. Lacking systematic frameworks for comparing multiple AI-generated proposals creates uncertainty, leading to suboptimal transformation outcomes.

E. Laurenzi et al. (Eds.): BIR 2026, LNBIP 601, pp. 511–519, 2027.
https://doi.org/10.1007/978-3-032-38498-0_34

Human–AI collaboration research emphasizes that AI should augment, not replace, experts—humans retain final decisions, especially in high-stakes, uncertain domains [4–7]. Organizations can move beyond ad-hoc, expert-only judgments using task- and context-based frameworks that: 1) decompose work into granular tasks, 2) score automation potential, and 3) use structured templates/decision tools to select appropriate AI solutions. Task-specific templates translate attributes (data types, latency, accuracy, risk, integration needs) into requirements for selecting or adapting AI models (LLMs, classifiers, RPA bots, recommenders) [8].

This study introduces a framework using multiple LLMs as "synthetic experts" in a structured evaluation process, systematically applying diverse AI models to generate, evaluate, and optimize automation solutions. It aims to empirically validate this multi-LLM framework by examining how business professionals assess its effectiveness across organizational domains and process types. Business Process Management (BPM) encompasses planning, analysis, design, monitoring, and optimization of organizational processes [9–11]. Business Process Automation (BPA) uses technology to perform routine tasks, improving efficiency and reducing costs while freeing employees for strategic work [12–14]. BPA evolved into Business Process Management Systems (BPMS), offering broader end-to-end functionality [15, 16] ysolmaz et al. note that while critical success factors (management support, methodology, goal communication) matter for both BPM and BPA, their relevance differs—BPA requires greater methodological agility, BPM demands stronger business-IT synergy [17].

LLMs handle complex language tasks—summarization, classification, Q&A—reducing manual effort in documentation, reporting, and compliance. They support process comprehension, lifecycle management, and adaptive workflows, improving understanding, reducing complexity, and increasing agility [18, 19].

LLM-based agent systems have shifted from single-agent planning to collaborative multi-agent frameworks leveraging profiling, communication, and skill development [20, 21]. Multiple LLMs can collaborate effectively: GEDI incorporates voting mechanisms to enhance reasoning [22]. Additionally, frameworks like FORD use debate among LLMs to reach consensus despite inter-inconsistencies, employing advanced models like GPT-4 as authoritative judges [23]. Multi-LLM collaboration frameworks, such as those tailored for medical tasks, show that collaboration can boost reasoning abilities and reduce divergence among models [24]. Similarly, the integration of LLMs with multi-agent systems (MAS) enhances decision-making by leveraging the strengths of both domains [25].

While performance optimization traditionally required resource-intensive fine-tuning, prompt manipulation and chain-of-thought methods now achieve comparable results more efficiently [26]. AI-driven frameworks support large-scale decision-making involving multiple stakeholders and criteria [27]. MetaAgents assigns LLM agents different roles to form teams, showing rational assembly but limits in complex teaming [28]. Adversarial debate frameworks improve factuality via opposing debaters and judges [24, 29]. Game arena studies show LLM agents adapt toward Nash-like equilibria over repeated play, varying in rationality and convergence [30–34].

2 Methodology

The framework's six-stage process: (1) **Process decomposition** – parses descriptions into discrete activities via LLM-based NLP; (2) **Synthetic expert panel** – four LLMs generate three solutions each per activity (12 total); (3) **Cross-model evaluation** – LLMs rate all solutions (1–10) on suitability and feasibility; (4) **Optimal selection** – voting identifies top-rated solutions; (5) **Process optimization** – identifies redundancies and improvements; (6) **Documentation generation** – produces descriptions, comparisons, and implementation guidelines.

The system uses a modular, layered architecture ensuring traceability across all stages. Horizontal scalability comes from independent module scaling, while vertical extensibility allows component substitution—new LLM services can be added via connectors without altering existing architecture. This modularity supports selective updates, parallel development across teams, and independent feature additions without full redeployment. Eight modules handle discrete responsibilities: **User Interface** captures input via IPython widgets; **Input Processing** uses NLP to decompose narratives into normalized activity records; **Prompt Management** generates template-based LLM queries; **LLM Interface** asynchronously distributes prompts to four parallel LLMs, returning structured JSON solutions; **Response Processing** aggregates and normalizes these outputs; **Analysis Engine** cross-validates solutions via a scoring matrix, applying voting algorithms to select optimal automation pathways; **Output Generation** produces CSV and DOCX documentation; and **Storage** provides multi-tier persistence across formats, supporting checkpointing and lineage tracking.

The system integrates four distinct LLM services through their respective APIs, creating a heterogeneous expert panel: OpenAI, Anthropic, Google, and xAI. OpenAI's models serve as the primary process analyzer and solution coordinator, while Anthropic, Google, and xAI models are integrated as secondary agents for alternative solution generation and cross-validation. All providers except xAI support structured JSON response capabilities. Each agent operates independently, maintaining separate API connections with dedicated authentication and rate limiting mechanisms. Across three successive deployment cohorts, the study covered three generations of models per provider. OpenAI models used were GPT-4o, o1, and GPT-5.2; Anthropic models were Claude Sonnet 3.5, 3.7, and 4.6; Google models were Gemini 1.5 Pro, 2.5 Pro, and 3.1 Pro; and xAI models were Grok-beta, Grok-2, and Grok-4, totaling twelve distinct LLM versions evaluated across the study.

Empirical validation was by human feedback. 140 business professionals acted as test users and applied the tool to real-world business processes. Each user selected a process from their own practice. Test users were recruited from professional trainings and Master's level courses at the authors' university's business school. Business professionals' domains included services (62), production (32), IT (16), finance (11), hospitality (9), well-being (7), and public sector (2). 73 participants had previous experience in designing business processes and 67 had none.

Business processes were classified into six high-level categories: transaction processing (36); production & service delivery (32); service management (30); administrative (16); financial and contractual processes (16); and marketing & sales (10).

Empirical validation followed an 11-step protocol: a test user selected a business process (5–15 activities) from their domain, providing context and process details. The tool clarified and refined the activity list, then the user manually suggested automations before four LLMs independently generated three suggestions per activity (12 total). Both the user and the four LLMs scored each suggestion (1–10), yielding 48 AI scores per activity. The tool selected optimal solutions considering workflow context, redesigned the process to reduce redundancy, and generated formal documentation. Participants then rated model performance (1–5) across AI transformation quality, process optimization, and design.

Human ratings were averaged per user across evaluation dimensions—LLM performance (activity-level, 1–10 scale) and tool performance (1–5 scale, across AI transformation, optimization, and design). Descriptives (means, SDs) were computed for all variables. Group differences used Welch's-corrected independent t-tests (Levene's test checked variance equality beforehand), with Hedges' g (independent) and Cohen's d (paired) for effect sizes. Paired t-tests compared LLM providers at the activity level. Pearson correlations (Bonferroni-adjusted, $\alpha = .008$) examined relationships between LLM quality and tool performance. Generational trends were tested via Welch's t-tests across model versions and, for the third cohort, across all four providers simultaneously ($\alpha = .05$; Python).

3 Empirical Validation

General Model Performance. Model performance was examined across three successive deployment cohorts, enabling a within-provider generational comparison. Table 1 presents mean ratings (SD) for all twelve models on a 5-point scale.

Table 1. Model performance ratings across three cohorts (5-point scale), Mean (SD)

Provider	Generation 1	Generation 2	Generation 3
OpenAI	GPT-4o: 4.14 (1.38)	o1: 4.15 (0.84)	GPT-5.2: 4.22 (0.81)
Anthropic	Sonnet 3.5: 4.00 (1.05)	Sonnet 3.7: 3.95 (0.79)	**Sonnet 4.6: 4.46** (0.82)
Google	Gemini 1.5 Pro: 4.23 (1.21)	Gemini 2.5 Pro: 3.51 (0.88)	Gemini 3.1 Pro: 3.70 (1.12)
xAI	Grok-beta: 4.34 (1.11)	Grok-2: 3.41 (1.02)	Grok-4: 3.77 (0.92)
Cohort	I + II, N = 37	I + II, N = 39	III, N = 63

OpenAI showed stable performance across all three generations, with no significant differences between any model versions (all $p > .68$), though variability decreased markedly with each successive release. Anthropic was the only provider to show a clear and statistically significant generational improvement. Sonnet 3.5 and Sonnet 3.7 performed comparably ($p = .811$), but Sonnet 4.6 rated significantly higher than both Sonnet 3.7 ($t(100) = -3.10$, $p = .003$, $d = 0.63$) and Sonnet 3.5 ($t(98) = -2.44$, p

= .017, d = 0.50), making it the highest-rated model across the entire study. Google showed a significant drop from Generation 1 to Generation 2: Gemini 1.5 Pro was rated significantly higher than both Gemini 2.5 Pro ($t(74) = 2.97$, $p = .004$) and Gemini 3.1 Pro ($t(98) = 2.23$, $p = .028$). Generations 2 and 3 did not differ significantly ($p=.381$), suggesting partial recovery but not a full return to Generation 1 levels. xAI exhibited the most pronounced decline. Grok-beta was rated significantly higher than both Grok-2 ($t(74)=3.81$, $p<.001$, $d=0.87$) and Grok-4 ($t(98)=2.76$, $p=.007$). The difference between Grok-2 and Grok-4 was not significant ($p=.069$), indicating modest but inconclusive recovery. Within Generation 3 (N=63), Sonnet 4.6 and GPT-5.2 were the top-rated models and did not differ significantly from each other ($p=.104$). Both outperformed Gemini 3.1 Pro (Sonnet 4.6: $t(124)=4.37$, $p<.001$, $d=0.78$; GPT-5.2: $t(124)=3.01$, $p=.003$) and Grok-4 (Sonnet 4.6: $t(124)=4.44$, $p<.001$, $d=0.79$; GPT-5.2: $t(124)=2.92$, $p=.004$), while Gemini 3.1 Pro and Grok-4 performed comparably ($p=.696$).

Field of Activity. LLM performance varies somewhat across the organization's field of activity. Production received the highest ratings (M = 4.41, SD = 1.23), followed by service (M = 3.97, SD = 0.51), IT (M = 3.84, SD = 0.87), finance (M = 3.82, SD = 0.61), hospitality (M = 3.75, SD = 0.59), and well-being (M = 3.46, SD = 0.44). Public sector was excluded from comparisons due to insufficient sample size. Service showed the lowest variability, while production exhibited the highest, suggesting more heterogeneous experiences among manufacturing and production-related participants. Well-being scored lowest with minimal variance, indicating consistently modest ratings across that domain. The difference between the highest-rated field (production) and lowest-rated (well-being) was statistically significant ($p = .002$) with a large effect size ($g = 0.83$), suggesting LLMs perform better for production-related automation tasks.

Process Type. LLM performance across process types: marketing & sales rated highest (M = 4.28, SD = 1.38), followed by transaction processing (M = 4.17), financial/contractual (M = 4.02), production & service delivery (M = 3.98), service management (M = 3.89), and administrative processes lowest (M = 3.62). Marketing & sales showed highest variability; financial/contractual showed lowest. The difference between highest and lowest ratings was non-significant ($p = .197$), suggesting LLMs performed comparably across functions, though better suited to structured, transaction-based processes than open-ended administrative workflows.

Process Activities. Each test user was provided with output from four different models and individually evaluated each activity within the process pipeline. Anthropic scored highest (M = 7.70, SD = 1.29), followed by OpenAI (M = 7.55, SD = 1.37), xAI (M = 7.47, SD = 1.43), and Google (M = 7.25, SD = 1.71). Google exhibited the highest variability while Anthropic showed the lowest, indicating the most consistent perceived quality across participants. Anthropic rated significantly higher than Google ($t(136) = 4.17$, $p < .001$), OpenAI ($t(138) = 2.77$, $p = .006$), and xAI ($t(137) = 2.96$, $p = .004$). OpenAI also outperformed Google significantly ($t(136) = 2.75$, $p = .007$). The difference between xAI and Google approached but did not reach significance ($p = .056$), while OpenAI and xAI performed comparably ($p = .360$). These results suggest that while all providers delivered broadly adequate automation suggestions, Anthropic produced consistently higher-quality solutions as perceived by domain expert evaluators.

Tool Performance. The tool performed well across all three dimensions (5-point scale), with new process design scoring highest overall (M = 4.45). Transaction processing led in transformation and optimization; marketing & sales topped new process design with the most consistent transformation ratings (SD = 0.32). Administrative processes showed the greatest variability. Financial/contractual processes scored near-equally across dimensions. Production & service delivery scored lowest in transformation but recovered in new process design, following the general trend of new process design outperforming other dimensions. See Table 2.

Table 2. Tool's output's performance across different business process types, Mean (SD)

Process type	Transformation	Optimization	New process design
Administrative	4.36 (0.63)	4.13 (0.71)	4.36 (0.69)
Financial and contractual processes	4.34 (0.56)	4.24 (0.52)	4.35 (0.61)
Marketing & sales	4.40 (0.32)	4.12 (0.67)	4.62 (0.48)
Production & service delivery	4.27 (0.57)	4.25 (0.54)	4.45 (0.52)
Service management	4.32 (0.59)	4.24 (0.54)	4.49 (0.54)
Transaction processing	4.43 (0.48)	4.41 (0.57)	4.47 (0.48)
ALL TOGETHER	4.35 (0.54)	4.26 (0.58)	4.45 (0.54)

4 Discussion and Conclusions

LLMs accelerate business process digital transformation by automating text-centric work and augmenting decision-making, but require domain adaptation and hybrid architectures to address transparency and reliability limitations. Prior studies highlight bias, hallucinations, privacy concerns, and governance needs [1, 2, 35, 36]. Most BPM research uses single-LLM approaches rather than multi-model panels [18, 37–40].

This study introduced a synthetic expert framework using four LLMs as independent experts for process analysis and automation assessment, reducing single-model bias and expanding solution diversity. Cross-model evaluation enables robust, multi-perspective quality assessment, while the framework also identifies process-level optimization opportunities, offering a repeatable methodology across domains.

Multi-agent/multi-LLM setups are emerging in decision-support and operations, with agents assuming complementary roles, showing improved quality and robustness over single-agent baselines [36, 41–43]. Empirical validation with 140 business professionals confirmed the framework's practical applicability. All LLMs performed comparably, with no consistent top performer, and newer versions didn't always outperform predecessors. The framework worked best for production-related, structured, transaction-based processes, with more variability in administrative and well-being domains.

Supplementary Information. Download link to supplementary materials, including the dataset

References

1. Raza, M., Jahangir, Z., Riaz, M.B., Saeed, M.J., Sattar, M.A.: Industrial applications of large language models. Sci. Rep. **15**, 13755 (2025)
2. Chkirbene, Z., Hamila, R., Gouissem, A., Devrim, U.: Large language models (llm) in industry: A survey of applications, challenges, and trends. In: 2024 IEEE 21st International Conference on Smart Communities: Improving Quality of Life using AI, Robotics and IoT (HONET). pp. 229–234. IEEE (2024)
3. Raiaan, M.A.K., et al.: A review on large language models: Architectures, applications, taxonomies, open issues and challenges. IEEE Access **12**, 26839–26874 (2024)
4. Rosemann, M., vom Brocke, J.: The six core elements of business process management. In: Handbook on business process management 1: introduction, methods, and information systems. pp. 105–122. Springer, Cham (2014)
5. Trkman, P.: The critical success factors of business process management. Int. J. Inf. Manag. **30**, 125–134 (2010)
6. vom Brocke, J., Zelt, S., Schmiedel, T.: On the role of context in business process management. Int. J. Inf. Manag. **36**, 486–495 (2016)
7. Moreira, S., Mamede, H.S., Santos, A.: Business process automation in SMEs: a systematic literature review. IEEE Access **12**, 75832–75864 (2024). https://doi.org/10.1109/ACCESS.2024.3406548
8. Moreira, S., Mamede, H.S., Santos, A.: Business process automation in SMEs. In: Lecture Notes in Business Information Processing, pp. 426–437 (2023). https://doi.org/10.1007/978-3-031-30694-5_31
9. Moreira, S., Mamede, H.S., Santos, A.: Process automation using RPA-A literature review. In: Procedia Computer Science, pp. 244–254 (2023). https://doi.org/10.1016/j.procs.2023.01.287
10. Karagiannis, D.: BPMS: business process management systems. ACM SIGOIS Bull. **16**, 10–13 (1995)
11. Pourmirza, S., Peters, S., Dijkman, R., Grefen, P.: A systematic literature review on the architecture of business process management systems. Inf. Syst. **66**, 43–58 (2017)
12. Aysolmaz, B., Joshi, A., Stubhan, M.: Examining and comparing the critical success factors between business process management and business process automation. J. Global Inf. Manag. (JGIM) **31**, 1–27 (2023)
13. Kourani, H., et al.: Leveraging large language models for enhanced process model comprehension. Decis. Support. Syst. **200**, 114563 (2026). https://doi.org/10.1016/J.DSS.2025.114563
14. Bennoit, C., Greff, T., Baum, D., Bajwa, I.A.: Identifying Use Cases for Large Language Models in the Business Process Management Lifecycle. In: 2024 26th International Conference on Business Informatics (CBI), pp. 256–263 (2024). https://doi.org/10.1109/CBI62504.2024.00037
15. Guo, T., et al.: Large Language Model based Multi-Agents: A Survey of Progress and Challenges. In: IJCAI International Joint Conference on Artificial Intelligence, pp. 8048–8057 (2024)
16. Cao, Y., et al.: Survey on Large language model-enhanced reinforcement learning: concept, taxonomy, and methods. IEEE Trans. Neural Netw. Learn. Syst. **36**, 9737–9757 (2025). https://doi.org/10.1109/TNNLS.2024.3497992
17. Zhao, X., Wang, K., Peng, W.: An Electoral Approach to Diversify LLM-based Multi-Agent Collective Decision-Making. In: EMNLP 2024 - 2024 Conference on Empirical Methods in Natural Language Processing, Proceedings of the Conference, pp. 2712–2727 (2024). https://doi.org/10.18653/v1/2024.emnlp-main.158

18. Xiong, K., Ding, X., Cao, Y., Liu, T., Qin, B.: Examining Inter-consistency of large language models collaboration: an in-depth analysis via debate. In: Findings of the Association for Computational Linguistics: EMNLP 2023, pp. 7572–7590 (2023). https://doi.org/10.18653/v1/2023.findings-emnlp.508
19. Shang, K., Chang, C.-H., Yang, C.C.: Collaboration among Multiple Large Language Models for Medical Question Answering. In: Proceedings - 2025 IEEE 13th International Conference on Healthcare Informatics, ICHI 2025, pp. 388–396 (2025). https://doi.org/10.1109/ICHI64645.2025.00052
20. Sissodia, R., Dwivedi, V., Verma, T.: Advancements in Multi-agent large language model systems for next-generation AI. In: Advancements in Multi-Agent Large Language Model Systems for Next-Generation AI, pp. 1–32. IGI Global Scientific Publishing (2026)
21. Huang, D., Yan, C., Li, Q., Peng, X.: From large language models to large multimodal models: A literature review. Appl. Sci. **14**, 5068 (2024)
22. Ding, R.X., et al.: Large-scale decision-making: Characterization, taxonomy, challenges and future directions from an artificial intelligence and applications perspective. Inf. Fusion **59**, 84–102 (2020). https://doi.org/10.1016/J.INFFUS.2020.01.006
23. Li, Y., Sun, L., Zhang, Y.: MetaAgents: large language model based agents for decision-making on teaming. Proc. ACM Hum. Comput. Interact. **9**, 1–27 (2023). https://doi.org/10.1145/3711032
24. Luo, H., et al.: Toward Edge General Intelligence with Multiple-Large Language Model (Multi-LLM): Architecture, Trust, and Orchestration. ArXiv. abs/2507.00672, (2025). https://doi.org/10.48550/arxiv.2507.00672
25. Lu, S.E.: Game-theory behaviour of large language models: the case of Keynesian beauty contests. Econ. Bus. Rev. **11**, 119–148 (2025)
26. Guo, S., et al.: Economics arena for large language models. arXiv preprint arXiv:2401.01735 (2024)
27. Payne, K., Alloui-Cros, B.: Strategic Intelligence in Large Language Models: Evidence from evolutionary Game Theory. arXiv preprint arXiv:2507.02618 (2025)
28. Lu, S.E.: Strategic interactions between large language models-based agents in beauty contests. arXiv preprint arXiv:2404.08492 (2024)
29. Topsakal, O., Edell, C.J., Harper, J.B.: Evaluating large language models with grid-based game competitions: an extensible LLM benchmark and leaderboard. arXiv preprint arXiv:2407.07796 (2024)
30. Cheung, M.: A reality check of the benefits of llm in business. arXiv preprint arXiv:2406.10249 (2024)
31. Al Khaldy, M., Gheraibia, Y.: Evaluation and Mitigation of the Limitations of Large Language Models in Business Decision-Making. In: 2025 1st International Conference on Computational Intelligence Approaches and Applications (ICCIAA), pp. 1–6. IEEE (2025)
32. De Michele, W., Armas Cervantes, A., Frermann, L.: Automated business process analysis: An llm-based approach to value assessment. In: International Conference on Advanced Information Systems Engineering. pp. 62–69. Springer, Cham (2025)
33. Kourani, H., Berti, A., Schuster, D., van der Aalst, W.M.P.: Process Modeling With Large Language Models (2024).https://doi.org/10.1007/978-3-031-61007-3_18
34. Kourani, H., Berti, A., Schuster, D., van der Aalst, W.M.P.: Evaluating large language models on business process modeling: framework, benchmark, and self-improvement analysis: Softw. Syst. Model. 1–36 (2025)
35. Grohs, M., Abb, L., Elsayed, N., Rehse, J.-R.: Large language models can accomplish business process management tasks. In: International conference on business process management. pp. 453–465. Springer, Cham (2023)
36. Wang, Z., Zhang, J.: From Bits to Boardrooms: A Cutting-Edge Multi-Agent LLM Framework for Business Excellence. arXiv preprint arXiv:2508.15447. (2025)

37. Xia, Y., Dittler, D., Jazdi, N., Chen, H., Weyrich, M.: Llm experiments with simulation: Large language model multi-agent system for simulation model parametrization in digital twins. In: 2024 IEEE 29th International Conference on Emerging Technologies and Factory Automation (ETFA), pp. 1–4. IEEE (2024)
38. Pajak, E., Bahamdan, A., Hellgardt, K., del Río-Chanona, A.: Multi-agent LLMs for automating sustainable operational decision-making. Syst. Control Trans. 1824–1829 (2025)

Author Index

E. Laurenzi et al. (Eds.): BIR 2026, LNBIP 601, pp. 521–522, 2027.
https://doi.org/10.1007/978-3-032-38498-0

FSC
www.fsc.org
MIX
Papier | Fördert
gute Waldnutzung
FSC® C083411

Kolibri 360 GmbH
Ferdinand-Jühlke-Straße 7
99095 Erfurt, Deutschland
produktsicherheit@kolibri360.de